Systems of Psychotherapy
A Transtheoretical Analysis

Systems of Psychotherapy
A Transtheoretical Analysis

EIGHTH EDITION

JAMES O. PROCHASKA
University of Rhode Island

JOHN C. NORCROSS
University of Scranton

CENGAGE
Learning·

Australia • Brazil • Mexico • Singapore • United Kingdom • United States

**Systems of Psychotherapy:
A Transtheoretical Analysis,
Eighth Edition, International Edition**
James O. Prochaska and John C. Norcross

Publisher: Jon-David Hague

Assistant Editor: Sean Cronin

Editorial Assistant: Amelia Blevins

Managing Media Editor: Mary Noel

Senior Brand Manager: Elisabeth Rhoden

Senior Market Development Manager:
Kara Kindstrom

Art and Cover Direction, Production
Management, and Composition:
PreMediaGlobal

Manufacturing Planner: Judy Inouye

Senior Rights Acquisitions Specialist:
Dean Dauphinais

Photo Researcher: Q2A/Bill Smith

Text Researcher: Q2A/Bill Smith

Cover Image: © Philip Jones

International Edition:

ISBN-13: 978-1-285-17576-8

ISBN-10: 1-285-17576-X

Cengage Learning International Offices

Asia
www.cengageasia.com
tel: (65) 6410 1200

Australia/New Zealand
www.cengage.com.au
tel: (61) 3 9685 4111

Brazil
www.cengage.com.br
tel: (55) 11 3665 9900

India
www.cengage.co.in
tel: (91) 11 4364 1111

Latin America
www.cengage.com.mx
tel: (52) 55 1500 6000

UK/Europe/Middle East/Africa
www.cengage.co.uk
tel: (44) 0 1264 332 424

Represented in Canada by Nelson Education, Ltd.
www.nelson.com
tel: (416) 752 9100/(800) 668 0671

Cengage Learning is a leading provider of customized learning solutions with office locations around the globe, including Singapore, the United Kingdom, Australia, Mexico, Brazil, and Japan. Locate your local office at: **www.cengage.com/global**.

For product information and free companion resources:
www.cengage.com/international
Visit your local office: **www.cengage.com/global**
Visit our corporate website: **www.cengage.com**

Printed in the United States of America
1 2 3 4 5 6 7 17 16 15 14 13

To Jan and Nancy

Brief Contents

Detailed Contents

Preface

Welcome to the eighth edition of *Systems of Psychotherapy: A Transtheoretical Analysis*. Our abiding hope is that our book will inform and excite you. Inform you about valuable psychotherapy theories and excite you to conduct powerful psychotherapy for the enrichment of fellow humans.

Our book provides a systematic, comprehensive, and balanced survey of the leading systems of psychotherapy. It is designed, however, to be more than just a survey, as we strive toward a synthesis both within each psychotherapy system and across the various systems. Within a particular system of therapy, this book follows the integrative steps that flow from the system's theory of personality to its theory of psychopathology and culminates in its therapeutic process and therapy relationship. Across the various systems of therapy, our book offers an integrative framework that highlights the many similarities of therapy systems without blurring their essential differences. The comparative analysis clearly demonstrates how much psychotherapy systems agree on the processes producing change while disagreeing on the content that needs to be changed.

Systems of Psychotherapy: A Transtheoretical Analysis is intended, primarily, for advanced undergraduate and graduate students enrolled in introductory courses in psychotherapy and counseling. This course is commonly titled Systems of Psychotherapy, Theories of Counseling, Psychological Interventions, or Introduction to Counseling and is offered to psychology, counseling, social work, psychiatry, nursing, human relations, and other students. Our volume is intended, secondarily, for psychotherapists of all professions and persuasions seeking a comparative overview of the burgeoning field of psychotherapy. We have been immensely gratified by the feedback from readers who have used this text in preparing for comprehensive exams, licensure tests, and board certification as well as from those who have found it instrumental in acquiring a more integrative perspective.

Our Objectives

The contents and goals of this eighth edition embody our objectives as psychotherapy practitioners, teachers, researchers, and theorists. As practitioners, we appreciate the vitality and meaning of different clinical approaches. We attempt to communicate the excitement and depth of these psychotherapy systems. Accordingly, we avoid simple descriptions of the systems as detached observers in favor of immersing ourselves in each system as advocates.

As practitioners, we are convinced that any treatise on such a vital field as psychotherapy must come alive to do the subject matter justice. To this end, we have included a wealth of case illustrations drawn from our combined 75 years of clinical practice. (When one of us is speaking from our own experience, we will identify ourselves by our initials—JOP for James O. Prochaska and JCN for John C. Norcross.) We demonstrate how the same complicated psychotherapy case—Mrs. C—is formulated and treated by each system of psychotherapy. This and all of the case examples counterbalance the theoretical considerations; in this way, theories become pragmatic and consequential—relevant to what transpires in the therapeutic hour. The details of individual clients have been altered, of course, to preserve their privacy and anonymity.

As psychotherapy teachers, we recognize the complexity and diversity of the leading theories of psychotherapy. This book endeavors to present the essential concepts clearly and concisely but without resorting to oversimplification. Our students occasionally complain that theorists seem to have a knack for making things more complicated than they really are. We hope that as you move through these pages you will gain a deeper appreciation for the complexity of the human condition or, at least, the complexity of the minds of those attempting to articulate the human condition.

Our decades of teaching and supervising psychotherapy have also taught us that students desire an overarching structure to guide the acquisition, analysis, and comparison of information. Unlike edited psychotherapy texts with varying writing styles and chapter content, we use a consistent structure and voice throughout the book. Instead of illustrating one approach with Ms. Apple and another approach with Mr. Orange, we systematically present a detailed treatment of Mrs. C for each and every approach.

As psychotherapy researchers, the evidence has taught us that psychotherapy has enormous potential for impacting patients in a positive (and occasionally a negative) manner. In this view, therapy is more analogous to penicillin than to aspirin. With psychotherapy expected to produce strong rather than weak effects, we should be able to demonstrate the effectiveness of psychotherapy even in the face of error caused by measurement and methodological problems. We thus include a summary of controlled outcome studies and meta-analytic reviews that have evaluated the effectiveness of each therapy system.

Research and practice have further taught us that each psychotherapy system has its respective limitations and contraindications. For this reason, we offer cogent criticisms of each approach from the vantage points of cognitive-behavioral, psychoanalytic, humanistic, cultural, and integrative perspectives. The net effect is a balanced coverage combining sympathetic presentation and critical analysis.

As psychotherapy theorists, we do *not* endorse the endless proliferation of psychotherapy systems, each purportedly unique and superior despite the absence of research evidence. What our amorphous discipline *does* need is a concerted effort to pull together the essentials operating in effective therapies and to discard those features unrelated to effective practice. From our comparative analysis of the major systems of therapy, we hope to move toward a higher integration that will yield a transtheoretical approach to psychotherapy.

And from comparative analysis and research, we hope to contribute to an inclusive, evidence-based psychotherapy in which treatment methods and therapy relationships—derived from these major systems of therapy—will be tailored to the needs of the individual client. In this way, we believe, the effectiveness and applicability of psychotherapy will be enhanced.

Changes in the Eighth Edition

Innovations appear and vanish with bewildering rapidity on the psychotherapeutic scene. One year's treatment fad—say, neurolinguistic programming—fades into oblivion in just a few years. The volatile nature of the psychotherapy discipline requires regular updates in order for practitioners and students to stay abreast of developments.

The evolution of this book closely reflects the changing landscape of psychotherapy. The first edition in 1979 was relatively brief and only hinted at the possibility of integration. The second edition added sections on object relations, cognitive, and systems therapies. The third edition brought new chapters on gender-sensitive therapies and integrative treatments, as well as John C. Norcross as a coauthor. The fourth edition featured a new chapter on constructivist therapies and the addition of material on motivational interviewing, EMDR, and psychotherapy for men. The fifth edition brought more material on experiential therapies and on interpersonal psychotherapy (IPT). The sixth edition provided a separate chapter on multicultural therapies (formerly combined with gender-sensitive therapies), and the seventh edition featured new sections on dialectical behavior therapy and relational psychoanalysis.

This eighth edition, in turn, brings a host of changes that reflect trends in the field. Among these are:

- a new chapter on third-wave therapies, including acceptance and mindfulness approaches (Chapter 11)
- a reorganization of the chapter on experiential therapies (Chapter 6) to focus equally on Gestalt and emotion-focused therapy
- a new section on the emerging evidence-based family therapies (Chapter 12)
- more attention to attachment-based therapies in both the psychodynamic and experiential chapters
- enlarged consideration of the transtheoretical model (Chapter 17)
- updated reviews of meta-analyses and controlled outcome studies conducted on each psychotherapy system
- continued efforts to make the book student friendly throughout (see the following section)

With these additions, the text now thoroughly analyzes the 16 leading systems of psychotherapy and briefly surveys another 31, thus affording a broader scope than is available in most textbooks. Guiding all these modifications has been the unwavering goal of our book: to provide a comprehensive, rigorous, and balanced survey of the major theories of psychotherapy. Expanding the breadth of *Systems of Psychotherapy* has been accomplished only within the context of a comparative analysis that seeks to explicate both the fundamental similarities and the useful differences among the therapy schools.

Student and Instructor Friendly

The 30-plus years since the first edition of this book have repeatedly taught us to keep our eye on the ball: student learning. On the basis of feedback from readers and our students, we have introduced aids to enhance student learning. These include:

- a list of key terms at the end of each chapter to serve as a study and review guide
- a series of recommended readings and websites at the end of each chapter
- a student companion website at cengagebrain.com, which includes mini-chapters on transactional analysis and implosive therapy, as well as elements to help with review and mastery of the textbook material.
- a set of PowerPoint slides for each chapter (coordinated by Rory A. Pfund, Krystle L. Evans, and John C. Norcross, all at the University of Scranton)
- an expanded *Test Bank and Instructor's Resource Manual* coauthored by two exceptional teachers, Drs. Linda Campbell (University of Georgia) and Anthony Giuliano (Harvard Medical School). Available to qualified adopters, the manual lists filmed therapy demonstrations of the psychotherapy systems featured in the text, more than 400 activity/discussion ideas, and additional case illustrations for use in class or on

examinations. The manual also presents 2,000+ original exam items.

- an alternative table of contents as an appendix for those who wish to focus on the change processes cutting across theories, rather than the psychotherapy theories themselves
- a Theories in Action video, developed by Ed Neukrug (Old Dominion University), that presents short clips illustrating the systems of psychotherapy in action. Available to qualified adopters.

Acknowledgments

Our endeavors in completing previous editions and in preparing this edition have been aided immeasurably by colleagues and family members. In particular, special appreciation is extended to our good friends and close collaborators, Dr. Carlo DiClemente and Dr. Wayne Velicer, for their continuing development of the trans-theoretical approach. We thank Allison Smith for her contributions to the chapter on multicultural therapies (Chapter 14) in previous editions. We are indebted to Rory Pfund and Donna Rupp for their tireless efforts in word processing the manuscript and in securing original sources.

We are also grateful to the following reviewers of the eighth edition:

Sheli Bernstein-Goff, West Liberty University

David Carter, University of Nebraska Omaha

Melody Bacon, Argosy University

Mark Aoyagi, University of Denver

Barbara Beaver, University of Wisconsin–Whitewater

We are amused and strangely satisfied that reviewers occasionally find our book to be slanted toward a particular theoretical orientation—but then they cannot agree on which orientation that is! One reviewer surmised that we disliked psychoanalysis, whereas another thought we carried a psychoanalytic vision throughout the book. We take such conflicting observations as evidence that we are striking a theoretical balance.

Three groups of individuals deserve specific mention for their support over the years. First, we are grateful to the National Institutes of Health, the University of Rhode Island, and the University of Scranton for their financial support of our research. Second, we are indebted to our clients, who continue to be our ultimate teachers of psychotherapy. And third, we are appreciative of the good people at Brooks/Cole and Cengage Learning for seeing this new edition of *Systems of Psychotherapy: A Transtheoretical Analysis* to fruition.

Finally, we express our deepest appreciation to our spouses (Jan; Nancy) and to our children (Jason and Jodi; Rebecca and Jonathon), who were willing to sacrifice for the sake of our scholarship and who were available for support when we emerged from solitude. Their caring has freed us to contribute to the education of those who might one day use the powers of psychotherapy to make this a better world.

James O. Prochaska

John C. Norcross

About the Authors

James O. Prochaska, PhD, earned his baccalaureate, master's, and doctorate in clinical psychology from Wayne State University and fulfilled his internship at the Lafayette Clinic in Detroit. At present, he is Professor of Psychology and Director of the Cancer Prevention Research Consortium at the University of Rhode Island. Dr. Prochaska has over 45 years of psychotherapy experience in a variety of settings and has been a consultant to a host of clinical and research organizations. He has been the principal investigator on grants from the National Institutes of Health totaling over $90 million and has been recognized by the Association of Psychological Science as one of the most cited authors in psychology. His 50 book chapters and over 300 scholarly articles focus on self-change, health promotion, well-being, and psychotherapy from a transtheoretical perspective, the subject of both his professional book, *The Transtheoretical Approach* (with Carlo DiClemente), and his popular book, *Changing for Good* (with John C. Norcross and Carlo DiClemente). An accomplished speaker, he has offered workshops and keynote addresses throughout the world and served on various task forces for the National Cancer Institute, National Institute of Mental Health, National Institute of Drug Abuse, and American Cancer Society. Among his numerous awards are the Rosalie Weiss Award from the American Psychological Association (APA), Innovators Award from the Robert Wood Johnson Foundation, SOPHE Honorary Fellow Award from the Society for Public Health Education, Beckham Award for Excellence in Education and Inspirational Leadership from Columbia University, and the Fries Health Education Award from the Society for Public Health Education; he is the first psychologist to win a Medal of Honor for Clinical Research from the American Cancer Society. Jim makes his home in southern Rhode Island with his wife, Jan. They have two married children and five grandchildren living in California.

 **John C. Norcross, PhD, ABPP**, received his baccalaureate from Rutgers University, earned his master's and doctorate in clinical psychology from the University of Rhode Island, and completed his internship at the Brown University School of Medicine. He is Distinguished Professor of Psychology at the University of Scranton, Adjunct Professor of Psychiatry at SUNY Upstate Medical University, and a board-certified clinical psychologist in part-time independent practice. Author of more than 300 scholarly publications, Dr. Norcross has cowritten or edited 20 books, the most recent being *Psychotherapy Relationships That Work, Self-Help That Works, Leaving It at the Office: Psychotherapist Self-Care, Psychologists' Desk Reference, Handbook of Psychotherapy Integration*, and multiple editions of the *Insider's Guide to Graduate Programs in Clinical and Counseling Psychology*. He has also authored two self-help books, most recently *Changeology: 5 Steps to Realizing Your Resolutions and Goals.* He has served as president of the APA Division of Psychotherapy, president of the Society of Clinical Psychology, and Council Representative of the APA. He has also served on the editorial board of a dozen journals and was the editor of the *Journal of Clinical Psychology: In Session* for a decade. He is a diplomate in clinical psychology of the American Board of Professional Psychology. Dr. Norcross has delivered workshops and lectures in 30 countries. He has received numerous awards for his teaching and research, such as APA's Distinguished Contributions to Education & Training Award, Pennsylvania Professor of the Year from the Carnegie Foundation, the Rosalee Weiss Award from the American Psychological Foundation, and election to the National Academies of Practice. John lives, works, and plays in northeastern Pennsylvania with his wife, two grown children, and two new grandkids.

CHAPTER 1

Defining and Comparing the Psychotherapies

An Integrative Framework

The field of psychotherapy has been fragmented by future shock and staggered by over-choice. We have witnessed the hyperinflation of brand-name therapies during the past 50 years. In 1959, Harper identified 36 distinct systems of psychotherapy; by 1976, Parloff discovered more than 130 therapies in the therapeutic marketplace or, perhaps more appropriately, the "jungle place." Recent estimates now put the number at over 500 and growing (Pearsall, 2011).

The proliferation of therapies has been accompanied by an avalanche of rival claims: Each system advertises itself as differentially effective and uniquely applicable. Developers of new systems usually claim 80% to 100% success, despite the absence of controlled outcome research. A healthy diversity has deteriorated into an unhealthy chaos. Students, practitioners, and patients are confronted with confusion, fragmentation, and discontent. With so many therapy systems claiming success, which theories should be studied, taught, or bought?

A book by a proponent of a particular therapy system can be quite persuasive. We may even find ourselves using the new ideas and methods in practice while reading the book. But when we turn to an advocate of a radically different approach, the confusion returns. Listening to proponents compare therapies does little for our confusion, except to confirm the rule that those who cannot agree on basic assumptions are often reduced to calling each other names.

We believe that fragmentation and confusion in psychotherapy can best be reduced by a comparative analysis of psychotherapy systems that highlights the many similarities across systems without blurring their essential difference.

A comparative analysis requires a firm understanding of each of the individual systems of therapy to be compared. In discussing each system, we first present a brief clinical example and introduce the developer(s) of the system. We trace the system's theory of personality as it leads to its theory of psychopathology and culminates in its therapeutic processes, therapeutic content, and therapy relationship. We then feature the practicalities of the psychotherapy. Following a summary of controlled research on the effectiveness of that system, we review central criticisms of that psychotherapy from diverse perspectives. Each chapter concludes with an analysis of the same patient (Mrs. C) and a consideration of future directions.

In outline form, our examination of each psychotherapy system follows this format:

- A clinical example
- A sketch of the founder
- Theory of personality
- Theory of psychopathology
- Therapeutic processes
- Therapeutic content
- Therapeutic relationship
- Practicalities of the therapy
- Effectiveness of the therapy
- Criticisms of the therapy
- Analysis of Mrs. C
- Future directions
- Key terms
- Recommended readings
- Recommended websites

In comparing systems, we will use an integrative model to demonstrate their similarities and differences. An integrative model was selected in part because of its spirit of rapprochement, seeking what is useful and cordial in each therapy system rather than looking for what is most easily criticized. Integration also represents the mainstream of contemporary psychotherapy: Research consistently demonstrates that **integration** is the most popular orientation of mental health professionals (Norcross, 2005).

Lacking in most integrative endeavors is a comprehensive model for thinking and working across systems. Later in this chapter, we present an integrative model that is sophisticated enough to do justice to the complexities of psychotherapy, yet simple enough to reduce confusion in the field. Rather than having to work with 500-plus theories,

our integrative model assumes that a limited number of processes of change underlie contemporary systems of psychotherapy. The model further demonstrates how the content of therapy can be reduced to four different levels of personal functioning.

Psychotherapy systems are compared on the particular process, or combination of processes, used to produce change. The systems are also compared on how they conceptualize the most common problems that occur at each level of personal functioning, such as low self-esteem, lack of intimacy, and impulse dyscontrol. Because clinicians are concerned primarily with the real problems of real people, we do not limit our comparative analysis merely to concepts and data. Our analysis also includes a comparison of how each major system conceptualizes and treats the same complex client (Mrs. C).

We have limited our comparative analysis to 15 major systems of therapy. Systems have been omitted because they seem to be dying a natural death and are best left undisturbed, because they are so poorly developed that they have no identifiable theories of personality or psychopathology, or because they are primarily variations on themes already considered in the book. The final criterion for exclusion is empirical: No therapy system was excluded if at least 1% of American mental health professionals endorsed it as their primary theoretical orientation. Table 1.1 summarizes the self-identified theories of clinical psychologists, counseling psychologists, social workers, and counselors.

Defining Psychotherapy

A useful opening move in a psychotherapy textbook would be to define psychotherapy—the subject matter itself. However, no single definition of psychotherapy has won universal acceptance. Depending on one's theoretical orientation, psychotherapy can be conceptualized as interpersonal persuasion, health care, psychosocial education, professionally

Table 1.1 Theoretical Orientations of Psychotherapists in the United States

ORIENTATION	CLINICAL PSYCHOLOGISTS	COUNSELING PSYCHOLOGISTS	SOCIAL WORKERS	COUNSELORS
Behavioral	15%	5%	11%	8%
Cognitive	31%	19%	19%	29%
Constructivist	1%	1%	2%	2%
Eclectic/Integrative	22%	34%	26%	23%
Existential/Humanistic	1%	5%	4%	5%
Gestalt/Experiential	1%	2%	1%	2%
Interpersonal	4%	4%	3%	3%
Multicultural	1%	–	1%	1%
Psychoanalytic	3%	1%	5%	2%
Psychodynamic	15%	10%	9%	5%
Rogerian/Person-Centered	2%	3%	1%	10%
Systems	2%	5%	14%	7%
Other	2%	9%	4%	3%

Sources: Bechtoldt et al., 2001; Bike, Norcross, & Schatz, 2009; Goodyear et al., 2008; Norcross & Karpiak, 2012.

coached self-change, behavioral technology, a form of reparenting, the purchase of friendship, or a contemporary variant of shamanism, among others. It may be easier to practice psychotherapy than to explain or define it (London, 1986).

Our working definition of **psychotherapy** is as follows (Norcross, 1990):

Psychotherapy is the informed and intentional application of clinical methods and interpersonal stances derived from established psychological principles for the purpose of assisting people to modify their behaviors, cognitions, emotions, and/or other personal characteristics in directions that the participants deem desirable.

This admittedly broad definition is nonetheless a reasonably balanced one and a relatively neutral one in terms of theory and method. We have, for example, not specified the number or composition of the participants, as different theories and clients call for different formats. Similarly, the training and qualifications of the psychotherapist have not been delineated. We recognize multiple processes of change and the multidimensional nature of change; no attempt is made here to delimit the methods or content of therapeutic change. The requirement that the methods be "derived from established psychological principles" is sufficiently broad to permit clinical and/or research validation.

Our definition also explicitly mentions both "clinical methods and interpersonal stances." In some therapy systems, the active change mechanism has been construed as a treatment method; in other systems, the therapy relationship has been regarded as the primary source of change. Here, the interpersonal stances and experiences of the therapist are placed on an equal footing with methods.

Finally, we firmly believe that any activity defined as psychotherapy should be conducted only for the "purpose of assisting people" toward mutually agreed-upon goals. Otherwise—though it may be labeled psychotherapy—it becomes a subtle form of coercion or punishment.

The Value of Theory

The term **theory** possesses multiple meanings. In popular usage, theory is contrasted with practice, empiricism, or certainty. In scientific circles, theory is generally defined as a set of statements used to explain the data in a given area (Marx & Goodson, 1976). In psychotherapy, a theory (or system) is a consistent perspective on human behavior, psychopathology, and the mechanisms of therapeutic change. These appear to be the necessary, but perhaps not sufficient, features of a psychotherapy theory. Explanations of personality and human development are frequently included, but, as we shall see in the behavioral, constructivist, and integrative therapies, are not characteristic of all theories.

When colleagues learn that we are revising our textbook on psychotherapy theories, they occasionally question the usefulness of theories. Why not, they ask, simply produce a text on the actual practice or accumulated facts of psychotherapy? Our response takes many forms, depending on our mood at the time, but goes something like this. One fruitful way to learn about psychotherapy is to learn what the best minds have had to say about it and to compare what they say. Further, "absolute truth" will probably never be attained in psychotherapy, despite impressive advances in our knowledge and despite a large body of research. Instead, theory will always be with us to provide tentative approximations of "the truth."

Without a guiding theory or system of psychotherapy, clinicians would be vulnerable, directionless creatures bombarded with literally hundreds of impressions and pieces of information in a single session. Is it more important to ask about early memories, parent relationships, life's meaning, disturbing emotions, environmental reinforcers, recent cognitions, sexual conflicts, or something else in the first interview? At any given time, should we empathize, direct, teach, model, support, question, restructure, interpret, or remain silent in a therapy session? A psychotherapy theory describes the clinical phenomena, delimits the amount of relevant information, organizes that information, and integrates it all into a coherent body of knowledge that prioritizes our conceptualization and directs our treatment.

The model of humanity embedded within a psychotherapy theory is not merely a philosophical issue for purists. It affects which human capacities will be studied and cultivated, and which will be ignored and underdeveloped. Treatments inevitably follow from the clinician's underlying conception of pathology, health, reality, and the therapeutic process (Kazdin, 1984). Systems of therapy embody different visions of life, which imply different possibilities of human existence (Messer & Winokur, 1980).

In this regard, we want to dispute the misconception that psychotherapists aligning themselves with a particular theory are unwilling to adapt their practices to the demands of the situation and the patient. A voluntary decision to label oneself an adherent of a specific theory does not constitute a lifetime commitment of strict adherence or dogmatic reverence (Norcross, 1985). Good clinicians are flexible, and good theories are widely applicable. Thus, we see theories being adapted for use in a variety of contexts and clinicians borrowing heavily from divergent theories. A preference for one orientation does not preclude the use of concepts or methods from another. Put another way, the primary problem is not with narrow-gauge therapists, but with therapists who impose that narrowness onto their patients (Stricker, 1988).

Therapeutic Commonalities

Despite theoretical differences, there is a central and recognizable core of psychotherapy. This core distinguishes it from other activities—such as banking, farming, or physical therapy—and glues together variations of psychotherapy. This core is composed of **nonspecific** or **common factors** shared by all forms of psychotherapy and not specific to any one. More often than not, these therapeutic commonalities are not highlighted by theories as of central importance, but the research suggests exactly the opposite (Weinberger, 1995).

Mental health professionals have long observed that disparate forms of psychotherapy share common elements or core features. As early as 1936, Rosenzweig, noting that all forms of psychotherapy have cures to their credit, invoked the famous Dodo bird verdict from *Alice in Wonderland*, "Everybody has won and all must have prizes," to characterize psychotherapy outcomes. He then proposed, as a possible explanation for roughly equivalent outcomes, a number of therapeutic common factors, including psychological interpretation, catharsis, and the therapist's personality. In 1940, a meeting of prominent psychotherapists was held to ascertain areas of agreement among psychotherapy systems. The participants concurred that support, interpretation, insight, behavior change, a good relationship, and certain therapist characteristics were common features of successful psychotherapy (Watson, 1940).

If indeed the multitude of psychotherapy systems can all legitimately claim some success, then perhaps they are not as diverse as they appear on the surface. They probably share certain core features that may be the "curative" elements—those responsible for therapeutic success. To the extent that clinicians of different theories arrive at a common set of strategies, it is likely that what emerges will consist of robust phenomena, as they have managed to survive the distortions imposed by the different theoretical biases (Goldfried, 1980).

But, as one might expect, the common factors posited to date have been numerous and varied. Different authors focus on different domains or levels of psychosocial treatment; as a result, diverse conceptualizations of these commonalities have emerged.

Our consideration of common factors will be guided by the results of a study (Grencavage & Norcross, 1990) that reviewed 50 publications to determine convergence among proposed therapeutic commonalities. A total of 89 commonalities were proposed. The analysis revealed the most consensual commonalities were clients' positive expectations and a facilitative relationship. In what follows, we review the therapeutic commonalities of positive expectations, the therapeutic relationship, the Hawthorne effect, and related factors.

Positive Expectations

Expectation is one of the most widely debated and heavily investigated of the common (or nonspecific) variables. This commonality has been described as the "edifice complex"—the patient's faith in the institution itself, the door at the end of the pilgrimage, the confidence in the therapist and the treatment (Torrey, 1972).

A computer search yields more than 500 studies that have been conducted on patients' expectations of psychotherapy. The hypothesis of most of these studies is that the treatment is enhanced by the extent to which clients expect the treatment to be effective. Some critics hold that psychotherapy is nothing but a process of influence in which we induce an expectation in our clients that our treatment will cure them, and that any resulting improvement is a function of the client's expecting to improve. Surely many therapists wish on difficult days that the process were so simple!

The research evidence demonstrates that client expectations definitely contribute to therapy success, but is divided on how much (Clarkin & Levy, 2004; Constantino et al., 2011). Of the studies reporting expectation effects, most demonstrate that a high, positive expectation adds to the effectiveness of treatments. Up to one third of successful psychotherapy outcomes may be attributable to both the healer and the patient believing strongly in the effectiveness of the treatment (Roberts et al., 1993).

But psychotherapy can by no means be reduced to expectation effects alone. A sophisticated analysis of multiple outcome studies found that psychotherapy was more effective than common factors conditions, which in turn were more effective than no treatment at all (Barber et al., 1988). The ranking for therapeutic success is psychotherapy, placebo, and control (do nothing or wait), respectively. In fact, psychotherapy is nearly twice as effective as "nonspecific" or **placebo** treatments, which seek to induce positive expectations in clients (Grissom, 1996).

On the basis of the research, then, we will assume that expectation is an active ingredient in all systems of therapy. Rather than being the central process of change, however, a positive expectation is conceptualized as a critical precondition for therapy to continue. Most patients would not participate in a process that costs them dearly in time, money, and energy if they did not expect the process to help them. For clients to cooperate in being desensitized, hypnotized, or analyzed, it seems reasonable that most of them would need to expect some return on their investment. It is also our working assumption that therapists consciously strive to cultivate hope and enhance positive expectancies. Psychotherapy research need not demonstrate that treatment operates free from such nonspecific or common factors. Rather, the task is to demonstrate that specific treatments considered to carry the burden of client change go beyond the results that can be obtained by credibility alone.

Therapeutic Relationship

Psychotherapy is at root an interpersonal relationship. The single greatest area of convergence among psychotherapists, in their nominations of common factors (Grencavage & Norcross, 1990) and in their treatment recommendations (Norcross et al., 1990), is the development of a strong therapeutic alliance.

This most robust of common factors has consistently emerged as one of the major determinants of psychotherapy success. Across various types of psychotherapy, at least 12% of psychotherapy outcome—why patients improve in psychotherapy—is due to the therapeutic relationship (Norcross, 2011). To summarize the conclusions of an exhaustive review of the psychotherapy outcome literature (Bergin & Lambert, 1978): The largest variation in therapy outcome is accounted for by pre-existing client factors, such as expectations for change and severity of the disorder. The therapeutic relationship accounted for the second largest proportion of change, with the particular treatment method coming in third.

Still, the relative importance of the therapeutic relationship remains controversial. At one end of the continuum, some psychotherapy systems, such as the radical behavior therapies, view the relationship between client[1] and therapist as exerting little importance; the client change in therapy could just as readily occur with only an interactive computer program, without the therapist's presence. For these therapy systems, a human clinician is included for practical reasons only, because our technology in programming therapeutic processes is not developed fully enough to allow the therapist to be absent.

Toward the middle of the continuum, some therapy schools, such as cognitive therapies, view the relationship between clinician and client as one of the preconditions necessary for therapy to proceed. From this point of view, the client must trust and collaborate with the therapist before being able to participate in the process of change.

At the other end of the continuum, Rogers's person-centered therapy sees the relationship as *the* essential process that produces change. Because Carl Rogers (1957) has been most articulate in describing what he believes are the necessary conditions for a

---

[1]We will employ the terms *client* and *patient* interchangeably throughout this textbook because neither satisfactorily describes the therapy relationship and because we wish to remain theoretically neutral on this quarrelsome point.

therapeutic relationship, let us briefly outline his criteria so that we can use these for comparing systems on the nature of the therapeutic relationship.

1. The therapist must relate in a genuine manner.
2. The therapist must relate with unconditional positive regard.
3. The therapist must relate with accurate empathy.

These—and only these—conditions are necessary and sufficient for positive outcome, according to Rogers.

Then there are those psychotherapy systems, such as psychoanalysis, that see the relationship between therapist and patient primarily as the source of content to be examined in therapy. In this view, the relationship is important because it brings the content of therapy (the patient's interpersonal behavior) right into the consulting room. The content that needs to be changed is thus able to occur during therapy, rather than the person focusing on issues that occur outside of the consulting room.

In light of these various emphases on the role of the therapeutic relationship, it will be necessary to determine for each therapy system whether the relationship is conceived as (1) a precondition for change, (2) a process of change, and/or (3) a content to be changed. Moreover, in each chapter that follows, we will consider the relative contribution of the therapeutic relationship to treatment success, as well as the therapist behaviors designed to facilitate that relationship.

Hawthorne Effect

Psychologists have known for years that many people can improve in such behaviors as work output solely as a result of having special attention paid to them. In the classic Hawthorne studies (Roethlisberger & Dickson, 1939) on the effects of improved lighting on productivity in a factory, it was discovered that participants increased their output by simply being observed in a study and receiving extra attention. Usually such improvement is assumed to be due to increases in morale, novelty, and esteem that people experience from having others attend to them—a phenomenon that has come to be known as the **Hawthorne effect**.

One commonality among all psychosocial treatments is that the therapist pays special attention to the client. Consequently, attention has been assumed to be one of the common factors that impact the results of therapy. Anyone who has been in psychotherapy can appreciate the gratification that comes from having a competent professional's undivided attention for an hour. This special attention may indeed affect the course of therapy—including those occasional cases in which patients do not improve because they do not want to surrender such special attention.

Researchers have frequently found that attention does indeed lead to improvement, regardless of whether the attention is followed by any other therapeutic processes. In a classic study (Paul, 1967), 50% of public-speaking phobics demonstrated marked improvement in their symptoms by virtue of receiving an attention placebo intended to control for nonspecific variables such as attention. (In psychotherapy studies, an attention placebo control group receives a "treatment" that mimics the amount of time and attention received by the treatment group but that does not have a specific or intended effect.) Years of research demonstrate that attention can be a powerful common factor in therapy.

To conclude that any particular psychotherapy is more effective than an attention placebo, it is necessary that research include controls for attention effects or simply the passage of time. It is not enough to demonstrate a particular therapy is better than no treatment, because the improvement from that particular therapy may be due entirely to the attention given to the patients.

Several research designs are available to measure or control for the effects of attention in psychotherapy. The most popular design is to use placebo groups, as in Paul's study, in which control participants were given as much attention as clients in therapy but did not participate in processes designed to produce change. An alternative design is to compare the effectiveness of one treatment with that of another, such as psychoanalytic therapy with cognitive therapy. If one therapeutic approach does better than the other, we can conclude that the differential improvement is due to more than just attention, because the less effective treatment included—and therefore controlled for—the effects of attention. However, we do not know whether the less effective therapy is anything other than a placebo effect, even if it leads to greater improvement than no treatment. Finally, in such comparative studies, if both therapies lead to significant improvement, but neither therapy does better than the other, we cannot conclude that the therapies are anything more than Hawthorne effects, unless an attention placebo control has also been included in the study. To be considered a controlled evaluation of a psychotherapy's efficacy, studies must include controls for the Hawthorne effect and related factors.

Other Commonalities

In his classic *Persuasion and Healing*, Jerome Frank (1961; Frank & Frank, 1991) posited that all psychotherapeutic methods are elaborations and variations of age-old procedures of psychological healing. The features that distinguish psychotherapies from each other, however, receive special emphasis in the pluralistic, competitive American society. Because the prestige and financial security of psychotherapists hinge on their being able to show that their particular system is more successful than that of their rivals, little glory has traditionally been accorded to the identification of shared or common components.

Frank argues that therapeutic change is predominantly a function of common factors: an emotionally charged, confiding relationship; a healing setting; a rationale or conceptual scheme; and a

therapeutic ritual. Other consensual commonalities include an inspiring and socially sanctioned therapist; opportunity for catharsis; acquisition and practice of new behaviors; exploration of the "inner world" of the patient; suggestion; and interpersonal learning (Grencavage & Norcross, 1990). Many observers now conclude that features shared by all therapies account for an appreciable amount of observed improvement in clients.

So powerful are these therapeutic commonalities for some clinicians that explicitly common factors therapies have been proposed. Sol Garfield (1980, 1992), to take one prominent example, finds the mechanisms of change in virtually all approaches to be rooted in the therapeutic relationship, emotional release, explanation and interpretation, reinforcement, desensitization, confronting a problem, and skill training. We shall return to common factors approaches in Chapter 16 (Integrative Therapies).

Specific Factors

At the same time, common factors theorists recognize the value of unique—or specific—factors in disparate psychotherapies. A psychotherapist cannot practice nonspecifically; specific techniques and relationships fill the treatment hour. Indeed, research has demonstrated the differential effectiveness of a few therapies with specific disorders, such as exposure therapy for obsessive-compulsive disorder, parent management training for conduct problems, and systemic therapy for couples conflict. As a discipline, psychotherapy will advance by integrating the power of common factors with the pragmatics of **specific factors**. We now turn to the processes of change—the relatively specific or unique contributions of a therapy system.

Processes of Change

There exists, as we said earlier in this chapter, an expanding morass of psychotherapy theories and an endless proliferation of specific techniques. Consider the relatively simple case of smoking cessation: In one of our early studies, we identified more than 50 formal treatments employed by health professionals and 130 different techniques used by successful self-changers to stop smoking. Is there no smaller and more intelligible framework by which to examine and compare the psychotherapies?

The **transtheoretical**—across theories—model reduces the therapeutic morass to a manageable number of processes of change. There are literally hundreds of global theories of psychotherapy, and we will probably never reach common ground in the theoretical or philosophical realm. There are thousands of specific techniques in psychotherapy, and we will rarely agree on the specific, moment-to-moment methods to use. By contrast, the **processes of change** represent a middle level of abstraction between global theories (such as psychoanalysis, cognitive, and humanistic) and specific techniques (such as dream analysis, progressive muscle relaxation, and family sculpting). Table 1.2 illustrates this intermediate level of abstraction represented by the processes of change.

It is at this intermediate level of analysis—processes or principles of change—that meaningful points of convergence and contention may be found among psychotherapy systems. It is also at this intermediate level that expert psychotherapists typically formulate their treatment plans—not in terms of global theories or specific techniques but as change processes for their clients.

Processes of change are the covert and overt activities that people use to alter emotions, thoughts, behaviors, or relationships related to a particular problem or more general patterns of living. In fewer words, processes are how people change, within psychotherapy and between therapy sessions. These processes were derived theoretically from a comparative analysis of the leading systems of psychotherapy (Prochaska, 1979). In the following sections, we introduce these processes of change.

Consciousness Raising

Traditionally, increasing an individual's consciousness has been one of the prime processes of change in psychotherapy. **Consciousness raising** sounds so contemporary, yet therapists from a variety of persuasions have been working for decades to increase the consciousness of clients. Beginning with Freud's objective "to make the unconscious conscious," all so-called insight psychotherapies begin by working to raise the individual's level of awareness. It is fitting that the **insight** or **awareness therapies** work with consciousness, which is frequently viewed as a human characteristic that emerged with the evolution of language.

With language and consciousness, humans do not need to respond reflexively to every stimulus. For example, the mechanical energy from a hand hitting against our back does not cause us to react with movement. Instead, we respond thoughtfully to the information contained in that touch, such as whether the hand touching us is a friend patting us on the back, a robber grabbing us, or a partner hitting us. In order to respond effectively, we must process information to guide us in making a response appropriate to the situation. Consciousness-raising therapies attempt to increase the information available to individuals so they can make the most effective responses to life.

For each of the change processes, the psychotherapist's focus can be on producing change either at the level of the individual's experience or at the level of the individual's environment. When

Table 1.2 Levels of Abstraction		
LEVEL	ABSTRACTION	EXAMPLES
High	Global theories	Psychodynamic, Gestalt, behavioral
Medium	Change processes	Consciousness raising, counterconditioning
Low	Clinical techniques	Interpretation, two-chair technique, self-monitoring

the information given a client concerns the individual's own actions and experiences, we call that **feedback**. An example of the feedback process occurred in the case of a stern and proper middle-aged woman who was unaware of just how angry she appeared to others. She could not connect her children's avoidance of her or her recent rash of automobile accidents with rage, because she kept insisting that she was not angry. After viewing videotapes of herself interacting with members of a psychotherapy group, however, she was stunned. All she could say was, "My God, how angry I seem to be!"[2]

When the information given a client concerns environmental events, we call this **education**. An example of therapeutic movement due to education occurred in the case of an aging man who was distressed over the fact that his time to attain erections and reach orgasms had increased noticeably over the past few years. He was very relieved when he learned that such a delay was quite normal in older men.

Defenses ward off threatening information about ourselves in response to education and feedback. These defense mechanisms are like blinders or the "rose-colored glasses" that some people use to selectively attend only to positive information about themselves and to ignore negative input. Cognitive blinders prevent individuals from increasing their consciousness without feedback or education from an outside party.

For example, my (JOP's) wife, who is also a psychotherapist, confronted me with the following information that made me aware of blinders I was wearing: We were trying to anticipate who would be on each other's list of sexually attractive individuals. I was absolutely sure that my first three guesses would be high on my wife's list. When I said a friend's name, my wife laughed and said that she knew I always thought that, but she wasn't attracted to him. She also said that she was now sure that his wife was on my list. My next two guesses were also wrong, but my wife was quickly able to guess that I found their wives attractive. I was amazed to realize how much I had been projecting over the years and how my projection kept me from being aware of the qualities in men that my wife found appealing.

How can our awareness of such information lead to behavior change? Think of our consciousness as a beam of light. The information unavailable to us is like a darkness in which we can be lost, held back, or directed without knowing the source of the influence. In the darkness, we are blind; we do not possess sufficient sight or light to guide us effectively in our lives. For example, without being aware of how aging normally affects sexual response, an aging man (or woman) would not know whether the best direction would be to admit he (or she) was over the hill and give up on sex, to eat two raw oysters a day as an aphrodisiac, to take Viagra, or to enjoy his or her present behavior without living up to some media stereotype of sexuality.

As we will see, many psychotherapy systems agree that people can change as a result of raised consciousness—increasing experiential or environmental information previously unavailable to them. The disagreement among these consciousness-raising psychotherapies lies in which concrete techniques are most effective in doing so.

Catharsis

Catharsis has one of the longest traditions as a process of change and refers to the therapeutic release of pent-up feelings and emotions. The ancient Greeks believed that expressing emotions was a superb mechanism of providing personal

---

[2]In the case of this woman, as with so many clients, we cannot demonstrate that the way we conceptualize the person's problems is, in fact, the way things really are. We cannot, for example, demonstrate in an empirical manner that this woman's problems were due to angry feelings that were outside of her awareness. Nevertheless, it is still useful in psychotherapy to make provisional assumptions about the origins of a client's problems. As case illustrations are presented throughout this book, they will be described in the manner that we found most helpful for the purposes of treatment, without assuming some ultimate validity of the clinical interpretations.

relief and behavioral improvement. Human suffering was, quite literally, let out and let go.

Historically, catharsis used a hydraulic model of emotions, in which unacceptable emotions—such as anger, guilt, or anxiety—are blocked from direct expression. The damming off of such emotions results in pressure from affects (or emotions) seeking some form of release, however indirect, as when anger is expressed somatically through headaches. If emotions can be released more directly in psychotherapy, then their reservoir of energy is discharged, and the person is freed from a source of symptoms.

In a different analogy, the patient with blocked emotions is seen as emotionally constipated. What these patients need to release psychological suffering is a good, emotional bowel movement. In this analogy, psychotherapy serves as a psychological enema that allows patients to purge their emotional blockage. The therapeutic process is aimed at helping patients break through their emotional blocks. By expressing the dark side of themselves in the presence of another, the individuals can better accept such emotions as natural phenomena that need not be so severely controlled in the future.

Most often, this therapeutic process has been at the level of individual experience, in which the cathartic reactions come directly from within the person. We shall call this form of catharsis **corrective emotional experiences**. As the term suggests, an intense emotional experience produces a psychological correction.

A fellow clinician related a cathartic experience several years ago when she was fighting off a bout of depression. She was struggling to get in touch with the source of her depression, so she took a mental health day off from work. Alone at home, she put on music and started to express her feelings in a free form of dance that she could perform only when no one else was present. After some very releasing movements, she experienced childhood rage toward her mother for always being on her back. She soon let herself express her intense anger by tearing her blouse to shreds. By the time her partner arrived home, she felt quite relieved, although her partner, looking at the destroyed blouse, wondered aloud whether she had flipped.

The belief that cathartic reactions can be evoked by observing emotional scenes in the environment dates back at least to Aristotle's writings on theater and music. In honor of this tradition, we will call this source of catharsis **dramatic relief**.

A patient suffering from headaches, insomnia, and other symptoms of depression found himself weeping heavily during Ingmar Bergman's movie *Scenes from a Marriage*. He began to experience how disappointed he was in himself for having traded a satisfying marriage for security. His depression began to lift because of the inspiration he felt from Bergman to leave his hopelessly devitalized marriage.

Choosing

The power of choice in producing behavior change has been in the background of many psychotherapy systems. The concept of **choosing** has lacked respectability in the highly deterministic worldview of most scientists. Many clinicians have not wanted to provide ammunition for their critics' accusations of tender-mindedness by openly discussing freedom and choice. Consequently, we will see that many therapy systems implicitly assume that clients will choose to change as a result of psychological treatment but do not articulate the means by which clients come to use the process of choosing.

With so little open consideration of choosing as a change process (with the exception of existential and experiential therapists), it is predictably difficult to suggest what choice is a function of. Some theorists argue choice is irreducible, because to reduce choice to other events is to advance the paradox that such events determine our choices. Human action is seen as freely chosen, and to say that anything else determines our choice is to show bad faith in ourselves as free beings. Few clinicians, however, accept such a radical view of freedom for their clients; they usually believe that many conditions limit choice.

From a behavioral perspective, choice would be a partial function of the number of alternative responses available to an individual. If only one response is available, there is no choice. From a humanistic perspective, the number of available responses can radically increase if we become more conscious of alternatives that we have not previously considered. For a variety of psychotherapy systems, then, an increase in choice is thought to result from an increase in consciousness.

The freedom to choose has traditionally been construed as a uniquely human behavior made possible by the acquisition of consciousness that accompanies the development of language. Responsibility is the burden that accompanies the awareness that we are the ones able to respond, to speak for ourselves. Insofar that choice and responsibility are possible through language and consciousness, it seems only natural that the therapeutic process of choosing is a verbal or awareness process.

The easiest choices follow from accurate information processing that entails an awareness of the consequences of particular alternatives. If a menopausal woman were informed, for example, that hormone replacement therapy (HRT) eventually caused cancer in all women, then her best alternative would be to follow the information she has just processed. With HRT, however, as with so many life decisions, we are not aware of all the consequences of choice, and the consequences are rarely absolute. In these situations, there are no definitive external guidelines, and we are confronted with the possibility of choosing an alternative that might be a serious mistake. Then our ability to choose is more clearly a function of our ability to accept the anxiety inherent in accepting responsibility for our future.

An example of so-called existential anxiety was seen in a college student who consulted me about the panic attacks she was experiencing since she informed her parents of her unplanned pregnancy. They insisted that she get an abortion, but she and her husband wanted to have the baby. They were both students, and entirely dependent on her wealthy parents for financial support. Her parents had informed her that the consequence of having a baby at this time would be disinheritance, because they believed she would not finish college once she had a baby. In 21 years she had never openly differed with her parents, and although she was controlled by them, she had always felt protected by them as well. Now, after just a few psychotherapy sessions, she became more aware that her panic attacks reflected her need to choose. Her basic choice was not whether she was going to sacrifice her fetus to her family's fortune, but whether she was going to continue to sacrifice herself.

At an experiential level, then, choosing involves the individual becoming aware of new alternatives, including the deliberate creation of new alternatives for living. This process also involves experiencing the anxiety inherent in being responsible for which alternative is followed. We will call this experiential level of choosing a move toward **self-liberation**.

When changes in the environment make more alternatives available to individuals, such as more jobs being open to gays and lesbians, we will call this a move toward **social liberation**. Psychotherapists working for such social changes are usually called advocates.

Conditional Stimuli

At the opposite extreme from changing through choosing is changing by modifying the conditional stimuli that control our responses. Alterations in conditional stimuli are necessitated when the individual's behavior is elicited by classical (Pavlovian) conditioning. When troublesome responses are conditioned, then being conscious of the stimuli will not produce change, nor can conditioning be overcome just by choosing to change. We need, literally, to change the environment or the behavior.

Again, either we can modify the way individuals behave in response to particular stimuli, or we can modify the environment to minimize the probability of the stimuli occurring. Changing our behavior to the stimuli is known as **counterconditioning**, whereas changing the environment involves **stimulus control**.

Counterconditioning was used in the treatment of a woman with a penetration phobia who responded to intercourse with involuntary muscle spasms. This condition, known as vaginismus, prevented penetration. She did not want to modify her environment, but rather to change her response to her partner. As in most counterconditioning cases, the procedure involved a gradual approach to the conditioned stimulus of intercourse while learning an incompatible response. She learned relaxation, which was incompatible with the undesired response of anxiety and muscle spasms that had previously been elicited by intercourse. Counterconditioning is learning to do the healthy opposite—relaxation instead of anxiety, assertion instead of passivity, exposure instead of avoidance, for example.

Stimulus control entails restructuring the environment to reduce the probability that a particular conditional stimulus will occur. A high-strung college student suffered from a host of anxiety symptoms, including considerable distress when driving his car. Whenever the car began to shake in the slightest, the student would also begin to shake. He attributed this particular problem to a frightening episode earlier in the year, when the universal joint on his car broke with a startling noise. Not once but three times it broke before a mechanic discovered that the real cause was a bent drive shaft. Because the problem appeared to be a function of conditioning, a counterconditioning approach was deemed

the treatment of choice. Before the treatment was under way, however, the student traded in his car for a van. Because his anxiety response did not generalize to his van, he solved his problem through his own stimulus control procedure. Eliminating or avoiding environmental cues that provoke problem behaviors is the core of stimulus control.

Contingency Control

Axiomatic for many behavior therapists is that behavior is controlled by its consequences. As most of us have learned, if a response is reinforced, then the probability of that response is increased. If, on the other hand, a punishment follows a particular response, then we are less likely to emit that response. As B. F. Skinner demonstrated, changing the contingencies governing our behavior frequently leads to changed behavior. The extent to which a particular reinforcer or punisher controls behavior is a function of many variables, including the immediacy, saliency, and schedule of the consequences. From humanistic and cognitive-behavioral points of view, the individual's valuing of particular consequences is also important in contingency control.

If behavior changes are made by modifying the contingencies in the environment, we call this **contingency management**. Desirable, healthy behaviors are followed by reinforcement; in select cases, undesirable, pathological behaviors are followed by punishment.

For example, a graduate student with a bashful bladder wanted to increase his ability to use public restrooms; he also wanted more money to improve his style of living. Therefore, he made a contingency contract with me (JOP) that earned him two dollars for each time during the week he urinated in a public restroom. I am pleased to say that I lost money on that case.

Seldom have behavior therapists considered the alternative, but there are effective means to modify our behavior without changing the consequences themselves. Modifying our internal responses to external consequences without changing those consequences will be called **reevaluation**.

A very shy man continued to desire a relationship with a woman but avoided asking anyone out because of his anticipation that he would be rejected. After several intensive discussions in psychotherapy, he began to accept that when a woman turns down a date, it is a statement about her and not about him. We do not know whether she is waiting for someone else to ask her out, whether she doesn't like mustaches, whether she is in a committed relationship, or whether she doesn't know him well enough—we simply don't know what her saying no says about him. After reevaluating how he would interpret being turned down for a date, the fellow began asking out women, even though he was rejected on his first request for a date. The external consequences of his behavior were the same, but he reevaluated their personal meaning.

Initial Integration of Processes of Change

A summary of these processes of change is presented in Table 1.3. The processes of consciousness raising, catharsis, and choosing represent the heart of the listed traditional insight or **awareness psychotherapies**, including the psychoanalytic,

existential, and humanistic traditions. These psychotherapy systems focus primarily on the subjective aspects of the individual—the processes occurring within the skin of the human. This perspective on the individual finds greater potential for inner-directed changes that can counteract some of the external pressures from the environment.

The processes of conditional stimuli and contingency control represent the core of **action therapies**, including those in the behavioral, cognitive, and systemic traditions. These psychotherapy systems focus primarily on the external and environmental forces that set limits on the individual's potential for inner-directed change. These processes are what the existentialists would call the more objective level of the person.

Our integrative, transtheoretical model suggests that to focus only on the awareness processes of consciousness, catharsis, and choice is to act as if inner-directedness is the whole picture and to ignore the genuine limits the environment places on individual change. On the other hand, the action emphasis on the more objective, environmental processes selectively ignores our potential for inner, subjective change.

An integrative model posits that a synthesis of both awareness and action processes provides more balanced and effective psychotherapy that moves along the continuous dimensions of inner

Table 1.3 Change Processes at Experiential and Environmental Levels

AWARENESS OR INSIGHT THERAPIES	ACTION OR BEHAVIORAL THERAPIES
Consciousness raising	**Conditional stimuli**
Experiential level: feedback	Experiential level: counterconditioning
Environmental level: education	Environmental level: stimulus control
Catharsis	**Contingency control**
Experiential level: corrective emotional experiences	Experiential level: reevaluation
Environmental level: dramatic relief	Environmental level: contingency management
Choosing	
Experiential level: self-liberation	
Environmental level: social liberation	

to outer control, subjective to objective functioning, and self-initiated to environmental-induced changes. Integrating the change processes afford a more complete picture of humans by accepting our potential for inner change while recognizing the limits that environments and contingencies place on such change. In Chapter 17, we will summarize the research evidence for these processes of change and our transtheoretical model.

Before leaving the processes of change, we would offer two additional comments about them. First, please do not confuse the change processes with components of specific therapy systems. Consciousness raising, contingency control, and the other processes are not methods suggested by specific theories. Rather, they are generic change strategies that cut across many theories. Second, the names of many of the change processes are probably new to you. But rest assured that you will become familiar and comfortable with them as you move through the remainder of the book.

Therapeutic Content

The processes of change are the distinctive contributions of a system of psychotherapy. The content to be changed in a particular therapy system is largely a carryover from that system's theory of personality and psychopathology. Many books purportedly focusing on psychotherapy frequently confuse content and process. They wind up examining the content of therapy, with little explanation about the change processes. As a consequence, they are actually books on theories of personality rather than theories of psychotherapy.

The distinction between process and content in psychotherapy is fundamental. As we shall see, psychotherapy systems without theories of personality are primarily process theories and have few predetermined concepts about the content of therapy. Behavioral, integrative, systemic, and solution-focused theories attempt to capitalize on the unique aspects of each case by restricting the imposition of

formal content (Held, 1991). Other systems, such as Adlerian, existential, and culture-sensitive therapies, which adopt change processes from other therapy systems, primarily address the content of therapy. Many systems of therapy differ primarily in their content, while agreeing on the change processes.

Put differently, theories of personality and psychopathology tell us *what* needs to be changed; theories of process tell us *how* change occurs.

Because psychotherapy systems espouse many more differences regarding the content of therapy, it is more difficult to bring order and integration to this fragmented field. A refreshing guide is Maddi's (1996) comparative model for personality theories. We have adapted parts of Maddi's model in synthesizing and prioritizing the vast array of content—the what—in psychotherapy.

Most systems of therapy assume a conflict view of personality and psychopathology. Some conflict-oriented systems believe psychopathology results from conflicts within the individual. For these, we shall use the term *intrapersonal conflicts*, indicating that the conflicts are competing forces within the person, such as a conflict between desires to be independent and fears of leaving home. Other therapy systems focus on interpersonal conflicts, such as chronic disagreements between a woman who likes to save money and a man who likes to spend money. Another group of therapies focuses primarily on the conflicts that occur between an individual and society. We shall call these individuo-social conflicts; an example is the tension of an individual who wants to live an openly gay life but is afraid of the ostracism that may result from society's bias against homosexuality. Finally, an increasing number of therapies are concerned with helping individuals go beyond conflict to attain fulfillment.

In our integrative model, we assume that patients' dysfunctions emanate from conflicts at different levels of personality functioning. Some patients express intrapersonal conflicts, others evidence interpersonal conflicts, and still others are in conflict with society. Some clients have resolved their principal conflicts and turn to psychotherapy with questions as to how they can best create a more fulfilling existence.

Because different patients are troubled at different levels of functioning, we will compare the psychotherapy systems in terms of how each conceptualizes and treats typical problems at each level of conflict. At the intrapersonal level, we will examine how each therapy system addresses conflicts over anxiety and defenses, self-esteem, and personal responsibility. At the interpersonal level, we will consider problems with intimacy and sexuality, communication, hostility, and interpersonal control. At the individuo-social level, we will compare their perspectives on adjustment versus transcendence and impulse control. At the level of transcending conflicts to fulfillment, we will examine the ultimate questions of meaning in life and the ideal person that would emerge from successful psychotherapy. Table 1.4 summarizes the **therapeutic content** occurring at different levels of personality.

Honest differences abound over whether particular problems—such as addictive, mood,

and relationship disorders—are most profitably conceptualized as intra- or interpersonal conflicts. Thus, we expect disagreement over our assignment of problems to a particular level of personality functioning.

Any viable theory of personality can reduce all psychopathology to a single level of functioning that the theory assumes to be critical. For example, an intrapersonal theory can marshal a convincing case that sexual disorders are primarily due to conflicts within individuals, such as conflicts between sexual desires and performance anxieties. By contrast, an individuo-social theory could summon a coherent argument that sexual disorders are primarily due to the inevitable tensions between an individual's sexual desires and society's sexual prohibitions. Our integrative assumption is that a comparative analysis of psychotherapies will demonstrate that particular systems have been especially effective in conceptualizing and treating problems related to their level of personality theory.

In comparing psychotherapy systems, we will discover that a theory's level of personality will largely dictate the number of people in the consulting room and the focus of the therapeutic transaction. If a theory focuses on intrapersonal functioning, then the therapy is much more likely to work solely with the individual, because the basic problem is assumed to lie within the individual. If, by contrast, a theory concentrates on interpersonal functioning, then it is more likely to involve two or more persons in conflict, such as a couple or family members.

Psychotherapies focusing on individuo-social conflicts will work to change the client, if the therapist's values are on the side of mainstream society. For example, in working with a pedophile who experiences no inner conflict over having sexual relations with children, a therapist will try to change the client, in that the therapist's values converge with society's values that this sexual behavior is unacceptable. However, if the therapist's values are on the side of the individual in a particular conflict,

---

Table 1.4 Therapeutic Content at Different Levels of Personality

1. Intrapersonal conflicts
   a. Anxieties and defenses
   b. Self-esteem problems
   c. Personal responsibility
2. Interpersonal conflicts
   a. Intimacy and sexuality
   b. Communication
   c. Hostility
   d. Control of others
3. Individuo-social conflicts
   a. Adjustment versus transcendence
   b. Impulse control
4. Beyond conflict to fulfillment
   a. Meaning in life
   b. The ideal person

such as a Hispanic/Latino wanting to freely express his ethnicity in a White-dominated workplace, then a therapist is far more likely to work for the client and to support movements that are transforming society. In comparing psychotherapy systems, then, we will examine which level of personality functioning is emphasized and whether such an emphasis leads to working primarily with an individual, with two or more people together, or with groups seeking to alter society.

The Case of Mrs. C

Psychotherapy systems are not merely static combinations of change processes, theoretical contents, and research studies. The systems are, first and foremost, concerned with serious disorders afflicting real people. In comparing systems, it is essential to picture how the psychotherapies conceptualize and treat the presenting problems of an actual client. The client selected for comparative purposes is Mrs. C.

Mrs. C is a 47-year-old mother of six children: Arlene, 17; Barry, 15; Charles, 13; Debra, 11; Ellen, 9; and Frederick, 7. Without reading further, an astute observer might be able to discern Mrs. C's personality configuration. The orderliness of children named alphabetically and of childbirths every 2 years are consistent with obsessive-compulsive disorder (OCD).

For the past 10 years, Mrs. C has been plagued by compulsive washing. Her baseline charts, in which she recorded her behavior each day before treatment began, indicated that she washed her hands 25 to 30 times a day, 5 to 10 minutes at a time. Her daily morning shower lasted about 2 hours with rituals involving each part of her body, beginning with her rectum. If she lost track of where she was in her ritual, then she would have to start all over. A couple of times this had resulted in her husband, George, going off to work while his wife was in the shower only to return 8 hours later to find her still involved in the lengthy ritual.

To avoid lengthy showers, George had begun helping his wife keep track of her ritual, so that at times she would yell out, "Which arm, George?" and he would yell back, "Left arm, Martha." His participation in the shower ritual required George to rise at 5:00 A.M. in order to have his wife out of the shower before he left for work at 7:00 A.M. After 2 years of this schedule, George was ready to explode.

George was, understandably, becoming increasingly impatient with many of his wife's related symptoms. She would not let anyone wear a pair of underwear more than once and often wouldn't even let these underwear be washed. There were piles of dirty underwear in each corner of the house. When we asked her husband to gather up the underwear for the laundry, we asked him to count them, but he quit counting after the thousandth pair. He was depressed to realize that he had more than $1,000 invested in once-worn underwear.

Other objects were scattered around the house, because a fork or a can of food dropped on the floor could not be retrieved in Mrs. C's presence. She felt it was contaminated. Mrs. C had been doing no housework—no cooking, cleaning, or washing—for years. One of her children described the house as a "state dump," and my (JOP) visit to the home confirmed this impression.

Mrs. C did work part-time. What would be a likely job for her? Something to do with washing, of course. In fact, she was a dental technician, which involved washing and sterilizing all of the dentist's equipment.

As if these were not sufficient concerns, Mrs. C had become very unappealing in appearance. She had not purchased a dress in 7 years, and her clothes were becoming ragged. Never in her life had she been to a beautician and now she seldom combed her own hair. Her incessant washing of her body and hair led to a presentation somewhere between a prune and a boiled lobster with the frizzies.

Mrs. C's washing ritual also entailed walking around the house nude from the waist up as she went from her bedroom bath to the downstairs bath to complete her washing. This was especially upsetting to Mr. C because of the embarrassment it was producing in their teenage sons. The children were also upset by Mrs. C's frequently

(continued)

nagging them to wash their hands and change their underwear, and she would not allow them to entertain friends in the house.

Consistent with OCD features, Mrs. C was a hoarder: she had two closets filled with hundreds of towels and sheets, dozens of unused earrings, and her entire wardrobe from the past 20 years. She did not consider this hoarding a problem because it was a family characteristic, which she believed she inherited from her mother and from her mother's mother.

Mrs. C also suffered from a sexual arousal disorder; in common parlance, she was "frigid." She said she had never been sexually excited in her life, but at least for the first 13 years of her marriage she was willing to engage in sexual relations to satisfy her husband. However, in the past 2 years they had had intercourse just twice, because sex had become increasingly unpleasant for her.

To complete the list, Mrs. C was currently clinically depressed. She had made a suicide gesture by swallowing a bottle of aspirin because she had an inkling that her psychotherapist was giving up on her and her husband was probably going to commit her to a psychiatric hospital.

Mrs. C's compulsive rituals revolved around an obsession with pinworms. Her oldest daughter had come home with pinworms 10 years earlier during a severe flu epidemic. Mrs. C had to care for a sick family while pregnant, sick with the flu herself, and caring for a demanding 1-year-old child. Her physician told her that to avoid having the pinworms spread throughout the family, Mrs. C would have to be extremely careful about the children's underwear, clothes, and sheets and that she should boil all of these articles to kill any pinworm eggs. Mr. C confirmed that both she and her husband were rather anxious about a pinworm epidemic in the home and were both preoccupied with cleanliness during this time. However, Mrs. C's preoccupation with cleanliness and pinworms continued even after it had been confirmed that her daughter's pinworms were gone.

The C couple acknowledged a relatively good marriage before the pinworm episode. They had both wanted a sizable family, and Mr. C's income as a business executive had allowed them to afford a large family and comfortable home without financial strain. During the first 13 years of their marriage, Mrs. C had demonstrated some of her obsessive-compulsive traits, but never to such a degree that Mr. C considered them a problem. Mr. C and the older children recalled many happy times with Mrs. C, and they seemed to have kept alive the warmth and love that they had once shared with this now preoccupied person.

Mrs. C hailed from a strict, authoritarian, and sexually repressed Catholic family. She was the middle of three girls, all of whom were dominated by a father who was 6 feet, 4 inches tall and weighed 250 pounds. When Mrs. C was a teenager, her father would wait up for her after dates to question her about what she had done; he once went so far as to follow her on a date. He tolerated absolutely no expression of anger, especially toward himself, and when she would try to explain her point of view politely, he would often tell her to shut up. Mrs. C's mother was a cold, compulsive woman who repeatedly regaled her daughters about her disgust with sex. She also frequently warned her daughters about diseases and the importance of cleanliness.

In developing a psychotherapy plan for Mrs. C, one of the differential diagnostic questions was whether Mrs. C was plagued with a severe obsessive-compulsive disorder or whether her symptoms were masking a latent schizophrenic process. A full battery of psychological testing was completed, and the test results were consistent with those from previous evaluations that had found no evidence of a thought disorder or other signs of psychotic processes.

Mrs. C had previously undergone a total of 6 years of mental health treatment, and throughout this time the clinicians had always considered her problems to be severely neurotic in nature. The only time schizophrenia was offered as a diagnosis was after some extensive individual psychotherapy failed to lead to any improvement. The consensus in our clinic was that Mrs. C was demonstrating a severe OCD that was going to be extremely difficult to treat.

At the end of the following chapters, we will see how each of the psychotherapy systems might explain Mrs. C's problems and how their treatment might help her to overcome these devastating preoccupations.

Key Terms

action therapies

awareness (insight)
    therapies

catharsis

choosing

common (nonspecific)
    factors

consciousness raising

contingency
    management

corrective emotional
    experiences

counterconditioning

dramatic relief

education

expectation

feedback

Hawthorne effect

integration

placebo

processes of change

psychotherapy

reevaluation

self-liberation

social liberation

specific factors

stimulus control

theory

therapeutic content

transtheoretical

Recommended Readings

Castonguay, L. G., & Beutler, L. E. (Eds.). (2006). *Principles of therapeutic change that work*. New York: Oxford University Press.

Frank, J. D., & Frank, J. (1991). *Persuasion and healing* (3rd ed.). Baltimore: Johns Hopkins University Press.

Lambert, M. J. (Ed.). (2013). *Handbook of psychotherapy and behavior change* (6th ed.). New York: Wiley.

Nathan, P. E., & Gorman, J. M. (Eds.). (2007). *Treatments that work* (3rd ed.). New York: Oxford University Press.

Norcross, J. C. (Ed.). (2011). *Psychotherapy relationships that work* (2nd ed.). New York: Oxford University Press.

Norcross, J. C., VandenBos, G. R., & Freedheim, D. K. (Eds.). (2010). *History of psychotherapy: Continuity and change* (2nd ed.). Washington, DC: American Psychological Association.

Maddi, S. R. (1996). *Personality theories: A comparative analysis* (6th ed.). Pacific Grove, CA: Brooks/Cole.

Prochaska, J. O., Norcross, J. C., & DiClemente, C. C. (1995). *Changing for good*. New York: Avon.

Zeig, J. K., & Munion, W. M. (Eds.). (1990). *What is psychotherapy? Contemporary perspectives*. San Francisco: Jossey-Bass.

Journals: *American Journal of Orthopsychiatry; American Journal of Psychiatry; American Journal of Psychotherapy; Archives of General Psychiatry; Brief Treatment and Crisis Intervention; British Journal of Psychotherapy; Clinical Case Studies; Clinical Psychology and Psychotherapy; Clinical Social Work Journal; Counselling and Psychotherapy Research; International Journal for the Advancement of Counseling; Journal of Child and Adolescent Psychotherapy; Journal of Clinical Psychology: In Session; Journal of College Student Psychotherapy; Journal of Consulting and Clinical Psychology; Journal of Contemporary Psychotherapy; Journal of Counseling and Development; Journal of Counseling Psychology; Journal of Infant, Child, and Adolescent Psychotherapy; Journal of Mental Health Counseling; Pragmatic Case Studies in Psychotherapy; Journal of Psychosocial Nursing and Mental Health Services; Journal of Psychotherapy in Independent Practice; Psychotherapy; Psychotherapy and Psychosomatics; Psychotherapy Networker; Psychotherapy Patient; Psychotherapy Research; The Scientific Review of Mental Health Practice; Voices: The Art and Science of Psychotherapy*.

Recommended Websites

American Association for Marriage and Family Therapy:
www.aamft.org

American Counseling Association:
www.counseling.org

American Psychiatric Association:
www.psych.org/

American Psychiatric Nurses Association:
www.apna.org/

American Psychological Association:
www.apa.org/

National Association of Social Workers:
www.naswdc.org/

Society for Psychotherapy Research:
www.psychotherapyresearch.org/

CHAPTER 2

Psychoanalytic Therapies

Sigmund Freud

National Library of Medicine

Karen was to be terminated from her nursing program if her problems were not resolved. She had always been a competent student who seemed to get along well with peers and patients. Now, since beginning her rotation on 3 South, a surgical ward, she was plagued by headaches and dizzy spells.

Of more serious consequence were the two medical errors she had made when dispensing medications to patients. She realized that these errors could have proved fatal and was as concerned as her nursing faculty that she understand why such problems had begun in this final year of her education. Karen knew she had many negative feelings toward the head nurse on 3 South, but she did not believe these feelings could account for her current dilemma.

After a few weeks of psychotherapy, I (JOP) realized that one of Karen's important conflicts revolved around the death of her father when she was 12 years old. Karen had just gone to live with her father after being with her mother for 7 years. She remembered how upset she was when her

father had a heart attack and had to be rushed to the hospital. For a while it looked as though her father was going to pull through, and Karen began enjoying her daily visits to see him. During one of these visits, her father clutched his chest in obvious pain and told Karen to get a nurse. She remembered how helpless she felt when she could not find a nurse, though she did not recall why this was so difficult. Her search seemed endless, and when she finally found a nurse, her father was dead.

I don't know why, but I asked Karen the name of the ward on which her father had died. She paused and thought, and then to our surprise, she blurted out, "3 South." She cried heavily as she expressed how confused she was and how angry she felt toward the nurses on that ward for not being more available, although she thought they had been involved with another emergency. After weeping, shaking, and expressing her rage, Karen felt calm and relaxed for the first time in months. My psychoanalytic supervisor said her symptoms would disappear, and sure enough they did. He knew we would have to go much deeper into what earlier conflicts this adolescent experience represented, but for now, Karen's problems in the nursing program were relieved.

A Sketch of Sigmund Freud

Early in his career, Sigmund Freud (1856–1939) was quite impressed by the way some of his patients seemed to recover following cathartic recollections of an early trauma. But he soon discovered that more profound, lasting changes required changes in his own approach. Over time, he switched from hypnosis, to catharsis, and finally to a dynamic analysis that radically increased not only the consciousness of his clients but also the consciousness of his culture.

Freud's genius has been admired by many, but he complained throughout his life about not having been given a bigger brain (Jones, 1955). Freud himself believed that his outstanding attribute was his courage. Certainly it took tremendous daring and inquisitiveness to descend into the uncharted depths of humanity and then to declare to a strict Victorian culture what he had discovered. Freud once observed that scientific inquisitiveness is a derivative of the child's sexual curiosity, the sublimation of anxiety-laden questions of "Where do I come from?" and "What did my parents do to produce me?" These questions exercised a particular fascination for Freud and later assumed a central position in his theory of personality because of his own intricate family constellation. His mother was half his father's age, his two half-brothers were as old as his mother, and he had a nephew older than he (Gay, 1990). He was the prized "golden child" born into a lower-class Jewish family.

For years he struggled for success. From his entry in 1873 into the University of Vienna at age 17, to his work as a research scholar in an institute of physiology, to earning his MD in 1891 and his residency in neurology, he expected that his hard work and commitment would result in recognition and financial success. He had never intended to practice medicine, but he found the rewards of research to be quite restricted and the opportunities for academic advancement for a Jew to be limited. Finally, after marrying at age 30, he began to develop a rewarding private practice. Yet Freud was willing to risk his hard-earned financial success to communicate to his colleagues what his work with patients had convinced him of: The basis of **neurosis** was sexual conflict—or, more specifically, the conflict between the id's instinctive desires and society's retribution for the direct expression of those desires.

Freud's profound insights were met with professional insults, and his private practice rapidly declined. For months he received no new referrals. For years he had to rely on his inner courage to continue his lonely intellectual pursuits without a colleague to share his insights. During this same period of the 1890s, he began his painful self-analysis, in part to overcome some neurotic symptoms and in part to serve as his own subject in his studies of the **unconscious**. Surprisingly, Freud was not particularly discouraged by his professional isolation. He was able to interpret the opposition he met as part of the natural resistance to taboo ideas.

Finally, in the early 1900s, Freud's risky work began to be recognized by scholars, such as the dying William James, as the system that would shape 20th-century psychology. Shape it he did, along with the incredibly brilliant group of colleagues who joined the Vienna Psychoanalytic Society. Most of these colleagues contributed to the development of psychoanalysis, although Freud insisted that as the founder he alone had the right to decide what should be called psychoanalysis. This led some of the best minds, including Alfred Adler and Carl Jung, to leave the Psychoanalytic Society to develop their own systems. Freud's insistence may also have set a precedent for a dogmatism that relied more on authority than on evidence in revising psychotherapy theories. Freud himself, however, continued throughout his lifetime to be critical of his own theories and would painfully discard selected ideas if experience contradicted them.

Success did not diminish Freud's commitment to his scholarly work or to his patients. He worked an 18-hour day that began with patients from 8:00 A.M. until 1:00 P.M., a break for lunch and a walk with his family, patients again from 3:00 P.M. until 9:00 or 10:00 P.M., dinner and a walk with his wife, followed by correspondence and books until 1:00 or 2:00 A.M. His dedication to his work was remarkable, although it is also striking that this man, dedicated to understanding sex and its vicissitudes, left little time or energy for his own sexuality.

Having emigrated from Vienna to London before World War II, Freud continued to work despite suffering from the ravages of bone cancer. At age 85 he died of probable physician-assisted suicide (Gay, 1988), leaving the most comprehensive theory of personality, psychopathology, and psychotherapy ever developed.

Theory of Personality

Freud's theory of personality was as complex as he was. He viewed personality from six different perspectives:

- The topographic, which involves conscious versus unconscious modes of functioning
- The **dynamic**, which entails the interaction and conflict among psychic forces
- The **genetic**, which concerns the origin and development of psychic phenomena through the oral, anal, phallic, latency, and genital stages
- The economic, which involves the distribution, transformation, and expenditure of psychological energy
- The **structural**, which revolves around the persistent functional units of the id, ego, and superego
- The adaptive, implied by Freud and developed by Hartmann (1958), which involves the inborn preparedness of the individual to interact with an evolving series of environments

We will focus primarily on his dynamic, genetic, and structural perspectives because these are most directly related to his theories of psychopathology and psychotherapy.

From all these perspectives, psychoanalysis is a conflict model leading to **compromise formation**. The mind is embroiled in constant conflict between conscious and unconscious forces, between what the individual immediately desires and what the society deems acceptable. In the end, mature human behavior represents a compromise between these warring factions. The id will demand instant gratification of food, sex, bodily relief, and adoration, but the superego will deny these earthly and immediate pleasures. So we invariably compromise—we wait until the acceptable time and place to eat, defecate, have sex, and secure undivided attention. We mentally compromise all day long.

Freud believed that the basic dynamic forces motivating personality were Eros (life and sex) and Thanatos (death and aggression). These complementary forces are **instincts** that possess a somatic basis but are expressed in fantasies, desires, feelings, thoughts, and most directly, actions. The individual constantly desires immediate gratification of sexual and aggressive impulses. The demand for immediate gratification leads to inevitable conflicts with social rules that insist on some control over sex and aggression if social institutions, including families, are to remain stable and orderly. The individual is forced to develop **defense mechanisms** or inner controls that restrain sexual and aggressive impulses from being expressed in uncontrollable outbursts. Without these defenses, civilization would be reduced to a jungle of raping, ravaging beasts.

Defense mechanisms keep individuals from becoming conscious of basic inner desires to rape and ravage. The assumption here is that if individuals are unaware of such desires, they cannot act on them, at least not directly. The defenses serve to keep the individual out of danger of punishment for breaking social rules. Defenses also keep us from experiencing the anxiety and guilt that would be elicited by desires to break parental and social rules. For defenses to work, the person must remain unconscious of the very mechanisms being used to keep sexual and aggressive impulses from coming into awareness. Otherwise, the individual is faced with a dilemma akin to keeping a secret from a 3-year-old child who knows you have a secret—the constant badgering to know what is being hidden can be overwhelming.

The core of the Freudian personality is the unconscious conflict among sexual and aggressive impulses, societal rules aimed at controlling those impulses, and the individual's defense mechanisms controlling the impulses in such a way as to keep guilt and anxiety to a minimum while allowing some safe, indirect gratification (Maddi, 1996). The difference between a normal personality and a neurotic one, of course, is simply a matter of degree. It is when the unconscious conflicts become too intense, too painful, and the resultant defense mechanisms too restrictive, that neurotic symptoms begin to emerge.

Although all personalities revolve around unconscious conflicts, people differ in the particular impulses, anxieties, and defenses in conflict. The differences depend on the particular stage of life at which an individual's conflicts occur. For Freud, the stages of life are determined primarily by the unfolding of sexuality in the oral, anal, phallic, and genital stages, as summarized in Table 2.1. Differences in experiences during each of these stages are critical in determining the prominent traits and personalities that ensue.

Oral Stage

During the first 18 months of life, the infant's sexual desires are centered in the oral region. The child's greatest pleasure is to suck on a satisfying object, such as a breast. The instinctual urges are to passively receive oral gratification during the oral-incorporative phase and to more actively take in oral pleasure during the oral-aggressive phase. Sucking on breasts or bottles, putting toys, fingers, or toes in the mouth, and even babbling are representative actions a child takes to receive oral gratification. As adults, we can appreciate oral sexuality through kissing, fellatio, cunnilingus, or oral caressing of breasts and other parts of the body.

Table 2.1 Summary of Freudian Psychosexual Stages

STAGE	AGE	LIBIDINAL ZONE	LIBIDINAL OBJECT	DEVELOPMENTAL CHALLENGES
Oral	Birth to 1	Mouth, thumb	Mother's breast, own body	Passive incorporation of all good through mouth; autoerotic sensuality
Anal	2–3	Anus, bowels	Own body	Active self-soothing and self-mastery; passive submission
Phallic	3–6	Genitals	Mother for boy Father for girl	Oedipus and electra conflicts; identification with same-sex parent; ambivalence of love relationships
Latency	6–11	None	Largely repressed	Repression of pregenital forms of libido; learning shame and disgust for inappropriate love objects
Genital	12+	Genital primacy	Sexual partner	Sexual intimacy and reproduction

SOURCE: Table content courtesy of Dr. Robert N. Sollod.

The infant's oral sexual needs are intense and urgent, but the child is dependent on parental figures to provide the breasts or bottles necessary for adequate oral gratification. How the parents respond to such urgent needs can have a marked influence on the child's personality. Parents who are either too depriving or too indulgent can make it difficult for a child to mature from the **oral stage** to later stages of personality development.

With deprivation, the child can remain fixated at the oral stage: Energies are directed primarily toward finding the oral gratification that was in short supply during childhood. Deprivation likely leads to pessimism; the mental set from the start is that one's needs will not be met. Suspiciousness comes from a feeling that if parents cannot be trusted, there are few whom one can trust. Self-belittlement derives from an image of having been awful, if one's folks could not care less. Passivity follows from the repeated conclusion that no matter how hard one kicks or cries, parents will not care. Envy is an inner craving to have the traits that would make one lovable enough for people to provide special care.

With overindulgence, the child can also become fixated at the oral stage but energies are directed toward trying to repeat and maintain the gratifying conditions. Overindulgence typically leads to preverbal images of the world and oneself that result in traits on the right side of each pair. Optimism comes from an image that things have always been great, so there is no reason to expect that they will not continue to be so. Gullibility derives from the experience of finding early in life that whatever one received from people was good, so why not swallow whatever people say now. Cockiness ensues from having been something super for parents to dote on. Manipulativeness relates to the mental set that comes from getting parents to do whatever one wants. Finally, admiration results from feelings that other people are as good as oneself and one's parents.

Fixation due to either deprivation or overgratification leads to the development of an oral personality that includes the following bipolar traits: pessimism/optimism, suspiciousness/gullibility, self-belittlement/ cockiness, passivity/manipulativeness, and envy/admiration (Abraham, 1927; Glover, 1925).

Besides these traits, fixation at the oral stage brings a tendency to rely on more primitive defenses when threatened or frustrated. **Denial** derives from having to finally close one's eyes and go to sleep as a way of shutting out the unmet oral needs. On a cognitive level, this defense involves closing off one's attention to threatening aspects of the world or self. **Projection** has a bodily basis in the infant's spitting up anything bad that is taken in and making the bad things part of the environment. Cognitively, projection involves perceiving in the environment those aspects of oneself that are bad or threatening. **Incorporation** on a bodily level includes taking in food and liquids and making these objects an actual part of oneself. Cognitively, this defense involves making images of others part of one's own image.

The well-defended **oral personality** is not considered pathological but rather an immature person, like all of the pregenital personalities we shall discuss. There certainly are many people who are overly optimistic, gullible, and cocky without considering themselves or being considered by others as pathological. Likewise, there are many people who believe it is wise to be suspicious, expect too little from this world, and perceive selfishness in others. These people are also rarely judged to be pathological.

Anal Stage

In a society that assigned functions of the anus to the outhouse and gagged at the sight or smell of the products of the anus, it must have been ghastly to think that a physician like Freud believed that this dirty area could be the most intense source of pleasure for children between the ages of

18 months and 3 years. Even in our ultraclean society, many people still find it difficult to imagine that their anuses can be a source of sensuous satisfaction. In the privacy of their own bathrooms, however, many people admit to themselves that the releasing of the anus can be the "pause that refreshes." As one of our constipated patients said, it is his most pleasurable time of the week.

Children in the **anal stage** are apt to learn that urges to play with the anus or its products bring them into conflict with society's rules of cleanliness. Even the pleasure of letting go of the anus must come under the parental rules for bowel control. Before toilet training, the child was free to release the sphincter muscles immediately as soon as tension built up in the anus. But now society, as represented by the parents, demands that the child control the inherent desire for immediate tension reduction. In Erikson's (1950) terms, the child must now learn to hold on and then to let go. Not only that, but the child must also learn the proper timing of holding on and letting go. If the child lets go when it is time to hold on—trouble; and if the child holds on when it is time to let go—more trouble!

The anal stage involves all kinds of power struggles, not solely those associated with toilet training. What to eat, when to sleep, how to dress, whom to kiss—all of these struggles during the "terrible twos" represent the child's efforts to negotiate societal and parental rules and to assert themselves. The child is most likely to become conflicted and fixated at the anal stage if the caretakers again are either too demanding or overindulgent. The bipolar traits that develop from anal fixation are stinginess/overgenerosity, constrictedness/expansiveness, stubbornness/acquiescence, orderliness/messiness, punctuality/tardiness, precision/vagueness (Fenichel, 1945; Freud, 1925).

Freud was concerned with overdemanding or overcontrolling parents who forced toilet training too quickly or too harshly. The individual receiving this caretaking style was more likely to develop an **anal personality** dominated by holding-on tendencies. The child was frequently forced to let go when the child didn't want to let go. Then when the child did let go, what did the parents do with the gift to them? Just flushed it down the toilet. Now such individuals react as if they will be damned before they again let go against their will. So these personalities hold tightly to money (stinginess), their feelings (constrictedness), and their own way (stubbornness). Again, a well-defended anal character is considered immature, not pathological; anal people typically take pride in their neatness and punctuality and even may be admired by others for these traits.

Overindulgent parents who are lackadaisical about toilet training more likely encourage a child to just let go whenever any pressure is felt. This route to an anal personality results in people who easily let go of money (wasteful), let go of feelings (explosiveness), and let go of their wills (acquiescent). Lack of concern with such a basic social rule as proper toilet training is assumed to encourage a child to be generally messy, dirty, tardy, and vague.

For Freud, conflicts during the anal stage resulted in the development of particular defenses. **Reaction formation**, or behaving the opposite of what one truly desires, develops first as a reaction to being very clean and neat, as the parents demand, rather than expressing anal desires to be messy. **Undoing**, or atoning for unacceptable desires or actions, occurs when the child learns that it is safer to say, "I'm sorry I let go in my pants," rather than saying, "I like the warm feeling of poo in my pants." Isolation, or not experiencing the feelings that would go with the thoughts, emerges in part when the child has to think about an anal function as a mechanical act rather than an instinctual experience. **Intellectualization**, or the process of neutralizing affect-laden experiences by talking in intellectual or logical terms, is partly related to such experiences as talking about the regularity of bowel movement as being soothing to one's gastrointestinal system.

Phallic Stage

The name of this stage, which refers specifically to male genitalia, reflects Freud's problem of theorizing too much about men and then overgeneralizing to women. For both, the sexual desires during the **phallic stage** are thought to be focused on the genitalia. From ages 3 to 6, both sexes are fascinated by their own genitalia and increase their frequency of masturbation. They are also very interested in the opposite sex and engage in games of "doctor and patient" in which they examine each other to satisfy their sexual curiosity.

The conflict for youngsters is not with their genital desires, because theoretically they and other kids could satisfy these desires. The conflict is over the object of their sexual desires, which in this stage is the parent of the opposite sex.

The boy's desire for his mother is explained as a natural outgrowth of the mother's serving as the major source of gratification for his previous needs, especially the need for sucking. Therefore, the son will naturally direct his genital sexual desires initially toward his mother and would expect her to gratify him. The **oedipal conflict**, of course, is that the father already has the rights and privileges of enjoying the mother. The son's fear is that the father might punish his rival by removing the source of the problem—the son's penis. This **castration anxiety** eventually causes the son to repress his desire for his mother, repress his hostile rivalry toward his father, and identify with his father's rules, in the hope that if he acts as his father would have him act, he can avoid castration.

Why a girl ends up desiring her father rather than her mother is more difficult to explain, given that the mother is presumed to be the main source of instinctual gratification for daughters as well as sons. Freud asserted that girls become hostile toward their mothers when they discover that their mothers cheated them by not giving them a penis. Why Freud assumed that females would conclude that there was something wrong with them because they lacked a penis, rather than vice versa, has always been a mystery. For example, a non-Freudian colleague tells the story of his 5-year-old daughter's discovery of her 3-year-old brother's penis. Rather than envying his penis, she went yelling, "Mama, Mama, Andy's 'gina fell out."

Nevertheless, and in spite of understandable protest by enlightened women, many classical psychoanalysts still assume that girls initially envy penises, that they become enraged toward the mother, and that they turn their desires to the father in part to be able to at least share his phallus.

Again, the critical issue is how the parents respond to the genital desires of their children. Both overindulgence and overrejection can produce fixations at the phallic stage, resulting in formation of the following bipolar traits: vanity/self-hatred, pride/humility, stylishness/plainness, flirtatiousness/shyness, gregariousness/isolation, brashness/bashfulness.

Overrejection, in which parents give their opposite-sex children little affection, few hugs or kisses, and no appreciation of their attractiveness, is likely to lead to the following self-image: "I must be hateful if my parent wouldn't even hug or kiss me. Why flirt, dress stylishly, be outgoing or brash, or take pride in myself if the opposite sex is sure to find me undesirable?" On the other hand, people who had overindulgent parents, whether seductive or actually incestuous, can more readily develop feelings of vanity. They feel they must be really something if daddy preferred them over mommy, or vice versa. The flirting, stylishness, pride, and brashness would all be based on maintaining an image as the most desirable person in the world.

Conflicts over sexual desires toward a parent are not solely due to how the parent reacts, however. The child must also defend against society's basic incest taboo. These conflicts lead to **repression** as the major defense against incestuous desires. By becoming unaware even of fantasies about one's opposite-sex parent, the youngster feels safe from incest and the consequent castration or taboos that would accompany it. However, as with all conflicted desires, the impulse is omnipresent and can be kept at bay only by unconscious defenses.

Latency Stage

In classical psychoanalytic theory, this stage involved no new unfolding of sexuality, but rather was a stage in which the pregenital desires were largely repressed. Freud associated no new personality development with the **latency stage**, believing that all pregenital personality formation had been completed by age 6. Latency was seen primarily as a lull between the conflicted, pregenital time and the storm that was to reemerge with adolescence—the beginning of the genital stage.

In more recent psychoanalytic formulations, latency is a time for ego development and learning the social rules of being a citizen. These gains enable the child to psychologically enter adolescence and to navigate the genital stage when it hits.

Genital Stage

In the **genital stage**, the libido reemerges—this time in the genitals. Having largely completed the challenges of the phallic and latency stages, the adolescent must now find appropriate objects for sex (love) and aggression (work).

In Freudian theory, an individual does not progress to the genital stage without at least some conflict between instinctual desires and social restraints. Some individuals will be fixated at the oral, anal, or phallic stage and will demonstrate the related personality type. Others will experience conflicts at each of the stages and will demonstrate a mixed personality that combines traits and defenses of each stage. But no one becomes a fully mature, genital character without undergoing a successful psychoanalysis. Because such a personality is the ideal goal of analysis, we will delay discussion of it until the section on this theory's ideal individual.

Theory of Psychopathology

Because all personalities contain some immaturity due to inevitable conflicts and fixations at pregenital stages, all of us are vulnerable to regressing into psychopathology. We are more vulnerable if our conflicts and fixations occurred earlier in life, because we would be dependent on more immature defenses for dealing with anxiety. In addition, the more intense our pregenital conflicts are, the more vulnerable we are, as more of our energy is bound up in defending against pregenital impulses, and less energy is available for coping with adult stresses. Well-defended oral, anal, phallic, or mixed personalities may never break down unless exposed to horrendous stress, which would then lead to symptom formation and intensification of immature defense mechanisms.

Stressful events—such as the death of a loved one, an offer of an affair, or a medical illness—stimulate the impulse that individuals have been controlling all their lives. They react on an unconscious level to this current event as if it were a repetition of a childhood experience, such as rejection by a parent or a desire for taboo sex. Their infantile reactions lead to panic that their impulses may get out of control and that the punishment they have dreaded all their lives, such as separation or castration, will occur. These individuals feel that they are "falling apart"—their very personality is threatened with disintegration. Like children, they are terrified that their adult personality will break down and that they will become dominated by infantile instincts. These individuals reexperience at an unconscious level the same infantile conflicts that caused their personality development and now threaten to cause their personality disintegration.

In the face of such threats, the person is highly motivated to spend whatever energy is necessary to keep impulses from coming into consciousness. This may translate into an exacerbation of previous defenses to the point which they become pathological. For example, a married woman who has been offered an affair and has an intense desire for taboo sex may rely more heavily on repressing such desires. Soon she is entirely fatigued and may show other symptoms of fatigue and depression, but at least she does not have the energy to act on an affair even if she wanted to. Although she constantly complains about her fatigue, for her it is better to be tired than to be in terror of acting out her infantile desires. A woman who did not have such intense fixations and conflicts over taboo sex might simply decline the offer or might accept if she thought it was worth the risks.

When a person overreacts to life's events to such an extent that symptoms develop, Freudians believe the symptoms are defending against unacceptable impulses and childish anxieties. In many cases, the symptoms also serve as indirect expressions of the person's unacceptable wish. An example: Karen's symptoms of headaches, dizziness, and medical errors diverted her attention from emerging rage toward the nurses on 3 South and the accompanying anxiety. Her medical errors also provided some expression of her hostile wishes without her being conscious that she was even angry, to say nothing of being threatened by internal rage.

When symptoms serve both as defenses against unacceptable impulses and as indirect expressions of these wishes, then the symptoms are doubly resistant to change. Other benefits from symptoms, such as special attention from loved ones or doctors, are secondary gains and make symptoms even more resistant to change.

But why does a person like Karen overreact in the first place to an event like being assigned to 3 South? Why did she respond to the current 3 South as if she were 12 years old again? Why didn't she just make the logical discrimination between an old 3 South and the current 3 South? Obviously, Karen was unaware of responding to

3 South as if she were 12 years old. If her response to 3 South was primarily on a conscious level, then she could indeed have made such logical distinctions based on her conscious, **secondary process**. But unconscious responses like Karen's follow **primary-process thinking**, which is alogical.

Logical thinking includes reasoning from the subjects of sentences, as in: (1) All men are mortals; (2) Socrates was a man; therefore, (3) Socrates was mortal. In primary process, reasoning frequently follows the predicates of statements, so that we think: (1) The Virgin Mary was a virgin; (2) I am a virgin; therefore, (3) I am the Virgin Mary. Or in Karen's case: (1) The ward where they let my father die was 3 South; (2) the ward where I am now is 3 South; therefore, (3) this 3 South is where they let my father die.

When Karen responds on an unconscious level, she does not systematically proceed through any reasoning process; rather, her primary-process reaction is automatically alogical. Primary-process responding is also atemporal, with no differentiation among past, present, and future. Therefore, on an unconscious level, Karen's response makes no distinction between the 3 South of 10 years ago and the 3 South of now. On an unconscious level, all is now, and so the same impulses and anxieties are elicited that were present 10 years ago.

Another characteristic of primary-process thinking is **displacement**, which involves placing the energies from highly charged emotional ideas onto more neutral ideas. In this case, Karen displaced the intense anger she felt toward her father for leaving onto her image of the more neutral people responsible for 3 South. Primary-process thinking is also symbolic, which means *pars pro toto*, that any part of an event represents the total event; thus, the name 3 South became a symbol for the many feelings stirred up over the death of Karen's father.

Finally, primary-process experiencing includes both **manifest** and **latent content**: The content that is conscious, or manifest, is only a minor portion of the hidden, or latent, meaning of events. Karen was thus originally aware of only the manifest event of becoming upset on her new ward; she was not even aware of the latent significance of the name 3 South until it was uncovered in psychotherapy.

With this understanding of primary-process responding, we can more fully appreciate why Karen's unconscious response to being placed on the present 3 South appeared to be irrational, or alogical. We can also appreciate why she was reacting like an angry child and why her response involved much more energy and meaning than could be understood from a relatively neutral situation like the name of the ward, 3 South.

If we went even deeper into the latent meaning of this event for Karen, we would probably find that her experience at age 12 represented her original loss of her father (through divorce) when she was 5. The rage that threatened to break out toward the nurses on 3 South may have been in part displaced from her original rage toward her mother, whom Karen imagined caused her father to leave at an age when she so desired him. Working on 3 South may also have threatened to bring to awareness feelings of sexual desire for her father mixed with hostility for his leaving when she needed him so. Even the fantasy that she might wish his death could damage Karen's image of herself as the caring daughter who would have saved her father if she had been a nurse 10 years before. To protect her image of herself, to protect herself from acting out dangerous impulses, and to protect herself from all the anxiety and guilt such impulses would elicit could be the reasons for her symptoms as defenses of last resort.

In this sense, as William Faulkner wrote, "The past is never dead. It's not even past." The unconscious remains alive and present in our primary processes, apt to be reactivated at any time in our lives.

Psychoanalytic theory offers a diagnostic alternative to the static, symptom-based *Diagnostic and Statistical Manual of Mental Disorders* (*DSM*). Starting with childhood development and acknowledging unconscious motivation, psychoanalytic diagnosis provides a richer, multidimensional portrait of personality style, mental functioning, and relational capacities. Five psychoanalytic organizations collaborated to publish the *Psychodynamic Diagnostic Manual* (*PDM*) to complement the *DSM*. In this way, psychoanalysis and the *PDM* provide a comprehensive profile of an individual's mental life. If the essence of psychopathology lies at an unconscious level and if the person has no awareness of the psychological significance of precipitating events, the impulses being elicited, the anxieties threatening panic, and the defensive yet gratifying nature of symptoms, then how can individuals be helped to overcome their disorders?

Therapeutic Processes

For Freud, only one therapeutic process could succeed in making the unconscious conscious. Before we can respond to environmental events in a more realistic manner, we must first be conscious of how our pathological responses to the environment derive from our unconscious, primary-process associations. To remove symptoms, we must become conscious of our resistance to letting go of those symptoms because they both defend against and give partial release to unacceptable impulses. We must gradually recognize that our impulses are not as dangerous as we thought as children and that we can use more constructive defenses to keep our impulses in control, in part by allowing more mature expressions of our instincts. Finally, to prevent future relapses, we must use our conscious processes to release our pregenital fixations so that we can continue to develop to mature, genital levels of functioning. Such radical increases in consciousness require considerable work on the part of both patient and analyst.

Consciousness Raising

The Patient's Work

The work of **free association** sounds simple enough—to freely say whatever comes to mind, no matter how trivial or repulsive. If patients could let their minds go and associate without defending, then their associations would be dominated by instincts. Because the instincts are the source of all energy and therefore the strongest forces in the individual, and because the instincts are always pressing to emerge into consciousness, patients would immediately associate to thoughts, feelings, fantasies, and wishes that express instincts.

However, free association is anything but easy or simple. Our earliest lessons in life were that such direct, uncontrolled expressions of instincts are dangerous. Humans also learned at the time symptoms developed that a loosening of defenses can be terrifying and can lead to pathology. Now, just because the psychoanalyst has asked the patient to lie on the couch and say everything that comes to mind does not mean that the patient can do so without considerable resistance or defensiveness.

To help the patient work in the face of potential terror and resulting defensiveness, the analyst must form a **working alliance** with the part of the patient's ego that wants relief from suffering and is rational enough to believe that the analyst's directions can bring such relief. Through this alliance, patients also become willing to recall in detail dreams and childhood memories, even though such material brings them closer to threatening impulses.

The Therapist's Work

The therapist's work begins with evaluating the patient to determine whether he or she is indeed a suitable candidate for psychoanalysis. As Greenson (1967, p. 34) succinctly puts it, "People who do not dare regress from reality and those who cannot return readily to reality are poor risks for psychoanalysis." This generally means that patients diagnosed as schizophrenic, bipolar, schizoid, or borderline personalities are considered poor risks for classic psychoanalysis.

If psychoanalysis does proceed, the therapist uses four procedures—confrontation, clarification, **interpretation**, and **working through**—in analyzing the patient's resistance to free associating and the transference that emerges as the patient regresses and expresses instinctual desires toward the analyst (Bibring, 1954; Greenson, 1967).

Confrontation and Clarification

The first two are fundamentally feedback procedures. In analytic confrontation, the therapist makes sure patients are aware of the particular actions or experiences being analyzed. For example, in confronting a particular transference, the analyst might give the patient the following feedback: "You seem to be feeling angry toward me," or "You seem to have sexual feelings toward me."

Clarification, which frequently blends with confrontation, is sharper and more-detailed feedback regarding the particular phenomenon that the patient is experiencing. Greenson (1967, p. 304) gives an example of how, after confronting a patient with his hatred for the analyst, he helped the patient clarify the exact details of his hatred:

> He would like to beat me to a pulp, literally grind me up and mash me into a jelly-like mass of bloody, slimy goo. Then he'd eat me up in one big "slurp" like the god damned oatmeal his mother made him eat as a kid. Then he'd shit me out as a foul-smelling poisonous shit. And when I asked him, "And what would you do with this foul-smelling shit?" he replied, "I'd grind you into the dirt so you could join my dear dead mother!"

Interpretation

Confronting and clarifying a patient's experiences prepare patients (or analysands) for the most important analytic procedure: interpretation. Greenson (1967, p. 39) defines interpretation in such a way as to make it almost synonymous with analysis itself:

> *To interpret means to make an unconscious phenomenon conscious. More precisely, it means to make conscious the unconscious meaning, source, history, mode, or course of a given psychic event. The analyst uses his own unconscious, his empathy and intuition as well as his theoretical knowledge for arriving at an interpretation. By interpreting we go beyond what is readily observable and we assign meaning and causality to a psychological phenomenon.*

Because interpretation goes beyond the experience of the patient, it is more than feedback to the patient. The meaning and causality assigned to psychological phenomena are determined, at least in part, by psychoanalytic theory. Therefore, the information patients are given regarding the meaning and causality of their responses is partly an education on how psychoanalysis makes sense of people and their problems. This is not to say that interpretations are given in theoretical terms. They certainly are personalized for the individual, and in that respect are feedback. Nevertheless, through interpretations patients are taught to view their conscious experiences as caused by unconscious processes, their adult behavior as determined by childhood experiences, their analysts as if they were parents or other significant figures from the past, and so on.

Psychoanalytic therapists assume that patients accept such teachings because the interpretations hold true for the patient. After all, it is the patient's response that verifies an interpretation. If patients gain **insight**—that is, if they have a cognitive and affective awakening about aspects of themselves that were previously hidden—then analysts have some evidence for the validity of their interpretations. The most critical response for verifying interpretations is whether the interpretations eventually lead to a change for the better in the patient.

The problem with patient improvement as the criterion for the verification of interpretations is that improvement in psychoanalysis is expected to be a slow, gradual process. First, the analyst and the patient must interpret the repeated **resistance** the client throws up against becoming conscious of threatening forces from within. The client misses appointments, comes late, recovers dramatically and wants to leave therapy, wants to leave because of not recovering, represses dreams, and does a million other things to shore up defenses. Then, as blind resistance is gradually reduced through insightful interpretations, the client begins to release hidden instincts toward the therapist.

The patient satisfies frustrated sexual and aggressive impulses by displacing them onto the analyst, and gradually a neurotic transference develops in which the patient relives all of the significant human relationships from childhood. For weeks or months, the therapist may be experienced as the nongiving, miserly mother who does not care about the patient; then the analyst is the lecherous father who wants to seduce the patient; or the wonderful, wise parent who can do no wrong; or the stupid fool who is always wrong. Transference reactions serve as intense resistances: Why mature further when you feel so good beating on your therapist or feel so safe with such a wise, caring parent? Painfully, through repeated interpretations, the patient must realize that these intense feelings and impulses come from within and represent the patient's pregenital conflicts, not realistic feelings elicited by the relatively blank-screen analyst.

Working Through

The slow, gradual process of working again and again with the insights that have come from interpretations of resistance and transference is called working through. In this last and longest step of psychotherapy, patients are acutely conscious of their many defensive maneuvers, including symptoms. They are undeniably aware of the impulses they have tried to defend against and the many ways in which they are still behaviorally expressed. They realize that they need not fear their impulses to the degree they once did as children, because in transference relationships they expressed impulses in intense words and were not castrated, rejected, or overwhelmed. Gradually the person becomes aware that there are indeed new and more mature ways of controlling instincts that allow some gratification without guilt or anxiety. Gradually the patient channels impulses through these new controls and gives up immature defenses and symptoms. The use of new defenses and the radical increase in consciousness are seen by Freudians as structural changes in personality, in which energies once bound up in pregenital conflicts are now available to the more mature ego of the individual.

Other Processes

Most psychoanalysts accept that corrective emotional experiences can lead to temporary relief of symptoms, especially for traumatic neuroses. Catharsis, however, even if used by an analyst, is not considered part of the psychoanalytic process. There is only one fundamental change process in analysis, and that is to increase consciousness; all the steps in analysis are part of that process.

Therapeutic Content

Intrapersonal Conflicts

Psychoanalysis obviously focuses on intrapersonal conflicts in therapy. The patient's inner conflicts among impulses, anxiety, and defenses represent the central concern. Problems may be acted out at an interpersonal level, but the understanding and resolution of such problems are achieved only through an analysis of each person's intrapsychic conflicts.

Anxieties and Defenses

We have already discussed anxiety due to threats of separation and castration. The Freudians also postulate **primal anxiety**, which is due to the assumed birth trauma of being overwhelmed with stimulation. Primal anxiety is the bodily basis for panic, which is the adult threat of being overwhelmed with instinctual stimulation. Moral anxiety, or guilt, is the threat that comes with breaking internalized rules.

In psychotherapy, anxiety may drive a person to seek relief because of its aversive properties. Once in therapy, however, an analyst must be careful not to uncover impulses too quickly lest the person panic and either flee therapy or feel psychotically overwhelmed. Anxiety is one of the central reasons therapy moves slowly—partly because anxiety signals the person to shore up resistance when dangerous associations are being approached, and partly because analysts feel that immature egos cannot hold up under high anxiety.

Defenses or resistance, as defenses are called when they occur in psychotherapy, are half of the content of psychoanalysis. Almost any behavior in therapy can serve defensive functions—talking too fast or too slowly, too much or too little, feeling good toward the therapist or feeling hostile, focusing on details or avoiding details. So the analyst is never without material. It is just a matter of which defenses are most likely to be acknowledged by the client as resistance, such as missing appointments or not recalling dreams. The analytic goal is not to remove defenses, but rather to replace immature and distorting defenses with more mature, realistic, and gratifying defenses.

Self-Esteem

Self-esteem has not been a major content area for psychoanalysis. It seems to be taken for granted that patients will experience conflict over self-esteem. Some will hold unrealistically low self-esteem—deprived oral characters who engage in continual self-belittlement or rejected phallic characters who feel ugly and undesirable, to name but two. Other patients will hold unrealistically high self-esteem, such as overindulged oral characters who are cocky or overindulged phallic characters who are vain and brash. Pregenital personalities cannot feel fundamentally good about themselves as long as they are dominated by infantile desires to be selfishly taken care of, hostilely controlling, or seductively narcissistic.

Lack of genuine self-esteem results from personality problems, rather than causing such problems. As such, analysts do not treat esteem problems directly. Acceptance of infantile characteristics may bring temporary relief, but what the pregenital personality really needs is a personality transplant. The best that can be done is to help patients consciously restructure their personalities into a more genital level of functioning. Only then can individuals experience a stable sense of self-esteem.

Responsibility

In a deterministic system such as psychoanalysis, how can we talk about individual responsibility? In practice, the analyst expects the patient to be responsible for the bill, to keep appointments three to five times a week, and to free associate. But theoretically, there is no freedom and no choice in psychoanalysis and, therefore, no responsibility. How can we hold a person responsible for any action, whether it be murder, rape, or just not paying a bill, if all pathological behavior is determined by unconscious conflicts and pregenital fixations? This difficulty in holding an individual responsible for his or her actions is one of the reasons why Mowrer (1961) said that Freud freed us from a generation of neurotics and gave us a generation of psychopaths.

Freud was a determinist, yet his theory is a psychology of freedom (Gay, 1990). His **psychic determinism** held that just as there is no event in the physical universe without its cause, so there is no mental event or mental state without its cause. Nothing is chance in the psychological world. Yet psychoanalysis is ultimately designed to make us more aware of our repressed conflicts and mental defenses, and thereby free us from the tyranny of the unconscious.

Interpersonal Conflicts

Intimacy and Sexuality

Intimacy, the authentic revealing and sharing between people, is fundamentally impossible for an immature personality. The problem of intimacy is basically a transference problem. The pregenital personality cannot relate to another person as the other person really is, but distorts the other according to childhood images of what people are like. In Piaget's terms, the person's earliest interpersonal experiences with parents result in internalized schemas that are primitive concepts of what people are like. Any new experience of a person is assimilated into this schema through selective attention to that person's actions.

Whereas Piaget (1952) suggests children's schemas of people change to accommodate new experiences, the Freudian concept of **fixation** suggests that pregenital personalities do not evolve in their schemas of people. Rather, immature individuals distort their perceptions of other people to fit internalized images. For example, a repeatedly abused child views people as untrustworthy and rejecting. That child becomes an adult who attends to the slightest reason for mistrust and the smallest sign of rejection as evidence that a new, potential intimate is the same as the abusers in childhood.

A thorough psychoanalysis is the premier method to mature to a level which people can perceive each other with the freshness and uniqueness each deserves. It is only by being fully aware of how we have distorted our relationships in the past that we can avoid destructive distortion in the present.

Sexual relationships for immature people also reflect transference relationships. Two immature people can only engage in object relationships in which the other is seen as perhaps finally being the one who will satisfy ungratified pregenital instincts. So the oral character may relate sexually with a clingy and demanding manner that smothers a spouse. The anal personality may relate sexually in a very routinized manner, such as every Wednesday night when the 11:00 television news is over rather than when sex is spontaneously desired. The phallic character may relate as the teasing, seductive person who promises so much in bed but has so little to give. The ability to relate to another as a mature, heterosexual partner results only after a satisfying working through of one's pregenital fixations. Otherwise we are reduced to two objects bumping in the night.

Communication

Most interpersonal communication between two immature people is interlocking monologue, not a genuine dialogue. Immature personalities are locked into their egocentric worlds, in which others are only objects for their gratification. They do not respond to what the other says, but rather to their own selfish desires. They do not talk to each other, but rather speak to their internal images of what the other is supposed to be. The messages they send have a manifest content that is also directed at hiding what the person really wants to say. If it takes an analyst years of "listening with the third ear" (Reik, 1948) to interpret what the person truly means, how can a spouse with two blocked ears be expected to hear? From a classical Freudian viewpoint, attempts at couples therapy between two immature personalities will only produce absurd dialogue best left to modern playwrights.

Hostility

The violence in our society, according to Freudians, reflects the hostility inherent in humans. Just as the work of ethnologists such as Tinbergen (1951) and Lorenz (1963) suggested that animals instinctively release aggression, the work of Freud suggested that the human animal possesses aggressive instincts to strike out and destroy. But humans also desire to live in civilized societies, and the stability of social organizations—relationships, families, and communities, to name a few—is continually threatened by the hostile outbursts of poorly defended personalities.

With paranoid personalities barely controlling their rage, defenses must be strengthened through supportive therapy or medication rather than uncovered by analysis. With overcontrolled neurotics, the best we can expect is to rechannel hostility into more socially acceptable outlets such as competition, assertiveness, or hunting. Otherwise, we will all be hunters and the hunted.

Control

Struggles over interpersonal control are frequently struggles over whose defenses will dominate the relationship. The more rigid the defenses, the more likely it is that individuals will insist on others conforming to their view of the world and their ways of acting. The person who repeatedly projects hostility onto the world, for instance, is likely to put considerable pressure on others to see the world as a hostile place. Conversely, if a person defends with repressive, rose-colored glasses, then interactions will be focused on only the cheery aspects of the world. If two people with incompatible defenses try to interact, there will be conflict. An insignificant matter, such as deciding which movie to see, can turn into a heated battle for control when it involves a spouse with rose-colored glasses who wants to see a light comedy and a hostility-projecting spouse who wants to see a war flick.

Individuals also expect to control relationships when they experience the other person as nothing more than an object that exists to gratify their infantile desires. Each pregenital type of personality has its unique style of controlling others: Oral characters control by clinging, anal characters control through sheer stubbornness, and phallic characters control through seductiveness. The most intensely controlling people seem to be anal personalities who have come from overcontrolling families. They feel they were once forced to give in on the toilet and thereby lost control over their bodies. Now they act as if they are determined never to give in again.

An anal-restrictive woman was raised by a governess who seemed to enjoy giving her cold-water enemas to force her to let go when she was 2 years old. She married a man who was toilet trained at 10 months of age. He was complaining that his wife could never let go and enjoy their sexual relationship. She went along with his demands for sex but seemed unable to let go to have an orgasm. The trauma that brought them into psychotherapy followed the wife's decision to solve her problem. She read Masters and Johnson's sex therapy book and reserved a hotel room in New York so they could have a sexual holiday. Once in New York, she became very aroused as she approached her husband, but he was now unable to get an erection. He was so determined to control their sexual relationship that he shut off his penis to spite his wife.

In treatment, the analyst must be keenly aware of how a patient is trying to control. The analyst will recognize when controlling behavior is serving defensive purposes of resistance or gratifying purposes of transference. The analyst must confront and clarify the patient's attempts to control and then interpret the meaning and causality of controlling maneuvers. The analyst's most effective method of countercontrol is silence: No matter what response the patient insists on, the analyst can respond with silence. It is like trying to fight with a partner who clams up—it can be terribly frustrating because the quiet one remains in control.

Individuo-Social Conflicts

Adjustment versus Transcendence

Freud (1930) believed there was a fundamental and unresolvable conflict between an organized society's need for rules, on the one hand, and an individual's desires for immediate, selfish gratification, on the other. This represents, in a nutshell, the superego versus the id, the reality principle versus the pleasure principle. Freud argued that

cultures did not need to be as oppressive about childhood sexuality as was his Victorian age; in fact, Freud, more than any other individual, was responsible for our modern sexual revolution. Nevertheless, Freud accepted the idea that culture must be repressive to some degree. Being the civilized individual that he was, he threw his weight behind civilization and was willing to treat its discontents.

Some radical post-Freudians argue that individuals need not be repressed. All of the destructive expressions of the death instinct, such as violence, materialism, and pollution, result from repeated frustration of the life instinct. If we adopt more childlike, spontaneous lifestyles, in which we give free expression to playing in bed and in fields, then we would not be frustrated and so aggressive. Those who assume a radical Freudian view usually accept sexuality as an instinct but see aggression as the product of the repression of our desires for spontaneous sexuality. Radical Freudians generally believe that individuals should be encouraged to transcend their particular cultures and find fulfillment by following their own unique paths in the face of possible social ostracism. But Freud himself, as radical as he was in many ways, was convinced that even the most conscious individuals must compromise with the culture in which they live and leave fantasies of transcendence to the angels.

Impulse Control

Freud was convinced that human sexual and aggressive impulses must be controlled. We are animals covered with a thin veneer of civilization. For psychotherapists to encourage the removal of that veneer is ultimately to encourage raping and rioting in the streets. Some believe that Freud himself contributed to removing this thin veneer. They see sexuality and aggression as out of control in our post-Freudian society. Dependency on drugs, alcohol, and food is rampant; violence seems to dominate the streets. Freud, however, was one of the earliest to recognize it is much easier for therapists to loosen the controls of neurotics than to produce controls for impulse-ridden personalities. He did not preach removal of the thin veneer of controls; instead, he believed that the best hope for individuals and society was to replace the rigid but shaky infantile veneer with a more mature set of controls.

Beyond Conflict to Fulfillment
Meaning in Life
Freud once said that, "The intention that Man should be happy is not in the plan of Creation." He believed we could not go beyond conflict, but he did suggest that we could find meaning in life in the midst of conflict. Meaning is found in love and work (*lieben und arbeiten*). Work is one of society's best channels for sublimating our instincts; Freud himself could sublimate his sexual curiosity into his work of analyzing his patients' sexual desires. **Sublimation** is a mature ego defense that allows us to channel the id's energy into more acceptable substitute activities: Oral sucking can become cigar smoking, anal expression can become abstract art, and so on.

Freud's embrace of the value of work came mainly from his total involvement in his own work. His voluminous productivity could come only from a person with a passion for work. A clearer source of meaning is love—the atmosphere that allows two people to come together, the most civilized expression of sexuality, and therefore the safest and most satisfying. Obsessive ruminating about meaning in life can come only from someone too immature to love and to work.

Ideal Individual
The ideal individual for Freud, and the ultimate goal of psychoanalysis, is a person who has analyzed pregenital fixations and conflicts sufficiently to attain, and maintain, genital functioning. The genital personality is the ideal. The **genital personality**

loves sex without the urgent dependency of the oral character, is fully potent in work without the compulsivity of the anal character, and is satisfied with self without the vanity of the phallic character. This ideal individual is altruistic and generous without the saintliness of the anal character, and is fully socialized and adjusted without immeasurable suffering from civilization (Maddi, 1996).

Therapeutic Relationship
There are two parts of the patient–analyst relationship, and they serve two different functions in treatment. The working alliance is based on the relatively nonneurotic, rational, realistic attitudes of the patient toward the analyst. This alliance is a precondition for successful analysis, because the rational attitudes allow the patient to trust and cooperate with the analyst even in the face of negative transference reactions.

Transference, by contrast, represents the patient's neurotic, unrealistic, and antiquated feelings toward the analyst. In transference reactions, the patient experiences feelings toward the analyst that do not befit the analyst but actually apply to significant people in the patient's childhood. Feelings and defenses pertaining to people in the past are displaced onto the analyst. These transference reactions represent the conflicts between impulses and defenses that are the core of the person's pregenital personality.

Repeating these impulses and defenses in relation to the analyst provides the content of psychopathology for analysis. The person does not simply talk about past conflicts, but relives them in the current relationship with the analyst. Relationship expectations from there and then are reenacted in the here and now of the consulting room. Manifesting transference reactions is not a curative process per se, because the essence of the transference is unconscious. Patients know they are having intense reactions toward the analyst but are unaware of the true meaning of their reactions. It is the analysis, or making conscious the unconscious content of the transference reactions, that is the therapeutic process.

The analyst's own reaction to the patient constitutes a delicate balance between being warm and human enough to allow a working alliance to develop, yet neutral and depriving enough to stimulate the patient's transference reactions. The stereotype has emerged that an analyst is just a blank screen and therefore cool and aloof. Even such an orthodox analyst as Fenichel (1941), however, has written that above all the analyst should be human. Fenichel was appalled at how many of his patients were surprised by his own naturalness in therapy. In order for the patient to trust the analyst and believe the analyst cares, the analyst must communicate some warmth and genuine concern.

Freudians disagree with Carl Rogers's (1957) assumption that it is therapeutic to be genuine throughout therapy. If analysts become too real, they will interfere with the analysand's need to transfer reactions onto them from people in his or her past. Patients can transform a blank screen into almost any object they desire, but it would take a psychotic transference to distort a three-dimensional therapist into an object from the past.

Although psychoanalysts agree with Rogers that it is best to adopt a nonjudgmental attitude toward a patient's productions to allow for a freer flow of associations, they do not respond with unconditional positive regard. Frequently, neutral responses such as silence are more likely to stimulate transference reactions, and thus an analyst's reactions to the patient's productions are best described as unconditional neutral regard.

Analysts would agree with Rogers that accurate empathy is an important part of therapy. Empathy is a prime source of useful interpretations, after all. Psychoanalysts also agree that an analyst must be healthier or, in Rogers's terms, more congruent than patients.

Analysts must be aware of their own unconscious processes, as another source of accurate interpretations and as a guard against reacting toward their patients on the basis of **countertransference**—the analysts' desires to make clients objects of gratification of their own infantile impulses. For example, the analyst must be able to analyze hostile withholding of warmth or support because a patient reminds the analyst of an annoying sibling. Likewise, an analyst must be able to recognize that giving too much of oneself to a client may represent encouragement to the patient to act out sexual desires with the analyst. In short, the analyst must be healthy enough to discriminate what is coming from the patient and what the analyst is encouraging, because a patient in the midst of transference reactions cannot be expected to make such crucial discriminations.

Practicalities of Psychoanalysis

In order for psychoanalysts to accurately analyze their own countertransference reactions, they must be psychoanalyzed by a training analyst and must have graduated from a psychoanalytic institute—a process that takes 4 to 6 years, depending on how much time is spent per week at the institute. Early on, most analysts in the United States were psychiatrists, because it was very difficult for nonphysicians to be admitted to analytic institutes—even though Freud supported the practice of lay analysis, which is analysis by a nonphysician. In the past three decades, however, nonmedical mental health professionals have been routinely accepted into formal psychoanalytic training.

"But where and how is the poor wretch to acquire the ideal qualifications which he will need in this profession? The answer is in an analysis of himself, with which his preparation for his future activity begins." So asked and answered Freud (1937/1964, p. 246) in enjoining psychoanalysts to complete personal analysis themselves.

Research has indeed found that 99% of psycho-analysts and approximately 90% of psychoanalytic psychotherapists have undergone personal therapy themselves and that their therapy experiences are typically lengthier than psychotherapists of other persuasions, averaging 400 to 500 hours (Norcross & Guy, 2005).

Although classical analysts prefer seeing patients four or five times per week, treatment can still be considered psychoanalysis if it occurs at least three times a week. Psychoanalysis currently costs between $120 and $200 per 50-minute session, with the cost varying according to the city and the reputation of the analyst. Theoretically, analysis has been considered inter-minable, in that there is always more in the unconscious that could be made conscious, but the actual work with an analyst is completed in an average of 3 to 5 years.

In orthodox analysis, patients agree, if possi-ble, not to make any major changes—such as mar-riage or relocation—while in analysis. Above all, they should make no important decisions without thoroughly analyzing them. At times, patients are asked to give up psychotropic medications and chemicals such as alcohol or tobacco.

The psychoanalysis itself involves the patient (or **analysand**) and the analyst interacting alone in a private office. The patient lies on a couch with the analyst sitting in a chair at the head of the couch. The patient does most of the talking; the analyst is frequently silent for long periods of time when the patient is working well alone. Patients are subtly encouraged to associate primarily to their past, their dreams, or their feelings toward the analyst. The analyst keeps self-disclosures to a minimum and never socializes with patients. Needless to say, the analyst becomes a central fig-ure in the patient's life, and during the neurotic transference, the analyst is *the* central figure. Fol-lowing termination, the analyst remains one of the most significant persons in the patient's memory.

Major Alternatives: Psychoanalytic Psychotherapy and Relational Psychoanalysis

Variations in the standard operating procedures of psychoanalysis have occurred throughout its his-tory. At times, the innovations resulted in rejec-tion of the unorthodox analyst by more classical colleagues, and the innovator has gone on to establish a new system of psychotherapy. A case in point is Carl Jung and his subsequent deve-lopment of analytical psychology (considered in Chapter 3). At other times, variations in orthodox analysis have been seen as a practical necessity, because particular patients lacked the ego or finan-cial resources to undergo the stress of long-term, intensive analysis. Cases in point are the deve-lopment of psychoanalytic psychotherapy and relational psychoanalysis.

In practice, most contemporary followers of Freud lean more heavily on psychoanalytic psychotherapy than on classical psychoanalysis. Furthermore, many psychotherapists consider themselves Freudians although they have been trained in settings other than psychoanalytic institutes—including social work, clinical psychol-ogy, and counseling training programs.

Anna Freud (1895–1982), Sigmund's youngest child, devoted nearly 60 years to adapting psycho-analysis to children and adolescents. Her work tried to address the unfinished problems bequeathed by her father. She enlarged the bound-aries of psychoanalysis with direct considerations of ego functioning without abandoning the bed-rock of psychoanalytic instinct theory. Indeed, Anna is rightfully known as one of the "mothers" of ego psychology (which is also considered in Chapter 3). Anna systematized and expanded our understanding of defense mechanisms. Her classic monograph (1936), *The Ego and the Mechanisms of Defense*, legitimized interest in both the ego and defenses (Monte, 1991).

Establishing more flexible forms of **psychoanalytic therapy** as truly acceptable alternatives within psychoanalysis has usually been credited to Franz Alexander (1891–1963) and his colleagues at the Chicago Institute of Psychoanalysis. Alexander and French (1946) argued that orthodox analysis had been developed by Freud to serve as a scientific means of gathering knowledge about neuroses, as well as a means for treating neuroses. Once the fundamental explanations for the development of personality and psychopathology had been established, however, there was no justification to proceed with all patients as if each analyst was rediscovering the oedipal complex. With a thorough understanding of the psychoanalytic principles of psychopathology, therapists could begin to design a form of psychoanalytic therapy that fit the particular patient's needs, rather than trying to fit the patient to standard analysis.

Some patients do indeed require classical analysis—namely, those with chronic neuroses and character disorders. But these patients are in the minority. Much more common are the milder chronic cases and the acute neurotic reactions resulting from a breakdown in ego defenses due to situational stresses. Clients with milder and acute disorders can be successfully treated in a much more economical manner than previously thought. Alexander and French (1946) reported 600 such patients who were treated with psychoanalytic therapy that lasted anywhere from 1 to 65 sessions. The therapeutic improvements they reported with their abbreviated therapy were previously believed to be achievable only through long-term, standard psychoanalysis.

Following the principle of flexibility, psychoanalytic therapy becomes highly individualized. The couch may be used, or therapy may proceed face-to-face. Direct conversations may be substituted for free association. A **transference neurosis** may be allowed to develop, or it may be avoided. Drugs and environmental manipulations will be included when appropriate. Therapeutic advice and suggestions will be included along with dynamic interpretations.

Because daily sessions tend to encourage excessive dependency, psychotherapy sessions are usually spaced over time. Daily sessions can also lead to a sense of routine in which the client fails to work as intensely as possible because tomorrow's session is always available. As a rule, sessions are usually more frequent at the beginning of therapy to allow an intense emotional relationship to develop between client and therapist, and then sessions are spaced out according to what seems optimal for the individual client. After therapy has progressed, it is usually desirable for the therapist to interrupt treatment to give clients a chance to test their new gains and to see how well they can function without therapy. These interruptions also pave the way for more successful termination.

Transference is an inevitable part of any psychoanalytic therapy, although the nature of the transference relationships can be controlled. A full-blown transference neurosis is usually what accounts for the length of standard analysis, so briefer psychoanalytic therapy will frequently discourage a transference neurosis from developing. A negative transference can also complicate and extend therapy, and so may be discouraged with particular clients. When the transference relationship is controlled and directed, and when the therapist relies on a positive transference to help influence clients, therapy can usually proceed more rapidly. A client with a positive father transference toward the therapist, for example, is much more likely to accept the therapist's suggestions to leave a destructive marriage or change to a more constructive job than would a client involved in a negative transference.

The nature of the transference can be controlled through the proper use of interpretations. If it has been decided that a transference neurosis is unnecessary or perhaps even damaging, the interpretations will be restricted to the present situation, because interpretation of infantile conflicts encourages regression and dependency. Regression to early stages of functioning can also be interpreted as a means of avoiding dealing with present conflicts. Attention to disturbing events in the past would be used only to illuminate the motives for irrational reactions in the present.

The psychoanalytic psychotherapist can also control the transference by behaving less of a blank screen and more the type of person that clients expect to find when they seek assistance for behavioral disorders. When the therapist is more real and empathic, neurotic transference reactions will be more clearly seen as inappropriate to the present situation and will be less likely to develop. Countertransference reactions in the therapist can also help foster a stronger therapeutic alliance. Such reactions in the therapist need not be analyzed away; rather, the therapist must consciously decide which reactions will be helpful to therapy and must express those reactions. If a client had a very rejecting father, for example, then remaining a blank screen may engender a negative transference, whereas expressing more accepting attitudes could foster a more therapeutic relationship.

The development of a safe and trusting therapeutic relationship determines whether clients can express the troubling feelings that have been blocked off because of early conflicts with parents. The expression of previously defended feelings, such as anger, erotic desires, and dependency, is what leads to therapeutic success. A **corrective emotional experience** occurs when patients reexperience the old, unsettled conflict but with a new, healthier ending within the therapeutic relationship. Corrective emotional experiencing, then, is a more critical process than the consciousness raising stressed in orthodox analysis. Of course,

a flexible attitude toward therapy does not see the process as an either/or issue. Psychoanalytic psychotherapy at its best should involve corrective emotional experiences integrated into conscious ego functioning through intellectual insights into the history of troubled emotions.

In recent years, psychoanalysis has undergone a paradigm shift from drive reduction to the relational model. **Relational psychoanalysis** posits that the therapist is unavoidably embedded in the relational field of the treatment; the pulls and feelings of the therapist are regarded as related to the patient's dynamics and as providing potentially useful information (Mitchell, 1988, 1993). Instead of transference being assigned entirely to the patient, relational psychoanalysts regard it as an interactive process *between* patient and therapist. Instead of assiduously avoiding countertransference, interpersonal psychoanalysts accept it as an invaluable source of information about the patient's character and difficulties in living. Stephen Mitchell (1988, p. 293) captures this idea in a passage from his book, *Relational Concepts in Psychoanalysis*:

> *Unless the analyst affectively enters the patient's relational matrix or, rather, discovers himself within it—unless the analyst is in some sense charmed by the patient's entreaties, shaped by the patient's projections, antagonized and frustrated by the patient's defenses—the patient is never fully engaged and a certain depth within the analytic experience is lost.*

This relational or **intersubjective** evolution in psychoanalysis functionally means that it has progressed from a one-person psychology to a two-person psychology (Chessick, 2000). The therapist is always as much a participant in the interaction as the patient.

Relational psychoanalysis focuses upon desires, not sexual and aggressive drives. A major desire is for close, satisfying relationships. The corresponding theory of mind is not Freud's structural perspective of id, ego, and superego, but rather a mind socially constructed from interactions with others and the external world. Both the important content and the curative method of relational psychoanalysis are human relationships.

The relational model of psychoanalysis assumes that both insight and corrective emotional experiences are necessary to produce deep and enduring change. Thus, the relational analyst has an expanded repertoire of change processes at his or her disposal: interpretation remaining one, but complemented by the power of the novel interaction within the therapy relationship (Gold & Stricker, 2001).

The locus of change for Freud was inside the patient's head; for relational psychoanalysts, the locus is between people. The analyst's role is thus transformed from lofty, cerebral detachment to concerned, active involvement. The importance assigned in classical psychoanalysis to abstinence, neutrality, and anonymity gives way in relational psychoanalysis to responsiveness, reciprocity, and mutuality. The relational analyst creates a different emotional presence to get the patient to hear and experience him or her in a different way. In this engaging manner, the patient undergoes a corrective emotional experience and learns new skills within the context of an empathic relationship. (We will have much more to say about the relational trends in psychoanalysis in our coverage of psychodynamic therapies in Chapter 3.)

Effectiveness of Psychoanalysis

Although psychoanalysis has concerned itself with the distortions emanating from transference for more than 110 years, it has not been nearly as concerned about scientifically controlling for the distortions involved in analyzing its own effectiveness. Freud viewed experimental support of psychoanalytic propositions and treatments as unnecessary. In a letter to early researcher Saul Rosenzweig, he wrote that psychoanalytic assertions were "independent of experimental verification." For its first 90 years, the effectiveness of psychoanalysis was supported almost entirely by case studies and clinical surveys reported by enthusiastic analysts. Such case studies and clinical surveys are the empirical starting point for all psychotherapy systems, but they are too biased and uncontrolled to scientifically establish the efficacy of any system (Meltzoff & Kornreich, 1970).

One of the earliest and best-known psychoanalytic survey studies is that of Knight (1941), who surveyed dispositions of patients who stayed in psychoanalysis for at least 6 months. The data involved the analysts' judgments of whether patients were "apparently cured," much improved, improved, unchanged, or worse when analysis was terminated. This survey study had the advantage of being cross-cultural, in that it included data on patients seen at psychoanalytic institutes in Berlin, London, Topeka, and Chicago. Dividing patients by diagnostic category, Knight reported the results shown in Table 2.2. Across patient diagnoses, approximately half of the patients completing classical psychoanalysis were apparently cured or much improved.

Subsequent surveys on the outcomes of psychoanalysis show similarly positive results (e.g., Bachrach et al., 1991; Fonagy & Target, 1996; Freedman et al., 1999). Improvement rates are typically reported by analysts to be 60% and better, depending on how improvement is measured (Galatzer et al., 2000). Naturalistic effectiveness studies of psychoanalysis, too, show positive effects (e.g., Blomberg et al., 2001). However, virtually all of that research entails retrospective, uncontrolled studies in naturalistic settings in

Table 2.2 Early Survey Results on the Effectiveness of Psychoanalysis by Patient Diagnosis

DIAGNOSTIC CATEGORY	NUMBER OF PATIENTS	CURED OR MUCH IMPROVED	NO CHANGE OR WORSE
Neuroses	534	63%	37%
Sexual disorders	47	49%	51%
Character disorders	111	57%	43%
Organ neurosis and organic conditions (e.g., colitis, ulcers)	55	78%	22%
Psychoses	151	25%	75%
Special symptoms (e.g., migraine, epilepsy, alcoholism, stammering)	54	30%	70%

SOURCE: Data from Knight (1941).

which the treatment was not standardized with respect to duration, technique, and so on. Such research is subject to considerable criticism, such as therapists not actually practicing the prescribed method, but it is a starting point for controlled experiments.

At the same time, the goals of psychoanalysis are not particularly amenable to quantification. How does one measure more joy in life or operationalize the capacity for love and work? Can resolved transference neuroses be gauged by a self-report checklist? Psychoanalysis is more ambitious than other therapies in that it hopes to impact fundamental personality organization—enduring **structural change**. Its treatment objectives are not easily specified in measurable, symptom-based outcomes. Many psychoanalysts believe that the extensive research via clinical surveys and natural effectiveness studies is sufficiently scientific and sensitive to document the multifaceted success of psychoanalysis.

Unfortunately, there are not any randomized clinical trials conducted on classical psychoanalysis or relational psychoanalysis, to our knowledge. Merton Gill (1994, p. 157), himself a passionate analyst, lamented before his death that

psychoanalysis is "the only significant branch of human knowledge and therapy that refuses to conform to the demand of Western civilization for some kind of systematic demonstration of its contentions." Thus, the effectiveness of classical and relational psychoanalysis has not been adequately tested.

Psychoanalytic Psychotherapy

Fortunately, several controlled outcome studies have been conducted on long-term psychoanalytic psychotherapy. Let us consider them, starting with a classic study.

The Menninger Foundation's Psychotherapy Research Project began in 1959 and lasted nearly 20 years. The study involved 42 adult outpatients and inpatients seen in psychoanalysis or psychoanalytic psychotherapy. Psychoanalysis lasted an average of 835 hours; psychotherapy lasted an average of 289 hours. The majority of patients improved on the Health-Sickness Rating scale, but there was no difference in improvement between those in psychoanalysis and those in psychoanalytic psychotherapy (Kernberg, 1973). Direct comparisons between the two treatments are difficult to make because patients were not randomly assigned but differed systematically between the two groups. Further limiting the conclusions on the efficacy of the two therapies was the absence of both a placebo therapy group and a no-treatment group.

In *Forty-Two Lives in Treatment*, Wallerstein (1986) extensively chronicles, over a 30-year span, the treatment careers and subsequent life changes of the patients seen in the Menninger project. Paralleling earlier reports, Wallerstein drew the following overarching conclusions from this extensive study: The traditional distinction between "structural change" and "behavioral change" is highly suspect; intrapsychic conflict resolution is not always a necessary condition for change; the supportive psychoanalytic therapy produced greater than expected success; and classical psychoanalysis produced less than expected success. The treatment results of psychoanalysis and psychoanalytic therapy in this study, as in others (Sandell et al., 2000), tend to converge rather than diverge in outcome.

Enough studies on psychoanalytic psychotherapy have appeared in recent years to enable a **meta-analysis**, a systematic evaluation of the results of several independent studies. One such meta-analysis located 27 studies of long-term psychoanalytic therapy, involving more than 5,000 patients and averaging 150 sessions (de Maat et al., 2009). The overall success rate was 64% of patients at termination and 55% at longer follow-up for moderate and mixed psychopathology. Those figures are quite similar to the numbers reported in the surveys of psychoanalysts, as reviewed earlier. When patients were compared from the beginning to the end of treatment, large effect sizes (1.03) were found for symptom reduction and medium effect sizes (0.54) for personality change.

Although favorable, such pre- to posttreatment effects tend to be inflated because they do not separate out the contribution of nonspecific factors (such as the value of attention and the passage of time) and because the psychoanalytic therapy is not directly compared to alternative (including briefer) treatments. A more rigorous meta-analysis of 11 controlled studies on the effectiveness of long-term psychoanalytic psychotherapy found the evidence to be limited and conflicting (Smit et al., 2012). The recovery rate from various mental disorders was the same for long-term psychoanalytic therapies as for various control treatments, including treatments as usual. That is, in controlled studies, psychoanalytic psychotherapy did not significantly outperform the control conditions.

In sum, there are multiple clinical surveys of psychoanalysts about the benefits of their craft and several naturalistic effectiveness studies of psychoanalysis, but no controlled outcome research attesting to its absolute or relative effectiveness. We can state with reasonable confidence that psychoanalysis is superior to no treatment at all, but we cannot safely conclude that psychoanalysis has proved itself more effective than a credible placebo therapy.

The conclusions from the growing research base on long-term psychoanalytic therapy remain decidedly conflicted. On the one hand, most of its patients do indeed profit from the beginning to the end of treatment. What's more, the evidence suggests that the outcomes of psychoanalysis and psychoanalytic psychotherapy tend to be quite similar. On the other hand, we cannot conclude that psychoanalytic psychotherapy outperforms less intensive and less expensive psychotherapies. (The considerable research conducted on short-term psychodynamic therapy will be considered in Chapter 3.)

Criticisms of Psychoanalysis
From a Cognitive-Behavioral Perspective

Behavioral criticisms of psychoanalysis have been frequent and intense. One set of criticisms revolves around the view that as a theory, psychoanalysis is much too subjective and unscientific. The psychoanalytic notions of unconscious processes, ego, and defenses are mentalistic, and incapable of direct observation in a way that can be objectively measured and scientifically validated. All too frequently, Freudians have reified rather than verified their concepts, such as the ego and the id. Freud's ideas about superego formation, female sexuality, dream interpretation, and other fanciful notions simply do not stand up under scientific scrutiny (Fisher & Greenberg, 1996).

The notion that "insight" itself is frequently therapeutic is another mentalistic fiction. As B. F. Skinner (1971, p. 183) wrote,

> Theories of psychotherapy which emphasize awareness assign a role to autonomous man which is properly, and much more effectively, reserved for contingencies of Psychoanalytic Therapies 51 reinforcement. Awareness may help if the problem is in part a lack of awareness, and "insight" into one's condition may help if one then takes remedial action, but awareness or insight alone is not always enough, and it may be too much. One need not be aware of one's behavior or the conditions controlling it in order to behave effectively—or ineffectively. On the contrary, as the toad's inquiry of the centipede demonstrates, constant self-observation may be a handicap.

But there is a more devastating reaction. Behaviorists do not argue with psychoanalytic theory; they ignore it. Why bother learning how psychoanalysis is supposed to work when there are no empirical data to demonstrate that it does work? The absence of any controlled experiments designed to evaluate the effectiveness of psychoanalysis after 110 years of practice is a scientific disgrace! Even a few experiments every decade would be slower than the average analysis. Freud himself can be excused as a genius too committed

to theory construction to gather controlled data, but surely not all of his followers can hide behind that excuse. Unless psychoanalytic researchers demonstrate scientifically that their treatment outperforms other bona fide psychotherapies, we will continue to ignore this once-dominant system as if it were a therapeutic dinosaur, too slow to survive.

From an Existential Perspective

In contrast to the behavioral view, psychoanalysis is much too objective for existentialists—not empirically, but theoretically and practically. Just look at the psychoanalytic conceptualization of humans. Psychoanalysis conceives of human beings as objects, mere bundles of instinctual and defensive energy. We are portrayed as neurotic collections of complexes, stages, defenses, and conflicts. This psychoanalytic conception has filtered into the very core of our self-concepts, becoming one of the dominant forces in our dehumanization.

Psychoanalysis is also much too deterministic for our tastes. Where are freedom, choice, and responsibility, the subjective experiences that allow humans the option of being different from all the objects of the universe? How can a system that has placed so much emphasis on consciousness as the process of freeing people from psychopathology not take freedom and choice seriously? We can freely choose to transcend psychoanalytic determinism and reductionism.

From a Cultural Perspective

Freud was indeed the grandfather of psychotherapy. He created psychoanalysis as a treatment for and by educated, middle-class Western Europeans. As is unfortunately true of many patriarchs, he legitimized intrapsychic (inside the mind) and androcentric (male-centered) biases adopted by generations of subsequent psychotherapists. Virulent attacks have been leveled over the years against psychoanalysis from a cultural perspective, which emphasizes the centrality of context, gender, and race/ethnicity.

For starters, the broader social context is practically ignored in psychoanalytic treatment. The exclusive focus on the intrapsychic makeup of the individual neglects the family, the culture, and the society. Disorders and fixations are attributed to internal conflicts rather than family dysfunction or social problems. An exemplar: Early on, Freud courageously attributed many of his female patients' disorders to the childhood sexual abuse they had encountered, but later he retracted this position and characterized these allegations as fantasies. As a result, generations of therapists treated childhood sexual abuse as an intrapsychic fantasy rather than an actual assault.

When psychoanalysts do venture from their internal psychopathological orientations to consider relationships, it is largely to engage in mother-bashing. One study (Caplan, 1989) analyzed a decade of psychological research to determine the nature and extent of mother-blaming. Of four categories—things that mothers do, things that mothers fail to do, things that fathers do, and things that fathers fail to do—only one regularly turned out to be viewed as problematic: things that mothers do. Mothers have been blamed for causing more than 70 different disorders in their children, including bedwetting, schizophrenia, and learning disabilities. The father's role is assumed to be peripheral. Psychoanalysts define "good enough mothering"; what about "good enough fathering?" (Okun, 1992). The impact of the father, the family, and the culture on the child are minimized, at least when development goes awry. Mothers must be to blame.

Freud's infamous declaration that "biology is destiny" represents an attempt to restrict women's power and status. A classic illustration of the sexist nature of classic psychoanalysis is penis envy. A girl, we are told, concludes that something is wrong with her because she does not have a penis and cathects with her father to share his phallus. Freud (1933/1965b, p. 124) wrote that "girls hold their mother responsible for their lack of a penis and do not forgive her for their being thus put at a disadvantage." How sexist is that? Note that the convoluted and unsubstantiated reasoning does not apply to boys. Why is there no vagina envy? Freud focused too much on sexual fantasy and not enough on sexist ideology.

Psychoanalytic theory is so clearly patriarchal and Eurocentric that much more could be criticized about it—the upper-class male values, the paucity of female psychoanalysts in Freud's inner circle, its historical orientation, its expensive and inefficient process, its focus on personality restructuring at the expense of behavior change, to name a few. All in all, we cast a mote in Freud's eye (Lerner, 1986).

From an Integrative Perspective

It is the essence of integration to seek what is of value in any therapy system, especially one as rich and complex as psychoanalysis. Some integrative therapists use a psychoanalytic approach, especially in their formulation of their clients' problems. Psychoanalysis presents one of the few theories with enough personality and psychopathology content to be the core of a diagnostic manual or the content of a Rorschach evaluation. Most integrationists will also use the concepts of resistance, defenses, and transference in their thinking about the content of therapy.

As a system of psychotherapy, however, classical psychoanalysis has become way too antiquated and dogmatic for integrative tastes. As in most systems, the disciples of a genius like Freud are usually less creative and, therefore, less flexible. With Freud, theory and therapy continued to evolve, but to many of the present practitioners of psychoanalysis, it seems more important to be orthodox than to be innovative and effective.

A Psychoanalytic Analysis of Mrs. C

During the early years of her marriage, Mrs. C apparently made an adequate though immature adjustment. As an obsessive or anal personality, she expressed such traits as excessive orderliness in the alphabetical ordering of her children's names, meticulousness in her concern with cleanliness, stinginess in holding onto unused clothes while buying no new ones, and constrictedness in never letting go of her sexual feelings and becoming excited. As time wore on and stress escalated, Mrs. C graduated into a full-blown obsessive-compulsive disorder (OCD).

These problems probably resulted from Mrs. C's interactions in the anal stage with overcontrolling and overdemanding parents. We know Mrs. C's mother was a compulsive person who was overly concerned with cleanliness and disease. Her father overcontrolled Mrs. C's expression of aggression and her interest in men. We can imagine that such parents would be quite harsh in their demands on issues such as toilet training and could produce many conflicts in their daughter over holding on and letting go of her bowels and other impulses. From psychoanalytic theory, we can hypothesize that Mrs. C's anal characteristics developed, in part at least, as defenses against anal pleasures such as being dirty and messy and against impulses to express anger.

Why did the experiences surrounding her daughter's case of pinworms precipitate a breakdown in Mrs. C's previously adaptive traits and defenses and lead to the emergence of a full-blown neurosis? Illness and fatigue from the Asian flu and from caring for so many sick children would place stress on Mrs. C's defenses. But the precipitating event was also of such a nature as to elicit the very impulses that Mrs. C had come to defend against since early childhood. First of all, how would anyone feel when a daughter brings home pinworms when the family is already down with the Asian flu and the mother is burdened with pregnancy and a toddler in diapers? Relatively unrepressed parents would be upset, even though they might not express their anger directly because the child did not intend to get pinworms. But Mrs. C was not free to express anger as a child and would probably have to defend against it as a parent.

A case of pinworms is also characterized by anal itching, with the pinworms locating in the anus. In fact, to confirm that the problem was pinworms, Mrs. C's physician directed her to examine her daughter's anus with a flashlight while her daughter was sleeping. So while on one level the pinworms were painful, on another level the possibility of contracting pinworms could tempt Mrs. C to exercise that secret pleasure of scratching an itchy anus. With defenses weakened by illness and fatigue, and with threatening impulses of aggression and anal sexuality stimulated by her daughter's pinworms, the conditions were set for the emergence of neurotic symptoms that both defend against and give indirect expression to Mrs. C's unacceptable impulses.

Look at how her neurotic symptoms provided further defense against her threatening impulses. The compulsive showers and hand washing intensify her long-standing preoccupation with cleanliness. If danger lies in being dirty, then wash! These compulsive symptoms are in part an intensification of her reaction formation of keeping clean to control desires to play with dirt and other symbols of feces. If desires to damage her daughter were also breaking through, then her washing could serve both as a means of removing Mrs. C from interactions with her daughter in the morning and as a means of undoing any guilt over aggression by washing her hands clean of such bloody thoughts. The underwear piled in each corner literally served to isolate Mrs. C and her family from more direct contact with anal-related objects.

How did Mrs. C's neurotic symptoms allow some gratification of her desires? The shower ritual is most obvious, because each time she lost her place in her ritual, she had to go back to giving herself anal stimulation. In the process of isolating dirty materials like underwear and items dropped on the floor, Mrs. C could also make a mess of her house. It does not take much of an interpretation to appreciate how Mrs. C was expressing her aggression toward her husband

(continued)

by making him get up at 5:00 A.M. and toward her children by not cooking or adequately caring for them.

Why was Mrs. C unable to express her feelings and desires directly and thereby prevent the need for a neurotic resolution of her conflicts? First, such direct expression would be entirely contrary to her core personality concerned with controlling such impulses. Second, the regression induced by her defenses' weakening would cause Mrs. C to react more on a primary-process level than on a rational, secondary-process level. At the unconscious primary level, Mrs. C would be terrified that loosening controls would result in her losing all control and being overwhelmed by her impulses. Being overwhelmed by instinctual stimulation produces its own panic, but Mrs. C would also panic about facing the wrath of her overcontrolling parents for being a bad girl who soiled her pants or expressed anger. At an atemporal, unconscious level, Mrs. C would not experience herself as the adult parent who is safe to express anger, but as the controlled little girl who had better not express any resentment.

In considering psychoanalysis for Mrs. C, an analyst would have to be quite confident that Mrs. C's problem was indeed obsessive-compulsive neurosis and not pseudoneurotic schizophrenia, in which the neurotic symptoms mask a psychotic process. Given how much she has already regressed and how much her life is dominated by defensive symptoms, there could be a real risk in encouraging her to regress further in psychoanalysis. If the analyst felt that further evaluation confirmed previous reports that Mrs. C. did not show evidence of a psychotic process, then psychoanalysis might proceed.

When directed to lie on the couch and say whatever comes to mind, Mrs. C would become quite anxious about having to give up some of her controls to the analyst. Obviously, she has to trust enough to believe that her analyst knows what to do and will not let her get out of control entirely. Resistance to letting her thoughts go would begin immediately. It might take the form of returning immediately to her obsession with pinworms whenever she became anxious. The analyst

would confront and clarify her pattern of talking about pinworms whenever she became anxious and then interpret this pattern in a way that would allow Mrs. C to become aware that she uses her obsession to defend against experiencing associations even more threatening than pinworms.

The psychoanalyst would, in addition, deal with Mrs. C's well-established defense of isolating her affect. The analyst would slowly confront her pattern of saying only what she thinks about events and not what she feels about them. The analyst would also be very sensitive to occasions when Mrs. C is being excessively warm and affectionate, because such expressions would likely be reactions to her true feelings of hatred and loathing for the nongiving, controlling therapist.

The psychoanalyst would slowly assist Mrs. C in understanding what her ritual cleaning is symbolically washing away. For which "dirty acts" is Mrs. C atoning? Sexual impulses, homosexual feelings, murderous urges toward her controlling father, and rage toward a burdensome family are all probable unconscious culprits. All were forbidden by her parents and society and all internalized into her punitive superego, but all are natural urges and curiosities of homo sapiens.

As Mrs. C gradually became aware of the defensive nature of her symptoms, she would gradually experience intensely the feelings that would be emerging toward the analyst. As she regressed, she might become aware of fears that her analyst was trying to control her sex life, just as her father seemed to want to control it when he followed her on a date during her teens. Even more threatening would be her desires to have her fatherlike analyst control her sexuality and thereby satisfy his and her desires together. As she regressed further, she might become aware of desires to have her fatherlike analyst satisfy her by having anal intercourse or to have her motherlike analyst pleasure her by wiping her anus.

Mrs. C's transference reactions would include considerable hostility displaced from both of her parents onto her analyst, so she would be frequently enraged that the analyst was demanding and controlling while being ungiving, as were both her mother and her father. But she could

(continued)

not become conscious of hostile and sexual impulses without also becoming conscious of fears that her parent/analyst was going to destroy her or reject her by sending her to a state psychiatric hospital. She would then become acutely aware of how frequently she would try to control both her anxiety and her impulses by expressing the opposite of what she felt, by apologizing, or in other ways undoing her reactions, or by isolating her impulses into more neutral thoughts.

As Mrs. C worked through the neurotic transference with her analyst, she would slowly gain insight into the meaning and causes of her neurosis. She would eventually become conscious of ways in which she could channel her dangerous impulses into more mature outlets that provide both controls and gratification for her desires, such as expressing her anger in words. Over many years, Mrs. C might consciously restructure her personality enough to give her ego some flexibility in expressing hostile and sexual impulses without having to panic when situations threatened to stimulate them.

We are much more at home with the flexibility of psychoanalytic psychotherapy and relational psychoanalysis. However, we are not comfortable with the fact that psychoanalytic psychotherapy, like psychoanalysis, has not been demonstrated to be more effective than any other form of therapy. One certainly cannot justify recommending classical psychoanalysis to clients when it is the lengthiest and most expensive alternative. Psychoanalysis may provide a rich source of therapy content, but it has yet to establish any real advantage in patient success.

Future Directions

Many psychotherapists in the past century have sounded the death knell for psychoanalysis. They are convinced that psychoanalysis will disappear as a body of knowledge and as a form of treatment. Allusions to psychoanalysis as a "dinosaur," "a relic," and a "gas-guzzler in an era of compacts" reflect this dismissive sentiment. However, we and many others agree with Silverman's (1976) assessment of psychoanalytic theory—borrowed from Mark Twain's famous quip when confronted with news reports of his own demise—that "the reports of my death are greatly exaggerated."

Although commentators periodically declare that Freud is dead, his repeated burials lie on shaky grounds. Central to contemporary psychoanalytic theory are a series of propositions that have received considerable research support and clinical consensus. Among these are—the unconscious is alive and powerful; the origins of many behavioral disorders are rooted in childhood; humans are in internal conflict and tend to produce compromise solutions; and mental representations of ourselves, others, and relationships profoundly impact our daily functioning (Westen, 1998). These are Freud's legacies.

At the same time, bewildering changes in practice confront the new generation of psychoanalysts. These include a diminishing number of patients for psychoanalysis proper; an increasing number of nonpsychoanalytically based psychotherapies; a societal retreat from insurance coverage for long-term psychotherapeutic care; a growing preoccupation with cost-effectiveness and cost containment; a rise in the use of psychotropic medication; and the increased use of managed care and accountability, with their inevitable infringements on the confidentiality of the therapeutic relationship (Rouff, 2000).

For all these reasons, the future of psychoanalysis probably lies in time-limited psychoanalytic therapy and briefer forms of relational psychoanalysis. The "gold standard" of psychoanalysis proper has given way to the "gold leaf" or copper of psychoanalytic therapy. Although there will always be classical psychoanalysis available to psychoanalysts in training and the wealthy in need, less than 1% of all patients receiving psychotherapy or counseling today receive psychoanalysis proper.

The future we foresee for psychoanalysis can be summed up by the terms *interpersonal* and *integration*. Although there is honest disagreement as to the permanence of the resurgence of psychoanalysis, almost all observers concur that this is attributable to its interpersonal and relational emphasis. New attention is being paid to the two-person or dyadic character of the therapeutic relationship. Both patient and therapist continually and reciprocally contribute to the therapeutic situation, which always contains real and transference elements. The notion of "pure" transference and the singular power of interpretation have proved illusions. The two-person, relational model is on the ascendancy.

In practice, few psychotherapists are "purists." Integration dominates the contemporary scene (see Chapters 16 and 17), and the modern psychoanalytic therapist demonstrates greater openness to tailoring treatment to the needs of the patient and adapting to changing circumstances. Many psychotherapists continue to embrace a psychoanalytic orientation while carefully integrating or assimilating methods from other systems of psychotherapy, especially humanistic and cognitive therapies. In fact, reviews of Freud's own treatment cases (e.g., Lynn & Vaillant, 1988; Yalom, 1980) indicate that the master used many "nonpsychoanalytic" methods, such as suggesting behavioral homework assignments and intervening with a patient's family on her behalf. Freud was an early integrationist.

Contributing to the renewed vitality of psychoanalysis is the tremendous interest in integrating advances in neuroscience. Neuroscientists are discovering that their biological descriptions of the brain may fit together best with the psychological theories Freud sketched a century ago (Solms, 2004). The term (and journal title) **neuropsychoanalysis** unites the previously divided fields of neuroscience and psychoanalysis.

If there were ever a Book of Genesis on psychotherapy, it would probably start out something like this: "In the beginning, there was nothing until psychoanalysis" (Scaturo, 2005). Freud had the formidable task of creating something from nothing and of structuring the structureless. He was *the* pioneer of psychotherapy. It is easy years later to contradict the pioneer, but it is not the function of the pioneer to say the last word but to say the first word (Guntrip, 1973). Psychoanalysis can no longer be simply identified with the original, classic psychobiology; Freud himself began the first major move beyond that starting point, when in the 1920s he turned his attention to the analysis of the ego. Freud was the courageous pioneer who opened up an entirely new field of systematic inquiry into the inner workings of human experience.

Key Terms

anal personality	incorporation
anal stage	insight
analysand	instincts
castration anxiety	intellectualization
compromise formation	interpretation
corrective emotional experience	intersubjective
	latency stage
countertransference	latent content
defense mechanisms	manifest content
denial	meta-analysis
displacement	neuropsychoanalysis
dynamic view	neurosis
fixation	oedipal conflict
free association	oral personality
genetic view	oral stage
genital personality	phallic stage
genital stage	primal anxiety

primary-process
   thinking
projection
psychic determinism
psychoanalysis
psychoanalytic therapy
psychosexual stages
reaction formation
relational
   psychoanalysis
repression

resistance
secondary process
structural
structural change
sublimation
transference
transference neurosis
unconscious
undoing
working alliance
working through

Recommended Readings

Fisher, S., & Greenberg, R. P. (1996). *Freud scientifically reappraised: Testing the theories and therapy.* New York: Wiley.

Freud, A. (1936). *The ego and the mechanisms of defense.* New York: International Universities Press.

Freud, S. (1900/1953). *The interpretation of dreams.* First German edition, 1900; in *Standard edition* (Vols. 4 & 5), Hogarth Press, 1953.

Freud, S. (1933/1965b). *New introductory lectures on psychoanalysis.* First German edition, 1933; in *Standard edition* (Vol. 22), Hogarth Press, 1965.

Gabbard, G. O., Litowitz, B. E., & Williams, P. (2012). *Textbook of psychoanalysis* (2nd ed.). Washington, DC: American Psychiatric Publishing.

Galatzer, R. M., Bachrach, H., Skolnikoff, A., & Waldron, S. (2000). *Does psychoanalysis work?* New Haven: Yale University Press.

Greenson, R. R. (1967). *The technique and practice of psychoanalysis* (Vol. 1). New York: International Universities Press.

McWilliams, N. (2004). *Psychoanalytic psychotherapy: A practitioner's guide.* New York: Guilford.

Mitchell, S. (1988). *Relational concepts in psychoanalysis: An integration.* Cambridge: Harvard University Press.

JOURNALS: *American Journal of Psychoanalysis; Bulletin of the Menninger Clinic; Contemporary Psychoanalysis; International Journal of Psychoanalysis; International Review of Psycho-Analysis; Journal of Clinical Psychoanalysis; Journal of the American Psychoanalytic Association; Modern Psychoanalysis; Neuro-Psychoanalysis; Psychoanalysis and Contemporary Thought; Psychoanalysis and Psychotherapy; Psychoanalytic Dialogues; Psychoanalytic Inquiry; Psychoanalytic Psychology; Psychoanalytic Quarterly; Psychoanalytic Review; Psychoanalytic Social Work.*

Recommended Websites

American Psychoanalytic Association:
   www.apsa.org
   www.teachpsychoanalysis.com
APA Division of Psychoanalysis:
   www.apadivisions.org/division-39/
International Association for Relational Psychoanalysis:
   www.iarpp.net/
Psychodynamic Diagnostic Manual:
   www.pdm1.org
Sigmund Freud and the Freud Archives:
   www.freudarchives.org

CHAPTER 3

Psychodynamic Therapies

Alfred Adler

Heinz Kohut

Max was preoccupied with getting into Harvard Medical School. He was convinced that acceptance at such a superior school was his only chance of demonstrating to others that he was not a clod. His own deep-seated feelings of inferiority were attributed to the fact that his younger brother had been favored at home and was superior at school. Max himself had always been a good student but never outstanding. He believed that his college performance was handicapped by his concern that other students were spreading rumors about his being homosexual. Max was afraid that he might one day reach out and grab the penis of one of his fellow students in his all-male college.

In spite of what others might think, Max was certain that he was not gay. He said he had never desired sex with a man and had experienced two fairly satisfying relationships with women. Max believed that his obsession to reach out and grab his fellow students was a hostile desire to strike back at those who were bothering him. His goal in psychotherapy was to extinguish his obsession with penises and with what fellow students thought, so that he could succeed in his quest for admission to Harvard.

One of Max's previous therapists, himself a Harvard MD, had assured Max that he was Harvard material. In spite of a glowing letter from the therapist, Max had failed to get into Harvard or any other medical school, for that matter. When I

(JOP) suggested to Max that his goals might be unreasonable and unnecessarily high, he didn't want to hear it. He was zealously doing postgraduate work to improve his scores on the medical school admissions test, and there was no holding him back. As our relationship developed, I expressed my admiration for his ambition but felt he was overly preoccupied with himself. He agreed, but countered that if he received his MD from Harvard, then he could really do something for others. Taking a lead from Alfred Adler, I challenged Max to prove that he cared about others. I challenged him to find a way to make at least one person a little happier each day for the next week.

That particular week, the staff at a state hospital happened to be on strike. Max met my challenge by volunteering each day to help care for some of the most troubled patients. Then he went even further. He became quite upset over the way the patients were treated in the hospital and began organizing the other volunteers and some patients to form a citizens' group for patients' rights. When he learned that such an organization already existed, he combined forces and was elected to the citizens' advisory board.

As his concern for others increased, Max's preoccupation with penises and his peers' opinions faded. He began an intense relationship with a woman volunteer who was also a strong advocate for patients' rights. His goal to get into Harvard, however, became even stronger, as he decided to eventually become a psychiatrist in order to make a meaningful impact on the state hospital system.

A Sketch of Freud's Descendants

Quoting Freud in psychotherapy is like quoting Newton in physics. Both men are assured of that permanent place in the history of thought that belongs to the genuine pioneer. Those who come after faithfully follow up and extend the original theory. We all warm our hands in Freud's fires.

Freud's direct descendants attempt to complete and expand all that he had left undone. These neo-analysts or neo-Freudians (*neo* meaning after or new) are now more commonly known as **psychodynamic therapists**. Although they are a diverse lot, psychodynamic therapists share similar directions away from classical psychoanalysis. These central revisions can be summarized as follows.

PSYCHOANALYSIS	PSYCHODYNAMIC
Id	Ego
Intrapsychic	Interpersonal
Defenses	Mastery, adaptation
Biological	Social

The classic psychoanalytic emphasis on the id (so-called **drive theory**) is transformed in psychodynamicism into an emphasis on the ego and its functioning, hence the term **ego psychology**. Whereas Freud was primarily concerned with intrapsychic (inside the person) conflicts, his descendants are more concerned with interpersonal (between people) conflicts. In fact, a major branch of psychodynamic therapy is known as **object relations**—*objects* meaning people (or their mental representations). Freud's original emphasis on biological forces and defense mechanisms shifts to social forces and coping or mastery experiences.

The dividing line between psychoanalytic therapies and psychodynamic therapies is hazy. Deciphering where one ends and the other begins is a genuine challenge but the differences are real enough. Adding to the confusion is the inconsistent use of terminology; some authors refer to all post-Freudian therapy as *psychoanalytic*, whereas others prefer the term *psychodynamic*.

In Chapter 2, we considered Freud's original drive theory of psychoanalysis and the newer relational psychoanalysis. In this chapter, we examine five variants of psychodynamic therapy: Adlerian therapy, ego psychology, object relations, supportive therapy, and brief psychodynamic therapy.

Of course, other prominent theorists have contributed to the evolution of psychodynamic therapy. As mentioned in Chapter 2, Anna Freud (1895–1982), Sigmund's daughter, made substantive contributions in her own right. Wilhelm Reich (1897–1957) was originally a member of Freud's inner circle but broke ranks when he rejected Freud's death instinct. Reich developed **character analysis** as an alternative to classical psychoanalysis.

Likewise, Carl G. Jung (1875–1961), once hand-picked by Freud as his successor and hailed as the "crown prince" of psychoanalysis, launched his own **analytical psychology**. Jung pursued a path different from Freud's when he found himself unable to accept the exclusively sexual nature of Freud's notion of libido. Jung relied extensively on the interpretation of dreams and symbols to access the patient's **archetypes** (inherited predispositions or models on which similar things are patterned). Jung was convinced of the existence of a **collective unconscious**, along with a personal unconscious. The collective unconscious contains primordial archetypes inherited from our past that record common experiences repeated over countless generations. Common archetypes include the hero, the shadow (or "dark side"), the Mother, and the trickster. These controversial propositions along with his word association test and the introvert-extravert distinction remain Jung's original contributions to the field.

Jung and Reich enjoyed tremendous popularity in the 1950s and 1960s; in fact, previous editions of this text devoted entire chapters to their theories. However, their influence has gradually waned, reflected in the repeated finding that less than 1% of psychotherapists designate themselves as Jungians or Reichians (see Table 1.1). As a result, we have condensed our presentation on them.

We begin this chapter, instead, with Alfred Adler. He is, arguably, the first and most prominent psychodynamic theorist whose impact continues to this day. Thereafter, we consider ego psychology, object relations, supportive therapy, and brief psychodynamic therapy.

A Sketch of Alfred Adler

Alfred Adler (1870–1937) was the first person to formulate how feelings of inferiority could simulate a striving for superiority, as evidenced by Max. Adler himself had striven to be an outstanding physician, in part to compensate for the frailty he had experienced as a youngster with rickets. As the second son in a family of six, he was further spurred to stand out by his rivalry with his older brother and his somewhat unhappy relationship with his mother. His strongest support, both emotionally and financially, came from his grain-merchant father, who encouraged him to complete his MD at Vienna University.

In 1895, Adler began as an ophthalmologist and then switched to general practice, which he maintained long after he became known as a psychiatrist. As a psychiatrist in Vienna, he could not help but consider Freud's theories, which were creating such a stir and generating so much criticism. Adler was quick to appreciate the importance of Freud's ideas, and he had the courage to defend the controversial system. Freud responded by inviting Adler to join his select Wednesday evening discussion circle.

Frequently cited as a student of Freud, Adler was actually a strong-minded colleague in harmony with Freud on some issues and in conflict on others. Adler's book *Study of Organ Inferiority* (1917) was highly praised by Freud. On the other hand, when Adler introduced the concept **aggression instinct** in 1908, Freud disapproved. It was not until long after Adler had rejected his own aggression-instinct theory that Freud incorporated it into psychoanalysis in 1923.

By 1911, the differences between Adler and Freud were becoming irreconcilable. Adler criticized Freud for an overemphasis on sexuality, although Freud condemned Adler's emphasis on conscious processes. At a series of tense meetings, Adler discussed his criticisms of Freud and faced heckling from the most ardent of Freud's followers. Following the third meeting, Adler resigned as president of the Vienna Psychoanalytic Society and soon resigned as editor of the society's journal. Later that year, Freud indicated that no one could support Adlerian concepts and remain in good standing as a psychoanalyst. Freud thus pressured other members to leave the society, at the same time setting an unfortunate precedent of stifling serious dissent.

Adler quickly established himself as the leader of an emerging system of psychotherapy. He called his system **individual psychology** to underscore the importance of studying the total individual in therapy. His productivity was interrupted by service as a physician in the Austrian army during World War I. Following the war, he expressed his interest in children by establishing the first of 30 child guidance clinics in the Viennese school system. Adler expressed his social interest by speaking out strongly for school reforms, improvements in child-rearing practices, and the rejection of archaic prejudices that persistently led to interpersonal conflict.

Adler's interest in common people was expressed by his commitment to avoid technical jargon and to present his work in a language readily understood by nonprofessionals. Unlike many intellectuals, he was eager to speak and write for the public, and his influence among the public probably spread further than his influence on mental health professionals of that era. As an indefatigable writer and speaker, he traveled extensively to bring his message to the public. His influence seemed to peak just prior to the advent of Hitler, when 39 separate Adlerian societies were established.

Adler saw the United States as a place of great potential for his ideas. In 1925, at a relatively late age, he was struggling to learn English so he could speak to American professionals and to the public in their own language. He became a professor of psychiatry at the Long Island School of Medicine and settled in New York in 1935. Two years later, at the age of 67, he ignored the urging of his friends to slow down and died from a heart attack while on a speaking tour in Scotland.

Adler's influence on people was as much personal as intellectual. Besides his serious compassion for those suffering from social ills, Adler showed a light side and loved good food, music, and the company of others. He entertained his guests and his audiences with his excellent humor. In spite of his own fame, he abhorred pomposity. He was committed both professionally and personally to expressing his commonality with his fellow humans.

Theory of Personality

Striving for superiority is the core motive of the human personality. To be superior is to rise above what we currently are. To be superior does not necessarily mean to attain social distinction, dominance, or leadership. Striving for superiority means striving to live a more perfect and complete life. It is the superordinate dynamic principle of life; striving for completion and improvement encompasses and gives power to other human drives.

Striving for superiority can be expressed in many ways. Ideals of the perfect life vary from "peace and happiness throughout the land" to "honesty is the best policy" to *Deutschland über Alles* (Germany above all). Perfection is an ideal created in the minds of humans, who then live as if they can make their ideals real. Individuals create their own fictional goals for living and act as if their personal goals are the final purpose for life. This **fictional finalism** reflects the fact that psychological events are determined not so much by historical circumstances as by present expectations of how one's future life can be completed. If a person believes that a perfect life is found in heaven as the reward for being virtuous, then that person's life will be greatly influenced by striving for that goal, whether heaven exists or not. Such fictional goals represent the subjective cause of psychological events. Humans evolve as self-determined participants who influence their futures by striving for internally created ideals. Each of us creates an **ideal self** that represents the perfect person we might strive to become.

What are the sources of this striving for superior ideals? Superiority strivings are the natural reaction to inescapable feelings of inferiority, an inevitable and virtually innate experience of all humans. Subjective feelings of inferiority may be based on objective facts such as **organ inferiorities**—physical weaknesses of the body that predispose us toward ailments such as heart, kidney, stomach, bladder, and lung problems. Organ inferiority can be a stimulus to compensate by striving to be superior. The classic case is that of Demosthenes, who compensated for his early stuttering by becoming one of the world's great orators.

Feelings of inferiority—or, more broadly, an **inferiority complex**—can arise from subjectively felt psychological or social weaknesses as well as from actual bodily impairments. Young children, for example, can be aware of being less intelligent and less adept than older siblings, and so they strive toward a higher level of development. To feel inferior is not abnormal. To feel inferior is to be aware that we are finite beings who are never wise enough, fast enough, or powerful enough to handle all of life's contingencies. Feelings of inferiority have stimulated every improvement in humanity's ability to deal more effectively with the world.

Feeling inferior and consequently striving for superiority applies to gender as well. Adler's notion of **masculine protest** refers chiefly to a woman protesting against her feminine role. Unlike Freud's proposal that a woman wishes to be a man and desires his anatomical structure, Adler recognized that a woman wishes to have a man's freedom and desires his privileged position in society. Status, not genitalia, is the real goal. A man, too, can suffer from masculine protest when he believes his masculinity is in some fashion inferior and consequently compensates by adopting hypermasculine behaviors. Preoccupation with big trucks, large guns, huge muscles, and other symbols of male power may reflect such compensation.

A person's particular feeling of inferiority influences the **style of life** that person chooses for becoming superior. Feeling intellectually inadequate as a child, for example, may lead one to become a superior intellectual. An intellectual style of life then becomes the integrating principle of the person's life. An intellectual arranges a daily routine, develops a set of reading and thinking habits, and relates to family and friends in accordance with the goal of intellectual superiority. An intellectual style of life is a more solitary and sedentary existence than is the active life of a politician, for example. A lifestyle is not the same as the behavioral patterns of a person's existence. All of a person's behavior springs from that individual's unique style of life. A lifestyle is a cognitive construction, an ideal representation of what a person is in the process of becoming.

People construct their lifestyles partly on the basis of early childhood experiences. The child's position in the family constellation—the **birth order** or **ordinal position**—is especially influential on his or her lifestyle. A middle child, for example, is more likely to choose an ambitious style of life, striving to surpass the older sibling. Second children, in particular, are born to rebel (Sulloway, 1996). The oldest child faces the inevitable experience of being dethroned by a new center of attention. Having to give up the position of undisputed attention and affection produces feelings of resentment and hatred that are part of sibling rivalry. The oldest child enjoys looking to the past when there was no rival and is likely to develop a more conservative style of life. The youngest child possesses older siblings who serve as pacemakers to goad development. Youngest children never have the experience of losing attention to a successor and are more likely to expect to live the life of a prince or princess.

Although objective facts such as organ inferiorities and birth order will influence the lifestyle a person constructs, they do not ultimately determine how a person lives. The prime mover of the lifestyle is the **creative self**. As such, the creative self is not easily defined. It is a subjective power that gives humans the unique ability to transform objective facts into personally meaningful events. The creative self keeps a person from becoming just a product of biological and social circumstances by acting on these circumstances to give them personal meaning. The creative self is an active process that interprets the genetic and environmental facts of a person's life and integrates them into a unified personality that is dynamic, subjective, and unique. From all the forces impinging on a person, the creative self produces a personal goal for living that moves that person toward a more perfect future.

Every style of life must come to grips with the fact that humans are social beings born into interpersonal relationships. A healthy style of life reflects a **social interest** in all human beings. A healthy personality is aware that a complete life is possible only within the context of a more perfect society. A healthy personality identifies with the inferiorities common to us all. The ignorance we all share, such as how to have peace in the world or how to be free from dreaded diseases, spurs the healthy personality to help humanity transcend these weaknesses. As Adler (1964, p. 31) wrote, "Social interest is the true and inevitable compensation for all the natural weaknesses of individual human beings."

Social interest is an inherent potential that can capture the commitment of any person, but it will not develop on its own. Social interest must be nourished within a healthy family atmosphere, which fosters cooperation, respect, trust, support, and understanding. The enduring values and action patterns of family members, especially the parents, make up a family atmosphere that can, if healthy, encourage children to reject purely selfish interests in favor of larger social interests. Healthy personalities are those encouraged by the prospect of living a more complete life by contributing to the construction of a more perfect world.

Theory of Psychopathology

Pathological personalities have become discouraged from attaining superiority in a socially constructive style. Pathological personalities tend to emerge from family atmospheres of competition, mistrust, neglect, domination, abuse, or pampering, all of which discourage social interest. Children from such families are more likely to strive for a more complete life at the expense of others. Children discouraged from social interest tend to choose one of four selfish goals for attaining superiority: attention seeking, power seeking, revenge taking, and declaring deficiency or defeat (Dreikurs, 1947, 1948). Although these selfish goals may be the immediate strivings of misbehaving children, they can also become the final traits that lead to pathological lifestyles.

A pampered lifestyle results from parents doting on their children, doing tasks for them that are well within the children's abilities to do themselves (Adler, 1936). The message the children receive is that they are not capable of doing things for themselves. If children conclude that they are inadequate, they develop an inferiority complex, which is more than just inferiority feelings; they acquire a total self-concept of inadequacy. Inferiority complexes lead pampered personalities to avoid tackling the basic life tasks of learning to work, relating to intimates, and contributing to a constructive society. Lacking adequate social interest, they attempt to compensate through constant attention seeking. The worldview of people with pampered lifestyles suggests that the world should continue to take care of them and attend to them even when they are noncontributing adults. A passive, pampered lifestyle results in laziness, in which the clear message is a dependent desire to be taken care of. Lazy adolescents and adults receive considerable negative attention from family and friends trying to steer them into a more constructive style of life. If being lazy or a nuisance fails to bring sufficient nurturance, the pampered person is likely to withdraw into angry pouting.

One of the most common neurotic styles to emerge from parental domination is the **compulsive lifestyle** (Adler, 1931). The constant nagging, scolding, deriding, and fault finding of dominating parents can lead to an inferiority complex in which the compulsive person feels powerless to solve life's problems. Afraid of ultimate failure in life's tasks, compulsives move into the future in a hesitating manner. When feeling powerless to handle their futures, they will hesitate, using indecision and doubt to try to hold back time. They may also resort to rituals to keep dreaded time from moving ahead. Besides giving a sense of timelessness by repeating the same act over and over, rituals serve as a safeguard against further loss of self-esteem. The compulsive can always say, "If it weren't for my compulsiveness, look how much I could have done with my life."

Compulsions as a compensatory means can render an almost godlike sense of power. The compulsive ritual is experienced as an epic struggle between the good and evil forces of the universe that only the compulsive has the power to control. Compulsives act as if they have the power to save other humans from harm, disease, or death, if only they carry out their rituals. So they check and recheck to see if the gas is off; they put knives on the table at just the proper angle; or they touch every classroom desk to make sure that no one has been hurt. To fail to repeat their compulsions is to risk evil consequences for the world. If compulsives feel they cannot succeed on the stage of life, they can at least create their own secondary theater of operations, their own dramatic rituals. The compulsive can ultimately declare a superior triumph: "See, I have succeeded in controlling my own urges."

Abused children are more likely to seek revenge on society than to help it. As adolescents and adults, these individuals often develop a vicious style of life that actively seeks superiority by aggressing against a society that seems so cold and cruel. More passive revenge can be taken by those who adopt a passive-aggressive style of life and hurt others through constant inconsiderateness.

Neglected children are apt to declare defeat as adults. They cannot expect to succeed in a society that does not care. The message in their withdrawal is that they are above needing others. To shore up their shaky sense of superiority, such isolates may denigrate others and convince themselves that they really have not lost anything of value. The more passive isolates despair and declare that, because of such overwhelming personal deficiencies, there is no way they can be of interest or service to others.

The destructive goals of pathological personalities are typically understandable, given the family atmospheres that encourage such goals. Though understandable, these goals are mistakes. Pathological personalities construct maladaptive goals by making such **basic mistakes** as generalizing about the nature of all human relationships on the basis of the very small sample they have experienced. Their particular parents or siblings may have acted cruelly, indifferently, or abusively. However, if it weren't for distorted perceptions, such troubled persons could find evidence of kindness and caring from more constructive relationships. Pathological personalities also make the basic mistake of forming conclusions about themselves based on distorted feedback from just a few people. Neglected children, for example, may erroneously conclude that they are unlovable because one or both of their parents were unable to care for them.

Therapeutic Processes

With their lifestyles created at a young age, most psychotherapy patients are too preoccupied following the details of their cognitive maps to be fully aware of the pattern of their lifestyles and the goals toward which they are directed. Many patients do not even want to think about the fact that their troubled lives are the result of their self-created styles of life. They prefer to experience themselves as the unfortunate victims of external circumstances. As a result, therapy must involve an analysis of the cognitive lifestyles of patients in order to help them become more fully conscious of how they are directing their own lives toward destructive goals.

Consciousness Raising

The Client's Work. Because the lifestyle is expressed in all that an individual does, clients cannot help but reveal their styles of life. Their behaving, speaking, sitting, writing, responding, asking questions, and paying bills all have the personalized stamp of a unique style of life. If the cognitive lifestyles are to be brought into bold relief and clear consciousness, then clients must be willing to reveal special phenomena in therapy, including their dreams, earliest memories, and family constellations. Besides revealing important information, clients are encouraged to participate actively in the analysis of their lifestyles.

Becoming more aware of one's lifestyle and disorder can be accelerated by reading books written by others, a process known as **bibliotherapy**. Adler and his followers were among the first psychotherapists to pen self-help books for the lay public, and their clients are frequently asked to read these and related works. The Adlerian goals for bibliotherapy are embodied in six "E's" (Riordan, Mullis, & Nuchow, 1996):

*E*ducate by filling in psychological knowledge and gaps

*E*ncourage by reading inspirational materials

*E*mpower by reviewing goal formation and attainment

*E*nlighten by increasing self- and other-awareness

*E*ngage with the social world through modeling and social mentoring

*E*nhance by reinforcing specific lifestyle changes addressed in psychotherapy

The Therapist's Work. In raising consciousness, Adlerian therapists rely on interpreting the important information that clients present. Adlerian interpretations are not concerned with making causal connections between past events and present problems. The past is connected to the present only to demonstrate the continuity of a patient's style of life. Interpretations are concerned mainly with connecting the past and the present to the future. Interpretations help clients become aware of the purposive nature of their lives, of how their past and present experiences are directed toward fulfilling future goals. Patients become aware of how all their behaviors, including their pathological behaviors, serve the goal of making real the fictional finalisms that were created early in life.

To become aware of the overarching pattern and purpose of a patient's life, the therapist must conduct a fairly complete evaluation of the lifestyle. A **lifestyle analysis** includes a summary of the client's family constellation. The order of birth, the gender of siblings, the absence of a parent, and the feelings of which child was favored are all crucial factors in a family constellation that can be interpreted as influencing the lifestyle. An interpretation of the client's earliest recollections (**anamnesis**) will give a picture of whether the client felt encouraged or discouraged to compensate for inferiority feelings in a socially constructive style.

A lifestyle analysis will also include an interpretation of the basic mistakes the client made in constructing a view about the nature of the world. The most common cognitive mistakes include (1) overgeneralizations, such as "nobody cares"; (2) distortions of life's demands, such as "you can't win at life"; (3) minimization of one's worth, such as "I'm really inadequate" or "I'm only a housewife"; (4) unrealistic goals to be secure, such as "I must please everyone"; and (5) faulty values, such as "get ahead, no matter what it takes" (Mosak & Dreikurs, 1973).

Unlike many therapists, Adlerians do not stop at analyzing their patients' problems. They are equally committed to giving clients feedback about their personal assets. Thus, a summary of a client's strengths is included as part of a lifestyle analysis, which is presented to the client in a teacher-to-student fashion. The lifestyle summary is offered as if the therapist were presenting at a case conference, but here the client has a chance to cooperate in the analysis. Clients can indicate whether they agree or disagree with the therapist's summary. Therapists can make necessary changes in their view of the client's lifestyle, or they can interpret the client's response as resistance to a more complete view of the lifestyle if clients are indeed resisting seeing themselves more completely.

The presentation of a lifestyle summary involves both feedback and education. Individual clients are given personal feedback about their unique family constellation, their personal feelings of inferiority, and their particular assets and basic mistakes. At the same time, clients are educated in a theory of lifestyle that emphasizes the creative self, social interest, and the striving for superiority. In interpreting life goals and demonstrating the basic mistakes in living for selfish values instead of social interests, Adlerians teach clients a new philosophy of life. In fact, Adlerians believe that psychotherapy is incomplete if it does not include an adequate philosophy of life (Mosak & Dreikurs, 1973).

Contingency Control

The Client's Work. As a cognitive approach to change, Adlerian therapy tries to weaken the effects of present contingencies by having clients reevaluate their future goals. By reevaluating their goals pertaining to power, revenge, and attention, clients decrease reinforcing consequences such as being the center of attention or controlling others. In the process of reevaluating selfish goals, patients may experiment with behaviors directed toward a social interest to experience the consequences that result from striving for social interest. After experiencing the good feelings that come from helping another person, clients can realistically compare and reevaluate the consequences that they had been receiving from a self-centered life.

The Therapist's Work. A technique to help a client reevaluate the consequences of selfish goals is to create images that capture the essence of the client's goals. Clients who are constantly striving to be the center of attention, for instance, may be asked to imagine themselves as Bozo the Clown, who becomes the center of attention by having people throw things at him, such as insults or sarcastic remarks. When clients find themselves playing the buffoon, they can imagine that they are like Bozo the Clown sitting in a dunk tank just egging people on to knock him down. These and related images encourage clients to laugh at their styles rather than to condemn themselves. Once clients can laugh about playing Bozo the Clown or Caesar the Conqueror, they can devalue the desire for attention or control.

Adlerians also assign tasks to patients designed to help them experiment with expressing a social interest. A therapist might assign a patient the task of doing something each day that gives pleasure to another person. In the process of completing such tasks, clients experience for themselves the valuable consequences that come from doing something for others.

As patient values change, therapists may still have to offer methods that help patients avoid slipping back into old habits of responding to selfish goals. **Catching oneself** is a technique that encourages clients to think about catching themselves "with their hands in the cookie jar." They should try to actually catch themselves in the process of acting out a destructive behavior—for instance, overeating or overdrinking. With practice, including the internal practice of anticipating "putting a hand in a cookie jar," clients can learn to anticipate a situation and to turn their attention to more constructive consequences rather than automatically responding to destructive goals.

Choosing

The Client's Work. Just as patients originally chose particular lifestyles as children, so too are they capable of choosing to radically change their lifestyles at a later age. Once they are more fully conscious of their fictional finalisms, and once they have evaluated selfish goals in comparison with social goals, clients are freer to choose to stay with their old styles or to create a new life. Some goals, such as holding power over others or craving excessive attention, are highly valued by many people, and there is no assurance clients will choose to give up such goals in the name of social interest. Clients may elect to stay with the security of an unsatisfying style of life because it is a known quantity or because many people value it in society. To consider choosing a radically new lifestyle can threaten security, and clients may opt to reaffirm their long-standing lifestyles.

The Therapist's Work. Rather than have clients face a sudden and dramatic decision to throw themselves into the darkness of an unknown style of life, therapists use techniques that encourage clients to experiment slowly with new alternatives for living. One such technique is the **acting "as if."** For example, a 35-year-old widow had decided that now, after having known the security of 6 years of relying only on herself, she valued the idea of developing an intimate relationship with a man. She had met a man to whom she was attracted at her Parents Without Partners group, but he had not asked her out. Because she had not been making any progress in pursuing her goal for more intimacy, I (JOP) suggested that she ask him if he would like to go for coffee after the meeting. She said she found that alternative exciting but insisted that she was not the kind of person who could do such a thing. Using an Adlerian technique, I suggested that she only act "as if" she were an assertive woman, rather than worrying about becoming such a person. With considerable courage, she acted as if she were assertive and got closer to the man. At the same time, she discovered that if she acted as if she were stronger, she could soon transform such fiction into reality.

For clients who insist that they would change if only they could control overpowering emotions, a **push-button technique** demonstrates that they can indeed choose to control their emotions. Using fantasy, clients are instructed to close their eyes and imagine very happy incidents in their pasts. They are to become aware of the feelings that accompany the scenes. Then clients are instructed to imagine a humiliating, frustrating, or hurtful incident and note the accompanying feelings. Following this, the pleasant scenes are imagined again. By pushing the button on particular thoughts, clients are taught that they can indeed create whatever feelings they wish by deciding what they will think about. After practicing cognitive control of emotions, clients are impressed with their enhanced ability to determine emotions. With an increased ability to choose whether to be angry or not, or depressed or not, clients are in the process of liberating their lifestyles from emotions that once seemed overwhelming.

Therapeutic Content
Intrapersonal Conflicts

Psychological problems are primarily intrapersonal in origin, reflecting the destructive lifestyle adopted at an early age. With its focus on the lifestyle of the individual, Adlerian therapy was traditionally carried out in an individual format. Nevertheless, Dreikurs (1959), a prominent student of Adler, is credited with being the first to use group therapy in private practice. Because destructive lifestyles are acted out interpersonally, a group setting yields firsthand information on how patients create problems in relating to others.

Anxiety and Defenses

However self-defeating a lifestyle may be, it at least provides a sense of security. When a therapist questions or threatens lifestyle convictions, anxiety is aroused and the client is ready to resist treatment. Anxiety can be used to frighten the therapist from pushing ahead, as when the patient threatens to panic if the therapist continues to probe. Anxiety serves a primary purpose, then, of keeping the client from taking action and moving ahead into the future. Anxiety can also serve as a secondary theater of operations, allowing clients to turn their attention from solving life's tasks to solving the considerable anxiety they are creating by their constant self-preoccupation. Psychotherapists need not worry about treating anxiety directly. However, they must be aware of the temptation to avoid directly analyzing a destructive lifestyle out of fear the client will create a tremendous amount of anxiety as an excuse for holding onto a secure but unsuccessful style of life.

The most frequent and powerful defense mechanism is **compensation**. Compensation serves not as a defense against anxiety per se but rather as a defense against the aversive feelings of inferiority. Compensation itself does not produce problems. It is the goal toward which a person strives to be superior that determines whether compensation leads to problems. A person suffering from intense feelings of organ inferiority might compensate and strive for superiority by becoming the community's most plagued hypochondriac. Or the same person could compensate by becoming the community's most revered physician.

The goal in psychotherapy is not to remove feelings of inferiority or to replace compensation with more effective coping mechanisms. Therapy is intended to help clients redirect their compensatory strivings from selfish, self-absorbing goals toward social, self-enhancing values.

Self-Esteem

Enough has been said about feelings of inferiority to indicate that problems with self-esteem are central in Adlerian therapy. The secret to solving problems of esteem is not to reassure maladjusted people that they are indeed well. Nor is self-esteem particularly enhanced through encouraging client self-absorption with the intricate details of their early years. The paradox of self-esteem is that it vanishes as a problem when people forget themselves and begin living for others. A solid sense of self-esteem can be secured only by creating a style of life of value to the world. Live a life that affirms the value of fellow humans, and the unintended consequence will be the creation of a self worthy of the highest esteem.

Responsibility

Those who would be free from psychopathology must have the strength to carry the double burden of personal responsibility and social responsibility. Clients are asked to assume the ultimate responsibility of choosing in the present those goals that will allow their most perfect future to unfold. Once clients accept responsibility for shaping their own lives, they must also accept the responsibility for the impact that their lifestyles exert on society. Will they, for instance, live a more complete life by creating a more perfect personality while at the same time producing a more polluted planet? The person who can hope to attain wholeness is one who can respond to the hopes of humanity.

Interpersonal Conflicts

Intimacy and Sexuality

Commitment to selfish interests prevents intimacy. Intimacy requires concern for a valued other above one's own immediate interests. Intimacy also requires cooperation with others in pursuing commonly shared goals. The inherent selfishness of psychopathology preempts such intimate cooperation. Yet so many people are surprised that they cannot have life both ways—they cannot dedicate themselves to a life of selfish competitiveness, for example, without that competitiveness eventually tearing apart their relationships or their families. People would like to pretend that a lifestyle can be fragmented into convenient parts, with competition, domination, and ruthlessness at work and cooperation, equality, and caring at home. This pretense may operate for awhile, but eventually the goals of selfish success will exact their toll on intimate relationships.

Communication

The innate preparedness of humans for language acquisition indicates that we are born to be social. Language alone, however, does not guarantee effective communication. Problems with communication are fundamentally problems with cooperation. Effective communication is, by its very nature, a cooperative endeavor. If one person is holding back information out of self-interest, or if another is sending misleading messages to gain a competitive advantage, then communication is bound to be conflicted. Couples suffering with competition conflicts, such as who makes the final decisions in their relationships, frequently complain of problems in communicating with each other, even though each is able to communicate effectively with a friend of the same sex. The task in therapy is not to correct communication patterns, but rather to help the couples reorient their values toward common goals so that their communications can be for shared rather than selfish interests.

Hostility

Adler originally considered the aggressive instinct to be the most important human drive. He later elaborated his position to include hostility as one expression of the basic will to power. Now we understand hostility as perhaps the worst of many mistaken paths of striving for superiority. For those discouraged from attaining perfection through social contributions, violence seems to provide a sense of superiority. To beat someone, to hold another person at gunpoint, to threaten someone's life can transform the most inferior-feeling individual into a godlike giant who can destroy another existence. To resort to hostility is to deny the value of another human being. Hostility is the worst expression of the belief that **self-interest** is of higher value than social interest. The tragic rise in violence in contemporary society may well be testimony to the prevalence of the belief that only the self, and never the society, is really sacred.

Control

All people have a need to control, to master certain situations and exercise restraint over others. Pathological personalities, however, are frequently preoccupied with dominating others. The most blatant controller was once dominated by parents and has subsequently committed to seek power over others in order to never again feel the intense inferiority that comes from being under another person's domination. The pampered personality represents a more subtle despot, using neurotic symptoms such as anxiety, depression, and hypochondriasis to get others to satisfy every whim. Pampered people are trained to use the services of others for solutions to problems rather than to become self-reliant. As adults, pampered people rely on symptoms to control others, including psychotherapists, in order to get others to care for them.

Control over others brings a sense of security, a position of superiority, and an exaggerated conviction of self-value. With these gains from control, many clients rely on subtle and not-so-subtle maneuvers to control treatment. Effective therapists will be aware of patients' efforts to control, and they can respond with countercontrol techniques. Patients who try to control therapy, for example, by insisting on how bad off they are and how unable they are to progress, may cry out in exaggerated self-worth, "I bet you've never had such a tough case as me before." The therapist may refuse to be impressed by responding, "No, not since last hour." The therapist is not attempting to win some control game, but rather to communicate that he or she is unwilling to cooperate with the client's maneuvers.

Individuo-Social Conflicts

Adjustment versus Transcendence

The tension between adjustment and transcendence should not pit the individual against society. Striving for transcendence is synonymous with striving for superiority; both entail finding fulfillment by transcending a present level of personal adjustment to attain a higher and more complete level of life. Healthy people will resist the discredited idea that fulfillment requires placing oneself against the system. Healthy people do not place self-esteem over social esteem in an attempt to rise above the society to which they are integrally related. Social transcendence is for snobs who can feel superior only at the expense of the commoners who surround them. Healthy people commit to helping the entire society transcend its present level of functioning to become a more perfect social system.

Impulse Control

The civilizing role of parents and clinicians is not to inhibit bad impulses but to strengthen social interest.

Children are not primarily biological beasts who must have controls imposed on destructive drives. Children are social beings who are prepared to cooperate if encouraged by parents and teachers. Accordingly, impulses must be directed toward prosocial goals as part of the total lifestyle. Impulses such as sex and aggression can be brought to completion for higher social interests, as in providing a pleasure bond between partners or aiding in the defense of a country against terrorists. Impulses become a problem for society only when the overall direction of a lifestyle is antisocial rather than prosocial in nature. Impulses threaten to break out of control not because of an excess of civilization but because some individuals lack dedication to civilization.

Beyond Conflict to Fulfillment

Meaning in Life

We create meaning in our lives by the lives we create. We are not born with intrinsic meaning in our existence, but we are born with a creative self who can fashion intrinsic meaning from our existence. From the raw materials of our genetic endowment and our childhood experiences, we shape the goals and the means to the goals that will give significance to our existence. If our vision is good enough and our goal is noble enough, then the lifestyles we construct may be valued works of art dedicated to the best in humanity. If, out of discouragement and distortion, we dedicate our lives to banal goals, then our lifestyle will reflect more basic mistakes than basic meaning. A basic mistake of many people is that existence can have meaning if it becomes a shrine to the self. The creative self seeks completion not by turning inward and drawing away from the world, but by reaching out to become connected to the greatest needs and the highest aspirations of humanity.

Ideal Person

Inspired by goals that transcend immediate wants or worries, the superior person is drawn to life with excitement and anticipation. Energies are not wasted on evasive defenses or on neurotic

patterns that provide ready-made excuses for failing to add to the world. The healthy person is at home in the world. The ideal person embraces *Gemeinschaftsgefühl*, the social interest that allows us to contribute to the common welfare. Social interest is not just an idealistic or inspirational value; it is also a pragmatic goal that produces mental health in life. The interests of the self and the interests of others do not conflict among those who care enough to find completion through cooperation. The ubiquitous social values of security and success are rejected in favor of the even higher social value of the common good. Healthy people are egalitarians who identify with the imperfections that we all share and with the aspirations of those who truly care.

Therapeutic Relationship

The therapeutic relationship is an integral part of the Adlerian process of helping clients overcome their long-standing discouragement so that they can reorient themselves toward a healthy social interest. Psychotherapists draw clients toward social interest by showing the personal interest they have for the well-being of their clients. In many ways, the therapeutic relationship is a prototype of social interest. The classical values of love, faith, and hope for the human condition are essential to both social interest and an effective therapeutic relationship. The therapist's positive regard for the patient reflects the love and caring of an individual dedicated to the well-being of human beings. The therapist's willingness to relate as a genuine equal communicates a faith in the client's ability to co-discover solutions to serious problems.

The therapist is not the doctor who acts on the client, no matter how helpless pampered clients act to persuade the doctor-therapist to take over their lives. The therapist is a teacher who exudes faith in the unused potential of the student-client to create a fulfilling style of life. The teacher-therapist is willing to recommend readings (bibliotherapy), assign homework experiments, and offer personal encouragement. The genuineness of the therapist reveals a willingness to make mistakes, to be perfectly human, which expresses the conviction that imperfect humans have the power to enhance life. The faith and love, which the patient experiences through the therapeutic relationship, give him or her hope that counteracts the discouragement that prevents meeting life head on. Support, faith, and hope from an empathic therapist make clients concretely aware of the intrinsic value that social interest from one human can have for another. With renewed hope and a vital awareness of the value of social interest, clients are provided fresh opportunities to break out of a self-centered existence and begin caring for others.

Practicalities of Adlerian Therapy

Adlerians are comparatively flexible and innovative in the formal aspects of psychotherapy. Formats vary from traditional individual sessions, to conjoint family sessions, to a multiple-therapist approach (two or more therapists working together with one patient), to group approaches with multiple therapists as well as clients. The multiple-therapist approach was originated by Dreikurs (1950) as a means of preventing serious transference or countertransference problems from interfering with therapeutic progress. The presence of two therapists also allows clients to become aware of how two individuals can differ and still cooperate.

The course of psychotherapy is expected to be relatively short-term, at least in comparison to classical psychoanalysis. The Adlerians were among the first to advocate time-limited treatment and to develop active methods to accelerate the therapeutic process. In fact, many methods embraced by brief therapists—clinician flexibility, group and family sessions, homework assignments, psychoeducational materials, lifestyle analysis, optimistic perspective, and collaborative relationship—were pioneered by the Adlerians (Sperry, 1992).

As part of the educational orientation toward solving or preventing emotional problems, Adlerian workshops have become a popular format for teaching parents how to raise children to cooperate, to care, and to strive as individuals. Similar workshops are available for couples, who can attend the educational sessions and either sit back and learn from others or come to center stage and discuss conflicts in their relationships, with the audience giving considerable support and positive suggestions. Adlerians have also established social clubs to foster social interest both within and outside of psychiatric hospitals. Within the social clubs, the strengths of individuals are stressed, as they are encouraged to enjoy the social aspects of the clubs rather than focusing on their weaknesses.

Adlerian therapy is also flexible with regard to fees and activities. As a reflection of their own social interests, clinicians are encouraged to provide a significant contribution to the community without charge. This *pro bono* service may be done through free evening couples workshops, free workshops for parents, or some private therapy hours for patients unable to pay.

Although Adlerians have traditionally worked with a full range of clients, they are especially active in working with delinquents, criminals, families, and organizations. The resurgence of Adlerian activity in these areas reflects a concern with social relationships in danger of disintegrating because of excessive self-interest. Following Adler's original example, Adlerians are heavily involved in school settings, especially with guidance counselors eager to help students clarify their values to find constructive goals for their energies. Adlerian principles and methods have been increasingly applied to workplace problems and organizational changes (Barker & Barker, 1996; Ferguson, 1996).

The Adlerian movement is now largely centered in the United States, with several training institutes that offer certificates in psychotherapy, counseling, and child guidance. Becoming an Adlerian therapist is more a matter of the individual's social values than of formal credentials—at least as compared to the countervailing priorities in other psychotherapy systems of psychotherapy. As a consequence, Adlerian institutes have been receptive to educators, clergy, and even paraprofessionals, as well as to members of the traditional mental health professions.

Ego Psychology

Adlerian therapy emerged as one of the earliest and most influential psychodynamic therapies, but assuredly not the only one. To appreciate the evolving orientation of the neo-Freudians, we now turn to a discussion of four other forms of psychodynamic therapy: ego psychology, object relations, supportive therapies, and brief psychodynamic therapy.

Classical psychoanalysis was based primarily on an id psychology, in which the instincts and conflicts over such instincts are seen as the prime movers of personality and psychopathology. Although id psychology (or the drive theory) remains the theory of choice of some analysts, others have followed the lead of Hartmann, Kris, and Loewenstein (1947), Erikson (1950), and Rapaport (1958), who established an influential ego psychology. Freud himself began a move beyond the id, when in the 1920s he turned his attention to the analysis of the ego.

Whereas id psychology assumes the ego derives all of its energies from the id, ego psychology assumes there are inborn ego processes—such as memory, perception, and motor coordination—that possess energy separate from the id (Rapaport, 1958). Whereas id psychology assumes that the ego serves only a defensive function in balancing the ongoing conflicts between instincts and the rules of society, ego psychology assumes that there are **conflict-free spheres** of the ego (Hartmann et al., 1947). That is, for Heinz Hartmann and other ego psychologists, there is an **autonomous ego**, an ego that functions independently of the id drives. These involve the individual's adaptation to reality and mastery of the environment (Hendricks, 1943).

The ego's striving to adapt to and master an objective reality motivates the development of personality. Ego analysts certainly do not deny that conflicts over impulses striving for immediate gratification influence our development. Rather, they assume that the separate striving of the ego for adaptation and mastery is an equally important influence.

Although development of impulse control is regarded as one of the early ego tasks, it is by no means the only task. Individuals are also striving to be effective and competent in relating to reality (White, 1959, 1960). The emergence of effectiveness and competence requires the development of ego processes other than defense mechanisms. Individuals are motivated to master visual-motor coordination, discrimination of colors, and language skills, for example, all independent of longings for sexual or aggressive gratification. With its own energies, then, the ego becomes a major force in the development of an adaptive and competent personality. Failure to adequately develop ego processes, such as judgment and moral reasoning, can lead to psychopathology just as readily as can early sexual or aggressive fixations. The person with inadequate ego development is, by definition, poorly prepared to adapt to reality.

Once the ego is assumed to have its own energies and developmental thrust, it becomes clear that more is involved in maturation than only the resolution of conflicts over sex and aggression. The psychosexual stages of Freud are no longer adequate to account for all of personality and psychopathology. Development of the conflict-free spheres of the ego during the first three stages of life is just as important as defending against the inevitable conflicts over oral, anal, and phallic impulses. Furthermore, the strivings of the ego for adaptability, competency, and mastery continue well beyond the first 6 years of life. As a result, later stages of life are as critical in the development of personality and psychopathology as are the early ones.

Erik Erikson (1950) broadened Freud's psychosexual stages to **psychosocial stages** that begin in infancy and extend through life to old age. The life cycle is described in terms of eight discrete crisis periods. The oral stage, for example, is critical to the child's development of trust versus mistrust. The latency stage, as another example, is seen by Erikson as critical in the development of a sense of industry, which involves learning to master many of the skills used in work. Freud, on the other hand, saw the latency stage as a quiet time-out during which no new personality traits developed. From Erikson's point of view, some individuals fail to develop a sense of industry not because of unconscious conflicts but because their culture discriminates against people of particular races or religions and fails to educate them adequately in the tools of that culture's trade. Failure to develop a sense of industry leads to a sense of inadequacy and inferiority. A sense of inferiority can lead to symptoms such as depression, anxiety, or avoidance of achievement. Thus, individuals can develop problems later in life even if they have developed a healthy personality during the first three stages of life. Of course, serious conflicts from early stages make it more difficult for later stages to progress smoothly. A person with serious dependency conflicts from the oral stage, for example, will probably have more problems developing a sense of industry than would a person free from such conflicts.

The essential point for psychotherapy here is that ego analysts concern themselves equally with early developmental stages and later developmental stages. By no means are all problems reduced to repetitions of unconscious conflicts from childhood. The adolescent stage, in particular, brings the massive challenge of developing ego identity versus ego diffusion (Erikson, 1950). Young adults must use their maturing ego processes if they are to move toward intimacy rather than lapse into isolation. Mid-adulthood involves the ego energies in creating a lifestyle that brings a sense of generatively, creating something of worth with one's life lest a sense of stagnation take over. And aging adults must look back over their lives to see whether they can maintain ego integrity in the face of death, whether they can look back and affirm their entire life cycle as worth living. If not, they are drained by despair.

Achieving identity, intimacy, and ego integrity are critical therapy goals of ego analysts. Much of therapy is focused on such contemporary struggles of patients. Treatment delves into history only as far as necessary to analyze the unresolved childhood conflicts that might be interfering with the person's present adaptation to life. Clearly, the content of **ego analysis** will differ from the content of classical analysis. The process of ego analysis may, however, be quite similar to the classical process, with long-term intensive therapy and use of free association, transference, and interpretation. On the other hand, most ego analysts tend to follow the more flexible format of psychodynamic psychotherapy.

Object Relations

Psychodynamic therapy has evolved by new theorists emphasizing different aspects of personal development as the core organizing principles for personality and psychopathology. Freud emphasized conflicts over gratification and control of id processes as the central organizing principle of people's lives. Ego analysts emphasized the ego as the central organizing principle; the resolution of ego challenges such as basic trust, autonomy, and initiative, determines an individual's way of life. **Object relations** theorists, including Fairbairn (1952), Kernberg (1975, 1976, 1984), and Kohut (1971, 1977), emphasize relationships between the self and other people as the major organizing principle in people's lives. David Winnicott, a child psychoanalyst and prominent theorist of object relations, once risked the remark, "There is no such thing as a baby…. A baby cannot exist alone, but is essentially part of a relationship" (Winnicott, 1931/1992; also Monte & Sollod, 2003).

Object relations are the mental representations of self and others (the objects). **Object** is the term Freud (1923) used for other people, because in id psychology others serve primarily as objects for instinctual gratification of pleasure rather than as authentic individuals with needs and wants of their own. Object relations are intrapsychic structures, not interpersonal events (Horner, 1979). Object relations are strongly impacted by early interpersonal relationships, which profoundly impact later interpersonal relationships.

The key difference between Freud's id model and the object relations model is aptly captured by the dictum, "libido is object seeking, not pleasure seeking." Freud saw the id as relentlessly pursuing pleasure alone, even at the expense of other people. But object relations therapists see us seeking other people to secure attachment and nurturance.

Object relations theorists differ somewhat on the importance of id forces in the relationship between child and parent. Otto Kernberg (1976) views object relations as partly energized by basic instincts, especially aggression, whereas Heinz Kohut (1971) deemphasizes id impulses in early relationships. Kohut (1971) assumes that children have inherent needs to be mirrored and to idealize. These needs obviously require others who can serve as objects that reflect the developing self and as objects that the self can idealize as models for future development.

The self develops through stages that differ from the classic oral, anal, phallic, and genital stages proposed by id and ego psychologies. According to the influential theorist Margaret Mahler (1968), the first stage of self-development is **normal autism**, which comes in the first few months of life. In this primary, undifferentiated state, there is neither self nor object. Fixation at this stage results in the severe pathology of primary infantile autism, which is characterized by a failure of attachment to objects and a failure of mental organization due to a lack of self-image (Horner, 1979).

Through the process of **attachment**, described by Mahler (1968) and Bowlby (1969, 1973), the child enters the stage of **normal symbiosis**. In this stage, there is confusion in the child's mind as to what is self and what is object, because neither is perceived as independent of the other. This stage normally lasts 2 to 7 months.

The child then enters the differentiation period, during which the child practices separating and individuating from significant others (Mahler, 1968). Crawling away from parents and then crawling back, walking away from parents and then running back, and even playing peekaboo, in which the parent disappears for a moment and then reappears, are patterns of physical play that allow children to mentally differentiate themselves as separate from the parents to whom they are attached. A failure to differentiate can result in **symbiotic psychosis**, reflecting a fixation at the symbiotic stage. In Mahler's (1968, p. 35) words, "The salient feature in childhood psychosis is that individuation, i.e., a sense of individual identity, is not achieved."

Under normal conditions, the stages of differentiation shift at about 2 years of age into an integration stage. Through integrating processes, the self and object representations, which have become independently perceived, are now fit into relationships with each other. Parent and self are perceived as both separate and related. When all goes well, children at this stage can learn to relate without having overwhelming fears of losing their autonomy, their individuality, or their sense of self.

During the integration stage, the child also begins to integrate the good and the bad self-images into a single, ambivalently experienced self. Similarly, the child needs to integrate the good and the bad object images into a single, ambivalently experienced object. Experiences that originate from within the person that were not integrated into the early self-representation, such as the image of oneself as capable of anger, continue to be split off from the sense of self. If these experiences are evoked later in life, they can produce a state of disintegration, with the person's sense of self falling apart.

The task of development is not only differentiation but also the emergence of identity. In the earliest stage, children vacillate between different ways of thinking and acting, expressing first one part of themselves and then another. This instability is due to **splitting**, a defensive attempt to deal with being overwhelmed by more powerful parents (Kernberg, 1976). If the child splits off bad self-images, such as the angry self, then there is less to fear from punitive parents. Similarly, if children can split off bad object images, such as the angry mother, then the object becomes less threatening.

The next step in identity development involves **introjection**, which is the literal incorporation of objects into the mind. This tends to occur during symbiosis: Mother can be experienced as less threatening if mother and child are one. A more mature identity, however, requires the process of identification, in which objects have influence but need not be "swallowed whole." With a more mature sense of identity, individuals can value both autonomy and community; they are open to influence from others without the fear of being overwhelmed by others.

Throughout all of these stages of identity development, the role of attachment is paramount. Winnicott (1965) stressed the centrality of "good enough" mothering in a **holding environment**. Such an environment makes the child feel taken care of, protected, understood, and loved. Transitional objects, known to parents as the security blanket, help to cultivate the child's internalization of the continuing presence of parental love. Years of a holding environment facilitates the child's capacity to be alone and, eventually, leads to independence. In Kohut's **self psychology**, the

ideal identity is an **autonomous self**, characterized by self-esteem and self-confidence. Secure in this identity, the person is not excessively dependent on others and is also not merely a replica of the parents. Developmentally, the ideal situation is for children to have both their need to be *mirrored* (appreciated and respected) and their need to idealize met through interaction with the parents.

Who the parents are is more important than how the parents intend to interact. If the parents have accepted their own needs to shine and succeed, then their children's exhibitionism will be accepted and mirrored. If the parents have adequate self-esteem, then they can be comfortable with their children's needs to idealize them. If, during the stages of self-development, the parents are not able to meet the child's needs to be mirrored and to idealize, the child will develop a troubled identity.

Kohut (1971) focuses on different types of **narcissistic personalities** that result from insufficient **mirroring** or idealizing. Mirror-hungry personalities, for example, are famished for admiration and appreciation. They incessantly need to be the center of attention. These people tend to shift from relationship to relationship, performance to performance, in an insatiable attempt to gain attention. Ideal-hungry personalities are forever in search of others whom they can admire for their prestige or power. They feel worthwhile only as long as they can look up to someone.

From Kohut's self-psychology perspective, narcissistic personalities cannot be treated by classical psychoanalysis, in which the analyst alternates between being a blank screen and raising consciousness through verbal interpretations. Psychoanalysis is successful when patients are able to project emotions toward others onto the therapist by means of transference experiences. Persons with self disorders, however, cannot project emotions and images consistently, because they are too personally preoccupied. These clients must be mirrored and must be permitted to idealize the therapist.

To be idealized, therapists must let themselves be known rather than remain shadows for the clients' projections. By combining Rogers's emphasis on empathy and positive regard (mirroring) and the existential emphasis on being authentic (idealizing), the object relations therapist can fill the void that clients experienced in childhood. By meeting some of the clients' unmet narcissistic needs, they enable clients to develop either a mirroring transference or an idealizing transference. After such transferences are developed, the self-psychology therapist can use the traditional consciousness-raising technique of interpretations to help patients become aware of how they try to organize their lives around narcissistic relationships. Clients can then begin to participate in the development of a more autonomous self.

In his famous 1979 article, "The Two Analyses of Mr. Z," Heinz Kohut (1913–1981) vividly presented the clinical differences between classical psychoanalysis and his self psychology. Kohut treated Mr. Z initially with classical psychoanalysis, but some 5 years later, Mr. Z was treated for a second time with self-psychology therapy when Kohut was deeply immersed in the writing of *The Analysis of the Self* (1971). As seen in the classical dynamic-structural terms of the first analysis, Mr. Z was suffering from overt grandiosity and arrogance due to an imaginary oedipal victory. The psychoanalytic goal—only partially accomplished—was to access and resolve the patient's repressed castration anxiety and depression due to an actual oedipal defeat. As seen in self-psychology terms of the second treatment, Mr. Z was suffering from overt arrogance and isolation on the basis of persisting merger with the idealized mother. The therapy tasks here occurred in two stages: The first was to help Mr. Z confront fears of losing his merger with the mother and thus losing himself as he knew it. The second stage was to assist Mr. Z in confronting traumatic overstimulation and disintegration fear as he became conscious of the rage, assertiveness, sexuality, and exhibitionism of his autonomous self. To oversimplify, the case formulation moved from a purely intrapsychic matter dominated by the patient's id drives and deficiencies to a fuller interpersonal configuration considering the patient's competencies as well. And Kohut's stance evolved from a relatively detached, cerebral analyst to a more empathic, involved, mirroring therapist.

Object relations therapists believe that traditional psychoanalysis can effectively treat neurotic patients who can develop normal transference relationships. But patients with severe self disorders, such as those suffering from borderline personality disorders or narcissistic personality disorders, cannot be effectively treated merely with interpretations of transference and resistance. Borderline patients can develop psychotic transferences and can thus experience the therapist as the split-off "bad parent." Profound fears of being overwhelmed, uninhibited, rejected, or abandoned can cause such patients to leave therapy or can prevent the development of a working alliance.

Otto Kernberg (1975; Clarkin et al., 1998; Kernberg et al., 1989) and James Masterson (1976, 1981), who specialize in the treatment of borderline disorders, combine limit setting and emotional support in this exhausting work. Setting limits on telephone calls, on acting out aggression toward the therapist, and on how often the therapist can be seen are critical with borderline patients. Setting limits on acting out will provoke anxiety that helps to clarify the underlying meaning of the acting out. Only by setting clear limits with such clients will the therapist maintain the opportunity for interpretations to be effective. In a therapeutic relationship that offers both sustained empathy and boundary setting, patients can gradually become conscious of the parts of themselves that have been split off. Without clear limits, the split-off parts of self and objects can threaten to produce disintegration within the individual or within the therapeutic relationship.

Supportive Therapy

The broad expanse of psychoanalytic (Chapter 2) and psychodynamic therapies (this chapter) can be arranged along a continuum of expressive-supportive treatment. At the one end is psychoanalysis proper with its emphasis on the patient's expression, free association, and regression along with the therapist's interpretation of transference, defenses, and unconscious conflicts. At the other end of the continuum is **supportive therapy** informed by psychodynamic concepts. Supportive therapy aims to strengthen the patient's coping, provide encouragement, and prevent regression. Rather than dissecting defenses, supportive therapy bolsters defenses. Direct support and suggestion are favored over insight and interpretation.

Supportive therapy is widely practiced, particularly in counseling, in psychiatry, and in concert with medication management (Rockland, 2003; Sudak & Goldberg, 2012). It is generally indicated when the patient does not possess the requisite psychological-mindedness or financial resources for an intensive, insight-oriented therapy, which is still preferred by most psychodynamic therapists on the conviction that insight exercises a more lasting impact than suggestion and support alone. Given constraints in the patient or the setting, the therapist actively reinforces the patient's adaptive behaviors in order to reduce the intrapsychic conflicts that may produce or aggravate psychiatric symptoms. As in psychoanalytic psychotherapy and object relations therapies, the therapist engages in an encouraging and engaging relationship with the patient as a method of furthering healthy relationships. In this respect, supportive therapy moves toward an integrative therapy (Chapter 16) that incorporates methods from the person-centered, cognitive-behavioral, interpersonal, and solution-focused therapies.

Supportive therapy may be used as the entire treatment or as a portion of the treatment. For example, I (JCN) was seeing a patient in expressive-exploratory psychotherapy for his cranky, mistrusting, and withholding personality pattern. We were uncovering and processing multiple traumatic experiences early in his life and his ensuing insecure attachment style. Then, about the eighth session, his home burned to the ground. We immediately transitioned into a supportive mode to strengthen his defenses, enlist his coping skills, and assist his recovery from the crisis.

In practice, psychodynamic therapy constitutes an admixture of both expressive/exploratory and supportive interventions. Long ago, Freud (1919, p. 167) recognized the inevitability that the "pure gold of analysis" would be mixed "freely with the copper of suggestion." Not all patients are capable of, or benefit from, the expressive, insight-oriented treatment. The trick is to determine which patients respond best to the expressive side and which best to the supportive side.

Brief Psychodynamic Therapy

Continuing the evolution of Freud's original theory, recent decades have witnessed a proliferation of brief psychodynamic therapies. Leading theorists and practitioners in this vein include Lester Luborsky (1984; Luborsky & Crits-Cristoph, 1990), James Mann (1973; Mann & Goldman, 1982), and Hans Strupp (1992; Levenson, 1995; Strupp & Binder, 1984). These psychodynamic treatments are united by several characteristics:

- Setting a time limitation on treatment, typically 12 to 40 sessions
- Targeting a focal interpersonal problem within the first few sessions
- Adopting a more active or less neutral therapeutic stance
- Establishing a rapid and strong working alliance
- Employing interpretation and transference interpretation relatively quickly
- Emphasizing the process and inevitability of terminating treatment

As direct descendants of psychoanalysis, all short-term psychodynamic therapists incorporate the cardinal psychoanalytic principles, including the presence of resistance, the value of interpretation, and the centrality of a strong working alliance. But all have also responded to the empirical research that strongly questions the value of lengthy over briefer psychodynamic psychotherapy and to the socioeconomic constraints on the number of psychotherapy sessions permitted by insurance carriers.

Briefer therapy requires thorough case formulation and planning. Calling on all that is known about a particular client and all that is known about the dynamics of psychopathology, the psychodynamic therapist plans a more precise treatment that fits the needs of a particular client. Modest and achievable goals are set, such as an improved interpersonal pattern, greater attunement to feelings, or a resolution of a specific conflict (Messer & Warren, 1995). Where standard psychoanalysis might let the treatment take its own course, the short-term dynamic therapist decides whether it should be oriented primarily toward supporting the ego, uncovering the id impulses, or changing the external conditions of the client's life. Not all details of treatment can be planned, of course, so the therapist will rely on conscious use of various techniques in a flexible manner, shifting tactics to fit the particular needs of the moment.

The brief dynamic therapist is obviously more active and directive in procedure and more interactive in the relationship than are orthodox psychoanalysts. In classic psychoanalysis, the therapist allows the transference to emerge slowly over time, with gradual and frugal interpretations. In short-term dynamic treatment, the therapist actively engages the patient early in the process, focuses on a core interpersonal theme, and offers frequent transference interpretations regarding links among the patient's behavior toward the therapist, current life figures, and significant past figures.

For example, a transference interpretation might concern a patient's frequent stomach cramps for which no medical reason could be identified and for which she presented to psychotherapy. These cramps are experienced only in the presence of her mother in the past, in the presence of her boyfriend in the present, and now in the presence of the therapist in the consulting room. One interpretation is that the cramps are the patient's habitual way of dealing with her difficulty in expressing aggression; instead of expressing her anger directly, she swallows it and turns it against herself (Messer & Warren, 1995).

Even as short-term psychodynamic therapists are more active and eclectic in practice than psychoanalysts, they continue to employ distinctive psychoanalytic methods. Comparative psychotherapy research (Blagys & Hilsenroth, 2000) reveals that seven themes and techniques characterize brief psychodynamic therapy:

- A focus on patients' expression of emotions
- An exploration of patients' attempts to avoid topics or engage in resistance
- The identification of repetitive patterns in patients' lives and relationships
- An emphasis on past experiences
- A focus on a client's interpersonal experiences
- An exploration of patients' wishes, dreams, and fantasies
- An emphasis on the therapeutic relationship

The latter theme refers to the therapist actively establishing a facilitative **therapeutic, or working, alliance** with the client. This alliance is characterized by conscious collaboration and explicit consensus, in contrast to the unconscious distortion of the relationship between therapist and client. The alliance is typically measured as agreement on the therapeutic goals, consensus on treatment tasks, and a relationship bond (Bordin, 1976). It is two people who like and respect each other working together toward mutual goals.

The positive relation between the therapeutic alliance and treatment outcome is one of the most robust findings in psychotherapy research. Among both adult (Horvath et al., 2011) and child (Shirk & Karver, 2011) clients, the quality of the alliance contributes to and predicts therapy success. Indeed, the success rate increases from 37% to 63% in low versus high alliance cases.

By emphasizing the therapeutic alliance, psychodynamic therapists become more empathic, more humanistic in the tradition of Carl Rogers (Chapter 5). Confrontation and interpretation give way to clarification and support, as illustrated in these contrasting statements (McCullough, 1997, p.13). A psychoanalyst might offer this interpretation:

> You are avoiding my eyes right now as I ask about your feelings. And now you're drumming your fingers on the table. This silence erects a barrier between us. What will happen if you continue to evade these issues in treatment?

A brief psychodynamic therapist might address the same phenomena by offering more empathy and mutuality:

> As I ask about your feelings, you often look away and become silent. Are you aware that this is happening? Is this topic painful for you to look at? Is there some way that I can help you make it more bearable to face?

Some brief psychodynamic treatments go by the name of **supportive-expressive therapy**. As systematized by Lester Luborsky and colleagues at the University of Pennsylvania, supportive-expressive psychotherapy assists patients in identifying the recurrent themes in their lives that have negatively impacted their relationships with other people. The therapist uses collaborative psychodynamic methods to establish a supportive relationship and then uses interpretative techniques to encourage patients to express and come to understand their core conflictual relationship patterns. Thus, it has two main components: providing support in an understanding relationship (supportive) and stimulating insight via clarifications and interpretations (expressive).

In short, brief dynamic therapists seek the best of both the theoretical and methodological worlds.

In theory, they rely on the comprehensive and guiding knowledge afforded by psychoanalysis and its contemporary variants. In method, they flexibly apply a host of techniques, most rooted in the psychoanalytic tradition, and pragmatically emphasize the therapeutic alliance, a pantheoretical concept.

Effectiveness of Psychodynamic Therapies
Adlerian Therapy

Adler (1929) did not conduct or favor controlled studies on the effectiveness of his individual psychology, preferring instead to relate cases. "Experiments," he wrote, "look only like a shadow of reality." Although many of Adler's seminal concepts—ordinal position, earliest childhood memories, social interest, to name a few—have been extensively investigated (Watkins, 1982, 1983, 1992), little empirical research has been conducted on the actual effectiveness of Adlerian therapy. Early major reviews (e.g., Smith et al., 1980) located only four controlled studies of Adlerian therapy. The average treatment results in the admittedly small set of available studies were just slightly better than the results of placebo treatments. Similarly, literature reviews fail to locate any substantial body of controlled outcome research on Adlerian therapy on either adults (e.g., Grawe et al., 1998) or children (e.g., Weisz et al., 2004).

A handful of controlled studies, all with different foci, is inadequate to draw any firm conclusions about the efficacy of Adlerian therapy. Perhaps the most we can say at this time is that it is superior to no treatment and, when compared with alternative treatments, it has been found to be as effective as client-centered therapy and psychoanalytic therapy in several studies.

Object Relations Therapies

We and others are unable to locate any controlled outcome studies on Kohut's self-psychology psychotherapy, but can report on several controlled outcome evaluations of Kernberg's object relations treatment, called **transference-focused psychotherapy** (Yeomans et al., 2002). The first study was a nonrandomized trial comparing transference-focused psychotherapy (TFP) and treatment as usual (TAU) for patients diagnosed with borderline personality disorder. TFP was superior to TAU on virtually all indices of effectiveness (Clarkin et al., 2001).

Subsequent studies were more rigorous, randomized controlled trials comparing the effectiveness of TFP to alternative therapies. In one such study, TFP, dialectical behavior therapy (Chapter 11), and supportive therapy were compared for 12 months among patients diagnosed with borderline personalities. At posttreatment, patients receiving any of the three therapies were improved, but patients receiving TFP fared slightly better on most measures (Clarkin et al., 2007). Another controlled study was conducted in multiple community mental health centers in the Netherlands. It compared TFP to schema-focused therapy in 88 patients suffering from borderline personality disorder. Both treatments proved effective in reducing borderline symptoms and in improving quality of life. Among all patients beginning treatment, schema-focused seemed slightly more effective; among those actually completing treatment, about the same percentage of schema-focused patients and TFP patients recovered or evidenced clinical improvement (Giesen-Bloo et al., 2006).

The composite results from these studies and from general reviews of treatment for borderline pathologies (Oldham, 2002) indicate that specific, structured psychotherapies are superior to unstructured TAUs. TFP has demonstrated its effectiveness in treating this severe disorder in several studies, but whether it is slightly more effective or slightly less effective than other treatments has not been conclusively determined. In the meantime, the balanced conclusion remains that psychodynamic and cognitive-behavioral therapies are of comparable effectiveness in the treatment of these personality disordered patients (Leichsenring & Leibing, 2003).

Supportive Therapy

The effectiveness of supportive therapy in controlled studies has been most frequently evaluated in the treatment of adult depression, with and without medication. A meta-analysis of 31 studies on supportive therapy found it was effective in the treatment of depression (ES = 0.58) compared to control conditions. Supportive therapy was mildly less effective than other psychological treatments, but this difference was no longer present after controlling for researcher allegiance (Cuijpers et al., 2012).

In an analysis of three randomized clinical trials (de Maat et al., 2008), short psychodynamic supportive psychotherapy was as effective as medication for depression. Combined treatment (supportive therapy plus medication) was more effective than either alone according to independent observers, patients, and therapists. In short, supportive therapy has proven itself effective for depression.

Psychodynamic Therapies (General)

The effectiveness of psychodynamic therapies has been extensively studied in controlled research. This body of research has been summarized in recent years through **meta-analysis**, a statistical technique that quantitatively combines the results of many different studies.

The results of meta-analyses are typically presented as an **effect size (ES)**. As shown in Table 3.1, an ES is a quantitative index of the magnitude and direction of therapy effects. Higher effect sizes indicate greater effectiveness. Each ES can be thought of as reflecting a corresponding percentile value; that is, the percentile standing of the average treated patient after psychotherapy relative to untreated patients.

Effect sizes can be calculated by a variety of methods, but the typical ES is reported as d—a difference between two groups or two different points in time. Throughout this book, we shall report effect sizes in terms of the d value or its equivalent in order to simplify explanations and to permit direct comparisons. In psychotherapy, the consensual rules of

Table 3.1 The Interpretation of Effect Size (ES) Statistics

EFFECT SIZE (ES OF D)	PERCENTILE OF TREATED PATIENTS	SUCCESS RATE OF TREATED PATIENTS	TYPE OF EFFECT	COHEN'S STANDARD
1.00	84	72%	Beneficial	
0.90	82	70%	Beneficial	
0.80	79	69%	Beneficial	Large
0.70	76	66%	Beneficial	
0.60	73	64%	Beneficial	
0.50	69	62%	Beneficial	Medium
0.40	66	60%	Beneficial	
0.30	62	57%	Beneficial	
0.20	58	55%	Beneficial	Small
0.10	54	52%	No effect	
0.00	50	50%	No effect	
−0.10	46	<50%	No effect	
−0.20	42	<50%	Detrimental	
−0.30	38	<50%	Detrimental	

SOURCES: Adapted from Weisz et al. (1995) and Wampold (2001).

ES interpretation are that 0 indicates no effect, 0.20 represents a small effect, 0.50 represents a medium effect, and 0.80 and above a large effect (Cohen, 1988).

A benchmark meta-analysis was undertaken by Smith, Glass, and Miller (1980; Smith & Glass, 1977) to examine the benefits of psychotherapy using a total of 475 studies. Approximately 29 studies were found at that time on psychodynamic treatments and 28 on psychodynamic-eclectic treatments, producing average effect sizes of 0.69 and 0.89, respectively. Patients treated with psychodynamic therapy (ES = 0.69) were, on average, more improved than 76% of the untreated patients. As also seen in Table 3.1, an ES of 0.69 or 0.70 translates in a success rate of approximately 66% among treated patients. When compared with effect sizes for other forms of therapy, the psychodynamic therapies were judged to be comparably effective to slightly less effective, depending on one's interpretation of the data.

Many meta-analyses have been conducted since the classic Smith, Glass, and Miller study in an effort to improve their design and include more recent studies. Meta-analyses on general psychodynamic treatments for youth and adults (Grawe et al., 1998; Shapiro & Shapiro, 1982; Weisz et al., 1995) converge in their conclusions. Psychodynamic therapy is effective, certainly more than no treatment or a wait-list condition. At the same time, several meta-analyses showed a modest but consistent superiority of behavioral and cognitive methods over psychodynamic therapies. This was a small difference; more treatment outcome could be accounted for by the type of patient problem being treated than by the type of treatment.

Much debate ensued over the meaning of these small differences uncovered by meta-analyses. Differences in effect sizes between psychotherapies can be due to a variety of factors, including the type of problems treated, the reactivity of the measures used, and the type of patients studied. Because the majority of comparative studies have been conducted by cognitive and behavior therapists, these therapists may consciously or unconsciously design studies that involve variables, measures, and clinicians that favor their preferred therapy. Relatively minor statistical advantages in such controlled studies do not necessarily mean that cognitive and behavior therapies invariably possess clinical superiority in real-world settings.

Research confirms that the researcher's own therapy allegiance impacts the results of treatment comparison studies. In many separate reviews of the literature, the most effective therapy tends to be that favored by the researchers conducting the study—the **allegiance effect** as it has come to be known. A review of treatment comparisons in adult therapy found that about two thirds of the variance in outcome differences between different psychotherapies was due to the researcher's own therapy allegiances (Luborsky et al., 1999). Another review of studies on child and adolescent therapy found that, when allegiance was controlled, there was no evidence of any outcome differences among various treatments (Miller et al., 2008). Cognitive-behavioral researchers tended to find better results for cognitive-behavioral therapies, whereas psychodynamic researchers discovered more impressive results for psychodynamic therapies. Such findings throw a wild card into interpreting treatment differences and remind us to temper any claims of the superiority of one therapy over another, unless the studies have been fairly conducted by theoretically neutral researchers.

When dispassionate researchers conduct the studies or control for the allegiance effect, most major therapies work about equally well for most disorders (Lambert, 2002; Wampold, 2001). Meta-analyses of comparative studies involving thousands of patients suggests that long-term psychodynamic therapy is as effective or perhaps a shade more effective than shorter forms of psychotherapy for complex mental disorders (Bhar et al., 2010; Leichsenring & Rabung, 2008, 2011). After long-term psychodynamic therapy, complicated patients on average were better off than 96% of the patients in the control groups. Such findings should also remind us, as Freud himself assuredly would, that our personal biases and emotional allegiances effect our conclusions!

Brief Psychodynamic Therapy

Multiple meta-analyses have been conducted on the effectiveness of brief psychodynamic psychotherapy with adults. In this section, we summarize those analyses, but first we begin by reviewing the results of a seminal study.

In a rigorous study conducted at Temple University, Sloane and colleagues (1975) compared the effectiveness of short-term psychodynamic psychotherapy with that of short-term behavior therapy. Thirty patients were randomly assigned to each of the therapy conditions, and 34 assigned to a waiting-list control group. Two thirds of the patients were diagnosed as neurotics and one third as exhibiting personality disorders. The therapists were matched for experience. Treatment lasted for 4 months, with an average of 14 sessions. The most striking findings of the study were that, at the end of 4 months of therapy, both treatment groups were significantly more improved than the no-treatment group, and neither form of psychological treatment was more effective than the other. On symptom ratings, 80% of the patients in each therapy group were considered either improved or recovered, compared to 48% in the control group. On ratings of overall adjustment, 93% of the patients in behavior therapy were considered improved, compared with 77% of the psychoanalytic psychotherapy group and 47% of the waiting list.

Consistent with the results of that single study, the efficacy of brief psychodynamic therapy with adults has been repeatedly confirmed by meta-analytic research. Meta-analyses (e.g., Abbass et al., 2009; Anderson & Lambert, 1995; Crits-Christoph, 1992; Driessen et al., 2010; Svartberg & Stiles, 1991) have all found large effects for brief psychodynamic therapy relative to wait-list controls. The average effect sizes are in the 0.85 to 1.0 range and compare favorably with the results of other therapies (Shedler, 2010). Translated into percentages, the average brief dynamic therapy patient is better off than 79% to 86% of wait-list patients. A couple of the meta-analyses found that short-term psychodynamic psychotherapy was slightly inferior to alternative psychotherapies at posttreatment, but the allegiance effect was probably at work here as well.

To address the controversial possibility of slightly inferior outcomes of brief psychodynamic psychotherapies, a meta-analysis was performed on 17 more recent, methodologically rigorous studies (Leichsenring et al., 2004). Short-term psychodynamic psychotherapy yielded significant and large pretreatment to posttreatment effect sizes for target problems (ES = 1.39), general symptoms (0.90), and social functioning (0.80). These effect sizes exceeded those of waiting-list controls and TAUs. No differences were found in outcomes between brief psychodynamic therapy and other forms of psychotherapy. That is, they evidenced equal effectiveness. The results of sensitive meta-analyses accounting for researchers' allegiance demonstrate that psychodynamic treatments produce comparable effects for specific disorders.

Short-term psychodynamic therapy may be especially well suited to personality disorders and somatic disorders. A meta-analysis examined the efficacy of both psychodynamic therapy (14 studies) and cognitive-behavioral therapy (11 studies) for personality disorders (Leichsenring & Leibing, 2003). Both treatments demonstrated effectiveness, with a slight edge to the lengthier psychodynamic therapy (also see Leichsenring & Rabung, 2008; Town et al., 2011). Another meta-analysis of the efficacy of short-term psychodynamic therapy examined 14 controlled studies involving 1,870 patients. The analysis yielded effect sizes of 0.69 for improvement in psychiatric symptoms and 0.59 for improvement in somatic symptoms, both equal to the effects of alternative psychotherapies found in other studies (Abbass et al., 2009).

A recent empirical thrust examines an old conviction that psychodynamic therapies may consolidate gains after treatment ends. That would lead to greater benefits and higher effect sizes at long-term follow-up than immediately at the conclusion of therapy. Five or six meta-analyses now support the notion that the benefits of psychodynamic therapy not only endure but also increase with time

(Shedler, 2010). In contrast, the benefits of other therapies tend to decay over time. This proposition of enhanced gains activates the allegiance effect as well: psychodynamic clinicians now claiming it as fact, and non-psychodynamic clinicians claiming it as a methodological artifact.

All in all, the controlled outcome research consistently finds that the measurable outcomes of psychodynamic therapy and its brief versions are superior to no treatment and TAU. Many non-psychodynamic clinicians still refer to the early meta-analyses suffering from the allegiance effect and argue for the superiority of their treatments, whereas psychodynamic clinicians cite the later research and argue for comparable effectiveness of their treatments. The question of "How good is brief psychodynamic therapy?" can now be answered with meta-analyses: It is definitely superior to no treatment and probably just as effective as alternative psychotherapies. But, as in all matters of the mind, the answer seems to depend on who is conducting the study and on who is interpreting the results.

Criticisms of Psychodynamic Therapies

From a Psychoanalytic Perspective

Freud anticipated that Adler's break with psychoanalysis would lead to the development of a superficial and sterile theory (Colby, 1951). In rejecting psychoanalysis, Adler rejected half of the human personality. The result is a one-dimensional theory that emphasizes the ego or self at the expense of the id, consciousness at the expense of the unconscious, social strivings at the expense of biological drives, and compensation at the expense of other defenses. Here we have a yin without a yang, half of the person presented as if it were the whole.

As a result of the holes in Adler's holism, there emerges a naive psychotherapy that suggests people can be helped with all types of cute gimmicks. Just ask a frightened, submissive woman to act "as if" she is assertive, and she will be liberated. Just push a button, and an embittered recluse can change his fantasies and feelings as fast as he can change the television channel. The power of positive thinking has been peddled as a lasting cure for centuries, when it is nothing but a temporary pep talk. People are not really locked into unconscious conflicts; they are only discouraged. Just have hope, faith, and charity, and that is the way to live successfully. Adler does indeed promise a rose garden to those willing to share his rose-colored glasses that filter out the dark side of life.

From a Cognitive-Behavioral Perspective

Adlerians cannot decide whether they are social-learning theorists who attribute maladaptive behavior to family constellations and other environmental conditions or mystics who attribute distorted lifestyles to an undeveloped creative self that sounds much like a soul. Why Adlerians feel the need to resort to the mythical concepts of choice and a creative self when observable behaviors of parental pampering, abusing, and ignoring would serve as explanations is unclear.

It is clear, however, that theoretical propositions concerning the effects of birth order can be defined and tested, whereas concepts such as striving for superiority and the creative self are vague and unamenable to scientific investigation. Perhaps Adlerians hold to such concepts in order to place the responsibility for change on the clients, because the therapy system has been unable to generate techniques powerful enough to produce adequate change in the behavior of clients. Whatever the reasons, the Adlerian school remains a strange combination of a theory that borders on scientific respectability and a religion that dedicates the soul to social interest.

From a Cultural Perspective

Give Adler and his psychodynamic colleagues credit for moving away from the overly sexual nature of Freud's drive theory and toward an appreciation of the broader family and cultural forces at work. But they do not go far enough. No matter how you repackage it, psychodynamic theory represents the same sexist, intrapsychic perspective in more social terms. Problems are still attributed to individuals,

not social ills. Intrapsychic forces of superiority and inferiority still rule the mental roost. The life-style analysis considers the impact of the family constellation, but the patient is still responsible for the illness and the cure. Psychodynamic therapy tries to change the sick patient, not the sick society.

Women fare a bit better under Adler than under Freud, but not much. Adlerian theory accepts psychotherapy as an extension of the socialization process. Be more socialized and civilized, and you will be free from psychopathology. That may be true for many men and children in need of socialization or resocialization, but what of the many women who are troubled because they are oversocialized? The ever-polite and passive client suffering from stress headaches will not be freed by striving to be more perfect. She needs to express her anger and resentment over always stifling herself for the sake of social harmony. The self-sacrificing spouse who experiences no sense of self because she has always lived for others doesn't need to be encouraged to make someone else happy once a day. She needs to know how to care for herself and to assert herself.

From an Integrative Perspective

There is much of value in psychodynamic therapies to those committed to integrating the psychotherapies. Alfred Adler broadened the exclusive reliance on insight and private knowledge to include action-oriented and psychoeducational processes in therapy. The therapeutic relationship was construed and offered as more egalitarian and more real than it was in psychoanalysis. Individuality and relatedness were accorded equal consideration in psychotherapy, reversing a trend toward self-contained individualism (Guisinger & Blatt, 1994). Adler and his followers were more flexible in their formats, innovative in their practices, and eclectic in their techniques than were Freud and his disciples. Not surprisingly, many contemporary eclectics, including Arnold Lazarus (see Chapter 16), have been heavily influenced by Adler's work and are enthusiastic about his psychotherapy.

On pragmatic grounds, systemization and evidence are sorely needed (Dryden & Lazarus, 1991). Although there are many interesting constructs and a prescribed lifestyle analysis, little systematic direction exists regarding which interventions should be used with which patients with which disorders. Just do the same thing for all patients—not a notion likely to be endorsed by any genuine eclectic! The empirical evidence on the effectiveness of Adlerian therapy, moreover, is far too scant for an eclectic to even consider wholly adopting its theory or its interventions.

On more theoretical grounds, it is ironic that Adler called his approach individual psychology, when he ultimately valued social interests over the interests of the individual. Adler attempted to resolve the inherent conflicts between society and the individual by suggesting the individual's best interests are really served by subjugating self-interest to the interests of society. Adlerian theory may indeed help balance therapeutic approaches that worship only the self at the expense of others. Nevertheless, it would be a mistake to conclude that a complete life can be found only in living for social interests and never for self-interest.

An Adlerian Analysis of Mrs. C

Mrs. C is a person almost entirely preoccupied with herself. Other people are mere shadows, minor characters who move in and out of her dramatic rituals. Her life has become a parody of a great epic. She is in a mortal struggle with the dreaded evil of pinworms, and only she can be powerful enough and perfect enough to prevent the pinworms from becoming the victors. She has obviously switched her striving for superiority from solving the primary tasks of life to a secondary theater of operations in which she can be the heroine, the star in her own style of life.

Mrs. C's dramatic dilemma is common to those with a compulsive personality. Having been raised under the constant castigation and derision of dominating parents, Mrs. C was discouraged from believing that she was capable of facing life's tasks successfully. She had indeed failed at the task of coming to grips with her own sexuality. She was in the process of failing at the work of caring for five children with a sixth on the way. The intense inferiority complex that she had accepted early in life was in danger of proving to be all too true. What she decided as a child was becoming a self-fulfilling prophecy: She was too inferior to find completion through life's tasks. Her solution was to switch the arena to a neurotic struggle that was more of her own making and more under her control.

Quickly Mrs. C became the perfect compulsive, the most complete washer others had ever known. What a special person she is, how unusual! She has already stumped several clinicians and a prominent psychiatric hospital. Her compulsive lifestyle serves, then, as a compensation for her inferiority complex of being unable to solve life's tasks, as a built-in excuse for not doing more with her life, as a means of freezing time by repeating the same rituals that seem to keep life from moving ahead, and as a dramatic struggle that proves how superior she is at holding back the evil forces of the world.

Progress in therapy would be a real threat to Mrs. C. She has judged herself as too inferior to progress in life. She has made a basic mistake of evaluating herself on the basis of early recollections of how her parents perceived her—as an inferior being, requiring constant control and domination. What distortions she may have added to these recollections may never be known. Did her parents never support her strengths or her strivings for independence? Did she encourage their domination because she found security in being protected from sex, disease, or boys? Were there not adults in her life, teachers or neighbors, who encouraged her, even if her folks were really such tyrants? Again, answers to such questions may never be known.

What must become known to Mrs. C is that she continues in her neurotic patterns because she

(continued)

concluded early in life that she was ultimately unable to succeed in life. She must come to understand that she is not special or disturbed because she has intense feelings of inferiority, but that she shares these feelings with all humans. Her disturbance is the result of striving to be special and trying to compensate for her inferiorities by investing all her energies in a completely self-centered life.

If Mrs. C continues to withdraw from living with and for others, she is indeed at high risk of becoming psychotically disabled. Her thinking and communication are of little social interest. They are almost entirely directed toward pinworms, toward her fears, and toward convincing others how special are her life circumstances. The social ties that connect thinking with social reality can break down if others continue to be of no interest to Mrs. C.

Given Mrs. C's intense self-preoccupation, it will be difficult to engage her with another human in the form of a psychotherapist. Because she has had considerable individual therapy, and because she seems only to have convinced herself of how special she is, it would be better to start Mrs. C in an Adlerian group. Although she would probably resist group therapy, on the grounds that she is too troubled and too in need of individual attention, a group would give the direct message that, in fact, she is not so special. She would have the opportunity to discover that others also have serious problems and serious feelings of inferiority, and yet many of them are moving ahead in life. Bibliotherapy would also advance this message. Finding herself unable to really care about others, Mrs. C might insist that if she were not so preoccupied with her own problems, then she could care about the others. The therapist and group members could correct such mistaken thinking by indicating that the reverse idea is really true: If she can begin to learn to care about others in the group, she can begin to forget about herself for awhile.

Mrs. C would also be encouraged to participate in a full analysis of her life script, including basic mistakes such as judging herself inadequate because she felt dominated by her parents. Her earliest recollections would be interpreted, as would her perceptions of her position in her family constellation. The group could be especially supportive in helping Mrs. C to become more fully conscious of her inferiority complex. Finding that others share intense feelings of inferiority can give Mrs. C the opportunity to rediscover a genuine interest in others.

Experiencing the caring of her therapist and of special group members can reorient Mrs. C from sheer self-interest to an emerging social interest. Tasks would be assigned to facilitate interest in others, such as assigning Mrs. C to call certain group members who are in a crisis to see how they are doing each evening. Mrs. C would be encouraged to step further out of her special drama back into the relational world by being assigned simple tasks to add pleasure to her children's lives, such as baking them a pie. Any reasons for avoiding these tasks would be interpreted as excuses. In the process of experimenting with such tasks, Mrs. C can become aware of the healing effect that caring for others can have on self-preoccupation.

Assigning tasks can help Mrs. C reevaluate the consequences of living for others versus living to ward off pinworms. Acting as if she is free, for the moment at least, to create something of value for others, even a simple pie, can demonstrate that she indeed has some choice in how she is going to continue living. Ultimately, she will have to confront the choice of whether to come off the stage of her limited theater of operations to reengage the world. After so many years of living for her own drama, Mrs. C may choose to hold onto the security and esteem of being the world's greatest container of pinworms, rather than risk creating a life that might be more useful to others, even if it is a bit more mundane.

Future Directions

Adler was clearly ahead of the learning curve in psychotherapy. His social recasting of Freudian theory initiated psychodynamic therapy; his task assignments foreshadowed the development of behavioral and other directive therapies; his techniques involving basic mistakes and "as if" anticipated the cognitive therapies; and his community outreach and psychoeducational programs foreshadowed community mental health. Many of Adler's ideas have quietly permeated modern psychological thinking, often without notice. It would not be easy to find another author from which so much has been borrowed from all sides without acknowledgment than Alfred Adler (Ellenberger, 1970, p. 645).

In some cases, success of a psychotherapy system begets more success and popularity. In other cases, success begets gradual disappearance as a distinct system and incorporation by other systems and the public. The fate of Adlerian therapy definitely seems to be following the second track.

The future impact of Adlerian therapy, then, will probably be more indirect than direct. Adler's influence will be represented in the cognitive and behavioral therapies it inspired. His system will be embodied, unknowingly in most instances, in the eclectic and integrative therapies it helped to spawn. The concepts of inferiority complex, superiority strivings, social interest, ideal self, and ordinal position, among others, have been widely incorporated, often without acknowledgment of Adler, into many psychotherapy systems and, indeed, into the public lexicon. Thus incorporated and assimilated, Adlerian therapy may gradually disappear as a distinct orientation as a result of its own success.

The principal direction for Adlerians is to go "on beyond Adler" (Manaster, 1987a, 1987b). What's needed are evolutionary Adlerians who will view Adler as an ancestor but who will do so critically, noting where they think he was essentially correct and where he may have missed the mark (Hartshorne, 1991). This evolution will certainly entail combining Adlerian techniques with those of other systems in a coherent brief therapy. "On beyond Adler" may well become the rallying cry of those who desire to avert the premature disappearance of Alfred Adler's seminal theory as a distinct system of psychotherapy.

The future of Freudian practice indisputably lies in psychodynamic therapy. In practice, most contemporary followers of Freud lean more heavily on ego psychology, object relations, supportive therapy, and brief psychodynamic therapy than on classical psychoanalysis. A case in point: When we asked hundreds of psychologists conducting psychotherapy to declare their theoretical orientations, only 2% identified themselves as psychoanalytic. But 18% identified themselves as psychodynamic (Bechtoldt et al., 2001). A decisive shift from psychoanalysis to psychodynamicism has occurred.

We offer four forecasts for the future of psychodynamic psychotherapy. First, and most assuredly, increasing attention will be paid to relational disturbances originating in infancy and early childhood (Strupp, 1992). Fueled by the object relations theorists and John Bowlby's (1969, 1973) seminal writings, **attachment styles** are serving as useful clinical guidelines. An insecure attachment style complicates a patient's later relationships, including the therapeutic relationship, whereas a secure attachment style predicts better relationships and therapy outcomes (Levy et al., 2011). The therapist can not only become an attachment figure for the client, but also respond differently depending on that attachment style. Indeed, *attachment* is quickly becoming a pantheoretical construct among child, couples, trauma, and psychodynamic therapists.

Second, the treatment focus will increasingly shift from the traditional neurotic disorders to more complex disorders, such as borderline and narcissistic personality disorders, multiple trauma, and somatoform disorders. The psychodynamic treatment of these conditions is now considered to be one of the treatments of choice. When other, typically shorter treatments fail, the discerning clinician will certainly consider the ambitious and comprehensive psychodynamic alternative.

Third, having now proved in the research that psychodynamic therapy represents an evidence-based treatment for multiple disorders, psychodynamic therapists will drill down to determine which form works best for which patient. When is long-term versus short-term psychodynamic therapy indicated? For which clients is supportive versus expressive therapy called for? The next generation of researchers will ask not only, "Does it work?" but "Does it work best for this particular patient in this situation?"

Fourth, future training will focus heavily on the preparation of brief psychodynamic therapists. Time-limited psychodynamic therapy reflects the ongoing march toward evidence-based and cost-effective treatments for specific disorders applicable to the largest number of patients. Guided by **treatment manuals**, analogous to a flight plan or a road map, training will ensure competence in appropriate therapist stances and techniques.

All of these future directions will provide needed specificity in training, research, and practice for the descendants of Sigmund Freud. And, all these directions will converge in enabling our clients to live fuller, deeper, more joyful lives with secure attachments and social interests.

Key Terms

acting "as if"	creative self
aggression instinct	drive theory
allegiance effect	effect size (ES)
analytical psychology	ego analysis
anamnesis	ego psychology
archetypes	fictional finalism
attachment	*Gemeinschaftsgefühl*
attachment styles	(social interest)
autonomous ego	holding environment
autonomous self	ideal self
basic mistakes	individual psychology
bibliotherapy	inferiority complex
birth order/ordinal	introjection
position	lifestyle analysis
catching oneself	masculine protest
character analysis	meta-analysis
collective unconscious	mirroring
compensation	narcissistic personality
compulsive lifestyle	normal autism
conflict-free spheres	normal symbiosis

object	striving for superiority
object relations	style of life
organ inferiority	supportive therapy
psychodynamic	supportive-expressive
therapists	therapy
psychosocial stages	symbiotic psychosis
push-button technique	therapeutic, or
self-interest	working, alliance
self psychology	transference-focused
social interest	psychotherapy
splitting	treatment manuals

Recommended Readings

Adler, A. (1927). *The practice and theory of individual psychology.* New York: Harcourt, Brace.

Carlson, J., Watts, R. E., & Maniacci, M. (2005). *Adlerian therapy: Theory and practice.* Washington, DC: American Psychological Association.

Kohut, H. (1977). *The restoration of the self.* New York: International Universities Press.

Luborsky, L. (1984). *Principles of psychoanalytic psychotherapy.* New York: Basic.

Rockland, L. H. (2003). *Supportive therapy: A psychodynamic approach.* New York: Basic Books.

Strupp, H. H., & Binder, J. L. (1984). *Psychotherapy in a new key: A guide to time-limited dynamic psychotherapy.* New York: Basic Books.

Summers, R. F., & Barber, J. P. (Eds.). (2009). *Psychodynamic therapy: A guide to evidence-based practice.* New York: Guilford.

Yeomans, F. E., Clarkin, J. F., & Kernberg, O. F. (2002). *A primer of transference-focused psychotherapy for the borderline patient.* Northvale, NJ: Jason Aronson.

JOURNALS: *Dynamic Psychotherapy; International Journal of Intensive Short-Term Dynamic Psychotherapy; Individual Psychology: Journal of Adlerian Theory, Research and Practice; International Journal of Psychoanalytic Self Psychology; Issues in Ego Psychology; Journal of*

Analytical Psychology; Journal of Analytic Social Work; Psychoanalysis and Psychotherapy; Psychoanalytic Dialogues; Psychoanalytic Inquiry; Psychoanalytic Psychology.

Recommended Websites

APA Division of Psychoanalysis:
  www.apadivisions.org/division-39

International Association for Psychoanalytic Self Psychology (Kohut):
  www.psychologyoftheself.com/
Journal of Individual Psychology:
  www.utexas.edu/utpress/journals/jip.html
North American Society of Adlerian Psychology:
  www.alfredadler.org
Society of Analytical Psychology (Jung):
  jungian-analysis.org/

CHAPTER **4**

Existential Therapies

Rollo May

James Bugental

Lilly entered psychotherapy haunted by the dread that she was dying from terminal failure. Her marriage had failed. Worse, she felt she had never really gotten to know her husband. Lilly didn't bother to get a divorce, so she wouldn't have to explain why she wasn't married in middle age. She also felt she failed by her inability to have a child, even though she cared deeply about her nieces and many of her students. But she felt, too, that she had failed in her career as a teacher. Lilly had to move from one part-time job to another, with colleges relying increasingly on temporary rather than tenured faculty.

Lilly had failed to live up to all the expectations of her family which once was famous. Worse, she failed to live up to her own expectations.

Lilly's finances were also failing to sustain her, especially in the face of her failing health. It turned out Lilly was dying from terminal cancer. But it wasn't the cancer that haunted her. It was the constant questioning about what had she accomplished with her life. It was an existential crisis. What had she achieved with all the time and talent she was given?

At a time of deep despair for Lilly, I (JOP) asked her to share with me the experiences she most loved in her life. Lilly came alive when she relived her adventures with different cultures, speaking foreign languages with people who became her friends. Lilly came alive when she recalled her favorite novels that took her back into earlier eras. She sometimes wished that she had lived in simpler times. She loved to paint watercolors of landscapes on the island where she lived in a small shingled shack by the sea.

Lilly could laugh, and she could cry. She had deep feelings and deep thoughts. As she shared these she gradually started to appreciate that her life was filled with rich experiences. How liberating it was for Lilly to choose that she would evaluate her life on what she had experienced rather than what she had achieved.

Lilly gave me a special painting of a flower. She also left me memories of a special life.

A Sketch of Early Existential Therapists

Most systems of psychotherapy emerge in a particular time and context in human events. Psychoanalysis, as we have seen, emerged near the end of the repressive Victorian era with a corresponding emphasis on sex. Cognitive therapy, with its focus on mind and sensory data, accompanied the dawn of computers and the Information Age (Miller & Hubble, 2004).

The developmental context of existential philosophy was the lost generation following the madness of World War I and the search for meaning following the destruction of World War II. The human species was capable of exceptional violence and cruelty; an estimated 61 million people were lost during World War II alone. People were understandably preoccupied with death, dread, and despair on a daily basis. The prospect of death and nonexistence was imminent for millions. What did it all mean? Was life meaningless? How does one grapple with death anxiety? How could people become free from oppression? How did people avoid responsibility for their heinous behaviors? Existentialism, first as a philosophy and then as a psychotherapy, addressed these fundamental questions of life, and of death.

Ludwig Binswanger (1881–1966) was one of the first mental health professionals to emphasize the existential nature of psychopathology and the therapeutic uses of the existential crisis that Lilly was experiencing. Binswanger believed that crises in psychotherapy usually represented critical choice points for patients. His commitment to a person's freedom to choose in therapy went as far as his acceptance of the suicide of one of his patients, Ellen West, who found death to be her most legitimate alternative (Binswanger, 1958).

Existentialists, like Binswanger, do not run from the dark side of life. Following the example of Kierkegaard (1954a, 1954b), the Danish philosopher, existentialists are willing to face aspects of life that are awful but meaningful at the same time.

Binswanger had originally struggled to find meaning in madness by translating the experience of patients into psychoanalytic theory. After reading Heidegger's (1962) profound philosophical treatise, *Sein und Zeit* (*Being and Time*), however, Binswanger (1958) became more existential and phenomenological in his therapy. The phenomenological approach enabled Binswanger to face directly the immediate experience of patients and to understand the meaning of such phenomena in the patient's language rather than in terms of the therapist's abstract theory.

Binswanger began applying his emerging existential ideas in the Sanatarium Bellevue in Kreuglinger, Switzerland, where he succeeded his father as chief medical director in 1911. After interning under the famous psychiatrist Eugen Bleuler, from whom he learned much about the symptoms of schizophrenia, he became intrigued with understanding the existence of the people experiencing psychopathological states. He worked on this for the rest of his life. Although he retired in 1956, he continued his work until his death in 1966 at the age of 85.

Medard Boss (1903–1991), a second early and influential existential psychotherapist, had a career remarkably similar to Binswanger's. Born in Switzerland in 1903, he also worked under Bleuler in

Zurich. Like Binswanger, he knew Freud and was heavily influenced by his thinking. Heidegger was his most important influence and, like Binswanger, Boss was concerned with translating Heidegger's philosophical position into an effective psychotherapy. Boss's particular concern was to integrate the ideas of Heidegger with the methods of Freud, as indicated in the title of his major work, *Daseinanalysis and Psychoanalysis* (1963). Boss worked for many years in the medical school as professor of psychoanalysis at the University of Zurich, which continues to be the European center of *Daseinanalysis* (being-there or existential analysis) even after his death in 1991 (Craig, 1988).

Although most existential therapists draw on the clinical formulations of Binswanger and Boss, neither dominates existentialism the way Freud dominated psychoanalysis or Rogers eclipsed person-centered therapy. One reason is that neither existentialist developed a comprehensive system or theory of psychotherapy. Boss, in fact, seems even antitheoretical. In a letter to Hall and Lindzey (1970), he wrote:

> I can only hope that existential psychology will never develop into a theory in its modern meaning of the natural sciences. All that existential psychology can contribute to psychology is to teach the scientists to remain with the experienced and experienceable facts and phenomena, to let these phenomena tell the scientists their meaning and their references, and so do the encountered objects justice.

The most influential existential therapist in the United States has been Rollo May (1909–1994). In contrast to the European context and medical training of Binswanger and Boss, May was born and raised in the United States and was trained in theology and clinical psychology. His immediate family consisted of five brothers and a sister, who later suffered from psychosis, and parents who endured a "discordant" marriage (May, 1989, p. 436). May's early life was lonely and conflicted; his childhood experiences sensitized him to the pain of loneliness and the inescapable anxiety associated with tumultuous family life (Monte, 1991). Following travel and a "breakdown" in Greece, May traveled to Vienna to study briefly with Alfred Adler, which strengthened his interest in psychodynamic psychotherapy. But returning to the states, he found that the psychology of the time was not investigating the profound questions of death, love, will, and hate that occupied his existence. Instead, May enrolled at Union Theological Seminary, where he began his lengthy friendship with theologian Paul Tillich. Thereafter, while trying to complete his doctorate in psychology at Columbia University, May came down with tuberculosis, then a killer disease. He was confined for the balance of 2 years at a tuberculosis sanatorium, where he needed to confront the possibility of his own death. May embraced an active stance toward his disease and found meaning that sustained him over the course of a productive and prolific career. May's own existential struggles have informed his books, among them *The Meaning of Anxiety* (1950/1977), *Existence* (May et al., 1958), *Love and Will* (1969), and *The Discovery of Being* (1983).

Like Binswanger and Boss before him, Rollo May never developed a formal system of existential therapy. In fact, May and colleagues (1958) defined existential therapy as an attitude that transcends orientation. Others have defined it as a dynamic therapy that addresses life's ultimate concerns (Yalom, 1980) or practically any antideterministic psychotherapy (for example, Edwards, 1982). Not surprisingly, then, the existential movement is a diffuse school of theorists and practitioners more aligned in their philosophical emphases than in concrete techniques or practical consequences. Put another way, existential therapy is more a philosophy about psychotherapy than a system of psychotherapy.

Several American psychotherapists have tried to pull together the many strands of existentialism into a coherent clinical approach. They combine the philosophical base of existentialism, as enunciated by Søren Kierkegaard, Martin Heidegger, Jean-Paul Sartre, and Martin Buber, among others; the clinical themes of the early existential therapists, principally Binswanger, Boss, and May; and their own therapy experiences into a recognizable system of psychotherapy. Central among these American systematizers are James Bugental (1965, 1987, 1990), Irving Yalom (1980), and Kirk Schneider (2007), from whose collective work we will also draw in this chapter.

Theory of Personality

Existentialists are uncomfortable with the term *personality* if it implies a fixed set of traits within the individual (Boss, 1983). For them existence is an emerging, a becoming, a process of being that is not fixed or characterized by particular traits. *Being* is a verb form, a participle, implying an active and dynamic process. Nor does existence occur just within the individual, but rather between individuals and their world.

Existence is best understood as **being-in-the-world**. The use of hyphens is the best we can do in English to convey the idea that a person and the environment are an active unity. Existentialists reject dualism that assumes a split between mind and body, experience and environment. Being and world are inseparable, because they are both essentially created by the individual.

Phenomenologically, the world is our own construction that to a greater or lesser extent reflects the construction of others, depending on how conventional we are. For example, a traditional Christian's world includes a Superior Being with which one can communicate, whereas the atheist's existence contains no such spiritual being. In therapy, a psychoanalyst experiences dynamics in patients

that a behaviorist would swear are figments of the Freudian imagination. The behaviorist might argue that eventually we will all respond to the same world once it is defined by the scientific method, but the existentialist argues that the scientific method itself is a human construction, inadequate for understanding the very reason that created it. Rather than reconciling differences in worldviews, the existentialist accepts that, to understand a particular human, is to understand the world as that person construes it.

We exist in relation to three levels of our world. In German these are called **Umwelt**, **Mitwelt**, and **Eigenwelt** (Binswanger, 1963; Boss, 1963; May, 1958). *Umwelt* connotes ourselves in relation to the biological and physical aspects of our world, and we will translate it as **being-in-nature**. *Mitwelt* refers to the world of persons, the social world; we will call it **being-with-others**. *Eigenwelt* literally means own-world and refers to the way we reflect on, evaluate, and experience ourselves; it will be translated as **being-for-oneself**.

Personalities differ in their ways of existing at each of these three levels of being. Imagine being on a beautiful, secluded beach by the ocean. One person might be afraid to set foot in the ocean because it is the home of sharks waiting to attack, whereas another person dives in, eagerly seeking refreshment in the cool waters. One person desires a lover in such a sensuous setting, whereas another feels all alone. One person walks along looking at the nearby land as a golden opportunity for a seaside housing development, but another feels sad about the encroachment of houses already under construction nearby. Still others feel at one with the ocean from which all life has come, whereas someone, somewhere wants to join the ocean to end life.

When we-are-with-others, we know that they are conscious beings who can reflect on us, evaluate us, and judge us. This may cause us to fear others and want to run from them. We may choose to clam up or to talk only about super-fluous topics such as the weather lest we reveal something about ourselves that others would dislike. Frequently, we anticipate what others are thinking or feeling about us, and we guide our observable behavior in order to have a favorable impact on them. This is the way, unfortunately, we typically are with others, a level of existence known as being-for-others. This mode of existence parallels the characterization of the modern personality as other-directed (Reisman, 1961).

Fortunately, there are precious times with special others in which we can let ourselves be, silly or sad, anxious or mad, without having to worry about what the other person is thinking about us. When we are being-for-ourselves, we are the ones who are reflecting on, evaluating, or judging our own existence.

Because self-reflection can be painful at times, we may choose not to be introspective. Or we may choose to think about ourselves only after having a few drinks or a few pills to deaden the pain. Or we may become incessantly introspective and have difficulty being with others. For existentialists, however, the risk of pain or self-preoccupation is the price we pay to achieve the considered, conscious life so important in creating a healthy existence.

In trying to create a healthy existence, we are faced with the dilemma of choosing the best way to be in-nature, with-others, and for-ourselves. With the emergence of consciousness, we realize how ambiguous the world is and how open it is to different interpretations. In this book alone, we are considering 16 different interpretations that could serve as guides for interpreting the natural, social, and personal aspects of our world. What is the existential alternative for living? The best alternative is not necessarily to choose to maximize reinforcements and minimize punishments, as some behaviorists would suggest, or to adapt our instinctual desires to the demands of our environment, as some Freudians would suggest.

The best alternative is to be authentic. For the existentialists, **authenticity** is its own reward. An authentic existence brings with it an openness to nature, to others, and to ourselves, because we have decided to meet the world straight on without hiding it from us or us from it. Openness means that authentic individuals are more aware, because they have chosen not to hide anything from themselves. An authentic existence also brings the freedom to be spontaneous with others, because we do not fear that we might reveal something about ourselves that contradicts what we have pretended to be. A healthy existence brings with it an awareness that any relationship we do have is authentic and that if anyone cares about us, it is really us they care about and not some facade constructed on their behalf. Authentic relationships allow us to truly trust others because we know they will be honest about their experience and not tell us what they think we want to hear.

An authentic existence is healthy because the three levels of our being are integrated, or in-joint, rather than in conflict. We experience ourselves as together: The way we are in nature is the way we present ourselves to others and also the way we know who we are. We do not get caught up in idealizing images about ourselves that prevent us from being intimate with others lest they tell us what we do not want to hear. Nor do we get so preoccupied with ourselves that we cannot get involved in the world around us. A healthy existence, then, involves a simultaneous and harmonious relationship to each level of being without emphasizing one level at the expense of others, such as sacrificing our self-evaluation for the approval of others.

With authenticity promising so much, why don't we all choose to be authentic? Why are so many of us terrified that if other people really knew us they wouldn't want to be with us? Why does the other-directed personality seem to be the stereotype of our time? What is the dread that comes with being more fully aware of ourselves and our world?

Theologian Paul Tillich (1952) outlined certain conditions inherent in existence that tempt us to run from too much awareness. These conditions fill us with a dread called **existential anxiety**. The first source of anxiety comes with our acute awareness that at some unknown time we must die: Being implies nonbeing. Death may be denied by our culture, including psychology, yet the fact that our total existence will end in nothingness can make us shudder. When we are honest, we are also aware that our most significant others can die at any time, ending not only their existence but also the part of our being that was intimately connected with them.

Many summers ago my wife and I were swimming with our young son and daughter in a salt pond near the ocean. A woman came over to borrow a paper cup, and when she turned around she immediately realized that her 4-year-old son was missing. She was convinced that he was in the water, so we began diving and diving and diving. The more we dove, the more anxious we became, hoping we would find him, then gradually hoping that we wouldn't. Two hours later, when the fire department pulled his lifeless body out of the deepest waters where no one expected him to be, all we could do was shudder and hold each other close.

Once we become conscious beings, we become aware that inherent in existence is a necessity-to-act. We must make decisions that will profoundly affect the rest of our lives, such as where we go to school, what career we choose, if and whom we choose to marry, and whether we have children. We must act, and yet in modern times, we are less and less certain about the basis for deciding. We cannot know beforehand with any degree of certainty how our decisions will turn out, and so we are continually under the threat of uncertainty and guilt. We must make decisions in relative ignorance of their ramifications, knowing that we will hurt people regularly without intending to.

In critical choices, we alone are responsible. Inherent in our responsibility is the anxiety of knowing that we will make serious mistakes, but not knowing whether this choice is one of those mistakes. For example, when I (JOP) was originally deciding whether to spend a year of my life writing the first edition of this book, I was quite anxious that such a decision might be a miserable mistake and might lead me to avoid other attractive pursuits. (Some of you may now believe that I had good reason to be anxious!)

The threat of **meaninglessness** is another contingency of human existence that produces anxiety. We all want to do something meaningful with our lives. The particular meaning may vary from love for one person, to sex for another, to faith for still another. But when we honestly question the significance of our existence, the issue becomes whether life itself means anything. We can rarely go to the theater or a modern museum or read a current novel without being confronted with this profound issue. For many of us, what we once believed in—our former religions, our former politics, or our former therapies—no longer seem as significant as they once did. This suggests that our current source of meaning may also disappear. All therapists see formerly vital marriages that have become entirely devitalized, with nothing left but deadly boredom. We see people trapped in previously gratifying jobs that are now nothing more than a means of structuring time, ruts that lead nowhere. Our clients become anxious, and so do we.

Part of our anxiety comes from knowing we are the ones who created the meaning in our lives, and we are the ones who let it die. Therefore, we must be the ones to continue to create a life worth living.

The prospect that existence has no significance whatsoever can be terrifying. The conclusion that one's existence is totally absurd can be immobilizing. This immobilization is exemplified by the main character in John Barth's (1967) *The End of the*

Road. If there is no meaning in life, then there is no basis on which to make a decision, so he could not act. His psychotherapist hatched the ingenious solution that because nothing mattered, he could do just as well by applying arbitrary principles when faced with the necessity to act. His principles for living included alphabeticity and sinistrality: When confronted with a choice in life, he would choose the option that began with the first letter of the alphabet or the option on the left.

Our **isolation**, our fundamental **aloneness** in the universe, is another condition of life that brings anxiety (Bugental, 1965). Regardless of how intimate I am with others, I can never be them, nor can they be me. We share experiences, but we are always under the threat of never totally understanding each other. Furthermore, we know that choosing to follow our unique direction and create our own meaning in life may lead to others' not wanting to be with us. The possibility of such rejection brings forth the anxiety of being literally alone.

These multiple sources of existential anxiety attest to the defining characteristic of the human condition: **finiteness**. Death reflects the finiteness of our time; accidents represent the limits of our power; anxiety over decisions reflects the inadequacy of our knowledge; the threat of meaninglessness, the finiteness of our values; isolation, the finiteness of our empathy; and rejection, the finiteness of control over another human being.

These contingencies of life have also been called the realm of nonbeing. These **existential givens** are matters of necessity—we must die, we must act—and hence are a negation of being, which is by definition open-ended and in the realm of possibility. Nonbeing is the ground against which the figure of being is created. Death is the ground that accents the figure of life in bold relief. Chance is the ground that determines the limits of our choice. Meaninglessness is the ground against which meaning can be seen. And isolation is the ground from which intimacy emerges.

Our being is conscious, chosen, and free, whereas nonbeing is without light, closed, and necessary. In daily living, we experience being as our "subjectness," in which we are the active subject or agent in directing our own lives; nonbeing is experienced as our "objectness," in which we are objects determined by forces other than our will.

Authentic being survives to the extent that it takes nonbeing into itself. It perishes to the extent that it attempts to affirm itself by avoiding nonbeing. Our self as a conscious, choosing, and open subject can *be* only through confronting and surviving the anxiety of existence. To avoid existential anxiety is to avoid nonbeing in its various forms. To avoid choice and its anxiety, for example, is to fail to be a choosing subject. An authentic personality is aware that existence is a constant flow from nonbeing into being and back into nonbeing again. This can be seen most clearly in the overall course of our existence, as we come from the darkness of having never been, live in the light of consciousness, and then return to the darkness of death. Our daily cycle is similar, as our present existence emerges from the yesterday that no longer exists into the being of the present and thrusts into the unconscious nonbeing of tomorrow. That is why authentic being is said to occur only in the present.

Theory of Psychopathology

Lying is the foundation of psychopathology. Lying is the only way we can flee from nonbeing, to not allow existential anxiety into our experience. When confronted with nonbeing, such as the drowning of the 4-year-old boy, we have two choices: to be anxious or to lie. We may choose to lie by telling ourselves that if we keep a constant eye on our family, we can prevent accidents. We hold close our children and our spouse, and when they are in sight we feel relaxed. The lie has worked. We have avoided an encounter with the existential anxiety of accidents, but nonbeing is always there, threatening to emerge into our consciousness. Lying always leads to a closing off of part of our world; in this case, we must close off any thoughts about the man who slipped right in front of his family and broke his neck. Consciousness of such events not only brings existential anxiety but also threatens to expose our lie.

Lying also leads to neurotic anxiety. If we become anxious, for example, just because our children are momentarily out of sight, we are experiencing neurotic anxiety. Neurotic anxiety is an inauthentic response to being, whereas existential anxiety is an honest response to nonbeing. Our children's leaving our sight is essential to many expressions of their own being; they do not exist to shore up our lies. We decide that they need to be in sight in order for us to be more comfortable; they decide to be away from us in order to exist more fully and freely.

We choose our lies, and are stuck with their consequences. The consequence now is that unless we are aware of our family at all times, we are anxious. Like a mother we saw in therapy, we may neurotically order our children to play in the living room at all times. We may choose to walk them to and from school, to go see them at recess and lunch time, or be anxious. We may telephone our spouse repeatedly, pretending to have something to say but wanting only to be reassured that our spouse is well. If we try not to call, the anxiety may become extremely intense. Thus, we tell ourselves we have no choice—we must call.

When neurotic anxiety leads to acting on that anxiety, we develop psychopathology, such as a compulsion to check on our family. By saying that we must check on our family, we have become an object that no longer has the choice to let our family be. Symptoms of psychopathology are **objectifications** of ourselves. In pathology, we experience ourselves as objects without choice or will. This can be terrifying, like the nightmares in which we are chased by someone and want to run, but no matter how hard we will it, we cannot run. We are trapped as a consequence of our own lies.

Psychopathology is also characterized by an overemphasis on one level of being at the expense of other levels of being. In this case, there is an overemphasis on being-with-others—namely, our family—at the expense of being-in-nature or being-for-oneself. We must be-with-others lest we become filled with neurotic anxiety.

Lying can occur at any level of existence. Hypochondriacs, for example, lie about the nature of illness and healing. They fabricate a theory that diseases can be avoided if only they see the doctor often enough and fast enough. Their bodies are constant sources of anxiety that send them scurrying to a doctor with every ache and twitch. "If only I run soon enough, I can outsmart nature at her games of chance," they lie. After convincing themselves they must run, trying not to run fills their being with neurotic anxiety. They have given up their will to their aches and their medicine man. "You take over, doctor," they seem to say. "This business of living is too scary for me." Lying-in-nature drastically reduces their freedom to be-with-others or to be-for-themselves, because all they can talk about or think about is their most recent attack of this or that.

People of a paranoid persuasion decide nature is filled with evil forces out to destroy them. The food, the water, or the air is poisoned, so we must constantly beware. Others of a more depressive temperament conclude that the world is falling apart, that the world is going to the dogs. The good old days are gone forever, and it is only downhill from here.

Perhaps the most common level of lying is for others. Early in life, we learn that we can misrepresent ourselves to others with some success. As children, we are smart enough to see that the option to lie can be a tremendous source of power. How to influence others by faking sad or mad or innocent, depending on their weak spot, is a lesson not missed by many. But, of course, every lie is accompanied by fear of discovery and the shame of being caught. Over the years, the impending shame builds and leaves us feeling that if people really knew who we are they would leave us alone. So we spend much of our time lying-for-others, seldom free to be-with-others.

Some brag of their ability to lie-to-others. Selling themselves, they call it—the royal road to success. People want them to smile, they smile; people want their egos built up, they build. The other people may be the customer, the boss, or the professor—it doesn't matter. The liars are happy to sell themselves—a small price for success, they think. The lie up their sleeves, of course, is that someday they will be free to be themselves. They promise themselves that once they get their graduate degree, then they will live their own lives—or maybe they better wait until they get their first job, or that final promotion, or that new position.

But "can this be pathological?" we ask. It is so common, so natural. The ability to delay gratification, even the gratification of being ourselves, is a necessary part of succeeding in society. The ability to play roles is essential for making it in the academic or mental health marketplaces. Those elitist European existentialists would reserve health for only the authentic few. But what they ask is that we not become so alienated that we equate statistically normal self-estrangement with health. If we are going to compromise ourselves away for others, then let us at least remain healthy enough to hurt about it, rather than hide behind the data that show we all do it to some extent.

Lying-for-ourselves is more complicated. First, we must consciously choose to lie; then at some point, usually beginning when we are children, we come to believe our own lies. For years, I (JOP) believed that I never got angry. I became depressed all right, but never angry. When I finally got tired of getting depressed, I became aware in my personal therapy that I could indeed get angry. To protect my idealized image of myself as a character who never lost his cool, I had to close off most of my feelings and be cold and depressed, but never angry.

The psychoanalysts would say that I was unconsciously repressing my anger. But the existentialists argue that in order to close off the "bad" parts of ourselves like anger, we have to first know that the anger is "bad." Sartre (1956) argues that all we need to assume is one conscious person who uses self-deception and chooses what aspects of the self to turn away from. Once we act on such **bad faith** in ourselves, we are faced with the impending guilt of knowing who we really are. As a result, our lying snowballs into symptoms, such as having to get depressed in order to never get angry.

Lying-for-oneself can occur in a wide range of pathologies. Many people are convinced they can attain perfection—be beyond criticism and, therefore, free from rejection—if they only work harder. So they become workaholics. Others protect their saintly self-concepts by turning their backs on their sexuality, modeling the Virgin Mary. Still others are convinced they are the perfect spouse and yet are afraid to come in for couples therapy. They send their partner. Once the psychotherapist straightens out their spouse, their marriage can be perfect again.

What we believe about our future critically affects how we act today. If we are overly objective, we may lose any basis on which to choose, and experience ourselves as being tossed and turned by the wind. Through lying, we may lose contact with the source of our personal direction, our **intentionality**. Intentionality is the creation of meaning, the basis of our identity. Sartre (1967) wrote that "man is nothing else but what he makes of himself. Such is the first principle of existentialism."

Our intentionality entails taking a stand in life. Our stance determines what we attend to—as when one person attends to the beauty of a beach, whereas another person attends to its business potential. The orientation we choose in life is the source of what our lives mean, and the source of the meaning we attribute to a beach. Lying, however, may convince us that our life is determined by a pathology that attacks us like an infectious disease—an accident over which we have no control.

Therapeutic Processes

Because lying is the source of psychopathology, honesty is the solution for dissolving symptoms. With authenticity as the goal of existential psychotherapy, increasing consciousness becomes one of the change processes through which people become aware of aspects of the world and of themselves that have been closed off by lying. Because lying also leads to an objectification of oneself in which the ability to choose is no longer experienced, therapy must involve processes through which individuals can again experience themselves as subjects or agents capable of directing their own lives through active choosing.

Techniques are slighted in existential therapy because technology is an objectifying process in which the therapist as subject decides the best means by which to change the patient as object. Although many patients want their therapists to fix them as a mechanic repairs a car, a technical focus only adds to patients experiencing themselves as mechanical objects. Existentialism encourages clients to enter into an authentic relationship with a therapist and thereby become increasingly aware of themselves as subjects, free to differ with the therapist even to the point of choosing when treatment will end. Although technique is deemphasized, we shall see that in practice the classical existentialists, such as Binswanger, Boss, and May, draw heavily upon psychoanalytic techniques, especially in the early stages of therapy.

Consciousness Raising

The Client's Work

If the explicit direction in psychoanalysis is to say whatever comes to mind, the implicit direction in existentialism is to be whatever you want to be. Patients are allowed to present themselves as they typically would relate to the world, with little intervention from the therapist early in therapy. Existentialists share the psychoanalytic assumption that patients will repeat their previous patterns of relating and will begin to form transference relationships. Whereas psychoanalysts assume that the transference is due to instinctual fixations,

existentialists see it as a result of the patients' objectification of themselves, which keeps them from being flexible and open to more authentic ways of being-in-the-world-of-therapy. Patients will impose their psychological categories onto therapy, so that if, for example, their experience of space with-others is a distant space, they will keep their distance from the therapist. If a patient is consumed with the past, then the patient will talk in therapy primarily about the past.

Patients are encouraged to engage in a process similar to free association but perhaps more appropriately called free experiencing. Patients are encouraged to express freely and honestly whatever they are experiencing in the present, although traditionally such "free" expression has been limited to expression through language, not action. In trying to freely experience, patients can become increasingly conscious that they are repeating the same patterns of being, such as being-in-the-past or being-for-the-future. They can become aware that there are parts of themselves and their world that they are not open to experiencing or expressing—for instance, their angry self or the reality of the therapist.

Patients will ordinarily try to maneuver the therapist into agreeing with their reasons for closing off such experiences, but because the reasons are lies, they will run into disagreement with the authenticity of the psychotherapist. For example, in saying "Don't you agree that it is immature to get angry?" the patient is pressuring the therapist for validation, but may instead meet with an honest response such as "No, I get angry at times, and I don't feel like a baby." Eventually the patient is encouraged to change from an egocentric experiencing of the process and person of the psychotherapy to a more authentic dialogue. By the time the client is able to enter into an ongoing dialogue, however, therapy is ready for termination.

The work of the patient in existential therapy requires enormous courage and honesty. Rollo May was convinced that we should ask more from our patients: "Their life is at stake" (Schneider et al., 2009). Broadening consciousness and enlarging experience is a hunk of life-changing work.

The Therapist's Work

Unfortunately, classical existentialists have not clearly identified their methods to increase the consciousness of clients. As with personality, many existentialists view existentialism as the philosophy they embrace in therapy and not as a system they use. As a result, many existentialists would oppose a systematic approach as contrary to an authentic encounter between the participants.

The writings of Binswanger (1963), Boss (1963), and May (1958), do give some idea of the variety of strategies traditional existentialists use in therapy. They agree that the therapist's work begins with understanding the phenomenal world of the patient. The **phenomenological method** focuses on the immediacy of experience, the perception of experience, the meaning of that experience, and observation with a minimum of a priori biases (Spiegelberg, 1972). The therapist attempts to experience the patient's unique construal of the world without imposing any theoretical or personal preconceptions onto the patient's experience. In understanding the patient's phenomenological world, most existentialists seem to use clarification, a type of feedback through which they illuminate the patient's experience, using the patient's own language rather than theoretical jargon. Such illuminating feedback helps patients to become more conscious of their being, including some aspects that have been closed off.

Once the therapist has gained a phenomenal understanding of the patient, the therapist chooses what techniques to follow. As Rollo May states, therapeutic technique follows understanding, in contrast to the more common, reverse order in which a clinician tries to understand a patient via the therapist's preferred theory. What is imperative is to avoid a gimmicky, quick-fix patch for the person; instead, in the tradition of Freud and his disciples, the therapist's work is to bring forth a new authentic person (Schneider et al., 2009).

Existentialists vary most at this step. Some, such as Boss (1963) and Bugental (1965), rely mainly on interpretation to analyze or make conscious the patient's transference reactions or repeated patterns of being. Although Boss and Bugental use psychoanalytic explanations of the patient's reactions when they fit, they also rely heavily on existential explanations, such as pointing out how the patient repeatedly runs from experiences related to death, decisions, or other aspects of nonbeing.

Other traditional existentialists seem to prefer a type of confrontation, in which the information they provide the patient is generated by the therapist's genuine reaction to the patient. **Existential confrontation** differs from psychoanalytic confrontation in that existentialists reveal their own experience of the patient and do not just reflect the patient's experience. The existentialist is by no means concerned with remaining a blank screen, because it is the therapist's honest feedback that can eventually break through the patient's closed world.

An example of such confrontation occurred when my (JOP's) wife, Jan, and I were conducting conjoint therapy with a couple in which the husband was complaining that his wife was refusing to have sex with him. At one intense point when the man insisted on dominating and degrading his wife, Jan told him, "You make me want to vomit." He was beside himself; he did not respond. He just fumed and the next morning came to see me individually, declaring that no woman had ever responded to him like that before. He couldn't imagine why, especially when the woman was a therapist. As I encouraged him to consider that stirred up similar feelings in his wife but she was afraid to express them because of his anger, he began to think that maybe, just maybe, he had something to do with his wife's feeling sick when he approached her sexually. His idealized image of himself had been shaken by Jan's intense confrontation, and he tried to shore up his lies by pressuring me into agreeing that a responsible therapist doesn't talk like that. When I encouraged him to face Jan's honest feedback, his lying-for-himself began to come out into the open. He began to see himself as the not-so-perfect man who perhaps had real trouble in being-with-women and not just with his "selfish" wife.

A literary example of existential confrontation is the haunting of Ebenezer Scrooge by the Ghost of Christmas Yet to Come in Charles Dickens's classic tale. The job of the Ghost, like the existential therapist, is to assist Scrooge in confronting the unpleasant truths about his life. By literally confronting his own death, Scrooge, like a patient, becomes instrumental in transforming his life (Yalom, 1980).

Although psychotherapy may begin with interpretations, for it to become existential, the therapist must eventually confront the patient with the therapist's own authentic being. If the therapist cannot be authentic, the patient may remain in a transference relationship, and this may be the reason psychoanalysis seems interminable. How can a patient be authentic with the therapist if the analyst remains an objectified blank screen?

By being authentic in the session, the therapist fosters a genuine encounter, which is a new relationship that opens up new horizons rather than a transference relationship that repeats the past (Ellenberger, 1958). Patients may continually try to freeze the therapist into the categories of their pathological world—keeping the therapist distant or casting her as a controlling authority figure, for instance. By being authentic, the therapist refuses to be frozen. By remaining authentic in the face of the patient's demands, the therapist confronts the patient, both verbally and experientially, with the patient's attempts at freezing the therapist and thereby keeping the patient frozen as a role or a symptom. Gradually the patient becomes aware that the therapist is taking risks to be honest and sees that the therapist can remain authentic in the face of such existential anxieties as being rejected by the patient or making mistakes. The patient becomes aware of a new alternative for being and is then confronted with the choice of changing his or her existence.

Choosing

The Client's Work

Clients are confronted with the burden of choosing from the very beginning of therapy, when they must decide whether they will commit themselves to working with a particular clinician. Patients are also confronted with having to decide what they will talk about in session and how they will be in therapy. The therapist will encourage clients to consider new alternatives for being, but the clients are expected to carry the burden of creating new alternatives in order for them to experience themselves as subjects capable of finding new directions for living. Once conscious of new alternatives, it is the client who must experience and exist with the anxiety of being responsible for which alternative to follow. The burden of choosing, then, is on the client.

This burden is perhaps most evident when patients are faced with **kairos**, critical choice points and momentous opportunities for deciding whether to risk changing a fundamental aspect of existence (Ellenberger, 1958), such as to be separate or partnered, to remain in the security of symptoms or to enter the anxiety of authenticity. The clients are the ones who must look deep into themselves to see whether they can muster up the courage to leap into the unknown future, knowing there is no guarantee that they will not fall flat on their faces. As an existential friend (Atayas, 1977) puts it, once clients become conscious that at least one person can be authentic, then they no longer have the choice of being a slave who is blind to better alternatives. The patient must now choose between being a coward and becoming a free person.

The Therapist's Work

The existential therapist takes every opportunity to clarify the choices that patients continually confront in their treatment, whether the choice pertains to what they should talk about each hour, how they should structure their therapy relationship, or whether they will return for future sessions. With such clarification, the patient becomes acutely conscious of being an active chooser, in spite of frequent protestations about being a patient, a helpless victim of psychopathology. The therapist also encourages patients to use their uniquely human processes of consciousness—their imagination, intellect, and judgment—to create rational alternatives to an apparently irrational way of being.

The therapist will remain with patients throughout their small choices and their kairos, empathizing with their anxiety and their turmoil. But the therapist knows that the road to being an authentic chooser rather than an objective symptom is basically a lonely one on which the patient alone must take responsibility for the choices. To jump in and rescue the patient, no matter how much the patient pulls on the therapist's rescue fantasies, would be to reinforce the lie that patients by definition are inadequate to direct their own lives.

Keen (1970, p. 200) provides the following example of an existential therapist confronting a patient with both the responsibility she has for choosing to change and the boring way that she is being.

Patient: I don't know why I keep coming here. All I do is tell you the same thing over and over. I'm not getting anywhere. [Patient complaining that therapist isn't curing her; maintenance of self-as-therapist's-object.]

Doctor: I'm getting tired of hearing the same thing over and over, too. [Therapist refusing to take responsibility for the progress of therapy and refusing to fulfill patient's expectations that he cure her; refusal of patient-as-therapist's-object.]

Patient: Maybe I'll stop coming. [Patient threatening therapist; fighting to maintain role as therapist's object.]

Doctor: It's certainly your choice. [Therapist refusing to be intimidated; forcing patient-as-subject.]

Patient: What do you think I should do? [Attempt to seduce the therapist into role of subject who objectifies patient.]

Doctor: What do you want to do? [Forcing again.]

Patient: I want to get better. [Plea for therapist to cure her.]

Doctor: I don't blame you. [Refusing role of subject-curer and supporting desire on part of patient-as-subject.]

Patient: If you think I should stay, okay, I will. [Refusing role of subject-who-decides.]

Doctor: You want me to tell you to stay? [Confrontation with patient's evasion of the decision and calling attention to how the patient is construing the therapy.]

Patient: You know what's best; you're the doctor. [Patient's confirmation of her construing therapy.]

Doctor: Do I act like a doctor?

Keen does not mention it, but if in fact the therapist acts like an omnipotent doctor or an authority figure who will cure the patient, then the therapist is lost. The patient's construal of therapy as a doctor-object relationship would be accurate, rather than a lie that allows her to run from her necessity-to-act as a responsible subject. With the therapist's authenticity, however, this is neither a game nor a battle. It is an honest confrontation between one person who experiences the potential of the other to choose and the other's desire to shore up the lie.

Therapeutic Content

Existentialism is a relatively comprehensive theory of existence concerned with the individual at all levels of personal functioning. Being-for-oneself is focused on intrapersonal functioning; being-with-others is the existential concept for interpersonal functioning; being-in-the-world includes, but is more than, the individual's relationship to society; and the search for authenticity reflects the goal of existentialists to go beyond conflict to fulfillment.

Intrapersonal Conflicts
Anxiety and Defenses
Anxiety is an ontological characteristic of every person, rooted in our very existence as a threat of nonbeing. The acceptance of freedom and the awareness of finitude will unavoidably result in

anxiety, or as Kierkegaard called it, the dizziness of freedom. Anxiety is not something we have, but something we are (May, 1977).

The existential approach retains Freud's basic dynamic structure but has a radically different content. The old Freudian formula of "instinctual drive produces anxiety which produces defense mechanisms" is replaced in existential therapy by "awareness of ultimate concerns produces anxiety which produces defense mechanisms" (Yalom, 1980). Accordingly, much of the focus is on the conflicts between the existential anxieties inherent in being and the lies that individuals use as defenses against such anxieties. As with psycho-analysis, anxiety is a central concept in existential therapy, but anxiety is viewed as a natural consequence of becoming conscious of nonbeing.

Rather than approach anxiety gradually in therapy, existentialists frequently confront it head on, especially during the periods of kairos. The only solution to existential anxiety is that suggested by Tillich (1952) in *The Courage to Be*: We must find courage within ourselves to accept existential anxiety as part of the price we pay for being uniquely human. In return, we can gain the excitement of becoming a unique and authentic human.

Because existential anxiety is a consequence of consciousness, the only defense against it is conscious lying—turning our attention away from threats of nonbeing by pretending to be something we are not, such as immortal, omnipotent, omniscient, or anything other than finite humans. We can give different names to different forms of lying if we prefer. Projection would be the lie that the responsibility for particular experiences belongs outside of us. Denial would be the lie of insisting that either we or the world are not what we honestly know them to be.

Over time, these and other defenses can become unconscious and habitual parts of our objectified selves. But defenses can remain frozen only if we continue to run from the anguish of being more open and authentic. Lying-for-others can succeed, for example, only when our lies are hidden from others. Choosing to let others, such as a psychotherapist, become aware of our pretenses removes the power inherent in lying.

Self-Esteem

In spite of what many behavioral scientists might say, **self-esteem** is not a function of how much other people value us. That is *social esteem*. If we make the same mistake as many behavioral scientists and base our self-esteem on social esteem, then we are reduced to being-for-others, which usually includes lying-for-others in order to win or maintain their approval. The fact that researchers report high correlations between how we value ourselves and how others value us just supports the existential conviction that we have indeed become a sick and other-directed society (Reisman, 1961).

An inner-directed person accepts that self-esteem occurs at the level of being-for-oneself and as a function of self-evaluation. An authentic person accepts that approval by oneself must come above approval by others. To strive to be free from what others think of us is romantic nonsense. We can be free, however, by caring more about what we think of ourselves than about what others think of us. When we are honest with ourselves, we know that we can feel genuinely good about ourselves only when we are genuine.

An existential therapist is not concerned with boosting a patient's shaky self-esteem. For example, if a patient becomes depressed over living an empty life, the therapist might say something along the lines of "It's natural that you are depressed. I would be worried about you if you could feel good about the way you've been living." The existentialist knows that all a therapist can do is boost a patient's social esteem through such measures as positive regard and positive reinforcements. In doing so, however, the therapist risks reinforcing the patient to remain a pigeon of other people—in this case, the therapist's pigeon. Self-esteem is the hard-earned natural response that patients can make only to themselves after struggling to be authentic.

Responsibility

Much has already been said about the centrality of responsibility in existential therapy. We have seen how, in choosing to be authentic, individuals are confronted with the existential anxiety of being responsible for who they become. We should also point out that to choose against authenticity—to lie, to conform, to avoid—makes us responsible for missing an opportunity to be ourselves, and we are faced with existential guilt (May, 1958). **Existential guilt** is a consequence of having sinned against ourselves. If our lives become essentially inauthentic—whether obviously pathological, as with the neurotic or psychotic, or normally pathological, as with the conventional conformist—we may at some time find ourselves faced with neurotic guilt. It is a more total self-condemnation for having abdicated our responsibility to become a genuine human being and not just a ghost of a person. Such self-condemnation can be so intense that some individuals may want to destroy their lives without their having really existed.

Guilt if we choose against ourselves and anxiety if we choose for ourselves—no wonder Sartre said that we are "condemned to be free." The existentialist insists a patient be strong enough to become more responsible and hence freer and more authentic.

Interpersonal Conflicts

Intimacy and Sexuality

Intimacy with others is an integral part of being human. The existential ideal for intimacy is poetically expressed in Buber's (1958) book, *I and Thou*. Intimate relationships involve the caring and sharing of what is most central in the lives of two authentic people. Although this is the ideal, the reality is that many people feel safe to relate only to objectified others and enter only into **I–it relationships**. Perhaps even more frequently, the interactions of two objectified people result in **it–it relationships**, which are at best two human objects relating as roles with each other. Such relationships are safe and predictable, but are devoid of giving or receiving anything unique to the two people involved. Any two people or even two robots could fill the roles, and it would make no essential difference to the relationship.

Sexuality is less of a concern for existentialists than is intimacy. The assumption seems to be that if individuals are free to be intimate, they will be free to be sexual if that is what they choose. Sexual conflicts are considered to the extent that the person's sexuality has been disowned or idealized in the process of self-objectification. In contrast to what psychoanalysts believe, sexuality is certainly not the essence of humanity. It is bad faith to say either that we must be sexual or that we cannot be sexual. We can be sexually free, which means the freedom to say yes to our own sexuality when we believe it is best to say yes, and the freedom to say no to our sexuality when it is best for us to say no. It is only in response to our repressive culture that we have adopted a perverted notion that sexual freedom means saying only yes. Existential sex therapy would help free people to say no in sexual relationships, whether to the demands of a spouse or to an internal calendar that says you are falling behind the national average of having sex. Existential sex therapy would be better described as sensual therapy, with clients encouraged to experience their whole body as sensual beings who enjoy touching and being touched from head to toe and not just genital to genital.

Communication

Existentialists suggest that conflicts in communication are almost inherent in our isolation. Because we can never enter directly the experience of another, we can never know fully what the other is attempting to communicate. Our own perspective is bound to do some violence to what the other is communicating; therefore, we again experience some existential guilt over our inability to fully be-with-others. Such guilt need not lead to withdrawal from others, but can motivate us to be more sensitive so that we do the least damage possible to another's experience. Guilt can also help us to be authentically humble as we recognize that, no matter how hard we try, we can never be smart enough or sensitive enough to know precisely what the other is experiencing. We cannot sit back smugly as we listen and say, "I know, I know, the same thing happened to me"—because it never did.

Problems in communication are inevitable also because of the meager way in which language reflects experience. Experience is so much richer than the abstraction that words usually relay. It is no wonder that existentialists sound like poets or novelists when they attempt to communicate the most significant experiences of themselves or their clients. The meagerness of words and the isolation of persons are no excuses, however, for a psychotherapy to omit experience from the realm of understanding. Communication through the medium of words can still present a rich enough picture of an individual's experience if the receiver drops theoretical decoders and listens with the openness of a trained phenomenologist.

Hostility

To experience hostility is to experience the threat of nonbeing, because hostility is one of the quickest and surest means to end life. This hostility can elicit existential anxiety and drive us to lie and tell ourselves or others we never get angry. The repression that follows can lead to our unwillingness to enter into intense relationships because such relationships are always potentially frustrating and thus may lead to hostility. To close off our aggression can also lead to depression and emptiness as we close off one of our body's sources of vital assertions.

Just as we lie if we say we cannot get angry, so too we lie if we say we cannot control our hostility. Some choose to be hostile to deny their finitude so they can play God and decide who will live and who will die. Once they tell themselves lies, they choose the power of violence, the power to end an existence. The people they choose to destroy will be those who threaten them of their nonbeing, such as by rejecting them. The killer says, in effect, "You cannot reject me if you no longer exist." Favorite targets for violence—Jesus Christ, John F. Kennedy, Martin Luther King, Jr., and Malcolm X, for instance—threaten to remind some individuals of how empty and inauthentic their own lives are in comparison.

For existentialists, however, violence is not always a pathological act. As Camus and Sartre learned from their meaningful days in the French resistance, one of their most authentic acts was to assist in the destruction of the Nazis. Camus (1956) later suggested, in his beautiful book *The Rebel*, that the first question of existence is suicide: To be or not to be is what we decide each day we go on living. The second is the equally violent question of homicide—to let another be or not. The power to kill, whether it be oneself or another, tells us just how free we can be. If freedom is our first principle, then nihilism is justified, and we are free to destroy others in the faith that something better may emerge. But if we are to control our freedom to kill, then our first principle is the affirmation of life, not freedom. Camus concludes that we can be free to kill if revolution is the only means available to remove the oppression that prevents others from being free.

Control

For Sartre, the attempt to control another person is psychologically the most violent thing we can do to the other. Because freedom is the essence of existence, to control other human beings is essentially to destroy them. Sartre (1955) is well aware, however, that most people have a strong desire to control others; this is one of the reasons for his saying, "Hell is other people." To control another person is to objectify that person, to deny that individual the freedom to leave us or hurt us or to remind us that we are not as special as we pretend to be.

The existential therapist teaches patients the futility of attempting to control others by remaining unwilling to be controlled. No matter whether the patient threatens to quit therapy, not pay a bill, or go crazy, the existentialist is enjoined to respond only out of honesty, never fulfilling a patient's desire to find false security through controlling others.

Individuo-Social Conflicts
Adjustment versus Transcendence

The only way a life based on adjustment might be healthy is if the society a person is adjusting to is basically honest. Few observers of our age would argue that honesty is a hallmark of our society. A majority of business managers admit to having surreptitiously broken the law in order to succeed; a large percentage of college students confess to having cheated in the classroom; practically all politicians routinely misrepresent themselves to their constituencies to get elected, to the point where we expect no less of them. How can one be sane in an insane society that does not discriminate between truth and delusion?

The only way to rise above the morass of lies and inauthenticity is to become conscious of how the forces of socialization and industrialization prefer to make us automatons, easily controlled. Once we become conscious of the pressures to sacrifice ourselves for success or security, we must take responsibility for becoming our own person rather than someone else's pigeon. Consciousness and choice are the uniquely human characteristics through which we can become uniquely human. We can still be-with-others and be-in-the-world without having to be owned by others or bought out by the world.

We must not delude ourselves into thinking we can transcend all that we have been thrown into. The givens of our life—our time in history, our native language, our genetic makeup—put real limits on our freedom. As Camus (1956) suggested, transcendence begins with choosing that which is necessary. To fight against our bodies, for example, trying to fly to the sun, can only destroy our limited freedom for rising above our society. *Freedom* is not just another word for nothing more to lose; it is a core commitment that nothing our society can give us is worth the loss of creating ourselves.

Impulse Control

Unlike psychoanalysts, existentialists do not fear that choosing one's own rules will precipitate dyscontrol over impulses because of a weakening of social controls. Some people may indeed choose a hedonistic lifestyle if that is most authentic for them. Other authentic individuals, such as Gandhi,

may choose to control even such a basic impulse as hunger for 40 days to express a stand for freedom.

To say that we must eat too much, drink too much, have sex too much, or get angry too much shows bad faith in our potential as self-directed individuals. People with impulse-control problems lie daily: "I'll just have one beer, or one potato chip"; or "Now that I've started, I may as well eat the whole thing"; or "You made me get angry." They tell themselves assorted lies rather than honestly acknowledge that they prefer to eat or drink rather than feel bored, anxious, or depressed. Impulses are not the dominant forces in humans, although many people let them become dominant. Consciousness and choice direct a mature person, so that being freer does not mean becoming a beast or a Dionysian irrationalist who is authentic only when expressing every spontaneous desire.

Beyond Conflict to Fulfillment
Meaning in Life

One does not discover meaning in life; one creates meaning out of life. The question is not what is the answer to life; the answer is that life is an ongoing process to be experienced, not a problem to be solved. The meaning of our existence emerges out of what we choose to stand for. Individuals can choose to take quite different but nevertheless authentic stances in their existences, and thus we find a multitude of conflicting meanings throughout history. Jesus stands for love, Marx stands for justice, Sartre stands for freedom, Galileo stands for truth, Picasso stands for creativity, Martin Luther stands for faith, Hitler stands for power, and Martin Luther King, Jr., stands for equality.

To know the meaning of our existence, we must ask ourselves: What do I stand for? Do I take a stand? Is what I am to become worth the price I pay, worth all the other possibilities I give up in choosing to be this particular person? These are questions of meaning that can haunt us but also motivate us to break out of the safe or successful route if what we see emerging is not significant enough to spend our existence on. If we do not break out during these critical periods of life, then we may at some later date break down because of the overwhelming depression, terror, or nausea that accompanies the awareness that we can no longer stand what we stand for. Many such breakdowns are the result of breakthroughs of the sense of meaninglessness; but rather than being just symptoms of an inadequate existence, they can be seen as fresh opportunities to begin a more meaningful life.

Ideal Individual

The ideal for living, and therefore for psychotherapy, is authenticity by making life choices that create meaning out of our existence. In Heidegger's terms, later borrowed by Sartre, an authentic life is one based on an accurate appraisal of the human condition and a fulfillment of one's potentialities. A person is authentic to the degree to which that person's being-in-the-world is unqualifiedly in accord with the givenness of his or her own nature and of the world (Bugental, 1976).

Authenticity requires awareness of one's self, relationships, and the world; recognition and acceptance of choices; and acceptance of full responsibility for those choices. To make choices requires the courage to be responsible for acting in the face of limited information on how our life may turn out. An authentic person must also find the courage to exist in the face of the fact that the very meaning we intend in our life can be negated at any time by the forms of nonbeing, such as death or isolation. The only value a person *must* follow to become authentic is to be honest, even in the face of nothingness.

Once a patient finds the courage to be basically honest, then we can no longer predict what that person will be. We can only predict what a conventional person will be, a reflection of the norms and expectations of the society, or what a pathological person will be, a reflection of the frozen past. To attempt to further define authentic individuals is to freeze them within the limits of our ideal. Authentic people refuse to be frozen, even by the ideals of their psychotherapists.

Therapeutic Relationship

The central task of the existential psychotherapist is to understand the client as a being-in-the-world. All technical and theoretical considerations are subordinate to this understanding. The therapeutic relationship is a direct relationship of two people, **I–Thou**, a sharing and experiencing together that leads to an elucidation of the patient's mode of being with an enlightened understanding of the implications for existence. The chief characteristic of the therapy relationship is a "being-together" of the therapist and client in the spirit of "letting be" (Hora, 1959, 1960). The concept of letting be means the authentic affirmation of the existence of another person.

The therapy relationship is both part of the process of change and the prime source of content for existential psychotherapy. In engaging a patient in an authentic encounter, the psychotherapist helps the patient become aware of the ways in which he or she avoids an encounter, such as insisting on remaining a patient rather than a person. The therapeutic relationship provides one of the best opportunities for patients to enter into a deep and authentic encounter, because the existential therapist is committed to responding authentically. If a patient has the courage to choose to be-authentic-with-the-therapist, then the patient has radically changed from lying-for-others or lying-for-self to being-with-another.

As a source of content, the therapy relationship brings into the here and now the patient's pathological style. For psychoanalytically inspired existentialists such as Boss (1963) and Binswanger (1963), pathology results in a transference relationship that is the first content to be analyzed or made conscious in order for a patient to enter an encounter. For other existentialists, the fact that the patient's lying-for-others or lying-for-self is occurring right in the consulting room allows patients to be confronted with their pathological ways of being. Patients cannot hide their pathological existence, because it is occurring in their immediate relationship to the existential analyst.

Patients will eventually be forced to become conscious of their running from the existential anxiety of responsibility by the therapist's remaining unwilling to take over for the patient.

In Rogerian terms, existentialists would agree that the therapist initially must be more congruent or authentic than the patient. Congruency on the therapist's part is necessary for the therapist to be genuine in session. If the patient is as congruent and genuine as the therapist, the two could have a rewarding encounter, but then there would really be no need for therapy. Existentialists also agree with Rogers's requirement of accurate empathy: The therapist strives to experience the world as the patient experiences it. **Dasein**—the therapist's literally "being there" with the patient—means an unconditional meeting of experience and relational presence (Bolling, 1995).

Existentialists do not agree, however, that a therapist must maintain unconditional positive regard toward the patient. To be authentic, the therapist can respond with positive regard only toward honesty and authenticity but never toward lying and pathology. That the therapist at first allows the patient to lie and objectify without overt judgment is accepted in order for the therapist to experience the patient's phenomenal world. But an authentic therapist can hold no positive regard for a patient's lying.

Practicalities of Existential Therapy

Existential analysts seem to be too unconcerned with mundane practicalities to write about them. Therapy schedules, fees, and formats are rarely broached in the existential literature. The impression one gathers is that much of existential analysis is similar to psychodynamic psychotherapy, except during times of kairos. That is, a regular appointment seems to last 50 minutes and is scheduled weekly. When a patient is in one of the critical crises, however, the existentialist seems to become much more flexible and may spend extended hours with the patient. Boss (1963),

for example, reports spending 4 days at the bedside of an obsessive-compulsive patient as the patient lived through a psychotic experience brought on by his repulsion at his own existence.

To our knowledge, traditional existentialists have no formalized criteria for judging the preparedness of someone to be an existential therapist. Existential work depends heavily on getting into the subjectivity of clients and thus calls extensively on the subjectivity of therapists. Enriching a therapist-to-be's own subjectivity would entail intensive personal psychotherapy, considerable life experiences in the larger world, extensive reading of both fiction and nonfiction portraying the human condition, and internships that nurture the sensitivities, skills, and innovation of the trainee (Bugental, 1987). Existentialists have been quite flexible about the formal educational backgrounds of their colleagues; medicine, psychology, education, and theology are just some of the disciplines represented among existential analysts.

Existentialists appear to be less amenable than other clinicians to the use of medication as an adjunct to psychotherapy. They prefer to have patients experience authentic, though acutely painful, emotions such as anxiety and guilt rather than pop a pill, thereby deadening the hurt. Medication also risks deadening themselves by treating themselves as objects that could be free from existential anxiety.

Who is to say whether existential therapy should be lengthy or brief? Why, the patient, of course. In a freely choosing relationship, the content, goals, and length of the psychotherapy will be largely determined by the client. In the spirit of "being together" and "letting be," the client is responsible for his or her choices. The existential therapist will weigh in with an honest and authentic opinion, but trying to control a freedom-enhancing psychotherapy would be antithetical to its purpose.

To the limited extent that one can generalize, existential analysis appears to be comparatively lengthy along the lines of psychoanalytic psychotherapy. At the same time, the major alternatives to existential analysis lend themselves more readily to briefer therapy. The centrality of choice, the

I–Thou relationship, the here-and-now orientation, and the imperative to act in the face of inevitable existential anxiety—all catalyze the therapeutic process (Ellerman, 1999). We now turn to these briefer alternatives to existential analysis.

Major Alternatives: Existential-Humanistic, Logotherapy, Reality Therapy

The focus of this chapter so far has been on traditional existential psychotherapy, also known as existential analysis, Daseinanalysis, and existential-analytic therapy. The early existential analysts, as we have seen, were originally trained in psychoanalysis and then created and converted to an existential orientation to clinical work. Subsequent generations of existential therapists, however, less frequently hail from a psychoanalytic background. Instead, they are likely to come from the humanistic traditions or to have been trained explicitly as existentialists.

Moreover, owing to existential therapy's paucity of technical procedures and practice guidelines, therapists committed to an existential stance have been free to choose from a variety of therapeutic systems compatible with the major tenets of existentialism. Although the traditional practice was to follow a psychoanalytic bent, there are those who prefer client-centered, Gestalt, Adlerian, or even cognitive-behavioral methods within an existential philosophy (for example, Denes-Radomisli, 1976; Dublin, 1981; Edwards, 1990; Maddi, 1978). These therapies are examined elsewhere in this volume. Here we will briefly consider existential-humanistic therapy, logotherapy, and reality therapy as three alternatives to classical existential analysis.

Existential-Humanistic Therapy

Clinical experience and published literature suggest at least two types of existential therapy: **existential analysis** and **existential-humanistic therapy**. Existential analysis, or Daseinanalysis,

can be viewed as an intermediate step between psychoanalysis proper and contemporary humanistic existentialism (Norcross, 1987). Existential-humanistic therapy operates at the interface of existentialism and humanistic theory and is closely allied with the "third force" in psychology (psychoanalysis being the first force and behaviorism the second; Maslow, 1962). A related, but not identical, distinction (Yalom, 1980) is that between the "old country cousins" (existential analysts) and their "flashy American cousins" (existential-humanistic therapists). Whereas the Europeans are more likely to discuss limits, acceptance, anxiety, life meaning, apartness, and isolation, the American existential humanists focus on potential, awareness, peak experiences, self-realization, I–Thou, and encounter.

A phenomenological study of the clinical practices of 22 self-identified existential-humanistic therapists and 11 self-identified existential-analytic therapists also supports the distinction (Norcross, 1987). Not surprisingly, the existential analysts reported using significantly more classic psychoanalytic techniques—analysis of the transference and interpretations, for instance—than did their existential-humanistic colleagues. By contrast, the existential-humanistic therapists reported substantially more physical contact (touching, embracing) with their patients and more Rogerian-type warmth and positive regard than did their existential-analytic counterparts. Limiting existentialists to two types may be a crude categorization, but these seem to accurately capture variation in existential practice.

James F. T. Bugental (1915–2008), a prominent American example, identifies himself as an existential-humanistic psychotherapist. The kind of existential psychotherapy he practices no longer carries the adjective "analytic," although it still owes much to the insights of psychoanalysis. Instead, he prefers to speak of it as "humanistic" to emphasize a value system less concerned with finding components (analysis) than with fostering the realization of human possibilities. For him, a goal of therapy is the increase in the true livingness of those who engage in the process (Bugental, 1991; Bugental & Bracke, 1992).

Following in the footsteps of his revered teachers, Jim Bugental and Rollo May, Kirk Schneider has systematized **existential-integrative therapy**. It represents an expansion of existential therapy as well as an integration with other therapeutic methods and modalities when in the needs of the patient and when in congruence with the tenets of humanism (Schneider, 2007; Schneider & May, 1995). It also signals a plea to the psychotherapy community to wake up and recognize existential dimensions of practice; without the existential awareness, clinical practice often devolve into adjustment rituals, gimmicky strategies, that quell but rarely transform.

Logotherapy

Of the forms of nonbeing, **logotherapy** is most concerned with meaninglessness (*logo* = meaning). After suffering through years in Nazi concentration camps in which his mother, father, brother, and wife perished, Viktor Frankl (1905–1997) became convinced that a **will-to-meaning** is the basic sustenance of existence (Frankl, 1967, 1969). Stripped to a bare existence, he experienced the truth of Nietzsche's dictum: "He who has a why to live for can bear with almost any how." But facing the horror of World War II and the madness of a nuclear future, more and more people find their lives becoming existential vacuums. Patients in greater numbers doubt the meaning of work, of love, of death, of life. Psychotherapies may be adequate for resolving discrete psychological disorders and mental conflicts, such as those between drives and defenses, but a relevant modern therapy must also be a philosophical therapy—a therapy of meaning for those confronted with the existential frustration of being unable to find a "why to live for."

Frankl himself survived Nazi concentration camps and the death of his family by creating meaning in his helping others face the ordeal.

In his classic *Man's Search for Meaning*, Frankl (1963) writes movingly of the terrifying deaths of his wife, parents, and brother, the brutality of his own imprisonment in four of the camps, and his encroaching apathy. In the midst of this seemingly overwhelming trauma, he found meaning by helping his fellow prisoners restore their own health. For Frankl and others, the search for meaning is the cornerstone of psychological well-being and the antidote to suicide.

"Why don't you kill yourself?" can be a threatening but effective question for beginning psychotherapy with some clients. After the initial startle, the person begins to realize that the reasons given for not committing suicide contain the seeds of a meaning that can blossom into a profound purpose for living. By facing each form of nonbeing, clients can become aware of a meaning for living. The accidents of one's genetic composition and family heritage place limits on who one can become, but also help form the contours of one's unique identity. Death is seen as a negation of being that also brings a responsibility for acting, because if life were endless, decisions could be postponed indefinitely.

Even in the face of fate, a person is responsible for the attitude assumed and choices made toward that fate. The victims of concentration camps, for example, could choose to die for the sake of a fellow prisoner, collaborate with the enemy for the sake of survival, or give meaning to the future by struggling to hold on for a better day (Frankl, 1963, 1978). "Between stimulus and response there is a space. In that space is our power to choose our response. In our response lies our growth and freedom" (Frankl, 1963).

The meaning of life is not an abstraction. People who are preoccupied with asking, "What is the meaning of life?" should realize that it is life that asks us what meaning we give to our existence. We can respond to life only by being responsible. We accept our responsibility when we accept the categorical imperative of logotherapy: "So live as if you were living already for the second time and as if you had acted the first time as wrongly as you are about to act now" (Frankl, 1963). Facing each moment with such acute awareness and with such responsibility enables us to find the meaning of life unique to us at this singular moment in our life.

Logotherapy is quite similar in content to existential therapy, although Frankl gives meaning an even more central position. Whereas existential analysis is similar in form to psychoanalysis, logotherapy is closer in form to the briefer psychodynamic therapies. Although philosophical issues will often be discussed in a warm, accepting manner, logotherapists will also confront, instruct, reason, and work in a variety of ways to convince a client to take a more conscious and responsible look at the existential vacuum that life has become. Therapy transcripts (Frankl, 1963, 1967) indicate that therapy techniques include interpretations and confrontations but also rely on persuasion and reasoning to a considerable extent. Logotherapy appears to be a form of consciousness raising that relies on a combination of personal feedback and persuasive education in a philosophy of existence.

In treating psychological problems, Frankl developed two special techniques. Clients with anxiety disorders are plagued by anticipatory anxiety. They anticipate dreadful consequences from feared encounters and struggle to avoid such encounters. In avoiding, however, they only increase their anxious anticipation of what will happen if they are forced into a feared encounter. To reverse this neurotic pattern, Frankl encourages clients to adopt an attitude of self-detachment and humor toward themselves and to intend to do the very thing they are dreading. With this **paradoxical intention**, clients find that the way they anticipated acting is rarely the way they in fact will act.

A student who was afraid that he would vomit if he went into the student union was instructed by me to go into the union and vomit intentionally. We joked about how he could explain his vomiting. With sufficient self-detachment he entered the union only to discover that when he intended that which he feared, he ended up having much more control over his anxiety than he had anticipated.

Anxious patients frequently use wrong activity in efforts to fight off obsessive ideas or compulsive acts. Instead of excessively attending and intending to control obsessive-compulsive behaviors, clients are instructed in **de-reflection**. In de-reflection, clients are instructed to ignore that which they are obsessed with by directing their awareness toward more positive aspects of life. By attending to a life full of potential meaning and value, clients substitute the right activity of actualizing personal potentials for the wrong activity of trying to fight off psychopathology.

Reality Therapy

Whereas logotherapy emphasizes a lack of meaning as the central concern, **reality therapy** emphasizes a lack of responsibility. Patients routinely prefer avoidance and blaming others, but reality therapists ask patients to choose their lives and insist that they assume responsibility for those choices.

Some readers may be surprised to find reality therapy presented in a chapter on existential therapy. However, the developer of reality therapy, Southern California psychiatrist William Glasser (1925–) did in fact derive many of his principles of therapy from Helmuth Kaisar, one of the first existential therapists in America. Furthermore, many of the central concerns of reality therapy parallel an existential approach toward personality and psychopathology. Glasser's (1975, 1984, 2001) approach to therapy is admittedly a unique blend of existential philosophy and behavioral techniques. For these reasons, several reviewers of this book suggested that reality therapy might be better placed in the behavior therapy chapter or in the eclectic chapter. On balance, though, we believe it is best suited for this chapter.

To attain our goals, we must have adequate control over our environment. According to Glasser (1984), the human brain functions like a thermostat that seeks to regulate its own behavior to change the world around it. All behavior is aimed at fulfilling the four psychological needs of belonging, power, enjoyment and freedom, and the physical need for survival. Successful satisfaction of these needs results in a sense of control.

The need for belonging motivates us to learn to cooperate and function as a unit, such as in couples, families, teams, clubs, or religious organizations. Power does not imply exploitation of others but rather achievement, competence, and accomplishment. These consequences provide a sense of control—we can make things happen. The need for fun or enjoyment balances our need for achievement. Life is meant to be enjoyed, not just endured. The need for freedom, independence, or autonomy implies that, to function in a truly human manner, we must have the opportunity to make choices and to act on our own. A successful identity develops from experiences of having the power and the pleasure of choosing to meet our own needs.

A failure identity is likely to develop when a child receives inadequate love or is made to feel worthless. Regardless of how cruel or unusual our early childhood, however, that is no excuse to avoid assuming responsibility for our present behavior. In fact, the only way we can transcend an early failure identity is to take responsibility for what we do now. Obviously the past cannot be changed. The past is closed and fixed, a part of nonbeing. The present and future are open to us, however, and can come more under our control if we will take responsibility for our present actions.

Troubled people are those who maintain a failure identity because they are unwilling to accept responsibility and face reality honestly. Mental disorder is the name we give to the variety of strategies that people use to ignore or deny reality and responsibility. People with grandiose delusions, who believe they are the Virgin Mary or Napoleon, are attempting to deny failure by creating a false identity. Other patients mistakenly attempt to develop worth by becoming

preoccupied with how special their symptoms are. Psychopathic patients believe they can ignore reality and succeed by breaking the rules, laws, and other realistic limits set by society. Once people begin to ignore or deny reality, they are more likely to repeat their failures. A person who has failed to gain adequate love, for example, might deny the need for love and withdraw from others, and by this withdrawal fail to find the love that could produce a sense of worth.

Another source of human misery is that people try to control other people. Glasser (1999) believes we misdirect our energy and depress ourselves when we try to force others to conform to our standards. The reality is that we cannot rule others. The only behavior we can control is our own. And when we realize that we can control only our own behavior, we can immediately redefine and enhance our personal freedom.

Reality therapy begins with helping clients become aware of what they are doing in the present to make themselves disturbed. The question for a depressed patient, for example, is not, "What's making you depressed?" but rather, "What are you doing to make yourself depressed?" If patients focus on past difficulties, the question is not why the person got into such difficulties, but rather why they didn't get into even more difficulty. Such a focus helps clients to become aware that even in the process of making difficulties for themselves, they still maintained strengths and responsibility that kept them from totally destroying their own lives or the lives of others. Clients are taught to focus on the strengths they have, not on the failures they had. With increasing awareness of their strengths, clients begin to realize that they can succeed without denying or ignoring reality.

Reality therapy is primarily present centered and choice focused. The past is important only as it relates to present actions. Obviously the present is where clients can choose to change. Blaming present problems on past abuses is one of the common client cop-outs that unfortunately has been reinforced all too often by traditional therapists. Reality therapists do not, however, point a cold, blaming finger at patients. Clients have already had enough coldness and condemnation. Therapy needs to be personal, with a warm, real, and caring therapist providing some of the love and confirmation missing in the client's early life.

The personal nature of reality therapy does not imply an all-accepting therapist. Value judgments must be made, but it is the judgment of clients that is critical. Having the therapist make the value judgments only serves to take responsibility away from clients. If clients are to succeed they must come to judge their behavior as acceptable when it is responsible, which means good for the client and for those with whom the client is meaningfully related. If clients are hurting themselves or others, then their hurtful actions are irresponsible and should be changed. Effective change comes only after there is a responsible awareness of how one's actions are destructive to self or others.

Choice is really the main process of change; in fact, Glasser (1999, 2001) now calls his **choice theory** the new reality therapy. Therapeutic change is the result of responsible choice based on the awareness of the hurt that one has been creating.

One of the therapist's tasks is to call clients on their cop-outs. Therapists should not engage in the irresponsible activity of excusing clients' misbehavior by blaming personal problems on the past actions of parents or on the present conditions of society. Successful people know they can work within the reality of society without being swallowed up by its immorality. The starting point for changing any immoral aspect of society is to accept responsibility for one's own actions.

Once a patient chooses to change irresponsible behavior, the reality therapist is available to help the person create specific plans for changing specific behaviors. The therapist serves as a guide for those failing to progress in reality. Plans must have a chance of succeeding from week to week, either in individual therapy or choice theory groups. If clients are taking on more than they can realistically accomplish within their present limits, then the therapist's task is to offer feedback and to help the clients design more realistic plans for the week. What clients need are experiences of success, not more experiences of failure. Reality therapists encourage a behavioral form of successive approximation in which a success identity is gradually established through weekly action plans that bring increasing consequences of success. Success comes not through the therapist's management of contingencies, but rather through the client's self-management of behavior.

Weekly plans are put in writing, frequently in the form of a contract. Putting a plan in writing is a clearer commitment to change. Written contracts also avoid the excuses of forgetting or distorting what was said. The therapist asks for details of the plan to see how realistic it is and how much chance it has for succeeding. Obviously plans, even written plans, are not absolutes. If a plan does not succeed, then it can be changed in response to feedback from reality. No excuses are accepted, however, if a plan does not work. The client takes responsibility, including the responsibility for choosing to change the plan. Most of us realize that things usually go wrong because people do not do what they said they were going to do. Blaming or deprecating does not help. The critical question is, "Are you going to fulfill your commitment or not? If so, when?" Or the therapist might say, "The plan didn't work. Let's change it."

Effectiveness of Existential Therapy

Our review of the existential literature and the psychotherapy outcome research revealed no controlled research to evaluate the effectiveness of existential therapy, traditional or otherwise. The standard meta-analytic studies, similarly, do not report on any outcome studies on existential therapy with children, adults, or older adults (Roth et al., 2005; Scogin et al., 2005; Weisz et al., 1995). Apparently, existential therapists do not tally conventional "success" rates, whether based on subjective or objective outcome criteria. To be sure, researchers have empirically investigated the existential givens of death, isolation, identity, and meaning (Koole et al., 2006). But the dearth of outcomes studies on existential psychotherapy have kept it on the fringes of mainstream, evidence-based practice (Keshen, 2006).

This resistance to standard empirical research is consistent with the existential distaste for ordinary "scientific" research. Objective research adds to the dehumanization of people by reducing their experience to test scores or aggregate data. The abstraction of people into numbers further objectifies patients, whereas existential therapy is committed to helping people experience their unique subjectiveness while giving up their escapes into self-objectification. Existential therapists, in particular, lead the charge against the "accountability" movement and the medical model (Elkins, 2009a, 2009b) underlying managed care that relies on objectification of emotions and that places a monetary value on human lives. On phenomenological principles, existentialists are opposed to contributing to the myth that the usual experimental methods of science can do justice to the study of humanity.

Logotherapy has experienced the same paucity of controlled outcome research (Batthyany & Guttmann, 2006). Many studies have been conducted on freedom, choice, and hope, of course, but we and others are unable to identify any controlled studies testing the effectiveness of logotherapy.

Frankl was an early proponent of paradoxical interventions, but was by no means the only or most systematic. Family systems therapists have been far more specific and prolific in examining the efficacy of paradoxical interventions. Meta-analyses of paradoxical interventions in general, not Frankl's paradoxical intention in particular, have shown they are as effective as, but no more effective than, typical treatment methods. The mean effect size for paradoxical interventions compared to no-treatment controls was 0.99; thus, on average, a treated patient would be more improved than 84% of the no-treatment group (Hill, 1987). Several meta-analyses also found that paradoxical interventions showed greater effectiveness than other methods with more severe and resistant cases (Beutler, Harwood, et al., 2011; Shoham-Salomon & Rosenthal, 1987). These results, we should reiterate, do not directly attest to the demonstrated efficacy of logotherapy, but to a broad class of techniques that includes Frankl's paradoxical intention.

Criticisms of Existential Therapy
From a Cognitive-Behavioral Perspective

With no controlled outcome studies, we fully understand why some existentialists consider their approach a philosophy about psychotherapy and not a system of psychotherapy. The title of the 2003 Society for Existential Analysis conference was the philosophy-friendly but research-oppositional "The (Im)Possibility of Research in Psychotherapy"!

But what kind of authentic philosophy would be unwilling to fall or stand on the basis of its effectiveness in helping patients overcome their pathologies? Let the existentialists use phenomenological methods if they prefer, but let them also demonstrate that such methods result in greater authenticity than do alternative approaches, including the placebo effect of expecting patients to be more open and honest.

As a theory, existentialism takes a giant step backward with such romantic-sounding ideas as love and will (May, 1969), which held back a science of humanity for so long. Not only is such philosophizing damaging to the human sciences, it is also, as Skinner (1971) so cogently argued, damaging to human societies. The continued emphasis on the myths of freedom and dignity can do nothing more than lead to the continued disintegration of our society. If existentialists are truly concerned with alienating phenomena such as the fragmentation of our communities, then let them use their eloquence in support of well-designed communities in which the contingencies are sane and the consequences of rule breaking severe. To sacrifice society in the name of the elitist authentic individual is a luxury we can no longer afford.

From a Psychoanalytic Perspective

How can existential analysis borrow so much of psychoanalytic technique and yet reject so much of psychoanalytic theory? How can existentialists be authentic and still act as psychoanalysts in therapy? Doesn't that violate their own principles, and doesn't it also show that effective therapy necessitates a relationship in which transference can be developed?

As a theory, existentialism does serious injustice to patients in the midst of unconscious conflicts by insisting that they are responsible for and even choose the very pathologies from which they struggle to extricate themselves. Can the existential therapist really believe that patients with severe compulsions to wash or psychotic delusions of persecution have any choice over what they are driven to do?

The logical but ludicrous consequence of the theory can be seen in Binswanger's (1958) analysis of the phenomenological meaning of his patient's suicide rather than his attempting to prevent her from lethally directing her hostility inward. Mowrer blamed Freud for giving us a generation of psychopaths, but existentialism is the more likely culprit. As a philosophy of our modern times, existentialism's emphasis on the freedom to choose and on individual rules for living is more responsible for the breakdown of social order than is psychoanalysis.

From a Humanistic Perspective

Lest anyone erroneously conclude that all humanists are sympathetic to traditional existential analysis, here is a quote from Abraham Maslow (1960, p. 57) regarding the concept of nonbeing:

I do not think we need take too seriously the European existentialist's harping on dread, on anguish, *on despair, and the like, for which their only remedy seems to be to keep a stiff upper lip. This [is] high I.Q. whimpering on a cosmic scale.*

From a Cultural Perspective

Dead white European men develop another elitist individual psychotherapy that ignores the realistic context of people's lives. Sound familiar? Existentialism has been roundly attacked by feminist, family-systemic, multicultural, and other therapists advocating a cultural position. The dearth of influential women in existential theory and the predictable neglect of their phenomenological worlds convey a distinct impression of existentialism as a bastion of male intelligentsia. In viewing each client as a unique essence, existential therapists fail to see or treat the family system as a whole. The passive stance of the therapist and the abstract nature of the concepts would make family therapy difficult in any case.

The lack of direction and concrete solutions make existential therapy particularly unsuitable for ethnic/racial minority clients seeking relief. Kairos brought on by poverty, racism, homelessness, and crime will surely not be solved by analysis of existential concerns, but such analysis might provoke a few more suicides in the face of the existentialist's benign neglect. The money and time would be much better spent in solving real problems in clients' *Umwelt* and *Mitwelt* than in interminable philosophizing about their *Eigenwelt*. Even if disadvantaged patients change internally, as existentialists maintain, they see little hope for—or have little choice or impact on—their external realities. Only in existentialism and the movies do people possess unlimited freedom, construct their own meanings, and execute boundless choices. Save it for the wealthy, worried well.

From an Integrative Perspective

Existentialism is rich in its appreciation of the human condition, yet meager in its therapy methods and outcome research. For example, the existential analyst focuses on the existential anxiety of responsibility at the expense of the other equally important forms of nonbeing. The existential analysts provide little insight into their therapeutic methods other than repeating much of psychoanalysis combined with a few slogans about therapist authenticity. The inadequate development of therapeutic procedures has proven May's (1958) fear that existentialism might degenerate into an anything-goes anarchy.

The existential rejection of scientific evaluation of psychotherapy has also encouraged an irrationalism in which many clinicians feel no responsibility to evaluate the effectiveness of their work. What criteria are we going to use to judge the honesty of different therapists? Are we left with a solipsism in which one person's truth is another person's lie? Existentialists would do well to recognize the truth in Bronowski's (1959) seminal book, *Science and Human Values*, that honesty is the fundamental value of science and that the scientific method is the most honest method we have. There is nothing inherent in the scientific method that says we cannot compare the phenomenological description of patients following different forms of therapy. Existentialists need to participate in the shared honesty of such comparisons, which can lead to the truth on which therapies are most effective with which patients and with which problems.

An Existential Analysis of Mrs. C

An existential analysis of Mrs. C is restricted by the case description, which contains just the facts and little of the subjective phenomena of her existence. From the facts, it looks as if Mrs. C's pre-pinworm existence was already heavily objectified. In sexual relations she was unable to be-in-nature, because she was nonorgasmic and thus unable to freely and fully enjoy the natural joys of sexuality. Because her mother had lied about sex being disgusting, Mrs. C at some point probably began to lie to herself that she was not sexual in order to close off anything about herself that would be experienced as disgusting. The original existential anxiety associated with sexuality was probably expressed in isolation in the form of rejection for being disgusting.

In everyday affairs, Mrs. C had also objectified herself by being so orderly, as exemplified by her cataloging her children alphabetically and scheduling them exactly 2 years apart. This orderliness suggests that she reduced her anxiety over the responsibility of having and naming children by placing the responsibility outside of herself onto an alphabet and a calendar. In spite of considerable objectification, Mrs. C is probably no more pathological than most conventional people who try to control their anxieties through arbitrary rather than authentic principles.

A crisis occurred when the Asian flu infected her family at a time when Mrs. C was tired from caring for five children and a sixth on the way. When the pinworms infested her daughter, an authentic response for Mrs. C would have been to experience the intense anxiety that no matter how hard she cleaned and cared for her children, they were still infected and were now faced with the possibility of additional infestation. Mrs. C had never been authentic at facing such threats of nonbeing, but under the additional stress of her own illness, she chose to lie to escape the anxiety related to the prospect of further diseases. The lie was ready-made in the form of the physician's orders for her to boil clothes and wash intensely. At this point she was not particularly responsible for the orders, but she was responsible for telling herself, "If I just wash enough, I can keep the nonbeing of diseases away from my children and myself." So she washed. With her washing based on this lying-about-nature, she was now faced with neurotic anxiety over not washing. Her conclusion was that she must wash, and her bad faith resulted in the objectification of herself into a human washing machine.

With full self-objectification in place, Mrs. C experienced herself as unable to keep from washing. Causality in her life was no longer intentional, but a compulsive drive like a motor that automatically switched on in the presence of dirt. With so much of her time and energy dedicated to washing, Mrs. C was bound to be faced with existential guilt over the many opportunities she was missing to be-for-herself and to be-intimate-with-her-family. Her washing also served as an attempt to cleanse herself of existential guilt. However, the longer she
(continued)

continued her washing compulsion, the less she was guilty over what she was doing and the more she was faced with the possibility of experiencing neurotic guilt for what she was becoming—a washing machine in human clothes.

After years of compulsive washing, to be confronted with the choice of not washing would raise tremendous existential anxiety over how meaningless her past decade had been. To face the choice of not washing would also be to face self-condemnation for having wasted precious years of her life and for having hurt her family. Better to hold onto the lie that she must wash! At least that way she is not responsible: She has not failed in life; her physician has failed her. When her psychotherapist said he was washing his hands of her case, she made a suicide gesture to force him to remain responsible for her by arranging for someone else to cure her. We can further see Mrs. C's desire to run from responsibility by the way she pressured her husband into assuming responsibility not only for the family but even for her very compulsion. "You tell me, George, what to wash next because I am so mechanical I cannot remember or decide what to wash" is the essence of her communication to her husband.

The reason Mrs. C began her washing ritual with her anus is that the anus was the locus of pinworms and was seen in her phenomenological world as a source of disease, as it is with many compulsive people. Even if Mrs. C could not control all the sources of illness in the universe, she could keep her own anus clean and could pretend that no germs would penetrate her immaculate body.

Mrs. C lived in a vigilant future where she kept an ever-watchful eye open for any signs of disease. Her space was surrounded by germs and worms, her symbols of nonbeing. She could be secure in such a dreaded world only if she remained clean, not only of dirt but also of any responsibility and, therefore, any guilt for having let her family down. In effect, she was attempting to literally wash her hands clean of the whole mess—a Pontius Pilate maneuver to absolve herself of responsibility and to avoid authenticity.

As with many obsessive-compulsive patients who devote their lives to making themselves into objects, it could be extremely difficult to engage Mrs. C in an authentic encounter. But this would be one of the few ways we would have to keep her from becoming totally washed up as a human being. To help Mrs. C experience her own subjectivity, an existentialist would look for every possibility of confronting her with choices in psychotherapy. For example, when Mrs. C stops at doors and waits for others to open them so that she can avoid contact with germs, the existentialist would confront Mrs. C with the choice of seeking help by opening a new door to therapy or returning to her secure but deadening patterns from the past.

Given the choice of what to talk about in therapy, Mrs. C would probably ramble endlessly about her preoccupation with pinworms and the details of her washing. At some point, her obsessive preoccupations would be interpreted as her means of remaining a patient so that she would not have to face her therapist as a person. The therapist might also choose to confront Mrs. C with the therapist's own feelings, for example: "I am tired of hearing the endless details about pinworms and washing. I want to see if you still exist within that laundromat you call a life. I know it will be scary and hurt like hell to open yourself up, but look, my hands are not clean either."

If Mrs. C could respond by sharing herself with the existential therapist, a kairos would occur during which Mrs. C would feel overwhelmed with guilt and anxiety. Both she and her therapist would recognize that one cannot face a decade of waste without being overwhelmed with the existential anxiety and guilt that are the authentic responses to such absurd waste. The therapist would do Mrs. C an injustice in trying to minimize her anxiety and guilt as only *feelings* of anxiety and guilt; she would *be* anxious and guilty. The only route to health would be to live through her confrontation of having not been authentic. The therapist can no more cleanse Mrs. C of her guilt and anxiety than she could cleanse herself. By remaining with her through such crises, however, the therapist can communicate that new options exist for the future and that Mrs. C can choose not to waste her options, including the chance to be-authentic-with-the-therapist.

Future Directions

Existentialism has a rich and established basis in psychology, sociology, education, and the humanities; as Medard Boss put it, existentialism has a potential voice in "everything with which human beings have something to do" (quoted in Craig, 1988). In the arts, the thriving Theatre of the Absurd attempts to convey the situation of humankind in a universe without meaning. In psychotherapy, the historical influence of existentialism is equally established, but its future is equivocal.

In many respects, existentialism's contemporary influence on psychotherapy is far greater than the small percentage of psychotherapists endorsing it as their primary theoretical orientation (see Chapter 1). The existential orientation frequently underlies clinical practice without explicit recognition (Norcross, 1987; Rubinstein, 1994). Core existential concepts—meaning, freedom, responsibility, individuality, authenticity, choice—have been incorporated into many contemporary systems of psychotherapy. Existentialism is a "strange yet oddly familiar" orientation to psychotherapy and life (Yalom, 1980).

What does this implicit but selective incorporation portend for the future of existential therapy? As long as there are philosophically inclined psychotherapists and angst-plagued patients, existential therapy will surely survive as a distinct orientation, but its overriding contribution to the 21st century will probably be as an indirect social force. It will serve as a vital counterbalance to the flourishing victimology in the world: When people convincingly deceive themselves into believing they are the unwitting, choiceless victims of fate, existentialists will confront them with the undeniable existence of active choice and personal responsibility. Existential therapy will promote the possibility and power of self-initiated change: When people delude themselves about the necessity of professional treatment, existentialists will challenge them with the efficacy of personal change and individual autonomy. These will be social forces more than therapeutic endeavors, but powerful correctives nonetheless.

Looking specifically at existential-humanistic psychotherapy, it promises to be valuable in, first, serving as a philosophical base for the majority of contemporary clinicians who integrate multiple methods (Chapter 16), and second, assisting a growing number of clients complaining of feelings of emptiness and lack of personal meaning (Bugental & Bracke, 1992). Integration of existential tenets with other psychotherapy systems, positive psychology, and the well-being/happiness movement will certainly intensify. Economic, technological, and social forces over the past decades have drastically assailed the capacity of being oneself, complicating the quest for freedom and authenticity. Existentialism offers fulfillment in an age of emptiness; it embraces authenticity in an era of medicalization; it addresses, in the words of Frankl's (1978) book title, *The Unheard Cry for Meaning.* Existential therapy, existential-integrative therapy, and logotherapy will help clients find meaning in their suffering, be it chronic pain, social ostracism, or posttraumatic stress disorder (Schulenberg et al., 2008). The meaning in trauma and terror can then be used for self-transcendent giving to the world, as in the case of Viktor Frankl himself (Lantz, 1992).

The rise of managed health care will threaten the affordability of insight-seeking therapy, but the short-term treatment offered by managed care may stimulate, paradoxically, a desire for more life-changing therapy in the existential-humanistic tradition. Patients' appetites for deeper self-exploration may be whetted by brief treatment, kindling a desire for more comprehensive exploration into their inner life. Although existentialists are probably overly optimistic about the paradoxical demand for long-term psychotherapy in an era of short-term treatment, the full impact of enhanced freedom from the information age and increased isolation from the technological revolution just may fuel a resurgence in the existential perspective on psychotherapy and, indeed, life.

Key Terms

aloneness/isolation
authenticity
bad faith
being-in-the-world
choice theory
Dasein
de-reflection
Eigenwelt (being-for-oneself)
existential analysis
existential anxiety
existential confrontation
existential givens
existential guilt
existential-humanistic therapy
existential-integrative therapy

finiteness
I–Thou (I–it, it–it) relationship(s)
intentionality
kairos
logotherapy
lying
meaninglessness
Mitwelt (being-with-others)
objectification
paradoxical intention
phenomenological method
reality therapy
self-esteem
Umwelt (being-in-nature)
will-to-meaning

Recommended Readings

Binswanger, L. (1963). *Being-in-the-world: Selected papers of Ludwig Binswanger.* New York: Basic.

Boss, M. (1963). *Daseinanalysis and psychoanalysis.* New York: Basic.

Bugental, J. F. T. (1965). *The search for authenticity.* New York: Holt, Rinehart & Winston.

Bugental, J. F. T. (1987). *The art of the psychotherapist.* New York: Norton.

Frankl, V. (1963). *Man's search for meaning.* New York: Washington Square.

Glasser, W. (1975). *Reality therapy.* New York: Harper & Row.

Glasser, W. (2001). *Counseling with choice theory: The new reality therapy.* New York: HarperCollins.

May, R. (1977). *The meaning of anxiety* (rev. ed.). New York: Norton.

May, R., Angel, E., & Ellenberger, H. (Eds.). (1958). *Existence: A new dimension in psychology and psychiatry.* New York: Basic.

Schneider, K. J. (2007). *Existential-integrative psychotherapy: Guideposts to the core of practice.* New York: Routledge.

Yalom, I. D. (1980). *Existential psychotherapy.* New York: Basic.

JOURNALS: *Existential Analysis*; *International Forum for Logotherapy*; *International Journal of Existential Psychology & Psychotherapy*; *International Journal of Reality Therapy*; *Journal of Humanistic Psychology*; *Journal of Phenomenological Psychology*; *Review of Existential Psychology and Psychiatry.*

Recommended Websites

Existential Therapy:
www.existential-therapy.com
International Society for Existential Psychology & Psychotherapy:
www.existentialpsychology.org/
Society for Existential Analysis:
www.existentialanalysis.org.uk
Viktor Frankl Institute (logotherapy):
logotherapy.univie.ac.at/
William Glasser Institute (reality therapy):
www.wglasser.com

CHAPTER 5

Person-Centered Therapies

Carl Rogers

William Miller

Marty was wealthy financially but impoverished emotionally. He rotated through glamorous houses in Miami, Phoenix, and the Hamptons, but his life was superficial. Golf, tennis, polo, parties, and dining out helped pass the time. But his wife, his children, and his friends were moving away from Marty. His superficial conversations, his sarcastic jokes, his negative attitude, and his limited feelings were causing others to seek more enriching relationships elsewhere.

At first, Marty was enraged at others. He blamed his increasing isolation on other people's self-centeredness or on the fact that he was no longer as important since selling his major company. Then, Marty tried to deny that being alone even bothered him. He preferred his independence; he had always been a lone wolf. Who needed others anyhow?

It wasn't until his wife separated from him and left him alone in the Hamptons that Marty's denial began to break down. He asked his wife to join him in psychotherapy, and he began to experience and express emotions. Instead of talking about his golf game or the polo match, Marty began to share his fantasies and his dreams. He dreamed about dolphins, and he believed they represented the type of person he wanted to become. The dolphins could jump for joy at the surface of the sea, but they could also dive to the depths of experience. They could communicate acutely with sounds and signals; they were sensitive and caring about each other's needs.

Through a caring and empathic therapeutic relationship, Marty discovered that he was not emotionally retarded, as he had originally feared. He discovered that he had learned to close off his feelings because of his mother's teaching that men don't show emotions. He had replaced genuine feelings with silly jokes. As an awkward teenager, he had defended himself with cutting comments and cognitive scanning for any signs of rejection. He had supplanted genuine relationships with social events.

In psychotherapy, Marty gradually reduced his defensiveness. He learned that men could exchange emotions without threat of becoming effeminate. He found that he could get close to his wife without being hurt by her. As all of this was occurring and as Marty was becoming more of the person he wanted to be, I (JOP) asked him what about therapy was the most helpful to him. He replied immediately: "You really listen, and you really care." Carl Rogers taught generations of psychotherapists the profound value of active listening and human caring. Later he added the importance of genuine sharing.

A Sketch of Carl Rogers

Carl Ransom Rogers (1902–1987) demonstrated a profound openness to change, beginning with his movement away from the fundamentalist Protestantism of his Wisconsin farm family to the liberal religion of Union Seminary in New York. His strict ascetic and religious family of origin allowed no drinking, dancing, card playing, or theatergoing. In his early upbringing, Rogers personally experienced the devastating effects on one's self-esteem of parents imposing conditions of worth on children. Foreshadowing his later research interests, he showed scientific interests early and became a serious student of agriculture at the age of 14, thus gaining an early appreciation of experimental design and empiricism (Sollod, 1978). After 2 years of preparation for the ministry, Rogers made a move common to a number of actual or potential clergy, toward training in psychotherapy. He received his PhD in clinical psychology in 1931 from Columbia in a highly Freudian program.

Beginning as an intern in 1927–1928, Rogers spent 12 years as a psychologist at a child guidance clinic in Rochester, New York. One of the later misconceptions about Rogers's approach was that it was largely useful to middle-class or upper-class adults with neurotic problems. Yet, the seeds of Rogers's ideas germinated in his work with lower-class children and their mothers (Barrett-Lennard, 1998).

During this time, he let his own clinical experience guide his theorizing and therapy. In the midst of a very busy but fertile schedule, he found time to put together his first book, *The Clinical Treatment of the Problem Child*, published in 1939. Rogers found both inspiration and confirmation of his views in the work of Otto Rank (1936), who emphasized the importance of the humanity of therapists rather than their technical skills in remedying human problems.

In 1940, Rogers moved to Ohio State University to train students in psychotherapy. As is so often true of students, they taught Rogers several important lessons. One of these lessons was that his ideas represented a new view of the nature of effective therapy and not a distillation of generally accepted principles, as Rogers had originally thought. Students also convinced him that if his new therapy was going to be accepted by scientifically minded practitioners, he would have to demonstrate its efficacy through controlled research. With his own strong commitment to the scientific method, Rogers began an extended series of outcome studies with his students both at Ohio State and later at the University of Chicago, where he moved in 1945.

The clarity of Rogers's clinical and theoretical writings in such books as *Counseling and Psychotherapy* (1942) and *Client-Centered Therapy* (1951) and the controls in his scientific research brought widespread recognition. For a humanistic psychologist, Rogers was tremendously successful in the traditional academic world, and in 1957 he returned to his home state at the University of Wisconsin. Here he was willing to make the acid test of any therapy, to see if his system could be effective in producing profound change in schizophrenic clients. During the 5-year study, Rogers and the other therapists found themselves becoming more actively genuine, disclosing more of their inner experiencing, which seemed to lead to greater improvement in such clients.

In 1964, Rogers moved to the Western Behavioral Sciences Institute in La Jolla, California, and began working with groups of normal individuals struggling to improve their interpersonal abilities. In 1968, Rogers and some of his research colleagues established their own Center for Studies of the Person in La Jolla. As a world figure in humanistic therapy, Rogers became as deeply involved in inspiring humanistic changes in education, business, marriage, and world relations (Rogers, 1970, 1977, 1983, 1987b) as he was in helping individuals to more fully realize their basic humanity. His longtime commitment to peacemaking led to many workshops between warring factions and culminated in the Rust Workshop on Central America in 1985 (Solomon, 1990). Enlarging the focus of his work from psychotherapy and clients to human interactions and all people was accompanied by a name change from the "client-centered" to the "person-centered" approach.

When Carl Rogers spoke, it was apparent that the audience was in the presence of a great man. The aura around him was warm and gentle, though his words were strong. He was willing to field any question and respond to even the most critical comments. When asked how he as a therapist could be both genuine and nondisclosing, he surprised us with his candor. He said that over the years of working first with psychiatric clients and then with growth-oriented groups, he had come to see that his model of a therapist as reflective and nondirective had been very comfortable for a person like him. For most of his life he had been rather shy and therefore nondisclosing. In the sunny climate of California, with its emphasis on openness in groups, he had come to recognize that too much of his former style was a convenient role that had protected him from having to reveal much of himself. Right until his death, Rogers was realizing more fully in psychotherapy, as in his life, the genuineness he had always valued but never fully actualized.

Theory of Personality

All humanity has but one basic motivational force, a tendency toward **actualization**. Rogers (1959, p. 196) defines the **actualizing tendency** as "the inherent tendency of the organism to develop all its capacities in ways which serve to maintain or enhance the organism." This includes not only the tendency to meet physiological needs for air, food, and water and the tendency to reduce tensions, but also the propensity to expand ourselves through growth, to enhance ourselves through relating and reproducing. It also refers to expanding our effectiveness, and hence ourselves by moving from control by external forces to control from within.

We are also born with **organismic valuing** that allows us to value positively those experiences perceived as maintaining or enhancing our lives and to value negatively those experiences that would negate our growth. We are born, then, with actualizing forces that motivate us and with valuing processes that regulate us. What's more, we can trust that these basic organismic processes will serve us well.

In relating to the world, we respond not to some "real" or "pure" reality, but rather to reality as we experience it. Our world is our experienced or phenomenal world. If others wish to understand our particular actions, they must try to place themselves as much as possible into our internal frame of reference and become conscious of the world as it exists within our subjective awareness. Our reality is certainly shaped in part by the environment, but we also participate actively in the creation of our subjective world, our internal frame of reference.

As part of our actualizing tendency, we also begin to actively differentiate—to see the difference between experiences that are part of our own body and functioning and those that belong to others. The special experiences that we come to own are self-experiences. We are able to become conscious of self-experiences by representing these experiences symbolically in language or other symbols. This representation in awareness of being alive and functioning becomes further elaborated through interaction with significant others into a concept of self. Our **self-concept** includes our perceptions of what is characteristic of "I" or "me," our perceptions of our relationships to others and to the world, and the values attached to these perceptions (Rogers, 1959, p. 200).

As our self-consciousness emerges, we develop a need for positive regard for that self. This need is universal in human beings, but we also learn to need love. This need for positive regard—the need to be prized, to be accepted, to be loved—is so addictive that it becomes the most potent need of the developing person. "She loves me, she loves me not" is the endless puzzle of the emerging individual who looks to the mother's face, gestures, and other ambiguous signs to see if she holds the child in positive regard. Although a mother's love is emphasized, positive regard from all others, especially significant others, becomes compelling.

Whenever another person, such as a parent, responds to a particular behavior with positive regard, our total image of how positively we are prized by the other is strengthened. On the other hand, let a parent respond to a behavior with a frown or another expression of negative regard,

and our total perception of how much we are loved by our parent is weakened. Consequently, the expression of positive regard by significant others is so powerful that it can become more compelling than the organismic valuing process. The individual becomes more attracted to the positive regard of others than to positive experiences that actualize the organism. When the need for such other-love becomes dominant, individuals begin to guide their behavior not by the degree to which an experience maintains or enhances the organism, but by the likelihood of receiving love.

Soon individuals learn to regard themselves in much the same way as they experience regard from other people, liking or disliking themselves as a total configuration for a particular behavior. This learned **self-regard** leads to individuals' viewing themselves and their behavior in the same way that significant others have viewed them. As a result, some behaviors are regarded positively that are not actually satisfying, such as feeling good about ourselves for getting an A after spending many dull hours memorizing tedious material. Other behaviors are regarded negatively that are not actually experienced as unsatisfying, such as feeling bad about masturbating.

When individuals begin to act in accordance with the introjected or internalized values of others, they have acquired **conditions of worth**. They cannot regard themselves positively as worthy unless they live according to these conditions. For some, this means they can feel good about themselves, feel lovable and worthy, only when achieving, no matter what the cost to their organism; others feel good about themselves only when they are nice and agreeable and never say no to anyone. Once such conditions of worth have been acquired, the person has been transformed from an individual guided by his or her own values to an individual controlled by the values of other people. We learn at an early age to exchange our basic tendency for actualization for the conditional love of others.

Theoretically, such a trade need not be made. As Rogers (1959, p. 227) states so clearly, "If an individual should experience only unconditional positive regard, then no conditions of worth would develop, self-regard would be unconditional, the needs for positive regard and self-regard would never be at variance with organismic evaluation, and the individual would continue to be psychologically adjusted and would be fully functioning." Unfortunately, such a hypothetical situation does not appear to occur in reality, except perhaps in psychotherapy.

Theory of Psychopathology

The more conditional the love of parents, the more pathology is likely to develop. Because of the need for self-regard, children begin to perceive their experiences selectively, in terms of their parents' conditions of worth, which have been internalized. Behaviors consistent with conditions of worth are allowed accurate representation in awareness. Children whose parents insisted on achievement, for instance, should be able to perceive and accurately recall experiences in which they were indeed doing well. Experiences that conflict with conditions of worth, however, are distorted in order to fit the conditions of worth, or may even be excluded from awareness. People who must achieve in order to feel good about themselves may, for example, distort their vacations into achievement times, as they count the number of historical sites, museums, or states they visit. Some workaholics may deny entirely that they have any desire to play or just lounge around. "Fun is for fools" is their motto.

As some experiences are distorted or denied, there is **incongruence** between what is being experienced and what is symbolized as part of a person's self-concept. An example of such incongruence was suggested earlier when I (JOP) indicated that I could not allow myself to experience anger and still feel good about myself. I perceived myself as one of those rare individuals who never gets angry. My wife has since told me that in situations where I would be expected to get angry, I would first begin to pucker my lips. If the frustration continued, I would then begin to whistle. I never allowed myself to become aware of these somatic clues of anger even though I was going around like a whistling teapot ready to explode.

For Rogers, the core of psychological maladjustment is the incongruity between the person's total experience and what is accurately symbolized as part of the self-concept. The incongruence between self and experience is the basic estrangement in human beings. The self is threatened. The person can no longer live as a unified whole, which is the birthright of every human. Instead, we allow ourselves to become only part of who we really are. Our inherent tendencies toward full actualization do not die, however, and we become like a house divided against itself. Sometimes our behavior is directed by the self we like to believe we are, and at other times behavior can be driven by those aspects that we have tried to disown. Psychopathology reflects a divided personality, with the tensions, defenses, and inadequate functioning that accompany a lack of wholeness.

Psychological maladjustment is a result of this basic estrangement of human beings. For the sake of maintaining the positive regard of others, we no longer remain true to who we really are, to our own natural organismic valuing of experience. At a very early age, we begin to distort or to deny some of the values we experience and to perceive them only in terms of their value to others. This falsification of ourselves is not the result of conscious choices to lie, as the existentialists would hold; rather, it is a natural, though tragic, development in infancy (Rogers, 1959).

As individuals live in a state of estrangement, experiences incongruent with the self are subceived as threatening. **Subception** is the ability of the organism to discriminate stimuli at a level below what is required for conscious recognition. By subceiving particular experiences as threatening, the organism can use perceptual distortions, such as rationalizations, projections, and denial, to keep from becoming aware of experiences, such as anger, which would violate conditions of worth. If individuals were to become aware of unworthy experiences, their concepts of themselves would be threatened, their needs for self-regard would be frustrated, and they would be in a state of anxiety.

Defensive reactions, including symptoms, are developed to prevent threatening experiences from being accurately represented in awareness. People who feel unlovable for getting angry, for instance, may deny their anger and end up with headaches. The headaches may not feel good, but at least most other people can love someone who is sick. Those who have self-regard only for success may develop compulsions to work. They may drive themselves into the late hours of the night with the aid of stimulants, feeling good about each success while their body experiences tremendous stress.

Some people are so threatened by sexual desires that they distort their perceptions to the point where they believe that they are pure and innocent and godlike, while others are trying to make them think dirty, rotten thoughts. A patient I tested at a state psychiatric hospital looked at the first Rorschach card I gave him, threw it down, and shouted, "Why the hell don't you go show these pictures to the goddamned communists? They're the ones that are perverting our kids with all of their sex education."

All human beings are threatened by some experiences incongruent with their self-concepts. To a lesser or greater degree, then, we all use some defenses or symptoms to preserve our self-regard and to prevent undue anxiety. Defenses help preserve positive self-regard, at a price. Defenses result in an inaccurate perception of reality due to distortion and selective omission of information. Early in my (JOP's) career, a 45-year-old man walked into my office and said, "Oh, you're younger. You must be in favor of open marriages. I won't be able to work with you." He requested a referral to another psychotherapist without even asking about my views on open marriage. In rigidly defending their views of the world and of themselves, people end up becoming rigid and inadequate in their styles of information processing. The more defensive and pathological the person, the more rigid and inadequate are that person's perceptions.

Some individuals suffer such a significant degree of incongruence between self and experience that particular events can prevent their rigid defenses from functioning successfully and can lead to personality disorganization. If the event threatens to demonstrate the degree of incongruence between self and experience, and if the event occurs suddenly or obviously, then such individuals are flooded with anxiety because their very self-concepts are threatened. With their defenses not working successfully, previously disowned experiences are now symbolized accurately in awareness. For these individuals, the organized self-images are shattered by unacceptable experiences.

Panic and disorganization were experienced by a sophomore who came to see me (JOP) following a bad trip with LSD. Before the experience, he had been convinced that he was a true follower of Jesus. He had seen himself as loving and kind and working for the well-being of others through a radical Christian movement. During his experience with acid, he saw himself as an egomaniac, misusing his leadership role in his Christian group to win a following of female admirers and to see his picture in the news. He said he kept running in a circle, trying to catch his picture of himself from the newspapers, but he had this eerie feeling that the picture was a stranger. He could not rationalize these self-perceptions as being due to LSD. He was so panicky and disorganized that he thought he might jump off a bridge to destroy his life in order to save his self. Fortunately, with the aid of crisis intervention from the counseling center and the support of friends, he decided to enter psychotherapy to begin the arduous process of reintegrating a sense of self that was more complete and less idealized.

Whether a person enters psychotherapy because of a breakdown, because of inadequate functioning due to perceptual distortions, because defensive symptoms are hurting too much, or because of a desire for greater actualization, the goal is the same: to increase the congruence between self and experience through a process of integration. Because Rogers conceptualizes the reintegration of self and experience as emerging from the therapeutic relationship, we will break with our standard chapter format and present Rogers's view of the therapeutic relationship before examining his theory of therapeutic processes.

Therapeutic Relationship

Rogers (1957, 1959) has stated very explicitly that the **necessary and sufficient conditions** for therapy are contained within the therapeutic relationship. Six conditions are necessary for a relationship to result in constructive personality change. Taken together, these conditions are sufficient to account for any therapeutic change. That is, these and only these conditions were hypothesized to produce therapeutic personality changes in all clients, in all therapies, and in all situations.

1. *Relationship.* Obviously, two persons must be in a relationship in which each makes some perceived difference to the other.
2. *Vulnerability.* The client in the relationship lives in a state of incongruence and is therefore vulnerable to anxiety because of the potential for subceiving experiences threatening to the self, or is anxious because such subception is already occurring. The vulnerability to anxiety is what motivates a client to seek and to stay in the therapeutic relationship.
3. *Genuineness.* The therapist is congruent and genuine in the therapeutic relationship. **Genuineness** means that therapists are freely and deeply themselves, with the actual experiences of the therapists being accurately represented in their awareness of themselves. It is the opposite of presenting a façade. This does not mean that therapists are always genuine in all aspects of life, but it is necessary when entering a therapeutic relationship. Rogers (1957, 1959) originally believed that within this condition there was no necessity for therapists to disclose their genuine experiences to clients overtly; it seemed necessary only that therapists not deceive clients or themselves. Following client-centered therapy with schizophrenic clients (Rogers et al., 1967) and work in human relations groups (Rogers, 1970), Rogers (1970) came to the conclusion that therapist genuineness includes self-expression.

The degree of self-disclosure by Rogers himself was rather minimal when compared with the extensive, spontaneous disclosure characteristic of many leaders of encounter groups. The following excerpt from a session with a schizophrenic client is an example that Rogers used to demonstrate his increased willingness to express his own feelings of the moment.

Client: I think I'm beyond help.

Rogers: Huh? Feeling as though you're beyond help. I know. You feel completely hopeless about yourself. I can understand that. I don't feel hopeless, but I realize you do. (Meador & Rogers, 1973, p. 142)

We shall see that other client-centered therapists go considerably further in disclosing their own immediate feelings.

4. *Unconditional positive regard.* The therapist must experience **unconditional positive regard** for the client. The client's incongruence is due to internalized conditions of worth. For the client to accept experiences that have been distorted or denied to awareness, there must be a decrease in the client's conditions of worth and an increase in the client's unconditional self-regard. If the clinician can demonstrate unconditional positive regard for the client, then the client can begin to become accurately aware of previously distorted or denied experiences

because they threatened a loss of positive regard from significant others. When clients perceive positive regard, existing conditions of worth are weakened or dissolved and are replaced by a stronger positive self-regard. When the therapist consistently prizes and cares about clients, no matter what the clients are expressing or how they are feeling, the clients become free to accept all that they are with love and caring.

5. *Accurate empathy.* The therapist experiences the client's inner world and endeavors to communicate his or her understanding to the client. Through **empathy** we sense the client's private world as if it were our own, without our own anger, fear, or confusion getting bound up in the experience. With this clear sense of the client's world, we can communicate our understanding, including our awareness of the meanings in the client's experience of which the client is scarcely aware.

   Without deep and accurate empathy, clients could not trust the therapist's unconditional positive regard. Clients would feel threatened that once the therapist came to know them more completely, there would be aspects of the client that would not be accepted with positive regard. With accurate empathy and unconditional positive regard, clients come close to being fully known and fully accepted (Rogers, 1959).

6. *Perception of genuineness.* The client perceives, at least to a minimal degree, the acceptance and understanding of the therapist. In order for the client to trust the caring and empathy of the therapist, the therapist must be seen as genuine and not as just playing a role.

Therapeutic Processes

Although Rogers wrote extensively about the conditions of the client–therapist relationship that facilitate positive change, he had less to say about the actual processes that occur in the interactions between client and therapist to produce such change. Throughout the 1950s, it seemed adequate to postulate that the three facilitative conditions of therapist genuineness, positive regard, and accurate empathy were all that was necessary to release a client's inherent tendency toward actualization. During the 1960s, Rogers and colleagues (1967) began to theorize that the curative process involved the direct and intense expression of feelings, leading to corrective emotional experiences. Later, client-centered theorists (e.g., Wexler, 1974; Zimring, 1974) began to view **client-centered therapy** as a process of expanding consciousness or awareness through the therapist bringing about more effective information processing in clients. Currently, then, the processes of change in client-centered therapy are most accurately conceptualized as a combination of consciousness raising and corrective emotional experiencing that occurs within the context of a genuine, affirming, and empathic relationship.

Consciousness Raising

The Client's Work

Given positive regard, clients are free to discuss whatever they wish in sessions. Clients, rather than therapists, direct the flow of therapy. This is the primary reason Rogers (1942) originally used the label **nondirective** to describe his therapy. Because clients come to treatment in distress, they can be expected to express personal experiences that are troubling them. The responsibility of clients, then, is to inform the therapist about their personal experiences and to be available for feedback from the therapist.

The Therapist's Work

Traditionally, the therapist's work in increasing the client's consciousness was seen as almost entirely composed of **reflection**. As a mirror or a reflector of the client's feelings, the therapist would communicate to the client messages that said, in essence, "You feel…." The specifics might be, "You feel disappointed in your father for leaning on alcohol," or

"You feel envious because your roommate has a special boyfriend and you wish you did." Through a commitment to understand the client with accurate empathy, the therapist is not dogmatically, authoritatively, or interpretively telling the client how or what to feel. The client-centered therapist is instead able to sensitively and exquisitely capture the essence of the client's expressions. The therapist can reflect so empathically and accurately because there is no distortion caused by interpretation or self-expression. The therapist is free to listen actively and reflect accurately the clients' feelings.

With such a caring and congruent mirror, clients become more fully conscious of experiences that previously were partly distorted or denied. These experiences, of course, include their feelings, or more importantly, their real feelings. Perhaps of even greater significance, clients become more fully aware of the You the therapist is reflecting—the You with increasing richness; the You who produced experiences once judged to be unworthy of self-regard, but which are now prized and shared by a significant other. Gradually the You of the therapist's empathic feedback is a richer and more congruent human.

More recently, person-centered therapists have recognized the mistake of equating the specific technique of reflection with the complex attitude of empathy. This error has resulted in limitations on the modes of empathic response (Bohart, 1993b; Bozarth, 1984). Rogers (1987a, p. 39) wrote later in his life, "I even wince at the phrase *reflection of feeling.*" He regretted that this simple intellectual skill was being (mis)taught as an accurate description of a complex interpersonal reaction. The evolving definition of empathy and the expanding role of the person-centered therapist emphasize the therapist's experiencing the world of the client by developing more active and idiosyncratic means of empathy predicated on the particular client (Bohart & Greenberg, 1997).

The contemporary view is that the therapist's work in raising consciousness involves more than just a feedback function. Part of the person-centered therapist's work is to help clients reallocate their attention so that they can make greater use of the richness in their feelings (Anderson, 1974). By more flexibly and fully attending to the client's feelings, the therapist helps clients break through their perceptual distortions in order to attend to the personal meaning of experiences that previously have not been processed into awareness. The client-centered therapist can thereby serve as a surrogate information processor.

In compensating for the client's more rigid and deficient style of information processing, the therapist first serves an attentional function. The client's experiences, especially threatening experiences, can be held in awareness for further processing. If the therapist did not reflect some of the client's threatening experiences, the client's selective attentional processes would cause such information to be lost in short-term memory, crowded out by other information receiving attention.

A case in point: In talking about her roommate's boyfriend, a shy sophomore was expressing a variety of feelings, including her close relationship to her roommate, her admiration of the boyfriend, and vague feelings of envy. Because envy was not a feeling she could accept, this client would have focused her attention on her admiration or her sense of closeness and would have lost the opportunity to become aware of feelings of envy that might be the source of her recent arguments with her roommate.

Because there is always more information impinging on a client than he or she can attend to, information from threatening experiences is most likely to be lost unless it is empathically reflected by the therapist and thereby kept available for further processing. By selecting out such threatening information to process into awareness, the person-centered therapist is, in fact, quite directive, but in a subtle and noncoercive style, and only by responding to information already in process in the client. In other words, person-centered therapists are relatively controlling of the process of therapy, but not its content.

As a surrogate information processor for the client, the therapist also helps the client adopt a more optimal mode of organizing information. As clients approach feelings that threaten self-regard, they typically become anxious, confused, or defensive, and may be unable to find adequate words for organizing and integrating such feelings into conscious experience. Some clients may anxiously search for language to organize their previously unacceptable feelings of anger or envy, whereas others will quickly give up and go on to something else. Therapists can move the work ahead by empathically organizing the information from a client's experience in a concise and accurate manner. Organized information is then more fully available to awareness.

An example of such helpful organization occurred with a 55-year-old woman who was expressing a variety of upsetting feelings toward her husband. She was angry because he wouldn't spend money to fix up the house for their daughter's wedding. She was depressed over how many years she had worked to make their restaurant a success, but now that they had money she still wasn't happy. She was trying to understand her husband's view that it would be better to remodel the house after they saved up the money rather than cash in one of their bonds. She said she felt torn and confused. When I (JCN) responded, "You feel impatient with his promises that someday the two of you are really going to live," she broke into tears and said, "Yes, that's it, that's it, that's what he's always been holding out in front of me."

Therapists help clients effectively process information by using symbols or words that are active, vivid, and poignant. All too frequently, the language and symbols of clients are conventional, repetitive, dull, and safe, reflecting the defensive ways clients process their experiences into awareness. Evocative symbols threaten to bring experiences into awareness that have previously been damaging to the client's self-regard. As clients become aware of how therapists can capture the client's own feelings in more vital and enriched language, they have the opportunity to use symbols that allow them to be conscious of how vital their lives can really be.

Zimring (1974) uses the philosophy of Wittgenstein (1953, 1958) to explain that as clients become aware of more vital, enhancing, and actualizing modes of expressing themselves, their experiences become more vital, more enhancing, and more actualizing. In Wittgenstein's view, expression and experience are a unity. Experiences do not exist somewhere in the organism, waiting to be expressed into awareness. Experiences are created by expression. Thus, the richer, the more potent, and the fuller the symbols that clients learn to use in expressing themselves, the richer, the more potent, and the fuller humans they become.

Catharsis

In the process of raising consciousness, person-centered therapists have emphasized the primacy of the client's feelings. The therapist's continual focus on "You feel…" helps clients to become more aware of feelings but also to release, express, and own their most powerful feelings. For Rogers (1959), feelings have both emotional and personal meaning components. In the previous section, we examined the expression, organization, and integration of the personal meaning, informational, or cognitive component of feelings. Now we will examine the cathartic release of the emotional component of feelings, which is equally important in the curative process. Although Rogers considered the expression of emotional and cognitive components of feelings as inseparable, we have taken the liberty of discussing them separately while recognizing their experiential unity.

The Client's Work

In the process of expressing themselves, clients usually begin by avoiding emotionally laden experiences. When feelings are talked about early in therapy, they are described as past experiences that are external to self (Rogers & Rablen, 1958). Clients will talk about emotional problems, but describe such problems as coming from outside themselves. "My partner is driving me up a wall"; "My folks are really on my back"; and "My studies are giving me a bad time" are some examples of early communications.

Gradually, in response to the therapist's empathy and positive regard, clients describe their feelings, but they are still primarily past emotions and thus lacking in intensity. As clients experience themselves as accepted, they can begin to describe present feelings more freely, but they are not yet fully living and expressing their emotional experiences. Part of the work of clients involves staying with emerging emotions even though anxiety is aroused and their defensive responses are mobilized.

Eventually, clients begin to fully express their feelings of the moment. These feelings are owned and accepted as coming from within the person. At the same time, emotional experiences that were previously denied are bubbling up. Rather than continue to deny all such feelings, clients gain more confidence that emotions can be valued and valuable. They discover that experiencing feelings with immediacy and intensity is a possible guide for living. They begin to trust their feelings and base more of their valuing on what they like or dislike, what makes them happy or sad, what produces joy or anger. With the release and owning of emotional experiences, clients get in touch once again with their inherent organismic basis for valuing their genuine feelings. The release and acceptance of such feelings are frequently vivid, intense, and dramatic as clients discover an internal basis for directing their own lives rather than having to be dominated, distorted, and threatened by the internalized values of others.

The Therapist's Work

Originally, the therapist's work seemed to be simply to allow clients to get in touch with their basic feelings by demonstrating an attitude of unconditional prizing of all the clients' feelings. Now, it is recognized that therapists help clients get in touch with and express threatening emotional experiences by continually redirecting the client's attention to the feeling aspect of whatever is being discussed. As the therapist explicitly reflects back to the client the essence of what the client is feeling implicitly, the client eventually attends to and feels the emotion and the meaning of experiences.

No relationship is completely unconditional, of course. Person-centered therapists genuinely express their conviction in, say, the value of life and safety. The early use of the term *nondirective* perpetuated the misperception that Rogers never disagreed with a client and passively consented to anything. Rogers would actively intervene if a client tried to kill himself or herself or tried to physically injure the therapist during a session (Patterson, 1985). But Rogers would always try to understand the client's destructive impulses and communicate this understanding in a way that would facilitate the client's self-exploration.

Many client-centered therapists follow Rogers's lead of directly expressing some of their own feelings. Especially in group work, therapists might express such emotions as, "I feel angry about the way you're attacking Tom," or "I feel deeply moved and saddened by what you've expressed," or "I really do care about you." The theoretical justification for person-centered therapists disclosing their own emotional experiences of the moment is that it allows for greater genuineness or congruence. Furthermore, if psychotherapists use nondirectiveness as an excuse to suppress their own annoyance because the weak client could not take it, an attitude of fundamental disrespect for the client's powers will be communicated (Barton, 1974).

The empirical justification for therapist self-expression is the discovery that therapists who speak genuinely out of their strong feelings tend to encourage and liberate clients to express their own emotional experiences (Rogers et al., 1967). In important respects, the self-expressing therapist may create emotional experiences in clients through such transactions, rather than releasing some feelings that are implicitly present within the client. The traditional view in client-centered therapy, however, is that threatening emotions are implicitly present in clients and are not being released because of the client's defensiveness. Through the therapist's emotional self-disclosure and, most importantly, empathic communication, clients are gradually freed from denying or distorting their emotions and can begin to speak and live out their strongest feelings.

Therapeutic Content
Intrapersonal Conflicts

Person-centered therapy is more of a process than a content theory, but it has had important things to say about many of the common content issues in treatment. As we have seen, person-centered theory has been especially concerned with the intrapersonal conflict between the client's self-concept and the total client's experience, which includes feelings that are threatening to the person's self-concept. Even in the movement toward group therapy and institutional consultation, person-centered therapists remain centrally committed to establishing an atmosphere of positive regard to help individuals overcome incongruence in order to be more fully functioning.

Anxiety and Defenses

Anxiety is not the cause of people's problems but the troubling consequence of a divided life. Although anxiety is frequently what drives people into treatment, our task is not to desensitize anxiety but rather to listen sensitively to the client's anxiety in order to discover more fully what organismic experiences are threatening to enter awareness.

In practice, person-centered therapists respect the potentially disorganizing effects of anxiety, and thus do not flood a client with threatening emotions. Instead, they allow a more gradual corrective emotional experiencing to occur. The person-centered style of catharsis may be slower and less dramatic than the exposure therapies (see Chapter 8), but it is also seen as less risky because anxiety can cause incongruent people to deteriorate.

The defense against anxiety-arousing experiences is either to deny them, banishing them from awareness entirely, or to use a whole range of distorting perceptions, such as projection or rationalization, that the experiences slant in favor of maintaining the person's self-concept. In Piaget's terms, distorting defenses involve the assimilation of new experiences into the schema of the self with no accommodation of the self-concept to those new experiences. The self is left unthreatened, but only at the expense of personal growth.

Self-Esteem

Rogers placed the need for self-esteem at the center of intrapersonal problems, only he called it *self-regard*. Low self-esteem is directly proportional to the gap between who we think we were and who we really are. The problem is not that we have too great concepts of ourselves that we cannot live up to; the problem is that our concepts of ourselves are too meager to let us be all that we were born to be.

Striving for self-esteem falls into an age-old trap. It keeps us locked into trying to actualize self-concepts created out of our parents' confining conditions of worth. The more restrictive our striving, the more we can feel good about ourselves only when we do not allow ourselves to feel much at all. Rogers's solution lies not in increasing self-esteem based on what we are supposed to be but rather in expanding our conditions of worth so that we can prize all that we can be.

Responsibility

Being the scientist that he was and having been educated in a time in which the behavioral sciences assumed determinism, Rogers did not include freedom and responsibility as core constructs in his original theory. In later years, however, he placed freedom and responsibility at the cornerstone of his work with committed couples, educational systems, and international relations.

In the context of the clinical setting, the troubled person is the victim needing parental regard that was all too conditional. The therapist is responsible for providing four of the six conditions necessary for effective therapy; clients provide themselves and a willingness to relate to the therapist. Even within this seemingly deterministic system, we can see that freedom is experienced in releasing a safe but restrictive self-concept to actualize the inherent tendencies to be all that we can be. Becoming responsible means learning again to respond to our natural organismic valuing rather than to the internalized values of others. The responsible person is the actualizing person who moves from **heteronomy**, or control by others and the environment, to **autonomy**, or inner control.

Interpersonal Conflicts

Intimacy and Sexuality

Intimacy is therapeutic, and therapy is intimate. In defining the necessary and sufficient conditions for a therapeutic relationship, Rogers presents an ideal for an intimate relationship: positive regard, accurate empathy, and interpersonal genuineness. The major difference between an ongoing intimate relationship and the therapeutic relationship is that in the former, both partners are, or at least become, relatively equal in their levels of congruence in order for the relationship to progress. In the latter, treatment is ready for termination when such a level of intimacy is reached, often to the sadness of both therapist and client.

Given the similarity between psychotherapy and intimacy, some incongruent people can make major strides toward actualization without receiving professional assistance. Unfortunately, truly intimate relationships are rare, in part because it is so difficult for us to grant to others what we withhold from ourselves: our love of our humanness, including our blemishes, our defects, our imperfections. To love and to feel intimate, most people must distort their perceptions of their partners to fit their conditions of what is worthy of love, just as they distort their perceptions of themselves. Eventually, when they discover who they are really relating to, they are likely to believe that the faults and the gaps in their relationship are due to their partner's incompleteness rather than to the narrow conditions of their own love.

Our society has traditionally placed narrow conditions on our sexual worth. These restrictive conditions have led too many people to disown the fullness of their sexuality so that they can hold themselves in high regard. In reacting to the plethora of prohibitions against being sexual, we may have gone to the opposite extreme of believing that to feel worthy we have to be sexually successful, to be routinely orgasmic or even multiply orgasmic, to always be aroused and maintain lubrication or erections, to never ejaculate too quickly but to always ejaculate. Much performance anxiety reflects the restrictive conditions of worth that say we must be sexually successful rather than sexually natural.

A more natural sexuality, one that is neither goal consumed nor performance oriented, is most likely to occur within an intimate relationship. In such a relationship, we are most likely to jettison either overly restrictive or overly demanding conditions of worth regarding either our own or our partner's style of sexual relating. When things go wrong sexually, as they will at times for nearly everyone, there is little threat of rejection in an intimate relationship. The atmosphere is present for the couple to work through their own sexual difficulties. Rogers (1972) himself revealed an intimate experience of how his wife's unconditional regard allowed him to work through a period of erectile dysfunction. If therapists focus only on sexual dysfunctions without cultivating more intimate relationships, they are liable to leave couples in relationships that will continue to need therapy when things go wrong.

Communication

At one time communication problems were believed to be inevitable, given the inadequacy of words to express feelings. With our enhanced awareness of accurate empathy, however, we now know that we can indeed understand the fullness of what another is communicating if we truly care to listen. The problem of communication is no longer a language problem; it is a problem in caring. The testimony of clients from many forms of effective therapy indicates how fully people feel they can communicate and be understood when someone really cares to listen. Just as we can train therapists (Truax & Carkhuff, 1967) and paraprofessionals (Carkhuff, 1969) to increase their ability to listen actively, so too have we learned how to train parents (Gordon, 1970) and teachers (Gordon, 1974) to listen actively and communicate effectively.

Hostility

From his humanistic orientation, Rogers sees the natural actualizing tendency as bringing people toward each other rather than driving them against each other. Hostility is not an inherent drive that must be controlled. It is, in part, a reaction to being overcontrolled by the restrictive conditions of parental regard. Hostility is our organismic way of rebelling against having to disown parts of our lives in order to be prized by others. It can also manifest itself when people cannot express angry feelings without feeling guilty or unworthy. There are individuals who use hostility against others with little caring, but such hostile individuals were most likely raised in dehumanizing atmospheres in which they themselves received little caring.

Control

Control becomes a problem in interpersonal relationships when individuals attempt to impose their conditions of worth on others. In subtle or not-so-subtle ways, such individuals communicate that they will continue to care only if others live up to their images of lovable human beings. Be nice, be a winner, be assertive, be deferential, be witty, be quiet, be sexy, and behave are just a few of the conditions that people place on their partners or their children. We let ourselves be controlled by others because we value maintaining their regard above what is organismically pleasing. We, in turn, act in restricted ways to control the positive regard of others. As long as our conditions of worth coincide, we tend to go on controlling each other without feeling conflict. Accusations of control become acute when conditions of worth conflict, as when some people can feel worthy only when they keep others waiting. To give up being controlled and to give up controlling, people must work hard in therapy at giving up their restrictive conditions of worth.

Individuo-Social Conflicts
Adjustment versus Transcendence

Going beyond one's internalized conditions of worth to become a whole person suggests transcending one's acculturation process. But once a person is in the process of becoming more congruent, there is no inherent conflict between being an actualizer and being part of a society. Rogers's (1959) view of the natural actualizing tendencies involves remaining in society in order to relate, to create, and to grow through the mastery of cultural tools. Rogers is certainly in favor of humanizing social institutions, such as couples, families, schools, universities, and businesses. Perhaps because so much of Rogers's professional life was spent in universities and growth-oriented centers, probably two of the most humane institutions of society, he seemed confident that autonomous clients can go out into society, be fully functioning, and still be at-home in the world.

Impulse Control

Natural organismic valuing provides inherent regulation over impulses. A person raised in a humanistic atmosphere will eat, drink, and relate sexually in a manner that is organismically enhancing and not organismically destructive. Attempts at bringing particular impulses under control through fancy techniques or faddish diets may produce short-term gain but little long-term maintenance, because they fail to enhance natural abilities for self-regulation. Once people feel good about who they are and are not under constant stress to be what others want, they will not resort to overeating, drinking, or smoking to feel good for the moment or to reduce stress. Acceptance of self begets control of impulses.

Beyond Conflict to Fulfillment

Meaning in Life

Meaning emerges from the process of actualizing our tendencies to become all that we are intended to be. Those convinced that there must be something more to life than natural living have probably not experienced all that there is to their lives. The haunting suspicion that there must be something "more" to life represents a subception that there is indeed a good deal more to life than what they are experiencing. What's missing is to be found within them and not outside them. There is no need to give life meaning for those in the process of living a congruent, complete life. The locus of evaluation, the source of meaning, is found within the individual. The person should be the center of his or her meaning, rather than having a meaning imposed by other individuals or society as a whole. The criterion for values is the actualizing tendency: Does this action or experience enhance the organism?

Ideal Individual

Rogers's (1961) ideal for the good life is found in a **fully functioning person**. This ideal type of individual would, of course, demonstrate organismic trusting. Being open to each new experience, the person would let all of the significant information in a situation flow in and through them and would trust in their eventual course of action. The person would not have to ruminate about decisions but would find the best decision naturally emerging as a result of not distorting or denying relevant information. The openness to experiencing indicates a person who is living primarily in the present, who is neither processing information that belongs to the past nor omitting information that belongs to the present.

The fully functioning person does not process experience through structured categories—through a rigid concept of self, for example. Instead, in what Rogers (1961) calls **existential living**, people let the self and the personality emerge from experience: They discover a sense of structure in experience that results in a flowing, changing organization of self and personality. Self is thus experienced as a process—a rich, exciting, challenging, and rewarding process—rather than a constricted structure that can process only what is consistent with internalized conditions of worth.

Organismic trusting, openness to experiencing, and existential living characterize the fully functioning person. He or she has the power to choose and direct life from within, regardless of the sad fact that actions may indeed be predictable on the basis of past experiences. The greatest sense of freedom comes in being creative, in producing new and effective thoughts, actions, and entities, because the person is in touch with the spring of life.

Practicalities of Person-Centered Therapy

The central focus of person-centered therapy on **self-authority** tends to mitigate against the use of psychometric tests and routine assessment in psychotherapy. Only three conditions suggest the use of tests in person-centered counseling: The client may request testing; clinic policy may demand that tests be administered; and tests may be administered as an "objective" way for the client and clinician to consider a decision for action, as in making vocational and career choices (Bozarth, 1991).

Because the person of the psychotherapist is more important than formal training in person-centered work, therapists from diverse backgrounds are welcomed. Counseling psychology, counseling, social work, and pastoral counseling have been especially well represented in the Rogerian approach.

Client-centered counselors have been among the most active in developing training approaches for paraprofessionals, such as students conducting peer counseling or laypersons facilitating self-help groups (Carkhuff, 1969). Through methods originally developed by Truax and Carkhuff (1967), students are trained through modeling, role-playing, videotaping, and feedback to learn the skills involved in becoming increasingly empathic, genuine, and positive in their regard. The bulk of paraprofessional counseling is performed according to Rogerian principles.

Personal therapy is seen as desirable, though not essential. In addition, aspiring person-centered therapists are strongly encouraged to participate in growth-oriented experiences. Any experience that enhances the sensitivity of the clinician and that fosters full functioning is regarded as valuable training.

Unfortunately, academic efforts to enhance trainees' empathy have become confused with mindless parroting or a sterile technique. In one of his last articles before his death, Rogers (1987a, p. 39) deplored the teaching of empathy as a cognitive skill: "Genuine sensitive empathy, with all its intensity and personal involvement, cannot be so taught." Training in empathy—or rather experiencing and witnessing empathy—will come about only in authentic, I–Thou relationships, including experiential groups and personal therapy.

Fees seem to follow the going rate for other forms of therapy in a given locale. The genuine therapeutic relationship typically translates into a face-to-face encounter, with no intervening desk.

The terms *brief* and *person-centered therapy* were rarely used in the same sentence during Rogers's lifetime. Rogers's own therapy cases almost always ran into tens of sessions and frequently went into hundreds. Although years of psychotherapy are unnecessary, due to the client's self-actualizing tendencies, the most common practice was to see clients individually, once a week for 6 to 12 months. Thus, little clinical or research attention was paid to brief or short-term person-centered therapy (Koss & Shiang, 1994).

Person-centered therapy (like most psychotherapies) has increasingly expanded into couple, group, and family therapy formats. Following Rogers's lead in moving from strictly individual work to more systems interventions, contemporary person-centered clinicians are active in group therapy, couple and family therapy (see August 1989 special issue of *Person-Centered Review* for an overview), and indeed entire communities and nations (see Levant & Shlien, 1984, for illustrations). Rogers has also exerted a profound influence on group treatment through his emphasis on the genuine encounter between people. Enlarging the scope of practice from the consulting room to planetary concerns, such as nuclear war and international relations, reaffirms the name change from *client-centered therapy* to **person-centered approach**.

A Major Alternative and Extension: Motivational Interviewing

William R. Miller (1947–) describes his **motivational interviewing (MI)** as Carl Rogers in new clothes. MI is a person-centered, directive approach that enhances intrinsic motivation to change by helping clients explore and resolve ambivalence

(Rollnick & Miller, 1995). As such, it combines elements of both person-centered style (warmth, empathy, egalitarian relationship) and person-centered technique (key questions, reflective listening). MI expands on person-centered therapy by incorporating therapist goals about desirable changes and by providing specific methods to move the patient toward behavior change (Moyers & Rollnick, 2002).

Some of our colleagues wonder whether MI ought to be classified as an extension of person-centered therapy or as an alternative to it. Those in the humanistic camp and Miller himself favor the former characterization, but many cognitive-behavioral colleagues insist that the operationalization of MI methods, its directive elements, and its voluminous research base distinguish it from the original Rogerian treatment. To accommodate both positions and to roll with the resistance, we will discuss MI as both an alternative to and an extension of person-centered therapy.

Miller (1978) began his career by applying behavioral self-control techniques to the treatment of problem drinkers. As a good scientist, he was struck (and annoyed) by his findings that the control group showed excellent improvement, comparable in magnitude to that of clients receiving 10 therapy sessions. The control group had received initial assessments, encouragement, advice, and a self-help book (Miller & Munoz, 1982).

Miller so disbelieved the results that he replicated them twice after increasing the intensity of therapy to 18 sessions (Miller et al., 1980). In one of the studies, the in-therapy behavior of the counselors was observed and rated on the empathy scale developed by Truax and Carkhuff (1967). Although the treatment group and control group showed comparable outcomes, the empathy ratings of the therapists could account for outcomes at 6 months ($r = .82$), 12 months ($r = .71$), and 2 years ($r = .51$). Therapist empathy, not the specific treatment method, strongly predicted client success. Miller concluded that the empathy and reflective listening advocated by Rogers must play a central part in any effective brief therapy.

Although he did not set out to create a new system of psychotherapy, Bill Miller faithfully followed the data and developed MI. He has now published more than 30 books and the Institute for Scientific Information lists him among the World's Most Cited Scientists. He is emeritus distinguished professor of psychology and psychiatry at the University of New Mexico. Fundamentally interested in the psychology of change, he has focused his research on the development, testing, and dissemination of treatments for addictions.

From his research and an analysis of effective brief therapies, Miller and Rollnick (1991, 2002) identified four principles of motivational interviewing.

- *Express empathy* by using reflective listening to convey understanding of the client's message and to express genuine caring for the person. At heart, MI fundamentally respects the client and understands his or her need for self-preservation.
- *Develop discrepancy* between the client's deeply held values and current behavior. Change is motivated by the perceived discrepancy. The client, rather than the clinician, should present the arguments for change. Clients literally talk themselves into changing.
- *Roll with resistance* by meeting it with reflection rather than confrontation. Resistance is simply understood as clients voicing the status quo side of their ambivalence. The therapist should avoid arguing for change; client resistance is a signal that the therapist should respond differently.
- *Support self-efficacy* by actively conveying the message that the client is capable of change. The therapist builds client confidence that change is possible and provides brief interventions that permit change and reinforce optimism. The client is the primary resource in finding answers and solutions.

In MI, therapists carefully avoid the classic confrontation in which the therapist asserts the need for change ("You must quit drinking!") while the client denies it. Therapists who respond to client resistance with confrontation or arguments are said to be exhibiting **counterresistance**. Direct confrontation is likely to escalate resistance rather than reduce it. MI methods leverage the inherent energy that resistance brings to the therapeutic interaction, seeking to redirect it in a manner that avoids a rupture in the therapeutic relationship and allows the emergence of client change talk. Just as a canoeist would probably not paddle upstream against a strong current, so too the motivational interviewer will not argue with clients. He or she will try to **roll with resistance** by using the energy in the current/ the client to steer the interaction (Moyers & Rollnick, 2002).

Instead of seeking to persuade directly, the therapist systematically elicits from the client and reinforces reasons for concern and for change. That is, the therapist actively facilitates the client's self-directed change. The therapist maintains a warm and empathic atmosphere that permits patients to explore ambivalent feelings about changing. Resistance is not confronted head-on but is skillfully deflected to encourage open exploration. Underlying this process is a goal of developing with the client a **motivational discrepancy** between present behaviors (real self) and desired goals (more ideal self). Evidence indicates that such discrepancy provides motivation that triggers behavior change (Miller & Rollnick, 1991).

Here is an exchange between a motivational interviewer and a client minimizing his alcohol abuse (from Miller & Rollnick, 2002, pp. 148–149).

Client: It sounds like (I'm drinking) a lot. I never really added it up before, but I don't think of myself as a heavy drinker.

Interviewer: You're surprised. [*Reflecting, instead of confronting.*]

Client: Yes! I know that when you were asking me how much I drink usually, it sounded like a lot. But I drink about the same as most of my friends do.

Interviewer: So, this is confusing for you. On the one hand, you can see that it's a lot, and this (test result) says it's more than 95% of adults drink. Yet, it seems about normal among your friends. How could both things be true? [*Expressing empathy for both sides and introducing discrepancy.*]

Client: I guess I can drink with the top 5%.

Interviewer: Your friends are pretty heavy drinkers.

Client: I don't know about "heavy." I guess we drink more than our share. Later in the same session:

Interviewer: So, what does this mean about your own drinking? What happens now? [*Asking open-ended key questions.*]

Client: Well, I want to do something. I don't want to just let this go on.

Interviewer: And what are the possibilities on that "do something" list? What's the next step? [*Avoiding the expert trap.*]

Client: I guess I have to do something about my drinking—either cut down or give it up.

Interviewer: One or the other.

Client: Well, I can't just let it go! If I keep drinking, won't all of this get worse?

Interviewer: Probably.

Client: Then something's got to change. I either cut down or quit.

Interviewer: But if it were clear to you that you had to quit altogether, then you could. [*Supporting self-efficacy.*]

Client: Sure. If I knew I had to.

Interviewer: How can you find out? [*Leaving solutions and decision to the client.*]

Client: I guess I try something and see if it works.

Four specific skills are used in MI to foster client safety, acceptance, and change. These skills are summarized by the acronym OARS:

- *Open questions* evoke change talk in the client and avoid closed questions by the therapist that would lead to the status quo (e.g., Why haven't you…?).
- *Affirmation* emphasizes the client's strength, efforts, and steps in the right direction; Rogers would call it positive regard or support.
- *Reflective listening* encapsulates the Rogerian skill of accurate empathy that allows the client to explore and experience the dilemma at hand.
- *Summaries* draw together the client's change statements and then deliver them back to the client for ever larger impacts.

The most recent version of MI (Miller & Rollnick, 2012; Miller & Rose, 2009) increasingly emphasizes the *spirit of MI*. Rather than a series of techniques for tricking ambivalent clients in changing, MI should be considered a collaborative and unfolding relationship respectful of client autonomy. As Carl Rogers (1980) said, it's more a way of being than a method. When you listen generously to people, they can hear the truth in themselves, often for the first time. That spirit allows the therapist to harness client ambivalence, develop a plan, and strengthen commitment to change.

MI was originally advanced for addictive disorders but has since been applied to a host of health-related behaviors (Arkowitz et al., 2008). MI has been effectively used with both typical mental health disorders—such as anxiety, depression, post-traumatic stress disorder, eating disorders—and broader social concerns—such as clean drinking water and the criminal justice system.

MI has at least three applications. First, it is used early in or as a prelude to treatment, in order to enhance client motivation for change. A client may be reluctant to engage in diabetes treatment, monitor his diet, or take his glucose readings; a therapist could use MI to explore the client's ambivalence toward treatment and to build his intrinsic motivation to participate in the treatments. Second, MI is used as a stand-alone brief intervention. For example, patients can be screened for alcohol abuse and then MI briefly applied in the context of primary health care. Third, MI is used with other treatments. It can be integrated into many systems of psychotherapy to reduce client ambivalence and to minimize the resistance (Miller & Moyers, 2005).

Once a psychotherapy system has been created and shown effective in controlled research, the treatment developer focuses on its **dissemination and implementation** (D and I). Dissemination refers to spreading the evidence-based treatment to professionals and the public; it's out there. The related process of implementation refers to practitioners using the treatment and thereby altering their clinical behavior; it's actually implemented. The usual means of D and I—writing books, publishing articles, giving talks—have largely proven ineffective in changing therapist behavior (Norcross et al., 2008).

Instead, treatment developers like Bill Miller have begun leveraging implementation science to widely install MI skills in health care professionals and programs. A network of MI trainers has been created, and most of the training resources have been placed online for public access (www.motivationalinterview.org). Further, a series of controlled studies has been performed to determine the most effective method for learning it. Miller and colleagues (2004) evaluated five training methods: clinical workshop only; workshop plus practice feedback; workshop plus individual coaching sessions; workshop, feedback, and coaching; or a wait-list control group of self-guided training. Licensed substance abuse professionals were randomly assigned to one of the five training methods, and their MI practice analyzed over 12 months. Professionals attending the workshop fared better than those training themselves. Feedback and coaching produced superior MI performance over and above the workshop alone. MI can be successfully disseminated through systematic training, ideally including coaching and feedback, with real-world substance abuse practitioners. But long-term implementation, as expected, takes longer to accomplish.

Effectiveness of Person-Centered Therapies

Carl Rogers consistently stood for an unusual combination of a phenomenological understanding of clients and an empirical evaluation of psychotherapy. He is widely regarded as one of the parents of psychotherapy research, particularly for initiating the rich tradition of **process research**. (Process research concerns the interactions between client and therapist, whereas outcome research tracks the success or effectiveness of therapy.) Rogers and his followers have demonstrated that a humanistic approach to conducting therapy and a scientific approach to evaluating therapy need not be incompatible.

In one of his last articles, which addressed the future development of the person-centered approach, Rogers (1986, pp. 258–259) continued to emphasize the need for empirical research:

> There is only one way in which a person-centered approach can avoid becoming narrow, dogmatic, and restrictive. That is through studies—simultaneously hardheaded and tender minded—which open new vistas, bring new insights, challenge our hypotheses, enrich our theory, expand our knowledge, and involve us more deeply in an understanding of the phenomena of human change.

The impetus given research by client-centered therapy is at least equal in importance to Rogers's theoretical contributions or the effectiveness of his

psychotherapy (Strupp, 1971). Two separate lines of research on the effectiveness of person-centered therapy have been pursued. The first concerns the veracity of Rogers's necessary and sufficient conditions hypothesis; the second line of research relates to the overall efficacy of person-centered therapy. We will consider each in turn.

The Facilitative Conditions

Rogers's (1957) provocative identification of purportedly "necessary and sufficient conditions of therapeutic personality change" precipitated scores of published studies, at least a dozen reviews, and even a "review of reviews" (Patterson, 1984). The empirical research on empathy, genuineness, and positive regard, which Rogers anticipated eagerly, has demonstrated that these facilitative interpersonal conditions are valuable contributors to outcome but are neither necessary nor sufficient. Dispassionate reviews conclude that "patients' positive perceptions of therapist facilitative attitudes have a modest tendency to enhance treatment gains" (Beutler et al., 1986, p. 279), and that "the evidence for the therapeutic conditions hypothesis [as necessary and sufficient] is not persuasive. The associations found are modest and suggest that a more complex association exists between outcome and therapist skills than originally hypothesized" (Parloff et al., 1978, p. 251).

Most person-centered therapists now concede the point and have reformulated the original hypothesis. One set of person-centered researchers conclude that the evidence, "although equivocal, does seem to suggest that empathy, warmth, and genuineness are related in some way to client change but that their potency and generalizability are not as great as once thought" (Mitchell et al., 1977, p. 481). Raskin (1992), an influential client-centered practitioner, summarizes his position on the original Rogerian qualities by saying they were not necessary, perhaps sufficient, definitely facilitative. Few researchers seriously suggest that these conditions are necessary and sufficient, even within person-centered psychotherapy (Bohart, 1993b; Kirschenbaum & Jourdan, 2005).

However, the facilitative conditions are facilitative. The accumulating research demonstrates that therapist qualities of positive regard, empathy, and genuineness are indeed effective for most people and most circumstances. As discovered by Rogers and rediscovered by Miller decades later, client perception of their therapist's empathy is the single strongest therapist determinant of successful psychotherapy (Bohart et al., 2002; Elliott et al., 2011). Although rarely sufficient for personality change, empathy is facilitative—in person-centered and all other systems of psychotherapy (Burns & Nolan-Hoeksema, 1992; Norcross, 2011). The facilitative conditions represent the core of the nonspecific or common factors across diverse forms of psychotherapy (as described in Chapter 1). Empathy is assuredly an evidence-based practice.

Person-Centered Therapy

The general pattern of early outcome research was that person-centered therapy outperformed no-treatment and wait-list control groups in samples of college students and mildly disturbed clients. In the early 1960s, Rogers and his colleagues (1967) courageously applied person-centered therapy to a group of institutionalized schizophrenics—one of the few psychotherapies then to be tested with this seriously disturbed population. Those results demonstrated little effectiveness.

Turning to the overall effectiveness of person-centered therapy with nonpsychotic clients, we shall review the conclusions of several meta-analyses on the subject. Aggregating about 60 studies, the Smith and Glass (1977; Smith et al., 1980) meta-analysis found that person-centered therapy showed an average effect size of 0.63. This was interpreted as a respectable and moderate effect, clearly superior to no treatment, but just barely

higher than the average effect of 0.56 for placebo treatment. Person-centered therapy was found to be comparable in effectiveness to psychodynamic and other insight-oriented therapies, but slightly below—some would say negligibly below—that of behavioral treatments (Shapiro & Shapiro, 1982). The one type of outcome measure on which client-centered therapy demonstrated higher change than a number of other orientations was in self-esteem, an area particularly prized by the person-centered approach (Rice, 1988).

A reassessment of the 17 published studies on client-centered therapy contained in the Smith, Glass, and Miller (1980) meta-analysis indicated that the apparent effectiveness of client-centered therapy was largely based on the treatment of problems that occur in academic settings (Champney & Schulz, 1983). Caution was recommended in generalizing the effectiveness of Rogerian therapy beyond academic problems and educational counselors to psychological problems and private practices.

More recent reviews of person-centered therapy show that it is definitely superior to no treatment and a placebo treatment. Whether it is as effective as or slightly less effective than other systems of psychotherapies brings us back to the **allegiance effect**, the tendency of the investigators to favor their own preferred treatment in conducting studies. The early meta-analyses found client-centered therapy to produce statistically significant benefits compared to wait-list or no treatment in over 90% of the studies (Grawe et al., 1998) and produce an average effect size of 0.95 compared to no treatment, a large impact to be sure (Greenberg et al., 1994). At the same time, in direct comparisons, client-centered therapy fared slightly poorly (Greenberg et al., 1994; Reicherts, 1998).

But then researchers began accounting for the allegiance effects in meta-analyses and discovered that most of these small, between-therapy differences began to fade away, leaving equivalent outcomes. Case in point is the treatment of depression.

When controlled for investigator allegiance, nondirective therapies worked about as well as cognitive, behavior, psychodynamic, and interpersonal therapies (Cuijpers et al., 2008). Direct comparisons revealed that the nondirective treatments were just slightly less effective ($d = -0.13$), a tiny difference. There are no large differences in efficacy between the major psychotherapies for mild to moderate depression.

Another case in point is the large controlled study, involving over 5,000 patients suffering from anxiety and depression, treated at one of the National Health Service primary-care centers in the United Kingdom over a 3-year period (Stiles et al., 2008). All treatment groups began with similar levels of distress, and all averaged marked improvement (pre- to posttreatment effect size of 1.39). Patients treated with person-centered, cognitive-behavioral, and psychodynamic therapies all achieved equivalent outcomes. When theoretically neutral investigators conduct the study, more times than not theoretically different approaches tend to show similar treatment outcomes.

One area in which person- or client-centered therapy appears not to achieve comparable effectiveness is with children and adolescents. One meta-analysis (Weisz et al., 1987) located approximately 20 controlled studies that included client-centered therapy. The average effect size was 0.56, which was smaller than those obtained for various behavioral treatments (ranging from 0.75 to 1.19). A subsequent meta-analysis of child and adolescent outcome research (Weiss & Weisz, 1995a, 1995b) identified six new studies testing the effectiveness of client-centered therapy. The effect size was again clearly better than no treatment but lower than that found for a variety of behavioral, cognitive, and parent-training interventions.

The emerging conclusions are that person- or client-centered therapy is effective for adults, just as or a tad less effective than alternative therapies. For children and adolescents, better than no therapy at all but probably not as efficacious than cognitive-behavioral treatments. Finally, the investigator allegiance effect remains a potent wild card when interpreting such differences.

Motivational Interviewing

There are now more than 200 randomized clinical trials investigating the success of MI. Its body of research, in fact, now surpasses the outcome literature on person-centered therapy. We shall review the results of a seminal study involving MI and then summarize its burgeoning body of outcome research.

In **Project MATCH**, one of the largest psychotherapy outcome studies in history, four sessions of an early form of MI was compared to 12 sessions of Cognitive-Behavioral Coping Skill Training and to 12 sessions of Twelve-Step Facilitation Therapy (Project MATCH Research Group, 1993, 1997). Two parallel but independent randomized clinical trials were conducted, one with 952 alcohol-dependent clients receiving outpatient psychotherapy and one with 774 clients receiving aftercare therapy following alcohol inpatient treatment. The first two sessions included MI and personal feedback based on intensive assessments of problems related to alcohol abuse. The last two sessions were basically booster sessions (Miller et al., 1992).

The briefer MI was just as effective at each follow-up as the lengthier and more established 12-step and cognitive-behavioral treatments. Of special note was that, at long-term follow-up, MI was more effective than Cognitive-Behavioral Coping Skills Training with patients who initially were less motivated to change as measured by being in earlier stages of readiness for change. Just as Carl Rogers predicted, clients can go a long way in a short time when provided with facilitative conditions, an accepting therapist, and considerable autonomy.

At least four meta-analyses have been conducted on the effectiveness of MI (Lundahl & Burke, 2009; Lundahl et al., 2010). The 2010 meta-analysis examined 119 studies on the effectiveness of MI relative to either a control group or a comparison treatment across multiple problems. Compared to wait-list or no treatment, the four meta-analyses found that MI produced average effect sizes between 0.27 and 0.40. One could expect that 14% to 20% of MI patients to do better than the untreated after only two or three sessions of MI. Compared to alternative active treatments, the four meta-analyses found that MI performed as effectively or a bit more effectively, with average effect sizes between 0.04 and 0.32 favoring MI. One could expect that 2% to 15% of MI patients to do better than patients receiving other therapies. Note, however, that MI was typically shorter (by two sessions) and less expensive than the alternative treatments. All told, MI has demonstrated large effects with small interventions (Burke et al., 2002).

Strongest support by far for MI efficacy is in the area for which it was originally designed: substance abuse among adults and adolescents (Jensen et al., 2011; Smedslund et al., 2011). MI, averaging just 100 minutes in length, showed clinical impact: 51% improvement rates and a 56% reduction in client drinking (Hettema et al., 2005). The meta-analytic results also support its effectiveness for smoking, but the results are not as dramatic as for drinking problems (Lai et al., 2010).

MI appears to be particularly effective with two populations: ethnic minority clients and resistant clients (Hettema et al., 2005; Lundahl et al., 2010). The meta-analyses report larger effects with samples composed primarily or exclusively of people from ethnic minority groups. The client-centered, supportive, and nonconfrontational style of MI may represent a more culturally respectful form of psychotherapy. MI also seems to be differentially effective with clients who are more resistant, angry, or less ready for change. This finding is consistent with the original intent of MI—enhancing clients' intrinsic motivation to change by helping them explore and resolve their ambivalence.

Hettema, Steele, and Miler (2005) made a challenging observation in their meta-analysis of 72 clinical trials spanning a range of target problems. They found that effect sizes comparing MI to control groups decrease rapidly and significantly over time. Across all studies, the effect size (d) was 0.77 at 0 to 1 month posttreatment, but dropped to 0.39 at 1 to 3 months. At followups longer than 12 months, a very small d of 0.11 was found. An interesting exception to this trend was in studies where MI was added to another therapy, like cognitive-behavioral therapy. Here the effects of the combined treatments remained consistent over time, with effect sizes hovering around 0.60. These results suggest that to produce durable effects over time, MI may need to be combined with another evidence-based treatment.

Criticisms of Person-Centered Therapies
From a Cognitive-Behavioral Perspective

Rogerians should be praised for their willingness to place person-centered therapy under scientific scrutiny. They must realize, however, that they were responsible for the many methodological errors in their original experiments. Fatal flaws in their studies include (1) omitting an untreated control group; (2) failing to control for placebo effects; and (3) neglecting the actual behavior and functioning of clients in favor of ratings of their subjective experiences. More recent controlled studies have corrected several of these faults, but the science is weaker than that demanded of evidence-based health care.

Even when sufficient controls and rigorous methods are employed, the general meta-analytic conclusion is that exposure, behavior, and cognitive therapies are as effective and probably more effective than person-centered therapy. The greater use of empathy and warmth by behavior therapists would probably prove useful, but the therapist's interpersonal behavior is rarely sufficient to conquer behavioral disorders. Don't stop with "touchy, feely" therapist qualities when specific, teachable behavioral methods have been found to be more effective and efficient. That's why we insist on putting some distance between the original person-centered therapy and the modern MI.

From a theoretical perspective, person-centered therapy is also open to serious question. Beneath all the rhetoric, Rogers is advocating a treatment based on a fuzzy form of extinction—the client's distress will gradually fade if the therapist ignores conditions of worth. Troubled responses are assumed to have been conditioned by the contingent love and regard of parents. The therapist is supposed to reverse the process by establishing a social-learning environment in which there are no contingencies, no conditions for positive regard. The client is allowed to talk on and on about troubled behavior without being reinforced or punished. Eventually, the absence of contingencies leads to an extinction of talking about troubles. Of course, we cannot determine from verbal extinction alone whether the client's troubled behavior itself has changed or whether the client has just quit talking about it. But why rely on extinction when it is necessarily lengthy and can lead to complications, such as spontaneous recovery of the extinguished responses? Further, when only extinction is used, there is no way of telling which new behaviors will be learned in place of the maladaptive responses being extinguished.

Rogers advocates trusting in a mysterious organismic actualizing tendency. This tendency is reminiscent of the ancient belief in teleology, which assumed that an acorn would grow straight and tall if we only kept our foot off it. Of course, we now know that the manner in which even an acorn develops is in part a function of how it is nourished by its ongoing environment.

From a Psychoanalytic Perspective

The Rogerian approach exemplifies how our perceptions can be distorted by the people we are most likely to see for psychological treatment. Person-centered therapy is an inspirational theory of humanity of enormous appeal to college students because it was based primarily on work with students. It is a theory and therapy for ambitious individuals whose typically American drive to achieve is mistaken for some inherent tendency to actualize. Where was such a driving tendency to actualize in the chronic schizophrenics that Rogers and his colleagues (1967) failed to make into fully functioning individuals?

What person-centered therapy actually provides is a transference relationship that has all the elements of an idealized maternal love. Clients are promised a rose garden in which all that they are, their worst as well as their best, will be met with unconditional love. The fact is that research (Truax, 1966) has demonstrated that even Carl Rogers made his responses to clients highly conditional on the clients' expressing feelings. When clients expressed particular feelings, Rogers was much more likely to show interest or express empathy. To pretend to be unconditional in our love is to do our clients a disservice; the real world is, in actuality, conditional with love. Such pretense can encourage clients to believe that, compared to the rest of the world, only a therapist could really love them.

From a Cultural Perspective

The person-centered disregard of the larger environment beyond the therapy relationship often leads to naiveté and ineffectiveness. The social milieu in humanistic theories is treated simplistically as an obstacle to self-realization, rather than as an arena in which the self will be either lost or realized. Downplaying external "reality" or the "real world," concepts Rogers often placed in quotation marks, can only confirm the public image of psychotherapy as unrealistic, self-indulgent, expensive talk about one's inner feelings and potentials. "Reality" consists of much more than emotions expressed in 50-minute sessions; family relationships, social institutions, economic considerations, and political power, to name just a few, routinely exert more influence on selfhood than person-centered therapists care to admit.

Rogers's preoccupation with selfhood, individuation, and self-actualization is culture specific. His position both reflects and reinforces the high value that Western culture places on individualism (Usher, 1989). Not all cultures share this emphasis on "self." In at least one culture, the term for "self" does not even exist (Pervin, 1993). Rogers's characterization of the ideal individual does not apply across cultures. Some ethnic groups favor an external (not internal) locus of evaluation and function quite well. Person-centered therapists may be comparatively nondirective in the content addressed in therapy, but the underlying values are anything but nondirective. The value on separateness and autonomy over interdependence and connectedness reflects a Western (and masculine) perspective.

Unlike Rogers, feminists insist it is not enough for a woman to alter her self-perception. "To imply that such an internal change would eliminate all cultural, economic, legal, and interpersonal obstacles to a woman's physical and psychological actualization is absurd" (Lerman, 1992, p. 15). Vigorous group advocacy, not gradual individual change, will better solve most of the contemporary problems plaguing women and minorities.

From an Integrative Perspective

We praise Rogers for his outstanding contributions to psychotherapy research and to articulating what constitutes a therapeutic relationship. The problem is, however, that he has gone too far and concluded that what may be necessary conditions for therapy to proceed are also sufficient conditions for therapy to succeed. His promise of facilitative therapist qualities

sounds like a Hollywood melodrama in which one unconditional love relationship comes along and emancipates a fully functioning person who lives happily ever after. What power he attributes to one caring relationship that meets only 1 hour per week! We are asked to believe that one special relationship alone is powerful enough to overcome the crippling effects of the conditional relationships that characterize our past and present lives.

Rogers's overemphasis on relationship qualities encourages the fantasy that an effective psychotherapist merely feels and relates without knowing much. His system suggests that anyone who is congruent, whether a peer counselor or a paraprofessional, can do effective psychotherapy with all patients and problems, without possessing knowledge about personality or psychopathology. Knowledge in Rogers's system is of little consequence; it certainly is not a necessary condition for effective therapy. Yet one wonders if it is sheer coincidence that master psychotherapists, such as Freud, Adler, May, and Rogers himself, have all been individuals with intense intellectual commitments as well as an enormous capacity for caring.

Finally, Rogers embodied unitary formulations and singular treatments for all clinical encounters (Norcross & Beutler, 1997). All clients suffer from the same essential problem of conditions of worth, and all require the identical treatment. For his avowed interest in an individualistic psychology, Rogers rarely managed to individualize his therapy to fit the particular client! Some patients thrive on a comparatively passive and unstructured form of psychotherapy, such as person-centered therapy, but other people do not. Instead, they require directive therapy and await active advice. History taking, confronting, teaching, interpreting, directing, and advising are all essential clinical activities in treating some clients with some problems. In these situations, person-centered therapy is contraindicated at best, poor practice at worst.

A Person-Centered Analysis of Mrs. C

Mrs. C was raised in an extremely rigid atmosphere in which her parents' conditions of worth centered on her being clean, germ-free, asexual, and meek. From her compulsive pattern of existence, we can imagine that her own internalized conditions of worth are just as rigid as those of her parents. The only experiences she lets herself possess are those in which she is obsessed with proving how clean and disease-free she is.

In her early years of marriage, Mrs. C had felt loved and regarded highly enough to be more flexible and better adjusted. Just what went wrong is open to speculation. Her family was struck with a severe flu, and then the possibility of a pinworm epidemic might have threatened her self-regard by confronting her with not having been clean enough and careful enough with her family. At a more central level, she may have been threatened by a subception that she could not really love her children when they were sick or dirty. Mrs. C may well have been experiencing the rigid limits of her love in relationship to her sick children and may have been threatened by doubts about the kind of mother she was if she could not really love her children when they needed her the most. But she had internalized her parents' lessons: love is contingent on cleanliness, love is too scarce to waste on the dirty or the diseased.

Although we do not know the exact experiences that were threatening to emerge into awareness, we do form the impression of a person who panicked, who was confronted with intense and undeniable experiences of being unlovable. Mrs. C's life became disorganized as she struggled to hold onto what little self-regard she could maintain by organizing her life around washing and avoiding germs. If we empathize with the communications contained in her symptoms, we may hear how desperately she cries out, "I am worthy. I am lovable. Look how clean I am. I am not diseased. Don't send me away. I will make myself more lovable, more worthy of your regard. I will work harder, be cleaner."

If she could express her genuine feelings, she might go on: "My therapist and my family can love me only if I stop washing; I can love myself only if I am clean and pure. I am in a trap where I gain their regard at the loss of my own, or hold onto what little self-worth I have by continuing to clean and risk losing the few people who have any regard left for me. Suicide seems like the only alternative in this no-win situation."

Is Mrs. C's view just the distorted perception of a troubled person? Do we not cast aside the dirty and the diseased? In our society, in which every major religious group values cleanliness more than mature love (Rokeach, 1970), should we be surprised that some people, like Mrs. C, base their existence on distorted social values and sacrifice their own organismic experiencing? Mrs. C is a tragic prototype of a culture so enamored with social values such as cleanliness as to be estranged from organismic values like love.

Mrs. C's family and therapist have indeed made their caring as rigidly conditional as she has. They say, "Don't wash and we will care about you"; she says, "Only when I wash can I care about myself." An effective psychotherapist must establish a relationship in which Mrs. C is held in high regard when she washes as well as when she doesn't, when she talks about washing as well as when she doesn't. When we appreciate that we are talking with a woman who is obsessed with maintaining the little self-regard she has left, we will not demand that she give up her one remaining source of esteem—her washing.

First, Mrs. C needs to experience the positive regard of those who care, whether she washes or not, whether she is obsessed or not. Then, and only then, can she begin to understand that being positively regarded is not contingent on either washing or not washing. Only then can she begin to gradually become a little freer to consider that maybe she, too, can love herself whether she washes or does not wash.

Caring is the fundamental issue, not cleaning. Mrs. C has been providing unconditional cleaning, cleaning whether it is warranted or not, when what she really wants is unconditional caring, caring whether she at this moment warrants it or not.

Future Directions

As with Adler and the existentialists, Rogers's major contributions have been gratefully incorporated by most practitioners whose preferred orientations are not Rogerian. Person-centered values and methods have become part of the therapeutic mainstream and assimilated into cognitive, self-psychology, feminist, experiential, and constructivist therapies. Rogers's lasting influences include the centrality of accurate empathy, the importance of the person of the therapist, the primacy of the relationship over technique, and the healing power of the therapeutic relationship. No wonder that, in national surveys of mental health professionals, Carl Rogers is routinely identified as one of the most influential psychotherapists in history.

Person-centered therapists can point with pride to the infusion of its principles into most systems of psychotherapy, but at the same time, this widespread assimilation has contributed to its slow decline in popularity (Lietaer, 1990). As a distinct, 70-year-old system, person-centered therapy is definitely on the wane in the United States (although it is more popular on the European continent).

In the past, person-centered therapy's historical strictures against authority, teaching, and telling have made clinicians hesitant to experiment with means to accelerate the therapeutic process. As Arthur Combs (1988, p. 270), a respected person-centered psychologist, humorously observed, "Anyone who has watched a group of person-centered counselors decide where to go on a picnic must surely have asked themselves whether there are not speedier ways of reaching good decisions." In the present, many practitioners of person-centered therapy argue for augmenting its process focus with specific, evidence-based methods from other orientations (Bohart, 1993b; Tausch, 1990). Facilitative therapist qualities can be profitably integrated with specific techniques from other systems of psychotherapy. There need be no inherent conflict between relationship and technique as long as the experience of the client remains the continuous touchstone for what is introduced by the therapist.

Many clinicians make a crucial distinction between the primary relationship conditions and the specialized therapist interventions that are indicated by certain **client markers** (Rice, 1988). These markers represent an expressed or inferred readiness for specific change tasks. Direct feedback, for instance, is particularly useful when a therapist picks up discrepant messages from the client. Offered in an accepting relational context, even feedback or confrontation can be an extension of accurate empathy (Norcross & Beutler, 1997; Sachse, 1990). Homework tasks outside the session can be mutually designed when a client expresses a desire to implement specific actions outside of the therapeutic relationship. By selecting those interventions missing in client-centered therapy, therapists could have the best of both worlds—the relationship and the technique.

Motivational interviewing has brought energy to person-centered therapy and kept it alive in new clothes. If you calculate the number of journal articles or professional books in psychotherapy, you will see the rapid interest in MI starting in the mid-1990s. MI has taken by storm not only the addictions field, but also health care generally by helping clinicians prepare ambivalent people for change. Decidedly brief and demonstrably effective for a multitude of disorders, MI has redirected our attention back to the curative powers of client autonomy and therapist empathy.

Empathy as a core of psychotherapy may be making a comeback (Bohart & Greenberg, 1997). As clients tire of technical interventions delivered in a few sessions by a hurried practitioner "managed" by an insurance carrier, they may hunger for a real human relationship, a genuine meeting of two individuals. As therapists reacquaint themselves with the relational world of their clients, they may discover an empathic perspective surprisingly similar to that of Rogers, as has been experienced in relational psychoanalysis, self-psychology, multicultural counseling, cognitive therapy, and yes, even in behavior therapy (Goldfried & Davison, 1994). Researchers too may return to the compelling awareness that psychotherapy is most fruitfully conceived and studied as a human relationship, rather than as a technical enterprise.

Person-centered therapies will appeal to new generations of helpers. Patient-centered training for medical professionals, especially physicians and nurses, should thrive in a consumer-oriented and holistic health care system. Executive coaches, wellness practitioners, and paraprofessionals will rely on the core Rogerian skills of accurate empathy, positive regard, and congruence in their daily work. Perhaps most importantly, person-centered therapies will need to maintain an openness to new theoretical ideas and to active, eclectic methods in the era of short-term treatments. This openness is exactly what Rogers's own life demonstrated and what his later writings (1986, p. 259) implored: "Open new vistas, bring new insights, challenge our hypotheses, enrich our theory, expand our knowledge, and involve us more deeply in an understanding of the phenomena of human change."

Key Terms

actualization
actualizing tendency
allegiance effect
autonomy
client markers
client-centered therapy
conditions of worth
counterresistance
dissemination and
   implementation
empathy
existential living
fully functioning
   person
genuineness
heteronomy
incongruence
motivational
   discrepancy
motivational
   interviewing (MI)
necessary and
   sufficient conditions
nondirective therapy
organismic valuing
person-centered
   approach
process research
Project MATCH
reflection (of feelings)
roll with resistance
self-authority
self-concept
self-regard
subception
unconditional positive
   regard

Recommended Readings

Arkowitz, H., Westra, H. A., Miller, W. R., & Rollnick, S. (Eds.). (2008). *Motivational interviewing in the treatment of psychological problems.* New York: Guilford.

Cooper, M., O'Hara, M., Schmid, P. F., & Wyatt, G. (Eds.). (2007). *Handbook of person-centered psychotherapy and counselling.* Hampshire, England: Palgrave Macmillan.

Farber, B. A., Brink, D. C., & Raskin, P. M. (Eds.). (1998). *The psychotherapy of Carl Rogers: Cases and commentary.* New York: Guilford.

Miller, W. R., & Rollnick, S. (2012). *Motivational interviewing* (3rd ed.). New York: Guilford.

Rogers, C. R. (1951). *Client-centered therapy.* Boston: Houghton Mifflin.

Rogers, C. R. (1961). *On becoming a person.* Boston: Houghton Mifflin.

Rogers, C. R. (1980). *A way of being.* Boston: Houghton Mifflin.

Schneider, K., Bugental, J. F. T., & Pierson, J. F. (Eds.). (2002). *The handbook of humanistic psychology.* Thousand Oaks, CA: Sage.

Journals: *Journal of Humanistic Education and Development; Journal of Humanistic Psychology; Journal of Phenomenological Psychology; Person-Centered Journal; Person-Centered & Experiential Psychotherapies.*

Recommended Websites

Association for Humanistic Psychology:
www.ahpweb.org/
Association for the Development of the Person-Centered Approach:
www.adpca.org/
Center for Studies of the Person:
www.centerfortheperson.org/

Motivational Interviewing:
www.motivationalinterview.org/
World Association for Person-Centered Psychotherapy:
www.pce-world.org/

CHAPTER **6**

Experiential Therapies

Fritz Perls

As long as sex was going well for Howard, all was well with the world. From ages 17 to 27, he had been very active sexually, with most of his time and energy spent in erotic adventures or in fantasizing about such adventures. Sexual relating was by far the most significant and satisfying activity in his life. No wonder he was so puzzled at the onset of his erectile dysfunction. Except for his first experience with a prostitute at age 17, he had never had any difficulty performing in bed. In fact, Howard loved to perform and prided himself on what a great lover he was. But now, no matter how hard he tried, he just could not succeed. Needless to say, he was quite depressed and anxious.

Fortunately, Howard had a special partner named Ginny, for whom he cared deeply. She wanted to be with him sexually in spite of his impotence, and was willing to join him in sex therapy. We began psychotherapy with the standard, Masters and Johnson (1970) method of **sensate focusing**, a series of couples exercises used to alleviate anxiety related to intercourse in which partners take turns exploring and massaging each

Leslie Greenberg

other's bodies (but not genitalia or breasts). The results were discouraging because of the amount of depression and anxiety Howard experienced in the nondemanding, pleasuring exercises. Because his erections remained inhibited when he was with Ginny, we decided to try systematic desensitization and then come back to sensate focusing. Although Howard progressed to the point of imagining intercourse without anxiety, he did not show much generalization to the actual sensate-focusing situation.

Finally, I (JOP) decided to use some Gestalt work to help Howard discover the significance of the intense, relentless pressure on his sexual drive. I asked Howard to imagine as vividly as he could that he was his penis and that his penis had something to say. As he got into the fantasy, I encouraged him to let the mouth of his penis say whatever it spontaneously desired, and here is what came out: "You're asking too much of me, Howard. You've been asking me to carry the whole meaning of your life on my back, and that's just too big a load for any one penis to carry. I'm bound to bend under such weight."

Such direct experiential work on a client's emotions is the *sine qua non* of the broad class of treatments known as the **experiential therapies**. **Gestalt therapy** emerged first and most prominently, so we devote the first part of this chapter to it. We then review a few other therapies in the experiential tradition, principally the influential **emotion-focused therapy** of Leslie Greenberg and colleagues.

A Sketch of Fritz Perls

Frederich (Fritz) Perls (1893–1970) was the developer of Gestalt therapy and the master of using Gestalt work to assist people to become deeply aware of themselves and their bodies. Perls did not start out with such an action-oriented approach, however. Like so many pro-creators of psychotherapy systems, his early career was heavily influenced by his studies of psychoanalysis with Freud. After receiving his MD in Berlin, where he was born, he studied at the Berlin and the Vienna Institutes of Psychoanalysis. He was analyzed by Wilhelm Reich, who had a profound influence on his development. Perls (1969b) said that if it had not been for the advent of Hitler, he probably would have spent his professional career doing psychoanalysis with a few select clients.

As an aware individual, he anticipated the horrors of Hitler, and in 1934, when Ernst Jones announced a psychoanalytic position in Johannesburg, South Africa, Perls accepted. Besides establishing a practice, he also began the South African Institute for Psychoanalysis. Over the next dozen years, he developed what he initially considered a revision and elaboration of psychoanalysis. In 1947 he published his first book, *Ego, Hunger and Aggression: A Revision of Freud's Theory and Method*. At that time Perls was still committed to an instinct theory but argued for the acceptance of hunger as an instinct as critical to the survival of the individual as the sexual instinct is to the survival of the species. In the face of the many revisions that Perls was suggesting for psychoanalysis, it became obvious that he was really beginning a new psychotherapy system. When he republished his first book in 1969 he subtitled it *The Beginning of Gestalt Therapy*.

With the rise of apartheid in South Africa, Perls again chose to leave a country heading toward unacceptable oppression. He emigrated to the United States in 1946, and with his therapist wife, Laura, began the New York Institute for Gestalt Therapy. There, Perls was probably influenced by Jacob Moreno, the psychiatrist who founded psychodrama and who insisted on combining action with the mentalistic talk of psychotherapy. In 1951, Perls coauthored *Gestalt Therapy: Excitement and Growth in the Human Personality*, an exciting and engaging presentation of Gestalt exercises.

As a person, Perls was similar to his writings: vital and perplexing. It was probably his many workshops with clinicians more than his writings that had such an impact on the psychotherapy profession. People saw him as keenly perceptive, provocative, manipulative, evocative, hostile, and inspiring. Indeed, it is difficult to separate Perls's personality from his method. Many professionals came away from an encounter with Perls feeling more alive and complete. Those who went out to spread the Gestalt gospel talked affectionately and almost worshipfully of Fritz. He certainly did not discourage such a cult. Believing that modesty is for modest people, Perls (1969b) wrote in his autobiography, "I believe that I am the best therapist for any type of neurosis in the States, maybe in the world. How is this for megalomania. At the same time I have to admit that I cannot work successfully with everybody."

Such unabashed egotism was fashionable in the 1960s, and many people flocked to Esalen in Big Sur, California, where Perls held court. If it was uniqueness, honesty, and spontaneity they sought in Fritz, they were not disappointed; if it was a grandfatherly positive regard they desired, they were frustrated. As a result of his personal impact and his professional writings, the Gestalt movement became a significant force in the last decade of Perls's life. He wanted to close out his life by building a Gestalt Training Center and Community in British Columbia, so he moved there just before his death in 1970.

With Fritz's death, Gestalt therapists lost their touchstone of just what Gestalt therapy can and should be. As one would expect from such a dynamic and spontaneous force as Fritz, there were many changes in his approach over the years. Consistency was not one of his strengths. Most Gestaltists, however, point to the 1969 publication of *Gestalt Therapy Verbatim* as the best representation of Perls's nature to Gestalt theory and therapy, and so that book serves as the main source for our presentation.

Theory of Personality

In spite of the centuries-old wish to disown our bodies, we humans must accept that we are basically biological organisms. Our daily goals, or **end-goals** as Perls (1969a) prefers to call them, are

based on our biological needs, which are limited to hunger, sex, survival, shelter, and breathing. The social roles we adopt are the means-whereby we fulfill our end-goals. Our role of psychotherapist, for instance, is a means-whereby we earn a living, which is a means-whereby we fulfill such end-goals as hunger and shelter. As healthy beings, our daily living centers around the particular end-goals that are emerging into awareness in order to be fulfilled. If we listen to our body, the most urgent end-goal emerges, and we respond to it as an emergency—that is, without any obsessive doubt that the most important action we can take at this moment is to fulfill the particular end-goal emerging into awareness. We then interact with the environment to select the substances we need to satisfy that end-goal.

End-goals are experienced as pressing needs as long as they are not completed; they are quiescent once they are given closure through an adequate exchange with the environment. If we are thirsty, for example, we experience a need to bring completeness to our thirst by responding to our need with an adequate supply of water from our environment. It is this continual process of bringing completeness to our needs, the process of forming wholes or **Gestalts**, that Perls posits as the one constant law of the world that maintains the integrity of organisms.

The serious concerns in living, then, lie in the completion of these organismic needs, as is well known by the millions of starving poor in the world. In a spoiled society such as the United States, we spend little of our time or energy in completing our natural needs. Instead we preoccupy ourselves with social games that are nothing more than social means to natural ends. Once we experience these social means as end-goals, we identify with them as essential parts of our ego, so that we act as if we must put almost all our energy into playing roles such as student, teacher, or therapist. Much of our thinking is involved with practicing how we can better act out our roles to more effectively manipulate our social environment and convince ourselves and others of the inherent value of our roles. As we repeatedly practice our roles, they become habits—rigid behavioral patterns that represent the essence of our character. Once we develop our social character and have a fixed personality, we have transformed our basic natural existence into a pseudosocial existence.

In a healthy natural existence, our daily life cycle would be an open, flowing process of **organismic needs** emerging into awareness. This process would be accompanied by a means-whereby we bring closure to the most pressing need of the moment, followed by the emergence of another end-goal into awareness. As long as we remain centered on what is occurring within us right now, we can trust our organic wisdom to select the best means-whereby we complete the most pressing need of the moment.

In a healthy existence, our entire life cycle involves a natural process of maturation in which we develop from children dependent on environmental support into adults who rely on self-support. Our development begins as unborn children entirely dependent on our mothers for support—for food, oxygen, shelter, everything. As soon as we are born, we have to do our own breathing at least. Gradually we learn to crawl, to stand on our own two feet, to walk, to use our own muscles, our senses, our wit. Eventually we have to accept that wherever we go, whatever we do, whatever we experience is our own responsibility and only ours. As healthy adults, we are aware that we possess the ability to respond, and to have thoughts, reactions, and emotions that are uniquely ours. This mature responsibility is fundamentally the ability to be what one is. For Perls (1969a), "responsibility means simply to be willing to say 'I am I' and 'I am what I am.'"

As healthy adults, we are simultaneously aware that other maturing organisms are equally able to respond for themselves, and the maturation process includes shedding responsibility for anyone else. We give up our childish feelings of omnipotence and omniscience and accept that others know themselves better than we can ever know them and can direct their own lives better than we can direct them. We allow others to be self-supporting, and we give up our need to interfere in the lives of others. Others do not exist to live up to our expectations, nor do we exist to live up to theirs.

The healthy personality does not become preoccupied with social roles. They are nothing more than a set of social expectations that we and others set for ourselves. The mature person does not adjust to society, certainly not to an insane society such as ours. Healthy individuals do not repeat the same old, tired habits that are so safe and so deadly. In taking responsibility for being all that they can be, such people accept Perls's attitude of living and reviewing every second afresh. They discover that there are always new and fresh means-whereby they can complete their end-goals. This freshness is what the creative cook discovers, what the joyful sex partner experiences, and what the vital therapist thrives on.

With these attractive possibilities emerging from the natural process of maturation, how is it that most people remain stuck in the immature, childish patterns of dependency? Several childhood experiences can interfere with the development of a healthy personality. In some families, parents withdraw needed environmental support before children have developed the capacity for inner support. The child can no longer rely on the safe, secure environmental support, nor can the child rely on self-support. The child is at an **impasse**. Perls's (1970) example of an impasse is a "blue baby" who has had the placenta severed and cannot rely on oxygen from the mother but is not yet prepared to breathe on its own—a very scary situation. Another example of an impasse occurs when parents demand that a child stand without support before the child's muscles and balance are adequately developed. All the child can experience is the fear of falling. Experiencing impasses can result in becoming stuck in the maturation process.

A more frequent source of interference comes from parents who are convinced that they know what is best for their children in all situations. In such families, children may fear "the stick," which is punishment for trusting their independent direction when it differs from what the parents believe is best. The child develops **catastrophic expectations** for independent behavior, such as "If I take the risk on my own, I won't be loved anymore or my parents won't approve of me." Perls (1969a) suggests that catastrophic expectations are frequently projections onto the parents of the child's own fears of the consequences of independence, rather than memories of how parents actually responded.

As we become more aware, we realize that marching to a different drummer can indeed be risky. If we act differently from our parents or peers, we may risk losing their love or approval. But they are not responsible if we choose to avoid the risks of being our own person. There are even more serious risks in our society if we refuse to play roles or to adjust to social expectations. We can lose jobs, friends, money, and even face crucifixion for being outside the boundaries of society. But we still cannot blame society if we refuse to take the risks of being healthy.

Fear of repercussions for independent behavior is a major cause of maturational delays, but it is not the most common. More people get stuck because they have been spoiled by parents who overindulged them as children. Perls believes that too many parents want to give their children everything they never had. As a result, the children prefer to remain spoiled and let their parents do everything for them.

Many parents are also afraid to frustrate their children; yet it is only through **frustration** that we are motivated to rely on our own resources to overcome what is frustrating us. By giving too much and not frustrating enough, parents establish an environment that is so secure and satisfying that the children become stuck in desiring to maintain constant environmental support. Perls's emphasis on being stuck by being spoiled is reminiscent of Freud's emphasis on overindulgence as one source of infantile fixations.

Perls does not blame the parents, however, for the spoiled child's remaining stuck. These children are still responsible for using all of their resources to manipulate the parents and others in the environment to take care of them. These children develop a whole repertoire of manipulations, such as crying, if that is what it takes to get support, or being the nice little child, if that is the role that gets others to respond. To allow immature personalities to blame their parents for their problems is to allow them to avoid responsibility for their lives, which is a critical part of the maturation process.

Theory of Psychopathology

The pathological person has become stuck in the natural process of growth or maturation. Accordingly, Perls preferred the term *growth disorders* rather than *neuroses* to refer to the common problems in living, although he frequently relied on the more traditional term *neurosis* when talking about psychopathology.

For Perls (1970), there are five different **layers or levels of psychopathology**: (1) the phony, (2) the phobic, (3) the impasse, (4) the implosive, and (5) the explosive. The **phony layer** is the level of existence in which we play games and enact roles. At this level, we behave as if we are big shots, as if we are ignorant, as if we are demure ladies, as if we are he-men. Our as-if attitudes require that we live up to a concept, live up to a fantasy that we or others have created, whether it comes out as a curse or an ideal. We may think it is an ideal to act as if we were Jesus, for example, but Perls would see it as a curse, because it is still an attempt to get away from who we really are. The result is that neurotic people have given up living in a way in which they can actualize themselves; they live to actualize a concept. Perls (1970) compares such pathology to an elephant that would rather be a rosebush and a rosebush that tries to be a kangaroo.

What we create in place of our authentic selves is a fantasy life that Perls (1969a) calls **maya**, from the Hindu for *illusion*. Maya is part of the phony level of existence that we construct between our real selves and the real world, but we live as if our maya is reality. Our maya serves a defensive purpose, because it protects us from the threatening aspects of ourselves or our world, such as the possibility of rejection. Much of our mental life is involved with making us better prepared to live in maya. Thinking, for example, is rehearsal for acting, for role-playing. This is one reason that Perls says he disesteems thinking. We become so preoccupied with our concepts, our ideals, and our rehearsals that soon we no longer have any sense of our real nature. In maya, things are not as they seem.

In the struggle to be something we are not, we disown those aspects of ourselves that may lead to disapproval or rejection. If our eyes cause us to sin, we cast out our eyes. If our genitals make us human, we disown our genitals. We become alienated from properties of ourselves that we and significant others frown on, and we create the holes, the void, where something should exist. Where the voids are, we build up phony artifacts. If we disown our genitals, for example, then we can act as if we are by nature pious and saintly. We try to create the characteristics that are demanded by our society for approval and that are eventually demanded by the part of ourselves that Freud called the superego.

In the process, we create our phony characters—phony because they represent only half of who we are. If the character we construct is mean and demanding, for instance, then we can be sure that below the surface is the opposite polarity of wanting to be kind and yielding. Our phony characters attempt to shield us from the fact that authentic existence involves, for each individual, facing personal **polarities** (Polster & Polster, 1973). We may rigidly adhere to being pious and saintly to keep from experiencing our opposite desires to be devilish and sexual. The healthy person attempts to find wholeness by accepting and expressing the opposite poles of life. Pathological individuals attempt to hide unacceptable opposites by pretending that their lives are composed entirely of their phony characters.

Perls called the most famous Gestalt polarities **Top Dog** and **Under Dog**. We experience Top Dog as our conscience, the righteous part of us that insists on always being right. Top Dog attempts to be master by commanding, demanding, insisting, and scolding. Under Dog is the slavish part of us that appears to go along with the bullying demands of Top Dog's ideals but in fact controls through passive resistance. Under Dog is the part of us that acts stupid, lazy, or inept as a means of trying to keep from successfully completing the orders of Top Dog.

Polarities are much more general and inclusive than Top Dog and Under Dog. Our psychological lives are dominated by polarities, be it connection/ separation or strength/vulnerability. In health, we creatively balance and continually recalibrate these polarities. But in neurosis, we keep one aspect out of awareness, and as a result, polarities lose their fluidity and become hardened into dichotomies. As long as people avoid accepting that they are also the opposite of what they pretend to be—that they are strong as well as weak, cruel as well as kind, and master as well as slave—they are unable to complete the Gestalt of life.

To try to face all that we are, to try to be whole, leads us to confront the **phobic layer** of our pathology. At this layer, we are phobic about the pain that ensues from facing how dissatisfied we are with parts of ourselves. We avoid and run from emotional pain, even though such pain is a natural signal that something is wrong and needs to change. The phobic layer includes all of our childish catastrophic expectations—that if we confront who we really are, our parents will not love us, or if we act the way we want to act, society will ostracize us, and so forth. These phobic responses frequently help us avoid what is really hurting; thus, most people come to therapy not to be cured but to have their neuroses improved.

Below the phobic layer is the most critical level of psychopathology: the **impasse**. The impasse is the very point at which we are stuck in our own maturation. It is what the Russians call the sick point. The impasse is the point at which we are convinced that we have no chance of survival because we cannot find the means within ourselves to progress when environmental support is withdrawn. People will not move beyond this point because of terrors that they might die or fall apart because they cannot stand on their own feet. But neurotics also refuse to move beyond this point because it is still easier for them to manipulate and control their environment for support. So they continue to play helpless, stupid, crazy, or enraged to get others to take care of them, including their therapists.

To experience the **implosive layer** is to experience deadness, the deadness of parts of ourselves that we have disowned. Neurotics would experience the deadness of their ears, or their heart, or their genitals, or their very soul, depending on what fundamental processes of living they have run from. Perls (1970) compares the implosive layer to a state of catatonia, in which the person is frozen like a corpse. The catatonia is due to the investment of energy in the development of a rigid, habitual

character that seems safe and secure but oh, so dead. To go through the implosive level, the person must be willing to shed the very character that has served as a sense of identity. The person is threatened with experiencing his or her own death in order to be reborn. That is obviously not easy.

To let go of one's roles, one's habits, and one's very character is to release tremendous energy that has been invested in holding back from being a responsible and fully alive human being. The person is now confronted with the **explosive layer** of neurosis, which entails an emancipation of life's energies. The size of the explosion depends on the amount of energy bound up in the implosive layer. To become fully alive, the person must explode into orgasm, into anger, into grief, and into joy. With such explosions, the neurotic has moved well beyond the impasse and the implosive and has taken a giant stride into the joy and sorrow of maturity.

Therapeutic Processes

Explosively breaking out of a neurotic life is an exciting, cathartic experience. The powerful release of the emotions of anger, orgasm, joy, and grief promises to bring a profound sense of wholeness and humanness. That's why so many people sought out Fritz Perls as he traveled throughout the country. But Perls quickly let people know that cathartic explosions could be attained only after increasing their consciousness of the phony games and roles they play and of the parts of themselves they disown. Patients need to become aware of how they are stuck in childish fantasies, of how they try to be something they are not.

Consciousness Raising

Consciousness raising in Gestalt therapy aims to liberate people from maya, from the phony, fantasy layer of existence. Because maya is an illusory mental world, a world of concepts, fantasies, and intellectual

- **May I feed you a sentence?**, in which the therapist asks permission to repeat and try on for size a statement about the patient that the therapist feels is particularly significant for the patient

Gestalt therapists do not interpret what clients say while participating in Gestalt work. Interpretation is seen as a representation of the traditional therapist's maya—the therapist's fantasy that the real meaning of a client and the client's world can be found in a favorite theory rather than in the client's present experience. It is just another form of one-upmanship. It is a way for therapists to convince clients that they should listen to the magnificent mind of the therapist rather than to their own senses. In practice, however, the use of *May I feed you a sentence?* comes awfully close to straight interpretations, although Gestaltists prefer to see this exercise as feedback in which the client is free to actively spit out the therapist's message if it doesn't fit.

Gestalt therapists raise clients' consciousness by allowing the clients' own eyes and ears to serve as a source of feedback. Clients are already aware of the sentences they have spoken, so Gestalt therapists do not reflect their clients' words as would Rogerian therapists. Gestalt therapists are more attuned to clients' nonverbal expressions—the quality of their voices, their posture, and their movements. Gestalt therapists feed back what they see or hear, especially what they see as bodily blocks to awareness. They ask clients not only to attend to their nonverbal expressions, such as their arms folded across their chest, but also to "become" their arms in order to express how they are tensing up the muscles to keep from opening up the feelings in their hearts. With the assistance of these action-oriented exercises, clients develop a deeper awareness that emerges from the depths of their bodies rather than off the top of their heads.

Catharsis

As clients become increasingly aware of their phony games, as they become more aware of their bodily resistances and phobic avoidance of the here and now, they are less likely to run from themselves. The fear of being themselves, however, can bring them to an impasse. They will want to communicate to the therapist that they are unable to continue on their own, that the therapist must take over for them or they will go crazy, panic, or terminate treatment. They try to convince the therapist that their catastrophic expectations are real and not just residual childhood fantasies. By pressing ahead, Gestalt therapists communicate through their actions that they believe clients do indeed have the inner strength to continue on past the impasse into their areas of deadness. Through sensitively selected exercises, clients begin to reown those parts of their personality that were sacrificed in the name of roles and games. Clients can begin to release all of the emotions that others will not love or approve of them if they are truly human.

The Client's Work

Cathartic releases require that clients take responsibility for continuing in therapy when they most want to run. The therapist will not try to talk them into staying in the hot seat if they feel it is getting too hot; they can and often do leave before the fireworks begin. If clients do stay in the hot seat, they must be responsible for throwing themselves into the suggested exercises and not playing passively.

If clients are prepared to take back and own what has been dead within, then they must be willing to participate in **Gestalt dream work**. Dreams are used in Gestalt therapy because they represent a spontaneous part of personality. Dreams are the time and place in which people can express all parts of themselves that have been disowned in the rat race to succeed at daily roles. For dreams to be cathartic, clients cannot just talk about their dreams; they must act them out. Clients are encouraged to "become" each detail of a dream, no matter how insignificant it may seem, in order to give expression to the richness of their personality. Only when we become as rich and as spontaneous as our dreams can we be healthy and whole again.

At a time when I (JOP) was preoccupied with my academic promotion and tenure, I found myself unable to experience any joy, not even the joy of sex. I sought the assistance of a friend who is a Gestalt therapist, and she asked me to conjure up a daydream rather than a dream. The daydream that emerged spontaneously was of skiing. She asked me to be the mountain, and I began to experience how warm I was when I was at my base. As I got closer to my top, what looked so beautiful was also very cold and frozen. She asked me to be the snow, and I expressed how hard and icy I could be near the top. People tripped over me there and were unable to cut through me because of how hard I was. But near the bottom people ran over me easily and wore me out. When we finished, I did not feel like crying or shouting; I felt like skiing. So I went, leaving my articles and books behind. In the sparkle of the snow and the sun, I realized again what Goethe had suggested through Faust: Our joy in living emerges through deeds and not through words. In my rush to succeed, I was committing one of the cardinal sins against myself—the sin of not being active.

Because catharsis in Gestalt therapy occurs primarily as a result of clients' expressing their inner experiences, such as their dreams, we can talk about the process as a form of **corrective emotional experiencing**. Gestalt therapy also entails **dramatic relief**, inasmuch as it is often conducted in groups or workshops; the corrective emotional experiences of the person on the hot seat serve as cathartic releases for the people who are actively observing what is occurring there.

The empty-chair dialogue pioneered by Perls and systematized by his followers demonstrates the therapeutic value of dramatic relief followed by a corrective emotional experiencing.

The empty chair is used when emotional memories of other people trigger the reexperiencing of unresolved emotional reactions: for example, **unfinished business** with a dead parent or unavailable ex-spouse. The client is to express feelings fully to the imagined significant other, such as an alcoholic parent, in an empty chair. This act helps remobilize the client's suppressed needs and give full expression to them, thereby empowering the client to separate emotionally from the other. The critical components of the resolution of the unfinished business appear to be the arousal of intense emotions, the declaration of a need, and a shift in the view of the other person (Greenberg et al., 1994).

The Therapist's Work

Because catharsis in Gestalt therapy can be very dramatic, we can conceive of the therapist's work as beginning with setting the stage for the event. The group waits with anticipation for someone to step forward to fill the emotionally charged hot seat. The therapist's attention is then focused like a spotlight on the client. The therapist suggests that the best scene for now is some particular exercise—let's say, dream work. The script is created mostly by the client, who decides which dream to act out. Once the client enters the scene, the therapist is like a director who is prepared to help the client live, rather than just play a part in, the dramatic exercise.

Like a good director, the Gestalt therapist will observe carefully and listen for a **process diagnosis**—the emergence of markers of particular types of affective problems with which the client is currently struggling, such as splits between two parts of the self (Greenberg, 1995). When a marker emerges, the therapist will suggest a specific in-session experiment or task to facilitate conflict resolution. Although Perls was able to do much of this automatically, contemporary Gestalt therapists have tried to delineate specific markers for specific in-session experiments. The emergence of splits is a marker for a two-chair dialogue, and a client expression of genuine vulnerability is a marker for empathic affirmation.

Gestalt therapists must also be aware of times when clients are trying to avoid the pain and fear of taking off their masks. Therapists try to block these avoidances by providing feedback and directing the client's attention to avoidance maneuvers, such as expressing important parts of a dream in a soft voice. If feedback alone does not produce change, then the Gestalt therapist will challenge clients to put more of themselves into the exercises, like a famous director challenging actors to give their best performance. Challenging clients to be more intense is especially effective in our competitive society, where people are so geared to meet any challenge. "OK, try it again with a fuller voice!" the Gestaltist might yell out. Such challenges also communicate the therapist's belief that clients do indeed have the inner resources to throw themselves more fully into the work, even when they are facing frightening or embarrassing scenes.

The Gestalt therapist can use other theater techniques to intensify the situation. Clients may be challenged to use the **repetition or exaggeration** game (Levitsky & Perls, 1970) until the true affect is expressed. Exaggeration or repetition is exemplified in the following excerpt from Perls (1969a, p. 293):

Fritz: Now talk to your Top Dog! Stop nagging.

Jane: (loud, pained) Leave me alone.

Fritz: Yah, again.

Jane: Leave me alone.

Fritz: Again.

Jane: (screaming it and crying) Leave me alone!

Fritz: Again.

Jane: (she screams it, a real blast) Leave me alone! I don't have to do what you say! (still crying) I don't have to be that good! I don't have to be in this chair! I don't have to. You make me. You make me come here! (screams) Aarhh! You make me pick my face (crying), that's what you do. (screams and cries) Aarhh! I'd like to kill you.

Fritz: Say this again.

Jane: I'd like to kill you.

Fritz: Again.

Jane: I'd like to *kill* you.

Gestalt therapists also direct clients to change their lines toward a more emotional and responsible direction, following the rule of using "I" language (Levitsky & Perls, 1970). Fritz Perls (1969a, p. 115) demonstrates this direction with Max.

Max: I feel the tenseness in my stomach and in my hands.

Fritz: *The* tenseness. Here we've got a noun. Now *the* tenseness is a noun. Now change the noun, the thing, into a verb.

Max: I am tense. My hands are tense.

Fritz: Your hands are tense. They have nothing to do with you.

Max: I am tense.

Fritz: You are tense. How are you tense? What are you doing?

Max: I am tensing myself.

Fritz: That's it.

An outstanding therapist like Perls is also able to use comic relief to reduce tension and humor to release joy. An example of comic relief occurred with a client who was plagued by an incredible inferiority complex. He felt uglier than everyone and more inadequate than anyone. After several sessions of tense psychotherapy he said, "I hope you don't misunderstand this, but I'm beginning to feel inferior to everyone but you." I (JCN) spontaneously responded, "That makes me feel real good." He laughed and I laughed and after awhile he said, "You don't know how good it feels to say that to someone."

The creative process in Gestalt therapy means the clinician will be an artist, not a scientist or a technician (Zinker, 1991). Fritz was admired for his artistic spontaneity, including his humor, which emerged in his workshops. Perhaps it is in humor that it is most obvious that a Gestalt therapist cannot predetermine the steps of effective therapy. For humor to be effective, the therapist must be free to be spontaneous, to capture the moment in creative humor.

Therapeutic Content
Intrapersonal Conflicts

The most important problems for Gestaltists are conflicts within the individual, such as those between Top Dog and Under Dog, between the person's social self and natural self, or between the disowned parts of the person and the catastrophic expectations that keep the person from expressing polarities that may meet with disapproval or rejection. Although Perls conducted Gestalt therapy in groups, his therapy was not a group treatment in which the important content is the relationship between people in the group. Perls's therapy was principally individual treatment occurring in a group setting. The important content occurs within the individual as he or she acts out Gestalt exercises that bring an enhanced awareness and a cathartic release. Other individuals in the workshop relate to the person on the hot seat vicariously rather than directly.

Anxiety and Defenses

Anxiety is the gap between the now and then, the here and there (Perls, 1969a). Whenever we leave the reality of now and become preoccupied with the future, we experience anxiety. If we are anticipating future performances, such as exams, speeches, or therapy sessions, then our anxiety is nothing more than stage fright. How will I perform on the exam? How will my speech go over? What will I do with that difficult client? We can also experience anxious anticipation over wonderful things that will happen: I just can't wait for that vacation to come! Many people fill this gap between the now and the future with all types of planned activities, repetitive jobs, and insurance policies to make the future predictable. These people try to replace anxiety with the security of sameness, but in the process they lose the richness of future possibilities. In a rapidly changing society, people clinging to the status quo become more and more panicky about the changing future.

For Perls, the solution to anxiety is obvious: Live in the here and now, not in the gap. By learning to be fully in the present, clients can transform anxiety into excitement.

Most people, however, avoid direct and immediate contact with the here and now through a variety of defensive maneuvers (Perls et al., 1951; Polster & Polster, 1973).

- **Projectors** distort experiences of themselves and their world by attributing the disowned parts of themselves to others in the environment. They avoid the excitement of their own sexuality, for example, by perceiving others, such as therapists, as being preoccupied with sex.
- **Introjectors** appear to take in the world, but in a passive and nondiscriminating manner. They never integrate and assimilate new experiences into their personal identity. They are the gullible oral characters who swallow anything others tell them.
- **Retroflectors** withdraw from the environment by turning back on themselves what they

would like to do to someone else, or by doing to themselves what they would like someone else to do to them. A woman who would have loved to chew out her mother, to take one example, avoided the risk of explosion by chronically grinding her teeth.

- **Deflectors** avoid direct contact by acting or reacting in a chronically off-target manner. They may go off on tangents when talking, speak in generalities to avoid emotion-laden specifics, or in other ways fail to get to the point of an interaction. Deflectors can avoid an impact from others, including therapists, by experiencing themselves as bored, confused, or in the wrong place.

Perls (1969a) emphasized how often thinking is used as a means of avoiding the here and now. Perls agreed with Freud's statement *Denken ist Probearbeit*—thinking is trial work, or as Perls prefers, thinking is rehearsing. Thinking is a means-whereby we prepare ourselves for social role-playing. Perls (1969a) suggests that most people play two kinds of intellectual games. The comparing game, or "more than" game, is a form of one-upmanship in which intellect is used to convince others that "My house is better than yours," "I'm greater than you," "I'm more miserable than you," "My therapy is better than yours," or "My theory is more valid than yours." The other intellectualizing game is the fitting game, in which we fit other people or other therapies into our favorite concepts of how the world is supposed to be. Or even worse, we may struggle to fit ourselves into our favorite concept of what we are supposed to be.

Self-Esteem

Shaky self-esteem is not the cause of neurosis but one of its consequences. As long as our esteem remains dependent on the approval and evaluation of others, we will remain preoccupied with what others think of us and with trying to meet their expectations. A solid sense of self-esteem is a natural reward of discovering that we have the inner strength to be self-supportive. Mental health professionals who perform supportive psychotherapy, which includes trying to shore up their patients' shaky self-esteem, in the long run contribute to the patients' low esteem by implicitly telling them that they do not have the inner resources to support themselves. On the other hand, the tough stance of the Gestalt therapist, who refuses to give unnecessary support even when the patient is crying for it, is implicitly telling patients that they have the inner strength to stand on their own. By tapping into that inner strength, clients will find a solid basis on which to feel good about themselves.

Responsibility

We have already seen that accepting responsibility for one's life is a critical part of being a healthy, mature human being. Developmentally, people avoid taking responsibility either because they were spoiled and find it easier to manipulate others into taking care of them or because they fear parental disapproval if they respond in a manner too different from what their parents expect. Unlike existentialists, Perls does not see avoidance of responsibility as deriving from inherent existential anxiety. For Perls, decisions about end-goals emerge naturally when one is centered as a natural organism. Problems with decisions occur only when people are not centered.

With a source of direction so natural, there is little need for existential guilt in the Gestalt system. Most of what people call guilt is actually unexpressed resentment. Guilt over premarital sex, for example, is frequently unexpressed resentment toward one's parents or church for trying to keep one from satisfying the natural sexual end-goals. Express the resentment either directly or in an empty-chair exercise, and the guilt will soon be gone.

Perls does not directly address the responsibility of living up to a commitment that one has made. He does make it clear that when he talks about responsibility he is not talking about obligations. Because a mature person does not accept responsibility for others, perhaps there are no obligations for a person who lives in the now other than to be true to oneself. For people living in the now, in the moment, making commitments is future oriented and foolish because we cannot predict that at some future point it will be most important to act on a commitment made in the past.

Interpersonal Conflicts

Intimacy and Sexuality

Genuine intimacy is exciting and plentiful from the Gestalt perspective (Luthman, 1972). Contrary to convention, intimate relationships begin with a commitment to ourselves, not to another. We are committed to presenting ourselves as we are, not pretending to be something the other expects or prefers. If who we really are is not liked by another, then it is best for us to learn that early rather than waste our time on a relationship that is bound to fail no matter how much we pretend otherwise.

As we relate, we accept differences as opportunities for growth, not as reasons for conflict. Differences are bound to bring frustration, but for Gestaltists frustration is welcome as a stimulus for further maturation. As we relate, we also accept that what we like and dislike is a statement about us and not a put-down of our partner. If we don't like our partner's cooking, for example, that is a statement about our taste and not a reason for saying that our partner is a lousy cook.

As differences emerge, we must be willing to stay with our feelings until all of them are out in the open. We can then make compromises up to the limits or boundaries of who we are as individuals. We cannot compromise ourselves away just to keep a relationship going, because such compromises will generate smoldering resentment that will eventually poison the relationship. Our limits

should not be seen as attempts to control the other person, but rather as the contours of who we are. We may find that once all of our feelings are in the open, neither of us can compromise far enough to allow the relationship to continue. Such a discovery is not a reason to blame or to hate, but rather to accept that we simply cannot make it together. On the other hand, if we do make it together, we can love even more because we are with a person who is strong enough to be authentic first and our partner second.

Although Perls has written little about sex, others (e.g., Otto & Otto, 1972; Rosenberg, 1973) have presented a series of exercises directed at helping sex to be a more total or holistic experience. The Gestalt emphasis on being in touch with our bodies, on getting back to our senses, and on breaking out of old habits and responding spontaneously with our whole organism are critical in freeing people to experience how sex can be so much more than genital orgasm. Learning more integrated breathing, more natural pelvic movements, how to make fantasies reality, how to enjoy the humor in sex, and how to explode into orgasm are part of making sex a total experience.

Communication

Because Perls worked mainly with individuals and not with ongoing relationships, he had little to say about communication conflicts. He does seem to suggest that most communication is part of social role-playing. People chatter away about how great they are, how important or miserable or meager their roles in life are. As an action-oriented therapist, Perls prefers to get away from so much talk and to let real feelings be expressed in action, such as dancing to communicate joy or weeping to express sorrow. Perls was certainly astute at helping people become aware of their nonverbal communication, of what their body was attempting to say in its various postures and movements.

When we must resort to words, conflicts can be kept to a minimum by following several rules of Gestalt therapy. First, we should communicate in the imperative form, because the demand is the only real form of communication for Perls (1970). When we ask someone a question, for example, we are actually placing a demand on that person. Instead of saying, "Would you like to go to the movies tonight?" we should be direct and say, "Let's go to the movies tonight!" When we use direct demands, the person with whom we are communicating knows exactly where we are and what we want. That person then can choose to respond directly to our demands, rather than to a question. Second, because what we have to say is really a statement about us and not about the other, we should own our statements by talking mainly in "I" language. Rather than say, "You really make me angry because of how rotten you treat me," we would say, "I am angry because I let you treat me so rotten. From now on, treat me with more consideration!"

Hostility

Problems with hostility are boundary problems. Those aspects of the world that we identify with and that we include within our ego boundaries are experienced as friendly, lovable, and open to our kindness. Those parts of the world that we experience as outside of our boundaries are alien, threatening, and subject to our hostility. White Americans who identify with white supremacy, for example, and exclude African Americans from their ego boundaries feel free to direct hostility toward blacks and to be at war with them. For other whites, who identify with the diversity and equality in our society, racists become enemies who are outside their ego boundaries and fair game for their hostility.

In intimate relationships, we expand our boundaries to include the other within our identity and create an experience of "we-ness." But even in intimate relationships, we usually cannot accept all aspects of another because we do not own all the aspects of ourselves. What we are most likely to be hostile toward in our intimates are their qualities that remind us of what we have disowned and projected outside of our boundaries. As the old saying goes, "We despise that in others which we fear most in ourselves." If we are hostile toward the tardiness of a friend, we should look within to see if we have disowned certain desires to not live our lives by the clock.

If we do not express resentments toward our intimates, we will begin to close off communication with them out of fear that openness might lead to expression of our hostility. We have failed to bring closure to an issue, and the resentment is an important signal that a Gestalt is pressing for completion. Unfinished business is then at hand. In psychotherapy, clients are encouraged to express intensely the hostility and resentment toward the empty chair that represents intimates with whom they are having trouble communicating. After releasing their hostility, clients begin to forgive their intimates for not being perfect so that they can begin to forgive themselves for not being perfect.

Control

Immature people are constantly involved in battles over interpersonal control. They either play a helpless, sick role, trying to manipulate others to take care of them, or play a perfectionist, Top Dog role in which they assume the responsibility for trying to get others to see the light and be more like them. They are acting out on an interpersonal level their intrapersonal pathology in which a constant struggle for control occurs between the Top Dog and Under Dog. Only with maturation and integration can people give up the constant struggle for control and live by the Gestalt creed (Perls, 1970, p. 1):

I do my own thing and you do your thing.
I am not in this world to live up to your
    expectations,
And you are not in this world to live up to mine.
You are you, and I am I,
And if by chance we find each other, it's beautiful.
If not, it can't be helped.

Individuo-Social Conflicts

Adjustment versus Transcendence

Gestalt is a therapy of transcendence. Adjustment to society might have been an acceptable treatment goal at some time in the past when society was more stable and healthy. But like many critics of modern society, Perls (1970, p. 23) says, "I believe we are living in an insane society and that you only have the choice either to participate in this collective psychosis or to take risks and become healthy and perhaps also crucified."

To some extent, all healthy individuals will experience themselves as outside the boundaries of society. They will experience themselves as aliens, always potential targets for the violence of society. Alienation is thus the condition of the mature person, of the fully aware person, as long as society remains insane.

To adjust to a brutalizing society means to give up more and more of yourself (Denes-Radomisli, 1976). To adjust to riding in the New York subways, for example, we are forced to give up our sense of humanity, deserving of courtesy and boundaries. To be relatively comfortable in such a situation, we have to cover or deny our awareness of being mistreated and of mistreating others. With successful adjustment, we will soon be unable to feel human at all and get along just fine as a role or a robot.

Unfortunately, the two alternatives for most people are alienation from society, in which the healthy person is one of the strangers in a strange land, and alienation from oneself, in which the unhealthy person is self-estranged. The final resolution for Perls was to seek transcendence by creating a Gestalt community in Canada in which a limited number of healthy individuals could both be themselves and be integrated within a community of whole people.

Impulse Control

Organismic impulses need not be controlled but need to be completed. Seeking food when hungry and sex when aroused are not dangerous to the individual; rather, completing these organismic needs is what creates an individual. These impulses are a biological source of motivation and direction that allow individuals to rise above being just a social role. These biological sources of self-direction are relatively culture-free, and individuals can trust in their bodies, rather than social conformity to an insane society, to lead them to a healthy life. If people were raised to trust their bodily messages, we could have a society of free and fulfilled people who let each other be rather than a society of rapists and ravagers.

Beyond Conflict to Fulfillment

Meaning in Life

The meaning that comes from living in the now is found in the awareness that every second in our one existence is being lived afresh. No fuller life can be imagined. No regrets occur among those jumping into the stream of the present, because regrets are the plague of those stuck in the past. There are no preoccupations about the future, because we trust that our healthiest future emerges out of a present in which we complete our most urgent Gestalts. There is only one authentic goal for the future: to actualize ourselves as responsible and whole human beings. If that is not meaningful enough, then why not try to be a kangaroo or a king?

Ideal Individual

The ideal outcome for Gestalt therapy is people discovering that they do not and never really did need a psychotherapist. Ideal clients accept that, despite all their manipulations to the contrary, they possess the inner strength to stand on their own and be themselves. Such individuals have discovered the center of their lives, the awareness of being grounded in oneself. In being centered, they take full responsibility for the direction of their lives and do not blame their parents or their past.

From their core they find the strength to take the risks of being spontaneous and unpredictable, including the risks of being ostracized or crucified if that is the ultimate consequence of being themselves. In return for risking, the ideal individual earns the freedom to be creative, to be funny, to dance with joy, to be overwhelmed with grief, to be outraged with anger, and to be totally engaged in orgasm.

Therapeutic Relationship

In Rogerian terms, Perls certainly endorsed the need for therapists to be more congruent—or, as he would prefer, more mature—than clients. If therapists are to be self-supporting enough to resist clients' pressures to rescue them, therapists must have developed adequate maturity in their own lives. It is also a rule of Gestalt therapy (Levitsky & Perls, 1970) that the relationship should be an *I–Thou* (*Ich und Du*) relationship (Buber, 1958), or what Rogers would call a genuine encounter.

In practice, however, Perls has been criticized by his colleagues (e.g., Kempler, 1973) for frequently playing the Top Dog, thereby forcing the client into an Under Dog or patient role. Kempler is certainly correct that in the available transcripts of Perls's work, the personal Perls, or Perls as an "I," is missing. The very format of the hot seat puts clients in an Under Dog position in which they are directed in exercises by the Top Dog therapist. When clients confronted Perls to look at his own behavior, he would counter with a psychoanalytic type of move that forced the clients to look at their own motives for making such suggestions.

Both in theory and in practice, Perls agreed with Rogers on the therapist's need to respond with accurate empathy. In Gestalt work, clinicians must be capable of experiencing the projections that clients are placing on them or the parts of the clients' personalities being disowned and then accurately feed back these blind spots.

Neither in theory nor in practice did Perls accept the Rogerian concept of unconditional positive regard. For Perls, such behavior on the therapist's part encourages infantilization. Patients must learn in treatment that if they act in immature or irresponsible ways, then mature people, including psychotherapists, will react with anger, impatience, boredom, or other negative responses. Put another way, Gestalt therapy is a **safe emergency** (Zinker, 1977). It is the place where a patient, in a relationship of safety and trust, is nevertheless challenged to destructure ingrained patterns of awareness and behavior. The Gestalt therapist prompts the patient to produce, not just talk about, a new self while dealing with a real therapist in the here and now.

At its best, the Gestalt therapeutic relationship is part of both the process and the content of therapy. As part of the process of being in the here and now, the therapist insists on remaining present-centered regardless of the patient's attempts to flee from the now. Therapists block immature efforts to make them take over the life of a client who is playing helpless, crazy, suicidal, or seductive. Through such frustrations in the relationship, clients are forced to grow, to become more aware of the games they are playing to remain unaware and immature. Gestalt therapists use their own awareness to realize when patients are attempting to avoid parts of who they are and to block avoidance by introducing exercises or exhortations designed to break through the patient's blocks.

As part of the content of Gestalt therapy, clients' projections of disowned parts of their personalities onto the therapist are centrally important. Patient enactments of developmental immaturities and their various defenses are also confronted and frustrated in the context of the relationship. In addition, to the extent that Gestalt therapists encourage a Top Dog/Under Dog relationship, they provide a here-and-now battleground for clients to fight out their conflicts with authority and with their conscience or internalized parent.

To the extent that Gestalt books suggest people can radically expand their consciousness and cathartically release their energies by participating in the prescribed exercises, the books imply a therapeutic relationship is not necessary. No one disputes that a mature relationship enhances the effectiveness of Gestalt work, but the relationship may not be essential for healthy growth to occur through Gestalt exercises. In part, disagreement on the necessity of the therapeutic relationship in Gestalt work revolves around the definition of "relationship." Gestalt work, as we have seen, does not require that the participants maintain a relationship in ongoing therapy together, nor that they have a therapeutic relationship before working together in a workshop. The requisite relationship, in Perls's eyes, is a state of common ground or attunement between a client and a therapist living in the here and now. This relationship or attunement *is* fundamental to the therapeutic process, and exercises without this relationship will likely be hollow, superficial, and even potentially harmful to the client (Forfar, 1990).

Did Perls desire an empathic and genuine bond to guide the appropriate use of technique? Absolutely. Did Perls insist that an ongoing relationship was necessary for growth? No.

Perls himself became concerned late in his life that many protégés were attempting only to learn techniques, instead of letting their work naturally emerge out of who they were and from an authentic therapist–client relationship (Kempler, 1973). But Perls had unwittingly contributed, both in his writings and in his workshops, to the belief that the Gestalt exercises were more essential to the content and process of Gestalt therapy than an authentic relationship was. And, as mentioned, so much of Perls's technique came from his idiosyncratic personality that it is hard to separate the two (Wagner-Moore, 2004).

More recent considerations of the Gestalt relationship have amplified the need for Perls's concept of authentic **contact** (Wheeler, 1990; Woldt & Toman, 2005). Contact is the appreciation of differences in direct exchanges between persons and groups of persons (Perls, 1969a). Unlike the psychoanalytic object relations theory (Chapter 3), contact does not yet designate an object or another person. Rather, the term designates a sensorimotor pattern, ways of feeling and moving, a going toward and taking from (Robine, 1991). This contact plays a huge part in the creation of the therapeutic bond—empathically sensing each other's emotions and existence, authentically responding to the other in the here and now, sensitively making a connection in the I–Thou tradition, revealing the personhood of the therapist, and respectfully acknowledging the differences between the two existences now in contact.

This renewed emphasis on contact in the Gestalt relationship softens the harsh, confrontational edge that some students experience in it and reminds us that Perls was capable of immense sensitivity to pain when clients confronted it directly. What's more, the emphasis on relational contact brings Gestalt therapy closer, in theory and in practice, to the desired therapeutic relationship of other systems in the humanistic tradition, particularly the person-centered and existential perspectives.

Practicalities of Gestalt Therapy

Perls said that to do his psychotherapy, all he needed was a chair for the hot seat, an empty chair for the client's role-play, a client willing to enter the hot seat, and an audience or group willing to participate in the work between therapist and client. Perls seldom saw clients in an office, especially in his most famous years. Most of his work was done in workshops, lectures, or seminars under the sun at Esalen. Many of his clients had only one clinical encounter with Perls, and yet the number of people who believed Perls had an impact on them is amazing. Apparently just watching Perls work with another person could produce a dramatic impact.

Gestalt therapists still prefer to conduct psychotherapy in a group setting, even though their work occurs primarily between the therapist and the person in the hot seat, not among group members. Our impression of the literature, however, is that the proportion of Gestalt therapy now conducted in an individual format far surpasses that performed in a group format. Increasingly, too, Gestalt therapists work with couples and families (see Greenberg & Johnson, 1988; Wheeler & Backman, 1994; Woldt & Toman, 2005).

Most Gestalt therapists tend to see their clients weekly, although as a rule they prefer at least 2 hours with a group and frequently longer, including marathon sessions. In Perls's workshops, clients did not pay extra for the therapy they received while in the hot seat, but rather just paid the entrance fee to the workshop or lecture. It was the client's responsibility to secure therapy by requesting or assertively taking the hot seat.

In terms of professional disciplines, Gestalt therapists include psychologists, social workers, psychiatrists, counselors, and educators. Although many tend to be more informal about their Gestalt training, the more respectable route includes a minimum of 1 year of intensive training at one of the Gestalt training institutes. Many major cities now have a Gestalt institute, the most famous probably being the Gestalt Institute of Cleveland, which was established in 1954 by Laura Perls, Isadore Fromm, and Paul Goodman.

As a group, Gestalt therapists are also more informal about patient screening and outcome follow-up, following Perls's precedent that it is the client's responsibility to decide to enter or terminate treatment. In fact, Perls and colleagues (1951, p. 255) wrote, "We present nothing that you cannot verify for yourself in terms of your own behavior."

The length of Gestalt therapy tends to vary considerably, from a single workshop session to weekly sessions for 6 months, but tends toward the briefer end. Several elements of Gestalt therapy contribute to its brief and focused nature (Harman, 1995). For one, initial development of a contract with the client narrows the focus on what conflicts the client would most like to resolve. For another, the here-and-now focus uses the present as the point of reference, as contrasted to extended analysis of the there-and-then. For still another, the active and directive techniques, such as the empty-chair dialogue to resolve unfinished business (Paivio & Greenberg, 1995), can bring conflicts into full awareness and move them toward resolution in just a few sessions. Brief Gestalt therapy appears to be the rule rather than the exception, just as it was originally with Perls.

Training in Gestalt is experiential. The medium is personal therapeutic work emphasizing individual awareness, emotional growth, and attendant personality change. The idea is that the individual grows as a result of contact with others, and this boundary contact nourishes and triggers a creative process. Personal development is thus integrated with professional training. Much of the learning occurs in therapy groups in which fellow students offer themselves as real-life clients to the therapists and the others to observe. This essentially comprises circular learning, in which individuals learn and teach each other by doing and observing (Napoli & Wolk, 1989). Some newer work attempts to teach the skills of Gestalt therapy in a more systematic fashion through a combined didactic-experiential and skill-training program (Elliott et al., 2004).

Experiential Therapies

Experiential therapy refers to a broad class of psychosocial treatments in the humanistic tradition that emerged in the 1960s, largely as a reaction against and alternative to the then-predominant psychoanalytic and behavioral perspectives. Gestalt is widely recognized as the earliest and most popular form of experiential therapy.

The core construct of personality and the central axis of change is therapeutic **experiencing** of emotions. Personality is understood in terms of potentials for inner "ways of being" or experiencing, which is a mode of apprehension characterized by its immediate, holistic, contextual, and bodily nature (Bohart, 1993a). Accessing deeper emotions and bodily states is the precious jewel of experiential therapy; it is what the patient can become, and it is the criterion for the success of experiential therapy (Mahrer & Fairweather, 1993).

The boundaries of experiential therapy are blurred at times—some include person-centered in this category—but we will restrict our coverage in this chapter to those therapies identifying themselves by the moniker "experiential." Among the prominent examples of experiential therapies are the symbolic-experiential family therapy of Carl Whitaker (Whitaker & Bumberry, 1988; Whitaker & Keith, 1981), the experiential therapy of Alvin Mahrer (1989, 1996), and the **focusing method** of Eugene Gendlin (1981, 1996).

Focusing therapy guides clients to enter a special kind of present-centered awareness, quite unlike our daily awareness. It is open, turned inward, centered on the present and on bodily sensations. When doing focusing, the client silently asks, "How am I now?" and stays attuned to that experience. Supported by a long series of research studies conducted by Gene Gendlin and colleagues at the University of Chicago, it bears a strong resemblance to the ideal consciousness prized by both Fritz Perls and Carl Rogers, with whom Gendlin studied and collaborated. They observed that the clients who did well in therapy could turn their attention inward to their body and label the impact of their feelings, beliefs, and worldviews. In so doing, clients could determine

what they genuinely sought and devise creative solutions to their problems. Teaching focusing, then, enables clients to recognize their felt meanings, process their experiences, and emerge with successful resolutions.

Emotion-Focused Therapy

By far the most researched and influential experiential therapy of late has been emotion-focused therapy (EFT), developed by Leslie Greenberg. In fact, it was originally known as **process-experiential therapy** as an alternative to Gestalt therapy.

Leslie S. Greenberg (1945–) worshipped math and physics, but once he became a mechanical and industrial engineer, he was unhappy. His early occupational dissatisfaction presaged his clinical belief that too many people cut themselves off from their feelings, from what makes them feel human and alive. Greenberg left Johannesburg, South Africa, for political as well as educational reasons and entered the counseling PhD program at York University in Canada. There, in the context of the inner exploration taking place in the 1960s, he became a student of Laura Rice, who had been trained at the Chicago Counseling Center with Carl Rogers.

Originally trained as a client-centered counselor, Greenberg subsequently trained as a Gestalt therapist at the Gestalt Institute of Toronto and as a family therapist at the Mental Research Institute in Palo Alto, California. His EFT combines elements of client-centered and Gestalt therapy, and his **emotionally focused couples therapy** applies his approach to couples and families. He spent 10 years as a professor at the University of British Columbia and then returned "home" to York University as professor of psychology. There, as a prolific author and leading voice of experiential therapy, Les Greenberg combines his passion for scientific investigation with his commitment to EFT for individuals and couples.

A system of psychotherapy begins with a theory of personality and psychopathology. EFT therapists believe humans are profoundly shaped and organized by emotional experiences and that emotion is the creative and organizing force in people's lives. Many psychotherapies help people suppress or manage their emotions, as though they are enemy combatants, but experiential theory values emotions as distinctive and growth-enhancing functions of homo sapiens. Emotions are the great captains of our lives (Greenberg, 2012).

The experiential theory of psychopathology stands in clear contrast to those of interpersonal therapy (Chapter 7) and cognitive therapy (Chapter 10). Interpersonal therapy contends that depression is caused by interpersonal problems, and the therapeutic emphasis is to restructure current interpersonal relations. Cognitive therapy contends that negative thoughts about the self, world, and future are the key determinants of psychopathology and that therapy should involve changing the thinking patterns. Although interpersonal and cognitive factors often are aspects of psychopathology such as depression, experiential therapy contends emotional processes underlie both of them. Thus, modifying negative beliefs and interpersonal interactions will be useful but not as useful as changing self-organization based on emotional processing. The emotional schema is the fundamental unit of experience.

EFT seeks to enhance client's emotional intelligence, which involves the recognition of one's own and others' emotional states to solve problems and regulate behavior. EFT also helps patients with **affect regulation** (cognitive, affective, and behavioral strategies used to increase adaptive emotions and decrease maladaptive ones) and with transforming their emotional memories. The goal is change in self-organization via increase in emotion utilization, enhanced affect regulation, and the transformation of emotion memory. More simply, EFT helps people become aware of what they are feeling, find better ways of coping with their feelings, and transform old emotional responses into new ones.

These goals are met in EFT through an interesting combination of consciousness raising, catharsis (corrective emotional experience), and choosing (self-liberation or a commitment to a new way of being). EFT blends a Rogerian, person-centered relationship with more active, Gestalt interventions, such as two-chair work and empty-chair dialogues. Both the therapeutic relationship and specific change processes are curative.

A warm, empathic relationship is crucial to accessing emotion and transforming it by new relational acceptance. From birth into adulthood, emotion is soothed by the presence of a responsive other. EFT therapists attempt to consistently validate clients, letting them know they have been heard. The therapist serves as an emotion coach (Greenberg, 2002), coaching clients to be more aware of their feelings, to regulate and transform them. To be a facilitative coach, the therapist must be rooted in listening and validating. Only from the base of empathy can the therapist know when to follow and when to suggest more active, Gestalt-based interventions.

Once a safe and strong therapeutic alliance has been established, therapists respond to particular client markers or verbal indications of specific conflicts. When the client presents a marker, such as self-critical conflicts, the therapist's work is to provide more directive methods. One client marker is the experience of splits, two parts of the self or personality in opposition, similar to what Perls called polarities of the self. The therapist will offer **two-chair work**—asking the client to alternate therapy chairs to express the oppositional emotions until a resolution of the split occurs. In the case of harsh self-criticism, the therapist guides one side of the client to express negative self-statements to the other side of the client, who then switches chairs and responds to the emotional criticism.

Another client marker is the expression of unfinished business with another person, now unavailable or deceased. Here, the therapist would use Perls's empty-chair dialogue to help the client resolve the unfinished business. The result is a nondirective, empathic relationship plus directive methods for specific emotional conflicts (Greenberg et al., 1993). EFT combines the styles of following and leading.

The clients' work is to experience, that is, to attend to their own bodily felt experiences and label their emotions. Clients who are cut off from their emotional experience are not as quick to complete therapy as those who enter with a capacity to experience. The number of sessions thus depends upon the person, but 16 sessions are probably the minimum dose for helping someone with depression through emotionally focused methods. More sessions, of course, are needed for patients with chronic and severe problems.

In the treatment of depression, EFT can be broken into four phases (Elliott et al., 2004). First is bonding, in which the therapist develops a strong empathic attunement with the client moment by moment. The person-centered relational conditions of empathy, genuineness, and positive regard are central in this phase. Second comes evoking and exploring emotions, the core of the emotion-focused work. Next comes constructing alternatives in which the participants generate adaptive emotions. Fourth and final is consolidation of new meaning. The client forms a new narrative based on experiential shift in core emotions.

In the 1980s, Greenberg and Susan Johnson expanded experiential therapy to relationships and formulated emotionally focused couples therapy. It focuses on the construction of the emotional experience and interpersonal drama of a distressed couple as it unfolds in the present moment. Johnson and Greenberg maintain that emotion organizes attachment bonds, and committed relationships are, of course, all about attachment (Greenberg & Johnson, 1988; Johnson, 2004).

Emotionally focused couples therapy distinguishes itself from other forms of couples work by its overriding emphasis on fostering two client capacities: attachment bond and emotions. Attachment is the fundamental unit of human relations, grounded in modern neuroscience and developmental psychology. Emotion is a powerful and often necessary agent of change, rather than a symptom to change. Thus, the overarching goals are to facilitate a more secure attachment bond and more constructive emotions that nourish both partners.

EFT for couples consists of three stages: de-escalation of the couple's negative cycle; restructuring of problematic interactions; and consolidation/integration (Johnson, 2004). The overarching goal is help couples become more aware of their negative interactions and to overcome them by establishing a more secure attachment. Each partner ultimately becomes a safety cue for the other, which reduces the experience of threat or vulnerability and enhances the ability to cope with stress. In this respect, the EFT therapist does not propose solutions but rather acts as a process consultant and emotional guide.

All told, Greenberg's EFT constitutes a vital and integrative therapy, emerging as a major alternative to Gestalt therapy but in the same experiential family. Particular advantages of EFT are that its operations have been codified in treatment manuals (Greenberg, 2002), it has been applied to couples therapy, it can be systematically taught (Elliott et al., 2004), and its effectiveness has been researched in several controlled trials.

Effectiveness of Experiential Therapies

As a humanistic approach, Gestalt therapy has not eagerly embraced the traditional scientific method of empirical research. As a growth-oriented approach,

Gestalt therapy has been evaluated largely for its enhancement of functioning, not recovery from symptoms. Compared to cognitive and behavioral treatments, there is little systematic research on the outcomes of Gestalt therapy, and the early research that has been conducted frequently concerns growth experiences, decisional conflicts, and nondiagnosable conditions.

Quantitative reviews conducted in the 1980s on the efficacy of Gestalt therapy are partially supportive. Across 475 studies examining various types of psychotherapy, Smith and colleagues (1980) found an overall effect size of 0.85, a large effect. Across 18 studies testing the efficacy of Gestalt therapy, the researchers found an effect size of 0.64, a number closer to the medium effect range. This effect size indicates that Gestalt therapy is consistently superior to no treatment but barely higher than placebo treatment (effect size = 0.56).

A series of careful meta-analyses over the years (Elliott et al., 2004, 2013) on the small amount of outcome research conducted on Gestalt therapy demonstrates it is superior to wait-list and no-treatment controls. No recent studies have compared it to an "active" placebo. In direct comparisons between Gestalt therapy and alternative psychotherapies, Gestalt therapy led to slightly lower gains (Greenberg et al., 1994). But when the investigator's theoretical allegiance is taken into account, those small differences fade away, and we are left with equivalent outcomes (Elliott et al., 2013).

Gestalt therapy has thus been found to be superior to no treatment but not to other tested systems of psychotherapy. Depending on one's perspective on the allegiance effect and clinical significance (as discussed in Chapter 3), Gestalt therapy is as effective or perhaps a bit less effective to tested cognitive and behavioral methods of therapy. Gestalt therapy has not been sufficiently researched with children, adolescents, or older adults to be included in those meta-analyses (Scogin et al., 2005; Weiss & Weisz, 1995a, 1995b; Weisz et al., 2004).

Turning to EFT, its results are consistently good compared to both no-treatment and alternative treatments (Elliott et al., 2013). In the early years, EFT and its earlier version, process-experiential therapy, were evaluated in studies concerning marital distress and decisional conflict, not diagnosable clinical populations (Reicherts, 1998). In recent years, randomized clinical trials have shown EFT is probably more effective than person-centered therapy and equally effective as cognitive-behavioral therapy in the treatment of clinical depression.

Two studies have reported that the addition of experiential methods to the client-centered relationship conditions resulted in greater patient changes at termination for depression (Goldman et al., 2006; Greenberg & Watson, 1998). At 18 months following treatment, EFT showed superior effects compared to client-centered therapy in terms of reduced symptoms and fewer depressive relapses (Ellison et al., 2009). Enhancing Rogers's empathic-relational therapy by adding specific experiential and gestalt-derived emotion-focused interventions definitely seems to lead to better results.

In a separate study, Watson and colleagues (2003) compared EFT and cognitive-behavioral therapy in a clinical trial of depression. The 66 clients' level of depression, self-esteem, and dysfunctional attitudes improved equally in both therapies after 16 sessions. Although outcomes were generally equivalent for the two treatments, there was a significantly greater decrease in interpersonal problems among clients receiving EFT than cognitive-behavioral therapy.

The effectiveness of experiential and Gestalt therapies remains a matter of controversy in academic settings. Many cognitive-behavioral faculty members assume that experiential therapies are inferior to cognitive-behavioral therapies on the basis of the earlier meta-analyses. But the small statistical superiority of cognitive-behavioral therapies is, in large part, the result of methodological factors—specifically the researcher **allegiance effect**

(Luborsky et al., 1999). That is, proponents of experiential therapies typically find substantial, positive effects compared to cognitive-behavioral therapies, whereas advocates of nonexperiential therapies typically find experiential approaches to be less effective than other approaches (Elliott et al., 2004). The researcher's theoretical allegiance is a strong predictor (effect size = 0.59) of whether experiential therapy is found to be as effective or less effective than alternative treatments. And when researcher allegiance is statistically controlled, differences between experiential and other therapies disappear (Elliott et al., 2004, 2013).

The effectiveness of emotionally focused couples therapy now seems established and beyond the dispute surrounding the allegiance effect. EFT with couples has been scientifically examined in at least eight studies, making it one of the most research-supported treatments for distressed couples. Couples receiving EFT experienced a 70% to 73% recovery rate from marital distress in 10 to 12 sessions. The controlled studies show that emotionally focused couples therapy is much more effective than no treatment and control groups (Johnson, 2004; Johnson et al., 1999), although it has not been extensively compared to other forms of couples treatment yet. The effects for couples appear to be stable over time (Halchuk et al., 2010), and EFT is now recognized as an evidence-based treatment for couple distress.

The comparative effectiveness of Gestalt and experiential therapies will probably be determined in the future by programmatic research aimed at identifying the particular people for whom it is most indicated. For example, in a series of studies, Beutler and colleagues (2005) examined the efficacy of a Gestalt-based group treatment that encourages affective arousal by intensifying awareness and facilitating unwanted emotions (Daldrup et al., 1988). The Gestalt-based treatment was compared to both cognitive therapy and a supportive/ self-directed therapy in groups of depressed outpatients who met weekly over 20 weeks.

As expected, the three treatments did not differ in overall effectiveness. However, also as expected, differential effectiveness emerged when the three treatments were cross-matched to compatible patients. Specifically, depressed patients who cope by acting out and projecting (the externalizers) tended to fare best in cognitive therapy because their personality dispositions collided with the introspective and awareness methods of the other treatments. By contrast, depressed patients who cope by using intrapunitive methods (the internalizers) tended to do better with Gestalt-based therapy. As further predicted, the directive treatments (cognitive therapy and Gestalt/experiential) were of greatest benefit to patients who had low resistance, whereas the self-directed treatment was more effective with highly resistant patients. Ensuing meta-analyses confirm these patterns: externalizing patients tend to do better with CBT, skill-building therapies while internalizing patients do better with insight-oriented and interpersonal treatments (Beutler, Harwood, Kimpara, et al., 2011); low resistance patients respond better to directive therapies while high resistance patients respond better to self-directive therapies (Beutler, Harwood, Michelson, et al., 2011).

In sum, Gestalt-based therapies are most effective for internalizing, low-resistant, overly socialized clients. This research conclusion perfectly describes the typical patients with whom Fritz Perls worked and excelled during the development of his system of psychotherapy.

Criticisms of Experiential Therapies
From a Cognitive-Behavioral Perspective

We must recognize that, at a societal level, the ultimate outcome of Gestalt therapy would be anarchy. "You do your thing and I do my thing" may sound romantic, but it is a shallow slogan that reinforces the development of narcissistic and egocentric individuals who have little reason to be concerned with others. Perls states directly that his ideal individual would not take responsibility for anyone else. What happens, then, to the socializing responsibility of parents? Is there any evidence that humans can live in relatively harmonious and secure societies if social expectations are rejected as consequences for helping to direct human behavior? Perls seems to forget that his work at Esalen was appealing to those who had already gone through a socialization process and tended to reject violence or force as means-whereby they satisfied such organismic end-goals as sex. Let the Gestaltists test their psychotherapy with undersocialized individuals, such as psychopathic prisoners, to see what kind of community they would create.

If it is not bad enough that there is pitifully little controlled outcome research on Perls's Gestalt therapy, then consider the sobering conclusion of a review on negative outcome in psychotherapy. A review of 46 studies on negative effects for adult, nonpsychotic patients in psychotherapy found that expressive-experiential therapies produce higher rates of deterioration than other psychotherapies (Mohr, 1995). So let us get this straight: Few research findings attest to Gestalt therapy's effectiveness, and convergent findings suggest its higher risk for negative effects. Not our idea of an evidence-based therapy!

From a Psychoanalytic Perspective

Where ego was, let there be id! The naive Gestaltist would like to deny that there are indeed biological impulses that can overwhelm both the individual's mental well-being and the social order. How would Gestaltists treat paranoid and other patients whose ego processes are in danger of being overwhelmed by rage? Encourage more rage? So much talk about responsibility, and yet the Gestaltists encourage professional irresponsibility by suggesting to potential patients that if

they want to go crazy or commit suicide, that's up to them. Such a philosophy may work fine in workshops filled with growth-seeking normal people. But it is certainly dangerous as an approach to a typical caseload of patients that includes people barely able to hold onto their sanity, let alone able to be mature, self-supporting humans.

From a Cultural Perspective

The emphasis in Gestalt therapy on awareness, self-support, and responsibility magnifies the role of the individual *qua* individual, separate from other people, often with little attention to important ongoing relationships and cultural systems (Saner, 1989; Shepherd, 1976). Isolation and occasional dalliances with others are the probable results. Who will tend to families and communities? Surely not the Gestaltists! The Gestalt prayer (Perls, 1973) reminds us that "I am I, and you are you. I'm not in this world to live up to your expectations, and you're not in this world to live up to mine. I is I, and you is you." All the "I-ness" has driven out the "we-ness." No wonder Perls predicted that the ideal person would be socially alienated; such people are merely reaping the "I-ness" they have sown. When problematic relationships are not dismissed as inconvenient or fatalistic enterprises ("It can't be helped"), they are discarded as our projections.

Social problems aren't the real culprits, Gestalt therapy tells us. They are merely handy intellectual excuses for the failure to take responsibility for our own behavior. Perhaps that's true for mildly neurotic, wealthy people luxuriating on the idyllic beaches of Big Sur, California, but for most of us, the real social forces of poverty, illness, sexism, racism, and crime are contributing culprits. Where else but in California and when else but in the 1960s could one seriously promise a life full of integration, expression, and freedom? It is a major hunk of work for women to integrate all the social, political, and economic forces and to arrive at a harmonious personal sense of self in which no experience needs to be discriminated against as inadmissible or unworthy (Polster, 1974). But speaking of "disowned" parts and of getting in touch with "polarities" begins to erroneously locate the disturbance solely within a person and unrealistically suggests that emotionally expressive work will free her from these social forces. Not in most neighborhoods. The Gestalt injunction to accept individual responsibility for change quickly deteriorates into blaming the victim. Genuine liberation for the oppressed must also come from without, not only from within.

From an Integrative Perspective

Perls believed that he was following the existential heritage, which rejects the dualism that overvalues mind at the expense of body. However, Perls left us a reverse dualism that overvalues body at the expense of mind. Gestalt therapy is obviously in need of a cognitive theory to balance its overemphasis on biology. Many observers have suggested an integration of Gestalt with cognitive therapy. Until some integration is achieved giving equal weight to the cognitive capacities of human beings, Gestalt therapy will remain a movement that attempted to balance Descartes by speaking for the body but unfortunately ended up flipping the philosophical cart, with the body now the Top Dog.

Like most "true believers," Perls and his fellow Gestalt enthusiasts overextended the usefulness of the therapy into indiscriminate applications with promises that cannot be met. Gestalt work is most effective with overly socialized, restrained, and constricted individuals. With less-organized and more seriously disturbed individuals, Gestalt work becomes a risky proposition. And with individuals whose problems center on impulse dyscontrol—acting out, delinquency, explosive disorders—it is probably contraindicated (Beutler, Harwood, Kimpara, et al., 2011; Shepherd, 1976). The integrative directive is to selectively use what works, not to indiscriminately use it all the time.

A Gestalt Analysis of Mrs. C

Like so many people in our society, Mrs. C was raised to disown the socially unacceptable aspects of her body. For most of her life, she succeeded in disowning the sources of her sexual desires and the bodily basis for her angry feelings. Since the onset of her full-blown neurosis, Mrs. C has been trying to disown her entire body by washing it away. Fortunately, the biological basis of her existence will not just lie down and die; her body keeps sending out messages that remind her that she is human and therefore subject to diseases, anger, and sexual desires. Mrs. C refuses to listen to her body and instead keeps obsessing in her mind and compulsing in her actions, "Wash away body, wash away," until she is now little more than a washed-out dishrag.

Mrs. C reports that her childhood disowning of sex and anger was due to catastrophic expectations that her parents would punish her if she did not play the role of a good, clean little girl.

How much these catastrophic expectations were based on reality and how much on fantastic projections cannot be established from the record. The important point is that these fears were part of the phobic layer that motivated Mrs. C to spend most of her existence in the phony layer of playing the model child, model mother, and now model neurotic.

At the time her symptoms began, Mrs. C was probably becoming increasingly dissatisfied with how responsible she had to be for everyone else, with no time or energy to realize who she really was. Five kids and a pregnancy, diapers, dishes, disease, and pinworms on top of it all! Who wouldn't want to yell out in anger and in despair? But Mrs. C never had the guts to stand up for herself, to do what she really wanted to do, so why would we expect her to do it now? Instead, she projected the responsibility for her problems onto the pinworms and then proceeded to spend her life trying to wash away the pinworms and

(continued)

herself. If she had confronted who she really was—a person able to get angry, a person desiring to be free, and a person more egocentric than she ever dared to be—her childish catastrophic expectations would tell her that she would be rejected and hurt. So don't think about who you really are; think only about the pinworms and the washing!

The reason the pinworm episode represented an impasse, a sick point, was that Mrs. C had never become a mature person, never developed the capacity to be responsible for herself. Now there were clearly too many kids, too much illness, and too many demands for Mrs. C to move ahead on her own. With the development of dramatic symptoms, Mrs. C could get others, including her psychotherapists, to take care of her. It was also apparent that Mrs. C was using her symptoms to manipulate others, such as getting her husband to attend to her by keeping track of her shower ritual. Apparently Mrs. C was finding it easier to remain sick and manipulative than to become healthier and stand on her own.

To work through her impasse, Mrs. C would have to face the implosive layer of her neurosis. She would need to experience the deadness of her genitals, the total emptiness of her past 10 years, and the loss of her very center. Because she had projected the responsibility for her miserable life onto pinworms, it is no wonder that her life now centered around pinworms. Mrs. C had no energy left to feel alive, because her organismic energy was all tied up in the rigid, neurotic patterns that had become her life.

With almost all of her energy invested in neurosis, Mrs. C would need to experience some tremendous explosions to be born again. She would explode into grief over the loss of a whole decade of her life. She would release all of her anger toward her daughter, her husband, her parents, and herself for letting her play the role of such a good daughter and such a good mother. Mrs. C would also reach way back into the earliest years of her life to see if she could discover the bodily basis for her sexuality so that she could for the first time in her life explode with orgasm. Only with these potentially violent

explosions could Mrs. C ever again hope to experience the joy of living.

To face the fears of her catastrophic expectations, to cross the impasse and become responsible again, and then to undergo the tremors of emotional explosions and shed the totally clean character that had been the source of her identity would perhaps be too much for Mrs. C. She would strongly prefer a psychotherapy that promised to improve her neurosis by letting her go back to being Mrs. Clean without having to wash all the time.

Assuming that Mrs. C wanted more from treatment than to return to her former immature adjustment, a Gestalt therapist would ask her to stay in the here and now. Of course, she couldn't do it. She would continually return to talking about pinworms or washing. She would insist on playing the helpless patient role and would let the therapist know how grateful she would be if the therapist could pull her out of her misery. Such maneuvers would be aimed at turning the responsibility for her miserable life over to the therapist. One of the most effective Gestalt exercises could be to instruct her to end all of her statements about her problems and her life with "and I take responsibility for it." If she could be encouraged and directed into experiencing the possibility of being responsible for her neurosis, Mrs. C might begin to experience some of the grief she must face over her wasted life.

A Gestalt therapist would also encourage Mrs. C to use the empty-chair technique to role-play her relationship to pinworms. She would first speak for the pinworms, which might well come on like Top Dog, and then respond with her present feelings toward the pinworms. As they yell out at her, "You must wash or we'll eat you up," she might begin to experience her rage toward the pinworms for dominating her life. As she began to let more anger seep out, she would probably want to avoid, lest she be punished or rejected for being a naughty, angry person. She might become more conscious of how childish her catastrophic expectations are. She might also become increasingly aware of just how much she has projected the responsibility for her

(continued)

problems onto the pinworms. The Gestalt clinician would offer Mrs. C feedback about her variety of maneuvers to get her therapist to take more direct control of her life.

As the Gestalt therapist refused to be manipulated into rushing in to rescue Mrs. C, she might begin to experience increasing anger toward the therapist. That would constitute a breakthrough from preoccupation with pinworms to feeling angry in the here and now. As she stayed with her fears over being angry, Mrs. C would realize that her catastrophic expectations were indeed her projections—her therapist would not hurt or reject her, and she would not get pinworms.

To own back so much of her disowned personality, Mrs. C would probably have to participate in Gestalt dream work. Because almost all of her waking hours have been rigidly spent in obsessions and compulsions, her sleeping hours would be the only time in which her disowned self could be spontaneously expressed. It would be difficult to force Mrs. C to vividly attend to her dreams because of all the pain and grief that would come with awakening to memories of having once been a real person. However, the breakthroughs could be tremendous if she began to face how much she had given up for the security of washing. Probably only through Gestalt dream work could such an absolutely rigid, habitual character like Mrs. C begin the cathartic process of reawakening to and reowning all the vital organismic aspects of her existence.

Future Directions

In retrospect, behavior was the favored content and focus of psychotherapy in the 1970s and 1980s, and cognition was the favorite through the 2000s. In prospect, emotion is the probable winner in the 2010s. Adding affect into the therapeutic mix and facilitating emotional change will likely be major foci of psychotherapy practice, research, and training in the coming years. This should reenergize Gestalt and experiential therapies. Instead of being avoided and controlled, emotions are increasingly recognized as organizing processes that enhance adaptation and problem solving (Greenberg et al., 1993). Having regained "the mind" during the cognitive revolution in psychotherapy, mental health professionals will rediscover "the feeling" after a 50-year drought since the 1960s heyday of Fritz Perls and the encounter movement.

We foresee experiential therapy's continued influence in at least three spheres: psychotherapy integration, couples work, and specific client presentations. Any satisfactory integrative therapy must incorporate more than words and ideas. Whether they label it Gestalt, experiential, affective, or emotion-focused, integrative practitioners seek methods to evoke emotions and to precipitate intense experiences. Emotion—the allegedly crazy, irresponsible part of the psyche—is almost always necessary to drive and achieve lasting behavior change. At the same time, emotional work is not always enough, and experiential therapists will increasingly seek other orientations—psychodynamic, cognitive, and systems, in particular—to balance and complete their own perspective (Tonnesvang et al., 2010). Back in 1976, contributors to *The Handbook of Gestalt Therapy* (Hatcher & Himelstein, 1976) were demonstrating the complementarity of Gestalt and other methods of psychotherapy. Gestalt therapists know that growth is by assimilation (Yontef, 1988).

That assimilation is embodied in the experiential, systemic, attachment-based couples therapy of EFT. When you begin using a host of adjectives and hyphens to describe a treatment, you know you are in the presence of integration. When you begin confronting the torrent of anger, hurt, and betrayal in couple sessions, you know you will be grateful for the systematic EFT conceptualization of emotions as unmet attachment needs and for its guidance in transforming those emotions into corrective experiences and secure connections. EFT couples work is an exciting, research-supported development that can be, will be, widely applied for relationship distress, depression, and trauma.

In their review of research on the experiential psychotherapies, Greenberg and colleagues (1994, p. 533) wisely conclude, "Probably the most obvious trend that emerges from this review is the shift away from the practice of offering a uniform treatment to all clients and toward adapting experiential treatments to specific disorders or problems." Certain disorders and patient presentations would seem to virtually require experiential work along the lines suggested by Perls and other experientialists. Words and ideas alone are typically insufficient to heal the emotional ravages of chronic pain, personality disorders, sexual abuse, and post-traumatic stress disorders. Recent handbooks on Gestalt and experiential therapy (Greenberg et al., 1998; Woldt & Tolman, 2005) devote the bulk of their pages to treatments of various disorders.

A concomitant evolution in recognizing that emotionally expressive work is not the treatment of choice for all people is occurring. Clients high in autonomy or resistance will probably respond negatively to more directive elements, and practicing Gestalt with them may partially explain the higher risk of negative effects. We will be increasingly able to pick our moments of using experiential work on the basis of clinical experience and research evidence, such as the demonstrations of the superiority of awareness-oriented experiential therapy for overcontrolled, internalizing patients. In doing so, we will have traveled full circle and returned to the reasonably healthy, oversocialized patients on whom Gestalt therapy was constructed and with whom Fritz Perls was so successful.

Key Terms

affect regulation
allegiance effect
catastrophic
  expectations
contact
corrective emotional
  experiencing
deflectors
dramatic relief
emotion-focused
  therapy
emotionally focused
  couples therapy
empty chair
end-goals
experiencing
experiential therapy
explosive layer
focusing method
frustration
Gestalt dream work
Gestalt therapy
Gestalts
here and now
hot seat
impasse
implosive layer
introjectors
layers or levels of
  psychopathology
"May I feed you a
  sentence?"
maya
organismic needs
own the projection
phobic layer
phony layer
playing the projection
polarities
present-centered
process diagnosis
process-experiential
  therapy
projectors
rehearsals
repetition or
  exaggeration
retroflectors
reversals
safe emergency
sensate focusing
Top Dog/Under Dog
two-chair work
unfinished business

Recommended Readings

Gendlin, E. T. (1996). *Focusing-oriented psychotherapy: A manual of the experiential method.* New York: Guilford.

Greenberg, L. S. (2002). *Emotion-focused therapy: Coaching clients to work through feelings.* Washington, DC: American Psychological Association.

Greenberg, L. S., & Johnson, S. M. (2010). *Emotionally focused therapy for couples.* New York: Guilford.

Greenberg, L. S., Watson, J. C., & Lietaer, G. (Eds.). (1998). *Handbook of experiential psychotherapy.* New York: Guilford.

Hatcher, C., & Himelstein, P. (Eds.). (1976). *The handbook of Gestalt therapy.* New York: Jason Aronson.

Perls, F. (1969). *Gestalt therapy verbatim.* Lafayette, CA: Real People Press.

Perls, F. (1973). *The Gestalt approach and eye witness to therapy.* Palo Alto, CA: Science & Behavior Books.

Polster, E., & Polster, M. (1973). *Gestalt therapy integrated.* New York: Brunner/Mazel.

Woldt, A. S., & Toman, S. M. (Eds.). (2005). *Gestalt therapy: History, theory, practice.* Newbury, CA: Sage.

Zinker, J. (1977). *Creative process in Gestalt therapy.* New York: Brunner/Mazel.

JOURNALS: *British Gestalt Journal; Gestalt; Gestalt Review; Folio: A Journal for Focusing and Experiential Therapy; Journal of Humanistic Psychology; Person-Centered & Experiential Psychotherapies.*

Recommended Websites

Association for the Advancement of Gestalt Therapy:
www.aagt.org/
Emotion-Focused Therapy Clinic:
www.emotionfocusedclinic.org/
Focusing Institute (Gendlin):
www.focusing.org/
Gestalt Therapy Page:
www.gestalt.org/
International Centre for Excellence in Emotionally Focused Therapy:
www.iceeft.com/
World Association for Person-Centered and Experiential Psychotherapy:
www.pce-world.org/

CHAPTER 7

Interpersonal Therapies

Courtesy of Drs. Gerald Klerman and Myrna Weissman

Gerald Klerman & Myrna Weissman

"I am not myself and I will never be myself again." That's what Marilyn was coming to believe. She was not functioning well in her career as a consultant and was functioning even worse with her family, especially her husband, Ed.

Their chronic disputes over their roles had deteriorated into an impasse. Marilyn was chronically angry and withdrawn; for his part Ed pursued intense intimacy and dependency. While Marilyn resented the fact that Ed refused to be the primary parent and house helper, she also felt ambivalent because she had been socialized to be a superwoman who could balance career, marriage, children, and home. Marilyn had been able to handle all of these responsibilities for years, but now she had to travel more and her two teenage daughters had become more demanding. Ed knew that his career as a middle-school teacher was not as demanding as his wife's job, but in his family his father was relatively free from demands at the end of a day of exhausting factory work.

This couple had sought couples therapy because they knew that if they didn't renegotiate

their relationship it would end in dissolution and divorce. What Ed wanted most was more intimacy, both physically and emotionally. What Marilyn wanted most was more support, both emotionally and physically, such as more help with their children and home. Ed also hoped his wife would obtain immediate relief from medications, because the frequent T.V. commercials had convinced him that antidepressants could be part of the solution. For some time Marilyn felt that anger was her only emotional problem, but her problems with sleeping, eating, energy, and sex made it hard for her to deny that she was not depressed. But she knew that medications alone would not solve her interpersonal problems.

This couple was not yet ready to restructure their relationship, but they were actively searching for all of the benefits that could come from such change, including better feelings about themselves and their marriage, better role models for their teenagers, more energy for their careers, and inspiring relationships with their friends and extended family. Such sharing helped them to pull

173

together rather than push apart. Ed felt the medication was also helping. While Marilyn agreed, she was concerned that her medications might lead her to be more accepting and less ambitious. But she also was coming to believe that it was time to let go of her self-image as Superwoman, in part to help Ed become more proactive as a father and a partner.

The Heritage of Interpersonal Therapies

Interpersonal therapy is rooted in the interpersonal psychodynamic approaches of Harry Stack Sullivan and Adolph Meyer and is informed by the attachment theory of John Bowlby. The leading proponent of the **interpersonal school of psychoanalysis**, Sullivan (1953a, 1953b, 1970, 1972) was an influential American psychiatrist who found abnormal behavior to be rooted in impaired interpersonal relationships and believed it could be ameliorated by an interpersonal variant of psychodynamic therapy. The therapist was a **participant-observer** in treatment, employing a mixture of reflectiveness and engagement in the therapy hour.

Known for founding the interpersonal school and for his "psychobiological" approach, Meyer (1957) emphasized the patient's current psychosocial environment and posited that many forms of psychopathology represented misguided attempts to adjust to the environment, particularly under stressful circumstances or in a stressful environment. As mentioned in Chapters 2 and 3, John Bowlby (1973, 1977) was convinced attachment in early life largely determines subsequent interpersonal relationships. Our relationship patterns are profoundly shaped by our **attachment styles**—secure, anxious, avoidant—established early in life, and the interpersonal therapist strives to move them toward more secure and hence more satisfying connections.

Several contemporary interpersonal therapies hail directly from the psychodynamic heritage (Horowitz & Strack, 2011). Cases in point are the relational psychoanalytic therapies (Chapter 2) and interpersonal psychodynamic therapies (Chapter 3). Another case in point is Lorna Smith Benjamin's (2006) **Interpersonal Reconstructive Therapy (IRT)**, designed to address complex cases with multiple disorders that have shown little benefit from previous treatments. These "nonresponder" clients usually involve one or more personality disorders and usually pose serious clinical risks, such as suicide. IRT focuses on the patient's troubling symptoms and relationship patterns and links them to key attachment figures. Early research suggests the suicide attempts and rehospitalizations are significantly reduced if patients have the opportunity to understand the interpersonal meanings of their suicidal behaviors during IRT (Critchfield et al., 2012).

Other contemporary interpersonal therapies, however, do not hail from the psychodynamic heritage and, in fact, take pains to distinguish themselves from it. The terminology becomes confusing for even the most conscientious of students: "You say that some interpersonal therapies are derived from the psychodynamic tradition, but other therapies using the same title of 'interpersonal' disavow the psychodynamic tradition?!" Yes, that is puzzling and true (but let's not blame the authors/messengers).

This chapter considers two psychotherapies identified as "interpersonal" that do *not* associate with the psychodynamic heritage. We first examine in detail the newer and more influential system known simply as **interpersonal psychotherapy (IPT)**, beginning with a sketch of its founders. We then consider, as a major alternative, the older and declining system of **transactional analysis (TA)**. (Expanded consideration of TA in the form of a complete chapter can be accessed online at www.cengagebrain.com.)

A Sketch of IPT Founders

IPT itself was developed in the early 1970s as part of a collaborative research program on depression by Gerald L. Klerman, MD, in New Haven and then in Boston, and by his New Haven collaborators, Myrna M. Weissman, PhD, Bruce J. Rounsaville, MD, and Eve S. Chevron. Their initial studies concerned the role of psychotherapy in relation to the use of antidepressant medication in maintenance treatment of depressives after recovery from an acute episode. Although Klerman did not believe he would find psychotherapy effective, the first maintenance study did, in fact, demonstrate its efficacy. Klerman, Weissman, and colleagues then began to more fully describe the treatment, termed it interpersonal therapy, and conducted a series of treatment studies on medication alone, IPT alone, and in combination. From the beginning, IPT was grounded and tested in **randomized clinical trials (RCTs)**.

The culmination of their research was their 1984 classic book, *Interpersonal Psychotherapy of Depression* (Klerman et al., 1984). The positive results of their clinical trials led to the NIMH Collaborative Treatment Study of Depression, which tested medication, IPT, and cognitive therapy for acute depression. The ensuing years have seen IPT thoroughly researched as a treatment for depression in all age groups and successfully applied to other mental disorders (Klerman & Weissman, 1993). In fact, when speaking of IPT today, the presumed reference is to Klerman and Weissman's IPT.

Klerman himself would not live to see the popularity of IPT. He died in 1992. However, Myrna Weissman (Klerman's wife) and John Markowitz (Klerman's last trainee) compiled the new studies on IPT and updated the treatment manual in the *Comprehensive Guide to Interpersonal Psychotherapy* (Weissman et al., 2000) with Klerman listed as a posthumous coauthor.

Today, IPT, spearheaded by Myrna Weissman and John Markowitz, is a leading system of psychotherapy. Formerly a professor at Yale, Weissman relocated to Columbia University, where she is now a Professor of Epidemiology and Psychiatry and Director of Clinical and Genetic Epidemiology at the New York State Psychiatric Institute. In addition to her groundbreaking work on IPT, she is a renowned epidemiologist, particularly in mood and anxiety disorders. In the tradition of Klerman, she continues to demonstrate via RCTs that the combination of psychotherapy and medication is more effective in the treatment of major depression than either alone.

Theory of Personality

Psychotherapy systems are beginning to lose their personalities, literally. Older systems, such as psychoanalysis, existentialism, and person-centered therapy, possess fully developed and rich theories of personality and human development. But newer systems of psychotherapy, including IPT, have typically eschewed detailed explanations of personality and development.

IPT substitutes stable interpersonal patterns for stable personality patterns. Therapy is designed to alter interpersonal patterns developed early in life. Healthy interpersonal relationships (or attachments) early in life predispose individuals to healthy interpersonal relationships later in life. Troubled attachments early in life predispose individuals to develop disorders that get expressed through troubled interpersonal relationships in the present.

Theory of Psychopathology

Depression and other disorders occur within an interpersonal context. Interpersonal life affects mood (and all other human behavior), and mood affects how the individual handles his or her interpersonal roles (Markowitz, 1997). The interpersonal approach to understanding depression reflects an undoctrinaire position that integrates the psychoanalytic emphasis on early childhood experiences with the cognitive-behavioral emphasis on current environmental stressors.

This connection occurs in the following way (Halgin & Whitbourne, 1993): A person's failure in childhood to acquire the emotional nurturance, cognitive operations, and behavioral skills needed to develop satisfying relationships leads to despair, isolation, and resultant depression, as demonstrated in Bowlby's attachment research. Once a person's depression is established, it is maintained by poor social skills, overreaction to loss, and impaired communication, all of which lead to further rejection by others. Environmental stressors make a bad situation worse.

For instance, a woman predisposed to depression by early parenting failures suffers the loss of her husband. In a prolonged grief reaction, she may become so distraught over an extended period of time that she alienates her friends and family members and thereby isolates herself. In time, a vicious cycle becomes established in which her behavior causes people to stay away, and because she is so lonely and miserable, she becomes even more difficult in interactions with others. Interpersonal disruptions, in this view, are both a cause and a consequence of depression.

Four major interpersonal problems produce depression and other forms of psychopathology: interpersonal loses, disputes, transitions, and deficits. Let us consider each in turn.

Loss and Grief

When a loved one dies, it is normal to react with grief. Although normal grief shares some features with depression, such as a sad mood and social withdrawal, it does not generally require treatment. Indeed, most people who experience grief do not seek treatment, and the symptoms of grief begin to decrease in a matter of a few months as the grieving individual comes to terms with the loss.

Abnormal grief reactions, however, may complicate this pattern and lead to depression and other pathologies. For example, in delayed grief reactions, individuals who experienced a prior loss but who did not complete a normal grieving process may subsequently exhibit a profound grief reaction when faced with a less significant loss or with a reminder of the original loss. This delayed grief reaction may not be accurately diagnosed because it is occurring much later than the original loss.

Role Disputes

Role disputes occur when the patient and significant other hold incompatible expectations in their relationship. Klerman, Weissman, and colleagues (1984) observed that unresolved and repetitious role disputes tend to be related to the onset, maintenance, or exacerbation of depressive symptoms. Patients may feel that they do not have control of their relationships, or may be afraid of losing a relationship with a significant other.

Role disputes generally fall into one of three stages: **renegotiation**, in which both parties are aware of the dispute and are trying to bring about a solution; **impasse**, in which negotiation has stopped between the two parties, leaving only an unspoken hostility; and **dissolution**, in which the relationship is damaged beyond recovery. In renegotiation, the patient needs to utilize more adaptive communication patterns in the relationship. In the case of an impasse, the patient may attempt to reopen negotiations in hopes for a successful resolution of the dispute. And with dissolution, the patient needs to see the relationship is over and they need to seek other interests and relationships to fill the void created by the lost relationship.

A specific role dispute may be indicative of a more general pattern of functioning also present in past disputes of a similar nature. Some people repeatedly create interpersonal disputes or conflicts with significant others in authority, such as a parent, teacher, boss, or police officer. If this is the case, then possible explanations for the repetitive dispute include an examination of what the patient may gain from such a pattern.

Role Transitions

A large literature has linked depression and other disorders with stressful life changes. Many of these changes are associated with a transition in the social role in which individuals find themselves. Although negative **role transitions** (such as losing a job) may understandably be associated with depression, it is critical to recognize that even seemingly positive role transitions may also lead to depression and other disorders. For example, having a baby may be accompanied by the stress of the new responsibility, the anxiety of failing as a parent, or the fear of being unworthy of such a wonderful baby. The most common role transitions are those associated with changes in the life cycle, including biological changes such as menopause, and those that involve changes in a social role, such as a marriage, childbirth, or retirement. In general, role transitions associated with psychological disorders are characterized by feelings of helplessness in coping with the transition, by the loss of members in the social support network, and/or by the need to develop new social skills. Klerman and colleagues (1984) report that in most cases, patients are aware of the transition and of the stress it is causing.

Interpersonal Deficits

Some clients may not have a specific interpersonal problem—a death, role transition, or dispute—causing their disorder. They may, instead, demonstrate a pattern of isolation that suggests interpersonal deficits are the source of the disorder. Clients with interpersonal deficits have generally had trouble throughout their lives in forming and maintaining relationships. An individual with adaptive interpersonal functioning maintains close relationships with family and intimate others, comfortable relationships with friends, and appropriate relationships with work acquaintances. An individual with interpersonal deficits, by contrast, tends to be socially isolated, anxious around other people, and maintains few, if any, meaningful relationships (Gotlib & Whiffen, 1991).

Single-Parent Families

Interpersonal therapy for adolescents (IPT-A) adds a fifth interpersonal problem to the four causes contained in adult IPT: the single-parent family. In addition to grief, role disputes, transitions, and interpersonal deficits, many troubled adolescents are dealing with the separation from or loss of a parent and with the authority conflicts that can accompany the single-parent family (Mufson et al., 2004a).

Therapeutic Processes

IPT acknowledges the profound impact of early developmental experiences on later interpersonal relations but focuses on improving current interpersonal relations. Rather than reconstructing and analyzing the "there and then," IPT strives to restructure and improve the "here and now" of the interpersonal domain. Regardless of personality traits or biological vulnerability, depression occurs in a psychosocial and interpersonal context. What is essential for recovery from depression, then, is to examine the context associated with the onset of the depression and the possibility of renegotiating difficulties in current interpersonal contexts (Frank, 1991).

IPT is a short-term, present-oriented psycho-therapy focused mainly on the patient's current interpersonal relations and life situations. As such, it can be best understood in comparison to other psychotherapies (Klerman et al., 1984):

IPT IS:	IPT IS NOT:
time-limited	long-term
focused	open-ended
about current relationships	about past relationships
interpersonal	intrapsychic/psychodynamic
interpersonal	cognitive/behavioral
improving relationships	achieving insight
identifying assets	identifying defenses
learning how to cope	curing the problem

The change processes of IPT occur in three phases of treatment, typically over 12 to 16 sessions. During the initial sessions of the first phase, consciousness raising is the most heavily emphasized process. The IPT practitioner deals with the depression by reviewing symptoms, giving the syndrome a name, according the patient the "sick role," and evaluating the need for medication. The disorder is consciously related to the interpersonal context by determining the nature of interactions, clarifying expectations of significant others and whether these are fulfilled, and establishing the changes the patient desires in the relationships. The major problem areas related to the current disorder are then identified. And, finally, the IPT concepts and contract are explained.

The second phase of IPT covers the intermediate sessions and directly addresses the **primary problem area**: grief, interpersonal disputes, role transitions, or interpersonal deficits. Only one or two of these problem areas are addressed in therapy. Numerous problem areas will probably emerge, and these will be noted; however, the time restriction necessitates focusing on the most troubling area.

The therapeutic strategies differ somewhat depending on which interpersonal problem area has been targeted, but let us consider unresolved grief. Here the cathartic process is applied to facilitate the mourning process and to help the patient reestablish interests and relationships to substitute for what has been lost. Toward these goals, numerous strategies are employed: relating symptom onset to loss of the significant other, reconstructing the patient's relationship with the deceased, describing the sequences and consequences of events surrounding the loss, exploring associated positive and negative feelings, and considering possible ways of becoming involved with others.

When catharsis is completed, therapy will progress toward increasing reliance on the process of changing conditional stimuli. What are the conditions that stimulate depression and other common disorders? Empty time, being alone, feeling unwanted, frequent arguments, and criticism are some of the most common conditions that need to be changed if disorders are to be resolved and future relapses prevented.

With role disputes, for example, the therapeutic process can focus on renegotiating or restructuring the condition of the relationship to dramatically reduce interpersonal conflicts that can trigger depression, anxiety, substance abuse, and other disorders. With dissolution, the only alternative for changing the destructive interpersonal condition is to dissolve the relationship.

Unlike other forms of psychotherapy, IPT has no ideological hesitation about the use of medications and makes no universal generalizations to all disorders. This integrative specificity probably originates in IPT's singular focus on major depression, which frequently entails adjunctive pharmacotherapy and which frequently presents in a manner quite different from other psychological problems. The use of medication and the focus on depression stem from the goals of treatment: symptom reduction and relationship improvement. Because of its brief duration and low level of psychotherapeutic intensity, IPT is not expected to have a marked impact on the enduring aspects of personality and character.

The third phase of IPT addresses termination. Similar to other therapies, feelings about ending treatment are discussed, progress is reviewed, and the remaining work is outlined. As is also true of other intentionally brief therapies, the arrangements for termination are explicit and adhered to.

In sum, IPT relies on multiple processes of change. Consciousness raising in the form of education is used to name the patient's disorder and to connect it with one or more major interpersonal problems. Catharsis is employed to assist the client in emotionally releasing the loss and grief and in beginning anew. And conditional stimuli are brought to bear on modifying both the patient's environment and behavior in resolving the interpersonal problems.

Therapeutic Content
Intrapersonal Conflicts
Anxiety and Defenses
Anxiety may be located within a person, but it originates between people. The most disruptive anxieties are caused by interpersonal abandonment, rejection, abuse, neglect, and isolation. The earlier, more severe, and frequent the traumatic interpersonal events, the more likely they are to provoke clinical disorders, such as substance abuse and eating disorders.

The IPT concern is not with identifying how people defend against such anxieties. The concern is with identifying the interpersonal assets individuals have or need to have to prevent such anxiety-arousing events. Focusing on psychodynamic defenses can keep clients and therapists stuck in a depressing past. Focusing on assets, such as building better relationships and interpersonal skills, can help clients enjoy a more fulfilling present and future.

Self-Esteem
Self-esteem is a precious asset that can help prevent the reoccurrence of interpersonal rejection, abuse, and neglect. The better we feel about ourselves, the better others are likely to feel about us. Similarly, the better significant others feel about us, the greater our self-esteem is likely to be. Though self-esteem may exist within us, it has its deepest roots between us and significant others.

Responsibility
The life events most likely to precipitate depression and other disorders are those for which patients share responsibility. We need to differentiate between independent stressful events (that is, events over which we have no control and for which we have no responsibility, such as the death of a loved one) and dependent events (that is, events that may have been dependent on our behaviors, such as getting fired). Research has demonstrated that depressed individuals experience the same number of independent stressful events as do nondepressed individuals, but they experience a greater number of dependent events (Hammen, 1991). The good news is that psychotherapy can help us assume more responsibility for dependent events and to develop interpersonal assets that can reduce the likelihood of such distressing events from occurring.

Interpersonal Conflicts
Intimacy and Sexuality
The more intimate the relationship, the more hurt and distress it can produce. Marriage is supposed to be the most intimate of relationships, but couple distress has been linked to several psychological disorders, including depression, anxiety, and substance abuse (Gotlib & McCabe, 1990; Moos et al., 1982). Even when depression remits, marital difficulties tend to persist. This is all the more reason why the treatment and prevention of depression call for treatment of interpersonal relationships where intimacy and sexuality can thrive.

Communication

Interpersonal disputes and deficits are often due to communication deficits. It is difficult, indeed, to build and maintain fulfilling relationships with faulty communication. To counter communication failures, IPT includes an analysis of common communication difficulties, including ambiguous, indirect, nonverbal communication as a substitute for open confrontation; assuming one has communicated without checking it out; assuming one has understood without confirming the message received; and silence that closes off communication. Building communication assets by correcting faulty communication is one of the best ways to negotiate interpersonal disputes and counter interpersonal deficits. It is also one of the best ways to prevent relapse of depression and other disorders.

Hostility

Interpersonal disputes at an impasse and not renegotiated are likely to deteriorate into chronic hostility that can produce psychopathology. In fact, one of the strongest predictors of relapse is a phenomenon referred to as **expressed emotion (EE)**. Expressed emotion encompasses emotional overinvolvement and chronic criticism of the distressed individual by a spouse or family member. Living in high EE households has been found to predict rates of relapse for patients diagnosed with schizophrenia and with mood disorders (e.g., Roth & Fonagy, 1996; Simoneau et al., 1998).

Individuo-Social Conflicts
Adjustment versus Transcendence

People raised in relationships marked by abuse, neglect, rejection, abandonment, and isolation are at high risk of adjusting to such households. As children, what choice do they have? They might conclude that there is something wrong with them interpersonally, and such treatment is all they deserve. They are at high risk of repeating such patterns due to interpersonal deficits.

Depression and other disorders can be symptoms that such interpersonal conditions are pathological and must be changed. IPT does not pretend it can change a pathological past of mistreatment. IPT does hold hope that interpersonal deficits can be undone and healthier relationships can be built with proper treatment.

Impulse Control

When average Americans are faced with episodes of psychological distress (increased anxiety, depression, lowered self-esteem, and impaired cognitive functioning), they tend to cope with poor impulse control. They drink more alcohol, smoke more cigarettes, eat more junk food, take more over-the-counter drugs and under-the-counter drugs (Mellinger et al., 1978). Americans typically cope with emotional and psychological distress with some form of oral behavior. So what is one of the healthiest forms of oral behaviors? Talking! That's why psychological distress is the most common reason people seek psychotherapy. IPT accepts the research that social support through communicating is an effective buffer for distress.

Beyond Conflict to Fulfillment
Meaning in Life

Klerman, Weissman, and colleagues (1984, p. 50) communicate eloquently about meaning in modern times:

> With increasing urbanization and industrialization, the traditional social supports that have characterized societies since the dawn of civilization in Egypt, the Middle East, India and China—religion, the church, the extended family and close neighbors—are less valued and less effective. We live in secular and mobile societies, and religion is less accepted as the source of truth, purpose, and consolation, and the church is less available as an agency of social support, charity and welfare, recreation and education; where the extended family and close communal

ties of the immediate neighborhood are little more than nostalgic images to be revered at Thanksgiving and Christmas. In the midst of these profound changes, individuals seek other means of meeting their needs for attachment, self-esteem, and purpose. There are limits to the extent to which modern society can proceed to reduce or even destroy the previous support systems. For whatever reasons, biological, psychological or social, individuals need attachments to provide for emotional sustenance, reinforce self-esteem and provide for sexual satisfaction and the development of families and children. Thus, although the traditional forms of family and neighborhood are less important, substitutes are being developed to provide the emotionally relevant equivalence in modern urban life. Psychological attention to interpersonal relations and the growth of professional psychotherapies offer secular, scientific, and rational responses to these needs.

Much of modern theater addresses the search for meaning in societies where interpersonal relationships continue to shrink to a few significant others. Ibsen, the founder of modern theater, writes in A Doll's House of an exchange:

the last three years have been like an endless workday without rest for me. Now it's over....
My poor mother doesn't need me ... nor the boys either.
How free you must feel.
No ... only unspeakably empty. Nothing to live for now.

Therapeutic Relationship

Throughout the course of treatment, the therapist's role is one of patient advocate, not neutral commentator. The interpersonal therapist is active, not passive, at least in comparison to practitioners of long-term, insight-oriented psychotherapies. The therapeutic relationship is not conceptualized as a manifestation of transference; patient expectations of IPT assistance are seen as realistic. Interpretations of patient-therapist interactions are made only when they are disruptive to progress. On learning this stance, one of our colleagues summarized it as follows: "The interpersonal in IPT refers to analyzing the interpersonal origins of depression outside of psychotherapy, not to analyzing the interpersonal relationship in psychotherapy."

In Rogerian terms, the therapeutic relationship in IPT is one of empathy and warmth, but not unconditional acceptance. The therapist conveys the message that depression is a problem to be resolved, not accepted, and is a temporary, not permanent, feature of the patient's life.

Practicalities of IPT

IPT is designed to be conducted by mental health professionals of various disciplines who have attained a terminal degree in their profession and who have acquired at least 2 years of psychotherapy experience with ambulatory patients. In addition, IPT therapists should express a favorable attitude toward short-term treatment and interpersonal theory and, ideally, hold no rigid attachment to any psychotherapy system.

IPT has been operationalized in treatment manuals (Hinrichsen & Clougherty, 2006; Klerman et al., 1984; Mufson et al., 2004a), which have fostered considerable research (see following sections) and have guided clinical practice. Adherence to the treatment manual is distinctive to IPT. In some of their writings, Klerman, Weissman, and colleagues even characterize the therapist role as "strictly adhering" to the manual within a collaborative relationship with the patient. The focus is upon completing the manual-guided work in 16 or fewer sessions and moving steadily toward termination so that patient regression and intense transference reactions are avoided as much as possible.

As such, IPT is definitely a time-limited treatment with a predetermined 12- to 16-week duration. It is practiced as a weekly, face-to-face, present-oriented, and short-term therapy. Pragmatic interventions focusing on the current interpersonal context of a patient's life have been shown to facilitate recovery from the acute episode as well as to provide some protection against reemergence of symptoms (Frank & Spanier, 1995).

Compared to other systems of psychotherapy, IPT is pragmatic and ecumenical about its applications. IPT is enthusiastic about combining medication with psychotherapy in **combined treatment**, as previously noted. IPT is also positively disposed toward conducting treatment in more cost-efficient formats, such as group therapy, and with less expensive psychotherapists, such as masters-level nurses. IPT is expressly used both as a treatment of acute disorders and, as a maintenance treatment, to prevent relapse.

Diffusion of Klerman and Weissman's IPT beyond the United States and into disorders other than depression has occurred slowly. But training opportunities and research programs have exploded in the past decade. The first international conference on IPT was held in 2004, and the International Society for Interpersonal Psychotherapy is coordinating training in many countries.

A Major Alternative: Transactional Analysis

The interpersonal therapies converge on several premises. First, they view maladaptive relationship patterns as central causes of many psychopathologies. Second, interpersonal therapies aim to improve patient functioning in current or prospective relationships. And third, they make explicit use of the psychotherapy relationship— the interpersonal interactions between therapist and client—as a means of facilitating that change (Mallinckrodt, 2000).

IPT embraces these premises, but rarely makes explicit use of the psychotherapy relationship itself. Transactional analysis, on the other hand, makes extensive use of the interpersonal interactions between therapist and client within sessions. In particular, TA relies on careful analysis and correction of the Parent, Child, and Adult ego states in therapy.

Eric Berne (1910–1970), the founder of TA, first came upon the phenomenon of people relating as Parent, Child, or Adult when he decided to listen to his clients and not his teachers (Berne et al., 1973). He had been practicing psychoanalysis for 10 years and had learned to translate whatever clients were saying into the theoretical language he had gained from his teachers. Thus, when a client remarked, "I feel as though I had a little boy inside of me," Berne would typically have interpreted the little boy to mean an introjected penis, as Otto Fenichel did in a similar case. But instead of asking himself, "What would Otto Fenichel say in this case?" he asked the client what he thought about it. As it turned out, the client really did feel like a little boy, and this feeling was the most significant clinical fact in determining the course of the client's life. As therapy proceeded, Berne asked at an appropriate time, "Which part of you is talking, the little boy or the grown-up man?" (Berne et al., 1973, p. 371). At the moment of asking this question, TA was born.

Berne's influence was huge in the 1960s. The 40 members in his 1958 San Francisco seminars grew to an international association 6 years later. His theory attracted a growing number of adherents with the popularity of *Games People Play* (1964), which presented his theory of personality and psychotherapy to millions of readers.

Everything in TA stems from the premise that human personality is structured into three separate ego states: **Parent, Adult, and Child (PAC)**. These **ego states** are not theoretical constructs; they are phenomenological realities amenable to direct observation. An ego state is a consistent pattern of feeling and experience directly related to a corresponding consistent pattern of behavior. When people are in the Child ego state, they sit, stand, speak, think, perceive, and feel as they did in childhood. Behavior of the Child is impulsive and stimulus-bound rather than mediated and delayed by reason. Throwing temper tantrums, acting irresponsibly, and engaging in wishful thinking or daydreams are classic expressions of the Child. At the same time, the Child is the source of spontaneity, creativity, humor, and fun.

The Child ego state is essentially preserved intact from childhood. It is as if the Child has been recorded on a nonerasable tape in the brain and can be turned on live at any time. The Child is at most 8 years old and can be as young as a newborn infant.

The Parent ego state is also carried over essentially intact from childhood. The Parent is basically composed of behaviors and attitudes copied from parents or authority figures. Although much of the Parent is based on videotape-like recordings from childhood, the Parent can be modified throughout life as the person emulates new parental figures or changes as a result of parenting experiences. When the Parent is in control, people use the language of controlling parents: "should," "ought," "must," "better not," and "you'll be sorry" predominate. Gestures such as pointing a finger or standing impatiently with hands on the hips are common expressions of the Parent.

The Parent is the controlling, limit setting, and rigid rule maker of the personality, as well as the nurturing and comforting part of the personality. The Parent is also the repository of traditions and values and is, therefore, vital for the survival of civilization. In ambiguous or unknown situations, when adequate information is unavailable to the Adult, then the Parent is the best basis for decision making.

The Adult ego state is essentially a computer, an unfeeling organ that gathers and processes data for making decisions. The Adult is a gradually developed ego state that emerges as the person interacts with the physical and social environment over many years. The Adult acts more clearly on the basis of logic and reason and is the best evaluator of reality because it is not clouded by emotion. The Adult can realistically evaluate not only the environment but also the emotions and demands of the Child or the Parent.

Each ego state is adaptive when used in the appropriate situation. The Parent is ideally suited when control is necessary, such as control of children, fears, the unknown, and undesirable impulses. The Child is adaptive when creation is desired, such as the creation of new ideas or new life, and for fun situations, such as parties or celebrations. The Adult is ideally suited when accurate prediction is necessary, such as deciding on a marriage, career, or budget. The well-adapted personality, then, switches easily from one ego state to another depending on the needs of the present situation.

Ego states provide the structure of the personality but not the motivation. Motivation for behaving comes from biogenetic drives for survival, such as hunger for food, but also from psychological drives, such as hunger for recognition, structure, and excitement.

One of the most important psychological drives is the need for **stroking**. For young children, stroking needs to be in the form of direct physical contact by means of being held, soothed, and cuddled (Spitz, 1945). Adults learn to get by with only the stimulation that comes from recognition.

One of the most exciting ways to spend time is to exchange strokes with others. An exchange of strokes defines a **transaction**. The hunger for strokes and for excitement makes human beings inherently social animals. Transactions that are spontaneous, direct, and intimate can be exciting, threatening, and overwhelming. Such free and unstructured exchanges of strokes are generally avoided, especially in short-term social interactions, in favor of more structured and safer transactions.

The safest form of transaction is a **ritual**, which is a highly stylized interchange. There are informal rituals, such as greetings: "Hello, how are you?" "Fine, thank you, and you?" There are also formal rituals that become established as traditional ceremonies, such as weddings or funerals, which are entirely structured and predictable. Rituals convey little information and constitute signs of mutual recognition.

The riskiest and most exciting transactions that are still structured are the **games people play**. A game is a complex series of ulterior transactions that progress to a psychological **payoff**—a feeling such as guilt, depression, or anger. In an ulterior transaction, communication appears to have not only an overt, social meaning but also a covert, psychological meaning. For example, if a woman asks a man, "Why don't you come by my place to listen to my favorite CDs?" and the man responds, "I'd love to. I'm really interested in music," they may be holding a simple, candid interchange between two Adults beginning to share a pastime. In a game, however, both players are also communicating a message at a different level. They may, for example, be exchanging Child-to-Child messages like "Boy, I'd really like to get you alone in my apartment" and "I'd like to hook up with you."

For the payoff to occur, one of the players has to pull a **switch**. In this case, after a few drinks and sitting close on the couch listening to music, the woman still seems to be sending a seductive communication. The man's vanity convinces him to proceed, and he puts his hand on her leg, only to be rebuffed by a push away and an irate, "What kind of woman do you think I am?"

The couple has just completed a hand of "Kiss Off" or "Indignation." Besides gaining mutual recognition, excitement, and some structured time together, there is also an emotional payoff for each. The woman is able to profoundly affirm her position in life that she is OK, while feeling angry toward men for not being OK, just as her mother always said. The payoff for the man is to feel depressed and thereby reaffirm his conviction that he is not OK.

Games serve to reaffirm the life position that a person chooses early in life. Based on experiences in the first few years of life, children make a precocious decision about how they are in life compared to others around them. The life position contains a summary conviction of how I am and of how others are. The four possible **life positions** are (Harris, 1967):

I'm OK—you're OK

I'm OK—you're not OK

I'm not OK—you're OK

I'm not OK—you're not OK

The first and universal position of children is to be OK unless the civilizing process helps to convince them that they are not OK. Or, as Berne believed, children are born princes and princesses, until their parents turn them into frogs (Steiner, 1974).

Adoption of an unhealthy life position will obviously predispose people to troubled lives. People who decide "I'm OK—you're not OK," to take one example, predispose themselves toward lives of crime and sociopathy. To exploit others, cheat others, or succeed at the expense of others is further confirmation that the person was entirely correct in deciding "I'm OK and you're not." Who needs a conscience when I'm convinced that all I do is OK and anything that goes wrong must be the responsibility of those who aren't OK?

People who decide "I'm not OK—you're OK," are plagued with constant feelings of inferiority in the presence of those they judge as OK. Such a life position can lead to withdrawal from others, because it is too painful to remain in their presence and be constantly reminded of not being OK.

Withdrawal reaffirms the not-OK position but is even more self-defeating because it deprives the person of any chance of getting the adequate strokes from others that could lead to a belief of being OK.

People who conclude "I'm not OK and neither are you" are the most difficult to reach. Why should they respond to others who aren't OK? What hope is there in life when neither oneself nor others are OK? These people simply survive, if they do not commit suicide or destroy others and themselves. The extreme withdrawal of schizophrenia or major depression is their most common fate.

Transactional analysis typically begins with a **structural analysis**, through which patients become more fully conscious of ego states that were previously confused, contaminated, or excluded. The (first-order) structural analysis looks at how two people interact with each other from their respective ego states; second-order structural analysis looks at the interaction between one's own ego states and then how that plays out in relationship problems. Therapy then proceeds to TA proper, in which self-defeating transactions are made conscious, beginning with self-destructive games, leading to full awareness of the unhealthy life positions that have been plaguing patients.

With a curative increase in consciousness, clients are able to choose their ego states. With heightened awareness, they can also decide whether they will go on acting out tragic games, positions, and scripts or choose more constructive patterns of meeting their basic human hungers. In other words, the core change processes of TA are consciousness raising and choosing.

Consciousness raising in TA begins as an educational process. Clients are expected to become well informed about the language and concepts of TA, usually through **bibliotherapy** involving the books of Berne (1964, 1970, 1972), Harris (1967; Harris & Harris, 1990), and Steiner (1971, 1974,

1990). The education continues as clients are taught to apply the concepts of TA to their own lives, beginning with becoming aware of which ego state is being expressed. As clients analyze their own lives in TA terms, they will frequently look to the therapist or group members for feedback regarding the accuracy of their self-interpretations.

To encourage clients to reduce their own confusion, the therapist frequently asks clients such questions as "What ego state are you in?", "Which part of you is talking now?", "Which part of you made that gesture?" The clients then respond in terms of their own subjective awareness, which they can check against feedback from the therapist or other members in group therapy.

Consider two recent patients, both of whom had to work hard to become aware of their self-destructive ego states. A middle-aged man was almost always working and continually preached to his spouse about how she should take better care of the house. He was unable to find any fun or joy in life because his rigid Parent had successfully excluded both his Child and Adult from being expressed. On the other hand, consider another middle-aged man, the constant Clown, the prankster who is the life of the party but disgusts his wife because he can never be serious. He exhibited a dominant Child who avoided the serious aspects of life by not giving expression to his Adult or Parent ego states.

Becoming aware of the emotional impact of transactions is part of the analysis of games patients play. In the Kiss Off game, for example, the repartee between the mutually attracted Child and Child is crossed when the woman switches to her Parent and asks accusingly, "What kind of woman do you think I am?" Because the emotional impact of such a switch is the key payoff of a game, it is absolutely critical that patients become conscious of how they cross transactions to elicit feelings. Much of the work in analyzing games involves confronting clients with the repetitious nature of their games and then interpreting the payoffs of the games and how they reinforce the client's life position.

In the process of becoming more fully conscious of their ego states, games, and life positions, clients also become aware of an increase in volition. With a reduction in confusion or contamination, clients are increasingly empowered to choose their ego state at any particular time. After expressing a previously excluded ego state in a session, clients can choose to express the same ego state outside the session. Once they become aware that their self-defeating life positions were originally decisions in childhood based on inadequate information, they can make more informed choices as Adults to live constructive, self-fulfilling lives.

Transactional analysts encourage the volitional powers of patients right from the onset of treatment by making it a contractual arrangement. In the contract, the patient chooses which goals to work toward, and the therapist decides whether such goals fit within the therapist's value system. The therapist also lets clients know that they are free to renegotiate the contract at any time or to terminate therapy once the present contract is completed.

The therapeutic relationship is part of both the content and the process of TA. The games that patients play with therapists, for example, form a critical part of the content to be analyzed. Clients who show consistently late for sessions or who fail to pay their bills may be playing "Kick Me." The naive therapist may indeed relate with a kick rather than an analysis of the client's self-defeating games. At the same time, the relationship can be part of the process of therapy, as when the therapist relates as an Adult to hook and to strengthen the Adult of the client.

To be effective, transactional analysts must be genuine in therapy, because it is impossible to fake being an effective Adult, a humorous Child, or a caring Parent. Transactional analysts also believe in relating as equals with clients. The insistence on a therapeutic contract is an indication of the belief that therapist and client can relate as equals. The Adult of every individual is assumed to be equally effective in relating to the world; indeed one treatment objective is to have the client relate on an Adult-to-Adult level as quickly as possible.

Patients are not the only potential game players in a transactional analysis. Although psychotherapists should certainly be less apt to play games than are their clients, transactional analysts must be ever vigilant to enacting their own scripts at their clients' expense. "Burnout" is a typical racket system of professional helpers: Give so much to everyone until it hurts and you can give no more to anyone (Clarkson, 1992). So are "Top Gun" games, in which therapists compete with one another in a hostile manner (Persi, 1992). Ongoing self-analysis and securing strokes away from the office are required to combat these and other therapist games.

Group therapy is preferred in TA, in part because it allows a greater number of transactions, including more troubled transactions, than might ordinarily occur with an individual therapist relating primarily as Adult. A typical group is composed of about eight members who meet once a week for 2 hours. Clients should be able to see the whole body of other members in order to pick up bodily cues that reveal Parent or Child ego states. A videotape recorder should be available to assist clients in analyzing their ego states and transactions; a blackboard for diagramming transactions is also recommended.

TA can be conducted as either a lengthy or a brief psychotherapy. Berne tended toward a lengthy treatment consisting of psychoeducation, individual therapy, and group therapy involving several years. Contemporary versions of TA favor briefer treatment combined with methods culled from other systems of psychotherapy (Lapworth & Sills, 2011;

Tudor, 2002). But whether lengthy or brief, pure or integrated, TA always analyzes the PAC ego states of clients and fosters the life position of I'm OK— you're OK.

Effectiveness of Interpersonal Therapies

Turning first to TA, a review of the literature yields only a small number of controlled studies on TA's effectiveness. In their meta-analysis, Smith, Glass, and Miller (1980) located eight controlled studies investigating TA. The average effect size for TA was 0.67—slightly larger than the average effect size of 0.56 found for placebo treatments but slightly smaller than the average effect size of 0.85 for all psychotherapies. A meta-analysis on individual psychotherapy with adults (Grawe et al., 1998) located only four controlled studies covering 226 patients. There was an insufficient number of treatment-to-control comparisons to reach any reliable statements about TA's effectiveness. Although some attention has been paid to child therapy in the TA literature (e.g., Massey & Massey, 1989; Veevers, 1991), insufficient controlled research has been conducted on TA with children to make it into the meta-analyses.

The emerging conclusions are that TA with adults has been proven more effective than no treatment and usually more effective than placebo treatments. Depending on the study and the interpretation of "differences," TA produces outcomes at best comparable to other forms of insight-oriented psychotherapy and at worst inferior to other forms of psychotherapy. A related conclusion is that TA has not been sufficiently evaluated in a large enough number of controlled studies to reliably evaluate its relative effectiveness.

By contrast, Klerman and Weissman's IPT has been thoroughly researched in randomized clinical trials. We shall begin our research synopsis by reviewing the results of a seminal RCT and then proceed to the quantitative reviews and meta-analyses.

The groundbreaking National Institute of Mental Health (NIMH) Treatment of Depression Collaborative Research Program evaluated the effectiveness of IPT, cognitive therapy, imipramine plus clinical management, and placebo plus clinical management for treating unipolar depressed outpatients (Elkin et al., 1989). This study, widely known by the less cumbersome title **NIMH Collaborative Treatment Study**, was groundbreaking on many accounts. First, it was the first coordinated, multisite study initiated by the NIMH in the field of psychotherapy. Although collaborative clinical trials are frequently used in psychotherapy, it had rarely been employed in such a large study. Second, the sheer size of the undertaking—screening 560 patients, treating 239 of them, assessing their progress over 18 months, training 28 therapists, and coordinating four treatment conditions at three sites across the United States—was impressive in and of itself. Third, the NIMH Collaborative Study set a research standard for the precision and number of controls employed in comparative outcome research. These controls included standardized training for the therapists, careful monitoring of therapist adherence to the respective treatment manuals, rigorous screening of potential patients, appropriate use of multiple disorder-relevant outcome measures, and follow-up of clinical outcomes for 18 months posttreatment.

At termination, collaborative study patients in all treatments showed significant reduction in depressive symptomatology and improvement in functioning. Aggregating across the battery of outcome measures, the three clinical treatments generally did best and the placebo treatment did worst. The percentage of "completer" patients judged to be recovered at termination on the Beck Depression Inventory was 70% for IPT, 69% for imipramine, 65% for cognitive therapy, and 51% for the placebo treatment, which combined a pill-placebo with regular meetings consisting of support, encouragement, and if necessary, direct advice. On secondary analyses in which patients were dichotomized according to initial severity of depression, significant differences among the treatments were present only for the subgroup of patients who were more severely disturbed. Here, there was some preliminary evidence for the superiority of interpersonal therapy and strong preliminary evidence for the superiority of medication. In contrast, there were no differences among the three treatment groups for the less severely disturbed patients.

Recent meta-analyses (Cuijpers et al., 2008, 2011) included 38 controlled trials of IPT for treating depression, involving more than 4,000 patients. The overall effect size (*d*) for IPT compared to a control group was 0.63, a medium effect. IPT definitely outperforms no treatment or a waitlist for depressed adolescents, adults, and older adults. The effect size for IPT compared to other psychological treatments was 0.04 in one meta-analysis and 0.20 in another. IPT is as effective or slightly more effective than alternative therapies. The meta-analyses conclude that the results of IPT are comparable to those of cognitive therapy for depression (Jakobsen et al., 2012).

The effectiveness of IPT as a maintenance treatment has also been investigated in several RCTs. In an early study by Klerman and Weissman (1991), 150 acutely depressed outpatients who had responded positively to a tricyclic antidepressant (amitriptyline) received 8 months of maintenance treatment with drugs alone, IPT alone, or a combination of the two. The findings showed that maintenance drug treatment alone prevented symptom relapse but did little for interpersonal functioning, whereas IPT alone improved social functioning and interpersonal relations but had little effect on symptom relapse. No negative interaction between the drugs and psychotherapy

was found; on the contrary, the combination of medication and IPT was most efficacious, probably because of their differential effects (Klerman & Weissman, 1991).

These results are supported by the meta-analytic findings (Cuijpers et al., 2011) and by additional research by Ellen Frank and colleagues (Frank, 1991; Frank et al., 1989). They also examined the prophylactic (preventative) effectiveness of IPT in depressed patients. IPT exerted a positive therapeutic effect in patients discontinued from medication at the outset of maintenance. After 18 months of maintenance, patients receiving IPT alone or IPT plus placebo survived, on average, 10 months longer without recurrence of depression than did those patients receiving occasional medical contact in conjunction with placebo. The median "survival" time was 61 weeks versus 21 weeks. These and other results point to the value of IPT in maintaining treatment gains and protecting against early recurrence of depression. What gets depressed clients well keeps them well.

An interesting line of research continues to examine the comparative effectiveness of IPT alone to IPT plus medication. One study (Miller et al., 1998, 2001) examined the effectiveness of IPT plus medication in the treatment of depressed elders. More than 70 patients at least 60 years of age received an antidepressant medication (nortriptyline) and IPT with an experienced clinician. Fully 81% of the patients showed a full response to the combined treatment (psychotherapy and medication together). The most common problem areas were role transition (41%), interpersonal disputes (34%), and grief (23%).

The meta-analyses generally, but not always, conclude that combination treatment (psychotherapy and medication) prove more effective for severe depression (e.g., Cuijpers et al., 2009, 2011; Miklowitz, 2008). In conjunction, IPT and medication tend to work quicker and delay relapses better than either treatment alone. IPT seeks to prevent relapse from mood disorders by resolving one or two of the most common interpersonal problems, whereas medication prevents relapse by targeting neurotransmitter deficits at the synaptic level.

Although IPT was first introduced as a treatment for depression, it has been increasingly applied to other disorders. In eating disorders, for example, IPT targets interpersonal stress and current interpersonal relationships rather than dietary issues or body weight (Johnson et al. 1996). Binge eating often begins in the context of unsatisfactory interpersonal situations, and the anxiety from conflictual relationships often triggers binge eating, leading to a loss of control over food intake. In an RCT, IPT achieved equivalent effects in the reduction of binge eating and vomiting with over 90% reduction in symptomatology maintained at 1-year follow-up. IPT was a bit slower in securing these positive results than cognitive therapy or behavior therapy (Fairburn et al., 1993); however, at long-term follow-up, the eating disordered patients treated with IPT fared better than those treated with behavior therapy (Fairburn et al., 1995). A meta-analysis confirms that IPT is efficacious for bulimia nervosa and binging, particularly in the long run (Hay et al., 2009).

By contrast, patients suffering from opiate addiction or cocaine abuse are rarely helped by IPT (Weissman et al., 2007). The problem is the majority of addicts (66% in one study) drop out of IPT (Carroll et al., 1991). These negative outcomes for the treatment of substance abuse suggest IPT is not always the royal road to treating a disorder (Markowitz, 1997); in fairness to IPT, it never claimed to be a solution to all disorders. Future research is needed to determine for which other disorders IPT will prove effective.

All told, the results from the NIMH Collaborative Study, multiple RCTs, and several meta-analyses strongly support the effectiveness of interpersonal psychotherapy for treating depression and eating disorders. IPT uniformly outperforms no treatment and placebo therapy in both the acute and maintenance treatment for adolescents, adults, and older adults. IPT rightfully deserves its reputation as one of the most researched and most effective treatments for mood and eating disorders.

Criticisms of Interpersonal Therapies
From a Cognitive-Behavioral Perspective
Well, what's not to like about IPT? It is a short-term, problem-focused psychotherapy originating in randomized clinical trials. Klerman and Weissman were committed scientists who agree with us that RCTs are for testing and establishing the efficacy of all treatments. They carefully replicated their treatment studies, and only gradually expanded IPT to other disorders and populations. The development of IPT was indeed scientific, or as we would prefer to call it, cognitive-behavioral.

Our biggest gripe is with the IPT label. Read the IPT treatment manuals or watch a session of structured IPT and you will find a sophisticated form of cognitive-behavioral therapy wrapped in interpersonal language. Educating patients, letting them emote, and then teaching social skills and stimulus control is what we CBT practitioners do. Avoid the post-Freudian interpersonal vocabulary and concentrate on therapist behavior. Then you will be honest in your labeling and will declare IPT a close cousin, if not a sibling, of cognitive-behavioral therapy.

From a Psychoanalytic Perspective
IPT may be many things, but it is definitely not "interpersonal." That term rightfully belongs to the descendants of Harry Stack Sullivan, John Bowlby, and relational psychotherapists who actively prize and intensively work with complex patients. IPT does neither.

IPT is an interpersonal theory without a person. Patients do not have personalities; they just have grief and role transitions. IPT has no theory of the person, only a technology of change. IPT has no explanation for the driving forces of intrapsychic life, only role disputes and interpersonal deficits. IPT has no use for a therapy relationship that delves into in-session interactions, transference, and resistance, only a relationship that avoids them and externalizes the focus to outside of treatment. Patients are left relating to an expert manual and medications. IPT has no interest in character change, only symptom alleviation. In short, IPT has no interpersonal theory, relationship, or goal.

From a Humanistic Perspective

Transactional analysis is faced with the Humpty Dumpty dilemma. Once you assume human beings are broken into three separate parts, all the king's horses and all the king's men will never put humanity back together again. Instead of the traditional dualism of Western thought, TA divides us into a tripartite personality of PAC that can never know the beauty of being whole.

In an era when fragmentation and isolation drive increasing numbers to seek treatment, how can we even think of using therapeutic terms such as games and scripts? TA strengthens fragmentation by reassuring us that personality does indeed come in separate parts. Rather than recognize the phenomena of Parent, Child, and Adult as the social roles they are, TA would have us believe that these roles are the fundamental reality of human personality. Once stuck with this assumption of fundamental fragmentation, we can never hope to realize the holism essential to health.

From a Cultural Perspective

Interpersonal therapy fails to go far enough. Yes, interpersonal theory extended the clinical focus from intrapsychic conflicts to interpersonal patterns, but it stops short of the family system and the sociopolitical context. When boiled down, the presumed determinants of interpersonal problems are still situated within the individual rather than within cultural structures and socialization.

If we really want to look at games people play, how about looking at "spouse abuse," "children in poverty," "underpaid women in the workforce," "blame the minorities," and "government for and by wealthy white men." Let's analyze and modify those scripts!

IPT practitioners posit that a fundamental cause of depression is role disputes. The real problem is disputes about roles. Oppressive roles, such as traditional roles of women, are likely to become depressive. No wonder women suffer twice the rate of depression as men. The traditional roles of ethnic minorities have been too small for their selves. The problem is not to help clients adapt to roles that are too restrictive and too oppressive. The challenge is to create opportunities for individuals to be free from abuse, neglect, and oppression. But these opportunities cannot be created by simply focusing on fragmented units, such as isolated couples or nuclear families. We must help rebuild social networks that support communities filled with healthy and connected households.

From an Integrative Perspective

Presenting a psychotherapy in common language has the decided advantage of allowing people to appreciate and use that psychotherapy. At the same time, formulating a theory of psychopathology and psychotherapy in the language of everyday life brings with it the risk of producing a system lacking depth.

In the 1960s and 1970s, the popularity of TA suggested that people were taking advantage of its simple terms and trying to apply it to their lives. In fact, all too often TA sounded like a system of slick Madison Avenue slogans. "I'm OK—you're OK" sounds like a rating from an OK used-car lot. "Games people play" is a catch phrase more appropriate for a reality series on TV than for tortured human transactions. In the '00s, the popularity of IPT indicates that a research-driven, personality-less therapy can prosper by using ordinary language and pragmatic interventions. In addition, any psychotherapy that works well with medication is bound to succeed in the era of pharmaceuticals.

Interpersonal psychotherapies frequently come through as commonsense approaches without the requisite sophistication to articulate the mysteries of the human condition and the complexities of human change. Both IPT and TA are typically American in language and in pragmatics. Everyday language is best suited for articulating everyday events. If we are attempting to explain (and rectify) human pathology, then everyday language leaves us cold. The problem with IPT and TA is that they are too common and too cognitive, too far from the depth and the passion that make life vital.

An Interpersonal Analysis of Mr. and Mrs. C

The marriage of Mr. and Mrs. C is at a depressing impasse and will deteriorate into dissolution, if not divorce, unless interpersonal treatment is forthcoming. The Cs have replaced intimate companionship with compulsive rituals. Instead of reaching out to each other for closeness and caring, Mrs. C preoccupies her hands with cleaning and controlling. And Mr. C participates in their *folie-à-deux* (madness of two) rather than striving to become a fulfilling family of eight.

In psychotherapy we could easily regress to focusing on Mrs. C's family of origin to understand how her cruel and controlling father dominated her relationships inside and outside their family. We could also imagine a mother who supported cleanliness over closeness, working over relating, and seclusion over sexuality. But understanding the past won't change the present. Mrs. C has already wasted too much time in therapy resurrecting her past, as if she could find some unconscious key that could unlock her current compulsions.

If we are to find a key to the Cs' current conflicts, we need to analyze the patterns in their interpersonal relationships. Mrs. C is obsessed with washing her hands. But hands aren't meant for washing. They are meant for touching her toddlers and teens in tender ways and her spouse in intimate and sensual ways. Instead of isolating herself in her shower being cued by her husband about her compulsion, she will need to learn again how to share her shower with her spouse.

If Mrs. C could miraculously wash away her compulsions, what would be left? Emptiness? Or happiness? What would fill the void? For most people, the greatest meaning and fulfillment emerges from their interpersonal relationships. If Mr. and Mrs. C do not receive IPT in renegotiating and rebuilding their relationship, their shared compulsions could be replaced by shared depression and marital dissolution.

But maybe their interpersonal relationship is beyond repair. Maybe they will have to face the future through a depressing divorce. If so, they would need help with anticipatory grieving over an anticipated loss. Facing the prospect of divorce could move them toward reconciliation and restructuring.

If Mr. and Mrs. C are to have a chance of revitalizing their marriage and their family, they will have to draw on their strengths. On the surface there don't seem to be a lot of strengths. But look at how much time and effort this couple spends on maintaining their irrational rituals. If they spent just a fraction of that on maintaining their marriage, what might they accomplish?

To do so, Mrs. C will need to learn that the healthier we become, the more our problems emerge from our strengths. The less healthy we are, the more our problems emerge from our weaknesses. One of Mrs. C's core weaknesses is

(continued)

her fear of dirt and disease. We also expect that she has irrational fears of intimacy and sexuality. She needs help to start facing her fears. Some of that help can come from medication. Antidepressant medications are now known to be effective for reducing compulsions as well as for depression. Combination treatment would be optimal for Mrs. C.

Mrs. C can also be helped to face her fears of intimacy and sexuality. Together, they can renegotiate how they can support each other's strengths rather than their neuroses. They can gradually begin sensate focusing in which they slowly begin to touch each other in sensitive and sensual ways. Mrs. C can start to own her hands and body as a means of relating rather than a way of controlling.

Mrs. C will need help to accept that her role is not to control. In healthy relationships we do need to be important sources of influence; Mr. and Mrs. C should be so with their six children. But unlike social control, interpersonal influence flows both ways. So they need to be open to being influenced (and changed) by their children. And their children could be sources of interpersonal strengths. Children want their parents to be healthy and happy. The children could become a growing source of fulfillment and fun. But the Cs will have to start to let go of their compulsive needs to control.

Even with the best IPT, the Cs will continue to experience problems. No matter how hard she tries, Mrs. C cannot wash her hands free of problems. Not with six children. Not with her fears and her father. Mrs. C will gradually become healthier as her problems emerge from strengths like the commitment to interpersonal relationships in her large family.

Maintenance IPT will need to be available on an as-needed basis. As they struggle to restructure their marital and family relationships, there will be times that the long-standing rituals pull them back into compulsion and isolation. During such vulnerable times, Mrs. and Mr. C will need to reach out to their psychotherapist as a source of strength and support to prevent relapse.

Future Directions

After a public surge in the 1960s and 1970s, TA has faded as a prominent system of psychotherapy because of its arcane language and research inadequacy. In our recent poll of experts on the future of psychotherapy (Chapter 18), the use of TA was predicted to decrease the most of any of the 31 systems. Nonetheless, TA remains popular among students of psychotherapy and in several European countries.

IPT and the interpersonal variants of psychodynamic psychotherapy are hot, but the prospects for TA are not. The limited prospects for TA lie in its integration with other systems of psychotherapy. TA is frequently combined with systems theory in couples treatment, and many transactional analysts find themselves associated with the existential/humanistic and relational camps (Hargaden & Sills, 2002). TA's future path is integrative psychotherapy (Knapp, 1999).

Many features of Klerman and Weissman's IPT portend its increasing popularity. IPT has been clearly operationalized in treatment manuals; it has been rigorously evaluated in controlled research; it is short-term in nature; it has an underlying interpersonal orientation attractive to many practitioners; it is applicable to acute as well as maintenance treatment; and it is compatible with concurrent pharmacotherapy—all likely features of the immediate future of psychotherapy (see Chapter 18). IPT will also derive increasing popularity from its creative and widening applications to many disorders, dysthymic disorder, couples conflict, bipolar disorder, and traumatic grief, among them (see Weissman et al., 2007; Mufson et al., 2004a; Stuart & Robertson, 2012).

Especially notable are successful efforts to apply briefer IPT by telephone and by nurse practitioners to primary care patients and postpartum women, a large percentage of whom present with complaints directly related to anxiety, depression, and functional body ailments (Grote et al., 2004; Klerman et al., 1987). In this way, IPT will be offered to a wider audience than that presenting for formal psychotherapy.

IPT's efficacy compares favorably both to sophisticated pharmacotherapy and to psychotherapies with more elaborate theoretical underpinnings. Future challenges will be to broaden training opportunities in IPT, understand how (through what processes) interpersonal therapy exerts these salubrious effects, and to test its generalizability to other disorders (Frank & Spanier, 1995; Markowitz, 1997). In these ways, IPT can improve its impact and extend its scope to the interpersonal functioning of an enlarged share of humanity.

Key Terms

attachment styles
bibliotherapy
combined treatment
dissolution
ego state
expressed emotion
  (EE)
games people play
impasse
interpersonal
  psychotherapy
  (IPT)
Interpersonal
  Reconstructive
  Therapy (IRT)
interpersonal school of
  psychoanalysis
life positions
NIMH Collaborative
  Treatment Study

Parent, Adult, and
  Child (PAC)
participant-observer
payoff
primary problem area
randomized clinical
  trials (RCTs)
renegotiation
ritual
role disputes
role transitions
stroking
structural analysis
switch
transaction
transactional analysis
  (TA)

Recommended Readings

Benjamin, L. S. (2006). *Interpersonal reconstructive therapy.* New York: Guilford.

Berne, E. (1964). *Games people play.* New York: Grove.

Hinrichsen, G. A., & Clougherty, K. F. (2006). *Interpersonal psychotherapy for depressed older adults.* Washington, DC: American Psychological Association.

Horowitz, L. M., & Strack, S. (Eds.). (2011). *Handbook of interpersonal psychotherapy.* Hoboken, NJ: Wiley.

Klerman, G. L., Weissman, M. M., Rounsaville, B. J., & Chevron, E. S. (1984). *Interpersonal psychotherapy of depression.* New York: Basic.

Stuart, S., & Robertson, M. (2012). *Interpersonal psychotherapy: A clinician's guide* (2nd ed.). New York: Oxford University Press.

Sullivan, H. S. (1953). *The interpersonal theory of psychiatry.* New York: Norton.

Weissman, M. M., Markowitz, J. C., & Klerman, G. L. (2007). *Clinician's quick guide to interpersonal psychotherapy.* New York: Oxford University Press.

JOURNALS: *Psychiatry; Interpersonal and Biological processes; Transactional Analysis Journal.*

Recommended Websites

International Society for Interpersonal Psychotherapy:
  www.interpersonalpsychotherapy.org/index
International Transactional Analysis Association:
  www.itaaworld.org
Society for Interpersonal Theory and Research (SITAR):
  www.sitarsociety.weebly.com
United States Transactional Analysis Association:
  www.usataa.org/

CHAPTER 8

Exposure Therapies

Edna Foa

Francine Shapiro

Annique was living the good life in an off-campus house with three fellow graduate students. She had it all—a loving family, a strong self, a bunch of devoted friends, a promising career after her final year of graduate school—until "that day."

On a sunny afternoon after class Annique returned to their apartment to find a burglar ransacking her room. The burglar briefly threatened Annique with his knife and then fled with the loot, including Annique's irreplaceable jewelry, originally belonging to her grandmother. She was obviously shaken and rattled, but she and her housemates got through it together. Or so she thought.

Four weeks after the burglary, Annique could not sleep through the night. She felt anxious and jumpy all the time, began experiencing flashbacks to that night, and scanning the environment, half expecting a reoccurrence of the robbery every day. Annique sought assistance at the University Counseling Center, where a staff therapist accurately diagnosed acute PTSD (post-traumatic stress disorder) and sensitively conducted supportive therapy once per week. Annique found the therapist warm and the

sessions useful to air out her feelings, but her insomnia, numbness, and fears persisted for another month without relief. Annique couldn't function in class and was contemplating a medical leave of absence from her graduate studies.

She was referred to me (JCN) for an exposure-based therapy to confront her crippling symptoms. Offered either prolonged exposure or EMDR (eye movement desensitization and reprocessing), Annique chose the latter. In the sessions, Annique directly confronted in her mind that burglar and her fears. She courageously, repeatedly faced "that day" until it lost its power over her. Following four sessions of EMDR, Annique was freed from her PTSD and resumed her good life. As Annique eloquently put it, "I adored my social worker at the Counseling Center, but with this trauma I needed something more than friendly support."

A Note on Exposure Therapies

Directly confronting feared stimuli, such as the burglary, and activating intense emotions, such as Annique's crippling anxiety, are the distinctive characteristics of treatment approaches known as **exposure therapies**. Following considerable attention given to these therapies in the 1970s, their clinical popularity waned in the 1980s, but they have been revived to combat a host of intransigent anxiety and trauma disorders.

In this chapter, we begin with a synopsis of an influential precursor of exposure treatments: **implosive therapy**. We then examine two of the most evocative and provocative of these therapies: **prolonged exposure** and **eye movement desensitization and reprocessing (EMDR)**. This chapter sequence is intentional: It reflects the historical development of these therapies (from past to present) and their theoretical predilections (from purely behavioral to integrative).

As we will see, these exposure therapies vary considerably in the procedures used to directly confront and gradually reduce emotions. Implosive therapy presents a fantastic form of imagery; prolonged exposure offers both imaginary and actual confrontation to the fears; and EMDR promises desensitization by means of directed eye movements or hand taps. These approaches also vary considerably in their theoretical explanations of psychopathology and psychotherapy. Nevertheless, they share the common assumption that behavioral disorders

can best be treated by directly exposing the patient to the emotional pain.

Several readers have argued that exposure is largely a method of behavior therapy, and thus should be placed in the behavior therapies chapter. Although it is true that the early forms of exposure hailed from the behavioral tradition, it is *not* true of most or contemporary versions of exposure therapy. They have evolved into fairly complex, distinctive, and integrative systems of psychotherapy. We believe they merit a separate chapter.

To keep this chapter to a manageable size, the sections on personality theory and therapeutic content have been omitted. Furthermore, we group criticisms of the three therapies together to avoid redundancy. (Expanded consideration of implosive therapy in the form of a minichapter can be accessed online at www.cengagebrain.com.)

Implosive Therapy

Thomas Stampfl (1923–2005), the founder of implosive therapy, became convinced early in his career that avoidance is at the heart of psychopathology. He developed his system of psychotherapy in order to help people face their most frightening memories, feelings, and thoughts. Stampfl was inspired by both the psychoanalytic content of psychopathology and the learning theory processes of **avoidance conditioning** and **extinction**. He developed a treatment that would integrate psychoanalytic and behavioral therapy, and later became among the first behavioral researchers to demonstrate the efficacy of implosion in the laboratory and apply it in the consulting room.

The symptoms and defense mechanisms that characterize psychopathology represent **learned avoidance** that serve to reduce anxiety in the short term. Phobics avoid stimuli such as dogs, elevators, or heights; obsessive-compulsives may avoid dirt, disorder, or anger; schizophrenics may avoid close contact with people; hypochondriacs attempt to avoid disease. If troubled individuals did not use their symptoms and defenses to avoid these stimuli, they would be confronted with considerable anxiety that could take on panic proportions.

People learn to avoid particular stimuli in order to avoid the conditioned anxiety. Consider the case of a 24-year-old man entering psychotherapy to overcome his dread of getting close to people, especially women. His traumatic childhood was punctuated by a hostile mother and an alcoholic, abusive father. He recalled multiple memories of physical and verbal abuse, such as the time he was talking jubilantly at breakfast about a field trip at school, when suddenly his mother grabbed his hair and pushed his face into the hot cereal because he was talking too loudly. He could never predict when he might get smacked in the back of the head or punished for showing anger, enthusiasm, or sadness. All he could predict was that when people were around, particularly his parents, he was more likely to face a frightening encounter.

The stimuli that were conditioned to elicit anxiety were his parents specifically and, through the process of **generalization**, almost any person with whom he became emotionally involved. When he began to get close to someone, his classically conditioned anxiety would be elicited. When he then retreated and avoided interpersonal closeness, his anxiety would be reduced and his avoidance of people reinforced. Even though the new people he might approach would not shove his face into hot cereal or scream unpredictably, he was still responding with anxiety and avoidance.

If the cause of psychopathology is conditioned anxiety and avoidance, then the solution is to apply the most effective methods of extinguishing both avoidance and anxiety responses. *Extinction* is the gradual disappearance of the conditioned anxiety because it is no longer reinforced—in this case, no longer reinforced by avoidance. Implosive therapy

was created in response to the single question of what intervention would faithfully reflect the operations of experimental psychologists when they subject lower animals to extinction procedures in the laboratory (Stampfl, 1976).

Early on, experimental research studies (e.g., Baum, 1970; Black, 1958; Solomon et al., 1953) documented that avoidance can be effectively extinguished if an animal is blocked from avoiding in the presence of anxiety-eliciting stimuli. When the animal is blocked in the presence of anxiety-eliciting stimuli, intense emotional reactions are evoked. The animal will scramble about the cage, climb the walls or attack the barrier, freeze in the corner, and shake, all followed by more scrambling.

Response prevention, on an animal level, extinguishes anxiety by forcing the animal to remain in the presence of the conditioned stimuli. On a human level, response prevention entails extinguishing pathological anxiety by working to prevent clients from avoiding the anxiety-eliciting stimuli.

Implosive therapy places great demands on the mental health professional. It is definitely one of the most emotionally draining therapies to conduct. Following a few evaluation sessions, the implosive therapist must construct stimulus scenes that evoke the maximum level of anxiety. Stimuli most directly related to the client's symptoms will be first in the series of anxiety-eliciting cues, such as bugs for a person with a morbid dread of bugs. When implosive therapists ask clients to vividly imagine scenes about bugs, they have the person imagine the bugs as close to them as possible, crawling on their arms, in their hair, sleeping with them in bed, under the covers, all over their bodies, with their bug eyes popping out, their antennas touching the client's lips, as they come mouth-to-mouth with each other.

More challenging for the implosive therapist is to construct scenes that have been repressed or cognitively avoided. These repressed stimuli are similar to what psychoanalysts refer to as the dynamics of psychopathology, such as repressed feelings of rage. These dynamic cues are assumed to be the stimuli that elicit the most anxiety. Dynamic cues are based on psychodynamic theories of psychopathology and on the therapist's clinical interpretations. Such cues include fears of losing control over hostile or sexual urges, anal impulses, fears of responsibility and facing one's conscience, and anxiety over anxiety itself. Implosive therapists use their full imaginations to create the most evocative scenes possible.

As implosive scenes are presented, clients are observed for overt signs of anxiety, such as rapid breathing, sweaty palms, crying, gripping the chair, or curling up and covering their faces. When signs of anxiety are observed, the therapist uses this feedback to intensify or repeat the scene to elicit and thereby extinguish more anxiety. The polite person will typically terminate a discussion or image that another person finds objectionable; by contrast, the implosive therapist intentionally intensifies the image to make it more objectionable!

As if that were not enough, the implosive therapist must stay with a scene until the anxiety has been noticeably reduced and at least partly extinguished. If a session or scene were terminated while the client was highly anxious, the client could become even more sensitized to the conditioned stimuli and might increase his or her avoidance once the session had ended. The client could also have anxiety conditioned to the treatment setting and might avoid returning to therapy. Consequently, implosive therapists are trained to stay with scenes until the client is drained of most of the emotion connected with a particular scene.

Implosive therapy has few contemporary proponents, and most of them prefer to characterize themselves as exposure therapists. Nonetheless, implosive therapy initiated treatments that directly confront clients' sources of fear and provided the clinical and research foundations on which others built. We now turn to the two most clinically popular and empirically supported exposure therapies: prolonged exposure and EMDR.

Prolonged Exposure
A Sketch of Edna B. Foa

Many clinicians have contributed to the treatment designated as prolonged exposure therapy, but the most influential and systematic has probably been Edna B. Foa (1937–). Born in Haifa, Israel, she came to the United States for her graduate education. She completed her master's at the University of Illinois under the supervision of O. H. Mowrer. In the 1960s, the clinical program was one of the strongholds of behavior therapy; the faculty included many of the early leaders of behavior therapy, Leonard Ullmann, Leonard Krazner, and Gordon Paul, among them. After completing her PhD in 1970 at the University of Missouri–Columbia, Foa received an NIMH postdoctoral fellowship to work with the father of behavior therapy, Joseph Wolpe at Temple University, the Mecca of behavior therapy at the time.

Foa has spent her entire career in Philadelphia, first at Temple University then at the medical college of Pennsylvania, and since 1998, at the Department of Psychiatry at the University of Pennsylvania Medical School. In 1979, she founded the influential center for the treatment and study of anxiety. There, with the collaboration of many colleagues, she has been instrumental in examining the effectiveness of exposure therapy for many anxiety disorders, primarily obsessive-compulsive disorder (OCD), PTSD, and social anxiety disorder (SAD).

Foa began her research career by examining the efficacy of behavioral treatments for anxiety and mood disorders. She soon discovered the limitations of behavior therapy: not all patients were helped and many remained quite symptomatic. As a natural sequel, she extended her research to the study of what worked for anxiety disorders. That led to the refinement of exposure therapy and to the development of emotional-processing theory (Foa & Kozak, 1986), a framework that has elucidated the mechanisms involved in pathological anxiety and that has assisted millions in overcoming their fears.

Theory of Personality

Prolonged exposure may be considered a prototype of the newer therapies that eschew speculation about human personality and motivation. Instead, these newer therapies principally concern themselves with facilitating behavior change. Prolonged exposure therapy, in this vanguard, is a theory of psychopathology and treatment, not personality.

Theory of Psychopathology

In the behavioral tradition, exposure therapists view anxiety as a conditioned response controlled by the two learning factors. Both respondent learning and operant learning are involved in the development and maintenance of behavioral disorders. Conditioning accounts for the acquisition of the fear, and extinction (or habituation) accounts for the fear reduction.

O. H. Mowrer (1947) advanced a **two-factor theory of learning** to explain avoidance. The first factor is **classical** or **respondent conditioning**, through which an animal learns to fear a buzzer because it has been paired with shock. This conditioned fear is labeled anxiety. The buzzer becomes a conditioned stimulus capable of eliciting an automatic and autonomic conditioned response similar to fear. If the dog remains near the buzzer, the aversive anxiety increases in intensity. If the dog jumps over the barrier, the anxiety is reduced, and the dog's avoidance is reinforced by the powerful consequence of anxiety reduction.

The second factor in learning to avoid is called **operant** or **instrumental conditioning** because it is instrumental in minimizing the dog's anxiety.

The classically conditioned anxiety serves as the motivating or drive stimulus that activates the avoidance response, whereas the anxiety reduction provides the consequence necessary for reinforcement of the instrumental avoidance.

Mowrer coined the term **neurotic paradox** to describe this phenomenon: the failure of maladaptive anxiety to extinguish despite its self-defeating nature. The paradox is resolved by distinguishing between the short term and the long term. In the short term, obsessive thoughts and compulsive rituals actually relieve anxiety by avoiding confrontation with feared situations. The obsessive-compulsive who washes his or her hands five times in a row or checks the door locks five times is being reinforced through anxiety reduction: "whew! I avoided dirt and danger again." In the long term, however, such washing and checking invariably lead to more intense avoidance and more intense anxiety. Avoidance of an anxiety-producing situation—be it an exam, a confrontation, or a fear—brings relief immediately but more misery eventually.

Foa and exposure therapists conceptualize anxiety-based psychopathologies in terms of both the traditional behavioral theory and an **emotional-processing theory** (Foa & Jaycox, 1999; Foa & Kozak, 1986). Why do some rape victims, for example, recover and others develop chronic PTSD? The emotional-processing theory proposes that special efforts are required to process the traumatic event, and that the completion of this process is necessary for recovery. Chronic disorders are signs that this processing has not occurred and that the representation of the traumatic experience in memory contains pathological elements, such as erroneous estimations about the potential for harm and about one's ability to handle the intense anxiety. Accordingly, Foa's exposure therapy aims both to reverse the behavioral conditioning and to correct the patient's erroneous cognitive and emotional processes.

Therapeutic Processes

Successful exposure therapy activates the patient's pathological structure and, at the same time, introduces corrective information that can be incorporated into a new, more adaptive structure. The therapeutic strategy is to reverse the reinforcement contingencies or the neurotic paradox: intentional, prolonged contact with the feared stimuli (prolonged exposure) and the active blocking of the associated avoidance (response prevention). In the short term, patients will certainly experience increased anxiety, but through the process of extinction, they will with equal certainty experience reduced anxiety and avoidance in the long term.

Take, for example, the common fear that children develop toward large and unfamiliar dogs. The child will manifest anxiety—trembling, protesting, crying, sweating, among others—and resultant avoidance—turning away, leaving the area, refusing to enter the space occupied by the dog. To countercondition this fear, we could opt for several types of exposure therapy, as I (JCN) was forced to do when my son, Jonathon, developed a canine phobia resulting from a single unpleasant encounter with a stray dog.

One decision is whether to administer exposure in an intensive or graduated fashion. Jonathon could be exposed directly and immediately to the dog (intensive) or exposed slowly and incrementally (gradually) from the least feared to the most feared situation. In the former, we would place Jonathon directly next to an unknown dog, which, of course, would precipitate intense anxiety. In the latter case, we would slowly introduce Jonathon to the general area and take "baby steps" toward the dog.

A second decision is whether the feared dog is presented to Jonathon in his imagination (**imaginal exposure**) or in the real situation (**in vivo exposure**). In both cases, the feared stimulus can be presented in an intensive or gradual fashion. Exposure methods varying on these dimensions of exposure medium and arousal level are accorded different names. Systematic desensitization, for instance, is at the extreme of imaginal and minimally arousing exposure (see Chapter 9). At the other extreme would be intense, in vivo exposure.

A third decision is how much we might block Jonathon's attempts to avoid the feared dog. Total response prevention would entail prohibiting the child from leaving the dog until practically all anxiety was eliminated. Partial response prevention would settle for less and allow the child to leave the dog following diminution of anxiety.

All things considered, we decided to treat Jonathon with both imaginal and in vivo exposure in fairly intensive manner with partial response prevention. We taught Jonathon to relax and imagine dogs approaching him at home. Once he was able to comfortably do so, we ventured out to meet some neighborhood dogs, allowing him to pet them for a few minutes and then step away. The 2-hour "treatment" was highly effective, despite the arcane jargon and the psychologist father. In fact, what we did closely resembled what many parents routinely do to overcome their children's fears.

In the exposure treatment of obsessive-compulsive disorder (OCD), the target is the catastrophic fear that underlies the obsessions and compulsions. Each session is terminated after **habituation** (defined as 50% reduction in anxiety to fear-producing stimuli) is achieved. Response prevention is used to block compulsive rituals, such as washing, by instruction, encouragement, direction, persuasion, and other nonphysical means. Because the rituals serve an anxiety-reducing function, the patient must learn that the feared catastrophic consequences do not occur if the rituals are not performed (Turner, 1997).

Although imaginal and in vivo exposure treatments emerged from conditioning theories, the recent conceptualizations invoke the concept of emotional processing to explain fear reduction during exposure. Foa and colleagues (Foa & Kozak, 1986; Foa & Meadows, 1997) suggest that exposure corrects erroneous associations and evaluations. This process of emotional processing requires the activation of the fear structure through the introduction of feared stimuli and the presentation of corrective information incompatible with the pathological elements of the fear structure. Thus, exposure reduces symptoms by allowing patients to realize that contrary to their mistaken ideas (Foa & Meadows, 1997): being in objectively safe situations that remind them of trauma is not dangerous; remembering the trauma is not equivalent to experiencing it again; anxiety does not remain indefinitely in the presence of feared situations or memories; and experiencing anxiety does not lead to loss of control.

In the treatment of PTSD, Foa uses both desensitization and cognitive change. The early sessions entail a thorough assessment, education about common reactions to trauma, and **breathing retraining** (teaching clients to breathe calmly from the diaphragm). Before exposure begins, clients receive a clear rationale for the treatment method. Repeated exposure to the trauma is then achieved in the office through imaginal exposure, which enhances the emotional processing, and then through in vivo exposure, which enables the client to realize that the trauma-related situations are not dangerous.

The exposure therapist warns the client that, "the treatment involves confronting you with situations and memories which generate anxiety and urge to avoid," but the therapist also reminds the client of the rationale for exposure treatment, something along the lines of, "Confronting these horrible memories, rather than avoiding them, will decrease your fear. Although it is quite natural for you to want to avoid the fear associated with them, as we discussed, the more you avoid these painful memories, the more they disturb your life."

During imaginal exposure, the client is asked to recall the memories of the trauma—be it an assault, combat, or disaster. The client is instructed to "recall these memories as fully and vividly as possible. Don't tell me the story in the third person, but in the present tense, as if it were happening right now, right here." As the client gets into the memories and becomes fearful, the therapist reinforces the client's persistence, saying, for example, "stay with the memory; you are doing fine," and "you are being courageous. Let's keep going with the image." The exposure therapist comments on the gradually dissipating anxiety and reassures the client that the anxiety decreases if he or she stays with it long enough.

For in vivo exposure, the therapist might accompany the client to the scene of the actual trauma or ask the client to wear the same clothing as when the trauma occurred. In Foa's treatment, in vivo exposure is carried out as homework to be practiced between sessions. Clients are instructed to remain in the fearful situations for at least 45 minutes or until the anxiety decreases.

Parallel steps are taken in exposure therapy for OCD. Clients receive a rationale for the exposure treatment, are taught a form of relaxation or self-soothing, and then asked to gradually expose themselves to feared objects or activities. In the case of OCD, this typically encompasses fears of becoming contaminated by touching "dirty" objects or fears of going crazy if they do not engage in compulsive rituals, such as checking, washing, or ordering (Foa & Wilson, 2001). Therapists present clients with prolonged exposure to supposedly contaminated objects, first in their imagination and later in the real environment. The key task here is response prevention—to help the patient not engage in the checking, washing, or ordering ritual that has reduced their anxiety in the past. Over time, prolonged exposure and response prevention results in habituation to the previously feared object or activity.

For example, one of our obsessive-compulsive patients was deathly afraid of touching raw vegetables or uncooked meats. I (JCN) began exposure by having the client vividly imagine a series of situations, using a fear hierarchy, in which he would see, approach, and then briefly touch such objects. Once he was able to manage his anxiety to the imaginal exposure, I asked him to purchase a bunch of raw carrots and celery stalks and bring them into the session. He reluctantly did so—using rubber gloves when he bought and brought them into therapy—and he was successfully able to complete the in vivo exposure. As a testament to his courage and the treatment success, he went on to intensive "maintenance therapy" by working as a restaurant cook!

Similar processes are posited for the effectiveness of **cue exposure** in the treatment of addictive disorders. In substance abusers, cues related to alcohol use, such as the smell of beer or the sight of a vodka bottle, elicit conditioned responses, such as anticipated pleasure or physiological cravings. These conditioned responses are associated with a desire to resume substance abuse and a desire to avoid drug withdrawal.

Repeated exposure to preingestion cues in the absence of substance use might lead to extinction of conditioned responses and maladaptive cognitions, thus reducing the likelihood of substance abuse in the future. Early results of cue exposure treatment for alcohol dependence were promising (e.g., Drummond & Glautier, 1994; Monti et al., 1993; Sitharthan et al., 1997), but a meta-analysis of nine treatment outcome studies suggests little effectiveness for cue exposure as currently implemented (Conklin & Tiffany, 2002).

Therapeutic Relationship

In many ways an exposure therapist operates like an effective but firm parent. Trust is engendered. Confidence is modeled, demonstrating that the feared stimuli, both real and imagined, will not hurt. There is also a parental insistence that helps the client remain in the presence of the feared stimuli, rather than running like a frightened child. The relationship reflects a form of tough love that says, "Don't run away from your problems. Soon you will master it and have a future free from fear."

An abiding therapeutic relationship is essential for clinicians to help patients stay with the threatening material when they desperately want to run. The therapist must engender trust in patients in order for them to continue to cooperate in treatment and to tolerate repeating the fearful memories until anxiety is markedly reduced. Trust building starts at the beginning of the first evaluative session, as the therapist communicates a desire to understand and to assist the client.

Exposure therapists are not particularly concerned with being genuine; they are concerned with being effective. They offer empathy during the evaluation sessions and after the prolonged exposure, but during the exposure itself they insist that the client directly face the fear. Exposure therapists communicate positive regard to clients through the implicit and explicit convictions that clients are much stronger than they usually think. Clients possess the strength and courage to confront the worst fears imaginable as long as they know that their intense anxiety is being elicited by psychotherapy and not by some unknown and uncontrollable source. Interestingly, it is typically other mental health professionals—not patients—who are most resistant to exposure therapy.

Practicalities of Exposure Therapy

The practice of exposure therapy generally entails 8 to 12 individual sessions, each 1 to 2 hours in duration, in a relatively soundproof room in order to let clients emote fully. The sessions typically run longer than the standard 50 minutes because damage could be done to clients by stopping a session on the hour when they are in the midst of experiencing intense anxiety. If a session were terminated while the client was highly anxious, the client could become even more anxious and might exacerbate the behavioral avoidance once the session had ended. The client could also connect the anxiety to the treatment and avoid returning to therapy.

Homework is assigned between sessions. The client is asked to conduct self-controlled exposure by, for instance, listening to an audiotape of a previous session or by imagining the feared situation while relaxing. Clients are asked to expose themselves to the fearful situations for at least 45 minutes or until the anxiety decreases.

Training is widely available from behavior and cognitive therapists experienced in prolonged exposure and response prevention, or PE + RP as it is sometimes known. A special training challenge is to help exposure therapists overcome their own socialized tendencies to avoid producing anxiety in other people. Instead of immediately reducing anxiety, exposure therapists learn to intentionally provoke short-term anxiety in the interest of long-term relief. Their own anxieties must be addressed so that they can effectively facilitate prolonged exposure and response prevention.

Effectiveness of Exposure Therapies

Implosive therapy was researched and its efficacy reported in early meta-analyses. In a 1976 book chapter, Stampfl cited four controlled studies on the efficacy of implosive therapy with clinical patients. All four studies found implosive therapy superior to no treatment: in one study, implosion was more effective than desensitization and in another study, the two treatments were equally effective. An independent review of the research on implosive therapy concurred that, when implosion was compared with systematic desensitization, there were no consistent differences in the effectiveness of the treatments (Morganstern, 1973).

An early meta-analysis on controlled studies containing at least two treatment groups and one control group found 10 studies that evaluated implosion (Shapiro & Shapiro, 1982). The average effect size for all the psychotherapies was 0.93; the average effect size for implosive therapies was 1.12—a large effect in general, and a slightly larger effect than the other therapies to which it was compared. Many studies included in this meta-analysis were behavioral analogues conducted in the 1970s using student volunteers with minimal problems.

Although now largely replaced by prolonged exposure, implosive therapy did not recede in popularity due to an absence of supportive research. Implosive therapy was clearly shown to definitely outperform no treatment, consistently outperform placebo therapy, and generally perform in a comparable, if not superior, manner to alternative psychotherapies.

Prolonged exposure has received considerable attention in controlled outcome studies for the treatment of anxiety, principally PTSD, OCD, panic disorder, social anxiety disorder, and specific phobias.

Post-Traumatic Stress Disorder

In a representative study, Foa and colleagues (1991) randomly assigned 45 rape victims with PTSD to one of four treatment conditions: stress inoculation training, prolonged exposure, supportive counseling, and waitlist. Treatment consisted of nine biweekly, 90-minute individual sessions conducted by a female therapist. Multiple outcome measures were taken at termination and at 3-months posttreatment. All treatments produced improvement at termination and at follow-up. At termination, both stress inoculation training (reviewed in Chapter 9) and exposure produced significantly more improvement in PTSD symptoms than did support or waitlist. At follow-up, however, prolonged exposure produced superior outcome in PTSD symptoms. The interpretation offered for these results was that prolonged exposure creates temporarily high levels of arousal, as patients are asked to repeatedly confront the rape memory, but leads to permanent change in the rape memory and hence results in more durable gains.

Indeed, in multiple meta-analyses of exposure treatments for PTSD, investigators consistently conclude that exposure is efficacious, easily surpassing the effects of wait-list conditions and sometimes surpassing the results of alternative therapies (e.g., Bradley et al., 2005; Powers et al., 2010; Sherman, 1998). In particular, exposure results in decreased symptoms of intrusive images and physiological arousal. These and other meta-analyses indicate that more than half of PTSD patients who complete exposure therapy improve and maintain their improvement after termination of treatment. A meta-analysis (Van Etten & Taylor, 1998) of 61 studies found that exposure therapies (and EMDR) are the most effective treatments for PTSD, surpassing the outcomes of drug therapies and nonexposure treatments.

For sexually abused (Harvey & Taylor, 2010) and traumatized children (Gillies et al., 2012), psychological therapies have also proven efficacious, with cognitive behavior and exposure leading the way. Symptoms of PTSD, depression, and anxiety are significantly lower within a month of completing therapy compared to a control group. At this point, the best research evidence of effectiveness is for CBT and exposure—because more research has been conducted on them with youth—but there is no clear evidence for the superior effectiveness of one over the other in treating children suffering from PTSD (Gillies et al., 2012).

One of the persistent and noisy criticisms of prolonged exposure is that it might cause **symptom exacerbation**, which, in turn, will lead to premature termination or to inferior outcomes. But research on PTSD victims indicates this is rarely the case (Van Etten & Taylor, 1998). Only a minority of female assault victims, for example, exhibit more distress during exposure treatment (10% to 20% on average). What's more, those who did report such exacerbation benefited as

much from therapy as those who did not report symptom exacerbation (Foa et al., 2002). But exposure therapists do need to remind patients that some of them will experience brief symptom exacerbation—things may get worse before they get better.

Obsessive-Compulsive Disorder

Several meta-analyses have been conducted on the effectiveness of exposure therapy with OCD for children and adults (e.g., Abramowitz, 1996; Abramowitz et al., 2005; Eddy et al., 2004; Kobak et al., 1998; O'Kearney et al., 2006; Rosa-Alcazar et al., 2008), leading to several positive conclusions. First, exposure is indeed effective for the treatment of OCD. Prolonged exposure with response prevention leads to substantial improvement for 65% to 70% of patients. Second, exposure with response prevention is more effective than serotonergic antidepressant medications, particularly in alleviating rituals. The outcome research also favors exposure in terms of side effects, dropout, and maintenance, whereas one advantage of medication is that less time and effort are required by the therapist and patient. Third, therapist-supervised exposure is generally more effective than self-controlled exposure. And fourth, the addition of response prevention to exposure is associated with better outcomes than no response prevention.

A recurrent problem with outcomes studies is that they employ different measures and methods of determining treatment success. Some studies use "improvement" as the criteria for success, whereas others use the more rigorous criteria of "no distress" or "return to the normal range." This makes it difficult for the student of psychotherapy to draw firm conclusions about the absolute and relative efficacy of psychological treatments. One solution to different measures is to set a high and standardized bar of patient success, such as **clinical significance** (Jacobson et al., 1999). Relying on **statistical significance** alone tends to inflate small, insubstantial treatment gains; by contrast, using a measure of clinical significance ensures the magnitude of treatment gains is substantial and meaningful.

The difference between statistical significance and clinical significance in patient success was demonstrated in an analysis of various treatments for OCD. When patient success was defined as statistically significant improvement, exposure and response prevention appears the most effective treatment, with 50% to 60% of patients improved. However, when patient success was defined as clinically significant recovery, exposure therapy and cognitive therapy have equivalent and lower outcomes, approximately 25% recovered (Fisher & Wells, 2005).

The research on exposure therapy and medication for OCD underscores that demonstrably effective treatments, even so-called treatments of choice, are not panaceas. For starters, about 20% of OCD clients refuse to participate in exposure and response prevention. Another 20% or so of clients drop out. For those who complete treatment, reduction in their OCD symptoms averages about 48% (Wilhelm et al., 2004). OCD symptoms persist at moderate levels even following a successful course of treatment (Eddy et al., 2004). Medications typically provide only 25% to 50% symptom reduction at high doses and result in 80% to 90% relapse rates following discontinuation of the medications (Dougherty et al., 2004). None of this is meant to suggest the treatments are ineffective; rather, it is to say that OCD is a severe and challenging disorder for which we still have much to learn.

Panic Disorder

In a meta-analysis of 34 treatment studies on panic disorder with agoraphobia (Cox et al., 1992), exposure therapy secured large, powerful effect sizes—1.34 to 3.42—across a variety of outcome variables from the beginning to the end of psychotherapy. The treatment effects for antianxiety medication (alprazolam) were also significant for most patient outcomes, but exposure had the most consistent strong effect.

Such research, however, does not clearly establish the specific contribution of the individual techniques, such as prolonged exposure, cognitive therapy, relaxation training, and breathing retraining. A meta-analysis of 42 studies attempted to do just that (Sanchez-Meca et al., 2010). The results showed that, after controlling for methodological quality of the studies and the type of control groups, the combination of exposure, relaxation, and breathing retraining gave the most consistent evidence for treating panic. The inclusion of homework and the provision of follow-up or booster sessions also improved treatment effectiveness.

Social Anxiety Disorder

Exposure therapy has also proved effective in the treatment of SAD, previously known as social phobia. In 29 randomized studies, all of the psychological therapies produced a large effect (d) on both anxiety and depression measures of SAD patients (Acarturk et al., 2009). As expected, studies with waiting-list control groups had significantly larger effect sizes than studies with placebo control groups. This meta-analysis makes it clear that psychotherapy for social anxiety is effective in adults, but also clear that most therapies employ a combination of exposure, social skills training, cognitive restructuring, and applied relaxation. **Dismantling studies**—research designs to break down a psychotherapy into its constituent ingredients to determine which are the active ingredients—are sorely needed.

Specific Phobia

Some of the earliest applications of exposure therapy targeted specific phobias, the most common of anxiety disorders. These refer to marked, irrational fear of a specific object that causes life interference or distress; common examples include flying, heights, spiders, and blood.

Data from 33 randomized controlled studies were subjected to a meta-analysis to examine the effectiveness of psychotherapies for specific phobias (Wolitzky-Taylor et al., 2008). Exposure treatments produced large effect sizes ($d = 1.05$) relative to no treatment, medium effects (0.48) relative to placebo treatments, and also medium effects (0.44) relative to nonexposure treatments. Although the authors of the meta-analysis did not account for the investigator's allegiance, which probably led to less-than-credible nonexposure treatments in the studies (Bernish et al., 2008), the meta-analysis does document the overall effectiveness of exposure for phobias and the probable superiority of exposure therapy over other therapies for specific fears.

Virtual Reality

As we have seen, exposure can be conducted in various ways: imaginal (in imagination), in vivo (in real-life situations), interoceptive (in physical sensations), and now, with the assistance of computer technology, in virtual reality. **Virtual reality (VR)** exposure therapy integrates real-time computer graphics, visual displays, and other sensory input devices to immerse patients in computer-simulated environments that they find anxiety-producing, such as heights, public speaking, and air flight. Patients are immersed in the computer-generated environments using a head-mounted display that covers their eyes. This treatment provides safe exposure in which the patient can be introduced to the anxiety-producing situations.

The results of controlled research are promising, showing large effect sizes and presaging increased use. A meta-analysis found 52 studies examining the effectiveness of VR exposure, and of these, 21 studies (300 patients) met inclusion criteria. The meta-analysis revealed large declines in anxiety symptoms following VR therapy (Parsons & Rizzo, 2008). A meta-analysis covering overlapping studies reported similar results: large

average effect sizes ($d = 1.11$) across different types of outcome measures (for example, behavioral, psychophysiology, subjective distress). In vivo exposure was not more effective than VR exposure; in fact, there was a trend favoring VR over in vivo treatment (Powers & Emmelkamp, 2008).

All in all, exposure therapy has acquitted itself well in the treatment of the various anxiety disorders. Although it would be premature to hail it as the singular treatment of choice, it certainly is one of the treatments of choice. Exposure therapy consistently produces beneficial results, certainly more so than no treatment, typically more so than medications, and sometimes more so than alternative therapies.

EMDR
A Sketch of Francine Shapiro

The traumatic discovery that led to the 1987 development of EMDR began nearly 10 years earlier. In 1979 Francine Shapiro was completing a doctorate in English literature at New York University and was enjoying success in that field. Then, right before launching into her dissertation on the poetry of Thomas Hardy, she was diagnosed with cancer. This devastating diagnosis led to a watershed in her life: searching for solutions to cancer and to its ravaging psychological effects. She left New York City, enrolled in a doctoral program in clinical psychology, and serendipitously discovered in herself a method now widely used to treat other people's traumatic experiences (Shapiro, 1995).

While walking through the park one day, Shapiro stumbled onto the key of EMDR. She noticed that several of her disturbing thoughts suddenly disappeared. When she brought these thoughts back to mind, they were not as upsetting or as valid as before. Fascinated, she paid close attention and noticed that, when disturbing thoughts came to mind, her eyes spontaneously started moving very rapidly back and forth.

At that point, she started making the eye movements deliberately while concentrating on disturbing thoughts. Again, the thoughts disappeared and lost their charge. Later she experimented with this procedure with other people and found similarly positive results. Because the primary focus was on reducing anxiety in the behavioral tradition and because the primary method was directed eye movements, she called the new procedure eye movement desensitization (EMD).

In response to several successful cases and a controlled trial published in 1989, she began training fellow clinicians and modifying the procedure. The result was the realization that the optimal procedure entailed simultaneous desensitization and cognitive restructuring of traumatic memories. This development led her to rename the procedure eye movement desensitization and reprocessing (EMDR). More than just a change in name, this was a shift in perspective that would take EMDR beyond its original behavioral conceptualization as a desensitization treatment for anxiety to a new, integrative approach to psychotherapy (Shapiro, 1995, 2002c).

Francine Shapiro founded the EMDR institute in Pacific Grove, California, an organization responsible for training and credentialing EMDR practitioners, and the EMDR Humanitarian Assistance Program, an organization that coordinates disaster relief and provides free training worldwide. She and her associates have trained over 80,000 licensed clinicians in EMDR, making it one of the most rapidly disseminated psychological methods in history. Shapiro has written over 50 articles and book chapters on EMDR, as well as several books. *Eye Movement Desensitization and Reprocessing* (Shapiro, 1995, 2002b) is intended for the professional audience, whereas *EMDR* (Shapiro & Forrest, 1997) and *Getting Past Your Past* (Shapiro, 2012) bring the therapy to a mass audience.

EMDR and Shapiro have been mired in controversy from the beginning, for several reasons.

First, the early case reports and the first controlled study indicated EMDR could offer relief from PTSD in just a few lengthy sessions. This induced paradigm strain, if not downright incredulity, by promising therapeutic benefit in a substantially shorter period of time with PTSD, which was traditionally seen as recalcitrant to psychotherapy. Second, training in EMDR proceeded before several controlled outcome studies were available. Some saw this as offering a promising treatment for difficult disorders because little else was available; others saw it as irresponsible training in which public dissemination exceeded scientific validation. And third, psychotherapy remains a largely male-dominated profession, especially in psychology and psychiatry. An assertive woman, a newcomer to the field controlling access to training and offering a paradigm-straining treatment with historically difficult patients, would certainly engender resistance.

Theory of Psychopathology

Humans possess an inherent physiological system geared to process information toward a state of mental health. The information-processing system is intrinsic and adaptive. The assumption is that the system is configured to restore mental health in much the same way that the rest of the body is physiologically geared to heal when injured.

Briefly stated, psychopathology occurs when this information-processing system is blocked. Traumatic life experiences set in motion a pathological pattern of affect, behavior, cognitions, sensations, and consequent identity structures. The pathological structures occur because the information is not processed; instead, the traumatic information is static, unresolved, fixed at the time it was stored during the disturbing event. These earlier, disturbing experiences are held in the nervous system in state-specific form. The trauma is, metaphorically speaking, "trapped" or "locked" in the neurophysiology.

Psychopathology persists beyond the time of the trauma because daily stimuli elicit the negative feelings and beliefs embodied in these traumatic memories and cause the client to continue to act in ways consistent with the trauma. In other words, the lack of adequate processing or resolution means the client reacts emotionally and behaviorally in ways consistent with the trauma. Being held in a distressing, excitatory state-specific form, the trauma continues to be triggered by ongoing events and is expressed in nightmares, flashbacks, intrusive thoughts, and avoidant behavior.

Annique, presented at the beginning of the chapter, intellectually knows that she will no longer be victimized each day by a robber. But the trauma lives on and continues to dominate her daily functioning and interactions. She and her information processing are stuck in the past. Traumatic memories are primarily responsible for pathological personality characteristics via a blockage in the information-processing system. Accordingly, unblocking the system and transforming the memories will heal the person.

Therapeutic Processes

The original conceptualization of EMD was one of desensitization according to the behavioral model; the evolved conceptualization of EMDR is that of **adaptive information processing**. Shapiro (2002b) candidly acknowledges that the model is a working hypothesis; we do not yet know what transpires specifically at the physiological level of trauma.

Accessing the traumatic memories activates the information-processing system, which then takes the information to adaptive resolution. This system not only transforms traumatic memories and disturbing information but also concomitantly shifts feelings, thoughts, and sensations. Taken together, these constitute changes in identity.

Annique brought her traumatic experiences into her mind, thus activating her information-processing system. EMDR will accelerate her information processing toward more adaptive resolution: substantial reduction in distress, followed by a "liberation" of her mature cognitions to think more rationally about the robbery, and an eventual shift in her identity from a fearful, enraged victim to a resolved, mature woman. Desensitization and cognitive restructuring are by-products of the adaptive reprocessing taking place on a neurophysiological level.

The essential change process then is counterconditioning via desensitization, distancing, and cognitive restructuring. For the traumatized, the healthy alternative is desensitization instead of hyperarousal, distancing instead of intrusive thoughts, and realistic thinking rather than fear-based reactions. Although consciousness raising and catharsis operate to some extent, they are not the central mechanisms of change in EMDR.

The eye movements have garnered the lion's share of attention, but EMDR actually consists of multiple phases (Shapiro, 1995, 2002c). The first phase involves taking a client history and planning the treatment. Clients unable to tolerate high levels of distress and clients without sufficient social support, for example, are not suitable candidates for the treatment.

The second phase encompasses preparation, in which the clinician introduces the client to EMDR procedures, explains the rationale, and prepares the client for possible between-session disturbance. As in prolonged exposure, the clinician briefs the client on the technical procedures, preferably in person and in a handout, and offers several metaphors for the experience itself. Two popular metaphors are train travel—riding on a train and looking out the window, just noticing the traumatic experiences and memories—and movie watching—sitting at the movies while watching the traumatic pictures on the screen. Both metaphors build in distancing from the traumatic experience itself and afford some self-mastery over the resulting emotions. Clients are expected to be proficient in self-soothing and relaxation before moving on to the desensitization proper. If they are not, then several sessions may be devoted to training and practice in various relaxation procedures.

In the assessment phase, the EMDR clinician identifies the target and collects baseline data before desensitization. The client is asked to select one memory, typically the earliest or the worst, to work on in that session. Then he or she chooses a negative cognition that expresses a dysfunctional or unhealthy self-reference related to the traumatic experience. Annique might say, "I am dirty," "I cannot trust men," or "I cannot be at home alone." The client then is asked to nominate a positive cognition that expresses a healthy or adaptive self-reference related to the trauma that will later be used to replace the negative cognition during installation. Annique might nominate, "I am clean," "I can trust again," or "I am in charge of my home." This positive cognition is assessed on a seven-point **Validity of Cognition (VOC) scale**, where 1 is "completely false" and 7 is "completely true." Before treatment, most clients will, with their information-processing system blocked, hold to the negative cognition and assess the positive cognition as a 1, 2, or 3 (in the false range).

While holding the memory and negative cognition in mind, the client is asked to give an SUD rating for how it feels right now. *SUD* is an acronym for **subjective units of distress**, where 0 is no distress or neutral and 10 is the highest distress imaginable. At predesensitization, clients typically report a moderate to high level of distress, an SUD rating between a 5 and a 10.

This leads to the **desensitization phase**, the longest phase and the most arduous for the patient. The patient is asked to bring up the traumatic image, think of the negative cognition, and notice the feelings attached to it as he or she follows the therapist's hand with his or her eyes. The therapist generates eye movements from one side of the client's range of vision to the other as

rapidly as possible without causing discomfort. Typically, the therapist holds two fingers upright, palm facing the client, approximately 12 to 14 inches from the client's face. Fifteen to thirty bilateral eye movements constitute a set, after which the therapist instructs the client to "blank it out" or "let it go" and to "take a deep breath."

The client describes the feelings, images, sensations, or thoughts with purposefully broad prompts such as, "What do you experience now?" or "What comes up for you?" The client briefly describes the experience, say, "I see him coming after me" or "My chest is tightening up" or "Just very afraid and alone." The therapist refrains from empathic reflections or supportive comments, which would interfere with or delay the desensitization, and instead asks the client to "Go with that" or "Just think of that" as another set of eye movements is introduced.

Whatever the stimuli, the desensitization continues until near the end of the session or until the client reports an SUD rating of 0 or 1. Each target ordinarily takes several sessions to process fully.

The next phase of treatment is called **installation** because the objective is to install and increase the strength of the positive cognition. Once the SUD rating reaches 0 or 1, the client has obtained sufficient relief to allow a more realistic and adaptive cognition to emerge. The desired cognition is linked with the original memory by asking the client to hold the target and the positive cognition together in his or her mind's eye. Sets of eye movement (or alternate stimuli) are done to enhance the connection. This continues until the client reports a 6 or 7 (completely true) on the VOC scale, which along with the SUD rating, comprises valuable outcome data on the procedure.

At the end of a given session, the client is returned to a state of emotional equilibrium, whether or not the desensitization is complete. The client is asked to maintain a log of distressing thoughts, images, or dreams that occur between sessions and is reminded to employ the self-soothing and relaxation exercises reviewed earlier in the treatment.

These multiple phases comprise the standard EMDR treatment. Protocols have been developed for specific populations and problems, for example, children, phobias, grief, and somatic disorders. Considerable work has also been done in integrating EMDR with family therapy (Shapiro et al., 2007).

In other cases, the client's processing will be blocked, and the dysfunctional material will fail to reach resolution. When this occurs, the clinician employs the **cognitive interweave**: a proactive version of EMDR that deliberately interlaces clinician-derived statements with client-generated material, instead of relying solely on the client's spontaneous processing. Clients frequently require the clinician-initiated processing in four situations (Shapiro, 1995, p. 245): **looping** (repetitive thoughts that do not move and that block processing); insufficient information; lack of generalization; and time pressures. The cognitive interweave is to be used sparingly, in cases where the client's own processing proves insufficient.

An ongoing debate concerns the similarity between EMDR and prolonged exposure in their respective processes of change. Shapiro describes EMDR as an integrative therapy that relies on adaptive information processing. Part of that processing involves a dual process of attention—to the image of the trauma and to the bilateral stimulation (such as eye movements)—that leads to a distancing or more detached perspective from the trauma. A handful of studies (e.g., Lee et al., 2006) support that proposition, but many skeptics insist that EMDR simply represents exposure with distraction in the form of bilateral stimulation. Until more careful research is conducted, the debate will probably continue along theoretical lines.

Therapeutic Relationship

The clinician-client relationship in EMDR should be characterized by empathy, trust, and safety.

A traumatized client has typically suffered for years in fear, embarrassment, and silence. Sharing the worst experiences of one's life takes extraordinary courage, and EMDR clinicians are expected to communicate their respect for this courage and the client's willingness to tolerate short-term distress for long-term relief (Dworkin, 2005). Although empathic, the EMDR therapist must refrain from providing empathic or supportive statements during the trauma processing itself. To do so, as in other exposure treatments, can inhibit the patient's desensitization and retard his or her inherent tendency toward psychological self-healing.

The therapeutic relationship and treatment context must ensure client safety. EMDR confronts traumatic material and potentially encounters dissociation in clients. Building rapport, screening patients, teaching relaxation, preparing clients, reviewing a "stop signal" for them to suspend processing, and being available as necessary between sessions all create a safe haven for client and clinician alike.

Practicalities of EMDR

EMDR sessions typically run 75 to 90 minutes to allow ample time for emotional reprocessing and a return to emotional equilibrium. The lengthier sessions occasionally pose difficulties in billing insurance companies, but the smaller number of sessions (four to six for a single target) seems to compensate. EMDR has loudly advertised itself as a brief and comprehensive treatment for trauma disorders.

EMDR offers its recipients a couple of advantages over prolonged exposure treatment. Clients do not need to verbalize their painful memories, just think about them. Nor are EMDR clients asked to conduct between-session exposure homework, as they do in Foa's exposure therapy. Further, the cumulating research and practice indicate that EMDR averages a session or two fewer than prolonged exposure.

In practice, clinicians frequently combine EMDR with other treatment methods and omit select elements of the EMDR protocol. A study of 532 therapists practicing EMDR determined that they were typically integrative or cognitive/behavioral in orientation and that they used EMDR primarily for PTSD and other anxiety disorders (Lyhus, 2003). Although initially developed for adults, EMDR has been modified for children (Tinker & Wilson, 1999). Part of EMDR's flexibility is that it can be conducted by practitioners of different orientations and of all mental health professions.

The EMDR Institute recommends two weekend workshops and supervised practice for advanced competence in the approach. The two-day Level I workshop covers the basics, and the two-day Level II workshop addresses the cognitive interweave and advanced applications.

Probably more than other systems of psychotherapy, EMDR originators and practitioners have committed themselves to providing **pro bono** (free of cost) treatment and training in disaster areas. Through the EMDR Humanitarian Assistance program, thousands of clinicians have been trained for free and tens of thousands of hours of EMDR have been rendered at token cost or no cost. EMDR has been taken all over the world to help victims of civil wars (e.g., Darfur, Balkans), natural disasters (e.g., Louisiana Hurricanes, Asian tsunami), and regional trauma (e.g., World Trade Center bombing, San Salvador killings).

Effectiveness of EMDR

The debate over the effectiveness of EMDR recapitulates the developmental history of validating many psychotherapy systems. At first, the originator of the treatment and a few proponents publish case reports and a single controlled trial, and then issue early claims of magnificent outcomes not obtained by alternative therapies. Opponents then immediately point to the paucity of rigorous outcome studies and publicly complain the treatment enthusiasts have gone far beyond their data.

Controlled outcome studies are gradually published attesting to the effectiveness of the treatment compared to no treatment or placebo but not to the purported superiority over alternative therapies. Finally, the detractors begrudgingly acknowledge that the treatment does work but not as well as originally claimed. Both sides then declare victory: the treatment originators are vindicated with a new, evidence-based psychotherapy, and the early detractors are proud to have preserved the integrity of the scientific process.

As the dust settles on EMDR's outcome studies, we are left with the predicable end state: originators concluding that it works very well and detractors arguing that it does not work better than other exposure treatments. In its 25-year plus history, EMDR has garnered more controlled research than any other method used to treat trauma. Shapiro (2002a) reviewed the results of 13 controlled studies, encompassing some 300 patients, of EMDR in the treatment of trauma. In Shapiro's evaluation, EMDR clearly outperforms no treatment and achieves similar or superior outcomes to other therapy methods for trauma. All but one of the most recent EMDR studies with civilian populations found that between 77% and 100% of the single-trauma victims no longer met diagnostic criteria for PTSD after the equivalent of three, 90-minute sessions.

Shapiro's detractors weigh in with more caution. Some cognitive-behavioral therapists conclude that controlled experiments using objective and standardized measures have failed to support the efficacy of EMDR beyond that of its imaginal exposure component (e.g., Acierno et al., 1994; Taylor et al., 2003). Others found the effects of EMDR consistent with nonspecific factors (Lohr et al., 1998). Some still consider EMDR a form of exposure therapy that has triumphed in marketing. As a leading trauma researcher (McNally, 1999, p. 619) put it, "what is effective in EMDR is not new, and what is new is not effective."

In between these partisan reviews, half a dozen meta-analyses render more balanced and dispassionate conclusions: EMDR is certainly more effective than no treatment and likely more effective than treatments not using exposure to anxiety-provoking stimuli. In fewer sessions and without homework, EMDR is equally effective as prolonged exposure (Bradley et al., 2005; Davidson & Parker, 2001; Powers et al., 2010; Seidler & Wagner, 2006; Sherman, 1998; Van Etten & Taylor, 1998). The most recent Cochrane review of PTSD treatments (Bisson & Andrew, 2007) concluded, "Trauma focused cognitive-behavioral therapy and eye movement desensitization and reprocessing have the best evidence for efficacy at present and should be made available to PTSD sufferers."

Interestingly, the effectiveness of EMDR for PTSD appears to be higher in rigorous studies that closely follow the specific treatment protocol (know as **treatment fidelity**). As the methodology of outcome studies become more rigorous, the treatment effect of EMDR becomes larger (Maxfield & Hyer, 2002). This finding reminds us that therapist competency and actual adherence to the psychotherapy should be assessed in all treatment outcome studies.

Insufficient controlled research has been conducted on EMDR with behavioral disorders other than PTSD. Thus, we cannot reach any conclusions about its effectiveness in other domains. Unlike the extensive research history of prolonged exposure with multiple anxiety disorders (as reviewed earlier in the chapter), the research base for EMDR has been largely concentrated on trauma.

All involved in the ongoing controversy—originators, detractors, and dispassionate researchers—do agree on one finding: The eye movements are only one form of bilateral stimulation and may not be required for the therapeutic effect. Hand taps and repetition of auditory cues are widely used as alternate stimuli (Shapiro, 1995,

1997). The eye movements in EMDR have come under the greatest scrutiny and await empirical validation as a necessary component (Perkins & Rouanzoin, 2002; see www.emdr.com/gpyp).

Here the consensus ends: The EMDR enthusiasts interpret the extant research as supporting some form of bilateral stimulation as an integral part of the integrative treatment, while the EMDR detractors argue that the dual attention stimulation proves unnecessary for any exposure treatment. In this regard, the "eye movement" in the "EMDR" title may have proven unfortunate.

Criticisms of Exposure Therapies
From a Cognitive-Behavioral Perspective

Exposure therapy is rightly part of our behavioral tradition, and, of course, has considerable empirical verification. Let's call exposure therapy what it truly is—a cognitive-behavior therapy method—and dissociate it from other pseudoscientific evocative therapies. No need to create a new genre or school of therapy; prolonged exposure is one of dozens of CBT methods.

EMDR may qualify as an evidence-based treatment, but Francine Shapiro and her EMDR disciples got the proper sequence of treatment development backwards. A scientist first rigorously evaluates the effectiveness and safety of a new treatment, and then—and only then—trains fellow practitioners to use the method. By contrast, Shapiro proudly announces that 20,000 clinicians were trained in EMDR before the controlled outcome studies were complete. To make matters worse, the eye movements in EMDR might not even prove necessary for the therapeutic outcome. Scientists shouldn't name their treatments after benign, unnecessary parts of those treatments! If you want to be accepted by the scientific community, then play by the established rules of science.

From a Psychoanalytic Perspective

Over 90 years ago, Freud (1919) observed that, if the analyst actively induced the patient to expose him/herself to the feared stimulus, "a considerable moderation of the phobia" would be achieved. We have long recognized that exposure can alleviate phobic behavior. But what Freud anticipated then—and what exposure and EMDR therapists fail to recognize today—is that reducing phobic behavior is insufficient. The ultimate aim of psychotherapy should be to make the unconscious conscious, not only to make the fearful less fearful.

EMDR is half-a-loaf psychotherapy. The patient is eye stimulated or hand tapped into a neutral SUD state within a few sessions, but the real work of psychotherapy remains. Following EMDR the therapist still needs to undertake the lengthy and laborious work of resolving trauma and gradually integrating the healing experience into the patient's identity. There are quick therapies, but there are no quick fixes in the psychological world of trauma.

From a Humanistic Perspective

The eruption of emotion in exposure does not come from some intrinsically meaningful struggle within the person. Instead, exposure and implosion therapists evoke emotions from outside the person by artificial exercises and perverse imagery. Nor does the client play a central role in giving meaning to the feared scenes or events. The therapist imposes crass exercises on clients, who are expected to bow to the therapists' sovereignty conjuring images of *A Clockwork Orange*, the startling film in which behavioral reconditioning is employed to advance social improvement.

Exposure treatment brings into clear relief the philosophical conflict between "doing to" and "being with" in psychotherapy (Power, 1981). "Doing to" perfectly encapsulates the instrumentality and technology of exposure. We prefer "being with" trauma victims, witnessing and affirming their tortured experiences, instead of doing things to them. Anyone in the midst of crisis seeks a caring presence and a soothing attachment, not impersonal techniques and anxiety-intensifying assignments.

From a Cultural Perspective

Traumatized children and adults predictably suffering from anxiety disorders require our compassion and respect. In exposure therapy, by contrast, they receive reactivation of the trauma and intensification of the anxiety. Exposure therapists may claim they do so only in the interest of client improvement, but the ends-justify-the-means argument is difficult to accept. The cure might be worse than the disorder.

At the very least, we should expect tons of therapist empathy with the victims' horrors and with the traumatic context producing the anxiety. However, the exposure therapists' empathy and sensitivity in these treatments are purposely employed to cultivate *more* frightening scenes for an anxiety-torn human. Trauma victims in search of sensitivity, support, and empowerment are provided more, higher decibel pain. When there is no empathic and caring relationship between clinician and client, psychotherapy is not worth doing.

We should also expect exposure therapists (and other mental health professionals) treating victims of heinous crimes and unspeakable trauma to forcefully advocate for prevention of these crimes and trauma. Effective treatment is useful, of course, but don't we collude with a disturbed society by treating only the individual's symptoms rather than the social causes? Exposure is too little and too late in the causal sequence. Let's expose the citizenry and politicians with terror-filled images of war, rape, violence, poverty, and discrimination and then maybe we will address the underlying social causes, instead of mopping up after the carnage.

From an Integrative Perspective

EMDR has been advanced as an integrative treatment that incorporates numerous theories and methods. The therapeutic emphasis on psychological self-healing and the client leading is consistent with person-centered therapy; the use of free associations is compatible with psychodynamic therapy; imaginal exposure as a means of desensitization hails from behavior therapy; and the cognitive interweave is a hallmark of cognitive therapy (Shapiro, 1995). EMDR is indeed more than eye movements; it is a complex system of psychotherapy.

At least once a decade a miracle cure appears on the therapeutic scene. Examples include hypnosis, desensitization, implosive therapy, and now EMDR. Professionals sign up in droves for training, hoping that they will replicate the early dramatic claims of the method's effectiveness. Professionals and laypeople can become mesmerized by such magic. The magic is in the eye movements and the suggestions, say hypnotists; the magic is in the desensitization and reprocessing, say the EMDRists; or is it in the emotional bowel movements of implosive therapy?

The real magic will emerge from scientific movements that identify the most powerful processes of change across psychotherapy systems. Is catharsis the key construct in exposure therapies? Or is the key construct the choice to face fears that we have avoided for too long? Or is extinction actually a function of counterconditioning as traumatic cues are paired with healthier responses like relaxation, eye or hand movements, or some other form of mastery? As psychotherapists become more seasoned, they tend to become more integrative. It is encouraging to see such cognitive development within EMDR. Simple solutions for complex problems are not likely to stand the test of time or of science.

Exposure Therapy with Mrs. C

Mrs. C is actively avoiding the conditioned stimuli of dirt and pinworms. Dirty underwear, dirt from the floors, and even thoughts of dirt or pinworms elicit intense anxiety. Because washing removes Mrs. C from the presence of dirt or the possibility of pinworms, it reduces her anxiety. Her compulsive hand washing is clearly instrumental in producing the powerful reinforcement of anxiety reduction.

Mrs. C was classically conditioned to fear dirt and disease by an obsessive-compulsive mother. Although details of her conditioning history are not given, we can imagine that dirt on her hands or clothes was probably paired with threats, castigations, slaps, or spanks, until dirt automatically elicited anxiety. When punishment was administered, Mrs. C would most likely be thinking about the dirt that got her in trouble, so that even thoughts of dirt were conditioned to elicit anxiety. In order to avoid further painful punishment from her parents, she learned to quickly wash her hands or to rigidly clean her clothes. Washing and cleaning would produce rapid reduction in anxiety, and Mrs. C was thus becoming conditioned to be clean.

In an environment rewarding cleanliness, Mrs. C's rate of washing apparently remained within a normal range until the trauma of the pinworms. As far as Mrs. C knew, her daughter's pinworms were to be realistically feared. Her physician frightened her into boiling the family's clothes and bedding in order to avoid a pinworm plague. When Mrs. C was informed of the frightening aspects of pinworms, she would have been thinking about pinworms, so the very thoughts of pinworms were conditioned to elicit anxiety.

Mrs. C was especially vulnerable at this time to further conditioning. She was already anxious about her own and her family's health because they all had the Asian flu. Plague upon plague could raise her anxiety to intolerable levels. She would be eagerly seeking a response that could reduce her anxiety and avoid further disease. So when the physicians said washing was the answer, washing was her response.

(continued)

The washing continued, however, even after the realistic threat was gone. The shock had worn off and the pinworms were gone, but her anxiety was not extinguished. Both her childhood anxieties and her recently conditioned fear of pinworms remained. Her hand washing was both stimulated by her anxiety over dirt and disease and reinforced by the reduction of anxiety. If she tried to remain in the presence of dirt or a scratching child without washing, her anxiety would increase markedly, almost to panic. When her anxiety became unbearable, she would rush to wash, and her washing response would be even more strongly reinforced by the reduction of panic. Even thoughts of dirt or pinworms could elicit intense anxiety.

Before rushing into the exposure itself, Mrs. C will need to understand the rationale for this paradoxical therapy—becoming less fearful by approaching your worst fears! The exposure therapist will provide a rationale for the exposure treatment and then teach her relaxation skills to use during and between the exposure sessions. That will take a couple of sessions.

Prolonged exposure plus response prevention will mean that Mrs. C will remain in the presence of each of the anxiety-eliciting stimuli without washing or running. This method will, of course, evoke high levels of aversive emotion, and Mrs. C's natural response would be to avoid by washing or terminating treatment. The exposure therapist must work to keep her from avoiding. By remaining in the presence of these aversive stimuli, Mrs. C would be flooded with fear, but soon the anxiety would begin to extinguish. The pinworms are gone; her parents will no longer hurt her. All she has to fear is conditioned fear itself, and that can be extinguished rapidly if she does not run.

Mrs. C would first be asked to imagine her fears—say, pinworms—in session. She would be instructed to picture vividly that she is at home and infiltrated with pinworms. She may sense them crawling on her. Exposure is designed to evoke maximum anxiety, and Mrs. C will want to run and wash it all away. She wants to avoid them, but the therapist employs response prevention.

"You can tolerate it without washing. You are getting through it." It will prove difficult for both the exposure therapist and Mrs. C, but she will learn not to run but rather to face what she fears most.

Between her sessions, Mrs. C will be asked to complete homework. She will listen to a recording of her previous session, which will expose her again to the anxiety-eliciting situations for at least 45 minutes or until her anxiety decreases. She will also be practicing breathing retraining, relaxation methods, and other forms of self-soothing at home.

Once Mrs. C feels reasonably relaxed while imagining her fears, the therapist will expose Mrs. C to the actual feared objects. In this case, Mrs. C will be presented with supposedly contaminated underwear in the real environment. The therapist instructs Mrs. C: "Hold them, rub them, put two pairs on your arms." she does so for 50 minutes without washing. Throughout the therapist encourages: "Don't run away; you are mastering your fears." "See how the anxiety is dropping; the underwear cannot hurt you." Each session ends only after at least 50% of Mrs. C's anxiety dissipates.

Mrs. C graduates to more fearful situations both in session and at home. Holding two pairs of underwear on her lap for 50 minutes increases to wearing a dirty pair for three entire days without removing them or showering. Once unthinkable, now attainable. Her anxiety continues to recede, and concomitantly her thinking becomes more realistic. "Why did I let underwear ruin me for years? I don't need long showers to protect me." In confronting her worst fears, Mrs. C gradually discovers that the shock has indeed worn off, the external danger is gone. And with extinction of anxiety and improvement in her thinking, the internal danger is also disappearing. The anxiety that has both stimulated and reinforced her constant washing has habituated. Mrs. C will no longer need to avoid thoughts of pinworms, anger, or hands that are a little dirty. After all, what is a pair of dirty underwear on the floor after she has worn the same dirty pair for three straight days?

Future Directions

Based in theory, demonstrated in the laboratory, and now proven in the field, exposure therapy has experienced resurgence in the treatment of intransigent anxiety-based disorders, such as PTSD and OCD. The prolonged exposure and response prevention of Edna Foa and others is seen by many as the psychological "treatment of choice" for several anxiety disorders.

Like EMDR, prolonged exposure is gradually becoming more comprehensive or integrative by incorporating breathing retraining, therapist support, and cognitive restructuring methods into its treatment package. And we can confidently predict that its popularity will continue, particularly as it expands into virtual reality therapy (Krijn et al., 2004; Wiederhold & Wiederhold, 2005) for a plethora of anxiety disorders.

EMDR has been shrouded in such controversy that its future is not entirely clear. But several things seem certain: Increasing numbers of clinicians will be trained in the system; future research will examine the respective contributions of the various stimuli (eye movements versus hand taps versus no bilateral stimulation); and accumulated research and practice will yield consensual conclusions on its effectiveness with disorders beyond PTSD. Some clarity is already emerging with regard to its applicability: PTSD and traumatic experiences, yes; panic disorder, probably not (Goldstein et al., 2000).

The primary stumbling block to wider acceptance of the exposure therapies is psychotherapist resistance. Although patients typically accept the procedure because they experience its benefits firsthand, many mental health professionals are reluctant to employ the anxiety-inducing techniques associated with exposure. Directly activating intense emotional expressions is too disconcerting for staid practitioners of "talk" therapy. The solution may lie in recognizing the truth that therapeutic breakthroughs frequently require confronting pain encoded in memories; or in contemporary lingo, no pain—no gain.

Key Terms

adaptive information processing
avoidance conditioning
breathing retraining
classical/respondent conditioning
clinical significance (versus statistical significance)
cognitive interweave
cue exposure
desensitization phase
dismantling studies
emotional-processing theory
exposure therapy
extinction
eye movement desensitization and reprocessing (EMDR)
generalization
habituation
imaginal exposure
implosive therapy
in vivo exposure
installation
learned avoidance
looping
neurotic paradox
operant/instrumental conditioning
pro bono
prolonged exposure
response prevention
subjective units of distress (SUD)
symptom exacerbation
treatment fidelity
two-factor theory of learning (Mowrer's)
Validity of Cognition (VOC) scale
virtual reality (VR)

Recommended Readings

Abramowitz, J. S., Deacon, B. J., & Whiteside, S. P. (2011). *Exposure therapy for anxiety: Principles and practice.* New York: Guilford.

Foa, E. B., Keane, T. M., & Fiedman, M. J. (Eds.). (2008). *Effective treatment for PTSD: Practice guidelines from the International Society for Traumatic Stress Studies* (2nd ed.). New York: Guilford.

Foa, E. B., & Rothbaum, B. O. (2001). *Treating the trauma of rape: Cognitive-behavioral therapy for PTSD.* New York: Guilford.

Richard, D. C. S., & Lauterbach, D. (2006). *The handbook of exposure therapies.* Oxford: Elsevier.

Shapiro, F. S. (2002a). *Eye movement desensitization and reprocessing* (2nd ed.). New York: Guilford.

Shapiro, F. S. (Ed.). (2002b). *EMDR and the paradigm prism.* Washington, DC: American Psychological Association.

Stampfl, T., & Levis, D. (1973). *Implosive therapy: Theory and technique.* Morristown, NJ: General Learning Press.

Wiederhold, B. K., & Wiederhold, M. D. (2005). *Virtual reality therapy for anxiety disorders.* Washington, DC: American Psychological Association.

Journals: *Behavior Therapy; Cognitive Therapy; Cognitive & Behavioral Practice; Journal of Anxiety Disorders; Journal of Behavior Therapy & Experimental Psychiatry; Journal of EMDR Practice and Research; Journal of Traumatic Stress.*

Recommended Websites

Center for the Treatment and Study of Anxiety (Foa):
 www.med.upenn.edu/ctsa/
EMDR Institute:
 www.emdr.com
EMDR International Association (EMDRIA):
 www.emdria.org/
International Society for Traumatic Stress Studies:
 www.istss.org/
Virtual Reality Exposure Therapy:
 www.virtuallybetter.com

CHAPTER 9

Behavior Therapies

Joseph Wolpe

Donald Meichenbaum

Juan, a young salesperson living the California dream, had developed a chronic case of claustrophobia that handicapped him in a variety of situations. When trapped in omnipresent traffic, he would become panicky, which was leading him to avoid driving whenever he could. Elevators were aversive places that elicited anxiety and avoidance. Just sitting in a crowded airplane without a quick exit had become a nightmare for Juan, so flying was omitted from his response repertoire. Add in crowded restaurants, theaters, and churches, and you can see how limited Juan's California dream had become.

But Juan's biggest dread was going to the physician's office to undergo a medical exam. A crowded waiting room was bad enough, but Juan panicked at the prospect of having to enter an MRI machine. He knew that his family history placed him at high risk for serious cardiovascular disease and he should stay in close contact with his cardiologist, but Juan's anxiety and avoidance were preventing him from keeping appointments.

With an economic recession raging, Juan decided to give first priority to his driving phobia.

It was keeping him from calling on customers, and he couldn't afford to lose any business. Working with a combination of systematic and in vivo desensitization, Juan gradually extended the radius of his driving from only 10 miles to the freedom to travel throughout California.

Juan then had the creative idea to construct an apparatus approximating an MRI machine—"closely confined like a coffin," he joked. Facing his fears

217

both of confinement and of death, Juan practiced daily with his invention, using the deep-muscle relaxation he had already learned. His wife and daughter teased him at times about retreating to his dark dungeon, but they also reinforced the gains they could see him making as he began moving freely into crowded conditions. "Why fear a crowd after you've spent time in a coffin?" Juan jested about his creative behavioral cure for claustrophobia.

A Sketch of Behavior Therapy

No single figure dominates behavior therapy the way Freud dominated psychoanalysis or Rogers created person-centered therapy. Behavior therapists vary tremendously in both theory and technique. Traditionally, learning theory was seen as the ideological foundation for behavior therapy, although there was never agreement as to which learning theory (Pavlov's, Hull's, Skinner's, Mowrer's, or others). The rapid proliferation of behavioral and cognitive-behavioral techniques during the 1970s and the 1980s defied any attempt to restrict the term to a single theory or unitary group of techniques. As a result, current usage of the term **behavior therapy** generally denotes conceptual behaviorism, methodological behaviorism, or an ill-defined combination of the two.

Conceptually, the major characteristics of behavioral treatments concern the primacy of behavior, the importance of learning, the directive and active nature of treatments, the importance of assessment and evaluation, and the use of persons in everyday life (Kazdin, 1984). In a longer list, O'Leary and Wilson (1987) cite the following among the core characteristics of behavior therapy:

- Most abnormal behavior is acquired and maintained according to the same principles as normal behavior.
- Assessment is continuous and focuses on the current determinants of behavior.
- People are best described by what they think, feel, and do in specific life situations.

- Treatment is derived from theory and experimental findings of scientific psychology.
- Treatment methods are precisely specified and replicable.
- Research evaluates the effects of specific techniques on specific problems.
- Outcome is evaluated in terms of the initial induction of behavior change, its generalization to real-life settings, and its maintenance over time.

Although many concepts contained in these lists seem quite acceptable in today's light, they represented a radical departure from the medical model of psychopathology in general, and psychoanalysis in particular. For example, the maladaptive behavior itself is seen as the problem that needs to be changed. No longer is troubled behavior seen as a symptom of an underlying disorder; rather, this medical notion is rejected in favor of the assumption that the symptom is the problem and is the appropriate target for therapy. Such treatment does not risk the substitution of new symptoms or the return of old symptoms.

Methodologically, behavior therapy is an empirical endeavor that must be tested and validated by the same rigorous, experimental procedures used to investigate any scientific question. Techniques cannot be assumed to be effective simply because they are derived from a favored theory. They must be validated under controlled conditions that use reliable and valid measures. Baseline measures of target behaviors need to be established before therapy in order to determine whether the treatment is producing any change in the rate or intensity of responding.

Although behaviorists agree on approaching treatment as a data-based, experimental method, they disagree about just what the data or the experimental method should look like. Should the data be only overt responses that the experimenter/therapist can observe, for example, or are self-reports of subjective units of distress (SUD) acceptable measures of anxiety? Should experimental designs be based on **small-*n*** (small-sample) procedures, in which a few clients are studied rigorously, or should therapies be validated through group designs that include placebo and no-treatment control groups?

The point is that contemporary behavior therapy entails a vast array of clinical techniques, a set of conceptual assumptions, and many possible methods for testing treatment success. Although divergence can be a source of confusion and ambiguity for students, it is also the source of the creative work carried out in psychotherapy. While appreciating the divergences among behavior therapists, we will nevertheless attempt to impose some clarity on this complex system by emphasizing three major thrusts within behavior therapy. We affectionately call these the **3 Cs of behavior therapy**: **counterconditioning**, **contingency management**, and **cognitive-behavior modification**. (Cognitive therapies per se are covered in Chapter 10.)

The first thrust or C we will survey is best represented by Joseph Wolpe's **reciprocal inhibition** or counterconditioning therapy. Wolpe's approach has been based primarily on a **respondent conditioning** of anxiety-related problems. His approach follows directly from the work of Pavlov and his conditioning of dogs, as everyone who has taken Intro to Psych will remember. Therapists utilizing counterconditioning techniques, including the stalwarts of systematic desensitization and assertiveness training, are most comfortable being called *behavior therapists*.

The second thrust of contingency management has traditionally been labeled **behavior modification** and has focused on **operant conditioning**. This approach follows directly from the work of B. F. Skinner and, as you will also remember from Intro to Psych, is concerned with changing the contingencies that follow and control behavior. With Skinner as a model, behavior modifiers have been particularly rigorous in validating interventions through well-controlled small-*n* designs, while being less concerned with

theoretical explanations for effective techniques. In part because of the negative connotations that some politicians and some of the public have ascribed to the term *behavior modification*, the name **behavior analysis** is also attached to this therapy approach.

Cognitive-behavior modification, the third thrust or C, has a multifaceted heritage. It was initially led by Donald Meichenbaum and represents those behaviorists who use cognitive explanations and cognitive techniques for producing behavior change. These therapists, known popularly as cognitive behaviorists, draw on a diversity of procedures, including cognitive restructuring, stress inoculation, and problem solving. Psychotherapists who prefer the label *cognitive* to communicate their use of primarily cognitive and rational-emotive techniques will be considered in Chapter 10. We freely admit, however, that the boundaries separating cognitive-behavior therapy from cognitive therapy are quite hazy. The distinctions may in fact be "academic" (as befits a textbook of this nature!).

Although behavior therapy will be presented as three separate branches for simplicity's sake, we should emphasize that most contemporary behavior therapists work with techniques from each of these three viewpoints. Reflecting this multiplicity are the diverse members of the Association for Behavioral and Cognitive Therapies (ABCT): some characterize themselves as behavioral, some as cognitive-behavioral, and some as mainly cognitive (Craighead, 1990). The point, again, is that behavior therapists are not particularly enamored with theoretical unity or technical purity, but rather are driven to apply whatever methods are most effective and efficient in changing troubled behavior.

In an attempt to capture both the essence and the diversity of behavior therapies, we will modify our standard chapter outline. First, behaviorists have generally believed that environmental conditions are of much greater importance in controlling behavior than are internal personality traits (Mischel, 1968). Although many behavior therapists, especially in England, have at times talked in terms of traits, behavior therapy has not been concerned with constructing a comprehensive theory of personality. Consequently, this section is omitted from the chapter. Second, because the emphasis of behavior therapy has been on the processes of change rather than on the content to be changed, we will also omit the section on the therapeutic content.

We will consider, in turn, the theories of psychopathology and psychotherapy for each of the three thrusts or three Cs of behavior therapy. We will examine the behavioral therapeutic relationship from a modeling perspective. The controlled outcome research on behavioral treatments will be presented in the section on effectiveness, followed by criticisms of behavior therapy. Finally, Mrs. C will be analyzed through a comprehensive approach to behavior therapy that incorporates counterconditioning, contingency management, cognitive techniques, and the modeling view of the therapeutic relationship.

Counterconditioning
A Sketch of Joseph Wolpe

Joseph Wolpe's (1915–1997) book *Psychotherapy by Reciprocal Inhibition* (1958) is the most comprehensive approach to behaviorism based on counterconditioning. Wolpe came to a learning-based theory of therapy in a rather indirect manner. As a Jew raised in South Africa, he was influenced by his grandmother, who took on the responsibility of trying to make him into a pious believer. He read many Jewish writers, especially Maimonides, the 12th-century Jewish physician and philosopher. In his early twenties, he began investigating other philosophers, beginning with Immanuel Kant, moving on to David Hume, and progressing through several other thinkers to Bertrand Russell. By the time his own intellectual journey was completed, his theology had been replaced by a physical monism.

Because he viewed Freud as a rigorous materialist, Wolpe's view of humanity became increasingly more psychoanalytic during his middle twenties. He might have developed into a psychoanalytic psychiatrist except that he began reading studies suggesting that Freud's theory did not fit many facts. He was also struck by the fact that Russia, with a materialistic ideology, had rejected Freud in favor of Pavlov. Wolpe was impressed by Pavlov's research but found he preferred the theoretical interpretations of conditioning in Hull's *Principles of Behavior* (1943).

In 1947, he began research on animal neuroses for his MD thesis at the University of Witwatersrand in Johannesburg. Working with cats, he paired a buzzer with a shock and classically conditioned anxiety to the buzzer. When the buzzer was on, the cats were inhibited from eating. Wolpe reasoned that if conditioned anxiety could inhibit eating, then maybe under the right conditions, the eating response could be used to inhibit anxiety. Because the troubled cats would not eat in their home cages, he began to feed them in dissimilar cages where their fear was much less. Wolpe thus began to countercondition the animals' anxiety by substituting an eating response for the anxiety response. By gradually feeding the cats in cages that were increasingly similar to their home cage, he reduced their anxiety until they could eat in their home cages. In a similar manner, he was able to use the eating response to inhibit anxiety to the buzzer.

Wolpe was now convinced that the use of such counterconditioning procedures could serve as the basis for a radically new therapy. He began looking for responses in humans that could be used to successfully inhibit and eventually countercondition anxiety. The use of deep relaxation to inhibit anxiety became the basis for **systematic desensitization**; the use of assertive responses to inhibit social anxiety became the basis for assertiveness training; and the use of sexual arousal to inhibit anxiety became the basis for new approaches to sex therapy. At the University of Witwatersrand, Wolpe met frequently with colleagues and students who were excited about this new and effective way to treat anxiety disorders. Arnold Lazarus and Stanley Rachman were among this group, and they helped to spread Wolpe's systematic desensitization to Great Britain and the United States, where Wolpe himself moved in 1963 (Glass & Arnkoff, 1992).

Wolpe surveyed the effectiveness of his counterconditioning approaches to treating behavioral disorders and reported success with 90% of more than 200 clients. His research with animals and his success with humans were reported in *Psychotherapy by Reciprocal Inhibition* (1958), and his work received considerable attention from clinical psychologists who had been trained in learning theory during their graduate education.

Wolpe continued his behavior therapy and research program at the University of Virginia, Temple Medical School, the Eastern Pennsylvania Psychiatric Institute, and, at the time of his death, Pepperdine University as a distinguished professor of psychiatry. He was a central, if somewhat controversial, figure in helping to establish behavior therapy as a major movement in mental health through his writings and workshops, and through establishing and editing *Journal of Behavior Therapy and Experimental Psychiatry*. His influential text, *The Practice of Behavior Therapy* (1990), was published in four editions.

Theory of Psychopathology

Anxiety causes most behavior disorders. Anxiety is primarily a pattern of responses of the sympathetic nervous system when an individual is exposed to a threatening stimulus. Physiological changes include increased blood pressure and pulse rate, increased muscle tension, decreased blood circulation to the stomach and genitals, increased blood circulation to the large voluntary muscles, pupil dilation, and dryness of the mouth. These bodily changes are the basis of anxiety and can be elicited by unconditioned stimuli such as an electrical shock, a startling noise, or a physical beating.

Anxiety can also be learned. Learning is said to occur if "a response has been evoked in temporal contiguity with a given stimulus and it is subsequently found that the stimulus can evoke the response although it could not have done so before. If the stimulus could have evoked the response before but subsequently evokes it more strongly, then, too, learning may be said to have occurred" (Wolpe, 1973, p. 5). Thus, people can learn to respond with anxiety to any stimuli, including buzzers, dogs, people, sex, elevators, and dirt, even though these stimuli previously did not evoke anxiety.

Through **classical**, or **respondent**, **conditioning**, a neutral stimulus, such as a dog, can be paired contiguously with a threatening stimulus, such as being bitten. The anxiety evoked by being bitten is associated with the sight of the dog, and the sight of the dog can become conditioned to evoke anxiety. Similarly, being punished for sex play as a child can make sex a conditioned stimulus that evokes anxiety, or being spanked for playing with dirt can result in dirt's being able to evoke intense anxiety. Even the thoughts associated with threatening stimuli, such as sexual thoughts, can become conditioned to elicit anxiety.

Through the process of **generalization**, stimuli physically similar to the original conditioned stimulus, such as other dogs, can also evoke anxiety. The more dissimilar a stimulus is to the original conditioned stimulus, the less anxiety the dissimilar stimulus will evoke. Thus, a puppy will elicit minimal anxiety because it is dissimilar from the original large dog that bit the individual.

Stimuli can be ranked on a gradient of similarity that constitutes a **generalization gradient**, or an **anxiety hierarchy**, that goes from the original stimulus, which evokes maximum anxiety, to a very dissimilar but related stimulus that evokes minimal anxiety. Humans can form hierarchies based on similarities of internal effects through generalization. Thus, situations that are physically dissimilar, such as being turned down on a date, being made to wait, and missing a bus, can form a hierarchy or generalization gradient based on the internal response of feeling rejected. As a result of either generalization, most patients will report that their anxiety levels vary depending on the stimulus situations they are in. A person conditioned to fear authority figures may complain of physical upset at work where the boss is, for example, but report less anxiety at home, except when a spouse or child becomes bossy.

People suffering from generalized or free-floating anxiety seem to be responding independently of any specific elicitor. Anxiety, however, is always the consequence of the elicitor; the problem for these clients is that they have been conditioned to fear stimuli that are omnipresent. One example is a client who was constantly anxious, even when trying to sleep or shower, because he had been conditioned by severe parents to respond with anxiety to his own body, which is obviously omnipresent.

Anxiety is the primary learning problem in psychopathology. Once anxiety is established as a habitual response to specific stimuli, it can undermine or impair other behaviors and lead to secondary symptoms. Sleep may be disturbed by anxiety; tension headaches or stomach upsets may occur; irritability may increase; concentration, thinking, and memory may be impaired; or embarrassing tremors and sweating may occur. Over time, the chronic physiological reactions of anxiety may impair bodily functions and result in psychophysiological symptoms, such as gastrointestinal symptoms. These secondary symptoms themselves may elicit anxiety because of their painfulness, their association with learned fears of physical or mental disorder, or simply their embarrassing social consequences. If these secondary problems produce additional anxiety, then new learning may occur, and a "vicious circle" is created that leads to more complicated symptoms.

Conditioned anxiety frequently leads to avoidance. Physical avoidance, such as phobias, may be learned because avoidance leads to the automatic consequence of terminating anxiety. Thus, some patients complain of having to avoid doctors, airplanes, elevators, or social gatherings. Other patients learn to terminate anxiety by consuming alcohol, barbiturates, narcotics, or other drugs.

Over time, the primary complaint is no longer anxiety but the phobias and addictions patients have developed in order to avoid anxiety. Of course, an addiction itself can produce anxiety and can lead to further problems in order to reduce the new anxiety, and the vicious circle goes on. Patients' symptoms are highly varied, ranging from sexual dysfunctions, to phobias, to psychophysiological complaints, to interpersonal difficulties, to substance abuse. The same patient may have several complaints not necessarily related in some supposed dynamic pattern. For example, a patient may suffer from an elevator phobia and insomnia without the two being related, just as a medical patient may have a tremor entirely unrelated to a cold. The successful treatment of a phobia may have no effect whatsoever on the insomnia.

Symptoms result from anxieties elicited by particular stimuli. Therefore, the successful elimination of a specific anxiety and a specific secondary symptom will not lead to new symptoms. **Symptom substitution** or **symptom return** is a theoretical myth of those who see all behavior as interconnected by a single, underlying dynamic conflict. What is common to most behavior problems is the presence of conditioned anxiety that is highly specific in both the stimuli that elicit it and the consequences that result from it. Successful treatment thus calls for successful, and at times successive, elimination of specific anxiety responses.

Therapeutic Processes

Because anxiety is learned through conditioning, it can be unlearned through counterconditioning. As Wolpe discovered in his research with "neurotic" cats, two critical tasks comprise effective counterconditioning.

The first is finding a response that is incompatible with anxiety and that can be paired with the stimuli that evoke anxiety. The principle of reciprocal inhibition states that "if a response-inhibiting anxiety can be made to occur in the presence of anxiety-evoking stimuli, it will weaken the bond between these stimuli and anxiety" (Wolpe, 1973, p. 17). With enough pairings of the anxiety-inhibiting response with the anxiety-evoking stimuli, the new, more adaptive response is eventually substituted for the maladaptive anxiety response. In simplified terms, do the healthy opposite of the problem and the problem will disappear. There are many responses that can inhibit anxiety, but the ones most frequently employed by behavior therapists are relaxation, assertion, exercise, and sexual arousal, all of which are associated with a predominance of parasympathetic nervous activity.

The second important task in counterconditioning relates to the fact that a strong anxiety response will probably disrupt relaxation, assertion, exercise, or sexual arousal. Therefore, it is critical that counterconditioning begin with stimuli low on a generalization gradient or hierarchy. Stimuli low on an anxiety hierarchy, such as a small puppy versus a large German shepherd, will elicit much lower intensities of anxiety. Again, in simplified terms, begin with "baby steps" toward the eventual larger goal. With stimuli low on a hierarchy, deep relaxation, strong assertion, or another counterconditioning response will be able to inhibit the anxiety response. By repeating such pairings with stimuli low on a hierarchy, the anxiety at each level is deconditioned. With the anxiety level receding, the pairings can proceed to stimuli higher in the hierarchy, until eventually the anxiety responses to the entire stimulus hierarchy can be deconditioned.

We shall illustrate counterconditioning with five behavioral methods: systematic desensitization, assertiveness training, sexual arousal, behavioral activation, and stimulus control.

Systematic Desensitization

Here, progressive deep-muscle relaxation is the response that is incompatible with anxiety. Therapists first teach clients how to relax the muscles throughout their bodies (Jacobson, 1938), teaching clients how to discriminate between when their muscles are tensely contracted and when they are fully relaxed. The therapist might begin by having clients grip the chair and focus on the tension in their forearms. Clients are then encouraged to relax their arms and to feel the contrast between the tension and the relaxation. Clients are encouraged to actively let go of the tension in their forearms until each fiber in their arms is relaxing. Clients learn that relaxing is an activity that can come under their control as they tightly tense each muscle group and then actively let their muscles relax. Usually muscles are tensed for 10 to 15 seconds, followed by 10 to 15 seconds of relaxation. Each important muscle group in the body is tensed and relaxed, usually beginning with the hands and forearms. By moving step by step through the muscle groups, clients become more and more relaxed.

The next step in desensitization is to construct an anxiety hierarchy that ranks stimuli from the most anxiety arousing to the least anxiety arousing. The hierarchy is frequently constructed along some stimulus dimension—time or space, for instance—as the stimulus situations move closer and closer in time to an anxiety-arousing situation, such as a job interview, or closer in space to a feared object, such as an elevator. The stimulus situations are imagined by the client and ranked from the least to the most anxiety arousing. A typical hierarchy will have 10 to 20 scenes, spaced relatively equally along a 10- (or 100-) point scale from practically no anxiety elicited to intense anxiety elicited. The scenes are typically realistic, concrete situations related to the client's problem. Frequently, patients will have more than one hierarchy to work on, although the greater number of specific anxieties they have, the less likely it is that desensitization will be effective. Once the hierarchies have been constructed, clients are asked to think of one or two relaxing scenes, such as lying on the beach on a sunny summer day, that can facilitate relaxation during the presentation of items in the hierarchy.

Now clients are ready to begin the actual desensitization. When they are deeply relaxed, the therapist asks them to imagine a scene as clearly as possible and imagine only the scene presented. They are told that if they experience any anxiety, they should signal immediately by lifting their right index finger. The client signals when the scene is being clearly pictured and, if no anxiety is elicited, continues imagining the scene for 10 seconds. If anxiety is elicited, then the client is instructed to stop imagining the hierarchy scene and go back to imagining the relaxing scene. Once clients report being clearly relaxed again, they are instructed to imagine the scene again. If a scene fails to elicit anxiety, then it is repeated at least once again before moving to the next item in the hierarchy. When a scene repeatedly elicits anxiety, the therapist moves back to the anxiety-arousing scene. If the scene continues to elicit anxiety, then clients need to be asked if they are adding stimuli to the scene. If they are not, then new items may need to be added to the hierarchy in order to allow the client to continue to progress. Usually a session is ended by having the client successfully complete a scene. The next session begins with the client imagining the last item that was successfully completed.

A desensitization session typically lasts 15 to 30 minutes, as most clients find it difficult to sustain both concentration and relaxation for more than 30 minutes. For clients with more than one hierarchy, a session will include scenes from each hierarchy rather than treating the separate hierarchies sequentially.

When systematic desensitization is completed in the office, clients are encouraged to test its effectiveness in a gradual manner. They are frequently instructed to use **in vivo desensitization**, in which they approach previously feared stimuli in real-life situations. They approach stimuli in the environment that were low on their hierarchies before confronting stimuli of greater intensity.

Exposure therapies share similar procedures with systematic desensitization, and many observers would place exposure in the behavioral camp. However, exposure typically entails full and immediate confrontation to the disturbing stimulus, whereas systematic desensitization proceeds gradually along the anxiety hierarchy. As a consequence, we covered exposure therapies in Chapter 8, separate from the behavior therapies.

Assertiveness Training

Whereas desensitization is the treatment of choice for specific phobias, **assertiveness training** is the choice for most anxieties related to interpersonal interactions. Candidates for assertiveness (or assertion) training include people afraid of complaining about poor service in a restaurant because of anxiety over hurting the waiter's feelings, people unable to leave a social situation when it is boring for fear of looking ungrateful, people unable to express differences of opinion because they are afraid others will not like them, and people fearful to tell professors or authority figures that they do not like being left waiting because the authority figures might get angry. The meek will not inherit the earth. The meek will frequently find that all they inherit is bad feelings because they are inhibited by anxiety from standing up for their rights.

Assertiveness training is not solely for the meek and shy, however. People who respond too often with aggression or anger can frequently be helped by assertiveness training as they learn more effective control over social situations instead of feeling constantly angry over not being able to influence others. Also, people who keep from expressing admiration, praise, or positive feelings because they might feel embarrassed can learn to be more positive through being more assertive. Assertive behavior is defined by Wolpe (1973, p. 81) as "the proper expression of any emotions other than anxiety toward another person." Accordingly, people who are characteristically passive or aggressive in interpersonal situations are prime candidates for assertion training.

Assertion and anxiety are to a considerable degree incompatible. Actively expressing admiration, irritation, and appropriate anger can inhibit anxieties over rejection, embarrassment, and possible failure. By learning to assert themselves in situations that previously evoked anxiety, patients begin to decondition anxiety by substituting an assertive response. As patients become more effective in their assertive behaviors, they are reinforced not only by the reduction of anxiety but also by their enhanced ability to be more successful socially.

Assertion training is varied, but invariably includes teaching clients direct and effective verbal responses for specific social situations. Clients who, for example, feel irritated but do not say anything when people cut in front of them in line are taught such responses as, "This is a line, please go to the back of it," or "I and others here would appreciate your respecting the rules of waiting in line." Patients are also taught more assertive nonverbal expressions that can inhibit anxiety. Facial "talk" displays appropriate emotion when asserting, such as smiling when telling a partner, "You look so lovely this evening!" Appropriate smiling, eye contact, and voice volume are nonverbal responses that can inhibit anxiety in social interactions.

Patients are encouraged to rehearse their new assertive responses both covertly and overtly. Covertly, clients distinguish between passive, assertive, and aggressive behavior and then imagine being more assertive in situations in which they were either passive or aggressive. Overtly, the clients rehearse assertion through role-playing with the therapist or group members. The therapist may play a waiter or waitress while the client practices insisting both verbally and nonverbally that a dinner entree be taken back because it was improperly prepared. The therapist can provide resistance to the client's assertions, such as saying, "I know the meal isn't quite right, but if I take it back the chef will be angry." Clients can then practice thinking on their feet, such as saying, "That's a problem for you and the chef to resolve. My concern is that I get what I ordered." The behavior rehearsals provide deconditioning of anxiety as well as preparation to deal more effectively with

adversaries who previously would have inhibited them.

As anxiety is reduced through role-playing of assertive interactions, clients become more confident about their abilities to face real-life situations. Therapists then give **graduated homework assignments**, beginning with less frightening situations and are most likely to lead to successes for the client. Beginning with situations that are less anxiety arousing is like starting at the bottom of an anxiety hierarchy in desensitization. As the anxiety in these less-threatening situations is effectively deconditioned through assertion, the person will usually experience less anxiety when preparing to assert in a more stressful situation. Beginning with too threatening a situation is likely to lead to failure, which will punish rather than reinforce the client's attempts to be more assertive. "Challenging but not overwhelming" is a phrase that captures just the right amount of difficulty.

Special care is needed when clients desire to be assertive in situations in which assertion may lead to punishment. In the past, many behavior therapists used the rule of never encouraging assertive behavior when punishment is likely to follow. However, such a rule encourages maintenance of the status quo for many people, including women, racial minorities, and LGBT clients, who traditionally have been derided for aggression when they were in fact assertive (Goldfried & Davison, 1994). Nevertheless, most clients and therapists desire to minimize the risk that the assertiveness of clients will evoke punishment, especially hostility or violence.

Using a minimally effective response reduces the probability that assertion will be met with hostility or other potentially punishing responses (Rimm & Masters, 1974). Thus, in expressing hurt or anger, clients can express the minimum negative emotion required to attain a desired goal. If the client's goal is not to be kept waiting by a professor, the client can knock on the door and with minimal irritation inform the professor that it is 2 o'clock and they have an appointment. A minimally effective response is less likely to evoke anger in the other person, and thus punishing consequences are less likely to occur. If a minimally effective response does not lead to the desired goal, then clients can escalate their assertiveness and express more determination to have their rights respected.

Although Wolpe's theory is still the leading explanation for the effectiveness of assertiveness training, assertion trainers use techniques that involve more than counterconditioning. Many clients need to first reevaluate their attitude about what it means to be an assertive person. For some, this involves **cognitive restructuring** (literally, changing thinking), in which they realize their personal right to be assertive. Assertion training also entails operant conditioning as therapists reinforce clients for each attempt to become more assertive. Using the process of **shaping**, therapists reinforce clients' successive approximations to the finished goal of assertion. In the early stages, for instance, merely an increase in eye contact or an escalation in voice volume will be reinforced.

Assertion training is frequently conducted in groups so that group members can provide each other reinforcement, practice, and feedback. The very process of giving effective reinforcement allows clients to practice expressing positive emotions toward others. Assertiveness training involves a great deal of feedback, as clients are encouraged to become more cognizant of the verbal and nonverbal responses that fail to communicate assertiveness. Some therapists use videotapes, which allow clients to get direct feedback concerning such behaviors as failure to make eye contact or hunching over in a nonassertive manner. Other therapists rely on feedback from themselves or from group members to raise the client's awareness of what changes are needed to be more assertive.

Wolpe's original assertiveness training has spawned a number of counterconditioning applications to interpersonal behavior. **Social skills training** includes but surpasses the behaviors originally taught in assertiveness training and has been extensively applied to individuals suffering from psychotic disorders and developmental disabilities (Curran & Monti, 1982; Hollin & Trower, 1986). **Refusal skills training**, routinely taught in treatment programs for addictive and consumptive disorders, enables patients to politely but persistently refuse offers to partake of the troubling substance (Marlatt & Gordon, 1985). And **communications skills training**, to take a final example, consists of instruction, modeling, practice, role-playing, and homework in fundamental communication skills, such as active listening and constructive negotiation (see Bornstein & Bornstein, 1986). Although all these procedures entail cognitive mechanisms of change, all received impetus from the counterconditioning paradigm: Inappropriate social behavior is reciprocally inhibited by appropriate social behavior, accepting an abusive substance is incompatible with skilled refusal of it, and destructive arguments are counterconditioned by constructive communication.

Sexual Arousal

Another counterconditioning method of behavior therapy is the use of sexual arousal to inhibit anxiety. Most contemporary forms of sex therapy use counterconditioning as an integral part of treating sexual dysfunctions, based on the seminal work of Helen Singer Kaplan (1974, 1987) and Masters and Johnson (1970). Wolpe (1958) was one of the first to report that sexual dysfunctions, such as male erectile disorder and female sexual arousal disorder, could be successfully treated with counterconditioning.

Given the negative attitudes toward sex that have traditionally prevailed in society, it is not surprising that many people have been conditioned to respond to sexual situations with anxiety. If their anxiety is intense enough, it will inhibit their sexual arousal. Through counterconditioning the sexual response can be substituted for the disrupting anxiety.

Wolpe's (1958, 1990) approach to sex therapy is quite similar to his in vivo desensitization.

Clients are first asked to identify when in a potential sexual encounter they first feel anxious. They are instructed to limit their sexual approaches to that point where anxiety begins. Obviously the partner's cooperation is important, because it can be extremely frustrating for the partner to have to stop once becoming aroused. Actually, in most cases, anxiety is evoked when intercourse is about to begin, so the cooperative partner can still be provided a reasonable degree of sexual gratification through alternative means. It is essential, however, that the partner not mock or goad the inhibited person into progressing beyond the point at which anxiety begins. By stopping and just lying still or talking, the anxiety can subside and sexual arousal can intensify. Gradually the anxious person will find that more anxiety is being inhibited and counterconditioned by sexual arousal. Gradually the couple moves from lying in bed naked together, to caressing the nonerogenous areas of the body, to caressing genitals, to beginning intercourse, and continuing with intercourse to orgasm without anxiety.

Although premier sex therapists on the order of Masters and Johnson (1970) and Kaplan (1974) include techniques that involve counterconditioning of anxiety, they would think it naive to hold that counterconditioning is the only process involved in effective sex therapy. The technique that these sex therapists use for reducing anxiety involves **sensate focusing**—literally, focusing on the sensations instead of the sexual act itself. In these exercises, partners take turns pleasuring each other, beginning with sessions in which the genitals and breasts are avoided and the rest of the body is caressed. The person being pleasured gives verbal or nonverbal feedback about what does and does not feel good.

Once the couple is able to enjoy nonerogenous stimulation without anxiety, they give each other sensate pleasuring that includes genital caressing but with no demands to reach orgasm. If this step goes well, the couple is then able to proceed with sensate pleasuring that includes intercourse, but

with no concern for reaching orgasm. With the gradual decrease in anxiety and marked increase in sexual arousal, couples are eventually able to participate in relatively free and gratifying sexual experiences.

Behavioral Activation

Depressed people frequently withdraw from their environment, disengage from their daily routines, and begin to avoid even pleasurable events. Over time, this avoidance exacerbates their depressed mood as they lose opportunities to be positively reinforced through social opportunities and successful experiences. Depression is not simply a state of mind; it is behavioral withdrawal and social isolation. What is the healthy opposite, the counterconditioning technique for such depression? **Behavioral activation**—a combination of improving daily activity, increasing pleasurable events, and enhancing feelings of personal mastery.

A number of behavioral therapies for depression have grown out of this counterconditioning tradition. The popular Coping with Depression Course (Lewinsohn et al., 1992), self-management for depression (Rehm, 1984), and behavioral activation therapy (Jacobson et al., 2001) are probably the best known and the best researched.

Behavioral activation returns to behaviorism's roots and avoids the newer cognitive techniques. It breaks the cycle of depression by increasing the patient's daily activities. Patients are presented with graduated exercises to promote activities and people that are reinforcing. The first day might only entail taking a shower and making a sandwich; the twelfth day might require a shower, a sandwich, a meeting with friends, and several hours of productive work. As patients schedule and structure their daily activities, they are asked to rate the degree of pleasure in each activity, and thus learn which are indeed gratifying. Success then gradually begets more success. The therapist may role-play or train patients to address behavioral deficits, such as passivity or social skills problems. Avoidance is identified and treated as a root cause of the depressive cycle; activation is prized as its solution.

Simple and elegant in theory, behavioral activation is more difficult to implement with depressed, unmotivated patients in the office. Therapists must exhort, teach, encourage, model, and occasionally accompany patients in performing their daily activities. For this reason, behavioral activation sessions are generally held twice weekly in the early part of therapy. For this reason too, patients' significant others may also be involved in therapy sessions early on to assist in the activation. However, the significant others' obvious frustration with the depressed patient and their attempts to aversively control the patient must be closely monitored so that it does not worsen the problem.

Stimulus Control

A final counterconditioning technique of behavior therapy to be considered is **stimulus control**— avoiding stimuli that elicit the problem behavior and inserting stimuli that cue the alternative, adaptive behavior. If you want to reduce fat in your diet, then avoid fast-food restaurants and snack foods, and instead insert healthy reminders and foods at home. As explained in Chapter 1, we can change our behavior to the environment and we can also change our environment. Sophisticated behavior therapy will assist clients in doing both.

Stimulus control instructions for the treatment of insomnia harness the power of the environment. The instructions also adhere to the key principle of counterconditioning: Do the opposite of the problem behavior. For people who suffer from insomnia, the problem behavior is that they do not sleep but remain in bed anyway. Thus, the bed becomes associated with wakefulness and frustration, not restful sleep. Doing the opposite in this case means getting out of bed when sleep does not come quickly and strengthening the bed as a cue for sleep.

The following rules constitute the stimulus control instructions (Bootzin, 2005): Lie down intending to go to sleep only when you are sleepy. (This rule strengthens the bed and bedroom as cues for sleep.) Do not use the bed for anything except sleep; do not read, watch television, or eat in bed. (This rule weakens the association of the bed with activities that might interfere with sleep.) If you find yourself unable to fall asleep, get up and go into another room. (This rule dissociates the bed from the frustration and arousal of not being able to sleep.) Stay up as long as you wish and then return to the bedroom to sleep. Get out of bed if you do not fall asleep within 10 to 15 minutes. (The goal is to associate the bed with falling asleep quickly.) If you are in bed more than 10 to 15 minutes without falling asleep, get out of bed again. Do this as often as necessary throughout the night. Set your alarm and get up at the same time every morning irrespective of how much sleep you got during the night. (This rule helps the body acquire a consistent sleep rhythm.) Do not nap during the day.

Typically, stimulus control entails helping patients to avoid high-risk environments and people that historically have cued their problem behaviors. People in recovery from drug dependence are trained to avoid places, people, and things that encouraged their drug use. Stimulus control also involves creating new cues and reminders for adaptive, nonproblem behavior. Making sober friends, living in a drug-free environment, and reading materials on abstinence, for example. To paraphrase Pavlov and Wolpe, do the opposite of your problem behavior and make your environment work for you, not against you.

Contingency Management

Human behavior occurs in predictable order, just like A, B, C. First comes the A, the antecedent, which precipitates and triggers the B, the behavior. Pavlov, Wolpe, and counterconditioning primarily concern themselves with the A → B (antecedent prompts behavior due to classical conditioning). After B comes C, the consequences of performing that behavior. B. F. Skinner, behavior modifiers, and contingency management primarily concern themselves with the B → C (behavior is largely determined by its consequences due to operant conditioning).

Theory of Psychopathology

Human behavior—whether adaptive or maladaptive—is largely controlled by its consequences. People are continually labeled pathological as if they are an alien species or a strange breed, when in fact their behavior can be explained by the same operant principles that account for most human behavior. Thus, maladaptive responses, such as painful head banging, are likely to increase in frequency if they are followed by **reinforcements**, such as special attention given only when head banging occurs. Conversely, maladaptive responses are likely to decrease in occurrence if they are followed by contingent **punishments**—for example, withdrawing a special treat or introducing a noxious chore. Maladaptive behaviors are also likely to decrease in frequency when they are consistently unrewarded, and they will eventually extinguish if no reinforcement occurs.

Reinforcements and punishments made contingent on particular responses will impact not only the probabilities of maladaptive behaviors already in existence but also the development of new responses. To illustrate the acquisition of a new maladaptive response, let me relate an experience I (JOP) had as an undergraduate out to have fun at a carnival. Walking along with a female friend, I was spotted by a barker who wanted me to try my luck at his gambling game. If he had told me that the eventual response he wanted was for me to plunk down my money as fast as I could get it from my wallet, I would have kept on walking.

Over the years, the carnival barker had learned something about shaping human behavior. Thus he began with a **prompt**, which included challenging me to win a big, furry $50 stuffed animal for my female friend. Responding to his prompt, I asked what I had to do to win, and he said just put 50 cents down and spin the wheel. When the wheel stopped, I had gained 450 points, which was more than half of the 800 points I needed for a big prize. Winning points also gave me the opportunity to spin again, and this time I earned 100 additional points. The next spin was reinforced by 25 more points. When I failed to get any points on the next spin, he again used a prompt to encourage me to put down another 50 cents. After all, 675 points on one bet was certainly worth another try. This time my spin was followed by 50 points and then 10 points, and there was no way I could lose, he said. He had been **fading** the prompts, as my tendency to spin the wheel was becoming more reliable. Soon I was reaching for more money and winning 5 points here and 5 points there. My money, however, was going out faster than points were coming in. He had indeed shaped me into responding with rapid bets. Soon I lost the $19 in my wallet, and all I had to show for it was 785 points.

As a psychology major, I went away shaking my head, thinking that B. F. Skinner had nothing on this carnival man, and Skinner's pigeons had nothing on me. No wonder compulsive gamblers are fond of saying that if you lose the first time out the Lord is on your side, and if you win big the first time out the Devil is on your side.

Maladaptive behavior does not occur in a vacuum. Some environment or stimulus situation sets the occasion for the behavior. A man beats up his wife at home almost every weekend but apparently treats her politely when in public. A woman client steals only in fancy stores but never in a discount store. The control that environments can have over maladaptive behavior results, in part, from the fact that certain stimuli serve as signals that reinforcement is likely to follow a response when the response is emitted in that particular stimulus situation. These are called **discriminative stimuli**. Other stimuli serve to signal that reinforcement will not follow a response when made under these particular stimulus conditions. Hence, clients learn that aggressive behavior or stealing may be reinforced in one situation and not reinforced, or even punished, in a different stimulus situation.

A **behavioral**, or **functional**, **analysis** consists of specifying the stimulus situations that set the occasion for the maladaptive behavior (antecedents), operationalizing the behavior itself (behavior), and detailing the reinforcement contingencies that follow (consequences). This A → B → C sequence is known as the **behavior chain** and is the foundation for understanding and modifying contingencies.

Behavioral analysis indicates three categories of frequent problems: behavioral excesses, deficits, and inappropriateness. First, there are problems that involve an excess in responding, such as washing one's hands 30 times a day. The washing of hands per se is not maladaptive, but the washing of hands excessively can become maladaptive. Second are the behaviors that entail a deficit in responding, such as rarely interacting with people. Often with deficits the problem is a lack of learning, such as a failure of the social environment to teach the skills required for effective social interaction. In the early days, behavior therapists principally reduced maladaptive behaviors rather than increased adaptive behavior, but in contemporary practice, the two tasks have achieved a more reasonable balance.

The third type of problem involves responses that are inappropriate to a particular situation or time, such as a patient who occasionally drops his drawers in public. The problem here is not the rate or skill of disrobing, but the fact that the particular response is inappropriate to the particular situation. Frequently meant by "inappropriate" is that most adults would expect that the behavior in question would be performed in private or elsewhere. We have been led to expect that in this particular situation the behavior would not lead to reinforcement and might even be followed by punishment. For the person exhibiting the maladaptive behavior, however, the same situation seems to signal that reinforcement is likely to occur. Either the person has failed to discriminate the stimulus situation accurately, such as a person who is acutely inebriated or profoundly retarded, or there is indeed a powerful reinforcement occurring not readily apparent to the observer.

What we frequently forget as observers is that reinforcement is entirely an individual matter, determined by an individual's reinforcement history. Thus, a reinforcing consequence for one of us—say, chocolate—might be a relatively neutral or even aversive consequence for another—as in the case of a nasty allergy to chocolate or peanuts. A consequence can be judged to be a reinforcement only if it actually increases the probability a response will be repeated, not merely if it appears to be pleasant. Inappropriate behavior is typically surprising and unexpected until we conduct an individual behavior analysis and discover what is in fact a reinforcement. Almost always, the heretofore bewildering behavior, such as masochistic pursuit of pain, begins to make sense in light of the person's learning history.

Therapeutic Processes

Environmental contingencies are forever shaping, maintaining, and extinguishing our behavior. Behavior modification attempts to systematically control contingencies in order to shape and maintain adaptive behavior and to extinguish maladaptive behavior. Theoretically, the therapeutic process is straightforward: change the contingencies and the behavior will change. Technically, effective contingency management involves the following six steps (Sherman, 1973):

1. State the general problem in behavioral terms, including the maladaptive responses and the situations in which they occur. This step is known as **operationalizing the target behavior**.
2. Identify behavioral objectives, which includes specifying **target behaviors** and whether the

behaviors should be increased, decreased, or reinforced only when emitted in more appropriate situations.

3. Develop behavioral measures and take **baseline measures** in order to be able to determine whether treatment is effective. Baseline measures show the rate of responses prior to the initiation of treatment.

4. Conduct **naturalistic observations**, which involves observing patients in their natural environments in order to determine the existing contingencies and therefore the effective reinforcements for a particular patient.

5. Modify existing contingencies, which involves specifying the conditions under which reinforcements are or are not to be given, what the reinforcements will be, and who will administer them.

6. Monitor the results by continuing to chart the rate of responses and comparing the results to baseline measures to determine the treatment's effectiveness. Changes in treatment can then be made when necessary, and treatment can be terminated when the behavioral objectives have been met.

The application of contingency management varies somewhat according to the *who* and the *what*: who is most effectively able to control contingencies, and what type of consequence is being controlled. Contingency management procedures can thus be categorized according to (1) **institutional control**, (2) **self-control**, (3) **mutual control** or contracting, (4) therapist control, and (5) aversive control.

Institutional Control

This type of contingency management is indicated when the managers of institutions are most effective in modifying contingencies. In the past, hospitals for chronic psychiatric patients, training schools for delinquents, institutes for developmentally disabled people, and classrooms for troubled students frequently provided too few reinforcements. When they

delivered reinforcements, the institutions often did so noncontingently. Thus, television watching, recreation time, and field trips were given independent of the resident's daily behavior. Some reinforcements, such as special attention from the staff, often were given for maladaptive responses, such as self-abusive behavior or aggressive acting out. There was little incentive for residents to improve their living conditions, hygienic habits, or social behaviors because most reinforcements were given independent of the residents' efforts.

As operant principles began to be applied to maladaptive behavior, clinicians in charge of wards or classrooms began to make reinforcements contingent on particular behaviors through the use of **token economies**. Tokens are symbolic reinforcers, such as poker chips or points on a tally sheet, that can be exchanged for items of direct reinforcement, such as social outings, recreational activities, and favorite foods. An economy involves an exchange system that determines exactly what the tokens can be exchanged for and the rate of exchange, or how many tokens it takes to get particular items or privileges. The economy also specifies the target behaviors that can earn tokens and the rate of responding required to earn a particular number of tokens—for example, making one's bed earns one token, and two tokens can be exchanged for a night at the movies.

Although it may sound simple to establish a token economy, it is truly complicated (Ayllon & Azrin, 1968). A multitude of rules must be followed for an effective economy to work. The important considerations include staff cooperation and coordination, because the staff must be more observant and more systematic in their responses to clients than in a noncontingent system; adequate control over reinforcements, because an economy becomes ineffective if residents have access to reinforcements by having money from home or being able to plead an exception for movie night from a "nice-and-lenient" staff member; clear definition of behaviors to be changed, because any lack of specificity will provoke conflict as to what constitutes the criterion (as any parent knows about children making their beds!); and providing positive alternatives to problem behavior, because it is critical that residents be shown what actions they can take to help themselves, rather than relying on a negative set of eliminating responses.

Perhaps most important, tokens must be gradually faded as problem behaviors are reduced and adaptive responses are established, because clients must be prepared to make the transition to the larger society. Using an abundance of social reinforcers along with token reinforcers helps prepare clients for fading, so that positive behaviors can be maintained by praise or recognition rather than by tokens. Also, encouraging patients to reinforce themselves, such as by learning to take pride in their appearance, is an important step in fading out tokens. All these and other procedures promote generalization of the adaptive behaviors to situations other than those in which the behaviors were learned and maintenance of the behaviors well into the future. (*Generalization* refers to different settings; **maintenance** refers to future time.)

Self-Control

At the opposite extreme from institutional control is self-control. In order to serve as their own behavior therapists, clients must be taught the fundamentals of the experimental analysis of behavior. They need to realize that self-control problems are not due to a paucity of mystical willpower or moral character but to inadequate manipulation of antecedents and consequences that control behavior. Clients must appreciate the ABCs of behavioral analysis, including the cardinal rule that immediate consequences exert greater control over behavior than do delayed consequences. Obesity, smoking, alcohol abuse, sedentary lifestyle, and procrastinating involve behaviors that have immediate positive consequences but long-term negative consequences.

Following a baseline period that includes charting the antecedents that set the occasion for the maladaptive responses, clients can begin to redesign their environments. Obese patients, for example, can be taught self-control of eating behavior, which includes narrowing the stimulus situations for eating, from television watching, newspaper reading, and visiting with friends to eating only at the table with the television off. In beginning to narrow their eating responses to the table, clients reduce the number of occasions for overeating. Clients are also informed of the research (Schachter, 1971) that demonstrates that for most obese people the presence of food rather than hunger is the more important stimulus for eating. Clients can then restrict the availability of high-calorie foods in their environment.

Clients can also work to increase behaviors incompatible with eating—for example, walking, hiking, or biking. The more walking or biking, the less likely they are to be eating. To increase their walking or biking, they may make reinforcing activities, such as television watching, contingent on an increase in walking. Clients should also reinforce themselves for avoiding fattening foods, such as allowing themselves to call a friend if they limit their calories at dinner. They can also inform their friends of their changes in eating behaviors so that friends or family can provide social reinforcement for avoiding overeating.

Appreciating the importance of shaping principles, clients should be careful to provide reinforcement for small improvements, such as studying for 30 minutes, rather than withholding reinforcement until their ideal goal is attained. Immediate reinforcement for studying should also be provided—say, going for a fruit juice or listening to a CD for 15 minutes—because the positive consequences of studying are quite delayed.

Clients are instructed to intervene early in the fairly long behavior chain that is terminated by the problem response. For example, intervening when they are beginning to approach the cupboard rather than trying to stop eating after the first potato chip is gone. Rather than testing their will-power by seeing if they can win the bet that they can eat just one, clients should realize that so-called willpower usually means intervening early rather than late in a chain of events that lead to trouble.

Mutual Control

This form of contingency management is indicated when two or more people in a relationship share control over the consequences that each wants. Couples, to take a prominent example, share control over many of the interpersonal consequences that each would like from the relationship.

The most common form of mutual control of contingencies involves **contracting**. To form a contract, each person in a relationship must specify the consequences that he or she would like to have increased (O'Banion & Whaley, 1981). Each can then begin to negotiate what he or she would want in exchange for giving the consequences the partner desires.

Richard Stuart (1969), an early behavior therapist, worked with four married couples who were in family court to get divorced. The couples shared the common complaint that the wife wanted more intimate talking, whereas the husband wanted more frequent lovemaking. The couples then worked out contracts in which the husband would get a poker chip for each quarter hour of active talking that he engaged in with his wife. Once he had earned eight poker chips he would trade them in for a sexual encounter. Needless to say, the rate of talking increased dramatically. At the same time, the wives were much more responsive to lovemaking.

Some people might find this form of contracting artificial and unromantic, but the couples seemed to enjoy their talking and lovemaking more than ever, and each of the four couples was able to avoid divorce. What some people dislike is that contracting makes explicit in relationships the **behavior exchange theory**, which holds that we interact in order to exchange reinforcements (Jacobson & Margolin, 1979). As long as there is a fair exchange of reinforcements, people are likely to continue in a relationship and to feel satisfied with the relationship.

Therapist Control

In outpatient treatment, psychotherapists ordinarily have little direct control over the daily environmental contingencies of their patients. Therapists can, however, control social reinforcers, such as attention, recognition, and praise, that occur in treatment. Therapists can make their social reinforcers contingent on improvement in the client's behavior.

Greenspoon (1955) was one of the first to demonstrate that verbal reinforcers can influence the types of responses emitted by clients, such as an increase in the number of "I" messages as a function of verbal reinforcement from the therapist. Effective therapists make a point of managing their own verbal and nonverbal reinforcements to make sure they are encouraging adaptive behaviors. All too often, therapists give special attention only to maladaptive responses, such as leaning forward and listening carefully when clients begin to express self-hatred.

Psychotherapists can gain greater control over contingencies by forming contracts with clients. A client can be required, for instance, to deposit $100 and to earn the money back through making appropriate responses, such as losing weight each week. A contingency contract in which the client earns, say, $10 for each pound of weight lost adds to the effectiveness of a self-control package (Harris & Bruner, 1971). The therapeutic contract can also include a provision for **response cost**, such as the client's paying $5 for each pound gained. Even better, the $5 can be donated to the client's least favorite organization, such as the White Supremacists Party or American Civil Liberties Union.

Contingency management procedures have been applied with promising success to the treatment of substance abusers. Alcohol abusers can earn prizes for submitting negative Breathalyzer samples and by completing steps toward treatment goals—"Give them prizes and they will come" (Petry et al., 2000). Or marijuana-dependent patients can earn vouchers for retail items contingent on them submitting cannabinoid-negative urine specimens (Budney et al., 2000). Contingency management provides incentive for change, using positive reinforcement for abstinence and occasionally response costs for returning to drug use (Higgins & Silverman, 1999).

Of course, behavior therapists are not confined to their offices or clinics. As noted at the beginning of this chapter, behaviorists value direct observation and intervention in the patient's natural environment. Within the natural setting, therapists can help clients restructure the antecedents and consequences controlling their troubled responses. Working in the natural environment possesses the decided advantage of not having to worry about generalization from the office to the client's home. There need be no concern with transfer of training, because the training is done right in the troubled environment. When working with children, for example, the clinician can go into the home and train parents to function as therapist surrogates or behavior modifiers. Parents can be trained to manage contingencies more effectively by instituting a token economy, by contracting with their children, or by making social reinforcements made contingent on positive responses from the child while avoiding reinforcement of negative behaviors.

Aversive Control

There are rare occasions when the control of discriminating stimuli and the management of reinforcements fail to change the maladaptive behavior. At these times, the behavior therapist will carefully consider the use of aversive controls. Maladaptive behaviors traditionally labeled impulse control problems—sexual deviations, alcohol dependence, and repetitive self-abuse, for example—may respond to aversive controls when more positive

techniques have failed. This is an important point: Any behaviorist worth his or her salt will only attempt **aversive conditioning** after multiple efforts at positive alternatives have failed. When aversive controls are applied within contingency management, the emphasis is generally on the contingent use of punishment (when an aversive consequence follows a particular response).

Ample research has outlined the conditions in which punishment can be most effective in producing lasting effects on behavior. The guidelines for using punishment are as follows: Punishment should be *immediate*, because delay confuses the contingency and increases the person's anxiety. It should be sufficiently *intense*, because the more aversive the punishment, the more effective it is. It should be *salient* to that person, along the same lines that reinforcement is individually defined. Punishment should be delivered *early in the behavioral chain*, to catch the problem early on before it intensifies. It should be delivered on a *continuous schedule*, which is more effective than an intermittent schedule of reinforcement, because intermittent reinforcement makes a response even more resistant to extinction. It should be provided across *all stimulus situations*; otherwise, the person learns to avoid responding in punished situations but not in unpunished situations. It should be delivered in a reasonably *calm manner*, so that the anger of the punisher is separated out from the punishment of the behavior. Finally, punishment should be accompanied by demonstration and reinforcement of *alternative, adaptive behaviors*, such as teaching a child to use restraint and assertive skills instead of smashing a younger sibling.

Let us illustrate the cautious use of aversive conditioning and apply the principles of punishment to a case combining therapist control and aversive control. Susan was profoundly developmentally disabled but stood out because of her unnerving habit of smacking herself in the face with her fist. Four to five times a minute, 3,000 times a day, 1 million times a year, this youngster hit herself. Susan's head banging had begun when she was 3 years old. At first, anticonvulsants and tranquilizers had reduced it, but at age 7 she began to cry frequently. Her neurologist thought that perhaps her medication was excessive, so he reduced it on a trial basis. Unfortunately, her head banging intensified, and the crying remained the same. Increasing the medication and trying new drugs proved to be of no help. Other methods were just as fruitless, and out of a sense of desperation, the neurologist referred Susan to a clinic employing behavior modification when applicable (Prochaska et al., 1974).

We (JOP and colleagues) reviewed Susan's school records to discern what techniques other psychologists had tried in treating her head banging. Unfortunately, most of our ideas had already been tested and had failed, such as reinforcing an incompatible response like piano playing or trying to extinguish her head banging by paying no attention to it while giving considerable attention to constructive behaviors. We also felt limited by the fact that baseline records indicated that Susan's rate of head banging seemed to remain quite stable across situations, including in an isolation room where she was unaware of being observed through a one-way mirror.

We decided to experiment with aversive conditioning. After wiring electrodes to Susan's legs and taking 15-minute baseline readings, we gave her a 2.5-milliamp shock each time she hit herself. It soon became apparent that the contingent shock was reducing the rate of head banging in the clinic. Systematic recordings even indicated partial generalization to her school. Before long, however, Susan began to discriminate the stimulus that set the occasion for the shock. She would hit herself until the electrodes were attached, then she would stop. After awhile, she even learned that she could hit herself without receiving a shock as long as her therapist wasn't watching her. Now there was no generalization outside of the clinic. We had been outsmarted by this developmentally disabled 9-year-old!

Realizing that a punishment paradigm of aversive conditioning could be effective only if given on a continuous schedule, we decided to purchase a remote-control shocking apparatus that would allow us to shock Susan any time of the day in any setting without her being able to discriminate where, when, or by whom she was getting shocked. On the first day of the remote conditioning, Susan hit herself 45 times compared to the usual 3,000 times. The next day it dropped to 17 hits, followed by 6 hits. Then the apparatus malfunctioned and began giving noncontingent shocks. Following repairs, it took only 2 days with a total of 12 shocks to bring Susan's head banging down to none.

For months she didn't hit herself. We decided to take the apparatus off her arm, and to our surprise she came over to us and wanted it back on. But we kept the apparatus off, and she went for months without hitting herself. In fact, for the next 5 years she hit herself approximately 250 times, compared with the 5 million hits she might have delivered without the aversive conditioning.

The logistics of aversive conditioning and the guidelines for effective punishment reveal why the punishment paradigm can become practically unworkable. With a 27-year-old exhibitionist, for example, it would be logistically impossible to have a therapist available whenever the client might come across a school bus. In Susan's case, it was possible to have someone available in all situations, but it obviously would become a highly expensive treatment if her parents had to hire someone to follow her with a remote-control device throughout her waking hours. One alternative with some patients is to train them to deliver their own shock immediately following a maladaptive response.

The use of painful punishers also raises ethical and legal questions. In Susan's case, we spent 2 months convincing the Department of Mental Retardation that contingent shock was the best alternative available for treating Susan's self-abuse.

In many cases, such as with prisoners, the use of aversive paradigms has been ruled illegal and is thus unavailable. Although we now know that the contingent application of aversive stimuli can be a powerful modifier of behavior, much needs to be done to resolve the practical and ethical issues involved in its use.

The use of **covert sensitization** as an aversive technique has raised fewer objections, in part because it has frequently been conceptualized as a self-control approach to modifying behavior. In covert sensitization (Cautela, 1967), conditioning is done through the use of covert stimuli and responses, such as thoughts and images. The client is first taught deep-muscle relaxation and then encouraged to imagine a scene that the therapist describes. A 30-year-old pedophile was asked to imagine approaching a 10-year-old boy to whom he was attracted. As he approaches the boy to ask him to come up to his apartment, he feels his stomach becoming nauseated. He feels his lunch coming up into his esophagus, and just as he goes to speak to the boy he vomits all over himself and the boy. People on the street are staring at him, and he turns away from the boy and immediately begins to feel better. He begins walking back to his apartment, feeling better and better with each step he takes. He gets back to his apartment, washes up, and feels great.

After teaching this man the covert scene, we had him practice it overtly, including making vomiting noises and gestures. To make the scene even more vivid, we had him sit in his apartment window, and when he saw a boy on the street whom he would like to approach sexually, we had him go to the bathroom and stick his fingers down his throat and vomit as he imagined propositioning the young boy. Within 2 months, this chronic offender was no longer feeling the urge to approach young boys, and he had followed through on our assertiveness techniques for forming adult relationships.

Because covert sensitization works with thoughts and images, it could just as readily have been categorized with the cognitive-behavior therapies considered next.

Cognitive-Behavior Modification

Behaviorism was established as a radical alternative to mentalistic theories of psychology, which attempted to account for human behavior in terms of cognitive or emotional constructs. Conditioning replaced cognition as the critical determinant of human behavior. Cognitive processes were not denied; they were viewed as less relevant to an effective analysis of behavior disorders.

However, as experimental psychologists conducted more research on cognitive processes and as behavior therapists treated more adults with complex problems, cognitive conceptualizations of behavior became respectable again. Most contemporary behavior therapists are comfortable with the incorporation of cognitive techniques and the label "cognitive-behavioral." They argue that once we go beyond treating young children or developmentally disordered individuals, we must take into account the cognitive processes critical in changing complex adult behavior. Estes (1971, p. 23), a prominent learning theorist, states emphatically:

> *For the lower animals, for very young children, and to some extent for human beings of all ages who are mentally retarded or subject to severe neurological or behavior disorders, behavior from moment to moment is largely describable and predictable in terms of responses to particular stimuli and the rewarding or punishing outcomes of previous stimulus response sequences. In more mature human beings, much instrumental behavior and more especially a great part of verbal behavior is organized into high-order routines and is, in many instances, better understood in terms of the operations of rules, principles, strategies, and the like, than in terms of successions of responses to particular stimuli. Thus, in many*

situations an individual's behavior from moment to moment may be governed by a relatively broad strategy which, once adopted, dictates response sequences rather than by anticipated consequences of specific actions. In these situations it is the selection of strategies rather than the selection of particular reactions to stimuli which is modified by past experience with rewarding or punishing consequences.

Theory of Psychopathology

As a hybrid of cognitive and behavioral parentage, cognitive-behavioral theories of psychopathology and psychotherapy are less distinctive than either of their parental contributors. Some cognitive behaviorists take their theories and techniques from the behavioral side and occasionally add a cognitive element. Other cognitive behaviorists begin with the cognitive theories of Albert Ellis or Aaron Beck and then throw in the behavioral element.

Lacking a consensual cognitive theory of psychopathology unique to behaviorists, we will adopt a cognitive model of maladaptive behavior that parallels the contingency model of maladaptive behavior. That is, psychopathology is due to deficits, excesses, or inappropriateness in cognitions.

Some maladaptive behaviors reflect a deficit in cognitive activity. Autonomic nervous system disorders—such as essential hypertension, tension headaches, and chronic anxiety—were traditionally assumed to be outside cognitive control because there is an inherent deficiency in psychological information available to the individual trying to control autonomic responses. With little or no feedback available, individuals are unable to use cognitive processes to gain voluntary control over disruptive autonomic responses.

Other problems are characterized by an excess of particular cognitive responses, as in the case of a hypochondriacal client who was constantly ruminating over the possibility of having cancer. Here the problem is that the same cognition is occurring repeatedly and interfering with the client's ability to use cognitive processes to solve other problems and to relate effectively with the environment. In such cases, what is needed is a reduction in particular cognitive responses, such as a decrease in the frequency of thinking about cancer.

Perhaps the most common problem is the use of inappropriate or ineffective cognitive responses. For some clients this involves inappropriate labeling, such as a client who mislabels sex as dirty and then responds to a sexual encounter with disgust. Other clients develop cognitive expectancies that are mistaken, such as a graduate student who expected all people in authority to act harsh, cold, and condemning and thus experienced difficulty in dealing with professors and supervisors in even the most routine matters. From a cognitive perspective, these clients experience trouble because they are not responding to the actual stimuli and consequences that occur in their environments. Instead, the clients are responding primarily to the labels and expectancies used to process environmental events. If their labels and expectancies are inaccurate, then their behaviors are bound to be maladaptive.

At a more complex level, some clients have developed ineffective strategies for solving problems. In a rapidly changing society, it is important to be cognizant of effective methods for attacking common problems, such as dealing with an upsetting boss, handling one's money, solving the inevitable conflicts of relationships, and living with the anxieties of adolescents facing an uncertain future.

If people learn ineffective strategies for approaching routine behavioral problems, they are likely to make serious mistakes that will lead to frustration, depression, and other emotional upsets. Clients who try not to think about problems in hopes that they will go away, frequently wait until the problem is out of control before taking action. Other clients, who are frequently labeled as dependent, may have adopted a strategy that involves rushing to an authority for the best solution. They may be unable to cope with even minor quandaries like what style of clothes to wear, what courses to take each semester, or how to study for an exam. These patients may do well when therapists give them specific directions on how to solve the particular quandary, but they are being reinforced in the short run for depending on a psychotherapist. What such clients actually need in the long run is more skills regarding the principles of effective problem solving.

Therapeutic Processes

If a patient's problem is the result of a deficit in information, then the solution is to increase the client's awareness by providing the necessary information. If clients are not aware, for example, that their blood pressure is increasing, then there is obviously no way they can consciously prevent the increase. In the case of maladaptive responses within the autonomic nervous system, the necessary information could not be given to clients until a technology was developed.

With the development of instrumentation over the past half century, it has become possible to give clients ongoing feedback about specific physiological activity occurring within their bodies. These **biofeedback** techniques allow clients to become conscious of changes in their blood pressure, pulse rate, brain waves, dilation of blood vessels, and other biological functions. When clients are wired to a biofeedback apparatus, they can receive physiological information that offers an increase in cognitive control over autonomic responses.

In the past decade, there has been a great deal of interest in **neurobiofeedback** or EEG feedback, particularly for the treatment of attention-deficit hyperactivity disorder (ADHD). In this form of biofeedback, information about brain wave activity (as opposed to muscle tension or blood pressure) is communicated to the patient. Specifically, electrodes are attached to the patient's head to amplify brain waves. The brain waves are transmitted to a computer, which translates the brain waves into a computer game or visual display. The patient is then taught to alter brain activity by focusing on and manipulating the computer game. The goal of neurobiofeedback is to train the individual to increase the neural activity associated with paying attention, while decreasing the neural activity associated with distraction.

When confronted with trying to change mistaken labels and expectancies, behaviorists frequently rely on techniques derived from Ellis's rational-emotive therapy and Beck's cognitive therapy, which are considered in detail in Chapter 10. Emotionally upsetting labels, including "awful" and "terrible," are challenged through techniques of cognitive restructuring. So too are catastrophic expectations challenged, not only for the realistically low probability of their occurrence, but also for the exaggerated negative consequences that they bring.

Another alternative to challenging mistaken cognitions has emerged from the social-psychological research on attribution theory. An **attribution** is an explanation for an observed event or an account of what caused something to happen. In their classic research on attributions, Schachter and Singer (1962) gave research participant injections of epinephrine (adrenaline) and told one group that the emotional arousal they would experience could be attributed to the drug they were given. Other participants were not informed of the effects of the drug and were placed in situations designed to evoke particular emotions, such as with a stooge modeling anger toward the experiment. Participants who were able to attribute their arousal to the drug demonstrated less emotional responding than those who were not aware of the effects of the drug.

Misattributions can exert devastating psychological effects, but there are several ways in which patients can be helped toward more accurate or more benign attributions (Goldfried & Davison, 1976, 1994). Clinical assessments, for example, are attributions made by clinicians, and the assessments can vary in the emotional upset they evoke. A client who attributes erectile dysfunction to unconscious conflicts over possible homosexual impulses will probably be relieved of considerable anxiety to learn that situational tension combined with alcohol can produce the observed problem. A client with physical symptoms, such as a man with chronic headaches who is highly anxious because he attributes his headaches to a brain tumor, may be immensely relieved if he learns that the accurate attribution is that the headaches are due to anxiety over health. The expectations that clients have for future events can be dramatically changed if their attributions over past or present events are significantly altered.

Martin Seligman and associates (1979) developed further the measurement and treatment of maladaptive attributions. They have consistently identified the three **attributional styles** of stability, internality, and globality (Peterson & Villanova, 1988; Peterson et al., 1982). Optimal performance and mental health are associated with a stable, internal, and global attributional style toward good events; that is, when positive events occur, we assign them a permanent, personal, and pervasive quality. The situation is reversed with bad events: Optimal performance and mental health are associated with a temporary, external, and specific attributional style. That is, when dreaded events occur, we should think of them as temporary, atypical events caused by external forces.

If you perform well on an exam, for instance, then the optimistic attribution is to tell yourself it will always happen (permanent), it was your responsibility (personal), and it will happen in other academic courses and life situations (pervasive). But if you perform poorly on an exam, then the optimistic attribution is that it was a rare fluke (temporary), it was the professor's or the situation's fault (external), and it will not happen in other courses or situations (specific). The point is that attributions are learned behaviors; learned behaviors can be unlearned. The resulting cognitive-behavioral

therapy assists patients in modifying their pessimistic attributions and adopting **learned optimism** (Seligman, 1990).

In creating **self-instructional training**, Donald Meichenbaum (1977, 1986) was a pioneer in cognitive-behavior modification (CBM). Meichenbaum works with patients to reduce their self-statements that produce maladaptive emotions and, at the same time, works to develop self-statements that facilitate adaptive self-control. In other words, decrease the hurtful thoughts and increase the helpful thoughts.

Impulsive and aggressive children have been of special concern to Meichenbaum and associates (Meichenbaum, 1977; Meichenbaum & Goodman, 1969, 1971). His early contributions laid the groundwork for the popular and manualized cognitive-behavioral treatments of childhood and adolescent disorders, especially attention-deficit, defiant, and impulsive disorders (e.g., Barkley, 1991; Kendall & Braswell, 1992).

To help children develop better self-control through self-instruction, the therapist performs a task while talking out loud to him- or herself. The child then performs the task with guidance from the psychotherapist. Next, the child performs the task while giving self-instructions aloud. The child then whispers the self-instructions while going through the task. Finally, the child carries out the task employing covert self-instructions. The child's behavior comes increasingly under the control of covert self-speech. Self-statements thus exert control over the individual's behavior in much the same way as statements coming from another person.

Meichenbaum and Goodman (1971, p. 117) illustrate what the therapist might say aloud at step 1 while copying line patterns.

Okay, what is it I have to do? You want me to copy the picture with the different lines. I have to go slowly and carefully. Okay, draw the line down, down, good; then to the right, that's it, now down some more and to the left. Good, I'm doing fine so far. Remember, go slowly. Now back up again. No, I was supposed to go down. That's okay. Just erase the line carefully.... Good. Even if I make an error I can go on slowly and carefully, I have to go down now. Finished. I did it!

By internalizing constructive and deliberate self-statements, impulsive children can learn to instruct themselves to slow down when performing a task and to correct themselves without becoming upset. Not only do these self-instructions replace irrational ideas that can lead to emotional upset, but they also provide coping skills for directing children in more adaptive behaviors.

Meichenbaum's (1986) CBM with adults proceeds in three phases. The first phase, conceptualizing the problem, is concerned with helping patients understand the nature of their problems and enlisting their active collaboration in formulating a treatment plan. The second phase, trying on the conceptualization, helps clients explore, sample, and consolidate this mutual view of the problem behavior. With this preparatory work complete, in phase three, modifying cognitions and producing new behaviors, the cognitive-behavioral therapist assists patients in modifying their internal dialogues and in enacting new behaviors to be performed in vivo. This third phase is designed to realign the ongoing reciprocal interactions among cognition, affect, behavior, and environment into more adaptive directions for the patient.

These phases of CBM have been successfully applied to children and adults in **stress inoculation** (Meichenbaum, 1985, 1996). This treatment is analogous to an inoculation in medicine wherein a small amount of an active virus is introduced into the body in order to mobilize a healthy response from the immune system. Instead of just learning to control anxiety in stressful situations, individuals can develop covert cognitive skills and overt behavioral skills that can inoculate them against stressors. Previously anxiety-provoking events—such as school or

work evaluations, public speaking, and interpersonal confrontations—can be reevaluated as challenges and learning opportunities. Such challenges can be mastered through a flexible combination of behavioral and cognitive skills rather than automatically construed as threats that must be avoided.

Stress inoculation is frequently used to help young clients complete scary medical procedures. Children facing the anxious prospects of surgery, dialysis, or chemotherapy are brought to the hospital before their medical procedures in order to receive a small dose of the forthcoming stress. First comes education. The children receive specific information on what to expect—what will happen during the procedure, where their parents will wait, who will be doing what and when. Second comes rehearsal. The children are safely exposed to the medical procedures—practicing the pinch of needles, for example—and taught relaxation skills and coping thoughts to combat the anxiety. Third comes the implementation, actually carrying out the medical procedures, but now with more prepared and less anxious children.

Although individuals vary in how they solve problems, there is a remarkable degree of agreement on the operations involved in effective problem solving (D'Zurilla & Nezu, 1999). **Problem-solving therapy** can be taught to clients who need more effective strategies for approaching problems. Therapists begin by educating clients in a philosophy that encourages independent problem solving. Clients are taught to define problems operationally in terms of the stimuli, responses, and consequences involved. Once all aspects of the problem situation have been defined concretely, clients are able to formulate the problem more abstractly, such as a conflict between two or more goals or between a goal and the available means to the goal.

A student came to me (JCN) for advice about whether she should drop out of college. She had just found out her father was having an extramarital affair and her parents were planning to divorce.

She was experiencing difficulties with concentration and studying, and was therefore contemplating dropping the remainder of her college education. In formulating her problem, it became evident that her major conflict was between her goal to advance herself and her desire to help her younger siblings. With the problem formulated, the next step is to generate alternatives. The client is encouraged to generate a range of possible responses to the situation. Principles of brainstorming (Osborn, 1963) are encouraged during this stage: withhold criticism of any alternative; freewheeling is welcomed, the wilder the idea the better; the more alternatives the better, increasing the probability that effective ideas will occur; combine and improve alternatives into better ideas.

With a variety of alternatives generated, the problem then moves into the stage of decision making. Obviously, the person is trying to choose the best, feasible alternative from those available. The student, for example, might choose to stay in school while taking out a loan, and thereby help herself educationally and her family financially; however, a loan might not be available. Another of her alternatives—to live at home, work, and attend college part-time—might resolve her conflict and also be feasible.

Many people get bogged down in decision making when they should realize that few decisions are irreversible. They need to make their best bet on one alternative and then move to the stage of verification, in which they begin to test the validity of their alternative. In taking action, such as moving home while continuing in college, the student observes the consequences of her decision in order to verify its effectiveness. If the consequences of her action seem to match her expectation, then she has exited from her problem. If the consequences do not adequately match her expectations, then she can always return to an earlier stage, such as generating new alternatives or deciding on a previously discarded alternative.

Therapeutic Relationship

The importance of the therapeutic relationship in behavior therapy varies according to the particular method and clinician. With systematic desensitization, for example, the relationship is not nearly as consequential as in CBM; the former has been successfully applied in large groups and with computers, whereas the latter emphasizes the active collaboration of patient and therapist. Similarly, the relationship assumes greater importance in some of the operant methods, especially if the therapist is using social reinforcement, and in cognitive-behavior therapy, especially if the therapist is treating complex psychopathology. Under such conditions, the more valuable the psychotherapist is to the client, the more effective a social reinforcer the therapist can be.

And behavior therapists can indeed be social reinforcers, leading clients to perceive them as empathic and warm. The educational and collaborative nature of the therapeutic relationship leads to patient ratings on therapist empathy, understanding, and warmth generally comparable to other, relationship-oriented psychotherapies (Glass & Arnkoff, 1992). A case in point is the oft-cited study of Sloane and colleagues (1975), who compared behavior therapy and psychoanalytic psychotherapy. From tape recordings, psychoanalytic therapists and behavior therapists were found *not* to differ on degree of warmth or positive regard. There were significant differences, however, on accurate empathy and genuineness. The behavior therapists were rated higher on both.

Many behavior therapists prefer the operational term **validation** to the person-centered *empathy* in describing their relationship goals. Validation occurs when the therapist communicates to the patient that her responses make sense and are understandable within her current life context. There are multiple means of validating clients in session: listening and observing, accurately reflecting, articulating the unverbalized, reinforcing progress, validating as reasonable in the moment, and treating the person as important and valid (Linehan, 1993b). Validation is an end in itself, but it also facilitates client change. And all of these therapist skills can be identified, rated, and taught—in contrast to the fuzzy notions of therapeutic presence or empathy.

If there is any general value to the relationship, it is certainly not in terms of the criteria Carl Rogers suggested. The behavior therapist would do clients an injustice to pretend to be unconditional in positive regard, because social reinforcements, including positive regard, are in reality contingent. The behaviorist is less concerned with accurate empathy than with accurate treatment. Nor is the therapist particularly concerned with being genuine; what clients need is a competent therapist, not one who is self-preoccupied with authenticity.

If there is any general value to a therapeutic relationship, it lies in establishing a secure precondition for psychotherapy and in therapist modeling. The behavior therapist must provide sufficient validation and invoke sufficient credibility, trust, and positive expectancies for clients to engage in the work expected of them during the session and in between sessions. The behavior therapist must also invoke **modeling**—observational learning in which the behavior of the therapist (the model) acts as a stimulus for similar thoughts, attitudes, and behaviors on the part of the client (Perry & Furukawa, 1986). In assertiveness training, for example, the therapist serves directly as a model who teaches clients more effective methods of being assertive. Modeling is such a critical part of assertiveness training that therapists who are not genuinely assertive would probably not be competent as assertion trainers.

Modeling occurs with most other forms of behavior therapy as well. A desensitizer, for example, models a fearless approach toward phobic stimuli, teaching clients that such stimuli can be mastered if approached in a gradual and relaxed manner. We cannot envision a snake-phobic therapist successfully assisting a snake-phobic patient! The contingency contractor models a positive approach toward problem solving and teaches clients that conflicts can best be solved through compromise and positive reinforcement rather than through criticism and punishment.

Modeling can serve many important functions in changing behavior (Bandura, 1969; Perry & Furukawa, 1986). Through observation, clients can acquire new behaviors; for example, clients observe a competent asserter for the first time and then begin to acquire the essentials of effective assertion. Modeling can facilitate adaptive behaviors by inducing clients to perform behaviors that they are capable of performing but have not been performing in appropriate ways, such as expressing positive feelings toward a spouse after the therapist has been observed to express similar feelings. Modeling can disinhibit behaviors previously avoided because of anxiety, as when clients learn to talk openly about feelings because the therapist has been direct about them. Finally, modeling can lead to vicarious and direct extinction of anxiety associated with a stimulus, such as when children extinguish fear of dogs because they have observed the therapist's children having fun with dogs.

The essential point is this: Considerable research demonstrates how beneficial modeling can be and also how modeling can be most effective. If behaviorists make therapeutic relationships a part of the process of change, then they must attend closely to what they are modeling and how effective a model they are becoming.

Practicalities of Behavior Therapy

Behavior therapists show considerable variation in the practical aspects of their work. Therapists using counterconditioning and cognitive-behavioral techniques are most likely to work in an office setting. Treatment is typically conducted in an individual or, increasingly, a group or couple format. Many of the behavioral and cognitive-behavior techniques, including assertiveness training, relaxation training, and problem solving, are applied in a group format for the sake of cost efficiency and group processes, including modeling, rehearsal, and group reinforcement.

Some behavior analysts are critical of therapists' staying in their offices; they suggest interventions performed in the natural environment are not plagued with the same generalization or transfer-of-training problems as those performed in the office. Certainly when behavior therapists are managing contingencies on a larger scale, as with token economics, they work directly in the environment of clients. Unfortunately, because of exaggerated fears of brave-new-world phenomena, behavior modification has been frowned on in some environments, the most noteworthy being prisons under the auspices of the federal government.

Much of behavior therapy, in fact, is conducted by caseworkers, teachers, technicians, and counselors working in institutions where behavior management is practiced. The systematic use of reinforcement is employed in most day care centers, child treatment clinics, adolescent residential facilities, partial hospitalization programs, and nursing homes. The question is not whether to use contingencies; the question is *how* to use contingency management most effectively in a treatment program.

Behaviorists commit to time-efficient, evidence-based treatments. In one of our studies (Norcross & Wogan, 1983), behavior therapists reported seeing clients less frequently and for a shorter duration than psychotherapists of all other persuasions; only 7% of their clients, on average, were seen for more than a year. Of course, particular clients will require more extensive treatment when warranted by their needs, not the therapist's theoretical orientation. The entire movement in psychotherapy toward cost efficiency and evidence-based treatments is old news to behavior therapists.

Behavior therapists and their cognitive-behavioral cousins are quite comfortable with technology as a part of treatment. The equipment can vary from a simple reclining chair for relaxation to remote-control aversive stimulators to complex biofeedback equipment. Additions to the technology arsenal include computer programs and smart-phone applications for collecting data and for administering treatments to clients in their natural environments.

Behavior therapists continually test the limits of their techniques and consequently have worked with a wide range of clients, probably the widest range of any psychotherapy system. Counterconditioning has been used most often with verbal adults who suffer from neurotic, health, and personality disorders. Cognitive-behavioral techniques are most often used with adults and adolescents, although problem solving and self-instruction are employed extensively with children. Contingency management techniques have been applied to disorders that have been most difficult for verbal therapies, such as impulse-control problems, addictive disorders, children's dysfunctions, and the problems of developmentally disabled and psychotically regressed patients.

Behavior therapists represent the full range of mental health professions but psychologists are two to three times more likely than members of other mental health professions to endorse behaviorism (Glass & Arnkoff, 1992). This is probably because they are more likely to have been trained in learning theories and in empirical research. Especially noteworthy is the role that experimental psychologists have played in the development of behavior therapy, because they traditionally have not been a direct part of any therapy system.

Behavior and cognitive-behavior therapists are at the forefront of competency-based education in psychotherapy. The behavioral mandate is to demonstrate competency in scientifically established methods.

To this end, behaviorists are heavily involved in creating treatment manuals and documenting evidence-based practice for the purposes of enhancing professional training and treatment selection. Treatment manuals attempt to operationalize therapeutic procedures, typically session by session, in such a way that other therapists can learn and replicate the procedures. Evidence-based practice, discussed in Chapter 18, is an emerging trend to identify health care interventions that have been empirically tested and supported as more effective than active placebos or alternative treatments. Such evidence-based practices are those that should be favored in treating patients and training students (Task Force on Promotion and Dissemination of Psychological Procedures, 1995).

Personal therapy is not deemed a particularly valuable prerequisite for conducting behavioral treatment. In fact, only about one half of behavior therapists report ever having experienced therapy themselves, a figure consistently the lowest among the theoretical orientations studied (Norcross & Guy, 2005). Interestingly and controversially, when behavior therapists do take their troubles to someone, that someone tends *not* to be a fellow behaviorist (Geller et al., 2005; Lazarus, 1971c; Norcross & Prochaska, 1984).

Effectiveness of Behavior Therapy

More controlled outcome research has been conducted on behavior therapy and cognitive-behavior therapy than on any other system of psychotherapy. About two thirds of the controlled outcome studies on psychotherapy with children and adolescents have been conducted on behavioral treatments (Kazdin, 1991; Weisz et al., 2004), and a majority of controlled outcome studies on psychotherapy with adults pertain to behavioral and cognitive-behavioral treatments (Grawe et al., 1998; Wampold, 2001).

It would take an entire book to review all the literature on the efficacy of behavior therapy. Our plan in this section, therefore, is to summarize the findings of multiple meta-analyses on the effectiveness of behavior therapy generally and then for selected behavioral methods and a few particular disorders. We review the effectiveness of closely related cognitive therapy in Chapter 10 and exposure therapy in Chapter 8.

Small-*n* Designs

Our research summaries and meta-analytic reviews on treatment effectiveness consider only controlled research using group designs. However, many behavior therapists have argued persuasively that there are legitimate research alternatives to the traditional multigroup design that uses placebo and/or no-treatment control groups. They argue that well-controlled case studies or studies with a small-*n* can yield valid data when techniques such as multiple baseline or ABAB designs (see following) are used.

In the **multiple baseline design**, several of the client's behaviors (not only the behavior being directly modified) are measured initially. The therapeutic intervention is then introduced for one of the behaviors, while measurement of all the behaviors continues. If the intervention produces improvement in the target behavior but not in the other behaviors, it is argued that there is something about the specific relation between the target behavior and the environmental modification that has produced the improvement. The assumption is that other behaviors would have been equally subject to nonspecific effects, such as the passing of time and the relationship with the therapist. Although there is much to recommend about this design, one problem is that we cannot say just which changes in the environment produced the behavior changes. Was it changes in concrete contingencies, for example, or was it the result of experimenter demands or expectations?

A similar dilemma arises with ABAB types of designs. In the **ABAB (reversal) design**, the person receiving the treatment is measured repeatedly: before intervention (baseline, A); during the time when the intervention is in effect (B); during a subsequent period when the intervention is temporarily discontinued (return to baseline, A); and again under the influence of the therapeutic intervention (B). The rationale behind this design is that if the client's behavior improves during the periods when treatment is administered and is worse during the initial period and at any other time when treatment is withdrawn, then the treatment itself is presumed to be causally responsible for the change. Here again we cannot determine precisely what in the treatment package accounts for the behavior change. Was it the client's expectations, the therapist's special attention, the treatment itself, or another uncontrolled variable?

Small-*n* designs are excellent vehicles for examining the efficacy of new procedures and are superb models for conducting clinical research when only a small number of patients are available. At the same time, small-*n* designs lack the power and control afforded by more traditional research designs. For these reasons, our review will not concern itself with the thousand plus small-*n* studies published to date.

Behavior Therapy with Children

Weisz and colleagues (1987, 2004; Weisz, Donenberg, et al., 1995) have conducted several meta-analyses on the effectiveness of psychotherapy with children and adolescents. They statistically examined 236 published randomized trials on treatment for youth (3–18 years). Across various outcome measures, the average treated youngster was more improved after treatment than about 80% of those not treated. They concluded that behavioral treatments proved more effective than nonbehavioral treatments regardless of client age, therapist experience, or problem type.

The behavioral methods, number of treatment groups, and average (unweighted) effect sizes in two of the meta-analyses were as follows (recall

that an effect size of 0.50 is considered medium and 0.80 a large effect in the behavioral sciences):

BEHAVIORAL METHOD	NUMBER OF TREATMENT GROUPS		EFFECT SIZE	
	1987	1995	1987	1995
Operant (e.g., reinforcement)	39	19	0.78	0.69
Desensitization/relaxation	17	31	0.75	0.70
Modeling	25	12	1.19	0.73
Social skills training	5	23	0.90	0.37
Cognitive-behavioral	10	38	0.68	0.67
Multiple behavioral methods	10	35	1.04	0.86

These effect sizes demonstrate the superior effectiveness of behavioral methods over no treatment and placebo treatment. The meta-analyses also indicate that behavior therapy is typically more effective than alternative treatments, such as play therapy and insight-oriented therapy.

The latter conclusion—the apparent superiority of behavioral treatments relative to nonbehavioral treatments in the treatment of children—has been critically questioned. Several researchers (e.g., Shirk & Russell, 1992; Wampold, 2001) argue with some data that the reported differences may be due to (1) differences in methodological quality between behavioral and nonbehavioral treatment studies, (2) investigator allegiance effects favoring behavioral treatments, and (3) a lack of treatment representativeness among nonbehavioral treatments.

Careful re-analyses of the data provide conflicting conclusions. One set of researchers (Weiss & Weisz, 1995a, 1995b) found little support for either argument (1) or (2) in the outcome literature on children. Another set of researchers (Miller et al., 2008) found that researcher allegiance (2) was strongly associated with differences in effectiveness in the outcome literature on children. In fact, once allegiance was controlled, they found no evidence for any outcome differences among treatments.

However, with regard to (3), all partisans agree that research evaluations of child therapy are unrepresentative of the real-life practice of child therapy. Research studies are particularly weak in **clinical representativeness**—their similarity to the actual clients, therapists, and settings in real-life clinical practice (Weisz et al., 2004). In particular, certain nonbehavioral forms of child therapy, such as play therapy and psychodynamic therapy, are not adequately represented in the research studies.

Behavior Therapy with Adults

In their classic meta-analysis, Smith and colleagues (1980) located 101 controlled studies on systematic desensitization, 54 on behavior modification, and 34 on cognitive-behavior therapy. The mean effect sizes were 1.05, 0.73, and 1.13, respectively, all substantially better than the 0.56 effect size for placebo treatments.

Shapiro and Shapiro (1982) replicated the Smith, Glass, and Miller study with an improved design. They included only studies over a 5-year period that contained at least two treatment groups and one control group. Most of the 143 studies evaluated behavioral therapies. The behavioral methods, number of treatment groups, and average effect sizes were as follows:

BEHAVIORAL METHOD	NUMBER OF GROUPS	EFFECT SIZE
Rehearsal and self-control	38	1.01
Covert behavioral	19	1.52
Relaxation	42	0.90
Desensitization	77	0.97
Reinforcement	28	0.97
Modeling	11	1.43
Social skills training	14	0.85

All of these effect sizes are considered large, and all are superior to those found for no treatment and placebo treatment. The differences among treatment outcomes have more to do with the problem type than with the psychotherapy system, but Shapiro and Shapiro (1982) concluded that their study revealed a modest superiority of behavioral and cognitive methods and a corresponding inferiority of psychodynamic and humanistic methods.

Similarly, in a massive meta-analysis of controlled outcome studies (Grawe et al., 1998), behavioral therapies achieved large and positive effect sizes. In studies covering 3,400-plus patients, statistically significant effects over control treatments were found for social skills training in 45 of the 61 comparisons. In studies involving 1,556 patients, stress inoculation outperformed the control in 30 of the 39 cases. And in studies involving 775 patients, problem-solving therapy proved superior to control treatments in 27 of the 29 studies. When all was studied and done, the behavioral and cognitive-behavioral treatments were superior to client-centered and psychodynamic treatments in direct comparisons. As discussed in Chapter 3, the clinical relevance of these statistically significant differences remains controversial.

One intriguing study (Bowers & Clum, 1988) examined the relative contribution of specific and nonspecific treatment effects. They conducted a meta-analysis of 69 studies comparing forms of behavior therapy with placebo conditions to obtain an estimate of the incremental contribution of specific interventions to the nonspecific effects of placebo. Their comparison indicated that the specific effects of behavior therapies are twice as great as the nonspecific (or common) effects.

Behavior Therapy with Couples and Families

Several meta-analyses (e.g., Dunn & Schewebel, 1995; Hahlweg & Markman, 1988) have been performed on the effectiveness of **behavioral marital therapy** (BMT). The treatment components are typically **communication skills training**, problem-solving training, and modifying dysfunctional relationship expectations and attributions. BMT produced significant changes in behavior, as compared with control couples. These gains were generally maintained over time. Cross-cultural comparisons of BMT found equal benefits for couples in the United States and in Europe.

A meta-analysis (Shadish & Baldwin, 2005) summarized results from 30 randomized clinical trials with distressed couples that compared BMT with no treatment. Results showed that BMT was significantly more effective than no treatment ($d = 0.58$). Interestingly, the findings also suggested that **publication bias** exists in the BMT literature whereby small sample studies with small effects are systematically missing compared with other studies. Meta-analyses using only large, published studies are likely to overestimate the actual effectiveness of psychological treatments.

The moderate to large effects found for behavioral family therapy are reviewed in Chapter 12 (systemic therapies). Suffice it to say here, behavioral family therapy has consistently demonstrated its superiority over no treatment and control treatment and, depending on the review, occasionally over alternative, nonbehavioral forms of family therapy.

The effect sizes of behavioral marital and family therapy are in some respects faceless numbers and thus difficult to translate into improved behavior and recovered lives. The results of one controlled family therapy study demonstrate in concrete human terms what an effect size means. Alexander and Parsons (1973) compared contingency contracting–based family therapy ($n = 46$ families), client-centered family therapy ($n = 19$), and no therapy ($n = 10$) in the treatment of adolescent delinquency. Results indicated that at a 6-month follow-up the contingency contracting group had a 26% recidivism relapse rate, compared with 47% for client-centered therapy, and 50% for no treatment. At the end of therapy, the behavioral group talked more and showed more equality in terms of who talked. Compared to no treatment, the behavioral, contingency contracting treatment allowed about twice the number of families to progress without their adolescent returning to delinquency. In essence, this is what the faceless numbers of effect sizes mean.

Specific Behavioral Methods
Relaxation Training
Different forms of **relaxation training** have been experimentally tested for decades. An early meta-analysis (Hyman et al., 1989) identified 48 experimental studies of relaxation techniques used to treat a variety of clinical symptomatology. The effect sizes ranged from 0.43 to 0.66 for the pre- to posttreatment of health-related symptomatology and were largest for nonsurgical samples with hypertension, headaches, and insomnia.

Another meta-analysis investigated the effectiveness of relaxation training for both generalized anxiety disorder (GAD) and panic disorder (Siev & Chambless, 2007). For GAD, relaxation training and cognitive therapy were both quite effective and equivalent in their outcomes. For panic, however, cognitive therapy outperformed relaxation training. The authors of the meta-analysis conclude that the pattern of results is evidence for the specificity of treatment to disorder, even within the behavioral and cognitive-behavioral tradition, as relaxation training was designed to treat the diffuse anxiety of GAD but not for panic.

Autogenic training, a specific self-relaxation procedure, has been extensively used in German-speaking countries but less so in English-speaking nations. Like other types of relaxation training, autogenic training is used to treat physical disorders, such as tension headaches and hypertension, as well as psychological disorders, such as anxiety and functional insomnia. A meta-analysis of 60 studies on autogenic training showed medium effect sizes, both pretreatment to posttreatment and in comparison to control conditions (Stetter & Kupper, 2002). Autogenic training worked as well, no better or worse overall, than other psychological treatments for the same disorders.

Social Skills Training

An early meta-analysis (Corrigan, 1991) examined the effectiveness of social skills training in 73 studies for four adult psychiatric populations: developmentally disabled, psychotic, nonpsychotic, and legal offenders. The effect sizes were large across various outcome measures. Patients participating in social skills training broadened their repertoire of skills, maintained these gains several months after treatment, and showed diminished psychiatric symptoms related to social dysfunctions.

Looking specifically at skills training for people with schizophrenia, another meta-analysis (Kurtz & Mueser, 2008) examined the effectiveness of social skills training in 22 controlled studies, including 1,521 clients. Results revealed a large effect for content-mastery exams ($d = 1.20$), a moderate effect size for performance of social and daily living skills (0.52), a moderate effect size for community functioning (0.52), and a small effect size for relapse prevention (0.23). That is, social skills training is effective in improving psychosocial functioning in schizophrenia but less so in preventing relapse.

Social skills training for children with emotional and behavioral disorders has also been extensively investigated. The results of six meta-analyses suggested that social skills training for such youth is effective, showing a 64% improvement rate relative to controls (Gresham et al., 2004). Social skills training was effective across a broad range of behavioral difficulties, including aggressive externalizing behaviors and internalizing disorders.

Stress Inoculation

A meta-analysis (Saunders et al., 1996) determined the overall effectiveness of stress inoculation training devised by Meichenbaum (1985). The analysis was based on a total of 37 studies involving 1,837 clients. The overall effect size of 0.51 on performance anxiety and 0.37 on state anxiety revealed moderately powerful effectiveness. Thus, stress inoculation treatment has been shown to be effective in reducing both performance and state anxiety and far better than no treatment or control treatments.

Biofeedback

Several researchers have meta-analytically examined the efficacy of biofeedback for treating various conditions. With respect to migraines, biofeedback produced a medium effect size ($d = 0.58$) and proved stable over an average follow-up phase of 17 months. Biofeedback was more effective than no treatment and placebo (Nestoriuc & Martin, 2007). Biofeedback with home training was found to be more effective than therapies without home training. With respect to tension headaches, biofeedback produced medium-to-large effect sizes ($d = 0.73$). Biofeedback proved more effective than headache monitoring, placebo, and relaxation therapies (Nestoriuc et al., 2008).

Behavioral Activation

The efficacy of behavioral activation was compared with cognitive therapy and antidepressant medication in a large, controlled trial with 241 adults suffering from major depression. Among more severely depressed patients, behavioral activation was comparable to antidepressant medication, and both outperformed cognitive therapy (Dimidjian et al., 2006). When followed for 2 years after the initial treatment, patients receiving behavioral activation and cognitive therapy experienced similar outcomes (Dobson et al., 2008). Patients treated with medication but withdrawn onto pill placebo suffered more relapses than patients receiving either psychotherapy. Both therapies proved less expensive and longer lasting than medication in the treatment of depression.

Several subsequent meta-analyses of randomized clinical trials (RCTs) support the effectiveness of behavioral activation for depression. One analysis included 17 RCTs and 1,109 clients (Ekers et al., 2008); another analysis included 34 overlapping RCTs with 2,055 clients (Mazzucchelli et al., 2009). In both analyses, behavioral activation outperformed no-treatment controls and proved equal in effectiveness to cognitive therapy for depression. Such findings have led many behaviorists to wonder whether the addition of the cognitive restructuring adds anything to the treatment; sometimes "less is more." Behavioral activation is a well-established and efficacious therapy for mood disorders.

Self-Statement Modification

Meta-analyses have been performed on the effectiveness of self-statement modification separately for children and adults (Dush et al., 1983, 1989). The **self-statement modification** was oriented explicitly around Meichenbaum's self-instructional training. For children, results of 48 outcome studies showed that self-statement modification surpassed no treatment and placebo treatment by roughly half a standard deviation. The average effect was 0.47. For adults, results of 69 studies showed that self-statement modification evidenced considerable gains beyond no treatment. The average effect size of 0.74 can be viewed as analogous to shifting the average treated client from the 50th percentile of control subjects to the 77th percentile. Alternative therapies shifted patients to the 67th percentile, on average (effect size = 0.49).

Contingency Management

A novel application of contingency management is to addictive disorders. The method aims to systematically increase reinforcement for nondrug-related activities and to remove such reinforcement for drug use. Research can tell us whether it works, but cannot tell us whether society should pay people to stop abusing drugs—a controversial political question (Higgins et al., 2007).

The results of three meta-analyses converge in their conclusions: Contingency management is effective in reducing use of opiates, cocaine, other drugs, and to a lesser extent, tobacco (Griffith et al., 2000; Mayet et al., 2004; Prendergast et al., 2006). Based on 47 studies, the overall effect size was 0.42, a medium magnitude. Contingency management clearly improves the ability of clients to remain abstinent, thereby allowing them to take fuller advantage of other treatment components. One of the meta-analyses (Griffith et al., 2000) reported an intriguing pattern. Larger and more immediate reinforcers led to better treatment results—as any behaviorist would predict.

Behavioral Parent Training

Several researchers have independently canvassed the large body of controlled research on **behavioral parent training** in the treatment of children's conduct disorders and antisocial behavior. There are at least 61 treatment groups, 48 control groups, and 3,592 participants available for analysis (Lundahl et al., 2004). The overall effect sizes in the 0.80 to 1.0 range indicate that the average child whose parents participated in parent training was better adjusted after treatment than approximately 85% of children whose parents did not (Kazdin, 2005; Serketich & Dumas, 1996). The large effects of behavioral parent training appear to generalize fairly well to both children's classroom behaviors and parents' personal adjustment. In the words of two reviewers of this vast literature, "perhaps no other technique has been as carefully documented and empirically supported as parent management training in treating conduct disorders" (Feldman & Kazdin, 1995, p. 4).

Behavioral parent training has certainly proven successful, but less so with fathers than with mothers. A meta-analysis of 28 studies shows that while such training has a large positive effect on mothers' parenting practices, it exerts a smaller effect on fathers (Fletcher et al., 2011). In the future, behavioral parent training will need to demonstrate comparable effectiveness with all parents and address the sociopolitical reality that mothers are still overwhelmingly the primary caretakers of children.

Problem Solving

A meta-analysis of 31 studies (2,895 participants) examined the efficacy of problem-solving therapy in reducing mental and physical health problems. Problem-solving therapy emerged as significantly more effective than no treatment ($d = 1.37$) and attention placebo ($d = 0.54$), but just barely more effective than other bona fide treatments offered as part of the study ($d = 0.22$). Assigning homework seemed to increase the effectiveness of the problem-solving treatment (Malouff et al., 2007)—as any behaviorist would attest.

Looking specifically at depression, 13 controlled studies of problem-solving therapies were subjected to a meta-analysis (Cuijpers et al., 2007). The average effect size of 0.83 indicated that short-term problem-solving therapy can be an effective treatment for depression, certainly more so than waiting list, pill placebo, or psychological placebo. At the same time, as with any treatment, problem-solving therapy was less effective with patients who suffered from more severe depression.

Behavior Therapy for Specific Disorders

Obsessive-Compulsive Disorder

Several meta-analyses have been published on the effectiveness of psychological treatment for obsessive-compulsive disorder (OCD). A review of the literature (86 studies in all) concluded antidepressants, behavior therapy, and the combination of antidepressants and behavior therapy were significantly more effective than placebo treatment (van Balkom et al., 1994). On patients' self-ratings, the meta-analysis indicated that behavior therapy was significantly more effective than the antidepressants and that the combination of behavior therapy and antidepressants tended to be more effective than the antidepressant medication alone. The overarching finding of this and other reviews (Eddy et al., 2004; Kobak et al., 1998) is that

behavior therapy, with or without adjunctive medication, is a premier treatment for OCD. (More detailed meta-analyses focusing on exposure as a treatment for OCD are reviewed in Chapter 8.)

Panic Disorder

Several meta-analyses have compared the effectiveness of cognitive-behavioral, pharmacological, and combined treatments for another anxiety disorder—panic disorder with or without agoraphobia. The largest meta-analysis (Mitte, 2005a) analyzed 124 studies, involving 10,653 patients. Behavior therapy was demonstrably superior to no treatment and a placebo control, as was pharmacological treatments. Adding cognitive methods to the behavior therapy did not improve effectiveness for the anxiety and panic, but additional cognitive methods seemed to improve the associated depressive symptoms of panic. Behavior therapy was at least as effective as pharmacotherapy and, depending on the type of analysis, even significantly more effective. The results clearly bear out that multiple forms of behavioral, cognitive-behavioral, and exposure methods are effective in the alleviation of panic.

Trichotillomania

Both medication and behavior therapy have been used to treat this disorder characterized by compulsive hair pulling. A meta-analysis of seven controlled studies demonstrated that **habit-reversal therapy** (ES = 1.14) was quite effective and more effective than medication (Bloch et al., 2007). Habit-reversal therapy (Azrin & Nunn, 1973) is a multicomponent behavioral intervention that combines self-monitoring of the problem, competing response training in which a healthy alternative is applied until the hair-pulling urge dissipates (a form of counterconditioning), and social support to increase motivation and treatment compliance.

Developmental Disability

A meta-analysis was conducted of 482 empirical studies on the treatment of problem behaviors of individuals with the developmental disability of mental retardation (Didden et al, 1997). Treatment effectiveness was examined for 1,451 comparisons between baselines and treatments as well as for 64 different treatment procedures. Contingency management procedures were significantly more effective than were other procedures. Interestingly, the analyses found that performing a formal behavioral or functional analysis increased treatment effectiveness.

That and other meta-analyses (Prout & Nowak-Drabik, 2003) demonstrate the probable superiority of behavioral and cognitive-behavioral therapies over other, less studied psychotherapies in the treatment of developmental disabilities. Individual treatment, as opposed to group treatment, employing contingency management seems to produce the most positive results.

Eating Disorders

A series of meta-analyses across the years (Hartmann et al., 1992; Lewandowski et al., 1997; Thompson-Brenner et al., 2003; Whitbread & McGowen, 1994) have investigated the effectiveness of pharmacological and psychological treatments of bulimia nervosa and have reviewed overlapping studies: 18, 19, 26, and 26 studies, respectively. The results revealed that psychotherapy leads to large improvements from baseline. In one meta-analysis (Thompson-Brenner et al., 2003), 44% of patients receiving individual behavior therapy recovered and 48% of patients receiving individual cognitive-behavior therapy recovered. Individual therapy showed substantially better effects than group therapy. Individual psychological treatments outperformed pharmacological treatments, mostly antidepressants. Overall, the results of these meta-analyses suggested that the use of behavioral (and cognitive-behavioral therapy) resulted in favorable treatment outcomes.

Attention-Deficit Hyperactivity Disorder

The Multimodal Treatment Study for ADHD (MTA Cooperative Group, 1999a, 1999b) was probably the largest clinical trial conducted with behaviorally disordered children. A total of 579 children with ADHD (combined type), aged 7 to 10 years, were randomly assigned to one of four, 14-month treatments: stimulant medication, intensive behavioral treatment (entailing parent training, teacher consultations, and therapeutic summer camp), the two treatments combined, or standard community care. All four treatments produced sizable reductions in symptoms over time.

On many outcome measures, combined treatment proved superior to the intensive behavioral treatment. For most ADHD symptoms, children in the combined treatment and medication groups showed significantly greater improvement than those given intensive behavioral treatment.

However, subsequent analyses revealed that the behavioral treatment alone was equally effective to the combined treatment on 82 of the 87 measures *when* the behavioral treatment was being intensively applied. But as the intensive behavioral treatment was slowly withdrawn, the medication continued—and that accounted for its greater improvement in the study over time (Pelham et al., 2000).

These findings and a host of research reviews (including at least seven meta-analyses; see Purdie et al., 2002) show that behavior therapy and stimulant medication result in clinically meaningful improvement with ADHD children. The combination of these two treatments is also effective and may result in incrementally greater improvements than either treatment alone.

Controlled group studies examining the effects of neurofeedback have found positive results among people suffering from ADHD. A white paper (Monastra et al., 2005) critically examined the empirical evidence, and concluded that EEG biofeedback was "probably efficacious" for the treatment of ADHD. Significant clinical improvement was reported in approximately 75% of the patients in the published research studies. Thus, behavior therapy, psychostimulant medication, and neurofeedback are all effective treatments for this malady.

Schizophrenia

An early meta-analytic review of 27 studies on social skills training with schizophrenics revealed that such training had a strong, positive impact on behavioral measures of social skill, self-rated assertiveness, and hospital discharge rate. However, the effects of social skills training on broader symptoms and functioning were quite modest (Benton & Schroeder, 1990).

A more recent meta-analysis updated the controlled outcome studies on psychosocial treatments for schizophrenia, including but not limited to social skills training (Bustillo et al., 2001). Results showed that, again, social skills training improved social skills but had no clear effects on relapse prevention, general psychopathology, or employment status. That is, social skills training has a positive impact, but only a modest degree of skill generalization (Roth & Fonagy, 1996).

Anger Disorders

Several meta-analyses have summarized the effectiveness of behavioral and cognitive-behavioral treatments on anger disorders. In the treatment of anger among adults (DiGiuseppe & Tafrate, 2003), research from 50 studies indicated that patients who received treatment were better off than 76% of controls. In all, 83% of patients improved in comparison to pretreatment. The overall effect size of 0.71 suggests moderate treatment gains for self-instructional training, cognitive restructuring, behavioral skills training, assertiveness training, biofeedback, systematic desensitization, and relaxation training.

In the treatment of anger among children (Sukhodolsky et al., 2004), analysis of 21 published and 19 unpublished studies indicated a mean effect size of 0.67, similar to that found for adults. Skills training and multicomponent treatments were more effective in reducing aggressive behavior and improving social skills, whereas problem-solving treatments were more effective in reducing subjective anger.

The emerging conclusions are twofold. First, a variety of behavioral and cognitive-behavior treatments for anger in children and adults show medium to large effects. Second, certain treatment methods are probably more effective for specific anger problems. Skills training is recommended for improving social skills. Relaxation training is recommended in cases of state anger. Cognitive restructuring is recommended for road rage and trait anger (DelVecchio & O'Leary, 2004).

Cigarette Smoking

Meta-analysis was used to cumulate the results of 633 studies of smoking cessation, involving over 70,000 subjects (Visweswaran & Schmidt, 1992). No treatment resulted in a 6% quit rate, and self-change programs produced a 15% quit rate, on average. Both of these were significantly less effective than formal treatment. Among the most effective methods were smoke aversion (31% quit rate), other aversive techniques (27% quit rate), instructional methods in work sites (30% quit rate), and hypnosis (36% quit rate).

Nocturnal Enuresis

Dozens of studies have examined the effectiveness of psychological and pharmacological treatments for nocturnal enuresis (bed-wetting at night). A quantitative integration of the research found that, at the end of treatment, an average of 57% of the children receiving psychological treatments ceased bed-wetting and 37% receiving pharmacological treatments ceased bed-wetting, compared to only 12% and 10% for placebo controls and no-treatment controls, respectively (Houts et al., 1994). Although both psychological and pharmacological interventions had outcomes superior to those observed in the control groups, children receiving psychological treatment were more likely to have stopped their bed-wetting at both posttreatment and follow-up than children given medications. The most successful treatment was that of the **urine alarm**, an old behavioral method of conditioning introduced in 1938 by Mowrer and Mowrer. A plastic pad underneath the child or a small sensor attached to the pajamas detects moisture from urination and starts an alarm to wake the child.

Hypertension

A meta-analysis on the clinical effectiveness of various treatments for essential hypertension used 166 studies (Linden & Chambers, 1994). Weight reduction ($d = 0.57$), physical exercise (0.65), and individualized cognitive-behavior therapy (0.65) were particularly effective and were of equal value to drug treatments in reducing systolic pressures. The individualized cognitive-behavior therapy was more effective than single-component behavior therapy, such as relaxation training, autogenic training, or biofeedback.

Migraine Headache

A review (Holroyd & Penzien, 1990) integrated the results from 25 clinical trials evaluating the effectiveness of propranolol and 35 clinical trials evaluating the effectiveness of relaxation/biofeedback training (2,445 patients, collectively). The meta-analysis revealed substantial, but very similar improvements in recurrent migraines treated with these methods. Both treatments resulted in 43% reduction in migraine headaches when assessed by daily recordings and in 63% reduction when assessed by other measures. By contrast, placebo medication (14% reduction) and no treatment (essentially 0% reduction) were inferior to both propranolol and relaxation/biofeedback.

Insomnia

At least six meta-analyses support the efficacy of behavior therapy for the treatment of insomnia. One of those meta-analyses (Murtagh & Greenwood, 1995) was conducted on 66 outcome studies. Generally, psychological treatments produced considerable enhancement of both sleep patterns and subjective experience of sleep. All of the active treatments, largely behavioral in nature, were superior to placebo

therapies. The following effect sizes were found at posttreatment: 0.81 for progressive muscle relaxation, 0.93 for other forms of relaxation, 1.16 for stimulus control, and 0.73 for paradoxical intentions. These are large and convincing effects; the largest effect sizes are generally those for stimulus control instructions (Morin et al., 1999, 2006; Okajima et al., 2011).

The meta-analyses further demonstrate that behavior therapy and pharmacotherapy (medication) have the same general effectiveness for persistent insomnia (Smith et al., 2002). However, behavior therapy results in greater reduction in sleep latency (the amount of time to fall asleep), does not have the negative side effects and addictive potentials of sleep medications, and lasts longer than the effects of medication, especially when the medications are discontinued. In the long run, then, stimulus control instructions and other behavioral treatments are generally more effective than sleeping pills.

Irritable Bowel Syndrome

A meta-analysis was conducted on 17 controlled studies examining the psychological treatment of irritable bowel syndrome, a chronic gastrointestinal disorder with a prevalence of 10% to 20% (Lackner et al., 2004). The effect sizes for reduction of bowel dysfunction, depression, and anxiety were generally in the medium range; the psychological treatments were effective in reducing both physical and psychological symptoms compared to control conditions. There were insufficient numbers of studies to determine whether any particular type of psychological treatment was more effective than others. However, practically all treatments were behavioral and cognitive-behavioral in nature—progressive muscle relaxation, self-instructional training, biofeedback, cognitive restructuring, and multicomponent treatments were the most prevalent.

The controlled research converges on the conclusion that behavioral and cognitive-behavioral therapies are frequently effective in reducing somatic symptoms (e.g., bowel dysfunction, hypertension, migraine headaches) as well as psychological symptoms (e.g., depression, anxiety, eating disorders). Such findings support the application of psychological treatments to health conditions in addition to mental disorders.

Criticisms of Behavior Therapy
From a Psychoanalytic Perspective

For a system priding itself on its empiricism, behavior therapy certainly is disappointing. In place of quality research, we get quantity. If numbers are good, then more numbers must be better. But what about the conceptual foundations of a problem that determine whether a study is even worth conducting? So what if desensitization can reduce a college coed's fear of spiders? Does that have anything to do with the devastating problems that therapists confront daily in their clinical practices? Most behaviorists would do themselves a service when planning a study if they asked the key clinical question for any outcome research—the so-what question. So what if having college students imagine vomiting in their lunches leads to a loss of a pound a week? Perhaps behavior therapy researchers could use a little insight into the motives that lead to their voluminous but inconsequential research.

Behavior therapists would like us to believe that somewhere there are compelling data that demonstrate the consistent superiority of behavior therapy. But where are the data? Certainly the classic study by Sloane and colleagues (1975; reviewed in Chapter 3) provides little solace. Their rigorous comparison of comprehensive behavior therapy with brief psychodynamic therapy found no significant differences in their effectiveness. Even with time-limited therapy, the psychodynamic therapists held their own.

The results of number-crunching meta-analyses might occasionally—but not consistently— demonstrate the superiority of behavior therapy in terms of symptom relief. However, if one looks under the cover of behavioral "objective methodology," one discovers a preoccupation with short-term success and behavioral outcome measures that stack the cards in the behaviorists' favor. Even a prominent behaviorist like Alan Kazdin (1991) concedes that the purported superiority of behavioral methods begins to disappear when the type of outcome measure and when the credibility of the alternative treatment are controlled. And the statistically significant differences fade further when we consider the researcher's allegiance effect (discussed in Chapter 3), which accounts for up to two thirds of the purported superiority of behavior therapy.

Researchers from other psychotherapy systems may at times be naive about methodology, but that is nothing compared to the behaviorists' naiveté about the purpose of psychotherapy. Symptom relief is one important goal, but not the only or principal goal for adults seeking psychotherapy. Where are the controlled studies of the effects of behavior therapy on enhanced insight, improved object relations, deeper self-awareness—the things that matter most to people? What most behavior therapy research demonstrates is not the superiority but the superficiality of the behavioral view of humanity. Dig a little deeper, behaviorists.

From a Humanistic Perspective

Examine the criteria for success in almost all the behavior therapy studies and it is apparent what is missing. Only a handful of studies clearly assessed the patients' feelings of happiness and harmony as criteria for successful treatment. And guess what? Electric shock did not help homosexuals find happiness (Birk et al., 1971). What's missing from behavior theory and therapy is humane values that can help us to decide what is a significant outcome for therapy. Significance in life is not determined by a .05 level of probability of changing symptoms. In an era when many people are suffering from a collapse in their sense of significance, behavior therapy strives only for symptom relief.

What behavior therapy offers to people seeking happiness and harmony in a dehumanizing world is a bunch of gimmicks. Do people who have been manipulated all their lives to believe that cigarettes can make them cool and attractive need to have hot smoke blown in their faces? Do people who overeat need to chart each bite of food to rid themselves of the boredom or the anxiety that gnaws away at them? Do we need people who are desensitized of all their anxiety, or do we need people who are anxious about all the insensitivity that surrounds them? Do we need to teach people to exchange poker chips to encourage talking, or should we help people find the intrinsic meaning that comes in sharing their most basic feelings? A gimmick a day will not keep the doctor away.

The alienating technology of Western society that has removed people from their roots is no longer seen as a problem; it is now seen as part of the therapy. Does it not make us shudder to realize how readily patients and therapists alike can reduce themselves to fit a hollow and mechanical model of human beings? Have we become so alienated that we no longer realize that having a controlling therapist and a packaged treatment manual is part of a much larger process of dehumanization? We create our cures to match the image of who we think we are and what we believe plagues us. Behavior therapy reflects an image of humanity as directed by conditions outside our control. Is the solution to our contemporary problems to be found in submitting ourselves to even more mindless conditioning?

From a Cultural Perspective

Who defines what is adaptive and what is maladaptive behavior? Who and what has to change? Are behavioral techniques being used to encourage clients to conform to normative standards of the dominant social group? In attempting to be explicit content-free methodologists, behaviorists risk becoming implicit content avoiders (Kantrowitz & Ballou, 1992).

Psychotherapists invariably must make decisions about the appropriateness of target behaviors, treatment goals, and outcome criteria. Sure, clients should have a larger voice in making these decisions, but behaviorists can't simply wash their hands of the mutual responsibility and absolve themselves by insisting "It's the client's decision."

When the therapist's values are hidden from view, implicit standards are used to determine what and who is in need of change. These nonconscious ideologies are likely to reflect mainstream, White, middle-class, heterosexual, masculine values. How many "rebellious" adolescents, "acting out" racial minorities, "confused" homosexuals, "sexless" wives, and "misbehaving" children have been "B-Modded" at the behest of the "man of the house" in the name of value-neutral, content-free technology? Psychotherapy is an undeniably value-laden enterprise. Won't you at least come out and publicly endorse your values?

The behavioral focus on individual skill training can neglect social causes and support dominant group values. Consider the ostensibly benign case of prescribing assertiveness training for a woman who has been sexually harassed in the workplace. On one hand, assertiveness training is an evidence-based treatment that will probably meet with the woman's approval. On the other hand, by focusing on a woman's skill deficits, neither aggressive sexuality nor boundary violations are addressed. Nor is the social norm of women's duty to protect themselves seriously questioned. The individual woman's distress may be temporarily reduced, but the social status quo is firmly protected.

In broader strokes, this is precisely the systemic complaint about behavior therapists: They fail to see that the entire family system, not the symptomatic person, is the therapeutic unit for achieving change. Ironically, the oft-touted "environmentalism" of behaviorism stops short of the family and the culture. A culture-sensitive treatment must alter the behavior patterns of both the self and the system.

From an Integrative Perspective

Welcome to the club, behaviorists! Most people who are in this business long enough recognize that no one treatment or single theory is complete enough to match the complexities of our clients. Certainly there is no unifying theory behind what is called behavior therapy. There are merely a series of techniques and a unifying commitment to determine which methods work best with which problems. This sounds like classical eclecticism rather than classical conditioning.

Even though prominent behaviorists such as Cyril Franks (1984) and Hans Eysenck (1970) criticized eclectics early on for muddying the therapeutic waters, the proliferation of behavioral techniques without an integrating theory is adding more complexity than clarity. Eclectics, however, have never had trouble living with ambiguity, even the ambiguity of a psychotherapy system that is supposedly united yet includes diverse methods such as desensitization, covert sensitization, biofeedback, cognitive restructuring, token economies, self-control, and dialectical behavior therapy. These techniques are about as alike as an eclectic's bag of tricks. Of course, there is really no criticism intended here. We don't mind being called behaviorists if you don't mind being called eclectics.

A Behavioral Analysis of Mrs. C

Mrs. C is restricted by a broad range of maladaptive responses, so she will need a course of comprehensive, multicomponent behavior therapy if she is to regain a rewarding life. First, she suffers from conditioned avoidance of dirt and disease. Her particular mode of avoiding is to wash excessively whenever she feels she has been in contact with conditioned stimuli, such as pinworms or dirt. Avoidance of these stimuli has also led to maladaptive behaviors, including avoiding cooking and caring for her children. She also avoids sexual relations, which may be related in part to her avoidance of dirt and disease, but is probably more related to her mother's modeling of avoidance and repugnance toward sex. Mrs. C also has behavioral deficits in directly expressing her anger and in securing reinforcing and pleasant experiences.

Mrs. C's anxiety is pervasive and generalized, perhaps because it is elicited by stimuli such as dirt that are always present to some extent in the environment. Mrs. C learned an excessive fear of dirt and disease early in life from her mother's modeled behavior and attribution to them of exaggerated dangers. As an adult, Mrs. C was further conditioned to be anxious about dirt because of the excessive dangers that both she and her physician apparently attributed to pinworms.

Mrs. C's interpersonal relations are characterized by excessive control, especially control of her family in order to prevent a plague of pinworms. Mrs. C probably also receives considerable reinforcement by being the sick center of attention within the family.

The problems evoked by pinworms and dirt can best be treated by systematic desensitization and prolonged exposure, which in tandem are considered the behavioral treatment of choice for obsessive-compulsive disorders such as Mrs. C's. Training in deep relaxation would be followed by hierarchies made up of stimuli related to dirt and pinworms. Part of a hierarchy would include, for example, imagining buying brand-new underwear

(continued)

wrapped in cellophane, followed by touching brand-new underwear, then approaching freshly laundered underwear, and moving toward picking up underwear that are basically clean though worn. Mrs. C would actually approach stimuli such as dirty underwear only after the automatic and uncontrollable response of anxiety is no longer elicited because it has been counterconditioned by desensitization.

Over time, Mrs. C can be exposed to a broad range of cues that elicit anxiety and avoidance, such as clean underwear, dirty underwear, piles of laundry, dirty loads, and washing machines. During such exposure sessions, Mrs. C would be prevented from making her avoidance responses—for instance, washing or showering.

In a similar manner, in vivo desensitization and skill training would be employed to counter her lack of sexual responding and avoidance of sex. We would begin with sensate focusing, followed by the progressive steps of sex therapy. Both Mr. and Mrs. C would be encouraged to enjoy the pleasures of sensual touching with no performance demands. They could discover that such relaxing, sensual, and nondemanding conditions can become cues for sensual and sexual sensations without eliciting anxiety and avoidance.

Mrs. C's obsessive thoughts of pinworms can best be overcome by a self-control package that would include self-reinforcements for thinking more positive thoughts—sensual thoughts or thoughts of being with her family, for instance. Whenever she switched from pinworms to planning a party, for example, Mrs. C would reinforce herself with self-statements such as, "That's great! I'll take parties over pinworms any day," or "Doesn't it feel good getting free from pinworms?" After years of insight therapy, we may have to help Mrs. C attribute her problems to her learning history instead of to unconscious forces threatening to overwhelm her.

Modifying Mrs. C's interpersonal behaviors will involve the whole family, because they have unwittingly reinforced her tendencies to dominate the family's interactions. We could experiment with family assertiveness training to help them stand up to Mrs. C's unreasonable demands and also to help her express her frustrations more directly. It would be important, of course, to include expressions of positive emotions as part of the training, as this family seems to rely heavily on negative rather than positive means of mutual control.

It will also be critical to teach the family reinforcement principles in order to help them reward Mrs. C for constructive behaviors, such as cooking and playing with the kids, and to help them extinguish her maladaptive behaviors. Because Mrs. C has spent so much of her time washing, it will not be enough simply to reduce her washing through desensitization. She could be left with a rather empty day, which could increase her depression. Thus, both the therapist and the family need to implement behavioral activation—prompting, scheduling, and reinforcing constructive alternates that can replace the washing. These responses could include working, playing, relaxing, caring, and reconstructing a reinforcing approach to family and friends.

Throughout the course of this comprehensive treatment, the behavior therapist would model assertion, self-reinforcement, and risk-taking. Mrs. C would learn vicariously from the therapist's own interpersonal behavior, such as talking about dirt and disease without anxiety and avoidance, encouraging sensual pleasuring without shame or guilt, and taking charge of situations through assertion rather than symptoms. The therapist would also explain and model that consistent reinforcement of small steps gradually results in big strides toward extinguishing maladaptive responses and learning rewarding alternatives.

If Mrs. C can learn to calm herself in the presence of dirt, assert herself when angry, pleasure herself and her husband, use self-control with her pinworm preoccupation, and gain reinforcements from her family for caring rather than cleaning, then she will have a chance to return to behaviors that have some semblance of sanity. As it now stands, without an intensive and extensive program of behavior modification, Mrs. C is at high risk of being punished for her failures by being sent to the state psychiatric hospital.

Future Directions

Paralleling its growth over the past four decades, behavior therapy will continue to experiment and expand in the near future. *Experimentation* is deliberately used here in a double meaning: Behavior therapists will rely on experimental methodology to determine which methods work best with which disorders, and behavioral self-identity will experiment with its proper boundaries. By operating in the empirical tradition, behavioral work will necessarily become eclectic—using what works with a particular client (see Chapter 16).

However, this will push the other question of experimentation: How "cognitive" can a behaviorist become before being relegated to the mentalistic heap or the cognitive camp? Several traditional behaviorists, B. F. Skinner (1990) and Joseph Wolpe (1989) among them, argued that the introduction of cognitive concepts unnecessarily dilutes and weakens the field. Younger behaviorists, as a rule, are more comfortable with both the identity of cognitive behaviorism and the practice of cognitive techniques. In fact, behaviorists voted 4 to 1 to change the name of their organization to the Association for Behavioral and Cognitive Therapies. Still, not all agree on who should be sitting at the table marked "behavior therapists."

Behavior therapy will expand in numerous directions, but we foresee two of permanence. First, as health care costs continue to rise and as mental health professionals become increasingly involved in health care, behavioral self-help, relaxation training, coping skills, and self-instructional training will be further integrated into health care practice. Much of this work will be conducted with behavioral medicine disorders, such as headaches, chronic pain, asthma, tobacco smoking, hypertension, and obesity. But we will also witness behavior therapists routinely identifying, treating, and preventing medical problems that arise from poor health habits, such as poor compliance, excess fat consumption, and inadequate physical activity.

Behavior therapy will surely move beyond the treatment of psychological problems into all branches of health care, including pediatrics and cardiology. Not too far in the future, behavioral coping strategies may well be routinely taught to assist in recovery from illness, in coping with chronic disease, and in preparing for noxious medical procedures.

Second, the historical and explicit focus on behavior change in behavior therapy will be complimented by the value of **acceptance** (Jacobson & Christensen, 1998; Wilson, 1996). Having made adaptive lifestyle changes, patients will need to accept what can probably not be changed—in their body shape, in their partners, in their physiological arousal, and the like. As in dialectical behavior therapy and in acceptance and commitment therapy (reviewed in Chapter 11), clients will increasingly be taught active strategies for facilitating acceptance, such as mindful awareness, validating relationships, and meditation exercises. This is not to say that behavior therapists will settle for less, but that they are becoming more aware of what can and should be changed (Goldfried & Davison, 1994).

The explosion of new techniques that marked the early growth of behavior therapy has passed; instead, progress will probably focus on refining existing treatments, developing treatment manuals for different disorders, and improving the ways in which evidence-based treatments can be disseminated more broadly and implemented more efficiently. After four decades of explosive growth, behavior therapy will consolidate its gains, experiment with its self-identity, and expand more slowly, as befits one of the premier systems of psychotherapy today.

Key Terms

3 Cs of behavior therapy	anxiety hierarchies
ABAB (reversal) design	assertiveness training
acceptance	attribution
	attributional styles

autogenic training
aversive conditioning
baseline measures
behavior analysis
behavior chain (ABC
    sequence)
behavior exchange
    theory
behavior modification
behavior therapy
behavioral activation
behavioral marital
    therapy
behavioral parent
    training
biofeedback
classical (respondent)
    conditioning
clinical
    representativeness
cognitive-behavior
    modification (CBM)
cognitive restructuring
communication skills
    training
contingency
    management
contracting
counterconditioning
covert sensitization
discriminative stimuli
evidence-based
    practice
fading
functional (behavioral)
    analysis
generalization
generalization gradient
graduated homework
    assignments
habit-reversal therapy
in vivo desensitization
institutional control

learned optimism
maintenance
modeling
multiple baseline
    design
mutual control
naturalistic
    observation
neurobiofeedback
operant conditioning
operationalizing the
    target behavior
problem-solving
    therapy
prompt
publication bias
punishment
reciprocal inhibition
refusal skills training
reinforcement
relaxation training
respondent
    conditioning
response cost
self-control
self-instructional
    training
self-statement
    modification
sensate focusing
shaping
small-n designs
social skills training
stimulus control
stress inoculation
symptom substitution/
    return
systematic
    desensitization
target behaviors
token economy
urine alarm
validation

Recommended Readings

Barlow, D. H. (Ed.). (2013). *Clinical handbook of psychological disorders* (5th ed.). New York: Guilford.

Dobson, K. S. (Ed.). (2009). *Handbook of cognitive-behavioral therapies* (3rd ed.). New York: Guilford.

D'Zurilla, T. J., & Nezu, A. M. (2007). *Problem-solving therapy* (3rd ed.). New York: Springer.

Goldfried, M., & Davison, G. (1994). *Clinical behavior therapy* (rev. ed.). New York: Wiley.

Kazdin, A. E. (2005). *Parent management training.* New York: Oxford University Press.

Kazdin A. E. (2008). *Behavior modification in applied settings* (6th ed.). Pacific Grove, CA: Brooks/Cole.

Masters, W., & Johnson, V. (1970). *Human sexual inadequacy.* Boston: Little, Brown.

Meichenbaum, D. (1977). *Cognitive-behavior modification.* New York: Plenum.

Schwartz, M. S., & Andrasik, F. (Eds.). (2005). *Biofeedback: A practitioner's guide* (3rd ed.). New York: Guilford.

Spiegler, M. D., & Guevremont, D. C. (2009). *Contemporary behavior therapy* (5th ed.). Belmont, CA: Wadsworth.

Wolpe, J. (1990). *The practice of behavior therapy* (4th ed.). Elmsford, NY: Pergamon.

JOURNALS: *Advances in Behaviour Research & Therapy; Applied Psychophysiology and Bio-feedback; Behavior Analyst; Behavior Modification; Behaviour Research and Therapy; Behavioral Technology Today* (electronic journal); *Behavior Therapy; Behavioral Assessment; Behavioral Interventions; Behavioural and Cognitive Psychotherapy; Biofeedback; Child and Family Behavior Therapy; Journal of Applied Behavior Analysis; Journal of Behavior Analysis and Therapy* (electronic journal); *Journal of Behavior Therapy and Experimental Psychiatry; Journal of the Experimental Analysis of Behavior; Journal of Psychopathology and*

Behavioral Assessment; Progress in Behavior Modification.

Recommended Websites

Association for Behavior Analysis:
www.abainternational.org/

Association for Behavioral and Cognitive Therapies:
www.abct.org/home
Behavior Analysis:
www.auburn.edu/~newlamc/apa_div25/
The Melissa Institute (Meichenbaum):
www.melissainstitute.org/index.html

CHAPTER 10

Cognitive Therapies

Albert Ellis

Courtesy of Dr. Albert Ellis

Aaron Beck

Courtesy of Dr. Aaron Beck

"I never thought I would like myself again," wrote Ros to her psychotherapist. "When I got into that deep pit of depression, I didn't think I could find my way out. Everywhere I turned I saw darkness and dislike. My hair wasn't right, my clothes weren't right, my voice was too high, my height was too low. Oh, God was it awful, I couldn't escape from this self I couldn't stand. I'm afraid I can understand why someone could kill themselves in such a state. Who said 'Hell is other people'? In that place Hell is yourself and there seems to be no escape. The future is downhill; the past I messed up.

"It's still hard to believe I talked myself into that dark dungeon. Everywhere I turned I saw negative stuff. The old wine bottle wasn't just half empty; to me there wasn't a drop left. It's amazing what your mind can do to you.

"I really appreciate how you helped me find my way through my mental maze. It became fun trying to discover what I was telling myself to keep me down. Yes, it was depressing to have been divorced, but I couldn't focus on positive facts of still having my friends, my children, my writing, and my future. In the future I was constructing in my mind, the sun was never going to shine again.

"Thanks for helping me to use my writing as homework to straighten out my thinking. Before I came to see you, my writing sounded like Sylvia Plath—all darkness and despair. It's not that there's not a dark side of life—it's just that if all I think about is the dark side, then life becomes empty rather than full.

"One of the most helpful things about the work we did together is that I learned how to correct my own maladaptive cognitions. I learned how to search and destroy the automatic self-statement that said I was bad; situations were bad; the future was bleak; my biology was breaking down. As a writer, I appreciate how powerful words can be, but I never knew how we can create our own novel in our heads and then cast ourselves as the tragic characters destined to self-destruct.

"Just wanted to let you know that the new novel I'm writing in my mind is so much happier. It's not that everything is perfect. I still don't like my hair but that will probably always be an obsession with me, and I still am searching for a man to make my life more meaningful. I know I should think more independently but that's how women of my generation were raised to think. So sometimes I would rather change my situation than my thoughts about my situation. But at least I don't let the situations drag me down.

"Off to see my daughter in San Diego. Hope all is well with you."

—*Ros*

Ros could have been writing to practically any cognitive psychotherapist. In this chapter, we look in detail at the two most influential and prevalent cognitive therapies: Albert Ellis's rational-emotive behavior therapy and Aaron Beck's cognitive therapy. In the interest of saving space and reducing redundancy, we have omitted the section on therapeutic content for Beck's cognitive therapy as it is quite similar to that of Ellis's.

We should note again that the lines separating cognitive, cognitive-behavioral, and some behavior therapies are fading. As witnessed in Chapter 9, contemporary behavior therapy is progressively becoming more cognitive, and practically every cognitive therapy incorporates elements of behavior therapy. The overlap is considerable indeed. But as we will shortly learn, cognitive therapy is a distinctive system of psychotherapy. And no one was as distinctive as Albert Ellis.

A Sketch of Albert Ellis

Almost from birth, Albert Ellis (1913–2007) emerged as "an independent, my-kingdom-is-myself youngster" (Ellis, 2010, p. 24). He was precocious, brash, and self-absorbed from a young age. Ellis overcame a multitude of health problems: He was repeatedly hospitalized as a child for the treatment of nephritis, infections, headaches, and pneumonia; he then endured diabetes for most of his adult life. In retrospect, he observed that, "I could see that my revolutionary devotion was oriented toward making me King of the May and was at least partly based on my trying to make up for some of my own inadequacy feelings" (p. 269). His life illustrates the ancient rule that a person's source of success is at once the root of the problem.

Ellis was a man of and beyond his times. He was born in Pittsburgh, but was raised and lived in New York City the remainder of his life. His fascination with sex and philosophy began from a young age. His revolutionary political views gave way to advocacy of sexual freedom. His reading of the Greek philosophers in particular helped him to formulate the fundamental premise of cognitive therapies: It is not the external event that distresses us but our appraisal or interpretation of that event.

Ellis enthusiastically presented and defended his rational approach to therapy since 1957, when he first demonstrated his innovative system at the annual convention of the American Psychological Association. Before that, he had practiced various forms of psychoanalytic treatment, which he had learned while earning his PhD in clinical psychology from Columbia. From the late 1940s to the early 1950s, Ellis became increasingly dissatisfied with the effectiveness and efficiency of both classical analysis and psychoanalytic psychotherapy. He believed Freud was correct that irrational forces keep neurotics troubled, but he was coming to believe that the irrational forces were not unconscious conflicts from early childhood. Ellis had seen too many patients with incredible insights into their childhood and their unconscious who continued to keep themselves troubled. That something that Ellis saw was a continual reindoctrination of themselves in an irrational philosophy of life.

Ellis found free association to be too passive and historically oriented to seriously challenge patients' contemporary ideas about themselves and the world. He began to attack the clients' belief systems directly and pushed clients to work actively against their own irrational premises. Ellis found himself well suited to this rational approach to therapy. With his quickness of mind, clear and concrete articulation of abstract ideas, love of intellectual debate, hardheaded faith in the power of rational discourse, and excellent sense of humor for dissipating irrational anger or anxiety, Ellis (1957b) demonstrated greater effectiveness with his new approach than with his older, psychoanalytic approaches.

In 1959, Ellis established the Institute for Rational-Emotive Therapy in New York City as a nonprofit organization to provide educational courses in rational living, moderate cost rational-emotive therapy for patients, and intensive training in rational-emotive therapy for professionals. The clinic has more than 25 therapists at any one time. The Institute—renamed the Albert Ellis Institute—regularly offers workshops and seminars throughout the country. His Friday night workshops for the public were a Manhattan fixture for more than four decades.

In his workshops, as in his therapy sessions, Ellis was a directive therapist who got right to the heart of an issue without mincing his words because someone might get anxious or upset. That is the other person's problem. Ellis's problem is to convince people to use their cognitive processes to create a life that maximizes the pleasure and minimizes the pain

of existence. He was fond of stating, "The purpose of life is to have a fucking good time," but Ellis was a long-term hedonist, not an irrational, short-term hedonist who indulges every momentary desire at the expense of long-term suffering.

So I (JOP) once asked him, "If the purpose of life is to have a fucking good time, why is it that you haven't taken a vacation in 15 years?" Believing that Ellis was caught in an irrational contradiction between his philosophy and his life, I was surprised at how quickly he responded, "What is wrong with me really enjoying my work? I never said we all have to have a good time in the same way." Watching Ellis in action reveals a person who finds great pleasure in his profession.

Up until his death at the age of 93, Ellis still saw patients each week—in addition to running workshops and publishing more than 800 articles and 80 books. He tirelessly advocated for a rational-emotive approach to psychotherapy and to life.

In fact, Ellis continued to revise and expand his brand of cognitive therapy until the end. At an institute-sponsored conference entitled "A Meeting of the Minds" (Kernberg et al., 1993), he announced that he was changing the name of rational-emotive therapy (RET) to **rational-emotive behavior therapy (REBT)**. Although the original name is still used in the literature, we will employ in this chapter the newer and more accurate REBT name. Ellis (1999) himself believed REBT is a preferable and more accurate term than RET.

REBT Theory of Personality

A rational-emotive explanation of personality is almost as easy as ABC (Ellis, 1973, 1991b). At point A are the **Activating events** of life, such as rejection by a lover or failure to get into a graduate program. Point B represents the **Beliefs** that individuals use to process the activating events in their lives. These beliefs can be rational (rB), such as believing that the rejection was unfortunate and regrettable or that the failure was annoying and unpleasant. The beliefs can also be irrational (iB), such as thinking, "It was awful that I was rejected," "I will never be loved again," or "How terrible it is that I didn't get into graduate school; they have prevented me from ever being successful." At point C, the person experiences the emotional and behavioral **Consequences** of what has just occurred.

Most people and many psychotherapists assume that the critical emotional consequences of personality development are a direct function of the activating events to which an individual has been subjected. That is, A leads directly to C. The more benign the agents and activities have been in early life, the healthier the personality will be; the more aversive the activating events, the more emotionally troubled the person. But these people and therapists are just plain wrong, according to REBT.

As a cognitive theory, REBT points to processes within the person as the critical determinants of personality functioning. It is not the activating events (A) that are crucial but rather the person's perceptions and interpretations of the events. That is, B leads directly to C. So a person who processes a rejection or a failure through a rational belief may feel the appropriate consequences of sorrow, regret, annoyance, displeasure, and a determination to change whatever can be changed to prevent a recurrence of the unfortunate events. Another person confronting very similar events but processing the activating events through an irrational belief system can produce inappropriate consequences such as depression, hostility, anxiety, or a sense of futility and worthlessness.

The point is that individuals make themselves emotionally healthy or emotionally upset by the way they think, not by the environment. The "in here," not the "out there," actually determines our feelings. As the Stoic philosophers held 2,500 years ago (Ellis, 1973), there are virtually no legitimate reasons for rational people to make themselves neurotic, hysterical, or emotionally disturbed.

People can avoid emotional disturbances if they base their lives on their inherent tendencies to be logical and empirical. Look at the progress humanity has made in the physical and biological sciences by keeping assumptions about the world natural rather than supernatural or mystical. Empiricism and logic should be used to test our assumptions and develop a more effective construction of reality. How much more effective our relationship to ourselves and to others could be if we would rely on reason as our guide for living. Certainly reason is not godlike, and its limitations can disturb us at times, but there is no better basis for minimizing emotional disorders than to use rationality to process the personal and interpersonal events of our lives. Scientific thinking is a candle in the dark.

As rational human beings, we recognize that the world is not always fair, that unfortunate events will occur in any life. We will at times, then, experience valid emotions such as sorrow, regret, displeasure, and annoyance. Realistically, we know we are imperfect and will always have our failures and faults, but we will rebel at the irrational idea that anyone can ever treat us as worthless just because we are imperfect. Accepting our tendencies to put our self-interests first, we will nevertheless be determined to change unpleasant social conditions along more rational lines, because we recognize that in the long run it is in our own self-interest to live in a more rational world.

In a more rational world, we would accept our natural predispositions to be self-preserving and pleasure producing. We would be less likely to engage in such self-defeating activities as the short-term **hedonism** of smoking or overreacting, which provide immediate gratification at the expense of lessening our aliveness. We would actualize more of our desires to be creative, to use language effectively, to be sensuous and sexual, to love and be loved (Ellis, 1973).

We would not fall into the irrational trap, however, of thinking of these natural desires as dire necessities. Being respected and valued by others, for example, would make life happier, but we would not conclude therefore that we must be approved by others. The emotionally healthy person can live in the delicate balance between caring enough about others to be effectively related but not caring so much about others as to become a prisoner of their approval.

REBT Theory of Psychopathology

Just as human beings evidence a natural propensity to be uniquely rational and straight thinking, so too humans have an exceptionally potent propensity to be crooked thinking creatures (Ellis, 1973). Individuals differ in their inherent tendencies toward irrationality, and so in their tendencies to be more or less irrationally disturbed. Societies and families also differ in their tendencies to encourage straight or crooked thinking, although unfortunately most societies rear their children in a manner that exacerbates their strong propensities to disturb themselves by irrational beliefs. But even the best of inheritances and the best of socialization cannot remove our susceptibility to being self-defeating.

There are no gods among us. In spite of perfectionistic and grandiose wishes to be gods, any of us at any time can fall victim to procrastinate, to repeat the same mistakes rather than think things through anew, to engage in wishful thinking rather than responsible action, to be dogmatic and intolerant rather than probabilistic and open, to rely on superstition and supernaturalism rather than logic and empiricism, and to indulge in greedy, short-range hedonism rather than responsible, long-term hedonism. The only difference between those labeled

pathological and those labeled normal is the frequency and intensity with which they emotionally upset themselves by relying on irrational thinking.

The psychopathologies of everyday life can be explained by the **ABC model** of human functioning. In emotional disturbances, activating events are always processed through some irrational belief. A dozen of the most common irrational beliefs follow.

1. Equating needs with preferences. Many human desires, such as sex, are needs because we define them as needs, even though they are in fact merely preferences.

2. We cannot tolerate certain events, whether it is waiting in line, facing criticism, or being rejected, when in fact we can stand such events no matter how unpleasant they may be.

3. Our worth as persons is determined by our successes and failures or by particular traits, such as income, as if the worth of a human being can be rated like performance traits.

4. We must maintain the approval of parents or authority figures, as if our existence is dependent on them.

5. The world should treat us fairly, as if the world could conform to our wishes.

6. Certain people are wicked or villainous and should be punished for their villainy, as if we could rate the worthlessness of a human being.

7. It is awful or terrible when things do not turn out the way we would like them to be, as if an idea like "awful" were a definable term with empirical referents.

8. We would fail to act if we did not think things were awful or if we were not angry or anxious, as if we need to be emotionally disturbed in order to take rational actions that would make the world a more pleasant place.

9. Harmful things such as cigarettes or drugs can add to happiness in life or that such harmful things are needed, just because going without them may be unpleasant for a while.

10. Human happiness is externally caused and people have little or no ability to control their feelings.

11. One's past history is the all-important determinant of present behavior, as if something that once strongly affected one's life must affect it indefinitely.

12. Beliefs learned in childhood, whether religious, moral, or political, can serve as adequate guides for adulthood, even though the beliefs may be pure prejudices or myths (Ellis, 1972).

Later in the evolution of REBT, Ellis (1991a; Ellis & Dryden, 2007) recognized the rigidity of these original 12 irrational beliefs and distinguished between dysfunctional inferences and the core dogmatic musts from which they are usually derived.

What is common to these irrational beliefs is a demanding and absolute mode of thinking characteristic of young children. Translating desires into needs, for example, is a style of thinking that makes a want into a must, a wish into a command. Preferences can be denied, but needs demand gratification. Needs are also more absolute and are assumed to be true for all people in all places. That we must succeed, must have approval, and must be treated fairly are all forms of immature demands. That there are people who are absolutely bad, events that are absolutely awful, and religious or moral teachings that are absolutely true reflect an authoritarian mode of absolutism that leaves no room for quibbling. Such absolutes have a demanding quality about them, as if they were commands from God and thus not open to question.

The novelist Joan Didion (1968, p. 163) expresses this point eloquently: "Because when we start deceiving ourselves into thinking not that we want something, not that it is a pragmatic necessity for us to have it, but that it is a moral imperative that we have it, then is when we join the fashionable madmen, and then is when the thin whine of hysteria is heard in the land, and then is when we are in bad trouble." Preferences for new sneakers, different meals, and an A on an exam are only preferences, not biological needs or moral imperatives. To confuse preferences and imperatives is to become hysterical and indeed to be in bad trouble.

The **irrational beliefs (iBs)** and **dysfunctional attitudes** (DAs) that constitute people's self-disturbing philosophies, then, possess two main qualities (Ellis, 1991a). First, they have at their core rigid, dogmatic, powerful demands, usually expressed in the verbs *must, should, ought to, have to,* and *got to.* This is musturbatory thinking: "I absolutely must have this important goal unblocked and fulfilled!" Second, the self-disturbing philosophies, usually as derivatives of these demands, generate highly unrealistic and overgeneralized attributions. This is **catastrophizing**: "If I don't have my absolutely important goal fulfilled, then it's awful, I can't bear it, I'm probably worthless, and I'll never get what I want!" Molehills are made into mountains.

Processing activating events (A) through absolute beliefs (B) will inevitably produce dysfunctional consequences (C). These irrational beliefs can produce excessive upsetting consequences such as anger over having to wait in line, self-pity over an unfair world, depression over parental disapproval, hostility toward wicked people, or guilt over breaking a rule from a dogmatic morality. Just because emotional upsets occur daily in the lives of millions of people is no reason to accept the irrational illusion that such emotional disturbances are in any way healthy or necessary. Does extreme anxiety over final exams, for example, add anything to the education or happiness of students? Are the fitful sleep, the constant worry, the sweaty armpits, and the stomach distress appropriate to facing a final, or are these symptoms more appropriate to someone going to war? Is the insistence that one must do "A" work on every exam the voice of a rational adult or the thinking of a scared child afraid of losing parental approval?

Not only are emotional upsets unhealthy and unnecessary, but such emotions frequently interfere with performance. Most students believe that it would be better to not be so anxious about exams, but they blame their anxieties on external events such as the exam itself or a competitive society. They fail to examine their internal beliefs about their own worth, the probable consequences of doing poorly on one exam, or the possibility of parental disapproval.

Some students become enraged over grading and evaluation procedures. They insist that tests are unfair and that grades should be dropped. Until the educational world adapts to their demands, they refuse to compromise, either flunking out or getting by with the minimum. Other students become anxious about their test anxiety. They know anxiety frequently meets with social disapproval, so they become more anxious that people will know how anxious they are. They may condemn themselves for being so anxious over an exam and end up feeling worthless and depressed.

When anxiety leads to more anxiety or depression leads to more depression, the original, inappropriate consequence itself becomes an activating event. This, in turn, is evaluated by further irrational beliefs as being awful or terrible, and this produces further disturbing emotional consequences. The vicious cycle of emotional disturbance can continue as people condemn themselves for being emotionally upset, then condemn themselves for continuing the condemning, then condemn themselves for seeking psychotherapy, then condemn themselves for not getting better, then conclude that they are hopelessly neurotic and that nothing can be done (Ellis, 1973).

REBT Therapeutic Processes

As long as patients (and psychotherapists) continue to focus on either the activating events (A) or the disturbing consequences (C), little in the way of lasting help can be found. Yet traditionally, all too many therapists have focused on historical activating events, going further back in the patient's history, as if anything in the past could be changed. Or clinicians have focused on releasing the anxious and distressed feelings, as if emotional consequences will dissipate into thin air just because they have been expressed. Once the ABCs of psychopathology are properly understood, it becomes clear that the proper route to changing distressing consequences is neither through examining As nor by ventilating Cs; rather, it lies in directly modifying Bs.

In REBT, the ABC model of human disturbance is followed by D—the **Disputing** of people's irrational Beliefs when they feel and act in a self-defeating way. This process leads them to E, an **Effective new philosophy**—a sound and rational set of preferential beliefs (Ellis, 1991a).

The corresponding therapeutic process is to identify the irrational beliefs causing the presenting symptoms, to dispute them vigorously, and to replace them with more rational beliefs that constitute an effective new philosophy of life. As Plato said, in a well-ordered soul, reason has the whip hand over emotion. Clients and therapists work together to raise the clients' level of consciousness from a childish, demanding, and absolute style of thinking to the logical, empirical, and probabilistic style of processing information that characterizes the mature adult and the responsible scientist.

Before venturing into the therapeutic processes of rational-emotive behavior therapy, we should note that REBT has two major forms: general, or inelegant, REBT, which is practically synonymous with cognitive-behavior therapy; and specialized, or elegant, REBT, which adheres more precisely to Ellis's formulations. Ellis (1987a) lists nine ways in which specialized REBT differs from cognitive-behavior therapy (CBT). REBT, for example, always employs psychoeducational techniques, includes a humanistic outlook, and differentially stresses profound philosophical change in addition to symptom removal. Although we appreciate the many points of convergence between REBT and cognitive-behavior therapies, the following sections pertain to specialized REBT.

Consciousness Raising

The Client's Work

Because much of the consciousness raising in REBT is an educational process, the work of clients frequently resembles that of students. In the process of explaining their problems, clients are quickly challenged to defend the beliefs that underlie their emotional upsets. They are challenged to give evidence, for example, for the belief that they must be popular in order to be happy. Clients soon learn that their favorite beliefs and biases are not accepted by the teacher/therapist just because the client presents the belief in an absolute or demanding way. "Show me where it is written that you must be a success in order to feel good about yourself" is a common challenge to patients' dogmatism.

Clients soon become aware that they have irrational beliefs that they cannot defend logically or empirically. They become aware that they are indeed upsetting themselves emotionally by insisting on such nonsense as the belief that just because they as children were the king of their family, they must be king of their companies in order to be happy. Such foolishness is met with impatience in RET. Like honest and humble students, clients have a lot to learn about this business of living, but at the same time they are encouraged to maintain the appropriate belief that they have the human potential to be as rational and as clear headed as the teacher/therapist.

One hour a week in therapy, however, is like the tutorials of the British universities—a chance to review progress and ask questions. If patients are to progress with any efficiency, they will ideally complete the homework assigned to them. Homework frequently entails reading well-reasoned books and listening to logic-driven audiotapes, especially those produced by Ellis and his associates. Homework may also include listening to and critiquing tapes of their therapy sessions, so that clients can come to recognize their own absolute or demanding beliefs. Clients work to become aware of making "should" or "must" statements when statements of preference or desire would be more accurate.

For instance, if clients say they cannot stand to be rejected by a potential date, they will be given behavioral assignments to ask three different people out on dates to test the hypothesis. This and similar assignments are instrumental in providing evidence to refute irrational beliefs to which patients cling tenaciously despite the absence of proof. Through such homework assignments, clients become irrefutably aware that their irrational beliefs are not grounded in fact.

As clients become more skilled at consciously catching their own slips into childish cognitions, they can take turns teaching others in rational-emotive groups and seminars. One client will be called on to analyze the underlying beliefs that another client is using to produce emotional upset, or to critique a fellow client's conclusion that failure to get a date this week proves that the client is a worthless worm. As many graduate students discover when they begin to teach, you do not really understand something until you teach it to others.

The Therapist's Work

Because the propensity to engage in crooked thinking is so profound, the REBT therapist is prepared to use a multitude of cognitive, emotive, and behavioral techniques to teach clients to distinguish between mature, logical-empirical thought and the trouble-making foolishness that frequently passes for reason. The methods are both structured and unstructured, didactic and interpersonal.

The therapist begins in the first session to interpret the irrational beliefs that are producing the clients' emotional complaints. The active therapist does not wait for patients to articulate all of their irrational premises. Being educated in rational-emotive behavior theory and experienced with a variety of clients, the therapist can anticipate the nature of the underlying beliefs based on the activating events and inappropriate consequences. For example, rejection by a spouse (A) followed by an incapacitating depression (C) most likely involves the following irrational beliefs (B): (1) Rejection is awful, (2) the person can't stand it, (3) she should not be rejected, (4) she will never be accepted by any desirable partner, (5) she is a worthless worm because she was rejected, and (6) she deserves to be condemned for being so worthless (Ellis, 1973).

Therapists need not be obsessive about the timing of interpretations. When they are confident that they understand the nature of the underlying beliefs, they should present the information to the client directly and forcefully. REBT therapists are under no illusions that one well-timed interpretation will produce lasting insights. Interpretations and confrontations will be made over and over until patients become undeniably aware of their irrationalities.

Interpretations do not involve making conscious connections between present upsets and past events, but rather between current complaints and current beliefs that clients are using to upset themselves. In the process of giving clients feedback about their specific irrational beliefs, therapists teach the ABCs of REBT. Therapists also provide explicit information about the nature of scientific reasoning and how it can be used to solve personal problems. Through books, tapes, seminars, and frequent mini-lectures in therapy, clients are taught the essentials of rational-emotive behavior theory. Of course, as with any theory, students tend to understand and accept REBT more when it is made relevant to the explanation and solution of their personal problems.

In addition to providing interpretations and confrontations, therapists raise the consciousness of clients to a more mature, rational level through **refutations**. As effective debaters, therapists can point out inherent contradictions between the clients' beliefs or between beliefs and actions. For example, the therapist shows clients that they can stand to be criticized even though it is uncomfortable; they do not die or go crazy or run out of the room just because the therapist has criticized one of their demanding beliefs. If clients are afraid of Mideastern men wearing turbans and insist that Muslims are bad, the therapist may counter with objective information about Muslims and the Koran. More frequently, the therapist puts refutations in the form of the common questions: "What evidence do you have …?" or "Where is it written that you must …?"

Committed to active learning, therapists direct their clients to complete various homework assignments designed to refute irrational hypotheses or to enable them to practice more rational thinking. Writing a paper on more effective means of finding a job can help a patient practice a more rational consciousness. Encouraging patients to get a massage can begin to refute the belief that they are not sensuous or that they cannot enjoy pleasure without guilt. Assigning perfectionists to wear two different-colored socks or wrinkled slacks can help them to blow their own images and, in the process, practice their new insight that life can be pleasurable without having to be perfect.

REBT therapists use a multitude of techniques to encourage clients to become more rational in their emotions and behavior. Humor is a comparatively safe method for helping clients become aware of some of their foolishness. In treating anxiety disorders, Ellis might assign a patient to sing one of his rational humorous songs, such as this one called "Perfect Rationality" (Ellis, 1991b) to the tune of "Funiculi, Funicula" by Luigi Denza:

Some think the world must have a right direction,
And so do I! And so do I!
Some think that, with the slightest imperfection,

They can't get by—and so do I!
For I, I have to prove I'm superhuman,
And better far than people are!
To show I have miraculous acumen—
And always rate among the Great!
Perfect, perfect rationality
Is, of course, the only thing for me!
How can I ever think of being
If I must live fallibly?
Rationality must be a perfect thing for me!

Self-disclosure of the therapist's foibles can keep clients from falling back into the wishful thinking that anyone, including the psychotherapist, can be godlike. Ellis is particularly fond of telling the story of how, at the age of 19, he was determined to overcome his social anxiety by giving himself the homework assignment of going to the park every day in August and forcing himself to talk to 130 women on park benches (Ellis, 2005). He failed miserably to get a date: Out of 130 prospects, Ellis made only one date—and she didn't show up! But he saw philosophically that none of the women ran away and none called a cop. Behaviorally, his social anxiety was gone.

Contingency Management

Recognizing no absolutes, including his own theory, Ellis relies on other psychotherapy systems when his own approach reaches its limits. As a cognitive behaviorist, he is especially receptive to behavioral interventions. Ellis at times characterized himself as a behavior therapist with a strong cognitive orientation, and the name change to rational-emotive behavior therapy underscores this conviction. As we saw in Chapter 9 on behavior therapy, as behavior therapists move toward the cognitive direction, they in turn frequently incorporate the principles of REBT.

The Client's Work

If the client is failing to follow through on homework assignments in spite of the therapist's interpretations or exhortations, the client may be asked to make a contingency contract that seems workable for the client. A Democrat-hater, for example, might be required to give the therapist $100 and sign a contract stating that for each week the client fails to go on a date, the therapist will send a $25 check from the client to the Democratic National Committee.

The Therapist's Work

Rational-emotive behavior therapists also attempt to reduce the effects of contingencies by having clients reevaluate particular consequences. "What is the worst thing that can happen to you if you take a risk?" the therapist asks frequently, and "Is that consequence really awful or catastrophic or is it just inconvenient or unpleasant?" Consequences such as being laughed at, being turned down for a date, and not getting an "A" on an exam can be "de-awfulized," and thereby defused as controlling consequences. The therapist can de-awfulize consequences by having the group laugh at the client's foolishness, or having a female client assert herself by trying to convince a male in the group to kiss her. The therapist has clients confront the very consequences that seem terrible so that they can reevaluate the consequences and no longer be controlled by them. Similarly, the therapist can assign the client to imagine an expected consequence 10 times a day, until the imagined outcome no longer elicits much emotion; again, this can reduce the probable effects of contingencies. Finally, contingency controls are changed by having the client continue to ask, "But what is the objective probability that what I expect will really happen?" With a reevaluation of the objective probabilities that a particular consequence will occur, the client becomes more able to take the risks required to produce more pleasure in life.

Counterconditioning

In the interest of completeness, we should also note REBT's frequent use of counterconditioning procedures in the behavioral tradition. These largely follow the principles and procedures outlined in

Chapter 9. Engaging in the healthy behaviors counterconditions, or reciprocally inhibits, the unhealthy behaviors; the obvious example in REBT is that embracing rational beliefs interferes with holding irrational beliefs. In addition, Ellis and his associates routinely use rational-emotive imagery, role-playing, exposure, and in vivo desensitization (see Ellis & Dryden, 2007; Maultsby & Ellis, 1974).

The origins of Ellis's infamous **shame-attacking exercises** can be tracked to Ellis's own foibles (Ellis, 2010). Clients are asked to intentionally commit in public a foolish or shameful act, such as walking a banana down the street or breaking out in a show tune in the middle of a city block. The results of these behavioral experiments typically prove to clients that they don't need to feel shame or embarrassed. Shame is essentially a self-conscious thinking error, an irrational belief.

When a patient complains that the work of counterconditioning is difficult or makes him or her anxious, Ellis typically responds in three ways. First, to agree empathically with the patient that changing thinking and behaving *is* difficult. Second, to challenge the patient's expectation that psychotherapy *should* be easy. And third, to remind the patient of one of REBT's main rules: **PYA—push your ass** (Ellis, 2005).

REBT Therapeutic Content
Intrapersonal Conflicts

Psychological problems are intrapersonal in origin: Individuals produce emotional problems within themselves by irrational beliefs. REBT usually begins, therefore, with individual sessions focusing on the client's demanding thinking rather than on the relationship between client and therapist.

Anxiety and Defenses

Anxiety is an inappropriate consequence of irrational beliefs. When we examine the myriad of events about which people make themselves anxious, we see how widespread irrational cognitions are. Parents become unduly upset about their children's sexuality. If gays and lesbians are irrationally believed to be horrible, then communities become threatened by having a homosexual teacher in the schools. People tell themselves they must be perfect, then become anxious when confronted by criticism; they tell themselves they should be liked by everyone, then get tense when someone is angry with them. Anxieties such as these cannot be extinguished by desensitizing a person to a particular stimulus, but by disputing the irrational thoughts that a person has about stimulus events.

Defense mechanisms are examples of human irrational propensities. Projection is a clear example of people thinking that emotional upset is caused by external events. Repression is a reflection of the irrational belief that it is best not to think about unpleasant events. Probably the most common defense, rationalization reflects people's desire to convince the world that they have good reasons for behaving or feeling foolishly. To REBT therapists, defenses are not to be protected; they are to be challenged. Confrontations, interpretations, and refutations can weaken these irrational forces and allow patients to become more rational and emotionally healthy.

Self-Esteem

We can never prove our worth as human beings. To base our esteem on an ability to achieve, to love, to be approved, or even to be rational is to say that the value of the whole person is defined by the value of only a single part or behavior. To rate our worth by totaling the value of all our separate traits and performances—such as school grades, tennis scores, and annual incomes—represents a futile, irrational desire for a global report card that indicates where we stand in relation to the rest of the universe. Any grand conclusion about our worth or lack of worth is a self-defined identification that declares us on the team of the deity or the devil.

Unconditional self-acceptance (USA) is the key to being a natural and logical member of our own team. There is no empirical referent for self-worth, no objective criterion in the universe that can measure our worth. Self-acceptance, by contrast, is a logical and justifiable state. If self-worth is based on performances such as grades, for example, we can cause our moods to rise and fall with the latest exam rather than enjoy our education to the fullest. But when we adopt self-acceptance, we experience no dramatic rise and fall. When we finally accept ourselves unconditionally, warts and all, we can give up the elusive search for self-esteem and free up energy for the meaningful question of how we can most enjoy our life.

Responsibility

Patients can be held truly responsible for their troubled lives only if they have been instrumental in creating their personal problems. They cannot be responsible for how others treated them in childhood; they can be responsible only for how they currently construe their childhood. They cannot be responsible for their genetic makeup; they can be responsible only for choosing to rely on reason over nonsense.

Accepting responsibility for one's own problems does not involve blaming oneself. Blame is just another expression of the **tyranny of the should**: "You shouldn't have been so foolish; you shouldn't have been so demanding." The fact is, patient, you have been foolish, demanding, and dogmatic, and you continue to be so as long as you engage in the irrational guilt that comes with blaming yourself and insisting that you should have been different in the past. Ask yourself, "Are you willing to be mature and responsible enough right now to use your reason to find better alternatives for living? Or will you wallow in the guilt of self-blame or the resentment of parent bashing? Feel regret and sadness if you will, but even more feel the excitement that can come with accepting the responsibility for a more reasonable and pleasurable life."

Interpersonal Conflicts
Intimacy and Sexuality

Surely love and intimacy can add to the good life. Not being islands, nearly all individuals find it enjoyable to love and be loved by significant others. It is reasonable to want to relate well in interpersonal encounters. In fact, the evidence suggests that the better their interpersonal relationships, the happier people are likely to be.

That is not to say, however, that love and intimacy are necessary for human existence. As soon as we define love as an absolute necessity, we become anxious, demanding, or dependent lovers. If we must have love, we become prone to try to possess those who provide essential nourishment, jealous if they turn their love toward others, and threatened that someone will come along and take away the love we cannot live without. The clinging-vine wife, the jealous husband, the possessive partner, and the insecure spouse are examples of people defining love as a necessity. In spite of popular religious beliefs, we need not deify love in order to appreciate it. Love is a human phenomenon that adds to the pleasure and joy of living, not an absolute that can justify our existence or sanctify ourselves.

Sex also requires no sanctification. Sex is not some dirty desire that can be justified only by procreation, marriage, or love. As an outspoken advocate of *Sex without Guilt* (1958), Ellis was a rare rational voice for sexual freedom well before the sexual revolution began rolling in the 1960s. Recognizing that sex may be more enjoyable for many people when it occurs within an intimate relationship, it is still reasonable to ask, "Where is the evidence that sex and love must go together?" To insist that sex needs love to be good is apparently a human teaching that is really a moral wolf in sheep's clothing, a form of the old repressive morality that demands that sex be justified by some higher value than intrinsic pleasure.

Sex can be just for fun. Sex can be the clearest expression of the natural propensity of people to be pleasure producing. To be free to enjoy this profound pleasure is to ignore the irrational prohibitions of an antisexual society or the equally irrational demands of an achievement-oriented society that would judge the worth of individuals by the number of orgasms they achieve or the number of partners they have. Sex without guilt and without anxiety comes to those who are rational enough to express their natural sexual desires without concern for parental or performance demands.

Communication

Most of what are labeled communication problems are, in reality, thinking problems. People who communicate boring, bizarre, repetitive, or contradictory messages are actually revealing the boring, bizarre, repetitive, or contradictory character of their cognitions. Effective dialogue is rare because people who can think effectively are rare. If people are helped to become more rational in their style of thinking, they will generally also become more effective in their style of communicating.

Many stutterers, to take one example, may think straight but have such desires to be perfect speakers that they are horrified at making the normal disfluencies of everyday speech. They cannot accept the hesitations, the "you knows," "ohs," and "ahs" of us mortal mouths. They end up self-consciously selecting the words over which they are least likely to stumble. As a result, they stop and stammer, recycle their sentences, and do a number of other things that result in even more disastrous disfluencies. They have to quit making demands on themselves to be ultrafluent and just start stumbling along like the rest of us.

Hostility

Hostility is the irrational consequence of (1) an inborn, biological tendency to become aggressive; (2) some unpleasant or frustrating event; and (3) a tendency to think crookedly about the event and a persistent refusal to work against this crooked tendency (Ellis, 1973). All three of these variables must be present for hostility to occur. Human beings are not just reflexive animals that react to frustration with aggression; otherwise, most of us would be hostile most of the time. Frustrating events are almost always available to us, because the world we live in obviously is a frequently depriving, restraining, unfair place. In order for us to erupt into rage, we have to focus on the frustrations around us; exaggerate the meanings of these events into something awful, horrendous, or villainous; and insist that such frustrations should not exist and that we can no longer stand their existence.

The hostile person demands the removal of injustice, unfairness, and frustration immediately. With such impossible demands, hostile persons upset themselves unnecessarily. They are like children throwing temper tantrums because their demands are not being met immediately. There is no law that says hostile people must continue with such unrealistic, immature demands. Because we cannot remove inborn tendencies to become aggressive or prevent all frustrations from occurring, our best alternative is to assist hostile people in construing frustrations as unfortunate and inevitable events, not major catastrophes they cannot tolerate.

Control

A desire to control others is merely one expression of the irrational demand that the world conform to one's wishes. Tactics for gaining compliance from others include imposing the tyranny of the should on them and then trying to make them feel guilty if they do not act as we believe they should. This is a favorite tactic of parents, as they insist that their children should be polite, not talk back to them, be successful, and never disgrace the family name. Threatening to follow demands with anger is a less subtle controlling technique that works especially well with people who believe it is terrible to have someone angry at them.

Most controls work only if the people being controlled cooperate by allowing their irrational beliefs to respond: "You're right, I should feel guilty for not being polite." If the person responds rationally—"Don't make guilt; I have enough trouble disputing my own internal tyrannical shoulds without having to fight yours as well"—then the person attempting to control has his or her subtle irrational communications exposed by the light of clear thinking. The most effective countercontrol method is to dispute the irrational demands of others by asserting one's own rationality.

Individuo-Social Conflicts

Adjustment versus Transcendence

People who believe that they can in any meaningful way transcend the restraints, injustices, and frustrations of society will inevitably make themselves neurotics. Fighting the inevitable is one of the foolish ways of creating anxiety, anger, or depression. The fantasy to fly like Icarus far above the world represents the grandiose beliefs of irrational people that they can somehow be more than mere mortals. Like Icarus, superhuman people eventually fall on their foolish faces.

Before we take on irrational forces in society, we had better fight the irrational forces in ourselves. We have to first get our own heads on straight before we worry about setting straight the heads of state. To replace one set of irrational beliefs with demands that are equally irrational may be the history of much of the world, but it certainly is not progress. If we are to make significant strides toward making our communities more pleasant places to live, we will require a substantial number of people who are committed to solving social problems through logical and empirical methods rather than through the tired, old dogmatic demands that society must be more just and decent.

Impulse Control

Humans are unique creatures who can make almost any desire into a seemingly uncontrollable impulse. The common desire to gain large sums of money without working can lead to a "need" to gamble. The desire for tasty foods can become an "irresistible impulse" to eat excessively, even though overeaters know obesity can be the consequence. Impulses to steal, smoke, or exhibit one's genitals are just some of the many ways that people can turn desires into self-destructive demands. Such short-term hedonists ignore the realistic long-term consequences of their actions by insisting, "I should be able to eat all I want and not gain weight"; "I should be able to gamble against the odds and be a winner"; "I should be able to take what I want and not be punished." In reacting to such demands, most forces in society, including many systems of psychotherapy, foolishly attack the impulsive behavior rather than the stinking thinking that creates impulse-ridden characters. If we want to create a less impulsive world, then the one impulse we want to attack is the tendency to engage in irrational thinking, whether it occurs on an individual or a social level.

Beyond Conflict to Fulfillment

Meaning in Life

If we are searching for absolute meaning to life, we are bound to be disappointed. There are no absolutes except those we create. If by "meaning" we seek a belief that can justify our existence, forget it. The universe does not care that we exist; we do. If by "meaning," however, we are looking for that which makes life more enjoyable, then we can agree that it is best to maximize our pleasures and minimize our pains, because by definition pleasure is what we enjoy. The particular pleasure we seek is an individual matter discovered by each person in the process of living. The important thing is that our pleasures come from desires, not demands. There surely is more joy in doing what we want to do rather than what we must do.

The rational person does not expect life to be a rose garden. The rational person knows there are irritating thorns in each person's life but refuses to transform them into deathly ailments. In other words, mole hills remain mole hills—don't make unpleasant events any more unpleasant than they already are.

Meaning is, in simple terms, a value system. Thus, effective therapists would do well to have a good philosophy of life. Psychotherapists should be prepared to discuss deeply philosophic questions with patients, if they expect to get very far. As Ellis has repeatedly noted, many popular therapies mainly seek to help patients *feel* better (minimize their presenting symptoms), rather than *get* better. Getting better involves making a profound philosophical change, which is intimately tied to examining, clarifying, and perhaps replacing values.

Questions of values may masquerade as purely practical questions of how to become less anxious or depressed. But behind such clinical requests are value judgments that it is better to be less anxious or depressed (London, 1986). There are those who believe that the best life requires suffering and deprivation. A therapist with such values might try to convince clients to cherish their depression rather than to extinguish it. Clients are looking for a better life, in which they are free from current symptoms and powerful enough to remove new symptoms, and effective therapists are prepared to present at least one alternative that has worked well for themselves.

Ideal Individual

The scientist is an excellent ideal for humanity because scientists are committed to the rational life, a life of collecting data and applying logic to solving problems. Honesty and open communication are values inherent in science (Bronowski, 1959). True scientists welcome rational criticism of ideas and methods; they do not believe it is catastrophic if their favorite theories are eventually rejected for more elegant or effective explanations. Scientists are fascinated, not frustrated, by what is inevitable. They recognize their own limits and do not expect that science can answer all the philosophical questions of life. At their best, scientists are long-term hedonists who immensely enjoy their research into the unknown rather than puritans driven by demands that they must succeed. The revolutionary discoveries of science provide evidence for the value of a philosophy based on logic and empiricism.

REBT Therapeutic Relationship

Practically the polar opposite of person-centered therapy, REBT concurs only with the Rogerian idea that the therapist demonstrates unconditional acceptance of clients, even while challenging many of the clients' irrational beliefs. When patients do not complete homework or come late for sessions, the REBT clinician provides unconditional support of them as people. However, full acceptance of the client as a human does not mean that the therapist must demonstrate warmth or liking toward the client. Such warmth may feel good, but it is not necessary for successful treatment. Therapists try never to evaluate the client as a person, but they do evaluate the client's beliefs and behaviors.

REBT therapists are not particularly sympathetic with patient weeping or anger, but use such visible indications of upset to demonstrate to patients the irrationality of their beliefs. Nor is accurate empathy with emotions particularly helpful; such empathy is frequently a form of commiseration that only encourages the person to continue feeling bad, sad, or upset. REBT therapists are quite empathic in the sense of listening closely in order to understand what clients are probably telling themselves to produce their distressing emotions. Clients report feeling understood, not because the therapist is emoting with them, but because the therapist is bringing into awareness the cause of the client's problems.

REBT practitioners frequently behave in a genuine and open manner, directly revealing their own ideas, beliefs, and philosophy of life. They are more willing than most to reveal some of their own foibles in order to dispute the client's belief that anyone, even a therapist, can be more than human. Transference feelings are challenged, not encouraged, because these represent yet more examples of clients' trying to demand that the world be something other than what it is.

A combination philosopher/teacher/scientist, the REBT therapist views the therapeutic relationship primarily as a precondition for effective education. As long as the client remains willing to relate, the therapist can use hardheaded reasoning to teach the client how to actively dispute the irrational beliefs at the root of emotional problems.

The vigorous challenging of the patients' irrational ideas (but not the patients themselves) has led some observers to take issue with Ellis's hard-line, directive approach. They contend that Ellis's sarcastic and exaggerated tone in disputing patients' irrational ideas may cast REBT in an unfavorable light. They advocate gentler models of cognitive disputation. Ellis (1987b) concedes the point, but continues to believe that a forceful, debating style is often necessary, especially with resistant clients.

A Sketch of Aaron Beck

Like Albert Ellis, Aaron T. Beck (1921–) came to pioneer cognitive therapy from origins in childhood illness and psychoanalysis. He was the youngest of five children of parents who both emigrated from Russia. Beck almost died at the age of 7 after a broken bone became infected and he developed a life-threatening blood infection. The surgery itself was traumatic: He was separated from his mother without warning and put under the knife before the anesthetic had taken effect. This experience led to fears of abandonment and health-related phobias that, like Ellis, Beck mastered by testing the accuracy of his beliefs by intentionally exposing himself to the situations that he feared. In many respects, the seeds of his later theoretical innovations were sown by his early life experiences (Hollon & DiGiuseppe, 2011).

Trained as an undergraduate at Brown University and then as a medical student at Yale University, Beck was dissuaded initially from psychiatry because of the esoteric nature of psychoanalysis. He opted for neurology, but during his rotations, became intrigued by the psychodynamic psychiatrists and eventually moved to the Austen Riggs Center at Stockbridge, Massachusetts, where he underwent a personal analysis and became enamored with cognition, derived from ego psychology then in vogue.

Convinced that psychoanalysis offered important insights into mental disorders, Beck undertook research to validate psychoanalytic hypotheses. However, his findings from experimental work on dreams and ideational material led him to discard most psychoanalytic notions. As good scientists do, Beck literally and figuratively followed the evidence away from psychoanalysis to formulate a cognitive theory and therapy for mental disorders. Working simultaneously but independently from Albert Ellis, he discovered that, by teaching patients to examine and test their negative ideas, their depression began to improve.

Over the past 40 years, Beck has created a system of psychotherapy known simply as **cognitive therapy** that has attracted enormous attention and prompted extensive research. In order to implement his research, Beck developed a number of widely used instruments, including the Beck Depression Inventory, the Beck Anxiety Inventory, and the Scale for Suicide Ideation. His initial research and clinical focus was depression, spawning the classic *Cognitive Therapy of Depression* (Beck et al., 1979), but has broadened to anxiety disorders (Beck et al., 1985), substance abuse (Beck et al., 1993), personality disorders (Beck et al., 2004), and schizophrenia (Beck et al., 2008).

Acknowledging the salience of interpersonal as well as cognitive factors in emotional health, he wrote *Love Is Never Enough* (Beck, 1988), a mass-market book applying cognitive therapy to marriage and marital therapy. Recognizing the tragic upswing of societal violence, Beck (2000) wrote *Prisoners of Hate: The Cognitive Basis of Anger, Hostility, and Violence.*

Now in semi-retirement and 50-plus years into his own marriage, Beck is University Professor Emeritus of Psychiatry at the University of Pennsylvania and president of the Beck Center for Cognitive Therapy and Research in Bala Cynwyd, Pennsylvania. At the center, he continues to teach and write, sometimes with the two of his four children who are psychologists. Known for his wisdom, warmth, and signature red bow tie, Aaron "Tim" Beck continues his prolific contributions to cognitive therapy.

Although Beck developed his cognitive therapy independently from Ellis, there are numerous striking similarities in their approaches. First, both Beck and Ellis were originally trained in the psychoanalytic tradition and emigrated to cognitive psychotherapy as they became dissatisfied with the clinical results of psychoanalysis. Second, Beck and Ellis share the goal of helping clients to become conscious of maladaptive cognitions, to recognize the disruptive impact of such cognitions, and to replace them with more appropriate and adaptive thought patterns. Third, both are rather integrative in technique selection and empirical in theory revision, as is typical of cognitive behaviorists in general. Fourth, both forms of cognitive therapy are problem oriented, directive, and psychoeducational. Fifth, both Beck's cognitive therapy and Ellis's REBT view homework as a central and indispensable feature of treatment. And sixth, both are committed to bringing self-help resources to individual clients and the public at large. They believe that such resources—including Ellis and Harper's (1997) *New Guide to Rational Living*, Beck's (1988) *Love Is Never Enough*, and Burns's (1999) bestseller *Feeling Good: The New Mood Therapy*—plus newer computer-administered cognitive treatments augment traditional psychotherapy.

Cognitive Theory of Psychopathology

Beck's and Ellis's respective theories of psychopathology converge in most important respects, although the vocabulary differs. In place of Ellis's irrational beliefs, Beck is more inclined to speak of maladaptive cognitions, dysfunctional attitudes, or in the case of his early research on depression, **depressogenic (depression-causing) assumptions**. In their benchmark *Cognitive Therapy of Depression* (1979), Beck and associates identify a number of common cognitive errors that cause depressed feelings. Several of these are presented in Table 10.1; note the tremendous overlap with the REBT list of irrational beliefs.

Consider the case of one of our patients, a middle-aged small business owner, who consulted us for depression following the collapse of his business. His dysphoric feelings betrayed the entire litany of these depressogenic assumptions. "I'll never be able to run a successful company" (**overgeneralizing**). "All I can think about is this business failure. What else is there to my life?" (**selective abstraction**). "It's all my fault. I should have worked harder, not taken those 2 weeks of vacation last year, never purchased that expensive

Table 10.1 Several Depressogenic Assumptions

COGNITIVE ERROR	ASSUMPTION
Overgeneralizing	If it's true in one situation, it applies to any situation that is even remotely similar.
Selective abstraction	The only events that matter are the failures, which are the sole measure of myself.
Excessive responsibility	I am responsible for all bad things, rotten events, and life failures.
Self-references	I am at the center of everyone's attention, particularly when I fail at something.
Dichotomous thinking	Everything is either one extreme or another (black or white, good or bad).

computer" (**excessive responsibility**). "All our neighbors and friends know I screwed up, and they're laughing at me behind my back" (**self-references**). And "It's all hopeless; there is nothing salvageable from the business" (**dichotomous thinking**).

Psychopathology originates in the client's preconscious or preattentive constructions of reality. These constructions reflect the operation of the client's underlying cognitive organization, called **schemas**, in interaction with the current environment. As in REBT, life events are interpreted through cognitive lenses or structures, which then lead to distressing thoughts and disturbing behaviors.

In cognitive therapy, the underlying cognitions are assumed to vary specifically with the behavioral disorder of clients, an idea known as the **content specificity hypothesis**. Different pathologies are related to different cognitive content. A paranoid personality, for example, holds core beliefs that motives are suspect, that one must look for hidden motives, and that trusting others is dangerous. The resultant behaviors are to accuse, counterattack, and be wary. The histrionic personality, by contrast, adheres to core beliefs that people are there to serve or admire me and that I can get by on my feelings. Distinctive behaviors of histrionics are to use dramatics, charm, temper tantrums, and crying. Obsessive-compulsives, like Mrs. C, harbor the core beliefs that "I know what's best" and details are crucial.

They, in turn, apply rules of perfectionism, evaluation, control, and the "shoulds." Each disorder, then, has a specific cognitive content.

Depression is related to a different pattern of ideas than is paranoia, hysteria, phobias, or obsessive-compulsive disorders. The basic ideation in depression has three themes, which Beck (1970) terms the **cognitive triad**: (1) Events are interpreted negatively, (2) depressed individuals dislike themselves, and (3) the future is appraised negatively.

These fundamental ideas are viewed, in contrast to Ellis, not as necessarily irrational. Instead, Beck characterizes them as too absolute, too broad or extreme, or too arbitrary. The cognitive triad gives rise to maladaptive self-verbalizations, or possibly visual images, which are experienced as automatic thoughts by clients. Much of cognitive therapy involves assisting clients in ferreting out automatic thinking and, ultimately, in reevaluating faulty cognitions by testing them both logically and empirically.

Cognitive Therapeutic Processes

In general, Beck (1976, p. 217) posits that the successful client passes through several stages in correcting faulty cognitions:

First he has to become aware of what he is thinking. Second, he needs to recognize what thoughts are awry. Then he has to substitute accurate for inaccurate judgments. Finally, he needs feedback to inform him whether his changes are correct.

Although this sounds like a quote from Ellis, there are subtle but important differences between Beck's cognitive therapy and REBT. Beck himself has delineated several of the salient differences between these two premier cognitive systems (Hollon & Beck, 1994; Padesky & Beck, 2003). For one, Beck's therapy tends to emphasize the process of empiricism to a greater extent than does Ellis's REBT; clients in cognitive therapy are encouraged to treat their beliefs as hypotheses to be tested by way of their own behavioral experiments. Whereas Ellis strives for a philosophical conversion based on rationality and logic, Beck encourages a reliance on the evidence to alter existing beliefs. For another difference, cognitive therapy tends to be more structured and precise than REBT. With depression, for example, Beck generally limits therapy to 20 hours. He adheres to treatment manuals specific to each disorder—depression (Beck et al., 1979), anxiety (Beck et al., 1985), and substance abuse (Beck et al., 1993), among others. The cognitive therapist would also routinely administer brief symptom checklists, including the Beck Depression Inventory and the Beck Anxiety Inventory, before sessions to monitor the condition and progress of the patient. This structure encourages a problem orientation, discourages wasting time, and provides the client with a therapeutic rationale and direction.

In one of the early sessions of cognitive treatment, the therapist introduces the influence of cognitions on affect and behavior. That is, the therapist introduces the cognitive model to patients. Many patients can relate initially to a vignette that does not involve them personally. The following is a typical explanation of the cognitive model (Beck et al., 1979):

Therapist: The way a person thinks about events affects how he feels and behaves. For example, a man was home alone one night and heard a crash in another room. If he thinks, "There's a burglar in the room," how do you think he would feel?

Patient: Very anxious, terrified.

Therapist: And how might he behave?

Patient: He might phone the police or run for help.

Therapist: In response to the thought that a burglar made the noise, the man would probably feel anxious and behave in such a way to protect himself. Now, instead, let's say he heard the same noise and thought, "The window was left open and the wind caused something to fall over." How would he feel?

Patient: Well, he wouldn't be afraid. He might annoyed that one of the kids left the window open.

Therapist: And how might he behave?

Patient: He would probably go and see what the problem was. He certainly wouldn't phone the police.

Therapist: So, this example shows us that there are a number of ways in which you can think about or interpret the same situation. What's more, the way you interpret the situation affects your feelings and behavior.

As a leading authority on depression, Beck recognizes the need to sequence treatment goals. The first priority is to reduce severe symptoms such as suicidal impulses, insomnia, and weight loss. For symptom relief, Beck relies more on behavioral activation and contingency management, structuring assignments in such a way that clients will succeed and be reinforced for their efforts. The first assignment might be simply to boil an egg. As the client begins to feel better, a more challenging assignment is given that can bring greater reinforcement, such as cooking a meal for the family.

An intervention introduced early in therapy can be **activity scheduling**, in which specific daily activities are selected and evaluated strictly on the basis of how effectively they elevate mood. These activities are also rated by clients in terms of mastery and pleasure. Depressed clients who characteristically report that they can master nothing and enjoy nothing are thus confronted with feedback to the contrary. After symptoms begin to lift, the focus of treatment shifts to underlying cognitions.

Three basic approaches to **cognitive restructuring**—modifying the thinking process—are to ask, in various ways, (1) What's the evidence? (2) What's another way of looking at it? (3) So what if it happens? Applied to the depressed businessman: Where is the evidence that you will never succeed again, that you were the only one responsible for the failure, that your neighbors are laughing at you? What's another way of looking at this event, this time in your life, this opportunity during a crisis?

Consider the example of a depressed student who believed she would not gain admission into any of the competitive PhD programs to which she had applied. In the cognitive tradition, I (JCN) gently but persistently questioned the reasoning that led to her distressed feelings:

Therapist: You applied to 12 doctoral programs, all within your range of credentials?

Patient: Yes, that's right. But my GRE scores and grades were not as high as some of the students accepted last year.

Therapist: Hmmm. How did your scores and grades compare to the typical student admitted in recent years?

Patient: Well, I'm in the middle and higher.

Therapist: And so the evidence suggests …?

Patient: That I am competitive but not the highest.

Therapist: Yes, I see. Better than most PhD students admitted but not at the very top. In a typical year, your numbers would indicate what would happen to your application?

Patient: That I would be given serious consideration and probably accepted.

Therapist: (smiling) That sounds about right. What then accounts for your distress?

Patient: When I lose my thinking and I think the worst.

Therapist: When you catastrophize, you feel depressed and mope around. When you catch yourself—as you just did here—and think realistically, then you feel and behave how?

Patient: I feel confident and behave like myself.

Therapist: And if the worst happened and you did not get into a PhD program this year, what would happen?

Patient: Well, nothing terrible. I would get a job that would prepare me better for graduate school for a year and then reapply next year.

Therapist: A fine contingency plan. Does that sound so awful as to leave you feeling depressed?

Patient: (smiling) I guess not! It's "mind over mood" (the title of a cognitive therapy self-help book she was reading; Greenberger & Padesky, 1995).

The student was not deliberately trying to thwart me but had reached a negative and erroneous conclusion regarding her chances of admission. Her reasoning can be seen as an example of dichotomous, or "all-or-nothing" thinking, in that any entrance examination scores or college grades less than the best was viewed as a failure. She had elevated the possibility of rejection into the certainty of catastrophe.

A key objective is to teach patients the method of **distancing**. They learn to deal with upsetting thoughts objectively, reevaluating them rather than automatically accepting them. Our depressed businessman was asked to examine the faulty logic behind his overgeneralization and to establish criteria for "similarity" to all other situations. When gently coaxed to do so, he realized that this was his first failure in a career of owning three successful enterprises. When asked to gather evidence on the probability of small businesses failing, he went online and discovered that more than half of new businesses fail.

Likewise, clients are taught the **disattribution technique**, in which they disabuse themselves of the belief that they are entirely responsible for their plight. When asked not to automatically attribute all bad events to himself and to share the responsibility, our businessman quickly realized that the poor national economy, two new competitors in town, and production delays at one of his suppliers all certainly contributed to the demise of his business.

By becoming conscious of depressogenic assumptions and dysfunctional cognitions, clients begin to free themselves from debilitating expectations that they are doomed to depression and other forms of pathology. In the case of panic attacks, for instance, patients are taught to identify and modify their misinterpretations of bodily sensations. This entails a broad range of cognitive and behavioral interventions. Among the cognitive approaches are questioning patients' evidence for their misinterpretations, substituting more realistic interpretations, and restructuring their images. The behavioral procedures include inducing feared sensations (e.g., hyperventilating or focusing attention on the body) in order to demonstrate the true cause of the panic attack, stopping safety behaviors (such as holding onto solid objects when dizzy), and practicing exposure to feared situations in order to allow patients to disconfirm their negative predictions about the consequences of their symptoms (Clark & Ehlers, 1993).

These assorted cognitive-behavioral procedures have been successfully applied for decades with patients suffering from a host of neurotic disorders. But in recent years the clinical consensus is that personality disordered patients rarely succeed in changing their problematic cognitions through empirical analysis and logical discourse alone. As a result, cognitive therapy has been extended and adapted for the treatment of personality disorders, with **schema-focused psychotherapy** (Young et al., 2003) leading the way. Personality disorders are no longer seen as a collection of isolated symptoms and cognitive distortions, but rather as dysfunctional schemas and self-perpetuating, self-defeating behaviors. Rooted in cognitive therapy but drawing from attachment theory (Chapter 3) and emotion-focused therapies (Chapter 6), Jeffrey Young's schema-focused therapy emphasizes affective change methods, the therapeutic relationship, and limited reparenting more than standard cognitive therapy.

Limited reparenting flows directly from the assumption that early maladaptive schemas arise when core needs are not met. Schema therapy meets these needs by helping the patient find the experiences that were missed in early childhood that will resolve the damaging experiences that led to the maladaptive schemas. Limited reparenting, paralleling healthy parenting, involves the establishment of a secure attachment through the therapist, within the bounds of a professional relationship, doing what she can to meet these needs (www.isst-online.com/).

Cognitive Therapeutic Relationship

In contrast to Ellis's direct confrontational style, Beck primarily uses a **Socratic dialogue**. Clients are led to make personal discoveries by a tactful progression of questions. This approach is described as **collaborative empiricism**: The participants are on a shared mission to determine from the evidence they gather which thoughts may be dysfunctional and which avenues they might pursue to enhance those thoughts. Therapeutic interactions are structured so that clients discover for themselves those thoughts that are inaccurate. A woman who thinks men will reject her if she expresses her positive feelings toward the feminist movement, for example, might be encouraged to test this hypothesis on her next date. Homework assignments are, for the most part, mutual decisions in which the patient is asked for ideas to test out the logic or to gather evidence.

Cognitive therapists aspire to be empathic and warm in the Rogerian sense, but do not view the facilitative conditions as necessary or sufficient. A trusting relationship with a credible therapist is likely to improve treatment effectiveness. However, the active ingredients of cognitive therapy are the identification of problematic schemas and their remediation, not the relationship between client and therapist.

The ideal type of therapist support will engender responsible dependency in a patient. The skilled cognitive therapist maintains the expert role in directing the course of treatment and yet insists the patient be an active partner with commensurate responsibility for the implementation and ultimate success of the treatment. This dual stance is possible because it is the therapist who understands the general principles of cognitive therapy, but it is the patient who rapidly becomes the expert on how the application of the principles impacts his or her own functioning (Alford & Beck, 1997b). In this way, the cognitive therapist provides both support and direction.

Practicalities of Cognitive Therapies

As a no-nonsense approach in which active intervention begins in the opening session, REBT is designed to teach the ABCs of emotional problems in 1 to 20 sessions with most mildly to moderately disturbed patients. Patients with greater inborn tendencies toward irrational thinking, such as borderline or psychotic individuals, can be helped, but therapy is longer-term, running at least a year.

Cognitive therapists generally endorse brief treatment due to their active, directive, and structured style. Problems are diagnosed, goals are identified, principles of the cognitive model are taught, and homework experiments are designed in short order. Audiotapes, books, and handouts supplement the formal sessions. Manuals for Beck's cognitive therapy prescribe 12 or 16 sessions, spaced further apart as the patient recovers. Ellis's REBT offers not only quick change but also "better, deeper, and more enduring" change in 1 to 20 sessions (Ellis, 1995).

Once patients have the basic cognitive model down, they are often placed in group therapy to further refine and practice the rational philosophy that they are applying to their problems (Ellis, 1992). Groups serve as a microcosm of the larger world in which clients can practice reacting to criticism, rejection, or pleasure in more rational ways. In therapy groups, clients can also practice new behaviors, such as assertion, that follow from more logical attitudes toward life. Independent of how much psychotherapy is conducted in a group format, however, the focus is not on the relationships among group members but on the application of cognitive therapy methods.

Distinctive features of REBT are the widespread use of bibliotherapy and public workshops. Ellis was an extraordinarily prolific author, writing more than 80 books on a multitude of topics, and almost all clients are expected to read one or more of these books relevant to their presenting complaints. He was probably the most prolific workshop conductor in the history of psychotherapy, giving literally thousands of addresses, seminars, and workshops throughout the world.

In form, the cognitive therapies are like most other therapies, with 50-minute weekly individual sessions or 90-minute group sessions as the norm. At the institutes, attempts are made to keep fees moderate, but in regular private practice, fees seem to follow the going rates in the community.

Both forms of cognitive therapy have been applied to clientele of various ages and disorders. As shown in the following section on effectiveness, cognitive and cognitive-behavioral therapies have proven successful with children, adolescents, adults, and older adults. The area of best-documented achievement for cognitive therapies to date has been the neurotic disorders, particularly unipolar depression and anxiety disorders. REBT and cognitive therapy have been applied to couples, to families, to sex therapy, and to organizations (see Dattilio, 2009; Ellis & Dryden, 2007; Epstein & Baucom, 2002; Freeman, 1983).

Increasingly, cognitive therapy is being applied to and evaluated on more disturbed patients. Beck's cognitive therapy has been applied to bipolar depression (Basco & Rush, 2005; Newman et al., 2002), personality disorders (Beck et al., 2004), substance abuse (Beck et al., 1993), and psychotic conditions (Beck et al., 2008; Wright et al., 1992).

Both cognitive treatments are amenable to combination with psychotropic medication as indicated. Beck, in fact, was an early research pioneer in testing their separate and combined effects.

At all levels, education in cognitive and cognitive-behavioral therapies is ideally grounded in science. Like cognitive therapy itself, training should be evidence-based and competency-based. Formal guidelines do not prescribe particular courses, but rather a set of training policies and competencies. These include foundational work in the philosophy of science, ethical decision making, research designs, clinical methods, and treatment adaptations to multiple clientele and contexts (Klepac et al., 2012).

Training is widely available in graduate programs and from the Ellis Institute in New York City and Beck's Center for Cognitive Therapy and Research outside Philadelphia. Both facilities offer traineeships, postdoctoral fellowships, and extramural training opportunities, the latter offered regularly throughout the United States. Training is available to mental health professionals with terminal degrees in all disciplines. These cognitive therapies have now established themselves throughout the world; REBT has more than a dozen affiliated training institutes in the United States and another dozen or so overseas, and there are now literally hundreds of centers featuring Beck's cognitive therapy.

Effectiveness of Cognitive Therapies

A review of the outcome research on cognitive therapies would properly begin by considering the research conducted on behavior therapies, covered in Chapter 9. Both Ellis and Beck believe that their respective therapies fall under the general rubric of "cognitive-behavioral" treatments. In this section, we summarize the outcome research conducted specifically on REBT and Beckian cognitive therapy and generally on cognitive-behavioral therapies. Our summary is, of necessity, selective: There are now more than 1,000 controlled studies conducted on cognitive and cognitive-behavioral therapies.

Rational-Emotive Behavior Therapy

The first outcome research was conducted by Ellis (1957b), who took closed case files and compared his own success using psychoanalysis, psychoanalytic psychotherapy, and RET. He selected 16 cases from psychoanalysis, 78 from psychoanalytic psychotherapy, and 78 using RET. His results were as follows:

METHOD	CONSIDERABLE IMPROVEMENT	DISTINCT IMPROVEMENT	LITTLE OR NO IMPROVEMENT
Psychoanalysis	13%	37%	50%
Psychoanalytic psychotherapy	18%	45%	37%
Rational-emotive therapy	44%	46%	10%

Although Ellis concludes these results demonstrate the superiority of RET over psychoanalysis, all he has shown is that he was more effective later in his career with his own psychotherapy than he was at the beginning of his career with Freudian analysis. Further, his study does not include a no-treatment control group, nor were the treatments administered at the same time or for the same length of time. His early work is more accurately seen as a comparative survey in which he was the sole judge of outcome.

In the classic Smith, Glass, and Miller meta-analysis (1980) of 475 studies involving 25,000 patients, RET produced an average effect size of 0.68 and cognitive-behavior therapy a 1.13 effect size. This means that the average patient who receives RET is better off at the end of it than 75% of the persons who do not have treatment, whereas the average patient receiving cognitive-behavioral therapy is better off than 87% of those without treatment.

Since the 1970s, about 400 outcome studies (most of them not RCTs) have examined the effectiveness of RET/REBT with various disorders and populations (DiGiuseppe et al., 2010). An early meta-analysis (Lyons & Woods, 1991) resulted in a total of 236 comparisons of RET to baseline, control groups, behavior therapy, and other forms of psychotherapy. The overall effect size pre- to posttreatment for RET was 0.95, which translates into 73% of the treated patients demonstrating significant clinical improvement over those not receiving RET. This figure indicates that RET consistently outperforms control groups and no treatment. No general differences in outcome were found among behavior therapy, cognitive-behavior modification, and REBT.

Parallel conclusions were drawn in the most recent and exhaustive meta-analysis of REBT, involving 191 studies (DiGiuseppe et al., 2010). Results indicate that the average effect size (*d*) pre- to posttreatment was 0.89, REBT versus no treatment 0.57, and REBT versus alternative treatment 0.04. Overall, the results consistently support the efficacy of REBT and suggest that it is as effective as other psychological treatments in reducing symptoms.

REBT and associated cognitive therapies have also been found to be effective for older children and adolescents. In a meta-analysis of 150 outcome studies with children and adolescents (Weisz, Donenberg, et al., 1995), the 38 treatment groups involving cognitive/cognitive-behavioral therapy produced an average effect size of 0.67, a moderately large impact. (Recall from Table 3.1 that 0.20 is generally considered a small effect, 0.50 a moderate effect, and 0.80 a large effect.) The cognitive therapies outperformed the nonbehavioral therapies, such as client centered and insight oriented.

A specific meta-analysis of 19 studies on the effectiveness of REBT with 1,021 children and adolescents (Gonzalez et al., 2004) produced a slightly lower effect size of 0.50, signifying that RET with children was generally beneficial and of a respectable magnitude. REBT had its most pronounced impact on disruptive and conduct disorders. And, as found in the REBT research with adults (Lyons & Woods, 1991), effect sizes were higher when treatment was lengthier. As Al Ellis would surely remind us, it takes time and work to profoundly change our thinking.

Cognitive Therapy

Inarguably the most actively researched systems of psychotherapy over the past decade have been Beck's cognitive therapy and generic cognitive-behavioral therapy. We will approach this burgeoning literature by sampling the pertinent meta-analyses, beginning, as did Beck, with outcome studies on depression.

Depression

In 1989, Dobson published a meta-analysis on the effectiveness of Beck's cognitive therapy for depression. He identified 28 studies that used a common outcome measure of depression and made comparisons of cognitive therapy with other psychotherapy systems. The average effect size was quite high across various measures: The average cognitive therapy client did better than 98% of the untreated, control subjects. The results documented a greater degree of change for cognitive therapy compared with no treatment, pharmacotherapy, behavior therapy, and other psychotherapies.

This conclusion was apparently correct, as far as it went. A more comprehensive meta-analysis on psychotherapy for the treatment of depression located 58 controlled investigations (Robinson et al., 1990). Findings confirmed that depressed clients benefit substantially from psychotherapy, and these gains are comparable to those obtained with pharmacotherapy. Initial analyses suggested a superiority in the efficacy of cognitive and cognitive-behavioral therapies for depression, as found by Dobson (1989). However, once the effect of **investigator allegiance** was removed, there remained no evidence for the relative superiority of any single approach. The apparent superiority of cognitive over other forms of therapy was largely, if not entirely, the result of the researcher's theoretical bias in such matters as construction of the study, selection of the outcome measures, and differential expertise in the implementation of the psychotherapies consistent and inconsistent with the researcher's allegiance.

Revisiting the effect of investigator allegiance and cognitive therapy for depression, other investigators reanalyzed the same 28 studies as Dobson (1989) and another set of 37 similar ones published from 1987 to 1994 (Gaffan et al., 1995). Once again, about half the outcome difference between cognitive therapy and other psychotherapies was predictable from the researcher's allegiance. However, comparable analyses from the newer set of studies showed no effect of investigator allegiance. The allegiance effect may be a historical phenomenon, perhaps the result of early reports being written by pioneers and advocates who delivered cognitive therapy more powerfully.

Over time, the apparent magnitude of cognitive therapy's superiority over other treatments, particularly behavior therapy, has declined. At this point, the benefits of cognitive therapy for depression are approximately equal to the benefits of other tested, bona fide noncognitive psychotherapies (Cuijpers et al., 2008; Jakobsen et al., 2012; Wampold et al., 2002).

Several other meta-analyses looked specifically at the efficacy of cognitive therapies for depression among children (Weisz et al., 2006), adolescents (Lewinsohn & Clarke, 1999; Reinecke et al., 1998), and older adults (Payne & Marcus, 2008; Pinquart et al., 2007; Scogin & McElreath, 1994). Among children, cognitive therapies produced an average effect size of 0.35 and fared no better or worse than noncognitive treatments (Miller et al., 2008; Weisz et al., 2006). Among adolescents, cognitive-behavioral therapy yielded the large, impressive effect sizes of 1.02 and 1.27 pre- to posttreatment in the two meta-analyses. The results demonstrate that cognitive-behavioral therapy is more effective than no treatment, active placebo, and even antidepressant medications in treating depressed adolescents (Michael & Crowley, 2002).

Among older adults, the mean effect sizes (d) for individual and group cognitive therapy versus no treatment or placebo in three meta-analyses were 0.85, 1.06, and 1.12, again large and robust effects. The results indicated cognitive therapy was reliably more effective than no treatment on patient-rated and clinician-rated measures of depression. At the same time, again paralleling the earlier conclusions, cognitive therapy was equal in effectiveness to the other tested therapies in the treatment of geriatric depression.

A prevalent and costly problem in the treatment of depression is relapse. Over half of patients— actually 54%—who respond to treatment will relapse into depression within 2 years of completing treatment (Vittengl et al., 2007). In order to prevent relapse, many cognitive therapists have begun offering continuation treatment—booster sessions spaced several weeks apart—following the more aggressive, acute phase of therapy. A meta-analysis of 28 studies, involving 1,880 adults, revealed that continuation cognitive therapy reduced relapse recurrence by 21% to 29% (Vittengl et al., 2007). Many depressed patients will require, and benefit from, continuation treatment.

What can be safely concluded is that cognitive therapy is definitely superior to no treatment and placebo treatments for depression among children, adolescents, adults, and older adults. What can also be safely concluded is that continued cognitive therapy reduces the probability of later relapse or recurrence. What can be probably concluded is that cognitive therapy is as effective or perhaps slightly more effective as other bona fide psychotherapies for depression. Indeed, along with interpersonal psychotherapy (IPT; Chapter 7), cognitive therapy is widely recognized as one of the first-line "treatments of choice" for depression (Tolin, 2010).

Anxiety Disorders (General)

Turning to the anxiety disorders, just as Beck and his associates did following their classic studies on depression, we find considerable research on cognitive therapy. Quantitative reviews consistently indicate that cognitive and cognitive-behavior therapies for anxiety are more effective than wait-list, placebo control, and treatment as usual groups (Chambless & Gillis, 1993; Hofmann & Smits, 2008; Hunot et al., 2007; Thorp et al., 2009). Indeed, cognitive and cognitive-behavioral therapies for anxiety disorders are one of the great success stories in all of psychotherapy.

In order to determine whether the success of cognitive therapy established in well-controlled scientific trials generalizes to less-controlled, real-world circumstances, 56 effectiveness studies of CBT for adult anxiety disorders were located and synthesized by meta-analysis (Stewart & Chambless,

2009). All pretreatment to posttreatment effect sizes were large, suggesting that CBT for adult anxiety is effective in routine clinical practice. Moreover, the effect sizes from these effectiveness studies were in the range of those obtained in efficacy trials. The concern that the results of somewhat artificial efficacy trials conducted in laboratories might not apply to the messy world of routine practice was not supported, at least for cognitive therapy and anxiety disorders.

Another consistent finding among outcome studies in the anxiety disorders is that cognitive and CBT outperform medication in the long run. Both medications and CBT offer clear and typically comparable effectiveness to patients in the short run. But in the long run, the success of medication is reduced substantially once the medication is discontinued. At that point, CBT is associated with lower dropout rates and with greater maintenance of treatment gains (Gould et al., 1997; Hofmann & Spiegel, 1999; Mitte, 2005b).

Obsessive-Compulsive Disorder

Despite the widespread acceptance of exposure therapy as the treatment of choice for obsessive-compulsive disorder (OCD), the scientific research shows that cognitive therapy holds its own here, too. In meta-analyses of the controlled studies on OCD, cognitive restructuring alone proved as effective as exposure alone (Abramowitz, 1997; Feske & Chambless, 1995; Rosa-Alcazar et al., 2008). Again, too, cognitive therapy produced larger effect sizes and greater rates of clinical improvement compared to medication (Abramowitz et al., 2005).

Panic Disorder

In an early review of five controlled trials of cognitive therapy in panic disorder, Clark and Ehlers (1993) found that 86% of the patients completed the cognitive therapy and that 82% of the patients were panic-free at follow-up. Both numbers were generally higher than those for alternative treatments, including supportive psychotherapy and relaxation training. Subsequent meta-analyses of treatment outcomes for panic found that the most effective treatment was usually a combination of cognitive restructuring, exposure, and breathing retraining (Gould et al., 1995; Hofmann & Smits, 2008; Sanchez-Meca et al., 2010).

Similarly positive results have been reported by David Barlow and associates, whose **panic control therapy (PCT)** includes elements of cognitive therapy, behavior therapy, and exposure therapy (Barlow & Lehman, 1996). PCT consists of education about the nature and physiological aspects of panic, training in slow breathing, cognitive restructuring directed at negative cognitions related to panic, and repeated exposure to feared physical sensations associated with panic. As in many contemporary cognitive-behavioral treatments, the lines of distinction in PCT between behavior therapy, cognitive therapy, and exposure therapy are blurry, and the best one can do is to describe it as cognitive-behavioral therapy. By whatever name, the efficacy of PCT has been demonstrated in numerous clinical trials: On average, about 80% of PCT patients are panic-free at posttreatment compared with 40% of patients receiving relaxation training alone and 30% of patients on a waiting list (Barlow et al., 2000; Hofmann & Spiegel, 1999).

Effectiveness of a given treatment can also be evaluated in terms of its cost-effectiveness. An interesting study for all of Australia calculated the costs and benefits for a period of 1 year of all adults suffering from diagnosable anxiety disorders (Heuzenroeder et al., 2004). Compared to current practice, CBT would be the most cost-effective treatment for both generalized anxiety disorder and panic disorder. CBT results in greater total health benefit than medication for both anxiety disorders, although the implementation of CBT would require more widespread access to a sufficient number of therapists trained in cognitive-behavior therapy. In short, CBT is a treatment of choice for panic disorder.

Post-Traumatic Stress Disorder

At least a dozen meta-analyses have been performed on the effectiveness of psychotherapy for PTSD. The results, without exception, demonstrate that psychotherapy for PTSD leads to large improvement from pretreatment (Bradley et al., 2005). Across all treatments, the average effect size for pretreatment to posttreatment was 1.43, rendering them some of the most effective psychological treatments devised to date. Cognitive-behavior therapy was equally effective as exposure and EMDR (see Chapter 8) among children, adolescents, and adults (Bradley et al., 2005; Gillies et al., 2012; Taylor & Chemtob, 2004).

Cognitive processing therapy (CPT) was developed by Patricia Resick as an integrative cognitive treatment for trauma and has been extensively applied with trauma survivors (Resick et al., 2008; Resick & Schnicke, 1996). It is a 12-session structured program, delivered in either individual or group formats, that combines a written form of exposure with cognitive therapy. After an introduction to PTSD symptoms and CPT, clients are asked to write an impact statement of how their trauma has affected them. The narrative is used to understand how they may have distorted the cause of the event or overgeneralized its meaning, such that it has caused impairment. The therapist begins to challenge faulty thinking about the traumatic event with Socratic questioning and collaborative empiricism. In the last five sessions, clients are provided skills to assist them in thinking about themes—safety, trust, esteem, intimacy—that are commonly disrupted following traumatic events. Several large RCTs now support the effectiveness of CPT for traumatized children and adults (Resick et al., 2008).

Eating Disorders

Meta-analytic research has considered the effectiveness of both psychotherapy and medication for bulimia. One analysis included 9 double-blind, placebo-controlled medication trials (870 patients) and 26 randomized psychotherapy studies (460 patients). When compared to medication, cognitive-behavior therapy produced significantly larger effect sizes for all types of treatment outcomes (Whittal et al., 1999). Further, behavior changes produced by psychotherapy endure at follow-up in contrast to medication where relapse rates are high (e.g., Johnson et al., 1996; Thompson-Brenner et al., 2003). These quantitative results correspond to the results of a multicenter comparisons of cognitive-behavioral therapy and interpersonal therapy (Agras et al., 2000) in suggesting that CBT is a treatment of choice for bulimia.

Another meta-analysis of 38 studies confirmed that CBT outperformed both no treatment and pharmacotherapy (mainly antidepressants) for binge eating disorder. The authors concluded that cognitive-behavioral interventions should be recommended as a first-line treatment (Vocks et al., 2010).

Although cognitive therapy may enjoy a clinical and statistical advantage over other treatments, the long-term effects of all therapies on eating disorders are rather modest (Wilson, 1999). In the multicenter study of bulimia, for example, only 8% of patients completing IPT and 45% of patients completing CBT had stopped binge eating and purging by the end of treatment. If we also consider in the analyses those patients who started therapy but dropped out (**intent-to-treat analysis**), then the results are even more disappointing. Only 6% of those treated with IPT had stopped binge eating and purging by intent-to-treat analyses, compared with 29% of those treated with CBT (Agras et al., 2000). While CBT proves more effective than no therapy, medication alone, and perhaps some other therapies for eating disorders, it cannot rest on its laurels until success rates reach higher levels.

Chronic Pain

Multicomponent cognitive and cognitive-behavioral therapies are generally effective in the treatment of chronic pain. That is the conclusion of meta-analyses on randomized controlled trials of CBT for pain in adults (Hoffman et al., 2007) and children (Eccleston et al., 2002). Among adults, the 22 studies showed positive effects of psychological interventions, contrasted with control groups, on pain intensity, behavioral disability, and quality of life (ESs = 0.41, 0.23, and 0.41). Cognitive-behavioral and self-regulatory treatments were specifically found to be efficacious. Among children, the 18 studies provide strong evidence that brief cognitive-behavior therapy is effective in reducing the severity and frequency of chronic pain.

Body Dysmorphic Disorder

This disorder is characterized by an imaginary defect in appearance or an excessive concern with a slight physical abnormality. A meta-analysis of 15 studies compared the effectiveness of pharmacological and psychological treatments for the disorder (Williams et al., 2007). Antidepressant medications were indeed effective (ES = 0.92) but cognitive therapy was even more effective (ES = 1.78). Such findings are consistent with meta-analytic conclusions on other disorders that suggest a slight advantage of CBT over pharmacological treatments.

Personality Disorders

A meta-analytic review of the effectiveness of psychotherapy in the treatment of various personality disorders (Leichsenring & Leibing, 2003) found 11 studies using cognitive-behavior therapies. CBT, including Young's schema-focused therapy and Linehan's dialectical behavior therapy (Chapter 11), yielded large overall effect sizes (mean pre- to posttreatment ES = 1.0). The results of CBT were generally the same as for structured psychodynamic therapy; both are effective treatments of personality disorders.

Chronic Fatigue Syndrome

Several meta-analyses have examined the effectiveness of CBT for this common and debilitating health problem (Castell et al., 2011; Malouff et al., 2007; Price et al., 2008). In 15 or 16 controlled trials, the effect sizes for CBT all fell into the moderate range (0.33, 0.39, and 0.48) at the end of treatment and compared to control conditions. The average dropout rate from treatment was 16%. Forty to fifty percent of the patients who completed CBT showed a clinical response compared to 26% in usual care. Overall, the results of the three meta-analyses of virtually the same studies concluded that CBT for chronic fatigue syndrome is moderately efficacious, more so than no treatment or treatment as usual, and equally efficacious as graded exercise therapy. However, CBT tends to more effective than alternative treatments when patients have comorbid anxiety and depressive symptoms.

Pathological Gambling

A meta-analytic review investigated the short- and long-term effects of psychological treatments of pathological gambling (Pallesen et al., 2005). Most of the treatments were CBT or eclectic in nature. At posttreatment, the analysis indicated that psychotherapy was substantially more effective than no treatment, yielding a very large ES of 2.0. At follow-up (averaging 17 months), the corresponding ES was still a large 1.5. Psychological interventions for pathological gambling are quite effective, with CBT leading the way.

Psychotic Disorders

As cognitive therapy has matured, it has tackled more severe and complex disorders, such as personality disorders and psychotic disorders. At least a dozen meta-analyses have now appeared on the effectiveness of cognitive therapy and broader cognitive-behavior therapy in the treatment of psychoses. All of the meta-analyses report modest effect sizes, with the strongest evidence available for chronic patients and the negative symptoms of schizophrenia (Tarrier & Wykes, 2004; Wykes et al., 2008). Social skills training, psychoeducational

coping interventions with families, and cognitive-behavioral therapy emerge as effective adjuncts to pharmacotherapy (Pfammatter et al., 2006).

A typical meta-analysis (Rector & Beck, 2001) concludes that CBT produces meaningful clinical effects on measures of positive and negative symptoms of schizophrenia. Patients receiving both routine care (including medication) and CBT achieved gains above and beyond those obtained by patients receiving routine care (including medication) and supportive therapy. Follow-up analyses in four studies found that patients receiving CT continued to make gains over time (Gould et al., 2001). Of course, CBT does not "cure" schizophrenia, but it does appear to speed recovery in acute schizophrenia and delay reoccurrences. The critical question now becomes whether CBT produces any clear advantage over other, and sometimes much less expensive, therapies for people with schizophrenia (Jones et al., 2012).

Marital and Group Therapy

The evaluation of cognitive therapy has not been limited to individual psychotherapy. Cognitive-behavior marital therapy emphasizes overt attempts to identify and change partners' maladaptive cognitions concerning themselves, their partner, or the relationship. A meta-analysis of CBT marital therapy (Dunn & Schewebel, 1995) yielded mean effect sizes of 0.54 in terms of behavioral improvement in the relationship and 0.78 for cognitive improvements. Couples treated with cognitive therapy improved significantly more than untreated couples but did not improve more or less than couples receiving behavioral marital therapy or insight-oriented marital therapy.

A similar effect size emerges from a meta-analysis of group CBT (Petrocelli, 2002). The analysis involved 22 published studies and 8 doctoral dissertations that used CBT in group therapy to reduce general symptomatology. The overall pretreatment to posttreatment mean effect size was 0.77. That effect size translates into a 68% success rate with group CBT.

Domestic Violence

Lest we be accused of presenting only favorable reviews of cognitive therapy's effectiveness, we will mention the sobering results of a meta-analytic review of 22 studies evaluating the treatment efficacy for domestically violent men (Babcock et al., 2004). Overall, treatment effects on batterers were in the small range, meaning that current treatments have a minimal impact on reducing recidivism beyond the effect of being arrested. There were no differences in effect sizes between CBT and other psychotherapies; none were particularly effective for this refractory population (Smedslund et al., 2009).

Homework Assignments

Although the use of homework assignments or between-session experiments is not limited to CBT, the research on their effectiveness is. Several meta-analyses have investigated the effectiveness of homework assignments in cognitive and behavioral therapy (Kazantzis et al., 2000; Mausbach et al., 2010); the largest examined 46 studies encompassing 1,072 patients (Kazantzis et al., 2010). The meta-analysis found that homework assignments definitely produced greater outcomes than did psychotherapy consisting entirely of in-session work; the mean effect size ($d = 0.48$) was in the medium range. Homework assignments enhance therapy outcomes, and actual compliance with those assignments adds more benefit to treatment outcome (Mausbach et al., 2010).

Differential Response

A cardinal task of psychotherapy outcome research is to identify those particular disorders and patients for which a psychotherapy system is especially effective. A series of prospective studies by Beutler and colleagues (see Beutler & Harwood, 2000; Beutler, Harwood, Kimpara et al., 2011; Beutler, Harwood, Michelson et al., 2011) identified differential effectiveness of Beck's cognitive therapy as a function of a particular patient's coping style and resistance. Externalizing depressed patients improved more than internalizing depressed patients in cognitive therapy; cognitive therapy and CBT seem to work especially well with acting out and disruptive behaviors. Patients with low resistance improved more in cognitive therapy as well. Low resistance allows the cognitive therapist to be more active and directive. These results suggest patient characteristics can be used to selectively assign psychotherapies; in this case, cognitive therapy is particularly valuable with externalizing coping styles and low-resistance patients.

Criticisms of Cognitive Therapies
From a Behavioral Perspective

Although Ellis appropriately advocated the scientist as an ideal, he acted primarily as a rationalist and a philosopher. Of his hundreds of articles and books on REBT, only a handful report properly controlled experiments on its effectiveness. An examination of published outcome studies on REBT reveals troubling figures: In half of the studies, no information was provided on whether manuals were used to guide treatment; in half of the studies, no information was provided in how well the treatment adhered to REBT specifications; and in the vast majority of studies, no formal assessment was performed on the extent to which REBT could be distinguished from comparison treatments (Haaga et al., 1991). With such a widely touted therapy and with such a large number of REBT publications available, it is difficult to rationalize how a therapist advocating empirical solutions has himself produced so much dialogue and so little data.

The voluminous research on Beck's multicomponent cognitive therapy proves something in it works, but not how it works or how people become disordered. What data are there, for example, to support the Beck's central assumption that disorders are primarily a function of a person's beliefs about antecedent events rather than a function of the events themselves? Are we to believe that traumatic events such as being beaten by one's mother, molested by one's father, rejected by peers, and ridiculed by teachers are less significant in producing emotional disturbances in children than are the beliefs that children possess about these events? Are we to believe that emotionally disturbed people are primarily victims of their own dysfunctional thinking rather than products of dysfunctional environments? Target pathological environments and reinforcements, not pathological cognitions.

Finally, cognitive therapists should look at the data from their own studies. The hypothesis that the unique mechanism of action in cognitive therapy involves change in underlying cognitions (or schema) has *not* been supported by empirical studies. Instead, many therapies tend to produce cognitive change (Persons & Miranda, 1995). In several studies, the therapist's focus on the impact of distorted cognitions on depressive symptoms does *not* correlate with outcome at the end of treatment (Castonguay et al., 1996). Behavioral activation (Chapter 9) is probably the effective component of cognitive therapy, not the cognitive restructuring (Jacobson et al., 2001). Don't confuse cause and consequence: The behavioral techniques, not the cognitive techniques, in cognitive therapy probably cause the consequence of improved thinking.

From a Psychoanalytic Perspective

REBT replaces the irrational demands of a primitive and parental superego with demands from an authoritative clinician who teaches submissive patients to accept a questionable philosophy of life. Clients come to be cured, and instead they are converted. Using some of the oldest forms of converting people to a new faith, cognitive therapists systematically tear apart the patient's worldview.

Confronted by therapists adept in debate tactics and Socratic dialogues, patients are made even more confused as their own explanations for their problems are characterized as dysfunctional, irrational, and immature. As patients are made to feel defenseless by the onslaught of the therapist ramming away at their ego processes, they become more vulnerable to whatever the therapist is selling. In place of old defenses, the cognitive therapist offers intellectualization and rationalization. The cognitive therapist offers a philosophical system that is glamorized as logical and empirical but is in reality a grand word game.

From a Humanistic Perspective

Where have cognitive therapists been during the 21st century to not recognize that the problem for most people is that they cannot feel enough, rather than that they feel too much? Alienation, not a negative schema, is the syndrome of our age. Alienation includes the inability of many people to experience the strong emotions that are part of being human. Emotions like horror, awe, terror, and anger may be unpleasant, but they are not inherently dysfunctional.

Yes, it may be immature to feel awful about getting a C in a course rather than a B. But it is not inappropriate or immature to feel awful about genocide and global warming. It may be irrational to become enraged over missing a bus, but it is not irrational to be outraged over children dying from preventable diseases. Too many people have lost the ability to be outraged over the continuing injustices of society. Let's not think problems away; let's use our emotions to fuel constructive change. Feel more, not less!

From a Cultural Perspective

The focus in cognitive therapies is obviously on thinking as opposed to other human processes. "Rational thinking" and the scientific orientation may fit well with the preferred processes of White, male European Americans. However, they may neither fit nor respond to the diverse ways of knowing of non-Whites, nonmales, and non-Europeans. Ways of knowing associated with some feminist and multicultural orientations—intuition, spirituality, and connection, to name a few—are ignored or devalued in cognitive treatments (Kantrowitz & Ballou, 1992). Cognitive therapists would have us believe that reliance on rational thinking is the be-all and end-all of effective human existence, but many feel and intuit otherwise.

A cornerstone of cognitive therapy is the notion that thinking is the primary determinant of one's feelings. If you wish to alter distressing feelings, then you alter the belief system. But challenging beliefs does not fit well with some cultures and genders. Many Asians, for example, have been taught to create harmony and to avoid conflict. Must we pathologize these beliefs and challenge them simply because they do not fit cognitive therapy's narrow, rational framework? Indeed, the very terms of cognitive therapy—testing, challenging, disputing, restructuring—force a stereotypically masculine view of beating inaccurate beliefs into submission and may reinforce a woman's sense of inadequacy.

We should also note, as we have in criticizing all the intrapsychic therapies, that cognitive treatment maintains the internal, mentalistic locus of psychopathology. The problems with people and the way to fix them are located inside the individual's head, rather than out in the culture and in the world. Now that's an "irrational" belief!

From an Integrative Perspective

Cognitive therapies make the same mental mistake of many patients and many true believers—overgeneralization. Rather than assume a reasonable position that some patients distress themselves by thinking in demanding or absolute terms, cognitive therapies jump to the generalization that virtually all patients do so. Instead of positing that many patients will profit by modifying their "awfulizing" and "catastrophizing," cognitive therapists behave as though cognitive therapy is the treatment of choice for everyone. These overgeneralizations negate the tragic side of life and devalue the emotional side of humans. Reason can be used to help patients discriminate between truly tragic, catastrophic events in life and those unpleasant events that need not lead to emotional upsets.

Likewise, cognitive therapy overgeneralizes about the status of certain emotions. A case in point is the insistence that anxiety is neurotic and self-induced. Such a universal generalization can encourage people to be anxious about being anxious rather than accepting some anxiety as healthy and authentic, such as anxiety over major decisions or death. In the areas of values and morality, REBT insists that shoulds, oughts, and musts are immature and inappropriate. A value judgment that holds that a person must be clean and orderly to be decent may indeed be destructive. The generalization, however, that any moral imperative is foolish could be even more destructive of human morale. A judgment that Nazism was unfortunate or regrettable would have been less likely to inspire people to put their lives on the line than was the absolute belief that all that is decent in human nature demanded an end to the evil of Nazism.

A Cognitive Analysis of Mrs. C

With her compulsive desire for order, Mrs. C could appreciate an explanation of her problems that is as simple as ABC. She is already keenly aware of A, the activating event, which was the case of pinworms contracted by her daughter. She is equally aware of the C, the emotional consequences of that event—namely, her morbid dread of pinworms and her compulsive need to wash. Like most patients and even some psychotherapists, however, Mrs. C is relatively unaware of how B, her belief system, has transformed an irritating case of pinworms into a catastrophe.

Mrs. C may have difficulty accepting that she has actively produced and maintained her own miserable world. She has convinced herself that pinworms are a terrible and awful event. She may, however, be able to appreciate how totally she has condemned herself for having allowed diseases such as the Asian flu and pinworms to infect her family. Mrs. C may be able to agree that she does believe not only that the pinworms were terrible, but that she was horrible for letting them occur. What a worm she is for being such a careless mother: An ideal mother, a perfect mother, would never let such a terrible thing happen! But Mrs. C failed to adequately protect her children from disease, and she believes she deserves to be condemned like a worthless worm. What a deserving target she is for pinworms: lowly, lousy, and loathsome. No wonder she feels so vulnerable to being infested by worms.

Mrs. C has probably always had a strong propensity to think in absolutes, particularly the belief that she must behave perfectly in order to be worthwhile. Of course, her parents encouraged such irrational beliefs by their own absolutist demands that she be perfectly clean, free of disease and of desires. Nevertheless, Mrs. C took to such teachings as if they were true because of her predisposition to think that perfection is possible. Her perfectionist beliefs were evidenced in her desire for order as reflected in the alphabetical naming of her children and in her need to be clean even before her full-blown compulsions developed.

Irrational thinking was clearly present throughout her life; all it took to produce psychopathology was a stressful activating event like a series of illnesses to set off her absolute, catastrophizing tendencies.

After Mrs. C thought herself catastrophic, she further frightened herself into believing that she must do everything within her power to prevent a recurrence. She must work compulsively lest she or her family become recontaminated. We can predict that she also engages in frequent self-condemnation for being so terribly compulsive. What a worm she is for always washing and never caring for her children! What a wife she is for always showering and never loving! The vicious cycle of self-condemnation will progress to condemning herself as a failure for not improving after years of psychotherapy, for wanting to kill herself, and for letting her family and her therapist down. What better evidence for her worthlessness than the fact that her husband and her therapist are prepared to commit her to the state psychiatric hospital.

A closer look would probably reveal that Mrs. C may well be psychotic and a probable candidate for hospitalization if effective outpatient treatment is not forthcoming. Like most patients diagnosed as severe neurotic (Beck et al., 1979; Ellis, 1973), Mrs. C evidences many signs of a thinking disorder characteristic of borderline or ambulatory schizophrenic patients. For example, Mrs. C has problems in focusing on a realistic solution to her problems because she is overfocused on pinworms. She perseverates as she thinks over and over and over again about pinworms. She also magnifies the dangers of pinworms entirely out of realistic proportions, becoming almost delusional in her belief that she is constantly surrounded by pinworms waiting to infest her.

An accurate diagnosis of Mrs. C as an ambulatory psychotic would serve as a warning not to expect psychotherapy to make her entirely free of pathology. That diagnosis would also lead to evaluation for psychotropic medication to augment cognitive therapy. Nevertheless, she and her family would be quite satisfied with having her return to her pre-pinworm level of compulsive adjustment.

(continued)

To make such a return, Mrs. C will need to learn to dispute her intensely irrational beliefs and to restructure her obsessive-compulsive schema about the world. She will have to learn that the pinworm event was catastrophic only because she defined it as such. As the cognitive therapist gently challenges her to think about the worst thing that could happen as a result of her OCD, she can begin to see that although such consequences would be irritating and unpleasant, they are by no means terrible or horrible.

Nor is Mrs. C a worm because her daughter once had pinworms. Mrs. C's self-condemnation will need to be challenged repeatedly by the therapist until she can begin to recognize that nothing she has done or failed to do is deserving of such condemnation. She will be taught USA—unconditional self-acceptance. She can go on condemning herself to a compulsive existence if she continues to engage in demanding, absolutist thinking, or she can begin to rely more on what rational powers she possesses to work against the irrational beliefs that distort her world.

With strong propensities toward dysfunctional thinking, Mrs. C will have to work hard at disputing her OCD-driving beliefs. A variety of homework assignments is in order. For starters, Mrs. C will be instructed to familiarize herself with basic tenets of REBT by reading, for instance, *How to Stubbornly Refuse to Make Yourself Miserable about Anything—Yes, Anything!* (Ellis, 1988). She will be asked to review the tapes of her psychotherapy sessions to identify her frequent use of such demanding concepts as *must*, *should*, *necessary*, *have to*, and *ought to*. She will be assigned to practice substituting more rational terms such as *want to*, *prefer to*, and *it would be better* for the many demanding things she tells herself. She may also be assigned to research the idea that a good mother must keep her children free from any disease in order to be a worthwhile human being, as a means of challenging her self-condemnation. Her husband will also be given important homework assignments, such as reading *How to Live with a Neurotic* (Ellis, 1957a) or *Love Is Never Enough* (Beck, 1988), so that he can begin to deal with her rationally rather than colluding with her neurosis.

Eventually, Mrs. C may begin to correct her thinking and thus defuse the consequences of pinworms. She may become more fully conscious of the fact that pinworms may be a pain, but they are not the worst of all possible fates; they may be unpleasant, but they are not catastrophic. The therapist will interpret how dysfunctional beliefs have led Mrs. C to continue to upset herself emotionally. Mrs. C needs to become aware that the source of her problems is not pinworms, but rather the way in which she thinks about pinworms. Her problem is not her imperfections as a wife and mother, but rather what she believes her imperfections mean to her worth as a human being.

Only if Mrs. C can learn to actively dispute such beliefs (and that is a big if) can she become free to enjoy some of life rather than waste herself away on foolish washing. Mrs. C can find some joy in life if she learns to quit insisting on more order and perfection than the universe provides, when the best we can do is accept ourselves as imperfect beings who can live happily in an imprecise world.

Future Directions

The safest prediction about cognitive therapy's direction is that it is moving up. Cognitive-behavioral therapies in general, and Beckian cognitive therapy in particular, are the fastest growing and most heavily researched systems of psychotherapy on the contemporary scene. The reasons for its current popularity are manifest: Cognitive therapy is manualized, relatively brief, extensively evaluated, medication compatible, problem focused, and demonstrably effective. Its research support is unmatched in the history of psychotherapy. Let us put it this way: If we were forced to purchase stock in any of the psychotherapy systems, Beck's cognitive therapy would be the blue-chip growth selection for the next decade.

Ellis's stock seems to be declining, whereas Beck's is climbing. The reasons for this state of affairs are conjecture, but Beck is certainly less controversial than Ellis, who favored expletive-laced lectures on the advantages of atheism and sexual freedom. Beck is more collaborative, Ellis more confrontational. Cognitive therapy is more precise and empirically based; REBT is more general and philosophically based. Beck holds prestigious academic appointments, whereas Ellis has always lived outside the halls of academe. Beck and his followers have garnered more teaching positions, federal grants, and controlled research trials than Ellis and his followers. A colleague summed it up by observing that Ellis acts like an entertaining New York taxi driver, whereas Beck behaves like an Ivy-League university professor (which he is).

Two reasons for cognitive therapy's current popularity—commitment to psychotherapy integration and dedication to empirical evaluation—will characterize its future as well. Since its introduction in the 1950s, REBT has become increasingly eclectic in methodology and content (Ellis, 1987b). REBT clinicians adopt many types of techniques, particularly the active and directive ones, from disparate schools (Ellis, 1999; Ellis & Dryden, 2007). Beck's cognitive therapy is equally committed to the cross-fertilization of psychotherapy systems. In fact, the construction and stance of his perspective have led some to describe it as an integrative therapy (Alford & Beck, 1997a). Cognitive methods are commonly blended into other therapies, as reviewed in Chapter 16; in fact, one particular integration with psychoanalytic therapy, known as **cognitive analytic therapy (CAT)**, is quite popular in Europe (Ryle, 1990, 1995).

Moreover, the ongoing dedication to examining the effectiveness of cognitive therapy will keep it in good stead among the scientific, practitioner, and insurance communities in an era of evidence-based practice (see Chapter 18). The widening application of cognitive therapy to more disabling conditions—such as bipolar disorder, schizophrenia, health disorders, and personality disorders—will ensure its relevance to an increasing number of therapists and patients.

A word of caution needs to be raised about its future. Large effect sizes indicate that if patients are willing and able to be treated with CBT, they are likely to get better. But the majority of individuals suffering from anxiety disorders do not receive CBT (Gunter & Whittal, 2010). Research suggests that only 4% to 11% of individuals with anxiety disorders seek mental health treatment at all (Mojtabai et al., 2002; Young et al., 2001). Among those who do seek treatment and have access to trained cognitive therapists, initiation and retention are problematic. Pretreatment attrition among patients who are evaluated and diagnosed with anxiety disorders is between 30% and 52% (Coles et al., 2004; Issakidis & Andrews, 2004; Mancebo et al., 2011); the dropout among patients who actually begin treatment is between 20% and 30% (Mancebo et al., 2011; Swift & Greenberg, 2012). These findings highlight the pressing future need for evidence-based treatments, cognitive and otherwise, to become more accessible and more engaging. Otherwise, our most effective treatments will reach only a small percentage of the population in need.

Befitting its status as a premier system of psychotherapy, cognitive therapy is moving rapidly to train health care professionals in its methods. These dissemination and implementation efforts have penetrated the largest health care systems in the developed countries: the British National Health Service, which has committed more than $250 million to training and employing thousands of additional psychotherapists primarily in CBT, and the US Veterans Affairs health care system, which has undertaken a national effort to disseminate CBT (Karlin et al., 2012). These experiences attest that large numbers of therapists, practicing in both urban and rural settings, can be trained in CBT to competency and in a manner that promotes sustained delivery of the treatment well after the completion of training. And, since CBT has been shown cost-effective in low- and middle-income countries as well (van't Hof et al., 2011), dissemination will be increasingly going global.

What else is the future of cognitive therapy? Just look on the web or your smartphone. Computer-based psychological treatments and self-help programs are overwhelmingly in the cognitive-behavioral tradition (Norcross et al., 2013). Yep, there's an (CBT) app for that.

Cognitive therapy's commitment to computerized interventions, international dissemination, psychotherapy integration, and research evaluation keeps it growing. The intense interest in the **third-wave therapies** (covered in Chapter 11) represents a recent evolution, but it is premature to predict whether the third wave will make a lasting impression on the shoreline or be washed away in the next tide. However, we can confidently predict that cognitive therapy will continue to evolve and flourish.

Key Terms

ABC model
activating events (A)
activity scheduling
beliefs (B)
catastrophizing
cognitive analytic
   therapy (CAT)
cognitive processing
   therapy (CPT)
cognitive restructuring
cognitive therapy
cognitive triad
collaborative
   empiricism
consequences (C)
content specificity
   hypothesis
depressogenic
   (depression-causing)
   assumptions
dichotomous thinking
disattribution
   technique
disputing/disputation
   (D)
distancing
dysfunctional
   attitudes/cognitions
effective new
   philosophy (E)
excessive responsibility
hedonism
intent-to-treat analysis
investigator allegiance
irrational beliefs (iBs)
limited reparenting
overgeneralizing
panic control therapy
   (PCT)
PYA—push your ass
rational-emotive
   behavior therapy
   (REBT)
refutations
schema-focused
   psychotherapy
schemas (cognitive
   schemas)
selective abstraction
self-references
shame-attacking
   exercises
Socratic dialogue
third-wave therapies
tyranny of the should
unconditional self-
   acceptance (USA)

Recommended Readings

Barlow, D. H. (Ed.). (2013). *Clinical handbook of psychological disorders: A step-by-step treatment manual* (5th ed.). New York: Guilford.

Beck, J. S. (2011). *Cognitive behavior therapy: Basics and beyond* (2nd ed.). New York: Guilford.

Beck, A. T., Rush, A. J., Shaw, B., & Emery, G. (1979). *Cognitive therapy of depression.* New York: Guilford.

Dobson, K. S. (Ed.). (2009). *Handbook of cognitive-behavioral therapies* (3rd ed.). New York: Guilford.

Ellis, A., & Dryden, W. (2007). *The practice of rational-emotive behavior therapy* (2nd ed.). New York: Springer.

Ellis, A., & Grieger, R. (Eds.). (1986). *Handbook of rational-emotive therapy* (Vols. 1–2). New York: Springer.

Leahy, R. L. (2003). *Cognitive therapy techniques: A practitioner's guide.* New York: Guilford.

Weisz, J. R., & Kazdin, A. E. (2010). *Evidence-based psychotherapies for children and adolescents* (2nd ed.). New York: Guilford.

JOURNALS: *Behavior Therapy; Behavioural and Cognitive Psychotherapy; Cognitive Behaviour*

Therapy; Cognitive & Behavioral Practice; Cognitive Therapy and Research; International Journal of Cognitive Therapy; Journal of Cognitive Psychotherapy; Journal of Rational-Emotive & Cognitive-Behavior Therapy.

Recommended Websites

Albert Ellis Institute:
   www.albertellisinstitute.org

Association for Behavioral and Cognitive Therapies:
   www.abct.org/home/
Beck Institute for Cognitive Behavior Therapy:
   www.beckinstitute.org
International Association for Cognitive Psychotherapy:
   www.the-iacp.com
International Society of Schema Therapy:
   www.isst-online.com/

CHAPTER 11

Third-Wave Therapies

Steven Hayes

Marsha Linehan

A distinguished 84-year-old woman from Japan has worn polka dots every day for more than 50 years. All of her artwork is covered with polka dots as well. She says that her obsession with polka dots began with her childhood hallucinations as she stared into a pond near her house. She had an abusive father, and she left Japan for New York at a young age to pursue her art career. Now she is famous for her polka dot paintings, sculptures, and lighting displays. Her art is included in major museums around the world and her work sells for millions of dollars.

But she lives in a private psychiatric hospital in Japan. This artist has had the courage to accept her psychotic experiences as a source of inspiration and creativity rather than a source of fear that must be hidden or shame that must be avoided. This active artist is a striking example of how the third wave of behavior therapies, like **acceptance and commitment therapy (ACT)** and **dialectical behavior therapy (DBT)**, help people to accept challenging experiences and to commit themselves to act on their fundamental values.

Cognitive-behavioral therapy has steadily evolved from its early stirrings in strict behavior therapy (the first wave) to its contemporary manifestation in cognitive therapy (the second wave). It is now poised for its third wave, which incorporates acceptance and mindfulness into standard cognitive-behavioral therapies (Hayes et al., 2004; Segal et al., 2002).

Third-wave therapies like ACT, DBT, and several variants of mindfulness interventions represent a combination of Western and Eastern philosophy, science, and practice. From the West, they build on behavioral and cognitive therapies, including skill building, cognitive reframing, and exposure to fears. However, rather than teaching people to control their thoughts, feelings, memories, and other private events, they draw from the Eastern traditions of noticing, accepting, and enhancing private events, especially previously unwanted experiences.

In this chapter, we consider in detail the two most developed and popular forms of third-wave therapies: acceptance and commitment therapy and dialectical behavior therapy. We then review **mindfulness-based cognitive therapy (MBCT)** as an example of mindfulness approaches. Given that these three theories emerged from behavioral and cognitive therapies, the focus here will be on their innovative perspectives on psychopathology, therapeutic processes, and relationships without separate sections on personality and therapeutic content.

A Sketch of Steven Hayes

ACT emerged from early influences on its primary developer, Steven Hayes (1948–), who grew up in Southern California in the 1960s during the heyday of the hippie counterculture. He came to psychology with a keen interest in how this culture impacts human development, as represented in Maslow's self-actualization. In B. F. Skinner's (1948) utopian novel, *Walden Two*, Hayes found a way of combining his interest in well-being with science. In the context of the counterculture, he developed an interest in Eastern philosophy and lived for several months in an Eastern religious commune in Grass Valley, California (Waltz & Hayes, 2010).

Getting into graduate school was unusually difficult, because of a negative letter from a professor who described his hippie appearance. After 2 years of failure, he was accepted into the clinical psychology program at West Virginia University, a stronghold of behavior analysis, based heavily on Skinner's science (Chapter 9).

Early in his academic career, Hayes and colleagues were immersed in the cognitive therapy (CT) of Aaron Beck (Chapter 10). They focused on one treatment component, cognitive distancing, because it seemed to overlap with Eastern traditions and behavior analysis. The process of mining thoughts objectively is called **distancing**. Any technique that facilitates a client's ability to hold thoughts as hypotheses (distancing) rather than literal truth is considered useful in CT. The aim of distancing in CT is to gain greater objectivity when evaluating thoughts.

Hayes (1987) conducted a functional analysis on cognitive distancing in CT and found the concept to be unnecessarily narrow. In CT, cognitive distancing should be applied to each dysfunctional thought as it occurs (e.g., Can you hold that thought as a hypothesis rather than a fact?). But, behavior analysis of language indicates that there is nothing special about each particular dysfunctional thought. Thoughts alone cannot directly cause distress or ineffective behavior. In behavior analysis, thoughts and feelings are not treated as causes but as behaviors under contextual influence. To change the impact of thoughts and feelings, one needs to change their context. Distancing techniques can establish a less literal, concrete, or factual context that can weaken the impact of language on behavior.

A first-semester graduate student felt quite depressed over being lonely in a new place and not functioning effectively in class. His most troubling thought was, "I'm not myself and I will never be myself again." Taken as a fact, this thought would likely lead to feeling depressed and acting ineffectively. Viewed as only one lightly held hypothesis, however, the student is free to consider an alternative hypothesis: "Maybe I am not feeling like myself because I am feeling depressed, and if I commit to more effective action, I may feel more like the kind of self I want to be."

It was Hayes's own panic disorder that crystallized his development of ACT. He watched in horror as his panic grew rapidly, simply by applying his normal problem-solving skills to it. He tried lots of things to reduce the anxiety, but those efforts meant that he had to constantly evaluate the level of anxiety and fearfully check to see if it was going up or down as a result of his efforts. As a result, anxiety quickly became the central focus of his life. After 2 or 3 years of compounding his anxiety, Hayes experimented with acceptance and valued action instead of detecting and disputing his insides. Although not an instant cure, his life gradually opened up again and the panic dissipated. Twenty years of research later, largely through his professorship at the University of Nevada-Reno, ACT emerged as a system of psychotherapy.

ACT Theory of Psychopathology

Western psychology typically operates under the "healthy normality" assumption, which posits that by their nature, humans are psychologically healthy. ACT assumes instead that psychological processes of a normal human mind are often destructive. Rather than psychopathology being a function of some people having troubled minds, all people have minds that can produce troubling thoughts, especially when such thoughts are not processed effectively.

At the core of many psychological disorders is the attempt to alter unwanted private events (thoughts, feelings, impulses) even when decreasing their intensity, frequency, or duration causes behavioral problems. This struggle is seen as a functional class of behavior called **experiential avoidance** (Hayes et al., 1996). Such avoidance can persist because immediately distracting oneself can result in immediate reduction, which is reinforcing. But, these efforts increase the importance of such private events: "They are really scary, depressing or troubling, and I must avoid such experiences."

Western culture, in particular, often supports linguistic contexts that facilitate continued struggles with trying to avoid undesirable thoughts and feelings. The constant commands of teachers and parents to "be quiet, be still, be good, behave" can convince kids that any thoughts, feelings, or impulses to behave more expressively must be bad, troubling, or abnormal. Such controlling contexts produce **cognitive fusion**, which is the domination of private events that are taken literally.

Cognitive fusion leads to over control of language, including loss of contact with the present moment and the tendency to take stances about the self literally: "I am not myself and I never will be myself again!" This can interfere with the ability to behave in accord with one's values. Psychological health is a form of psychological flexibility: changing when change is needed and persisting when persistence is need to accomplish natural ends (Hayes et al., 2004).

ACT Therapeutic Processes

If psychopathology is primarily a function of experiential avoidance of private events and linguistic contexts that produce cognitive fusion (the domination by private events that are taken literally), then dysfunctional behavior can best be modified by changing the clients' contexts. This is best accomplished through processes like cognitive distancing, in which clients can take thoughts as hypotheses rather than facts to be feared and avoided. The focus is not on controlling or changing private events, but on how we process and react to such events.

Consciousness Raising

A **present-moment focus** allows us to be fully aware of the here and now, experienced with openness, interest, and receptiveness. This healthier present focus can help us to let our behavior be influenced more by the present context and less by shame, guilt, or anger from traumatic memories or fear of the future. This mindful approach also supports a context for the **acceptance** process, which allows thoughts and feelings to come and go in our consciousness without struggle. Learning cognitive diffusion methods helps clients shift from the context that takes thoughts and emotions literally, as facts that must be followed, to a context where such experiences can be taken as hypotheticals that need not control our behavior.

The Eastern philosophy of exercising self as perspective can facilitate clients accessing a transcendent sense of self, a continuity of consciousness that is unchanging. If my sense of self is narrow, concrete, and rigid, it will probably keep me stuck in narrow and rigid patterns of behavior. If my sense of self is "I am a schizophrenic," how much more confining is that than having self as a special perspective, like the artist who perceived her world through polka dot glasses. Her unique perspective transcended her abusive childhood, her rigid cultural context, and her visual hallucinations. Her continuity of consciousness existed across her lifespan, across the countries she lived, and across her artistic creations. Her self as special perspective has inspired and challenged so many people to view "reality" from the often beautiful but unusual perspective of polka dots.

Choosing

As individuals become freer to be—to live in the present, to accept their private experiences, and to not have to verify such experiences—they are constructing a foundation for choosing their behaviors rather than driven by their fears. On what basis will they make such choices once they are prepared to let go of their rigid past or anxious future? **Values.** Discovering what is most important to their true self is the next process that provides healthier behaving. Techniques like **values clarification** can help individuals decide which values provide the best context for choosing, rather than be controlled by their cultural context that requires they fill a rigid role, like a student, a teacher, a patient, a factory worker, or a farmer.

Committed action is the process of setting goals according to values and carrying them out responsibly. It needs to be recognized that clients can act on their personal values even if, or especially if, they continue to experience private events that can be evaluated as pathological. Witness again the polka dot princess who transformed her lifelong hallucinations into a sense of self that was committed to her values to create art that reflected her special perspective.

Catharsis

Steven Hayes would say let the feelings flow; let them come and go. Don't hold onto them, as if they are the most important experiences in life. Don't avoid them as if they are the most scary things in life that can cause you to behave badly. Accept the flow of feelings, as normal, like the flow of thoughts, images, and memories. At the same time, don't overvalue feelings as the experiential basis on which to act. Look to your core values that reflect your fundamental sense of self and let those values guide your committed actions.

Counterconditioning

How does ACT help clients counter their overlearned habits of avoiding private perspectives? By focusing on the present. That's what assists clients in learning to remain with their thoughts and feelings (even when unpleasant) with openness and interest. Acceptance of such experiences and inviting them to come and go can counter the teaching to avoid them. The healthy opposite of controlling and avoiding is accepting. Cognitive distancing can diffuse the fears that accompany reifying thoughts and feelings as the real causes of acting. Such acceptance can replace the avoidance, and then committed action based on true-self values brings healthier behaviors that can replace dysfunctional behaviors.

ACT Therapeutic Relationship

ACT therapists often relate to clients like experienced coaches or trainers who initially help clients to identify the private events that interfere with more effective action. Thoughts or feelings of being inferior, unlikeable or unattractive, for example, can lead to avoidance by turning to overeating, drinking, or sitting at home watching TV. The trainer asks **workability** questions, such as, how do such reactive behaviors work out for you? While they produce immediate avoidance and thus temporary relief from distressing feelings, clients can become aware of how poorly these behaviors work in the long run by leading to greater loneliness, anxiety, or depression.

Once aware of how avoiding such private events produces ineffective responses, clients are taught mindfulness techniques that help them stay in the present. As mindfulness trainers, therapists teach clients distancing or diffusion techniques that permit them to stay in the present and to accept private events as verbal behaviors that need not be verified, judged, or avoided. They are neither scorned nor esteemed; they just are and can be accepted without troubling consequences. "It is what it is," as the saying goes, often with a shrug of the shoulders.

As therapy progresses, ACT practitioners may function as a value clarification trainer, helping clients to identify values that are most important to their true self. Committing to action in the presence of the therapist strengthens client's commitments. Then like an accountable coach, therapists follow up to help hold clients responsible for their commitments.

While specifically addressing verbal behaviors as private events that retard effective action, ACT also recognizes that the lack of skills, like social skills, can be important barriers. Here ACT therapists function as behavior analysts, who can engage in skill training, using techniques from traditional behavior therapy (Chapter 9). Like an expert ski or music instructor, ACT therapists need to evaluate when clients are progressing enough to move from early more experiential phases of therapy, like staying in the present, to more behavioral phases, like values clarification and committed action based on such values. Along this journey, clients are encouraged to engage in acceptance and change work—not in the hope of feeling better—but instead, in the hope of living better.

A Sketch of Marsha Linehan

We now turn to the second of the third-wave or acceptance therapies: DBT, beginning with its influential founder. Marsha Linehan (1943–) developed DBT in the 1970s to more effectively treat clients who were chronically suicidal or self-injurious and often suffered from borderline personality disorder (BPD). Her work with such challenging clients grew out of her early self-image as a missionary who wanted to help the most miserable people in the world (Linehan, 2000). Her plan until her senior year of college was to become a psychiatrist and to work on the back wards of a state mental hospital, but at the last minute, she realized that there were few medical treatments for mental disorders that worked. She realized that she needed to become both a scientist and a practitioner, and received a PhD in experimental-personality psychology in 1971 at Loyola University of Chicago. A 1-year internship followed at the Suicide Prevention and Crisis Clinic in Buffalo, New York. She went on to postdoctoral training at State University of New York (SUNY) at Stony Brook and worked with Gerald Davison and Marvin Goldfried on clinical behavior therapy. Indeed, to this day,

Linehan prefers that DBT be categorized as an *expanded behavior therapy.*

Linehan wanted to apply behavior therapy with difficult-to-treat clients but found such clients were not always willing or able to cooperate. Many clients experienced attempts to change their behavior as invalidating, implying that something is wrong with them that they need to get rid of. Common responses were to argue with the therapist or drop out. Faced with such challenges, Linehan developed a psychotherapy that would create a **dialectic** between the thesis of behavior therapy (the client needs to change behaviors) and the antithesis (the therapist needs to accept me for who I am). In the end, clients would achieve a synthesis (balancing change and acceptance). Much of the dialectic was learned directly from her years of experience as a Zen student herself and as a scientist-practitioner at the University of Washington.

Much of DBT and Linehan's mission to assist the most miserable people in the world were forged from her own personal experiences. In 2011, Linehan gave a public lecture at the Institute of Living in Connecticut in which she disclosed her journey through the hell of mental illness and back, which began when she was admitted as a patient to the Institute of Living at age 17 for long-term residential treatment. She was admitted after injuring herself and for what would now be probably diagnosed as BPD. The years of treatment resulted in her subsequent efforts to return to hell to get others out of their misery.

DBT Theory of Psychopathology

Unlike ACT that views psychopathological thoughts and emotions as products of normal minds, DBT views borderline personalities as products of genetic and social abnormalities. Individuals with BPD have a biological predisposition for heightened sensitivity and reactivity (quick and strong reactions) to emotionally evocative stimuli, as well as delays in letting go of the emotional arousal. Individuals with such biological dispositions are especially vulnerable to social environments that invalidate the individual's expression of emotions and thoughts through punishing, ignoring, or trivializing such communications. Add environments with sexual, physical, or emotional abuse and you have pathological conditions that can generate BPD. Such individuals can get intensely angry, hurt, rejected, jealous, depressed, or anxious quickly in response to stimuli that would evoke mild reactions in most people. Such disruptive emotional reactions are likely to lead to serious disruptions in interpersonal relationships, including therapeutic relationships.

DBT Therapeutic Processes

When working with clients who are strongly reactive to communications perceived as critical, rejecting, or invalidating ("Let's talk about what you need to change"), Linehan recognized the need to balance principles of behavior change with principles of radical genuineness and unconditional regard from Carl Rogers's person-centered therapy (Chapter 5). To help clients accept and cope with powerful emotions they may feel when challenging their habits or exposing themselves to upsetting situations, Linehan turned to **mindfulness** and **meditation** derived from Eastern Zen Buddhist practices.

Given the high risk of disruptive events among suicidal and borderline patients, Linehan developed a structured protocol with three priorities. The first priority is for therapists to deal with threats of suicidal or other self-destructive behaviors. The second priority is to focus on threats to the therapeutic relationship, such as dropping out or disrupting treatment. The third priority is skill development, including behavior change skills from behavior therapy, like assertiveness and interpersonal training, and acceptance skills based on mindfulness.

To meet these multiple priorities, DBT is typically divided into individual sessions, for dealing with threats to the client and to treatment, and group sessions where clients can learn and practice more functional behaviors. The skill-based group therapy (Linehan, 1993b) helps each client practice the multiple skills they are learning over the course of ongoing individual therapy.

The overarching focus on the dialectical patterns moves the patient toward more balanced responses to life situations. In Buddhism, this is walking the "middle path" between such dialectical tensions as skill enhancement versus self-acceptance, affect regulation versus affect tolerance, and self-efficacy versus help-seeking.

Consciousness Raising

As with ACT, DBT calls on mindfulness as a core skill that facilitates the capacity to be more conscious of the present moment without judging or rejecting what one is experiencing. Clients learn to *observe* nonjudgmentally their internal and external environments to be more aware and understanding of what is occurring in any given situation. Without judgment statements, they *describe* what they are observing to help others be aware of what is being observed. They can learn to *participate* by focusing most fully on what they are doing and experiencing. By not judging internal and external events as good or bad, fair or unfair, they can begin to better accept events that historically would be emotionally or interpersonally disruptive.

Choosing

Like other third-wave therapies, DBT provides clients choices that go beyond altering distressing behaviors. These therapies train clients to be mindful and accepting of distressing events. The first noble truth of Buddhism is that life is suffering—it entails pain, loneliness, frustration, disease, and ultimately death. This irrefutable fact becomes useful and therapeutic because Buddhism explains how suffering can be coped with: Choose to accept it. Attempting to avoid all pain or distress is usually the single biggest source of suffering. As Buddhists advise, invite your troubles to sit beside you. Instead of trying to change what we don't like about ourselves, others, or the world, we can choose to be more accepting. We can appreciate and inhabit the present, rather than ruminating about our past mistakes and preoccupying ourselves with future anxieties.

Counterconditioning

DBT includes training in a broad range of skills that can reduce vulnerabilities to emotional dysregulation and interpersonal disruption. This approach is based on the premise that even when components of physiological and psychological reactivity are due to immutable genetic dispositions and early developmental experiences, they may still come under the control of the individual. For example, based on empirical evidence, the DBT PLEASE skills target:

- *PhysicaL* illness: If you are sick, get proper treatment
- *E*ating: Eat a healthy diet and in moderation
- *A*void mood-altering drugs that are not prescribed
- *S*leep: Enough but not too much
- *E*xercise: An effective amount of exercise improves body image and reduces distress.

DBT teaches skill sets for other major behavior changes related to **emotional regulation** (or distress tolerance): how to better regulate the intensity, duration, and frequency of intense negative emotions like anger, anxiety, and depression. Similarly, there are DBT skills for **interpersonal effectiveness**, including assertiveness training and communications training.

Probably the most unique set of skills taught in DBT concern **radical acceptance**. These skills require considerable practice, as they run contrary to the human desire to control the physical world and as many of us have been inculcated in the self-destiny worldview. To achieve a deeply attentive, radically accepting state of mind in the present moment is no easy task. DBT therapists thus train patients in mindfulness in and out of therapy sessions, in individual therapy, and in group therapy. Dozens of training activities can be used: becoming aware of bodily sensations, such as taking 5 minutes to experience the sensual pleasures of a single grape; appreciating the moment; practicing mindfulness meditations; and retraining breathing. Perhaps needless to say, DBT is inclusive and ambitious in the range of behavior changes to fulfill Linehan's original mission of helping BPD individuals who might otherwise be among the most miserable people in the world.

The DBT protocol requires that therapists participate in their own consultative and supervisory groups. No single individual should be treating BPD; it truly takes a supportive and coordinated group of professionals. The groups keep DBT therapists from burning out when working with clients who can be so demanding but also so rewarding when they are engaging in the dialectical process of accepting when needed and changing when possible.

DBT Therapeutic Relationship

Since patients with serious problems like BPD have so often been invalidated by parents who were critical, neglectful, rejecting, or abusive, DBT therapists often relate like healthy parental figures. They strive to be radically genuine and accepting, not afraid to genuinely validate such patients for whatever progress they are making. The series of DBT **validation strategies** sound like Rogerian facilitative conditions: responsiveness, self-disclosure, warm engagement, and genuineness (Linehan, 1993a).

Like effective parents, DBT therapists also are not afraid to help their patients set more effective limits on their intense emotional reactions that can disrupt treatment and disrupt relationships. This dialectic results in balancing communication styles as well: sometimes warm and empathic, and other times powerful and confrontational. DBT practitioners will express both omnipotence and impotence depending upon the situation (Linehan, 1993a), just like a responsive parent.

As therapy progresses, DBT therapists shift from parenting to teaching to consulting as the clients progress from accepting emotional and interpersonal events without disruption and as they learn skills that can enhance their emotional and interpersonal functioning. The relentless exposure to clients' disruptive emotions and intense reactions can burn out the best of DBT therapists. Thus, they ensure that they have supportive groups and supervisory consultations that can share the responsibility of caring for and about such patients.

Mindfulness Therapies

Mindfulness can constitute a separate system of psychotherapy or can serve as an important component of other systems, like ACT and DBT. Mindfulness techniques, like meditation, can also be an essential part of how one lives in Eastern spiritual traditions, such as Buddhism, and can be applied by integrative therapists for specific purposes, like managing stress more effectively. Mindfulness skills can be taught in classes or workshops without being part of formal psychotherapy.

Given the multitude of ways to apply mindfulness, it is debatable whether it should best be taught as a psychotherapy system or as a particular technique. What is clear is that mindfulness has enjoyed a long and rich tradition in Eastern views and is a major force in the third-wave therapies. In this section, we will discuss mindfulness in the context of **mindfulness-based cognitive** therapy (MBCT). MBCT began with Beck's (Chapter 10) cognitive therapy for depression, and then added an adaptation of the mindfulness-based stress reduction (MBSR) program developed by Kabat-Zinn (1990) at the University of Massachusetts School of Medicine.

MBCT was created to prevent relapse of major affective disorders, specifically, major depressive disorder (MDD). Individuals who are experiencing their third or greater episode of MDD have a 90% chance of a relapse or reoccurrence of MDD. While continuing with antidepressant medications can reduce the risks of relapse, many individuals do not choose to stay on such medications for a lifetime. When medications are discontinued, relapse is likely to occur relatively quickly.

Many forms of cognitive-behavior therapy have demonstrated effectiveness with depression, but relapse remains a major challenge. Teasdale (1988) studied relapse from a cognitive perspective examining the differential activation hypothesis, which posits that sad moods have the power to reactivate patterns of negative thinking. Even after the resolution of depressive episodes, the links between sadness and negative thinking persist and can lead to a downward spiral that initiates a depressive relapse. Research on this model has examined the construct of cognitive reactivity and has demonstrated the tendency of formerly depressed people to react to mild changes in mood with large changes in thinking.

A parallel line of research on people's styles of thinking also informs the MBCT model of depressive relapse. A ruminative style of thinking is the tendency to focus passively on the causes and consequences of one's problems and is associated with more severe depressive symptoms and impaired problem solving. Combining cognitive reactivity and a ruminating style produce high vulnerability to depressive relapse. At times of lower mood, old habitual patterns of thinking switch in automatically (Segal et al., 2002). Such thinking runs repeatedly around well-worn "grooves" (I'm not myself and I'll never be myself again). These grooves repeat patterns rather than finding effective ways forward out of depression and this thinking creates vicious circles of more intensive mood leading to more negative thinking.

The basic construct that guides mindfulness-based cognitive therapy centers on the metaphor of modes of mind. The *doing mind* strives toward a particular goal, such as avoid this sad mood. If effective action can be taken to achieve this goal, the person can exit the doing mode. However, if the desired end cannot be achieved (e.g., changing a serious mistake in the past) or if a solution cannot be readily found, the mind can be trapped in an endless loop of mental problem solving, such as ruminating about the past or worrying about the future.

The *being mind* represents a wholly different way of interacting with experience. In this mode, the focus is on welcoming and expressing the present moment rather than evaluating it in relation to the past and future. Instead of striving for a goal, the being mind takes in the present moment for exactly what it is and does not try to change it. From their visits to Kabat-Zinn's MBSR Clinic, the developers of MBCT came to appreciate how a mindfulness program could help both patients and practitioners to access their being mind.

Like ACT and DBT, MBCT employs the therapeutic processes of consciousness raising, choosing, and counterconditioning. To prevent relapse, MBCT therapists or instructors guide treatment first by helping clients become aware of the different modes of mind. Clients can become conscious about when they are in the mode of doing mind (e.g., trying to solve a problem, ruminating about the past, or worrying about the future). They frequently discover how little time they spend just being in the present, without automatically switching to the mode of doing. For many clients, they become enlightened, their mind is meant for more than just doing. They begin to discover living in the present.

Healthier lives involve increasing freedom to access more than one mode of mind. Those who always have to be doing, evaluating, achieving, or solving may not appreciate how much of living one can miss by ruminating about the past or worrying about the future. Such automatic overlearned styles can cause them to be stuck in grooves.

Because cognitive styles and reactivity are overlearned habits, they cannot be solved just by choosing the being mind. These strong habits need to be countered by MBCT trainers helping participants continually bring their focus back to the present moment through the use of in-session mindfulness practice, exercises, and assigned homework. Thus, treatment entails participants/patients learning to distinguish doing and being modes of mind (consciousness raising), choosing to access their being mind more, and acquiring the skills (counterconditioning) to disengage from automatic responses and engage their attention in a more direct and intentional manner.

Inquiry is the process by which the group therapist/leader engages participants in a conversation about the moment-to-moment experiences in mindfulness practice. "What do you find happening?" "What are you experiencing now?" "Can you notice how your thoughts turn away?" By its nature, the inquiry is collaborative and mutual, involving joint and interactive sharing. The therapist/leader both guides the practice of the group and pays attention to his/her experience in a fashion that parallels what the participants are asked to do. The therapist is, at once, a leader and a co-participant.

MBCT practitioners often call themselves instructors, as opposed to psychotherapists. They model spiritual leaders who enlighten people in modes of mind but they offer MBCT from a secular rather than spiritual perspective. MBCT, like meditation, yoga, and other mindfulness methods, is usually provided to groups. Thus, the center is

less on the individual relationship and more on the process of progressing to being in the moment. To be effective, the professionals must be sensitive, patient practitioners and not just providers of mindfulness. The professionals need to be present in the moment if they are to be effective models for the being mind.

Following the structure of Kabat-Zinn's (1990) MBSR, the formal MBCT program consists of eight weekly sessions. The initial four sessions teach participants the mindfulness skills of paying attention, noticing mind wandering, and directing attention to a single, relatively neutral focus. The final four sessions concentrate on ways to skillfully handle negative mood shifts, cultivate sustained wellness, and protect against relapse.

As a method of relapse prevention, MBCT was designed to reduce or delay the recurrence of individuals with chronic depression. Data from six large randomized clinical trials (RCTs) support its efficacy in doing so (Segal et al., 2002). MBCT significantly reduces the risk of recurrence of depression (risk ratio of 0.66 vs. 0.34 for treatment as usual). The relative risk reduction was 43% for participants with three or more depressive episodes, and proved as effective as maintenance antidepressant medication (Piet & Hougaard, 2011; see also Chiesa & Serretti, 2011).

The research to date has focused on treatment outcomes; the process and mechanisms of treatment are yet to be rigorously examined (Felder et al., 2012). Nonetheless, the mindfulness practices and the mutual inquiry seem to lie at the heart of its effectiveness.

Practicalities of Third-Wave Therapies

Third-wave therapies are performed in individual, couple, and group formats with adolescents, adults, and older adults. Linehan insists that DBT proper for borderline personality disorders should be conducted by specially prepared mental health professionals as a combination of intensive individual therapy and skills-based group therapy, but many practitioners seem not to be providing the concurrent groups. By contrast, most mindfulness and meditation sessions are offered in only group formats, frequently by instructors without advanced degrees in the helping professions.

Training in third-wave therapies is widely available in both graduate programs and continuing education. Hayes and associates offer multiple trainings and have placed their training materials in the public domain, principally through the massive website of the Association for Contextual Behavioral Science. Linehan established her own institute, which focuses on nurturing therapists and offering mindfulness for caregivers, as well as Behavioral Tech, which disseminates evidence-based treatments for difficult-to-treat disorders.

As psychotherapies mature, they branch out far from the disorders on which they were originally developed and tested. ACT, initially created for anxiety and depression in individual adults, has now been applied to children, adolescents, couples, body dissatisfaction, PTSD, eating disorders, and a host of other problems. DBT, initially created as an intensive outpatient treatment for personality disordered and chronically suicidal individuals, has been increasingly applied to such complex problems as deliberate self-injury, substance dependence, bipolar disorder, and eating disorders (Dimeff & Koerner, 2007).

Throughout all these new applications, the emphasis remains on teaching both the client and the clinician the requisite mindfulness skills. More so than most systems of psychotherapy, the third-wave therapies literally "practice what they preach." ACT, DBT, and MBCT therapists are expected to maintain their own meditative or mindfulness practices so that they can guide others' practices and inquiries from within. Self-practice allows therapists to share their own struggles, emphasize the common pursuit, cultivate the necessary self-soothing skills for working with highly resistant clients, and focus on being with difficulties rather than automatically (and ineffectively) trying to fix them.

Effectiveness of Third-Wave Therapies

We will first examine the treatment effects of third-wave therapies across disorders and then present results for a few specific disorders.

Across disorders, ACT consistently outperforms no-treatment and wait-list controls and performs as well as other bona fide psychotherapies. Two meta-analyses (e.g., Ost, 2008; Powers et al., 2010) of 13 and 18 controlled trials, respectively, both found an average effect size (d) of 0.68 when comparing ACT to control groups. Hayes and colleagues (2006) reported a similar effect size of 0.66 for ACT. There were no significant differences between ACT and alternative treatments, suggesting comparable effectiveness to established psychotherapies.

Across multiple disorders, DBT produces an average ES of 0.58 versus no-treatment control groups in 13 controlled trials and an average of 1.13 for within-treatment group changes (Ost, 2008). Those statistics indicate that DBT patients typically experience considerable improvement, much better than those not receiving any treatment. At the same time, in the few direct comparisons to other established treatments, patients receiving DBT tended to do no better (or worse).

Anxiety Disorders

Mindfulness and acceptance-based therapies have been increasingly applied to anxiety disorders. A meta-analysis examined 19 studies with 11 being uncontrolled (Vollestad et al., 2012). MBCT was the most frequent therapy (eight studies) and

MBSR the next most frequent therapy (four studies). Only two studies assessed ACT. Across these treatments, the overall between-group ES (*d*) was 0.83 for reduction in anxiety symptoms compared to no treatment.

Another meta-analysis (Chen et al., 2012) analyzed 36 RCTs using meditative therapies where most medical patients had anxiety as a secondary concern. They reported an overall ES of 0.59 in comparison to attention controls, 0.52 in comparison to wait-list controls, and 0.27 in comparison with alternative treatments. They found that studies conducted in Eastern countries (India, China, Japan) had a significantly larger effect (0.77) than those conducted in Western countries (0.46). This provocative finding may reflect greater acceptance of meditation therapies by patients in the East, greater expertise by therapists in the East, and/or greater researcher allegiance (and positive bias) toward meditation by researchers in the East.

Mood Disorders

Hoffman and colleagues (2010) examined the effectiveness of mindfulness-based therapies (MBCT and MBSR) in 39 studies with patients with a range of conditions, including generalized anxiety, depression, cancer, and other medical and psychiatric disorders. They found that from pre- to post-test within treatment groups, the therapies were moderately effective (ES = 0.63) for reducing anxiety. They also found from pre- to post-test within mindfulness treatment groups a moderate ES of 0.59 for reducing depression. In patients with both anxiety and mood disorders, larger effects were found for improving anxiety (ES = 0.97) and moods (ES = 0.95).

Stress

Ten studies assessed the effects of MBSR on stress in a variety of healthy groups, including undergraduates, medical students, nurses, college faculty, and pregnant women (Chiesa & Serretti, 2009). The interventions included the key components of the Kabat-Zinn program in group sessions and with homework for at least 45 minutes per day for 6 days per week, but the duration of the program varied from 4 to 10 weeks. The MBSR produced significantly larger within-group effect sizes (*d* = 0.74) for stress reduction and for increases in spirituality (*d* = 0.82) than within the control groups. These findings suggest that practicing mindfulness methods, like meditation, may be good for therapists as well as for their clients.

Personality Disorders

At least eight RCTs of Marsha Linehan's DBT have been conducted with patients suffering from BPD. Her initial controlled study compared 1 year of DBT to treatment as usual (TAU) in the community. After 1 year of treatment, patients receiving DBT had significantly fewer suicide attempts, higher treatment retention (DBT 83% vs. TAU 42%), fewer days of hospitalization, lower anger, and higher social and global functioning.

Meta-analytic results indicate that DBT is an effective and efficient treatment for BPD, one that certainly outperforms no treatment and usually outperforms TAU (Heard & Linehan, 2005). A review of 16 studies (8 RCTs, 8 neither randomized nor controlled studies) involving 794 patients found that DBT produced moderate effect sizes (*d*s of 0.37 and 0.56) for reducing suicidal and self-injurious behaviors (Kliem et al., 2010). The dropout rate was 27% pre- to posttreatment.

However, it is difficult to ascertain whether the improvement reported for patients receiving DBT derive from the specific ingredients of DBT or from general factors associated with expert psychotherapy. In order to address this question, Linehan and colleagues (2006) conducted a controlled trial comparing DBT with therapy provided by experts in treating BPD. Their dismantling study was designed to begin answering questions as to the unique effects of DBT. Patients were randomly assigned to either 1 year of DBT or 1 year of community treatment by experts nominated by mental health leaders. Compared to community treatment, DBT was associated with better outcomes: fewer suicide attempts, less treatment dropout, lower medical risk, and other indexes of success. Accordingly, the effectiveness of DBT can probably not be attributed to the common factors associated with expert therapy. Something unique to DBT seems to be effective in reducing suicidal behavior.

Chronic Pain

A meta-analysis of 22 studies was conducted on third-wave treatments for chronic pain (15 studies applying MBSR and 7 applying ACT; Veehof et al., 2011). Across all studies, moderate effect sizes were found for pain (0.47) and depression (0.64) when comparing pre- to post-test changes in treatment groups. When only the 10 RCTs were assessed, the effect sizes for treatment versus control groups were small for pain (0.25) and depression (0.25). It is important to note that therapies that emphasize acceptance rather than removal of private events, like pain and depression, may not produce as much reduction in such experiences. Remember that such therapies accord priority to living better rather than to feeling better.

Cancer Patients

Ten studies assessed the effects of MBSR on the mental and physical health symptoms in cancer patients (Ledesma & Kumano, 2008). For mental health outcomes (anxiety, depression, and/or stress), medium effects (0.48) were found for the MBSR treatments. For physical health outcomes (e.g., immunity levels, hormonal indices, and self-reported symptoms), the effects of MBSR were significant but small (0.18). Outcomes were assessed only at the end of MBSR, and more research is needed on the effects of long-term mindfulness on both mental and physical health.

Criticisms of Third-Wave Therapies
From a Psychoanalytic Perspective

Behaviorists, like B. F. Skinner, were the primary reason that psychology "lost its mind" and teetered on the edge of becoming a brave new world of technology. Fortunately, the new wave of behavior therapists has rediscovered the centrality of the mind for mental disorders. In fact, all of the third-wave therapies include mindfulness approaches that free patients to let their troubling thoughts, feelings, and memories flow more freely without judgment, disruption, or other defensiveness.

This approach is uncannily similar to our method of free association that has characterized psychoanalytic therapies for over a century. Patients are encouraged to say whatever comes to mind and let their consciousness flow wherever less conscious private events might take them. Not only are they staying in the presence of private events that typically cause them to defend (avoid?), but they are sharing these private memories with their psychoanalytic therapists. Since many patients experience their therapists as parental figures, sharing with accepting and understanding figures rather than criticizing and condemning certainly helps to reparent patients and let them accept private events that previously they disowned.

Third-wave therapists typically stop with clients accepting such private events, but this is where we psychoanalytic therapists begin. Analyzing these events can lead to more conscious understanding of the deep and prolonged conflicts that patients experience within themselves and with significant others. There is no reason to just accept such conflicts when psychodynamic therapies can reduce and resolve such conflicts. The new-wave behavior therapists must be shocked to discover that DBT is not the only approach that is effective with borderline personalities. Our structured psychodynamic therapies have been found to be just as effective in treating this frustrating condition (Chapter 3).

Given the reacceptance of the mind, we would encourage third-wave therapists to drop their identification with behavior analysis and to see themselves as a new wave of psychoanalysis. "Accept" the fact, ACT and DBT therapists; you are putting old psychoanalytic wine into new-wave bottles.

From a Cognitive-Behavioral Perspective

Although the third-wave therapies arose from the behavioral tradition, not all cognitive behaviorists have signed on to the expansion. Some CBT critics complain that the clinical practices have gotten ahead of the outcome data (Corrigan, 2001). ACT, in particular, does not seem to add much to the clinical results of established CBT with the same disorders. Why go adding new concepts and new methods that do not produce better outcomes? Whatever happened to our prized principle of parsimony?

Other behaviorists argue that ACT sounds more like a religion than a science. Lots of touchy-feely terms defy behavioral operationalization. Exactly why do we need a new system of psychotherapy or a new "wave" of behavior therapy to teach acceptance skills? Some dedicated cognitive behaviorists think that third-wave therapies represent overhyped, quasi-mystical methods wrapped in new-age packaging.

From a Humanistic Perspective

How encouraging it is that third-wave therapists are helping to humanize behavior therapies! They have accepted humanistic concepts like the mind, a unique self, core values, self-acceptance, and being in the here and now rather than the unchangeable past or unknowable future. It is unfortunate that they had to learn Eastern philosophies rather than study in graduate school humanistic and experiential therapies constructed to help individuals accept experiences of nonbeing, death, and disease. "Accepting that which is necessary" is what Nietzsche thought long ago to be a precondition of freedom.

It is also unfortunate that the third-wave therapies need to cover their more humanistic inclinations with science from behaviorism. Skinner would turn over in his Skinner box if he learned that behavior analysts were embracing epiphenomena like the mind, private experiences, the real self, and choosing to stay in the present. Eastern perspectives like Buddhism have a rich tradition of guiding entire cultures to healthier living. They certainly don't need to be dressed up in Western science to be acceptable and helpful.

From a Cultural Perspective

Encouraging clients to accept private experiences of abuse, neglect, and rejection seems to implicitly accept such social injustices. Abuse in all of its forms is generally the consequence of people with more power and privilege imposing their will and their way on those with less power and privilege. The world has become more aware of how parents and priests, teachers and bosses, can create private traumas for those without the position to prevent such mistreatment. The world has, in addition, seen how well-intentioned people trying to accept and appease abuse have unknowingly enabled the abuse of power to continue.

Why would being angry and outraged, resistant and resentful, depressed and demanding justice be seen as pathological? What the world has seen is that courageous individuals going public with private experiences of abuse have joined together to change the cultural contexts that previously permitted abusive behaviors to go unpunished. The world doesn't need more acceptance of the unearned privilege like that held by the 1% wealthiest in the United States. Needed are interventions at multiple levels that lead to much more equitable distribution of power that enable many more people to realize their potentials rather than accepting their present culture.

From an Integrative Perspective

If you hang around psychotherapy long enough, you see the same concepts reappear in different language. *Acceptance* and *mindful* are two of these recurring concepts. Psychoanalysts discussed the role of an "observing ego" in the 1940s, Carl Rogers emphasized "self-acceptance" in the 1950s, and the Beatles and the hippies introduced most of the West to Zen Buddhism in the 1960s. Indeed, as members of 12-step programs would remind us, the importance of being mindful and accepting goes back even further to the Serenity Prayer by Reinhold Niebuhr:

> *God, grant me the serenity to accept the things I cannot change,*
> *Courage to change the things I can,*
> *And wisdom to know the difference.*

It is gratifying that cognitive-behavior therapists are learning from other theoretical traditions and are painfully learning that not all behaviors can be, or should be, changed. Even the most complete of functional analyses and the most effective of behavioral technologies cannot conquer all that ails the human populace.

The fecal matter hits the fan, of course, when deciding what can be changed and what should be accepted. The uncontrollable problems, such as inclement weather and fateful accidents, are those we accept, while the controllable behaviors, such as exercise and avoidance, are those we can change. But exactly which can we control and thus change?

That's where the value of integrative therapy and clinical experience come in. Overestimating our ability to change leads to grandiose plans and behavioral wipeouts. Underestimating our ability to change results in apathy, resignation, and millions unnecessarily leading lives of compromised health and quiet desperation. Let's follow the Serenity Prayer and integrate both change strategies and acceptance strategies depending upon the individuality of the patient and the singularity of the situation. That's the time-honored integrative wave.

A Third-Wave Analysis of Mrs. C

Mrs. C could only accept experiences that were clean. She dreaded any thoughts, feelings, or memories that were dirty, disgusting, or diseased. But, look at how much her cultural context included under the construct of dirty: dirty language that communicated anger, disgust, or other intense emotions; dirty jokes that expressed sexual desires, fantasies, or memories; dirty hands that symbolized guilt, shame, or other transgressions; and dirty dealing that represented cheating, lying, or other ways of mistreating herself. Add to this Mrs. C's personal history with symbols of dirt, disgust, and disease: dirty diapers with seven children and disgusting pinworms that spread disease in her family.

The more preoccupied Mrs. C became with avoiding private events that had any dirty or disgusting connotation, the more she filled her public environment with objects that would cue more dreaded thoughts, feelings, or memories. Take the piles of underwear: What was hidden under there? Underwear designed to cover private parts and control private events denoted by shame and sin.

Mrs. C had avoided any awareness of private events that would fill her mind with dirty,
(continued)

disgusting, or dreadful experiences. But she encountered the paradox of change: trying to suppress unpleasant thoughts typically just makes them more entrenched. Troubling memories and feelings from the past kept increasing symptoms. Similarly, anxious and depressing obsessive thoughts about the future preoccupied her and led to compulsive behaviors, like washing her body. Piling more underwear kept her from feeling well or living well.

Third-wave therapists would agree that mindfulness was needed to help Mrs. C stay in the present. She needed help in distancing from private events, which lead to fusion and confusion about what was truly dirty or disgusting and what were linguistic representations of the past that did not have to be taken literally and responded to dreadfully. Diffusing such experiences as hypotheses that come and go can diffuse the control such events exert over her behavior. Accepting that emotional events can be pathological ways that normal minds work will lead Mrs. C to reduce their power over how she behaves.

Mrs. C might have embraced meditation as one method of mindfulness. Breathing has always served as a cornerstone of the Eastern traditions; it is immediately available and required for life. Mindful breathing embodies "being"' instead of "doing" or "fixing," and it creates distance from the immediacy of distressing obsessions.

As her breathing deepens, Mrs. C could calm herself and remember that she does not need to like or endorse OCD; rather, she could learn to radically accept it is what it is. The OCD, in reality, is not bad or good; it "just is." In this mindful way, she would eventually learn to become less disgusted, less damning, and less distressed.

As Mrs. C creates a growing sense of herself as a person with a healthier perspective on private and public events, she can identify values that represent her real self rather than remaining a self that has to be cleansed from the dark sides of life. Mrs. C might, for example, accept her commitment to the well-being of her children and family. Taking committed action may entail spending more time teaching her family the mindfulness skills that she uses to counter her anxiety and avoidance. That can get her freer from the guilt and shame of having exposed her children and husband to irrational demands, like endless showers and growing piles of underwear.

As she and they learn to live more in the mindful present, they can let go of a past preoccupied with dirt, disgust, and disease. The more they learn to live in the present and to act on fundamental values that reflect an alternative sense of self, they can grow. The C family can construct a future freer from pathological private events and filled with the meaningfulness of being fully present.

Future Directions

A new generation of acceptance-based, third-wave therapies is upon us. They moved behavior therapy from treating simple, discrete problems to addressing broadband, serious psychopathology. In fact, they transcended the simple label of "behavioral" and ventured into exposure (Chapter 8), cognitive (Chapter 10), constructivist (Chapter 15), and integrative (Chapter 16) methods. These newer treatments represent a more complex and complete psychotherapy firmly grounded in, but expanding cognitive-behavior therapy (Hayes, Follette, & Linehan, 2004).

Acceptance and mindfulness therapies have taken off in recent years. It's not uncommon these days to hear trainees describing their theoretical orientation as "cognitive-behavioral plus third wave." And it's not uncommon to hear therapists relating their weekly schedule of meditation classes or mindfulness practices. A recent review of the literature revealed 42 controlled studies conducted on ACT in 10 different countries (Woidneck et al., 2012). Linehan's (1993a, 1993b) book on treating borderline disorder and the accompanying skills manual are among the most frequently cited publications in mental health. DBT skills and workbooks, if not always the entire DBT protocol, seem to have permeated the landscape. We can confidently predict the ascension and expansion of the third-wave therapies in the next decade.

Several challenges await there. One is whether third-wave treatments demonstrate value added over and above existing cognitive-behavior therapies. Meta-analyses to date have not demonstrated that the third-wave therapies outperform the established therapies from which they emerged. Second, the flexible ACT and DBT protocols are employed across disorders and countries, and early indicators are that they are cross-culturally relevant. As with all therapies, they will also need to show that they are acceptable and efficacious to members of different cultures. Third, mindfulness-based therapies face the challenge of demonstrating that adding cognitive and behavioral methods based on Western science are more effective than mindfulness alone based on long traditions and applications in Eastern cultures.

Building on Eastern traditions, third-wave therapies are washing over thousands of cognitive-behavioral clinicians and attracting clinicians of diverse theoretical persuasions. In the short run, they will assuredly prosper. In the long run, whether they will grow or eventually fade remains to be seen. Like the waves that preceded, they could be preempted by another, fourth movement. The probable future is that third-wave therapies will shed their image as the "new treatments" and become firmly established within the ever-expanding, evidence-based context of cognitive-behavioral therapy.

Key Terms

acceptance
acceptance and
  commitment
  therapy (ACT)
cognitive fusion
cognitive reactivity
committed action
dialectic
dialectical behavior
  therapy (DBT)
differential activation
  hypothesis
distancing
emotional regulation
experiential
  avoidance
inquiry
interpersonal
  effectiveness
meditation
mindfulness
mindfulness-based
  cognitive therapy
  (MBCT)
mindfulness-based
  therapies
modes of mind
present-moment focus
radical acceptance
ruminative style of
  thinking
third-wave therapies
validation strategies
values
values clarification
workability

Recommended Readings

Baer, R. A. (Ed.). (2006). *Mindfulness-based treatment approaches.* San Diego, CA: Academic Press.

Hayes, S. C., & Smith, S. (2005). *Get out of your mind and into your life: The new acceptance and commitment therapy.* Oakland, CA: New Harbinger.

Hayes, S. C., Follette, V. M., & Linehan, M. M. (Eds.). (2004). *Mindfulness and acceptance: Expanding the cognitive-behavioral tradition.* NewYork: Guilford.

Hayes, S. C., Strosahl, K. D., & Wilson, K. G. (2011). *Acceptance and commitment therapy: The process and practice of mindful change* (2nd ed.). New York: Guilford.

Linehan, M. M. (1993a). *Cognitive-behavioral treatment of borderline personality disorder.* New York: Guilford.

Linehan, M. M. (1993b). *Skills training manual for treating borderline personality disorder.* New York: Guilford.

McKay, M., Wood, J. C., & Brantley, J. (2007). *Dialectical behavior therapy skills workbook: Practical DBT exercises for learning mindfulness, interpersonal effectiveness, emotion regulation, & distress tolerance.* Oakland, CA: New Harbinger.

Segal, Z. V., Williams, J. M. G., & Teasdale, J. D. (2012). *Mindfulness-based cognitive therapy for depression* (2nd ed.). New York: Guilford.

Recommended Websites

Association for Contextual Behavioral Science (ACT):
www.contextualpsychology.org/

Behavioral Tech Research (DBT):
www.btechresearch.com/

Linehan Institute:
www.linehaninstitute.org/

Mindfulness-Based Cognitive Therapy:
www.mbct.com/

Steve Hayes' Training Page:
www.contextualpsychology.org/steve_hayes

CHAPTER 12

Systemic Therapies

Virginia Satir

Salvador Minuchin

Kathy and Dan hailed from prominent extended families. Kathy and Dan, however, were from branches of their families that were in decline. Dan's parents were plagued by alcohol abuse, as was Dan. Kathy's family of origin was plagued with a multitude of dysfunctions, including substance abuse, depression, and physical abuse. Kathy herself was troubled by depression and passivity. Although they were both in their late thirties, Kathy and Dan were stuck in their career development, unable to complete their graduate degrees. Their modest inheritances were rapidly disappearing. They each seemed stuck in a deteriorating family system.

With the help of systemic therapy, Kathy and Dan became more aware and communicative about how they were repeating patterns from their families of origin. Dan was grappling with rules against succeeding. Kathy was struggling with rules against asserting. As part of her psychotherapy, Kathy traveled to different parts of the country to meet with her mother, sister, and brother. Instead of stepping into blame games, Kathy tried to communicate in a more objective and understanding manner. She was completing the process of differentiating herself from her family of origin while remaining emotionally connected to family members.

Kathy was not surprised that she was becoming more assertive, less depressed, and more successful. She was surprised, however, that her brother took dramatic steps to get off drugs; her sister entered family therapy to work on stopping her physical and emotional abuse of her children; and her mother began to feel her long-standing depression lifting. From her graduate studies, Kathy knew how family members can deteriorate as one member improves in treatment. She was pleasantly surprised to discover that an entire family system could improve as one member began to restructure her relationship to her family of origin.

The Context of Systemic Therapies

Systemic therapies maintain that individuals can only be understood within their social context. Systemic therapies, themselves, can best be understood within the context from which they emerged. Although people have probably been examining and listening to family problems as long as there have been families, systemic therapy was truly a 20th-century development.

The 1950s and 1960s were seminal years for the development of systems therapies (see Broderick & Schrader, 1991, for a review). These decades witnessed the emergence of **General Systems Theory (GST)** in biology and **cybernetics** in computer science. Rather than follow the traditional scientific method of reducing phenomena to their simplest elements—such as electrons, neutrons, and protons—General Systems Theory advocated studying the biological processes that lead to increasing complexity of organization of whole organisms (von Bertalanffy, 1968). Cybernetics advocated studying the methods of communication and control common to living organisms and machines, especially computer systems. In this chapter, we will first look at how systems are understood from these two perspectives and then see how this understanding has been applied to the treatment of troubled individuals, couples, and families.

To understand the functioning of whole organisms, we must study not only the separate elements of the organism, but also the relationships among them. A **system** is defined as a set of units or elements that stand in a consistent relationship with one another. A system comprises the separate elements as well as the relationships among those elements. A family system, for instance, comprises not only, say, four individuals but also the interrelationships among those four individuals and the entire context and rules of the family. Even the labels given to individual members, such as parent and child, suggest consistent relationships between them.

Organization and system are virtually synonymous. A system is a set of organized units or elements. Principles of organization suggest that when elements are combined in a consistent pattern, an entity is produced that is greater than the additive sum of each of the separate parts. This is the concept of wholeness. A marital system, for example, cannot be broken down simply into two separate individuals. Not only are there two individual subsystems, but there is also a consistent relationship between the individuals that creates a marital subsystem. In this case, 1 plus 1 equals 3.

Systems are also organized in such a way that relationships among elements create **boundaries** around the system and each of its subsystems. In biological systems, the boundaries may be easily identifiable, such as a cell membrane or an animal's skin. In human systems, boundaries are frequently more abstract. The rules of relationships delineate boundaries. The rules of monogamy, for example, help identify the boundaries of a traditional marriage; a spouse who is having an affair would be considered "out of bounds" or acting outside the rules of the relationship.

Boundaries may be too permeable, with unclear rules about who can interact with whom and how. In incestuous families, for example, the boundaries between the parental subsystem and the child subsystem are unclear and permeable to the point of pathological. Boundaries can also be too rigid, preventing adequate interactions among individuals in a system or between systems. Families with child abuse, for example, may be rigidly bound off from the larger social system and be unable to accept social support that could help prevent such abuse.

Systems are often conceptualized as hierarchically organized. Systems are related one to another according to a series of hierarchic levels. Each system is seen as being made up of component subsystems of smaller scale; conversely, each system is a component part of a larger system. A family system comprises individual subsystems, a partner/marital subsystem, a sibling subsystem, and a parental subsystem. The family system, in turn, is a component part of a larger neighborhood system, which is hierarchically related to even larger social systems, such as the community, the region, and the nation.

Controlled adaptation is the key to meaningful change. Controlled growth leads to differentiation and development of tissues, organs, and individuals. Uncontrolled growth, like cancer, leads to the disorganization and even death of a living system.

Homeostasis, or balance, explains how living systems control or maintain a steady state. Walter Cannon (1939), a physiologist, first described a set of mechanisms within the neuroendocrine system whose function was to maintain consistency of the internal environment of the organism, such as constant blood pressure, temperature, and water content. If changes in the organism exceed a set of safe limits, then control mechanisms in the hormonal and autonomic nervous system will be activated to help bring the system back into balance.

Family systems possess their own set of mechanisms whose primary purpose is maintenance of an acceptable behavioral balance within the family. Families have been found, for example, to maintain surprisingly stable rates of speech interaction (Reiss, 1977). High-interaction families maintain a high rate of speaking across sessions even though individual members vary a great deal in speaking across sessions.

Living systems are characterized as **open systems**, which means that energy can be freely transported into, within, and out of the system. Information is the most important type of energy in living systems, because it is an energy that reduces uncertainty. When information is packaged or programmed efficiently, it powerfully increases a system's ability to function in a highly complex and well-organized manner. Communication involves the process by which information is either changed from one state to another, or moved from one point to another in space. Cybernetics serves as a model for how information can be transformed or transmitted effectively within couple and family systems.

Because there is no single, unifying systems therapy, we will present four major systemic approaches—the communication/strategic, the structural, the Bowenian, and the new generation of evidence-based family therapies. Inasmuch as these systemic therapies focus on patterns of relationships within systems rather than on individual personalities, the sections on theory of personality will be omitted. Each systemic therapy does, however, have important things to say about the development and/or maintenance of psychopathology and how psychopathology in human systems can best be changed.

Over the years, the term **systemic therapies** has acquired two distinct meanings. First, systemic, therapy can refer to a **therapy modality** or **format**. Like individual therapy or group therapy, systems therapy denotes meeting with a certain number of people, in this case, a couple or family. Therapists can work with the family to help a distressed member. Second, systemic therapy can refer to treatment content or goal. The treatment deals with family systems content and works toward improving the family system. An individual is no longer the patient; the couple, the family, or another system is the patient. In this sense, it is quite possible to conduct systemic therapy without having the entire family present. As in the case of Kathy and Dan and as in the multigenerational family therapy of Murray Bowen, only one or two people may be in therapy, but the entire system is targeted for change. Therapists can see an individual's symptoms as belonging to the entire system.

In this chapter, we present systemic therapy primarily as a treatment content/goal—an alternative way of thinking about psychopathology and psychotherapy. However, much of the outcome research has been conducted on family therapy as a modality/format. Bear in mind that these two meanings are frequently interrelated and not easily separable in practice. A psychotherapist may invite several members of a family into the consulting room for family therapy because she desires both to assist a symptomatic member and to target the entire system as a treatment goal.

Communication/ Strategic Therapy

The communications approach to psychotherapy emerged from two interrelated organizations rather than from a single individual. The first organization was the Double Bind Communications Project begun in 1952 by Gregory Bateson, with Jay Haley and John Weakland as members of the project and Donald Jackson as consultant. The second organization was the Mental Research Institute (MRI) founded by Jackson in 1958 with Virginia Satir and Paul Watzlawick as two important members of the institute. The two organizations had unclear boundaries because Jackson participated in both projects. The Double Bind Project was located at MRI, and when the Double Bind Project terminated in 1962, Haley and Weakland joined MRI. It is not coincidental that both of these organizations were founded in Palo Alto, California, which is part of the Silicon Valley, one of the world's foremost centers of computer science.

What all these individuals shared in common was the conviction that communication is the key to understanding human behavior. The MRI group went so far as to assume all behavior is communication. Just as we cannot not behave, so, too, we cannot not communicate. Communication, then, involves both verbal and nonverbal behaviors.

The Double Bind Project originally focused on how conflicting communications could produce symptoms of schizophrenia. Initial research on double bind communications revealed interesting relationships between family dynamics and schizophrenic communications. In 1959, the project was divided into an experimental approach and a family therapy project. Family interactions were videotaped and attempts made to differentiate "schizophrenic" from "normal" communications. In the family therapy project, observations were made in natural settings, and various techniques based in part on communications theory were introduced.

The staff at MRI described a therapy format that focused on analysis of communication between individuals, and subsequently among family members. Interventions were then designed to change communication patterns between one individual and another and among all members of a family (Greenberg, 1977).

Gradually, the organization of these two groups began to change. Bateson's project ended in 1962, and he went on to advance a communication perspective on a broad range of human and animal behaviors until his death in 1980. Jackson died in 1968, ending a short but very creative career. Satir left to contribute to the human potential movement, which began in California and rapidly became a worldwide phenomenon; she later toured the country demonstrating and advocating for a humanistically oriented communication therapy, until her death in 1988. Haley relocated to the Philadelphia Child Guidance Clinic to participate with

Salvador Minuchin in creating a vital center for systems therapy and then codirected his own Family Therapy Institute outside Washington, DC, until his death in 2007.

Such a creative group of individuals would not be expected to leave behind a single, coherent theory of psychotherapy. They did, however, develop an innovative set of concepts for understanding psychopathology in systems and a set of therapeutic principles for helping systems change.

Theory of Psychopathology

Systemic therapists have frequently observed that decreases in psychopathology in one family member are often accompanied by increases in symptoms in another family member. Jackson, for example, treated a woman for depression and found that as her depression subsided, her husband began phoning to complain that his wife's emotional condition was worsening (Greenberg, 1977). The wife's continued improvement led to the husband's loss of his job and subsequent suicide.

Psychopathology is fundamentally an interactional process among family members, rather than an intrapersonal problem within one member. Psychopathology serves as a homeostatic mechanism to help families maintain an internal balance for family functioning. When a family is threatened, it can move toward balance through puzzling, psychotic, or other pathological behaviors. A family's status quo may be one in which the parents fight infrequently. When they do fight, if violence threatens to run out of control, a child can communicate concern by becoming symptomatic. These symptoms serve as a negative feedback loop that results in a halt in hostilities as the family develops a newfound concern with the **identified** (or index) **patient (IP)**. But the entire system should be the patient, not merely the individual who has developed symptoms to save the system.

A breakdown in family functioning occurs when the rules of relating become ambiguous. The rules of relationships provide a stable organization for family functioning. If the rules become ambiguous, the system becomes disorganized, and symptoms are likely to develop to restore order to the family. If the rules are clear, such as the rule that family members will not relate violently, then an argument between parents need not threaten the family's functioning, and a child will not have to develop symptoms to control a threat of violence.

The rules of relating in a family are best observed through the patterns of communication in the family. Who communicates to whom, how, and about what define the patterns of relationships that make up a family. Most families, for example, have a clear rule that when parents are communicating with each other in an angry manner, the children stay out of it. The spouse subsystem maintains clear boundaries or rules that prohibit children from becoming part of intimate arguments.

When communication patterns in families are unclear, then rules become more ambiguous and psychopathology is likely to develop. **Double bind communications** are among the most troublesome patterns of communicating because they involve two incompatible messages. A classic example of a double bind situation is presented by Bateson and colleagues (1956, p. 259):

> *A young man who had fairly well recovered from an acute schizophrenic episode was visited in the hospital by his mother. He was glad to see her and impulsively put his arm around her shoulders, whereupon she stiffened. He withdrew his arm, and she asked, "Don't you love me anymore?" He then blushed, and she said, "Dear, you must not be so easily embarrassed and afraid of your feelings." The patient was able to stay with her only a few minutes more and, following her departure, he assaulted an aide and was put in the tubs.*

Verbally the mother is communicating a wish to be close to her son, but nonverbally her tightening communicates a wish to be distant. When the son withdraws, the mother contradicts her nonverbal message by asking, "Don't you love me anymore?" The rules for relating are being communicated ambiguously. Are mother and son supposed to have a close or a distant relationship? The son clearly cannot win. If he relates closely, his mother tightens up. If he pulls back, she becomes upset. No wonder the son becomes confused and hostile.

Communication is a complex pattern of interactions frequently misunderstood by psychotherapists, let alone clients. In their book *Pragmatics of Human Communication*, Watzlawick, Beavin, and Jackson (1967) conceptualize communication in five axioms. First is the axiom already stated: It is impossible to not communicate. Silence is obviously communication, though it is frequently ambiguous communication open to interpretation and to misunderstanding.

The second axiom holds that, besides transmitting information, communication also implies a commitment and defines the nature of the relationship. Communication contains both a report, which is the content of the message, and a command, which defines how the communicators are to relate. Satir (1967) emphasizes that if the content and the command are congruous, then the relationship is defined as harmonious. If the two levels of communication are incongruous, as when the mother conveys a verbal wish to be close and a nonverbal tightening that commands distance, the relationship is likely to be characterized by disharmony and pathology.

The third axiom states that the nature of a relationship is contingent on how a communication sequence is punctuated. If a communication response cannot end with a period until the same person always has the last word, then such **punctuation** defines the person with the last word as exerting greater power in the relationship.

The fourth axiom states that humans communicate both verbally and nonverbally. Verbal communication is clearest in terms of content but does not provide much information about the relationship between the communicators. Nonverbal communication tells us more about the relationship but is still ambiguous about the nature of the relationship. For example, tears can be a sign of joy. The more families rely on nonverbal messages, the more ambiguous their relationships are likely to be and the more problems are likely to arise.

The fifth and final axiom states that all communication exchanges are either **symmetrical** or **complementary**, depending on the type of relationship. If equality exists and either party is free to take the lead, a symmetrical relationship exists. If one leads and the other follows, the relationship is complementary. Psychopathology can occur in either type of relationship.

In symmetrical relationships, competition can escalate into a runaway situation as each person struggles to have the last word in defining the nature of the relationship. Arguments can become endless. Pathology in symmetrical relationships is characterized by more or less open warfare, or a **schism** (Lidz, 1963). Marital schism is defined as a state of severe chronic disequilibrium, discord, and recurrent threats of separation. One parent is constantly undercutting the other. The competition leads to parents vying for the love of the children and the children in rivalry for the parents' affection. The rule being communicated in families with marital schism is mutual distrust and angry competition instead of cooperation.

Complementary relationships can rigidify and prevent adequate growth of family members. A parent who insists that a young adult relate as a child can disconfirm that young adult's sense of self as autonomous and equal. Such disconfirmation can lead to symptoms of depersonalization, confusion, or aggressive acting out. In marital systems that have become rigidly complementary, one partner must always be in overt control and dominate the family. There is a lack of reciprocity, of give-and-take, between the partners, and the marriage and the family are skewed in the direction of the controlling partner (Lidz, 1963). The weak partner allows the domination so that continuation of the marital and family system is not constantly threatened, even if it means domination by irrational or pathological ways of behaving. The rule of these families is accommodation, even if it means compromising oneself away.

Therapeutic Processes

If psychopathology is primarily a function of unclear or hostile communication that results in ambiguous rules for relating, then psychopathology can best be modified by helping individuals in systems to communicate more clearly and constructively about the rules of their relationship. The emphasis in **communication therapy** is not on the content of the communication, but rather on the relationship-defining aspects of communication. The emphasis is not so much on what people communicate as on how they communicate. The focus is on **metacommunication**—that is, communication about communication. Because people can only relate through communication, if they change how they communicate, they also change how they relate.

Homeostatic mechanisms in families, however, make family systems resistant to change. If therapists are to be effective in changing the family's ingrained rules for communicating and relating, then they will need to intervene with a definite strategy (and thus are also known as **strategic therapists**) powerful enough to disrupt the family's rigid resistance.

Consciousness Raising

Among the communication/strategic therapists, Jackson placed greatest emphasis on the importance of family members becoming more aware

of the dysfunctional nature of their current rules for communicating and relating. Jackson assumed that before change is possible, the family must understand rule functioning.

The client's task is not to develop historical insight into the family's rules of relating and communicating. The family's work is simply to relate in the here and now. Then, either by following the therapist's directives or by resisting such directives, they can begin to see how dysfunctional are their communication patterns and their rules for relating.

The first task for the Jacksonian therapist is to not become blinded by the content of communications. Focusing on a family's history, in particular, can be one of the quickest ways to miss how the family is interacting in the here and now. Because rules for relating are enacted in the present, the therapist's first task is to become more aware of who communicates to whom, about what, and how. In the initial sessions, the therapist will try to clarify the family's rules for functioning by asking about the family's expectations for each parent and about the role that each child plays in the family system. The therapist tries to open these areas up for clearer communication and, hopefully, for change.

Relabeling, or **reframing**, is a technique designed to make explicit the family rules and to describe them in a more positive manner. As an example, Jackson (1967) cites a situation in which a mother and daughter are talking and the mother begins to cry. Because the daughter has been labeled as aggressive, she is assumed to be the cause of her mother's crying. The daughter even confirms this unwritten assumption by saying that she did not mean to hurt her mother. The therapist intervenes by relabeling the hurt as a "touching closeness." This technique takes away the negative motivation of an act and labels it in a positive way. Under the family's rules of communication, the daughter is perceived only as aggressive and hurtful rather than as trying to touch her mother in a close way. Family members may define a relationship between two people in a negative way for years, so that all communications between them are interpreted negatively. If the therapist can suddenly define the communication in an affirming way, the family can begin to see itself in a new way.

Another means of making the family aware of dysfunctional rules is to produce a runaway in the system by **prescribing the symptom**. If the problem is that the parents are being too punitive, the therapist could recommend that they be even more punitive as a means of regaining control. The parents then have the opportunity to discover just how they are relating to their children. As their punitive communications increase, they threaten to produce a runaway, or breakdown, in the system. The parents then have the opportunity to gain genuine insight into how dysfunctional their punitive actions are for the family's well-being.

A technique similar to prescribing the symptom is **reductio ad absurdum**. This technique takes the complaint to an absurd extreme so that a client can become aware of how dysfunctional it is to relate in such a manner. If a mother is complaining about her daughter's aggressiveness, the therapist can commiserate with the mother regarding the daughter's acting out, emphasize the cross she has had to bear, suggest that anyone else would have been completely crushed by it, until finally the mother has to counter with "I didn't say it was *that* bad." In this way, the mother and the family come to realize that she is not as vulnerable to her daughter's acting out as she seems.

Choosing

Clients experience symptoms as outside of their personal control. They are "helpless" when it comes to choosing whether to be free from symptoms.

Symptoms are especially likely to emerge in family systems characterized by double bind communications. Double binds lead individuals to develop a sense of having no choice. They're damned if they do and damned if they don't. Double bind communications contain rules to relate in two incompatible ways—"Come close, but don't touch!" Double bind communications create symptoms, in part because they leave the receiver with no choices for resolving incompatible or paradoxical communications.

Communication/strategic therapists have been ingenious in liberating clients from double bind situations and from symptoms by creating **therapeutic double binds**. When constructed correctly, these **paradoxical techniques** liberate clients by giving them two choices: to cooperate with the therapist's directives or to refuse to cooperate.

The client's work is simple: Choose to follow the therapist's instructions, or choose to rebel. The therapist's task is more challenging. The therapist must create a paradox that will help liberate clients whether they follow or refuse the therapist's directive. The directive is structured so that it (1) recommends continuing the very behavior the patient expects to change, (2) implies that acting out the symptomatic behavior will produce change, and (3) thereby creates a paradox because the patient is told to change by remaining unchanged.

Patients are thus put in an untenable situation regarding their symptoms. If they cooperate and choose to carry out their symptoms, they no longer have the experience of "can't help it"; the behavior becomes choice behavior rather than symptomatic or helpless behavior. If the clients resist the directive, they can do so only by not behaving symptomatically, which is the goal of therapy. Therapeutic double binds give clients two choices, both of which liberate them from symptomatic or helpless behavior.

A therapeutic double bind presupposes an intense therapeutic relationship that has a high degree of survival value and expectation for the patient (Watzlawick et al., 1967). In addition, it must be communicated in such a convincing manner that the client cannot dissolve the paradox by commenting on it. If the client says, for example, "You're trying to trick me," the paradox is dissolved.

In the case of a couple who argued constantly, Jackson reframed the argument as a sign of emotional involvement and told them that this apparent discord only proved how much they loved each other. He recommended that they continue their fighting to express their love. No matter how ridiculous the couple may have considered this interpretation—or perhaps because it was so ridiculous to them—they set about proving to the therapist how wrong he was. This was best done by stopping their arguing, just to show that they were not in love. The moment they chose to stop arguing, they found they were getting along much better (Watzlawick et al., 1967).

Catharsis

Virginia Satir was unique among her Palo Alto colleagues in placing more emphasis on feelings than did the others. She combined systemic theory with ego psychology and humanistic theory. Satir agreed that troubled families need to communicate clearly. Most troubled families, however, have difficulty in communicating their feelings directly. If they cannot be clear about their feelings toward each other, they certainly would be more likely to have ambiguous rules for relating. Satir's (1967, 1972; Satir & Baldwin, 1983; Satir et al., 1977) approach to systemic work, therefore, accorded more importance to helping families express their emotions and thereby change rules that prohibit emotional relating.

The patient's task is to take the risk of communicating feelings more directly rather than indirectly through nonverbal actions. Clients first gain insight into which feelings they usually omit from their communications. Blamers usually omit feelings about the other person; placaters omit feelings about themselves; super-reasonable communicators omit feelings about the subject being discussed; and irrelevant communicators omit everything. Once aware of their pattern of communication, clients then struggle to become more congruent communicators by expressing the emotions they usually omit.

The therapist first uses consciousness raising to assist patients in becoming aware of which patterns of dysfunctional communication they typically use. Through feedback and interpretations, the Satir therapist helps clients become aware of the meanings contained in both their verbal and nonverbal communications.

As clients become aware of the deeper feelings that they are communicating only indirectly, the therapist encourages them to express their feelings more directly. Rather than communicating secondary feelings, such as anger or envy, the therapist would encourage clients to express the primary feeling of hurt. Secondary feelings such as anger can be dysfunctional for families, whereas expressions of hurt almost always help families to create more supportive and caring rules for relating.

Counterconditioning

Jay Haley was distinctive among the original MRI group for his therapeutic focus on **power**. Behind every communication is the command element or a struggle for interpersonal power. As he used the term, a person who has achieved "power" has established himself or herself as the one who determines what is going to happen. Power tactics are those maneuvers that people, including psychotherapists, use to give themselves influence and control over their social world and so make that world more predictable.

In his classic (and controversial) book, *The Power Tactics of Jesus Christ and Other Essays*, Haley (1986) does not concern himself with the spiritual message of Jesus or his ideas, but with how Jesus organized and dealt with people. Jesus was the first leader to lay down a program for building a following among the poor and powerless. His basic tactic was to define the poor as more deserving of power than anyone else to curry their favor.

Jesus was an expert in the **surrender tactic**, reportedly used by certain beasts of the field and birds of the air. When two wolves are in a fight, for instance, and one is about to be killed, the defeated wolf will suddenly lift its head and bare its throat to the opponent. The opponent becomes incapacitated; he cannot kill as long as he is faced with this tactic. Although he is the victor, the vanquished is controlling his behavior merely by standing still and offering the vulnerable jugular vein. Throughout his public life, Jesus preached the use of the surrender tactic—turning the other cheek and forgiving those who wrong you. Becoming helpless in the face of authority almost invariably wins and frustrates the opponent.

This analysis of power in systems guided Haley's (1976, 1980, 1990) directive, problem-solving therapy, in which he tries to quickly grab the upper hand in the family system. His typical procedures included clarification, reframing, and a host of directives that function as fuzzy forms of counterconditioning in which family interactions are restructured to be incompatible with the old, pathological interactions.

Having extensively studied the work of the famous hypnotherapist Milton Erickson, Haley (1973) delivers two types of **directives**. **Straight directives** are given when the therapist wants the family to do what the directive says—for example, telling a disengaged and overly serious family to play a fun game for at least 2 hours. **Paradoxical directives**, based on the theoretical foundations laid by Don Jackson, are given when the goal is for the family to oppose the therapist—for example, the "winner's bet," in which the therapist bets misbehaving adolescents that they will continue their misbehavior. The therapist takes the position that adolescents cannot control their behavior, thus casting them in a therapeutic double bind.

Haley (1984) also developed **ordeal therapy**, a systemic twist to the behavioral process of contingency management for extremely resistant patients. Here the strategic therapist imposes an ordeal appropriate to the person who wants to change—an ordeal more severe than the problem. The main requirement of the assigned ordeal is that it causes distress equal to or greater than that caused by the symptoms. It is a variant of the paradox: The cure is worse than the illness.

In one case, a woman in her early thirties was suffering from extreme anxiety manifested by regular outbursts of perspiration. Haley's strategy was to contract for an activity that she would dislike so much that she would give up her anxiety rather than do it. The contract: If she was anxious enough during the day to perspire abnormally, then she was to awaken at 2:00 in the morning to wash and wax the kitchen floor. She had to repeat it every night—even though it was wasted energy devoted to her most hated chore—until she did not perspire. The success of the trick, so to speak, depends on the patient's not dissolving the paradox by realizing that it is a trick. The Haley-like therapist must also cultivate an enormously powerful image for the contractual ordeal to continue without the patient simply dropping out of treatment.

Therapeutic Relationship

Even though Satir was active and directive with families, she emphasized the centrality of accurate empathy, positive regard, and genuineness in family systems. The therapist relates in such a way as to develop an atmosphere conducive to more congruent and functional communication. Functional communication requires an atmosphere in which anything can be discussed, anything can be raised, and there is nothing to hold a person back. This type of therapeutic context can best be achieved when the therapist relates to each family member in a caring, empathic, and congruent manner.

Rather than be nondirective, however, the Satir therapist needs to jump right in with the family and help direct them to the feelings that have been omitted from their incongruent communications (see Loeschen, 1997, for examples of Satir's relationship skills).

Haley, as we have said, concentrates on the command or power aspect of communications. The central question is which person is to govern the behavior of the other and thereby set the conditions for their relationship. Because the issue of who is in charge is critical to any relationship, it is also the central issue in a therapeutic relationship. In troubled systems, individuals avoid taking responsibility for defining the nature of their relationships. In a therapeutic system, it is necessary for the therapist to be responsible for defining the nature of the therapeutic relationship. The rule for relating is clear: The therapist is in charge and in control.

Giving directives is the means by which therapists can change the rules of relating and communicating in families. If a mother keeps intruding when father and son are communicating, the strategic therapist can directly change this pattern by giving the mother a directive to stop intruding. Directives also serve to intensify the relationship between the therapist and family. By telling people what to do, the therapist becomes involved in the action and becomes important to the patients. Whether the family follows straight directives or resists paradoxical directives at home, the therapist remains in their lives throughout the week.

As a serious student of Milton Erickson, Haley (1973) used direct and indirect techniques to control the therapeutic relationship. This is beautifully illustrated in the classic case of a bedwetting couple treated by Erickson. Erickson told the couple that the absolute requisite for therapeutic success would be their unquestioning and unfailing obedience to the instructions given to them. Erickson then commanded the bedwetting couple to deliberately wet the bed before getting into it each night for a period of 2 weeks. At the end of this time, they would be given one night off and would sleep in a dry bed on Sunday night. On the following Monday morning, they were to throw back the covers when they saw a wet bed; then, and only then, would they realize that they would face another 3 weeks of kneeling and wetting the bed. There was to be no discussion or debate, only silence and obedience.

The outcome was that each night the couple, with considerable distress, wet the bed. However, 2 weeks later when they awoke on Monday morning, the bed was dry! They started to speak but remembered the order to be silent. That night, without speaking, they "sneaked" into a dry bed and did so for the next 3 weeks.

Did the couple choose to change their behavior, or were they following the injunctions of the therapist? Were they conscious of the use of paradox, or did the therapist have an indirect hypnotic control over their behavior? In Haley's view of therapy as a power struggle, the processes of change are not really important. What is important is the outcome—who won the battle.

Practicalities

Communication patterns can best be observed and modified when a full family system is present. Communication/strategic therapists are flexible, however, and will work with marital subsystems or even an individual subsystem if necessary. Sessions usually last 1 or 1½ hours, but the therapist expects the family to continue its work at home as the members struggle with the therapist's directives.

Because so much is communicated through nonverbal behavior, communication/ strategic therapists find it valuable to videotape sessions, especially for training of novice therapists. Family therapists in general, and communication/strategic therapists in particular, are at the forefront of videotaping, direct observation, and supervision through a one-way mirror. Videotaping also permits the sessions to be used for research on communication patterns in families.

Strategic and communication therapies remain highly compatible with the contemporary emphasis on time-limited psychotherapy. Therapists limit their participation to the minimum necessary to set in motion the family's natural helping resources. Communications therapy was originally developed with schizophrenic families and would typically last a year or two. By contrast, MRI's newer Brief Therapy (Segal, 1991) and Haley's (1976) problem-solving therapy are short-term endeavors, lasting just a few weeks or months.

Fees have been a tricky issue for systemic therapists. Most health care insurance covers treatment for individual psychopathology but not couple or family problems. As a result, couples and family therapists can be forced to adhere to the notion of an identified patient, if only for insurance reimbursement. Families also wonder if fees will be greater because more people are being seen in therapy. This is sometimes the case, but typically systemic therapists charge a standard fee per session regardless of whether a family, a couple, or an individual is being seen.

Structural Therapy

Salvador Minuchin (1922–) learned about the diversity and adaptability of families while growing up in a Jewish family in rural Argentina and while living in Israel, where families from all over the world converged to build a new nation. He learned about the power that families have over psychopathology in the early 1960s, when he was conducting psychotherapy and research with delinquent youths at the Wiltwyck School in New York. Minuchin had been trained as a psychiatrist in traditional individual psychotherapies developed to fulfill the needs of verbally articulate, middle-class patients burdened by intrapsychic conflicts. The boys he was working with, however,

hailed from disorganized, multiproblem, poor families. Improvements achieved through the use of traditional techniques in the residential setting of the school tended to disappear as soon as the children returned to their families.

Minuchin and others were looking for effective alternatives with delinquents at a time when psychotherapy was becoming liberated from its preoccupation with individual psychopathology. Family therapy emerged in the 1950s, and Minuchin and others at Wiltwyck began applying this new perspective to *Families of the Slums* (Minuchin et al., 1967). Approaching delinquency as a systemic issue proved more helpful than defining it as a problem of the individual. At the same time, Minuchin and his colleagues recognized that even family therapy was not a panacea for delinquency, because psychotherapy does not have the answers to poverty and other social problems (Malcolm, 1978).

In 1965, Minuchin became director of the Philadelphia Child Guidance Clinic, where he developed structural family therapy with a wider cross-section of families. His **structural therapy** had considerable impact on diabetic and asthmatic children who were experiencing an unusually high rate of emergency hospitalizations because their conditions were being worsened by stress. Minuchin knew that he could not cure diabetes or asthma through family therapy, because these problems had a physical etiology. Minuchin (1970) believed that his therapy could best be tested with anorexia nervosa, because this eating disorder could be construed as being entirely due to emotional factors. By working to change the structure of families, Minuchin claimed that he was able to cure more than 80% of children with anorexia nervosa, a syndrome that had traditionally been attributed to individual psychopathology.

Further expansion and refinement of structural therapy occurred throughout the 1970s, when Minuchin brought in Braulio Montalvo from Wiltwyck and Jay Haley from the MRI group. This work culminated in the classic *Families and Family Therapy* (Minuchin, 1974), a fully developed account of the structural way of understanding and treating families. In 1976, Minuchin stepped down from the politics and administration of directorship and concentrated on the training of family therapists. He now does so from The Minuchin Center for the Family in New York City (Colapinto, 1991), where he completed his book, *Mastering Family Therapy: Journeys of Growth and Transformation* (Minuchin, 1997).

Theory of Psychopathology

Structural theory is more concerned with what maintains psychopathology than with what caused it. By the time therapists see patients with symptoms, the causes of the problems are part of history. These historical causes frequently cannot be empirically determined and certainly cannot be changed. What can be changed are the contemporary factors that maintain psychopathology. Whether or not it is caused by the intrapsychic dynamics of the individual, psychopathology is maintained by the interpersonal dynamics of the system. Thus, we should be concentrating on pathological family structures rather than searching for pathological intrapsychic structures.

Pathological family systems can best be understood in contrast with healthy family systems (Minuchin, 1972). An organized family will maintain clearly marked boundaries. The marital subsystem will have closed boundaries to protect the privacy of the spouses. The parental subsystem will have clear boundaries between it and the children, but not so impenetrable as to limit the access necessary for good parenting. The sibling subsystem will have its own boundaries and will be organized hierarchically, so that children are given responsibilities and privileges consistent with age as determined by the family's culture. Each family member is also an individual subsystem with a boundary that needs to

be respected. Finally, the boundary around the nuclear family will also be respected, although the extent to which kin are allowed in varies greatly with cultural, social, and economic factors.

The boundaries of a subsystem are the rules defining who participates in the subsystem and how. The boundary of a parental subsystem is defined, for example, when a mother tells her older child, "You aren't your brother's parent. If he is playing with matches, tell me and I will stop him." Healthy development requires that subsystems in a family be relatively free from interference by other subsystems. Clear boundaries or rules help maintain freedom from outside interference.

The rules that govern transactions within a family, though not usually explicitly stated, form a whole—the **structure** of the family. For a family to change its structure, it must change some of its fundamental rules for interacting.

Two major types of family structures are pathological and require changing. The first is the **disengaged family**, which has excessively rigid boundaries. In the disengaged family, there is little or no contact between family members. There is a relative absence of healthy structure, order, or authority. Ties between family members are weak or nonexistent. The overall impression of a disengaged family is distance and disconnect. The mother in this group tends to be passive and immobile. She feels overwhelmed, has a derogatory self-image, experiences herself as exploited, and almost always develops psychosomatic and depressive symptomatology. The children in such families are at risk of developing antisocial symptomatology.

The second type of troubled family is the **enmeshed family**; its boundaries are diffuse. The distinguishing quality of enmeshed families is a "tight interlocking" of its members, such that attempts on the part of one member to change elicit immediate complementary resistance on the part of others (Minuchin et al., 1967). Enmeshment is essentially a weakening of boundaries among family subsystems. Because the boundary between nuclear family and families of origin is not well maintained, in-law problems are likely to develop. The boundary separating the parents from their children is crossed frequently in improper ways, such as incest. The roles of spouse and parent are insufficiently differentiated, so that neither the spouse subsystem nor the parental subsystem can operate. Individual boundaries are not respected, so that individual subsystems are not able to develop adequate autonomy and identity. An anorexic adolescent, for example, may assert autonomy only by saying no to the family's demands to eat.

Families are open systems that continually face demands for change. These demands may come from changes in the larger environment, such as the death of a family friend. Demands may also come from developmental changes in the family, such as the birth of a baby or a child's attaining adolescence. Healthy families respond to demands for change by growth on the part of each individual in the family, each subsystem within the family, and the family as a unit. Dysfunctional families respond to demands for change in pathological ways, as when the mother in a disengaged family becomes more depressed or a child acts out. Usually one family member develops symptoms and becomes the identified patient, even though the basic problem is the family's inability to grow and adapt to change.

Therapeutic Processes

Because symptoms are manifested and maintained in family structures unable to adapt, the goal of therapy is to restructure families to free the members to grow and relate. Because the family structure reflects the rules for interacting, changing a family's structure involves changing its rules for relating. This typically entails changing the system's boundaries from rigid or diffuse to normal, from a disengaged or enmeshed family to a healthy family.

Consciousness Raising

Minuchin (1974) shares a view of consciousness unique to systems theorists: Consciousness is not just an intracerebral process, but also an extracerebral process. Individuals think and feel and exist within social contexts, and the events they experience in the family are crucial aspects of consciousness. If the family context transforms to a higher level of development, then the individual's consciousness will also be raised. Members of disengaged families, for example, are likely to perceive the social world as disconnected people with highly rigid boundaries between them. To conceive of people as interrelated and interdependent is against the family rules. By participating in a family context that becomes more engaged, that lowers the boundaries, the individual becomes mindful of how people are inherently related.

The client's work in this process is relatively simple: to attend the family sessions and be attentive in the sessions; to give feedback to the therapist when asked about changes that might be desired; and to perceive changes in relationship patterns as they occur in the family context. In a classic case with an anorexic girl, Minuchin (1974) asked the attentive adolescent about the family's rule against closed doors. Would she like to close her door in order to have more privacy? The girl said that indeed she would. She was thus helping the structural therapist to become more aware of the need for clearer boundaries around individual subsystems in this enmeshed family. By perceiving others in the family beginning to close their doors, including the parents closing their bedroom door for the first time, the clients could concretely see how a family can function better by having better boundaries.

In structural therapy, the therapist does much of the work. The therapist is active and directive. In order to direct actions in an effective way, the therapist must become conscious of the structure and the rules that govern a particular family. The therapist's attention is focused on the here and now, because family rules can best be perceived by observing who interacts with whom and how. Some of this increased awareness the therapist shares overtly with clients; other aspects are best perceived by changing the family context. The therapist will almost routinely reframe a presenting problem, for example, so that the family members can become more conscious of how symptoms are system events rather than individual events.

Minuchin (1974, p. 1) illustrates reframing in an opening session with Mr. Smith, who has been hospitalized twice for agitated depression, his wife, 12-year-old son, and father-in-law.

Minuchin: What is the problem?

Mr. Smith: I think it's my problem.

Minuchin: Don't be so sure. Never be so sure.

Mr. Smith: Well, I'm the one that was in the hospital.

Minuchin: Yeah, that still doesn't tell me it is your problem. Okay, go ahead. What is your problem?

Mr. Smith: Just nervous, upset all the time … seem to be never relaxed.

Minuchin: Do you think you are the problem?

Mr. Smith: Oh, I kind of think so. I don't know if it is caused by anybody, but I'm the one that has the problem.

Minuchin: Let's follow your line of thinking. If it would be caused by somebody or something outside of yourself, what would you say your problem is?

Mr. Smith: You know, I'd be very surprised.

Minuchin: Let's think in the family who makes you upset?

Mr. Smith: I don't think anybody in the family makes me upset.

Minuchin: Let me ask your wife, okay?

Instead of focusing on the individual, Minuchin focuses on the person within the family context. He helps the family conceptualize symptoms as systemic problems rather than individual disorders. Reframing the problem in this way will help family members raise their consciousness from a strictly individualistic ideology to a systemic perspective.

Frequently, reframing is used to interpret the role that symptoms play in maintaining homeostasis within a family. To the parents of a girl who had been hospitalized for a psychotic break, Minuchin expressed his concern that when they returned home with their daughter, she would go crazy again (Malcolm, 1978). The reason she would go crazy was to save their marriage. The psychotic symptoms were thus interpreted as the means by which a good daughter could help her family stay together, rather than the weakness of a bad daughter who falls apart. Reframing enables each family member to become more aware of how symptoms are an integral part of the family's functioning.

The therapist will encourage a family to enact family transactions rather than describe them. In **enactments**, the therapist explicitly directs family members to engage in a particular activity, such as "Discuss with your mother your curfew time and try to come to a decision." More dramatically, the therapist may arrange a lunch and have food brought to the session so the family can enact how they dine with an anorexic in their midst. Enacting transactional patterns helps family members experience their own reactions with heightened awareness. Enactment also allows therapists to see family members in action, and it is through such observations that the therapist becomes aware of the family structure.

Choosing

Structural therapy is relatively unique in that it emphasizes the process we have labeled **social liberation**. Social liberation occurs when a social system is changed to create more alternatives for healthy responding. Laws requiring equal opportunity for everyone in the workplace, for example, can enhance individual growth and social justice. The more alternatives in a system, the greater the freedom individuals have to choose responses conducive to their own growth. Structural therapists emphasize restructuring of family systems as the means by which subsystems in the family can become freer to respond and relate in healthier patterns.

The client's commitment to liberate the system from pathogenic rules begins with a formal or informal contract to participate in structural therapy. The contract includes rules of how often the family will meet, who will attend, how long sessions will last, and the initial goals of therapy. Implicitly, the family is also choosing to let an outsider, the therapist, join their system. Once therapy is under way, clients need to find the courage to try alternative ways of relating that the therapist recommends.

Restructuring assignments in the session and as homework can produce stress, because the assignments transgress rules that have bound the family together. By cooperating with such assignments, however, family members participate actively in creating a new set of rules that permit them to relate in a family that can foster growth rather than illness.

The first task of the structural therapist is to join the system to change it from within. But that is no small task, because family systems erect boundaries designed to exclude outsiders. Minuchin uses the common term **joining** to denote a host of techniques for entering a family system by engaging its members and subsystems. The therapist must learn to speak the language of the family, using its own metaphors and idioms. The therapist must also join all of the various subsystems in the family, lest the therapist be seen as the parents' agent or the children's agent. When joining with the parents, the therapist will speak the language of responsibility; when joining the sibling subsystem, the therapist will speak the language of rights.

Like anthropologists who join new social systems, systemic therapists must initially accommodate themselves to the rules of the system. If the family is hierarchically structured across four generations, the therapist might address the great-grandmother first. This type of **accommodation** involves maintenance of the family subsystems through planned support of the family structure. The therapist also accommodates to the family through tracking the context of the family's communication and behavior, by asking questions for clarification, making approving statements, or asking for amplification of certain points. Another accommodation technique is **mimesis**, which is imitating or miming important communication or behavior patterns of the family. In a jovial family, for example, the therapist becomes jovial; in a family with a restricted communication style, the therapist's communication becomes sparse.

Once the therapist and family have joined, they have in fact created a new therapeutic system. The therapist is the leader of this system, as expressed through the therapist's becoming more directive. The therapist's use of reframing, for example, communicates that the family will function at a systems level rather than focus on one identified patient. In the process of joining the family, the therapist avoids confrontation, lest the therapist risk being excluded by powerful subsystems of the family. Once all parties are joined, however, the therapist can confront and challenge the dysfunctional rules of the system.

Marking boundaries is one technique to restructure the family. Like a good leader, the structural therapist has created a psychopolitical map of the family terrain. The therapist needs to have an accurate idea of who relates to whom and how. Then the therapist can give assignments that will redraw the boundaries along healthier lines. If mother and daughter relate as siblings, for example, the therapist may put the mother in charge of the daughter's activities for a week. If the boundary that delineates an individual is not respected, the structural therapist may ask each person to think and speak only for herself or himself. If a clear boundary does not exist around a couple who spend all their time parenting, the therapist may ask them to go away together for a weekend without children.

The structural clinician can keep the therapeutic system functioning at home by assigning tasks for homework. The mother who follows through on her homework of supervising her daughter's activities for a week is responding at home to the healthier therapeutic system rather than to the old rules of relating that defined mother and daughter as sisters.

The use of enactment in the sessions not only increases consciousness about historical patterns of relating, but also permits the therapist to change patterns of relating in the here and now. The therapist may, for example, use a blocking technique that breaks up the usual communication patterns. Daughter may be blocked from communicating to father through mother and may be asked to relate to father directly. If mother and father consistently avoid clear boundaries around them by having a child sit between them, the therapist can block such transactions by directing the child to change seats with mother or father.

The therapist may use an exaggerated imitation of the family's style to point out a dysfunctional pattern. In a family with an overcontrolling mother who yells at her adolescent daughter, the therapist might yell louder. Manipulating such moods can force the mother to soften her interactions and thereby give the daughter more autonomy.

By accommodating and joining and then confirming, blocking, and challenging the family's patterns of interacting, the structural therapist is liberating the family from destructive rules of relating. In the process of helping a family restructure itself, the therapist frees its members from transactions that have created psychopathology.

Therapeutic Relationship

The structural therapist has a unique way of relating to clients. The joining process certainly includes accurate empathy, warmth, and caring. But once a therapeutic system has been created, the therapist relates as an authoritative leader. The therapist acts like a psychopolitician, advocating for the benefit of each family member against a social system that has developed a destructive structure. The therapist joins with each family subsystem to overthrow a set of rules that prevent the members from relating within and across healthy boundaries.

Without a relationship based on joining, the therapist would be impotent in helping families liberate themselves from enmeshed or disengaged transaction patterns. The relationship alone, however, cannot produce structural changes in family systems. The therapist must be willing to challenge, block, and disrupt a homeostatic system. Minuchin behaves like a charismatic director—flattering, mocking, encouraging, joking, commanding, cajoling, always leading. Only by using active, disruptive techniques can the family therapist give troubled families greater freedom to restructure themselves along healthier lines.

Practicalities

The format of therapy should be consistent with the function of therapy. If the goal is to observe how a family structures itself in space, then the whole family should be present. The room should be large and flexible enough to allow family members to sit initially wherever they choose, thereby revealing the family's rules. The therapist must also be flexible enough to restructure the seating as a means of restructuring the family. The practicalities of many therapies, such as the seating arrangements of clients, are part of the process of understanding and changing the structure of families.

A therapist who aims to strengthen the boundaries of the spouse subsystem may request to see only the parents for a session or two. If a therapist aims to restructure a multigenerational family, then it is most practical to have all generations present, rather than have the clients simply talk about the grandparents.

In practice, structural therapy has been used most often with families in which a child or adolescent is the identified patient. Such families are usually more willing to come in as a full family than are families in which an adult member is identified as the patient.

Structural therapy is designed as an active, short-term treatment that initiates the change process that helps restructure families. By releasing family members from their stereotyped positions, restructuring enables the system to mobilize its underutilized resources and to improve its adaptability. The structural therapist limits the number of sessions to the minimum necessary to set in motion the family's natural helping resources. Structural therapists were among the pioneers of brief therapy.

It may happen that, as a result of structural intervention, the family is helped not only to change but also to **metachange**. That is, in addition to overcoming its current crisis, the family will enhance its ability to deal with future events without external help (Colapinto, 1991). This high level of achievement is of course desirable, but more modest and practical accomplishments are still valuable. Families may well need to come back for help at times of future crises. The prospect of booster sessions is more practical, natural, and economical than the protracted presence of a therapist accompanying the family for years.

Bowen Family Systems Therapy

The audience was expecting Murray Bowen (1913–1990) to present a theoretical paper as part of a symposium at a professional convention. Instead, Bowen (1972) presented a "convention shattering" procedure that he had used to change his own family of origin.

Bowen was part of a large, extended kin group that had dominated a small southern town for many generations. At the 1967 symposium, Bowen revealed how he had intruded into most of the dominant triangles of his immediate family by means of a surprising strategy. He sent off letters that told various relatives about the unpleasant gossip that others were circulating about them. He signed these letters with endearing salutations such as "Your Meddlesome Brother" or "Your Strategic Son." He also announced an impending visit. Bowen then arrived as heralded, to deal with the predictably indignant reactions of his relatives. The effect on the family was dramatic. Many closed-off relationships were reopened. Once the initial fury against Bowen had subsided, his intervention created a warm climate of better feelings all around.

Bowen's intervention with his family of origin grew out of the **family systems therapy** he had been developing over the previous two decades. After serving as an army physician in World War II, he had trained at the Menninger Clinic in Topeka, Kansas. Like many of the early systems theorists, he was particularly enthusiastic about trying to understand and treat schizophrenia. It was not new to conceptualize schizophrenia as emanating from an unresolved symbiosis between mother and child. It was a radical innovation at a psychoanalytic center such as Menninger's, however, to actually bring the mother into the clinical picture as part of the investigation and treatment of schizophrenic patients.

Bowen's clinical work was followed by 5 years of family research, from 1954 to 1959, at the National Institute of Mental Health (NIMH) just outside Washington, DC. Bowen began by having a small group of schizophrenic patients and their mothers live together on a hospital ward. After a year of individual therapy for both patients and mothers, fathers were included and the family was treated as a single unit rather than treating individuals in the unit (Bowen, 1978).

Sensing that the NIMH was not particularly supportive of his new approach, which flew in the face of conventional individual psychotherapy, Bowen relocated a few miles away to Georgetown University, where he remained until his death. Here, Bowen (1978) formulated his cerebral and deliberate approach, known as family systems therapy, and here he completed detailed multigenerational research with a few families, including one case going back more than 300 years. Noting that one could spend a lifetime on only a few such family studies, Bowen made the seminal decision that his own family was most accessible for such a multigenerational study. From this study and the intervention with his own family, Bowen (1978; Kerr & Bowen, 1988) became convinced of the importance for both clients and therapists of differentiating themselves from their families of origin.

Theory of Psychopathology

Emotional illness arises when individuals are unable to adequately differentiate themselves from their families of origin. **Differentiation of self** is the ability to be emotionally controlled while remaining within the emotional intensity of one's family. Differentiation of self reflects the extent to which one can think objectively about emotionally loaded issues within the family.

Fusion is the phenomenon that interferes with differentiation of self from family. Fusion refers to two aspects of immaturity. First, there is the fusion of feeling and thinking when objective thinking is overwhelmed by emotionality and becomes its servant. What results then is rationalization or intellectualization to justify the acting out of emotional immaturity. Second, fusion refers to the absence of boundaries or the lack of individuality between two or more individuals, as in the case of symbiotic relationships.

Fusion in families results in an **undifferentiated family ego mass**, which is a quality of "stuck togetherness." Fusion leads to a conglomerate emotional oneness. The more threatened or insecure a family feels, the more they tend to fuse. The more stressed or distressed individuals feel, the more they seek the security of oneness that results from family fusion. Chronic distress can produce emotionally ill individuals unable to differentiate themselves from their family. They remain stuck forever in the family, and the family is stuck around them.

Fusion between any two people, such as a husband and wife, relieves tension by involving vulnerable third parties who take sides. Fusion thus gives rise to **triangulation**. Dyads are inherently unstable because they inevitably result in periods of insensitivity, abrasiveness, or withdrawal. The party who feels offended or rejected will attempt to triangulate a parent, child, neighbor, or partner for support.

Triangles are much more stable relationships; they are, in fact, the basic building blocks in any emotional system. Triangles can make differentiation from the family difficult because the parents need a child to maintain a stable system or because a child needs a parent for support against others. In couple conflicts, the most common triangles lead to in-law problems, affairs, or child problems.

Triangles in a state of calm consist of a comfortable twosome and an outsider. One of the classic triangles of this type is the close mother and child with a passive, withdrawn father. The favored position is to be a member of the close twosome rather than the odd one out. When tension mounts in the outsider, the predictable move is to try to form a twosome with one of the original members of the twosome, leaving the other one an outsider. Thus, the foci within the triangle shift from moment to moment and over long periods of time, as each member jockeys for a comfortable position. In this case, if father tries to get close to his child, the mother is likely to react with upset lest she be the odd one out.

When the triangle is in a state of tension, the outsider position becomes the preferred position. From this comfortable position the person can say, "You two fight and leave me out of it." In a state of tension, if it is not possible to shift the focus within the triangle, the members of the original twosome will form another triangle with a convenient family person, such as another child. In periods of very high tension, a system will triangle in more and more outsiders. A common example: a family in crisis triangulates neighbors, schools, police, and mental health professionals into the family problem. If the family is successful in getting others involved, then they can revert to a more comfortable homeostasis and let the outsiders fight.

Rather than resolve triangles through self-differentiation, most people use **emotional cutoff** to cope with their unresolved attachments to their families of origin. The cutoff consists of denial and isolation of the problems when living close to the parents, or physically running away, or a combination of the two. Whatever the pattern, the person yearns for emotional closeness but is allergic to it. People who use intrapsychic cutoff mechanisms to tolerate living closer to the parents generally function better. Those who put physical distance between themselves and the parents—the infamous "geographic cure"—tend to blame parents and act out impulsively in relationships. When problems develop in their own marriage or nuclear family, they tend to run from these as well.

Triangles tend to occur across generations, because a parent or child is often the most available and vulnerable person to be brought into a couple's conflict. If a wife is experiencing considerable discomfort about her marriage, she can regain its homeostasis or balance by projecting her anxieties onto a child. A **family projection process** pulls the parents together by creating a preoccupation with the child's problem. The child who is most vulnerable to this projection is the child who is emotionally closest or most fused with the parents. This child will tend to be the person who develops symptoms for the family. This child will also have little chance of differentiating an adequate self, because the family needs the child to maintain homeostasis in the parents' relationship. If the child becomes unstuck and matures through psychotherapy, for example, then the parents' marriage will be at risk of deterioration.

Because triangles typically occur across generations, severe psychopathology can develop from a **multigenerational transmission process**. A child who has been triangulated can emerge from the family with a lower level of self-differentiation. This child is likely to marry someone of a similar differentiation level, and their children are likely to have even lower levels of differentiation. After multiple generations, a child can emerge with such a low level of differentiation that a severe pathology, such as schizophrenia, is almost inevitable. Rather than an individual process, psychopathology is almost always a multigenerational transmission process.

Therapeutic Processes

Psychopathology arises from an inadequate differentiation of self from the family emotional system; consequently, the goal of Bowenian treatment is to increase differentiation of self. Because triangles interfere with differentiation of self, successful therapy will involve detriangulation of family members. Rather than work on all possible family triangles, the therapist has the advantage of knowing that a family is a system of interlocking triangles. Thus, change produced in one triangle will probably cause change in all the triangles.

A nuclear family is formed as the result of the fusion of a couple, typically a husband and wife. Accordingly, they are the most important members to increase their differentiation of self, even if it is a child who is manifesting the family's symptoms. Bowen (1978) thus preferred to work with the marital subsystem rather than have the children present in therapy. He was also convinced that successful therapy is possible by working with only one individual member who is motivated to mature and differentiate. When there is finally one member of a troubled triangle who can control his or her emotional responsiveness and not take sides with the other two, the emotional intensity within the twosome will decrease and both will move to a higher level of differentiation.

Unless the triangulated person can remain in emotional contact, however, the twosome will triangle in someone else. By helping only one member to become more differentiated and detriangulated, a therapist can help an entire family system to change.

Consciousness Raising

Differentiation of self requires thinking objectively about emotionally loaded topics in the family. Clients can think more objectively about themselves and their families by developing their powers of observation more keenly. Observation involves the ability to step back from an emotional interaction and perceive the events from an emotional distance. Observation helps control automatic and autonomic reactions.

When two or more members of a family system are present, the work of each patient is to observe what the other person is communicating. Observation can allow clients to become more objectively aware of what others are communicating rather than building an emotional rejoinder. Clients working alone can learn to use these same powers of observation as part of their homework. When they are home, their work is to

observe the role they play in family triangles and to observe the typical emotional reactions they exhibit in each triangle. Observation not only begets an objective perspective but also creates a unique perspective different from the perspective of family members who are too caught up in the family drama to see themselves and others clearly.

When two or more family members are present, the Bowenian therapist keeps the emotional system sufficiently toned down to allow clients to process conflicts objectively without undue emotional reactions. The therapist is active with constant questions, first to one spouse and then to the other. The therapist will subsequently ask the listening client to share his or her thoughts and observations about what was just communicated. Encouraging spouses to communicate directly to each other will only encourage them to react emotionally rather than objectively.

The therapist also uses education to teach clients about how family systems function and dysfunction. This education begins by helping clients become more aware of each other's family history and the role each played in the history of his or her family of origin. Often the therapist will create a **genogram**, a family tree of sorts, that illustrates the relationships of family members across several generations. The genogram will illustrate which family members were close, which were cut off, and which were conflicted. This genogram can be used to teach clients about triangles and how they interfere with differentiation of a more autonomous self.

Family system therapists emphasize observations rather than interpretations as the means to a differentiated consciousness. Interpretations are directed at the "why" of family interactions. Why people act the way they do is not open to direct observation, and interpretations about the motives of others tend to be subjective and emotional. Observations, on the other hand, focus on the who, what, when, and where of family relationships, which are more objective, observable facts.

Choosing

Patients can liberate themselves from the family system by choosing to respond in a more autonomous fashion. Autonomy involves responding from an "I" position rather than reacting from a "We" position. The "I" position derives in part from what "I" observe to be factual rather than what "We" as a family hope to be true. Enormous courage is required to choose to respond differently from the family ideology, because the individual risks the wrath or rejection of family members, just as Bowen risked the fury of his family when he chose to respond differently.

Choosing to respond autonomously does not mean returning to the family of origin and blaming one's parents or siblings for personal problems. That sort of blaming is simply another emotional reaction to the family system that will stimulate the blamed relative to triangulate in a third party for support. Autonomous responding is not intended to blame or to change the other person.

The differentiating person chooses the "I" position to communicate "This is what I think or believe" and "This is what I will do or not do," without imposing values or beliefs on other family members. The **responsible I** assumes responsibility for one's own experiences and comfort and leaves emotional and intellectual space for others to create their own happiness. A reasonably differentiated person is capable of genuine concern for others without expecting something in return. The togetherness forces of family fusion, however, treat differentiation as selfish and hostile.

People who choose to be different in significant ways from their families must be willing to behave reasonably rather than react emotionally to the predictable forces against differentiation. The predictable steps in the family reaction to differentiation are: (1) "You are wrong," (2) "Change back," and (3) "If you do not, you will be criticized, be ostracized, or be guilty of driving your parent or partner crazy."

The therapist's task is to respond autonomously to family forces rather than to react emotionally. The therapist remains differentiated rather than become triangulated into the family system. The therapist is differentiated enough to respond reasonably to clients' attempts to make the therapist feel guilty, angry, anxious, or overly responsible. The therapist responds from a well-differentiated "I" position rather than a "We" or "You" position.

When clients are ready to risk more autonomous responses in their families of origin, the therapist functions like a coach or consultant. The therapist clarifies that the client's goal is to differentiate oneself, not to blame or change others. The goal is not to win in a confrontation or to impose an interpretation, but simply to enhance one's differentiation. Clients can be reminded that they can behave differently in their family regardless of whether others change or not. Responding differently can indeed liberate relatives to change, but that is their responsibility, not the client's. Like a good coach, the therapist will check on the progress clients have made between sessions in their relationships to their family of origin.

Therapeutic Relationship

The Bowenian relationship is important as much for what the therapist does *not* do as for what the therapist does. Effective therapists do not allow themselves to be triangulated into family relationships. Even though clients will use all types of conscious and unconscious maneuvers to triangle the therapist into reacting emotionally, the differentiated therapist consciously chooses to respond reasonably. Unlike some family therapists who dive right into the family system to create strong emotional reactions, the Bowenian therapist prevents a transference reaction by maintaining an objective "I" position. Entering a triangled relationship with spouses may indeed allow them to reestablish a homeostasis that removes symptoms, but it does nothing to help them establish differentiated selves who can prevent future symptoms. The Bowenian therapist, in sum, acts as a model of autonomous, responsible, and differentiated behavior despite the inevitable attempts to ensnare him or her in triangles and emotions.

By maintaining an "I" position, the family system therapist relates in a genuine manner, which allows clients to differentiate their own beliefs and actions from the therapist's. The therapist relates in a calm, relaxed, and interested style that communicates caring, without trying to establish the unconditional positive regard that is more conducive to family fusion than self-differentiation. Finally, the Bowenian therapist depends on the powers of observation and objective thought rather than empathy to understand what is going on in troubled families.

Practicalities

Bowen's family therapy is more flexible than those systemic theories that insist on having all family members present. Actually, the more family members present, the more difficult it is to detriangulate the parents, because the energy and emotions can shift from one triangled child to the next. Bowen (1978; Kerr & Bowen, 1988) himself preferred to work with the spouses or with one motivated parent, rather than with the children present. Other Bowenian therapists, however, will work with entire families as part of their practice. Estimates are that about 25% of systemic practice is with entire families, 25% with spouses, and 50% with individuals (Aylmer, 1978).

Differentiation of self is a lengthy and often painful process before people become more autonomous adults in the presence of their parents. Psychotherapy can certainly facilitate this process. At the same time, many clients are seeking relief from symptoms rather than differentiation of self. Therapy will thus be briefer with many clients, but it will take several years of well-spaced sessions to complete a genuine growth process.

More so than other systems theorists, Bowen was a strong proponent of **family of origin therapy** for the psychotherapist. Because therapists must avoid becoming triangulated by the togetherness forces of the clients' systems, it is essential that Bowenian therapists participate in a lengthy personal therapy designed to differentiate themselves more fully from their own family of origin. Such therapy is a core component of training in the Bowen method and associated intergenerational therapies (Lebow, 2005).

Evidence-Based Family Therapies

The communication/strategic, structural, and Bowenian approaches to family therapy all grew out of clinical practice and theorizing in the 1950s and 1960s. By contrast, the so-called **evidence-based family therapies** all grew out of empirical research in the 1980s, 1990s, and 2000s. They are the new generation that build on the rich heritage of preceding systemic therapies and that, as their title proudly proclaims, favor research evidence.

These evidence-based family therapies include functional family therapy (Alexander & Parsons, 1982; Sexton, 2010), multidimensional family therapy (Liddle, 2009), and multisystemic therapy (Henggeler et al., 2009). We shall feature the latter given its clinical popularity and extensive research.

Multisystemic therapy (MST) is a highly directive, intensive family-based treatment based on systems, social-ecological, and social-learning theories (Henggeler & Schoenwald, 2003). MST was developed for treating families with serious clinical problems, typically youth with conduct disorders and substance abuse. The "multi" in

MST refers to the multiple targets of the treatment—the individual, the family, and the larger system—that contribute to the adolescent's problem. Multiple-level assessments of the individual, the family, and the social systems are built into the 2- to 4-month treatment.

Families mandated to MST typically come from clinical populations historically labeled as "resistant" (e.g., juvenile offenders, substance abusing youth) and who have typically experienced multiple treatment failures. It is assumed that treatment will not progress until the therapist and key family members (the youth's caregivers or other adults who have decision-making authority) are engaged and ready to work on important therapeutic tasks, such as defining problems, setting goals, and implementing interventions to meet those goals.

Family members collaborate with MST therapists in designing a tailored treatment plan. The plans build on the strengths in their lives, which makes it more likely the family will be successful with the plan, both during and after treatment. While the plan is particularized to fit the ecology of each particular case, the therapist is instructed to select only those assessment and treatment methods whose effectiveness has been amply demonstrated in controlled research.

MST therapists utilize several core clinical strategies to enhance collaboration with families. These strategies are culled from various theoretical orientations and help create a climate of engagement while behavioral and systemic interventions are being implemented. The most common engagement strategies used in MST entail going where the youth and family live (vs. always in an office), scheduling sessions frequently and as needed, expressing warmth, reframing negativity, maintaining a family (vs. a child) focus, harnessing family supports, and responding flexibly to these troubled families (Tuerk et al., 2012).

The systemic and behavioral interventions target the adolescents' entire system—family, friends, school, and neighborhood—to break the cycle of antisocial activities. These interventions include many of those reviewed earlier in this and the behavior therapy chapter: parent management training, conjoint family sessions to improve relations, tutoring and vocational counseling, involvement with friends who do not participate in criminal behavior, network therapy with extended family and friends to help the parents/caregivers maintain the changes, and contingency management to reward all of these positive behaviors.

No treatment is effective if it is not administered, and MST directly addresses the ubiquitous problem of missed sessions among low-income, "resistant" families. Using the five P's for resuming contact with clients can increase communication when treatment has stalled (Tuerk et al., 2012):

1. *Prepare.* Obtain releases of information for communicating with the client's social network early in treatment so that they can be contacted in case of client disengagement.
2. *Persevere.* Stop by a client's residence and leave notes to demonstrate that the therapist is committed to doing whatever it takes to keep the family in treatment.
3. *Practice the "foot in the door" technique.* Offer to bring food to the session or request a 5-minute check-in session at a time or place the client prefers.
4. *Provide positive reinforcement.* Strive to reinforce clients whenever re-contact is made (instead of scolding for missing), so that they feel warmly welcomed back.
5. *Promote urgency.* Coordinate a session through other systems working with the family, for example, the family's neighbor or the youth's probation officer, and then emphasize the genuine concern and desire to achieve treatment goals.

The therapeutic processes of change in multisystemic therapy are predictably multiple: consciousness raising, choosing, counterconditioning, and contingency management. The therapeutic relationship serves as both a precondition of change and a process of change. That relationship is distinctive in that the youth, the family, and the entire system are recipients of services. It is more accurate to speak of multiple collaborations rather than *the* therapeutic alliance.

Therapists on the MST team are on call 24 hours a day, 7 days a week. Such an intensive service is possible because they work with a limited number of families at any given time. Their aim is to break the cycle of criminal behavior by keeping kids at home, in school, and out of trouble.

Effectiveness of Systemic Therapies

The value of conventional research methodologies in assessing the effectiveness of systemic therapies is hotly contested in some circles. Although many defend the necessity of scientific evaluation, critics argue that most therapy research reflects the assumptions of logical positivism, which are antithetical to the principles of systems thinking itself. The critics argue that systems theory is characterized by **nonlinear dynamics**, by change that is not amenable to the linear cause-and-effect models familiar to behavioral scientists. Instead, chaos and complexity theory provide the best ways to understand systems theory and to advance more sophisticated methods for studying complex human systems (Warren et al., 1998).

According to those who espouse nonlinear dynamics, the assumptions of the scientific method are incompatible with the following underlying assumptions of systemic therapy (Goldenberg & Goldenberg, 2008):

- Multiple viewpoints exist regarding what constitutes reality and change (rather than a single, objective reality).

- Multiple causalities account for most events (not simple, treatment-causes-improvement sequences).
- The entire system should be the unit of study (rather than changes in individuals or smaller units to ensure rigor).
- The therapist should be searching for systemic connections (not explanations based on intrapsychic or linear causes).

For better or worse, however, proponents of nonlinear dynamics have not published controlled outcome studies using their own guidelines, so we are left to consider the published research conducted in the conventional manner.

Overall Effectiveness

At least 20 meta-analyses have been performed and published on the general effectiveness of couple and family therapy. These meta-analyses center on the format of family therapy, rather than the theoretical orientation of systemic therapy, but they are nonetheless relevant here.

Reviews of numerous meta-analyses (Carr, 2009a, 2009b; Shadish & Baldwin, 2003) generate these evidence-based conclusions:

- Couple and family therapies are indeed effective, with an average effect size across meta-analyses of 0.65 compared to no-treatment controls. This figure translates into a treatment success rate of 65% in couple and family therapies compared to 34% in untreated control groups.
- The treatment effects are slightly reduced at follow-up (after termination), dropping from an effect size of 0.65 to 0.52. Positive effects remain but taper over time.
- Family therapy and systemic interventions usually prove effective for both child-focused and adult-focused problems, which are among the most common and intractable behavioral health conditions.

- The average effects for couple therapy ($d = 0.84$) tend to be higher than the effects of family therapy. This number translates into a success rate of approximately 80% of treated clients versus 30% of untreated people.
- Direct comparisons of various couple and family therapies find small and usually insignificant differences among them. The possible exceptions are the relative inferiority of Satir and person-centered therapies and the relative superiority of behavioral marital therapy (see Chapter 9).
- Comparisons between couples/family therapy and other treatments consistently show that couples and family therapy works as well, and sometimes better, than alternatives, including individual psychotherapy and group therapy. The evidence suggests for now, a tie between the effectiveness of individual therapy and family therapy (Shadish et al., 1995).

Taken together, the outcome literature on marital and family therapies (MFT) is comparatively large and quite impressive: "[T]herapists and researchers should be pleased with the state of the MFT outcome research literature. It is generally as good or better than outcome research in most other areas of psychotherapy, and it demonstrates moderate and often clinically significant effects" (Shadish et al., 1995, p. 358).

Specific Disorders

As psychotherapy research matures, it graduates from the global question of "Does this psychotherapy work?" to the more narrow "Which psychotherapy works best for these patients and these disorders?" The outcome research on couple and family therapy has followed this progression, moving from an examination of its overall effectiveness to its effectiveness with specific disorders. In this section, we summarize the controlled outcome research on six disorders: alcohol dependence, drug abuse, conduct disorder, depression, childhood obesity, and schizophrenia.

Alcohol Dependence

A meta-analysis was conducted on 21 controlled studies of family-involved therapy for alcohol dependence (Edwards & Steinglass, 1995). Family therapy was definitely effective in motivating alcoholics to enter treatment; in fact, alcoholics whose family members were involved in therapy entered treatment at rates ranging from 57% to 86% across the four studies as compared with rates from 0% to 31% in the control groups. Once the alcohol abuser entered treatment, family therapy was only marginally more effective than individual therapy.

Drug Abuse

Several reviews have documented the effectiveness of family therapies in the treatment of substance abusers. A meta-analysis on 15 studies (1,571 cases) involved couple and family therapy for drug abuse (Stanton & Shadish, 1997). Clients receiving family therapy manifested significantly lower drug use after treatment than did clients in nonfamily therapy. Family therapy was shown to be as effective for adults as for adolescents and to be a cost-effective adjunct to methadone maintenance. The meta-analytic evidence favored family therapy over (1) individual psychotherapy, (2) peer group therapy, and (3) family psychoeducation for the treatment of drug abuse.

A meta-analysis of outpatient interventions for adolescent substance abuse located 31 randomized trials (Becker & Curry, 2008). The treatment approaches with evidence of superiority were family therapy, motivational interviewing (Chapter 5), and cognitive-behavioral therapy (Chapter 10). Family therapy is demonstrably more effective than no treatment and perhaps more effective than individual therapies for both adolescents and adults suffering from substance abuse.

Conduct Disorder

A recent meta-analysis summarized the results of 24 studies involving the newer, evidence-based family therapies in the treatment of adolescent substance abuse and delinquency (Baldwin et al., 2012). As a group, functional family therapy, multidimensional family therapy, and MST all substantially outperformed no treatment ($d = 0.70$) and modestly outperformed treatment as usual ($d = 0.21$).

In reviews of research-supported psychotherapies for children and adolescents, family-based approaches predominate, especially in the treatment of externalizing problems such as conduct disorder and delinquency (e.g., Chorpita et al., 2011; Weisz & Kazdin, 2010). We shall review the effectiveness of MST specifically in a few pages, but for now, we would highlight the success of these treatments in working with youth and families that many psychotherapy systems have neglected. Youth with conduct problems have high dropout rates from school, psychotherapy, and even life; single-parent status, economic disadvantage, minority status, and residence in low-income neighborhoods place them at a huge disadvantage (Gopalan et al., 2010). Yet, much in the tradition of Minuchin and colleagues, these new-generation family therapies have not only successfully engaged such families in treatment, but also proven effective in attenuating a range of serious clinical problems while improving family functioning.

Depression

A meta-analysis of eight controlled trials provided evidence for the effectiveness of family- and couple-based treatments for depression (Barbato & D'Avanzo, 2008). Couples therapy is comparable to individual therapies in reducing depressive symptoms ($d = 0.12$) and more effective than individual therapies in improving relationship satisfaction ($d = 0.60$). It comes as no surprise to systems advocates, but many individual therapists are surprised to learn that "individual" disorders are frequently best treated in couple and family treatments (Carr, 2009b).

Childhood Obesity

As psychotherapy has progressively blended into health care, more research has been conducted on psychological treatments for health behaviors. Case in point: family therapy for childhood obesity. Because children's diets and exercise are profoundly influenced by parental behavior, many clinicians have added family components to childhood weight-loss programs. A meta-analysis of 16 studies indicated that treatments containing a family-behavioral component produced larger effect sizes than the alternative treatments (Young et al., 2007). Childhood obesity is a family and systemic problem requiring family and systemic intervention.

Schizophrenia

A number of family treatments for schizophrenia have been initiated, partly in light of the high relapse rates for schizophrenia and partly because of the success of **expressed emotion (EE)** in predicting relapse. Studies demonstrate that relapse is far more likely if schizophrenic patients live with or have extensive contact with relatives who are excessively critical or overinvolved (that is, showed high levels of expressed emotion; Roth & Fonagy, 1996). Family therapy aims to improve functioning and to prevent relapse, as opposed to curing the illness.

The treatment outcome data on schizophrenia over the past 25 years point to the effectiveness of family therapy. One set of researchers (Huxley et al., 2000) identified 70 controlled studies on schizophrenic patients: 26 on group therapy; 18 on family therapy; and 11 on individual therapy. Sixty-one of the 70 studies included control groups, and all studies included medication in addition to the psychotherapy. Adjunctive psychotherapy augmented the benefits of medication and enhanced functioning in psychotic disorders. Family therapy demonstrated the most promising findings.

Several meta-analyses have specifically examined the outcomes of family treatment of schizophrenia. In a meta-analysis of 53 controlled studies, family treatment showed a consistent benefit in reducing relapse, decreasing readmission to the hospital, and improving medication compliance (Pharoah et al., 2011). The median relapse rates were 18% for family therapy and 44% for controls at 1 year and 33% for family therapy and 64% for controls at 2 years; the addition of family therapy cuts the relapse rate by almost half (Barbato & D'Avanzo, 2000). Other meta-analyses have also demonstrated that adding family therapy to medication in the treatment of schizophrenia reduces the probability of relapse and increases the patient's well-being (Lincoln et al., 2007; Pilling et al., 2002).

Communication/Strategic Therapies

Most communication therapists have not been involved in controlled assessments of their treatments. In an evaluation of her therapy effectiveness, for example, Satir (1982) reported that she had treated close to 5,000 families of nearly every shape, form, nationality, race, income group, religious orientation, and political persuasion. Although she believed that her approach had been generally useful to her clients, she indicated that she had done no formal research on her effectiveness. The few direct evaluations on the Satir approach have yielded small, even nonsignificant, effect sizes (Shadish et al., 1993).

The meta-analytic evidence (Shadish et al., 1993; Stanton & Shadish, 1997) for the effectiveness of strategic therapy is modest in general, but robust for treating substance abusers. The effectiveness of strategic therapy remains uncertain with schizophrenic, anxiety, and psychosomatic disorders, three conditions which it purports to treat successfully (Gurman et al., 1986; Sandberg et al., 1997). Beyond its demonstrated effectiveness with substance abuse, then, strategic therapies

have not been sufficiently evaluated to determine their absolute or relative effectiveness.

Structural Therapy

During the 1970s, Minuchin and his colleagues published a series of clinical surveys on four disorders in children: labile diabetes, anorexia nervosa, chronic asthma, and psychogenic abdominal pains. Very impressive gains were reported: For example, at follow-up, 88% of the treated diabetic children were judged to be recovered, meaning there had been no hospital admissions for acidosis after treatment and/or diabetic control had become stabilized within normal limits (Rosman et al., 1978). In another example, 86% of child and teenage anorexics, treated for between 2 and 16 months, were found at follow-up to have achieved normal eating patterns and a normal body weight (Rosman et al., 1978).

As with most uncontrolled research, these findings are difficult to evaluate or trust. The surveys were generally cumulative, with later reports including cases from previous surveys. In some reports (e.g., Minuchin et al., 1975), it sounds as if these impressive effects with anorexia are due entirely to structural therapy. In other reports (e.g., Liebman et al., 1975), the treatment for anorexia nervosa is described as an integration of structural therapy and behavior modification. Contingency control processes were used in such a way that the anorexic children could earn activity privileges in the hospital or at home only by gaining weight. Because these are survey studies, it is impossible to determine how much of the outcome is due to behavior therapy compared to structural therapy. Further, the absence of placebo control groups, no-treatment groups, or an alternative family therapy makes it unclear what is producing these impressive results.

Controlled outcome studies yield more definitive and trustworthy evidence of effectiveness, but only a few such studies have been conducted on structural therapy (Shadish et al., 1993). Structural therapy has been tested in the family treatment of substance abuse, psychosomatic disorders, and conduct disorders. With all of these difficult populations, structural therapy is judged to be probably effective (Sandberg et al., 1997; Stanton & Shadish, 1997)—definitely superior to no treatment and probably superior to individual treatment. However, its effectiveness is still untested in schizophrenia, mood disorders, anxiety disorders as well as most childhood disorders (Shadish & Baldwin, 2003).

Bowen Family Systems Therapy

To our knowledge—and to others' (e.g., Sandberg et al., 1997; Shadish & Baldwin, 2003)—there have been no RCTs conducted on the effectiveness of Bowenian therapy. One study has been conducted on an adaptation of Bowen systems therapy for drug abuse, using a combination of both family and individual sessions (see review by Stanton & Shadish, 1997). A few other studies have been open, uncontrolled trials (Nichols, 2003). The effectiveness of Bowen's family systems therapy is thus largely untested.

Multisystemic Therapy

MST has been evaluated in at least 15 RCTs, and the results show favorable treatment effects with chronic juvenile offenders that have generally been sustained (Henggeler, 2011). An early meta-analysis of 11 MST studies, involving 708 participants, reported an average effect size of 0.55 at the end of treatment (Curtis et al., 2004). Following treatment, youth and their families treated with MST were functioning better than 70% of youths and families treated alternatively. MST demonstrated fairly high treatment engagement and completion rates with difficult client populations.

A later meta-analysis of 24 studies on four of the new-generation, evidence-based family therapies, including MST, revealed a large effect size of 0.70 compared to no treatment and a small effect size of 0.26 compared to alternative therapies. There was insufficient evidence to determine whether any of the four "evidence-based" family therapies differed in their effectiveness to each other (Baldwin et al., 2012).

Put into financial terms, MST and functional family therapy show the highest cost savings when compared to other juvenile offender programs (Aos & Barnoski, 1998). They are cost-effective approaches to reducing delinquency. The cost savings to taxpayers and crime victims was $13,908 for MST and $21,863 for functional family therapy per adolescent treated (Sexton et al., 2003).

These and other reviews remind us of the effectiveness of including parents in the treatment of youth mental health disorders. The scientific findings counter many long-held notions that family therapy will not prove productive because parents hinder treatment in various ways. In fact, the family is key to treating substance abuse, health problems, conduct disorders, and other maladies of childhood (Diamond & Josephson, 2005).

At the same time, MST and the other evidence-based family therapies have not proven a panacea. There is no convincing evidence that MST outperforms other systemic therapies (Baldwin et al., 2012; Littell, 2008; Littell et al., 2005). But there is evidence that the effectiveness of MST has not easily generalized to some real-world settings and that cultural misalignments have occurred. Even the best of evidence-based therapies, we should remember, are not suited for all patients or all contexts.

A Final Caveat

Before concluding our review of the outcome research, we should remember that the majority of the controlled research has been conducted on the family treatment format, not on systemic therapy per se. This disconnect between the treatment format (the number of people in the room) and the therapy system (a systemic emphasis) frustrates students and confounds the interpretation of the outcome research. Was the therapy effective because it brought several clients into the room or because it targeted the entire system or because of both factors? Let us repeat what we said earlier: Systemic therapy has two, overlapping meanings— a therapy format and a treatment content/goal.

Criticisms of Systemic Therapies
From a Psychoanalytic Perspective

Minuchin's structural therapy is another in a long series of attempts to construct simple solutions for complex problems. It is simplistic, for example, to assume that all of psychopathology is maintained by structured relationships in current family living. What about more severely disturbed adults, like many borderline personalities, who live alone? What is the structural therapist going to do for a person who needs help in developing relationships, not restructuring them? Remember that roughly three quarters of patients receive individual psychotherapy. What does structural therapy have to offer to the majority of clients? There are only so many ways a therapist and client can restructure their seating arrangements. What structural relationships is the therapist going to observe, map, and rearrange with individual patients?

Simplistic also is the belief that the history of the family, patients' developmental histories, and their internal dynamics can simply be ignored. Just join the family and let the action begin. But the family never becomes aware of how problems developed, nor will they necessarily understand how the problems disappeared. All that is clear is that they were joined by an authoritative parent figure who rearranged the furniture and used metaphors about open and closed doors to settle boundary disputes. It certainly can shake things up and probably even help, but what happens when the family faces its next developmental crisis? There has been no systematic attempt to help the family gain insight into either the causes or the cures of their problems. No wonder the family is likely to have to return for more restructuring (or is it reparenting?) from an omnipotent mental health professional.

From a Cognitive-Behavioral Perspective

Bowen is pouring old wine into new bottles. The old wine is his psychoanalytic heritage; the new bottles are multigenerational families. Bowenian concepts have a distinctly Freudian flavor. Differentiation of self from family fusion sounds like differentiation of ego from id. The goal of having intellect control emotions sounds like the goal of having the ego control the id. Triangles are seen as the source of psychopathology; this sounds similar to the oedipal conflict as the key to psychopathology, with mother, father, and child in conflict. No wonder some psychoanalytic theorists claim Bowen as one of their own.

In therapy, Bowen is prepared to continue the same kind of archaeological expedition that psychoanalysis favors. Psychoanalytic therapists, at least, would only take the patient back to birth; Bowen is prepared to dig back through previous generations for further clues to contemporary problems. Unlike communications and structural therapists, Bowenian therapists don't stop when symptoms go away. They continue to restructure multigenerational relationships in search of an autonomous self, just as psychoanalysts restructure the psyche in search of an autonomous ego.

Like psychoanalysts, Bowenian therapists cannot serve as objective guides for such archaeological expeditions unless they have also undergone the almost interminable process of differentiating the self from the family of origin. Lest therapists be at risk of becoming triangulated in therapy (acting out the countertransference?), they need to undergo intensive therapy themselves.

Bowen tries to bridge two theoretical perspectives, psychoanalysis and systems theory, without appreciating that neither has a solid foundation in scientific research. The result is a shaky structure that has not undergone the rigorous tests of controlled experimentation. The result is also a theory that is shaky as to whether it is grounded in principles of individuals or systems. Look, for example, at how Bowen prefers to work with individuals instead of the whole family. Even when Bowen works with couples, he doesn't focus on their communications with each other.

And how can a true systems theorist believe in an autonomous self? Systems theorists are determinists who assume an individual component is defined and controlled by the organized system of which it is a part. Bowen's thesis stands systems theory on its head. Instead of the whole being greater than the sum of the individual parts, Bowen would have us believe that an individual can be greater and stronger than the sum of the whole family.

From a Humanistic Perspective

Communication/strategic therapists present us with too many paradoxes. First they create a theory based on how systems stay the same. Then they recommend this theory to help people change. Concepts of wholes, hierarchies, homeostasis, and feedback loops explain how systems maintain a stable relationship, not how they change. This theory teaches therapists to expect family resistance and encourages pessimism about potential for change. As a result, families are tricked into changing rather than treated with respect.

Paradoxically, it may be the therapist's technique that encourages resistance rather than the system's rules. Who wouldn't resist being treated like God, being told to deliberately wet one's bed, or having one's complaints reduced to absurdities? Such therapists can produce the very resistance they have been taught to expect. When such tricks

work, the therapist is so clever; when they fail, the family is so resistant.

Why should we believe that couple and family systems are so stable, when marriages are disintegrating at unprecedented rates? Communication and strategic theories may have been appropriate to the stable 1950s but not to the rapid changes of today. Change is now the norm, not stability. Future shock includes distress from too much change and too little stability in our social systems (Toffler, 1970). Less therapeutic disruption, fewer tricks, and more therapist genuineness and support will foster the greater stability required of contemporary families.

Do individuals matter in these families, or are they just mindless elements controlled by the rules of the system? Systemic therapists see the woods, but miss the trees. Who is responsible for these rules—the system, or the individuals in the system? And who will be responsible for changing the rules? Haley (1976, 1986) recognizes this paradox, but unfortunately he winds up delivering power to the therapist rather than according power to the clients. In power struggles, processes of change don't matter, only the outcome—does the therapist win the struggle? This ethos sounds dangerously close to the ends justifying the means. But how else can you justify manipulative techniques such as prescribing symptoms, mandating double binds, and assigning them ordeals? These techniques make for good theater of the absurd, but they fail to create a humane system for the troubled individuals, couples, and families of our day.

From a Cultural Perspective

The "fathers" of family systems therapies were just that—fathers with a masculine bias. With the exception of Virginia Satir, the pioneers of family therapy were white men trained originally in the 1940s and 1950s in the psychoanalytic tradition and inbred with a male-dominated orientation to psychotherapy.

Murray Bowen's perspective has much of value to feminists, but his concept of "differentiation" smacks of the politics of rational man. Bowen describes the differentiated person as "autonomous," "being-for-self," and "intellectual," whereas the poorly differentiated person is characterized as "seeking love and approval," "being-for-others," and "relatedness." What is valued in Bowen's system are those qualities for which men are socialized; what is devalued are those for which women are socialized. As is true of practically all social and philosophical schools from Socrates onward (Lloyd, 1984), Bowen elevates reason as a principle, associating it with men and their activities, and devalues emotion, associating it with women and their activities.

Salvador Minuchin tends to unbalance and restructure the family through the mother. Analysis of Minuchin's writings and videotapes shows that he treats the peripheral fathers with greater deference and less pressure to change (Luepnitz, 1988). Watching Minuchin's taped demonstrations, especially the one entitled "Taming Monsters," reminds us of the pervasive description of mothers in the "adequate" American family: obese, overwhelmed with responsibility, without access to the outside sources of activity and self-esteem that fathers have. Then to top it off, structural therapists tell the mothers that they must change! Structural family therapy may well recapitulate the mother-blaming of the larger social order.

Communication/strategic therapy seeks to perfect the unexamined life. The assumptions that action often precedes understanding and that changing patterns is more important than insight are not necessarily congenial to women and other oppressed groups. The dualism between action and insight is unfortunate, because women frequently seek both in psychotherapy and because empowerment typically entails some form of awareness. Assigning ordeals, intervening paradoxically, and employing tactics without mutual insight begin to feel a lot like social control, even if they are designed to be therapeutic.

Underlying most systems theory is a single normative model for healthy family functioning that transcends all class, cultural, and ethnic differences. In a pluralistic society, it is a constant struggle to help people understand that there is richness and strength in diversity, including diversity of family forms. After an intensive study of healthy families, Lewis and colleagues (1976) decided to title their book *No Single Thread*, communicating that they had discovered no single structure in the ways these families functioned.

Yet many family therapists continue to theorize about Ozzie-and-Harriet models of the family that include well-bonded spouse, parental, and sibling subsystems. No wonder that MST does not fit all families or cultures. The U.S. Census finds that less than 5% of the nation's households matched the stereotype of a working father, a nonworking mother, and two children. What about the large number of single-parent families, childfree families, extended families, cohabiting couples, gay-couple families, blended families, immigrant families? Inclusive theorizing and multicultural practice are required for pluralistic societies.

From an Integrative Perspective

Systems therapies are valuable additions to the psychotherapist's repertoire as long as they are kept within reasonable boundaries. For example, strategic therapists have created paradoxical interventions that can prove effective with highly resistant individuals, couples, or families. But most clients cooperate in treatment, and imposing a paradoxical intervention on these patients undermines the sanctity of the therapeutic alliance and perpetuates the image of therapists as manipulative control freaks. Structural therapy lacks an adequate theory and technique for dealing with intense resistance but would appear to be helpful with families motivated to help a child suffering from psychosomatic stress or anorexia. Bowenian therapy, on the other hand, seems better suited for young adults who are experiencing problems in separating from their families of origin. The newer evidence-based family therapies are certainly indicated for substance abusers and juvenile delinquents. Within such bounds, systemic therapies can become part of a more comprehensive approach to change.

Systemic therapies are out of bounds, however, when they try to construe every problem as a systems problem. It is true that in some cases, improvement in one family member can be accompanied by a worsening in another family member. However, it is even more often the case that when one family member recovers from substance abuse, anxiety, depression, and other forms of psychopathology, the whole family system improves. Just as the specter of symptom substitution threatened therapists for generations, systemic positions would make us believe that patient substitution—in which symptoms shift from one family member to another—is the rule rather than the exception. But there is no research to suggest that patient substitution is any more frequent than the old bugaboo of symptom substitution.

A Systemic Analysis of the C Family

For 6 years, individually oriented psychotherapists treated Mrs. C out of context. Mrs. C was treated as an isolated event, even to the extent of being removed from her family for a year in a psychiatric hospital. Blinded by the traditional ideology that psychopathology is an individual event, previous mental health professionals were unable to see how her symptoms were developed and maintained in a pathological family system.

The marital subsystem is characterized by a complementary relationship in which Mrs. C acts and Mr. C reacts. The entire family is skewed in the direction of Mrs. C's symptoms. Her obsession with cleanliness dominates the family's rules for relating. It is not surprising that Mrs. C's family of origin was skewed in the direction of her domineering father.

The C family system is pathologically enmeshed. Unclear boundaries abound, as Mrs. C runs around with bare breasts in front of her teenage sons. The children enjoy no space in their own home into which they can invite their friends. The boundaries between Mr. and Mrs. C are lost when he participates in the washing rituals. Mr. C arises at 5:00 A.M. to yell out "Right arm, Martha; left arm, Martha." And yet only Mrs. C has been identified as a patient. *Folie à deux!* The entire family lets silverware and underwear lie around the house until it looks like a dump. Yet only Mrs. C is going to be dumped in the state hospital. *Folie à famille!*

What threatened this family to the extent that it could regain balance only by developing puzzling and pathological behaviors? The family history suggests that the family health care system was threatened by a runaway of pinworms, Asian flu, and a sixth pregnancy. Apparently the family was unable to grow and adapt to the changes imposed by this crisis. The family physician prescribed washing, and Mrs. C washed and washed until she became the identified patient. But did other family members grow to help meet the tremendous demands on the family? Did Mr. C, for example, grow into a more complete parent to assist with the burdens of five children, illness, and an infestation of pinworms?

The boundaries of the enmeshed C family were becoming too permeable. The boundaries had already been permeated by pinworms and a foreign influenza. The system's preoccupation with cleanliness communicated a need to establish clearer boundaries. Mrs. C, for example, was becoming entirely enmeshed in her children's health and hygienic concerns, just as her father had been enmeshed in her personal concerns. In a desperate attempt to clarify her personal boundaries, Mrs. C would scrub her skin; Mrs. C was trying to clean the skin that defines the physical boundaries of herself as an individual.

The C family became organized around a set of compulsive rules for relating. Perhaps because there were already so many children in the family,

(continued)

these rules forbade any neighbor children from crossing the literal boundaries of the home. Mr. and Mrs. C related as a couple in the intimacy of their bedroom primarily around the compulsive shower. The shower set limits on Mrs. C's availability for relating to her children in the morning. She also set limits on her concerns by communicating only about their health and hygiene and not about friends and feelings.

For 10 years, the compulsive rules for relating served to cleanse and clarify many of the family boundaries. With the older children entering adolescence and adulthood, however, these rules were too rigid and constrictive to respond to the children's increasing needs for autonomy, intimacy, and privacy. In trying to restructure itself, the family was threatening to remove Mrs. C from the boundaries of the home. In return, she threatened suicide.

The C family is certainly in need of a powerful agent from outside the system who can join with the family to restructure their communication and boundaries. The entire family should be seen, including Mrs. C's parents if necessary. The therapist would first have to join with each of the subsystems in the family. With the children, the therapist would speak the language of greater autonomy and responsibility. The therapist might help the children to communicate a goal of inviting a friend to visit within the bounds of their own room. The therapist would open new areas of communicating, such as rules about dating, curfews, and working outside the home.

Once the systemic therapist had joined the family to create a new therapeutic system, she would begin to liberate the family from dysfunctional rules and structures by producing disequilibrium. Of course, there is no rigid way of restructuring a family system. A rigid set of rules for relating in therapy could present the paradox of substituting one compulsive set of rules for another. The therapist would relate in a flexible manner, responding more freely to pathological communications or structures than the family members respond. If the family insists on defining the problem as Mrs. C's problem, the therapist will reframe the compulsive symptoms into systems language. The compulsive rules of cleanliness can be reframed

positively as an expression of the family's desire to stay healthy together. Reframing the symptoms can produce cognitive disequilibrium that enhances family awareness of how the symptoms have served the family.

The therapist can liberate the family from compulsive rules by prescribing alternative ways of relating, both in the sessions and at home. If Mrs. C keeps her physical distance from her children in the sessions, the therapist may take a younger child's hand and say, "Come on, let's give Mama a big hug to show her we love her." As part of the concern about staying healthy together, the therapist may give the parents a homework assignment to spend one evening together cooking their children a hearty, healthy meal. This assignment could help to create better boundaries around the parents and could help the children to perceive them as more equal rather than complementary.

If the Cs prove to be particularly resistant to restructuring, the systemic therapist can always call on paradoxical techniques for liberating the family. The therapist may prescribe the symptom—say, a 2-hour shower in the morning. The rationale would be that the shower is one of the best ways that Mrs. C has for communicating her concern with staying clean for the good of her family. Also, the morning shower is one of the best ways that Mr. C has of showing his concern for his wife. Because the shower is one of their best ways for cooperating as a couple, a long, leisurely, warm shower is just what the doctor ordered.

Of course, prescribing a long morning shower would serve as a therapeutic double bind. This assignment would give Mr. and Mrs. C a choice: to cooperate or not with the assignment. If they choose to cooperate, then they are choosing to carry out their symptoms. The symptoms would no longer be out of control, because they would no longer have the experience of "I can't help it—I must wash, or I must keep track of my wife's washing." If they choose not to cooperate, then they are choosing not to carry out their symptomatic behavior. Either way, they begin to liberate themselves from a pathologically structured way of relating.

Future Directions

As a discontinuous break with past ideas of linear and intrapsychic causality, systems therapy remains an alternative to conventional wisdom rather than a part of it. The clinical concepts and therapeutic strategies associated with it are not yet considered part of the mainstream. At the same time, we and others find unambiguous signs that the systemic perspective is moving toward parity with more conventional and established perspectives, such as the psychodynamic, humanistic, behavioral, and cognitive traditions (Coyne & Liddle, 1992). The future of systemic therapies is thus filled with expanding opportunities, but it must pursue new directions.

One promising direction lies in the continuing application of systems theory to areas beyond the treatment of the nuclear family system. One of these areas is, paradoxically, the individual patient: to treat both the psyche and the system within the context of individual psychotherapy. Therapists have rediscovered the self in the family system (Snyder & Whisman, 2003).

Another application (and the title of a journal) is family systems medicine, in which family medicine and family therapy are integrated. The family treatment of alcohol dependence and drug abuse, as we have seen, is particularly effective, as is couple/family therapy with clients suffering from dementia, sexual problems, and cardiovascular disease (Pinsof et al., 1996; Snyder et al., 2006). Systems theory will continue to be applied to larger social systems as well, such as organizations and communities.

Another probable direction is the use of a consensual diagnostic system for dysfunctional families. Traditional diagnostic schemes, such as the DSM-V, locate the source of the disorder within the individual and neglect the relational context. No standard classification scheme for dysfunctional relationships has emerged, and as a consequence, systems therapists and their patients have been hampered by a variety of clinical, legal, and insurance difficulties. However, several organizations joined forces to compile a comprehensive typology of family diagnosis. Kaslow's (1996) monumental *Handbook of Relational Diagnosis and Dysfunctional Family Patterns* summarizes the typologies and provides the next steps for a truly interactional system of clinical diagnosis.

Within systemic therapy, there has been a decided breakdown of schoolism and a movement toward integration. In large surveys of family therapists, between one third and one half describe their theoretical orientation as eclectic; systemic therapy is far from monolithic (Jensen et al., 1990; Lebow, 1997; Rait, 1988). The growing contact between systems therapies and psychotherapy integration offers mutual benefits. The amalgamation of systems thinking with solution-focused and narrative therapies (Chapter 15) stands as a prominent exemplar of this movement.

In the past, systemic therapy had been like a car cruising on automatic control with the driver comfortably seated in the lotus position. Family therapy rested on the normative concepts of gender relationships and idealized conceptions of family cultures. Subtle bias was "cruising" along by exaggerating cultural and gender differences or ignoring them (Hare-Mustin, 1987). But no more. In the future, systemic therapies will create gender-sensitive and cultural-competent treatments (Boyd-Franklin, 2006; McGoldrick & Hardy, 2008).

Family therapists have been historically trained in the disciplines of psychology, counseling, psychiatry, or social work and then attended post-degree training programs or advanced workshops in couple and family therapy. But this equivalency training is gradually giving way to a requirement of academic training in marital and family programs. The once-open doorways to state licensure as a family therapist have become almost impassable for professionals without a degree from a family therapy program.

Ironically, most of the field's founders would be unable now to qualify as family therapists, as defined by the 50 states that license or regulate the practice of marriage and family therapy.

The wisdom of this change has been hotly debated, but it appears that family therapy as a profession will become similar in its exclusiveness to psychology, medicine, and other professions. Systemic therapies will remain a standard part of psychology, social work, and counseling training, even if their graduates are not formally licensed as "family therapists." As is true of most psychotherapy systems when they mature into adulthood, systemic therapies, once the innovative pioneers, have now become more institutionalized in terms of training and credentialing.

Despite their inevitable evolution, systemic therapies refuse to reduce complex systems to individual dynamics. Looking solely within an individual is woefully incomplete. Systems therapies will continue to embody the paradigm shift to a new way of conceptualizing human problems and their resolution.

Key Terms

accommodation
boundaries
Bowenian/family systems therapy
communication therapies
complementary
cybernetics
differentiation of self
directives
disengaged family
double bind communication
emotional cutoff
enactments
enmeshed family
evidence-based family therapies
expressed emotion (EE)
family of origin therapy
family projection process
fusion
General Systems Theory (GST)
genogram
homeostasis
identified patient (IP)
joining
metachange
metacommunication
mimesis
multigenerational transmission process
multisystemic therapy (MST)
nonlinear dynamics
open systems
ordeal therapy
paradoxical directives/ techniques
power
prescribing the symptom
punctuation
reductio ad absurdum
reframing
relabeling
responsible I
schism
social liberation
straight directives
strategic therapy
structural therapy
structure
surrender tactic
symmetrical
system
systemic therapies
therapy modality/ format
triangles/triangulation
undifferentiated family ego mass

Recommended Readings

Bowen, M. (1978). *Family therapy in clinical practice.* New York: Jason Aronson.

Goldenberg, I., & Goldenberg, H. (2013). *Family therapy: An overview* (8th ed.). Belmont, CA: Brooks/Cole.

Gurman, A. S., & Jacobson, N. S. (Eds.). (2008). *Clinical handbook of couple therapy* (4th ed.). New York: Guilford.

Haley, J. (1976). *Problem-solving therapy: New strategies for effective family therapies.* San Francisco: Jossey-Bass.

Henggler, S. W., Cunningham, P. B., Schoenwald, S. K., et al. (2009). *Multisystemic therapy for antisocial behavior in children and adolescents* (2nd ed.). New York: Guilford.

McGoldrick, M., Giordano, J., & Garcia-Preto, N. (Eds.). (2005). *Ethnicity and family therapy* (3rd ed.). New York: Guilford.

Minuchin, S. (1974). *Families and family therapy.* Cambridge, MA: Harvard University Press.

Satir, V. (1967). *Conjoint family therapy.* Palo Alto, CA: Science and Behavior Books.

Sexton, T. L., Weeks, G. R., & Robbins, M. S. (Eds.). (2003). *Handbook of family therapy.* New York: Brunner-Routledge.

Watzlawick, P., Weakland, J. H., & Fisch, R. (1974). *Change: Principles of problem formation and problem resolution.* New York: Norton.

JOURNALS: *American Journal of Family Therapy; American Journal of Orthopsychiatry; Contemporary Family Therapy; Family Process; Family Therapy; International Journal of Family Psychiatry; International Journal of Family Therapy; Journal of Family Psychology; Journal of Family Psychotherapy; Journal of Feminist Family Therapy; Journal of Marital and Family Therapy; Journal of Psychotherapy and the Family; Journal of Sex and Marital Therapy; Journal of Systemic Therapies; The Family Journal.*

Recommended Websites

Ackerman Institute for the Family:
www.ackerman.org/
American Association for Marriage and Family Therapy:
www.aamft.org/
Avanta—The Virginia Satir Network:
www.satirglobal.org/
Bowen Center for the Study of the Family:
www.thebowencenter.org/index.html
Minuchin Center for the Family:
www.minuchincenter.org/
Multisystemic Therapy:
http://mstservices.com/

CHAPTER 13

Gender-Sensitive Therapies

Mark Bowden/the Agency Collection/Getty Images

Laurie entered my office and sat as far away from me as possible. She was depressed, angry, and withdrawn. She was confused and said she didn't know what had caused her chronic disorders.

Laurie had come to psychotherapy because her husband was threatening to leave her. He couldn't get close to her. When they had sex, it was like she wasn't really there.

I asked Laurie if she had been abused. She burst out, "How did you know? I never told anyone—not even my mother, not my priest, not even my best friend. I am so ashamed," she sobbed.

"Laurie, who were you protecting?"

"My mother—she couldn't survive without my father. And my family, he threatened he would leave."

"How about your father?"

"No, I hated him—hated him—but we were so dependent on him. We couldn't survive without him."

"Can you survive without him now?"

"Of course I can!" she shouted angrily. "I haven't gone near him in years."

"What would you like to say to him?"

"I want to tell him I hate him. I want to let him know how he humiliated me—how he messed up my life. I want this dirty secret out in the open so I don't have to hide."

Laurie was getting ready to free her body and her self from her father and her family. The next session she sat in the chair next to my desk.

A Sketch of Sociopolitical Forces

Modern psychotherapy was created by White men in their own image. Since its earliest beginnings in Europe, psychotherapy has emphasized male society's definition of healthy mental states and has largely ignored the needs of the diverse populations it professes to serve. Most psychotherapy research, practice, and training have been historically conducted by men, even though women have comprised the majority of clients. The net result was that the preponderance of psychotherapy was **androcentric** (male-centered).

353

Female psychotherapists across the nation began dialogues in the late 1960s that both reflected and ignited the feminist therapy movement. In the 1970s, these women joined together to form a number of feminist mental health organizations, including the Association for Women in Psychology. Carol Gilligan's (1982) *In a Different Voice* was an early and influential work that contested the androcentric vision of psychological science and reframed it in more inclusive, feminist terms. Although the immediate focus of her work was moral development, her broader concern was to illuminate sexist bias in the design, conduct, and interpretation of psychology. Inspired by such writings, the ongoing Women's Rights Movement, and the United Nations Decade of the Woman (1976–1985), feminist therapy has grown by leaps and bounds since those early beginnings.

Feminism, the philosophical root of feminist therapy, is a commitment to equal social, economic, and political rights for men and women. Of late, there has been confusion and backlash over the use of the term *feminist* (Faludi, 1991). We will use the term descriptively and accurately as defined in the dictionary: A person who believes in and/or advocates the principle that women should have political, economic, and social rights equal to those of men.

Feminist therapy is based on the twin convictions that women share many of the characteristics of oppressed people and that women have been denied equal rights and an equal voice. The key to a healthy individual lies in recognizing the negative effects of a male-dominated society on women's self-concept and on establishing a more egalitarian power balance with men. In Gilligan's terms (1982, p. xxvi), the goal is "to bring women's voices into psychological theory and to reframe the conversation between women and men."

No single person is responsible for the creation or development of feminist therapy. Instead, it has been a collaborative endeavor involving hundreds, if not thousands, of clinicians, advocates, and theorists. Feminist therapy has truly been a group effort, in the best sense of that term and in the feminist tradition of interdependent collaboration, as opposed to promoting an autonomous individual.

In this chapter, we examine in detail feminist therapy. Then, we briefly explore psychotherapy for men, another gender-sensitive psychotherapy.

Theory of Personality

Feminist psychotherapy has its roots, paradoxically, not in psychology, but in the philosophy of the women's movement of the 1960s and 1970s. As a consequence, it has no consensual theory of personality. Nonetheless, a distinctive emphasis of feminist theory is the assertion that a person's identity is profoundly influenced by prevailing environmental pressures, such as gender roles and gender-based discrimination.

Gender influences cognitive structures and behavior patterns. Nancy Chodorow (1989) proposed that psychological differences between the genders are due mainly to the fact that children are raised primarily by women. A little girl's identity is founded on a sense of continuity in her relationship with her mother. She internalizes the personality messages her mother sends out and attempts to incorporate them into her own behavioral repertoire.

In contrast, a little boy's identity is formed through a discontinuity in his relationship with his mother. He learns to give up his identification with his mother and becomes masculine through his relationship with his father. Chodorow (1978) asserts that mothers connect more with their daughters and separate from their sons and that this produces a "division of psychological capacities" between girls and boys. Because girls learn to be affiliative and nurturant from their mothers, they grow up motivated for motherhood. Boys, however, because they actively avoid emulating their mothers, never learn to be nurturant. They typically model the aggressive, power-seeking nature of older male role models.

Power inequalities and gender-role expectations shape the cognitive structure from the moment a child comes into the world. From the first day of life, a child is constantly bombarded with messages of gender expectations. Consider an illustrative study (Smith & Lloyd, 1978): Mothers of first-born infants were presented with a previously unknown 6-month-old infant dressed in "gender-appropriate" or "cross-gender" clothing and instructed to play with the infant for 10 minutes. The results indicated that only the infant dressed as a girl was first offered a doll to play with, whereas only the infant dressed as a boy was first offered a hammer or a rattle. The infant dressed as a boy was also encouraged to be more physically active than the infant dressed as a girl.

Girls are typically expected to be sweet, sensitive, and docile, whereas boys are expected to be strong, stoic, and brave. Girls are socialized to cultivate attractiveness to men, and males are socialized to view women as objects of consumption (Luepnitz, 1988). Gender politics are deeply embedded in the fabric of American society and, thus, over the course of our psychological and social development, profoundly influence how we see ourselves (Meth & Pasick, 1992, p. 5). Gender-role expectations are deeply ingrained in adult personality.

Relational-cultural theory emerged from the Stone Center at Wellesley College in the late 1970s to explain female development throughout the life span. Personality is not defined by individual construction alone; personality is also built in response to societal marginalization and power imbalances. Relational-cultural theory holds that female identity, our personhood, is in large part culturally defined by the domination and subordination of women.

Most of our relational expectations are laid down early in life, but there exists enormous relational plasticity and resilience later in life. Although women may be born into a dependent role in a sexist society, they can become interdependent and connected in more complicated ways as they age (Jordan et al., 2004). Women are profoundly subject to early socialization in life but can transcend it later in life.

Theory of Psychopathology

Much of psychological distress is environmentally induced and **culturally determined**. Pathology occurs when the social structure is so rigidly defined that people are not permitted to grow and when relationships are unbalanced, as is the case with power inequalities between men and women. Distress is not solely the result of intrapsychic conflicts, but more likely the result of social and political factors. In fact, the term *psychopathology* is generally avoided in the feminist literature because it smacks of an underlying intrapsychic perspective; words such as *distress*, *pain*, or *problem* are preferred.

Definitions of normality and identification of psychopathology frequently reflect an androcentric bias. Although the predominant categorization of mental disorders, the American Psychiatric Association's *DSM*, describes clusters of real symptoms, it also represents the dominant attitudes of its membership (70% male) and overvalues stereotypically male behaviors of autonomy and control (Nikelly, 1996). Dependent personality, and passive-aggressive personality are offered in the *DSM* as female-predominant mental disorders, not as coping behaviors resulting from disadvantaged positions and exploitive situations that women cannot easily escape. But the *DSM* fails to consider exaggerated male traits as pathological. Where are the delusional dominating personality disorder, the greedy personality disorder, and the macho personality disorder?

Under the leadership of Jean Baker Miller, author of the influential book *Toward a New Psychology of Women* (1986), the Stone Center sought to better understand women's distress. Isolation was seen as a primary source of women's suffering; it occurs when one has suffered from chronic nonresponsiveness, ongoing humiliations, and more blatant violations from others. Such interactions produce a feeling of "not mattering," of not being relationally competent, of not making a difference in life.

Gender socialization shapes not only the prevalence, but also the expression of distress. The prevalence of various behavioral disorders differs between the sexes (Karpiak & Zaboski, 2013; Robins et al., 1984). Congruent with sex role stereotyping that leads women to internalize distress and men to externalize it, men show higher lifetime prevalence rates for externalizing disorders, such as alcohol and drug abuse and antisocial personality disorder. Women, on the other hand, show a higher prevalence of mood, phobic, obsessive-compulsive, and panic disorders—largely internalizing problems.

A multitude of interrelated sociopolitical factors place women at higher risk for these forms of behavioral distress. A short and incomplete list would include sex role stereotyping, gender-role expectations, role strain and conflict, sexual trauma, and gender-related economics. We shall briefly consider each of these.

Cultural messages are relayed routinely through newspapers, television, the Internet, educational systems, and religious institutions. These media instill in young children messages about gender inequality, stereotyped sex role behavior, and negative self-values. Textbooks generally depict little girls as passive and fearful, whereas little boys are adventurous and daring. Curriculum choices often encourage girls to pursue courses in humanities and home economics, but boys are encouraged to pursue courses in math and science. Teachers attribute the failures of girls to lack of competence, but attribute the failures of boys to lack of effort (Worell & Remer, 2002).

These social messages are facets of **internalized oppression**; the external messages become a part of how we think and feel. Little girls are scolded for wanting to play with trucks and trains, the so-called "boy toys," and told that their self-worth rests primarily on being pretty and proper. Girls are rarely encouraged to pursue activities that require autonomy or skill; they are told to play "dress up" and "house," whereas little boys are encouraged to play doctor or police officer. At an early age, girls begin to devalue themselves and their true desires as they begin to conform to the expectations of the larger society. One researcher (Seidenberg, 1970, p. 134) states emphatically, "No woman will treasure fame or glory she can achieve at the price of being called unfeminine. This below the belt blow sends most women into despair."

Gender-role expectations often generate a false sense of self. Women are forced to accept the "gender rules": Women are expected to be a lady, to never swear, hit, or get angry. They should strive to please men and, above all, never offend or best a man. These gender-role expectations, these double standards are captured in the offensive riddle: What do you call an assertive man? Successful. What do you call an assertive woman? Bitch.

The unquestioning acceptance of these rules leads many women to adopt roles they might not undertake if they were given a choice. After years of living a life that is false and unfulfilling, a woman's reservoir of anger and resentment builds and is often expressed through self-destructive behaviors.

Omnipresent sex role stereotyping limits the potential of all human beings. When individuals are forced to conform to gender-role expectations, they fail to achieve—or even try to achieve—skills in areas outside of their gender borders. Individuals, especially women, who subscribe to a traditional sex role orientation suffer from a higher incidence of depression and anxiety, lower self-esteem, and more social withdrawal than women who do not strictly adhere to traditional female roles and expectancies (Worell & Remer, 2002).

Ms. A came to therapy with an ultrafeminine appearance and not a hint of any so-called masculine traits (Lerner, 1986). She had never gone through a "tomboy" stage and had avoided aggressive play her entire life. She seemed to be a model of domesticity and femininity. Lately, her boyfriend and the feminist subculture had been pressuring her to become more liberated, but when she tried to change her appearance, even slightly, to include more masculine aspects, such as wearing jeans, she began experiencing feelings of depersonalization and unreality. Through psychotherapy, it became evident that Ms. A maintained her sexual identity primarily through strict conformity to behaviors ascribed to her sex that were clearly differentiated from those ascribed to men.

Women's distress also stems from stresses created by society's antagonism toward their changing roles. As women enter new roles, they develop a greater sense of self and independence, but the reluctance of society to change with them hampers their success. Women in new work roles frequently face poor child care options, resistant partners unwilling to become coequal in parenting and household responsibilities, and few employers willing to establish flexible shifts and job-sharing positions. Trying to balance work with a traditional household role leads many women to develop role overload and role strain.

Role strain involves conflicting demands from different roles. For example, a woman may work during the day, come home and care for her family in the evening, and then attend school at night. She has four distinct roles to perform (worker, mother, wife, and student). The strain of performing adequately in all these roles can be overwhelming.

Role conflict involves roles clashing with each other, as when the priorities of being a good mother conflict with the priorities of being a good student. The pressures of one role can take over and inhibit performance in other roles. Conflicted over "abandoning" children to day care settings, many women feel that they are forced to choose between being a good mother and a good worker. The fire fueling this guilt is associated with the messages society sends to women about proper child-rearing practices.

Mother blaming, or mother bashing, portrays mothers as responsible for virtually all the problems of their children. Psychology contains no concept of "acceptable" or praiseworthy behaviors for mothers (Caplan, 1989). If the family appears to be warm and loving, it is "enmeshed," and this is invariably considered to be the mother's fault. There is also a double standard in describing mothers and fathers. Mothers are described according to how they are, whereas fathers are described by what they do; if both parents behave in the same manner, the mother's behavior is described as "cold," but the father is "just that way."

Sexual trauma increases the vulnerability to all forms of psychopathology. Women who have experienced sexual violence as a child or as an adult see the world through different eyes than those who have not. They frequently express feelings of alienation, of being out of step with others, and of psychological distance (Walker, 1990). Violence against women is horribly common, and its devastating consequences can haunt women for the rest of their lives. Approximately one fourth of American women may have experienced some form of childhood sexual abuse. A history of childhood sexual abuse has often been found in adult women who suffer from eating disorders, substance abuse, post-traumatic stress disorder, and various dissociative disorders.

Women who have experienced sexual trauma are often victimized twice—once during the act and again by society and the law. About 60% of rapes are acquaintance rapes (Worell & Remer, 2002), but the men who commit these crimes are frequently let off the hook. Blaming women for rape is a way of denying the violent and traumatizing nature of the crime. Holding women responsible for rape by inferring that they broke the rules of society (the rules being to protect yourself at all times) keeps many women from reporting the act and also prevents them from experiencing the feelings of anger and loss at the violation. It is estimated that only 30% of rapes are reported; of those reported, only 30% of the perpetrators are found guilty. Instead, the victims are left feeling guilty, anxious, and angry.

Feminist therapists were among the pioneers in recognizing the trauma of the war at home—women survivors of sexual assault, domestic violence, childhood abuse, and workplace harassment (Brown, 2004, 2005a). In fact, they created names for the event-specific consequences of interpersonal trauma—battered women's syndrome (Walker, 1979), for one.

The lower economic status of women adds to the formation and maintenance of distress. Women continue to be clustered in lower paying, sex role occupations (U.S. Bureau of Labor Statistics, 2011); there is a distinct economic disadvantage to being female. The **feminization of poverty** is a pithy phrase that captures the realization that single and divorced women and their children constitute an increasing proportion of poor people, especially in the United States (Goldberg & Kremen, 1990). Gender gaps in wages at work and in child care at home conspire to keep women in economically fragile, and thus less powerful and more distressed, positions.

Women are typically paid less than men and are usually well below men in income level. The average female worker is just as well educated as the average male worker (median schooling of 12.8 years), but a woman makes only 81 cents for every dollar a man earns when they both work full-time year-round (U.S. Bureau of Labor Statistics, 2011). The gender wage gap has narrowed for most age groups, but it is a vicious patriarchal myth that it had vanished. The financial gap is even worse when women take interruptions in their work lives (Rose & Hartmann, 2004). Money does not guarantee mental health, but it does offer a buffer against life's strains.

The workplace, in general, can represent a harsh setting for women. Between 40% and 80% of all working women have been sexually harassed, depending on the definition. Harassment and the acceptance of harassment by a male-dominated society can leave women feeling powerless and with lowered self-esteem. It also reinforces the view of women as sex objects and denies that they are intelligent, contributing individuals.

Many career women suffer when they choose to have a child: Their companies assign them to the so-called "mommy track." Suddenly, promotions and important assignments begin to disappear (Paludi, 1992).

Also hindering advancement is the **glass ceiling**—the subtle barrier that women and minorities face in their climb up the corporate or power ladder. Although women can see the top of the hierarchy and are informed that with patience and persistence they can reach the apex, they rarely do. The glass ceiling frequently prevents women from moving into top positions: only 17% of the U.S. Congress member and only 16% of Fortune 500 board members are women (www.cawp.rutgers.edu, www.catalyst.org). If you need any more evidence, simply count the number of U.S. presidents or Catholic popes who were women!

Under these collective circumstances, women's problems in living are not necessarily psychopathological. Rather, they frequently represent reasonable and creative attempts to survive oppressive conditions. Resistance may be evidence of resiliency. For therapists to erroneously attribute women's problems to their pathological dispositions, instead of correctly to their oppressive situations, is to commit the **fundamental attribution error**. (The error is the tendency of attributing one's own behavior to the situation, while attributing other people's behavior to their dispositions.)

Whatever the distress, a cure becomes possible only when the cause is discovered. From the feminist viewpoint, the cause of dysfunctional behavior is principally related to gender, not through genes or neurotransmitters, but through the gender socialization processes, expectations, and discrimination. Corrective actions are thus frequently educational and political in nature.

Therapeutic Processes

The therapeutic process in feminist therapy is a gradual sequence of awareness (consciousness raising), decisions (choosing), skills (counterconditioning), and action (social liberation) within the context of an empowering and egalitarian therapy relationship.

Consciousness Raising

Consciousness raising is a vital part of feminist psychotherapy. An overarching goal is that clients develop a feminist consciousness (Brown, 1994), an awareness that one's suffering arises not from individual deficits but from cultural invalidation and exclusion because of one's status as a nondominant group in the culture. In order for a woman to escape the oppressive thumb of a male-dominated culture, she must first realize the negative impact these values and expectations have exerted on her life. She must first understand how sociopolitical and interpersonal forces influence her behavior. Both sexes are subject to gender-role expectations, but women often receive the more severe punishment if they refuse to acquiesce in role expectations (Hyde, 1991).

Women will gradually differentiate between what they have been taught is socially acceptable and what is actually healthy for them. Millions of women were raised to be "good girls"—docile and submissive—but later learned that such a passive style contributes to behavioral deficits and emotional distress. Women taught to be interpersonally passive instead of assertive, for instance, are likely to experience more depression, eating disorders, and sexual conflicts than their assertive counterparts (McGrath et al., 1990).

Consciousness raising helps uncover the underlying purposes of behaviors. Women come to realize that they often do things not because they want to, but rather because society expects them to. Connections between external situations and psychological problems often surface when a woman realizes that the reason she feels unfulfilled is because she has rarely done anything just for herself, that her actions have always been in response to the expectations of others.

Consider the case of Ms. J, a 30-year-old woman married to a financially successful husband and the mother of a young daughter (Lerner, 1988). She came for therapy complaining of depression, stating that her life was "going nowhere." Ms. J described her husband as a "brilliant workaholic" who engaged in repetitive cycles of distancing and dominating the family. He had not "allowed" her to work until their daughter entered kindergarten. The client was now bored and unfulfilled with her current job and wanted to return to graduate school, but she feared that her husband would never tolerate her competence or her involvement in anything that excluded him. In keeping with the dictates of culture and the prescribed complementarity of marriage, the client had dutifully underfunctioned, putting aside her own ambitions to bolster her husband and preserve harmony.

Consciousness raising about possible sex bias and sex role stereotyping in the *therapist* is the beginning of the therapist's work. Most mental health disciplines have adopted principles related to sex role bias. Responsible psychotherapists are enjoined to routinely examine their own practice and language for gender stereotypes and to recognize how their own socialization and attitudes about gender may affect the services they provide. Further, therapists engender their own consciousness about the characteristics of psychotherapy and strive to use gender-affirming practices in working with girls and women (American Psychological Association, 2007).

Feminist therapists enjoy a variety of options regarding consciousness raising. One task is to be a client's supporter, to encourage her in whatever she feels would be beneficial for her, but also to educate her on sexist social methods and individual cognitions. Therapists assist clients in uncovering the expectations they have been socialized to accept and in evaluating the influence of social norms on their problems. Through the use of self-disclosure and mutual support, therapists encourage clients to become more self-directed and autonomous. In consciousness raising, a feminist therapist can both educate and understand—something that is often difficult to accomplish in traditional psychotherapies.

Feminist therapists walk a tightrope: They demonstrate how women are subject to limitations imposed by a sexist society, but they also reinforce the idea that women must not accept the role of the passive victim. Too little or too much toward either side will probably retard improvement.

Therapists liberally refer clients to groups that endorse feminist principles and that aid in the therapeutic process. Women's groups, domestic abuse groups, assertiveness training, power analysis, and sex role analysis are just a sampling of the variety of educational groups. **Power analysis groups** are designed to increase women's awareness of the power differential existing between men and women and to empower women to have influence on the interpersonal and institutional externals in their lives. Similarly, sex role analysis groups are designed to increase women's awareness of how the sex role expectations of society adversely affect them and also to understand the ways in which men and women are socialized differently in society.

Consciousness-raising groups are an integral component of feminist therapy. These groups, initially an outgrowth of the women's movement, involve groups of women who meet regularly to discuss their lives as women. They share information about their lives and identify common threads in their experiences. A woman who is being abused by her husband may become involved in a consciousness-raising group and subsequently discover that several other members of the group have also been abused. The knowledge that she is not alone in her predicament may help the woman feel less isolated; moreover, group members' experiences and advice may prompt her to seek the help she desperately needs. Women come to understand that their experiences with discrimination and violence are not isolated incidents involving only themselves, but are universal experiences of women.

Bibliotherapy involves the client's learning about herself and her environment through reading. Reading books and articles relevant to therapeutic issues educates the client and reduces the knowledge differential between the therapist and the client. Popular examples are books related to assertion, sexual abuse, women's health, codependency, workplace discrimination, relationship conflicts, and family of origin concerns.

Choosing

Genuine choice is often a difficult concept for clients to understand. After being invalidated and silenced for years, the notion that they can choose to live and grow without the heavy weight of a gender-role albatross around their necks is both fascinating and frightening. The forces of society are strong, and old cultural norms are difficult to break. Once clients understand the sociocultural impact on their lives, they usually develop a genuine desire to adopt a healthier lifestyle.

Society, however, does not acclimate quickly or easily to "rocking the boat" and may resist her efforts. Throughout the process of choosing how to change, the client will probably face many obstacles, such as discrimination, belittlement, and discouragement, including from family and friends who feel that the client was "fine just the way she was," which usually means submissive and dependent.

Two major choices a client faces are the degree of change she wants to accomplish and whether she can achieve her goal without the support of a patriarchic society. The power a woman gains in changing her life may not be worth the pain of alienating her family in the process. Getting a prize, even the prize of power, may be worthless unless you have significant people in your life with whom to share it. In short, choosing in feminist therapy means choosing power and choosing how to use it.

A woman with knowledge of gender socialization can use its power to change. The feminist therapist encourages the client to make choices that will change her life for the better—not just to settle for what others are willing to give her, but to lobby for what she is truly entitled to. The therapist and the client agree on the parameters of treatment. Ideally, the therapy is free of constrictions based on gender-defined roles, and the options explored are free of sex role stereotypes. By empowering clients, therapists help them develop greater autonomy, self-confidence, and power. To choose something, rather than just passively accept current conditions, requires power, and power is what the therapist seeks to instill in clients. The term **empowerment** captures the essence of this process. Choosing is ultimately the responsibility of the client, but helping the client develop the power and the skill to choose wisely is in the hands of the therapist.

Counterconditioning

Feminist therapists are quite comfortable in teaching new skills as long as it is done within an empathic, empowering relationship. The principle of doing the healthy opposite applies to a multitude of gender-linked, cultural-induced distress: relaxation training for sexual anxiety, assertion training for passive behavior, cognitive training for patriarchal irrationalities, communication training for women who have not yet found their voice. Exposure, behavioral, and cognitive-behavioral methods are also assimilated into the feminist treatment of trauma (Herman, 1997).

Social Liberation

The change process known as **social liberation** entails increasing alternatives for social behaviors. These include advocating for the rights of oppressed populations, empowering clients to change their lives, and making policy interventions.

The interconnectedness of clients' "inner" world and their "outer" world is often ignored in traditional psychotherapy (Gerber, 1992). But through feminist therapy, clients come to realize the significance of the statement **The personal is political**. This feminist motto essentially means using understanding about oneself as a basis for understanding the oppression of all women. This motto expresses the feminist position that the source of psychopathology is not intrapsychic, but rather sociopolitical in nature. The intrapsychic influences on distress pale in comparison to the broader social and political forces that hold women captive in stereotyped expectancies and gender discrimination. Therapy, therefore, targets women's unhealthy external situations as well as internalized messages.

Feminists have looked at many behaviors traditionally viewed as personal—as simple interactions between individuals—and reconceptualized them as expressions of political power (Hyde, 1991). When a woman is sexually harassed in the workplace or is sexually assaulted in the dorm, society tends to view these acts as personal, individual acts—one person acting against another. Feminists, however, view these actions not only as personal attacks, but also as political expressions of men's power over women. The sexual assault is not simply a personal attack against that one woman; it is an act of power directed against all women by men who feel entitled to demean and abuse women.

By reflecting on their own experiences of discrimination and disempowerment, women come to understand that oppression does not affect only them; it affects everyone in society, women and men alike. Just because they have come to realize the effects of oppression, it does not disappear. Women need to become involved with the political process, to work to change social attitudes and political actions. It is not enough merely to understand that women possess unequal power; women must join together to liberate people from gender expectations that label people without trying to understand them.

Feminist therapists empower women to undergo a revolution from within as well as a revolution from without. Traditional therapies focus only on internal, individual psychological changes. Feminist therapy endorses this essential change but combines it with external, collective, and political transformations. A woman assisted in recovering from a sexual assault, for instance, may be encouraged to extend the healing process through co-leading therapy groups for assaulted women, volunteering at a women's resource center, educating the public about sexual abuse, or lobbying in the state capital for a bill protecting victims.

The feminist therapist strives to help women understand the need to continue fighting for their rights and to be a positive role model for involvement. Toward this end, therapists themselves form and join groups to initiate social change. Feminist therapists testify in court on behalf of their clients, promote legislation in statehouses on behalf of all women, advocate for adequate child care, and participate in a myriad of sociopolitical activities to free women from abuse.

At the same time, feminist therapists attempt to educate and liberate fellow mental health professionals. Since the 1980s, feminists have brought the attention of all psychotherapists to "the problems of violence and abuse in the family, to the strains of gender roles in a changing culture, to the ethics of practice and boundary violations, to precision and care in the application of diagnostic labels, to consideration of the need for fair and unbiased evaluations of all parties in marital and custodial disputes, and to the need for clients to have power over their actions and relationships" (Brown & Brodsky, 1992, p. 56).

Therapeutic Content
Intrapersonal Conflicts
Anxieties and Defenses

Anxiety reflects a woman's natural reaction to the forces of sexism, discrimination, and violence that try to keep her in a subservient position. Anxiety also results, in part, from the conflict between the desire to expand life experiences beyond those traditionally available to women and the need to maintain the ties and strengths that women receive from their group identity. Society's limitations feed women's distress and provoke their defensive reactions. This natural anxiety can stereotype women as unassertive, weak, and dependent, but when women fear walking alone and constantly guard against workplace discrimination, anxiety and defenses are adaptive forms of coping.

Self-Esteem

A large part of a woman's self-esteem is based on the creation and cultivation of close relationships. Woman typically derive immense satisfaction and fulfillment when the relational aspects of her life are in place, when she feels loved and accepted for who she is and who she wants to be.

In a broader context, women often view society as a collection of relationships. The nature of these relationships shapes self-esteem of the group as a whole. Many theorists view women's relational style as healthier than men's, but when unhealthy relationships arise, such a style can lead to low self-esteem and maladaptive behaviors among women.

For centuries, men have ingrained in women the belief that attractiveness, not character or achievement, is their most important attribute. What woman wants to hear that no matter how intelligent she is or how good she is at her job, the only thing that really matters is looking good and finding a husband? Research indicates that women tend to underestimate their abilities, whereas men tend to overestimate theirs (Worell & Remer, 2002). The tendency for women to make statements such as "I just don't have the ability" and "I can't" stems mainly from societal expectations. Society tends to attribute women's success to luck and men's success to skill—a damaging stereotypical message that cultivates a sense of inferiority, which in turn lowers self-esteem.

Responsibility

Many women feel responsible for everyone but themselves. They put the needs of others (parents, children, family, coworkers, supervisors) above their own. Women must come to appreciate the need for personal responsibility—to be happy and healthy themselves. Responsibility involves making time for oneself, nurturing the self in order to nurture others. Many women have to realize that in order to truly love and support others, they must first learn to love and support themselves.

Women must also accept responsibility for helping to break the cycle of oppression and powerlessness. Responsibility rests on the shoulders of all women to understand the negative impact of society and work for change. Women must understand the full meaning of the motto "The personal is political," appreciating the need to free not only themselves, but all marginalized people from the bonds of oppression.

Interpersonal Conflicts
Intimacy and Sexuality

Chronic disconnection is the source of most human suffering. Feminist therapy involves healing these disconnections and bringing people back into connection, back into intimacy with themselves and others.

Women can experience a distorted sense of intimacy and sexuality stemming from the fact that they are frequently seen, and react to being seen, as sexual objects. For many women, being sexual is also a way of being and of relating to men (Jordan et al., 1991). Male-dominated society equates sex with intimacy. Although women can typically establish intimate friendships with other women, it is difficult to establish these intimate bonds with men. Men have been socialized to view women as sexual objects of consumption, and these stereotyped expectancies are difficult to break.

Communication

Communication problems between the sexes exist because men and women have not learned to "speak the same language." Sometimes it seems as if men are speaking in Chinese while women are speaking in Russian, and there is no translator available to straighten out the mixed messages. Men tend to express their anger, whereas women tend to express their pain and needs. Men prefer communication that reports; women prefer communication that rapports. These two communication styles lead to a paucity of genuine communication. "You just don't understand" is the frequent refrain (Tannen, 1990).

To communicate effectively, men and women must be willing to learn to listen to each other, to stop thinking only of themselves, and to open themselves up to the other's communication style. Many women must learn to express anger and frustration effectively; in turn, many men must learn to communicate the whole gamut of feelings and needs.

Control

Central to the issue of control is power. Who holds the power, and how do they use it? The current power base of society rests in the hands of men, as it has for centuries. This power imbalance both reflects and reinforces male domination. Men perpetuate myths about women that undermine their self-confidence, distort their attributes, and in essence, keep them relatively powerless. Conditions of worth imposed on women dictate that women are not supposed to be powerful; they should be meek and deferential to men. If women express a desire for power and control, they are labeled as unfeminine and scorned by the androcentric society. Women must work to gain power to put them on an equal footing with men, because to gain power is to gain self-confidence and control.

Individuo-Social Conflicts

Adjustment versus Transcendence

The goal of feminist therapy is to enable the client to change the social, interpersonal, and political environment at the root of psychological problems. Simply adjusting to an oppressive society helps neither the client nor society; "adjustment" to a sexist society is the problem. For the self and society to advance, we must transcend—go beyond what we already know and accept—the patriarchal power structure to facilitate both women's and men's growth.

By achieving personal and social power, women will discover that adjusting to social expectations is unlikely to result in the contentment they desire. They must learn to live life for themselves, to move beyond the traditional and restricting conditions of society, and to exercise their newfound power to help free others caught in the web of society's control.

Beyond Conflict to Fulfillment

Meaning in Life

Women have traditionally defined themselves through attachment and found meaning through their relationships (Gilligan, 1982). Raising kids, supporting partners, tending to elderly parents, and serving as the emotional centers of the home were sources of life's meaning for centuries. However, the emphasis on relationships and responsibility is unnecessarily restrictive. Women may find meaning in having kids or remaining childless, devoting themselves to careers or home, deciding to marry or not. Once the shackles of patriarchy have been shed, women may make life meaningful in any way they can.

Ideal Individual

The ideal individual, woman or man, is one who is in touch with feelings and needs, is self-nurturant, and is interdependent. Interdependence involves the sharing and caring of two independent people. The ideal person possesses self-esteem and power but doesn't use these to control others. The ideal individual has progressed to a higher level of social and self-awareness and works toward social improvement.

Some feminist theorists have suggested that the ideal individual would represent an Aristotelian mean, an equal balance of stereotypically male and female characteristics, a concept known as **androgyny**. An androgynous individual possesses a large and flexible behavioral repertoire and exhibits a range of psychological characteristics depending on the situation. Androgyny has been prescribed by many as a way for women to become liberated from traditional gender-role traits and lead more fulfilling lives. Androgynous individuals tend to be more independent, flexible, and higher in self-esteem than stereotypically "feminine" women (Bem, 1975, 1977).

There are arguments against androgyny as a prototype for the ideal individual, however. By valuing an androgynous personality, society is setting up new expectations, an ideal that is incredibly demanding. Now people must be successful not only at their own prescribed gender role, but also at another. As Hyde (1991, p. 119) puts it, "In the good old days, a woman could be considered reasonably competent ('successful') if she could cook well. To meet new standards and be androgynous, she not only has to cook well, but also has to repair cars." Some feminists also argue that to become androgynous, women must add "masculine" traits to their behavior patterns, thus making women become more like men. Instead of urging women to emulate selected stereotypically male traits in an attempt to curry favor in a male-dominated society, society should learn to value qualities that women already possess.

Therapeutic Relationship

The client–therapist relationship in feminist therapy is characterized by two Es: empowerment and egalitarianism. *Empowerment* is the process whereby therapists help instill power, both social and individual, in the client. The power balance between the sexes in society is alarmingly disproportionate. For centuries, men have possessed the power advantage over women, from physical strength to academic and vocational advantages; women always seem to come in second in a two-gender race (de Beauvoir, 1961).

The therapeutic relationship models and offers power. When women are taught to achieve power and to use it appropriately, many psychopathologies will disappear. Through the therapist's own understanding of power and use of self-disclosure, the therapeutic dyad can transfer power to the client and serve as a role model for interactions outside of the office.

The second hallmark of the therapeutic relationship is **egalitarianism**—a comparatively equal relationship between the therapist and the client. Equalizing power will be manifested in many ways: reducing the knowledge discrepancy between the participants, generating mutual goals, increasing the clinician's self-disclosure, and demystifying the process of therapy. Reducing the discrepancy includes valuing the client's

perspectives and insights just as highly as the therapist's. Because therapy is a cooperative relationship, goals are mutually generated by the therapist and the client. Self-disclosure reduces the role distance and the power differential between the parties and aids in developing a trusting relationship. Because feminist therapy often focuses on sensitive women's issues—such as work discrimination, sexual harassment, and physical changes—therapist self-disclosure is a vital component in establishing a trusting and empathic alliance.

Therapy should be a demystifying process. Feminist therapy is a way of being, believing, and understanding; it is a perspective that allows fluidity, acknowledges interconnectedness, and encourages exploration. Avoiding dogma and jargon, feminist treatment is concerned with making the process accessible and comprehensible, rather than mystifying and mysterious (Walker, 1990).

The egalitarian relationship is centrally important in feminist therapy—first, because it minimizes the social control aspects of therapy and, second, because it does not reproduce the power imbalances women face in society. If directive therapy methods are employed, the therapy itself should not have the effect of maintaining or reinforcing stereotypic dependency of women. By becoming involved in a real relationship in which their opinions and feelings are validated, women will come to expect and enact this relationship style with others.

Above all, the therapeutic relationship in feminist therapy is characterized by a deep, personal, two-way communication between the therapist and the client. In the person-centered tradition, the ideal relationship is characterized by genuineness, warmth, equality, and empathy. Research has repeatedly confirmed that the client's perception of therapist empathy predicts successful treatment (Chapter 5; Bohart et al., 2002).

In relational-cultural theory, the ideal resembles mutual empathy (Jordan, 2010). That's not asking clients to take care of the therapist, but for the therapist to show emotional engagement and responsiveness. To promote change, clients must see, feel, and hear the therapist's empathy. Clients are helped by noting their impact on the therapist in a real, concrete relationship. The feminist therapist neither hides nor rabidly self-discloses; the feminist therapist demonstrates mutuality and becomes a real presence in clients' lives. Isolation is the glue that holds oppression in place. Feminist therapy heals isolation through mutual empathy, through moving disconnection to connection.

Practicalities of Gender-Sensitive Therapies

Feminist therapy is consumer oriented from the start. Clients are encouraged to shop around until they find a clinician they relate to comfortably. More than most practitioners, feminist therapists are inclined toward lower cost sessions and sliding fee scales to make their services available to a larger proportion of the population.

Feminist therapists invite clients and their families to ask questions about the services they will receive. Going beyond the typical informed consent for treatment, feminist therapists aspire to **empowered consent**, meaning that the client gains access to knowledge that the clinician possesses regarding, for example, risks and benefits of psychotherapy, the right to refuse any method, the ability to seek a second opinion, and the right to terminate treatment at any time. The distinctive emphasis on women's groups and bibliotherapy contributes to the demystification of psychotherapy and the value of social liberation.

Feminist therapy flexibly accommodates both long-term and short-term treatment. The length of therapy is largely determined by the patient, who is empowered and expected to make such critical decisions. She is to become the expert and authority on her own life, including her own psychotherapy. When the patient and therapist together decide to pursue the ambitious goal of both individual change and social change, the length of therapy increases accordingly. The development of feminist consciousness takes considerable time, but the success of feminist action takes even longer (Brown, 1994).

As a practical point, feminist therapists have pioneered nonhierarchical leadership approaches to therapy groups, community organizations, and professional associations. Leadership is itself "gendered" and is conducted within a gender context. Also known as women's leadership style, the non-hierarchical style emphasizes consensus building and inclusiveness. It is part and parcel of a more egalitarian sharing in the power of leadership.

For these and additional reasons, feminist therapists are strongly encouraged to undergo personal therapy. Personal treatment can limit the problem of projecting one's own problems with boundaries, hierarchies, and intimacy onto one's patients (Luepnitz, 1988). A course of personal treatment will also place therapists in the role of the client, thus sensitizing them to the power dynamics of therapy and increasing respect for their patients' struggles.

Feminist therapists endorse and conduct gender awareness training in mental health. Appreciation of gender in treating women requires understanding not only how girls and women are raised but also how psychosocial services respond to them (American Psychological Association, 2007; Walker, 1990). Graduate courses should be offered in gender and sex role development, gender analysis of contemporary society, counseling girls and women, and gender-sensitive supervision.

A final practical point is the gender of the psychotherapist. Almost all self-identified feminist therapists are female. Controversy abounds on whether male therapists can practice feminist therapy or merely profeminist therapy (Ganley, 1988; Jordan, 2010).

Male-Sensitive Psychotherapy

Traditional psychotherapy was designed by men primarily to treat women. It thus reflected male assumptions about female personality development. In recent years, feminist psychotherapists have enumerated the flaws in these assumptions and offered correctives. The next task is to design psychotherapy for men based on an accurate understanding of male personality development (Levant, 1990).

The feminist movement, although intended primarily to advance the cause of women, also sparked the realization that men are negatively affected by gender-role expectations and that they, too, suffer from role strain. Consider four stereotypes of "true masculinity" (Brannon & David, 1976):

- *No sissy stuff:* A truly masculine person avoids anything remotely "feminine."
- *The big wheel:* A masculine person is successful and looked up to; he is the breadwinner of the family.
- *The sturdy oak:* Masculinity involves exuding confidence, strength, and self-reliance.
- *Give 'em hell:* A masculine person is aggressive and daring.

In order to conform to stereotypes, men achieve these standards or accept the consequences of "failure." Uncritical acceptance and achievement of these expectations is a burden for men, but so also is the risk of being unmasculine and therefore ostracized. To negotiate between these two perils, men frequently hide their feelings behind a façade of toughness, resistance, and sometimes violence.

The privileged position of men in Western cultures has been, at once, a blessing and a curse. On the one hand, men have enjoyed advantages in education, ownership, politics, employment, and power. On the other hand, this masculine gender role entails inhibition of emotional expressiveness, reliance on aggression and control, as well as preoccupation with achievement and success (Eisler & Blalock, 1991). Many male problems—partner violence, rampant homophobia, objectification of women, neglect of health needs, and detached fathering, to name a few—are unfortunate byproducts of the typical male socialization (Levant & Pollack, 1995). Despite their many privileges, men continue to die 6 years sooner than women on average and continue to kill themselves three times more frequently than women.

The male gender role complicates psychotherapy. Men find it difficult to seek help because to do so would be to admit weakness, further threatening self-esteem. Many studies have demonstrated that men endorsing traditional masculine ideology hold more negative attitudes toward, and less frequently seek, psychotherapy (Addis & Mahalik, 2003). Men's reluctance to seek psychological help stands in marked contrast to the prevalence and severity of problems that afflict them.

Socialization also begets difficulty in identifying and expressing emotions, a condition known as **alexithymia**. Men are often genuinely unaware of their emotions. In the absence of such awareness, men tend to rely on their cognition and try to logically deduce how they should feel (Levant, 1990). If they are aware of their emotion, many men are also slow to express them. A clinical tale tells of a farmer who asked his son on Sunday afternoon how he was feeling. On Tuesday morning, the son grunted "fine."

Consider the case of Marc, who consulted me (JCN) in his early forties as he was embroiled in his third divorce and alienated from his three children. Marc was raised by a controlling mother and a distant father, who was frequently away from home on business. He was shown little nurturance as a youth, never receiving the modeling, skills, or inclination to be close and expressive. When he did express feelings, 95% of the time it was to express annoyance and anger. Following the traditional male script, Marc exuded strength, ignored feelings, and became a big wheel. He excelled at sports and scholastics, becoming a successful physician. In his first appointment, Marc asked "Why? Why can't I relate to women? Why do my kids dislike me? Why do I feel lonely all the time?"

One way of looking at Marc's life is anchored in the **gender identity paradigm**, in which there are two distinct and opposite identities of "masculine" and "feminine." Marc incorporated the traditional characteristics of the masculine sex role: no sissy stuff, the big wheel, the sturdy oak, and give 'em hell. According to the gender identity paradigm, healthy psychological adjustment depends on achieving a secure gender identity.

Another and newer way at looking at Marc's life is through the lens of the **gender role strain paradigm** (Pleck, 1995). Here, gender roles are seen as socially constructed and frequently problematic. According to the gender role strain paradigm, gender role norms are often inconsistent and contradictory. Social condemnation and stressful consequences commonly follow role violations, and many behaviors prescribed by gender role norms are dysfunctional (Good & Brooks, 2005).

The role of male had been unwittingly but destructively imposed on Marc by his parents, teachers, and peers, the cultural transmitters who subscribe to the prevailing gender identity. Marc had learned to overvalue autonomy and undervalue connections; he was limited in his ability to express intimate emotions and form mature attachments. Whereas the gender identity paradigm views psychological health as predicated on conforming to traditional gender role norms, the gender role strain paradigm asserts that conforming to traditional gender roles generates distress and dysfunction.

Treating men in therapy can be an arduous process. Perhaps the most daunting tasks occur at the very beginning: getting boys and men to avail themselves of psychotherapy and then trusting clinicians enough to form a therapeutic alliance (Good & Robertson, 2010). Men tend to fear intimacy, and the therapeutic relationship is certainly an intimate one. Men are typically reluctant to admit to their problems and share them with the therapist. For instance, one of my (JCN) male clients repeatedly protested at the slightest hint of empathy, declaring "I'm a big guy and don't need anyone holding my hand or feeling sorry for me." Attempts at empathic resonance were rejected as "unmasculine."

Plenty of men feel bewildered in the emotional-relational world of psychotherapy. They are uncomfortable with both the language and experience of therapy; "sharing emotions," "becoming vulnerable," and "connecting to your inner child" only intensifies their discomfort and shame at being in treatment. That's not the Guy Way of dealing with problems.

The profession has not done a good job of creating a user-friendly environment for male clients. We can either shoehorn men into a process that traditionally has been more user-friendly for females, or reshape what we do for males (Stosny, 2010).

Male-sensitive therapy seeks to help men understand the strong connections between gender beliefs and problematic behaviors. Through treatment, men come to recognize emotional needs, identify sources of beliefs, and recognize that these beliefs were not freely chosen but can be changed nonetheless. Men aim to change their "reality" about the meaning of masculinity to more functional and healthy ideals. For example, "real men" can express positive and vulnerable feelings, can be more openly nurturant in their relationships, acknowledge needs for interdependence and security, and learn alternatives to physical or intellectual responses.

The treatment formats for boys and men are more flexible than conventional, face-to-face individual psychotherapy. All too often, therapists attempt to help troubled males by using an approach that is incompatible with their relational styles (Kiselica, 2003). A male-sensitive therapist working with adolescent boys can adopt male-friendly practices, such as beginning therapy informally (e.g., tossing a football outside, playing checkers or chess), expressing humor because it is a common way for men to begin conversations about serious issues, sitting side by side instead of face to face to reduce self-consciousness, avoiding open-ended questions about feelings, and focusing on practical matters that are foremost on the young man's agenda. The key is for the therapist to discover how a particular boy relates to the world and then to adjust the treatment accordingly.

Group therapy is also a powerful and common treatment format for men. They are accustomed to bonding and cooperating in sports teams, scout troops, military units, and work units (Kiselica, 2003). Groups counter isolation and build trust over time. Although drum-beating retreats for men received much publicity years ago, more typical is an ongoing men's therapy group meeting every week or two (Andronico, 1996).

In recent years, increasing awareness of the special psychological concerns of men has opened up new discussions about treating men in psychotherapy. The Society for the Psychological Study of Men and Masculinity (SPSMM) and the American Men's Studies Association, as two organizational forces, promote the critical study of men and advances male-sensitive treatment. A deluge of books has focused on male issues in psychotherapy (e.g., Brooks, 1995; Good & Brooks, 2005; Horne & Kiselica, 1999; Levant & Pollack, 1995; Pollock & Brooks, 1998; Rabinowitz & Cochran, 2001). The emerging male-sensitive therapies acknowledge their historical debt to feminist scholarship for articulating the profound and pervasive impact of gender, on women and men alike.

Effectiveness of Gender-Sensitive Therapies

Many uncontrolled studies have been conducted on the effects of feminist therapy, consciousness-raising groups, and gender-sensitive psychoeducational groups. However, we cannot locate any controlled outcome research conducted on feminist therapy. It is not included in the various meta-analyses on the effectiveness of adult psychotherapy, youth psychotherapy, or couple psychotherapy. The effectiveness of feminist therapy, in both relative and absolute terms, has not been rigorously evaluated.

Available research suggests that female therapists, first, and therapists of the patient's gender, second, facilitate the treatment *process*, especially if these therapists present a nonstereotypic sexual viewpoint (Beutler et al., 1986). Enhanced empathy and increased satisfaction are commonly observed in same-gender dyads as compared to opposite-gender dyads. However, same-gender therapeutic relationships have not consistently produced differential treatment *outcomes* (Orlinsky & Howard, 1980). That is, there are no consistent effects of therapist gender or patient-therapist gender matching on therapy effectiveness (Bowman et al., 2001; Sue & Lam, 2002).

Traditional outcome studies on the effectiveness of feminist therapy may be more difficult to conduct than in other therapy systems because most evaluation research examines remission of symptoms, which is only part of the feminist therapy agenda. Feminist therapists are interested in changes in decision making, attitude, flexibility, and social advocacy. For example, studies using qualitative methodology report consciousness-raising groups have an enormous impact on female participants (Ballou, 1990). Researchers who ask women to report experiences, or who have participated themselves, using self-reports and participant observation, have found significant changes in social/political awareness, vocational interests, self-perception, sex roles, and ego strength. However, no significant changes are typically found on standardized measures of psychological symptoms in the consciousness-raising groups.

Criticisms of Gender-Sensitive Therapies

From a Psychoanalytic Perspective

Freud had a complicated, conflictual relationship with women—as do most men. Nonetheless, he was a pioneer far ahead of his time in recognizing the context of gender and in promoting the cause of women. His theories highlighted the interplay of gender in the family of origin and liberated women from repressive Victorian standards of sexuality. His psychoanalysis was among the first to accept women as trainees and to endorse nonmedical training for psychotherapists (as medical schools did not accept women in that era). Freud was a prefeminist therapist.

Feminists are correct in sharing Freud's emphasis on the deterministic forces operating on humans, but are incorrect in locating the source of that determinism. Social expectations and cultural practices contribute to neuroses to be sure, but the essential origins are intrapsychic, within us. Blaming society generates victims, not survivors. To paraphrase Shakespeare, "The fault, dear Brutus, is not in our stars (or society), but in ourselves."

The essential truth of psychotherapy is that an individual's struggle and ultimate capacity to adapt are fought from within the individual, not against an oppressive society. We say that the "Political is personal." Look inward, not outward, for solutions.

From a Cognitive-Behavioral Perspective

Science searches for universal laws applicable across diverse conditions. Many feminists would deny that such universal principles exist. They maintain that all truths are contextual. But is calculus any less valid for men than for women? Do the laws of physics vary from gender to gender, or are there universal truths of electronics and mechanics that can be applied by any person? Does each person have to construct his or her own principles of physics? Chaos would ensue if such extreme claims were true.

Psychotherapy as a science also involves the search for universal principles of behavior change. Is there any evidence that principles of contingency management hold for men but not for women? Certainly gender may affect what behaviors are reinforced or punished. But if people do not reinforce prosocial behaviors and punish antisocial behaviors, there will soon be no culture. If women have been conditioned by the dominant culture to adopt self-defeating behaviors, then they had best apply principles of contingency management, counterconditioning, and stimulus control to counter their conditions and control their contexts.

And, at the risk of sounding gender *in*sensitive, where are the randomized clinical trials on the effectiveness of feminist therapy? Is there any robust research that demonstrates feminist therapy effects client improvement as much as or more than cognitive-behavior therapy? Gender sensitivity may represent social progression, but the lack of solid outcome research represents scientific regression.

From a Humanistic Perspective

Traditionally, academics and mental health professionals have been ardent defenders of freedom of speech; today, however, in an era of political correctness, only certain types of free speech are allowed. Liberal feminists use their pulpits to promote their political agendas—pro-choice, pro-gay marriage, antiguns, antibusiness, and so on. What began as a liberating ideology for women has devolved into an oppressive ideology for society.

Feminist thought police on college campuses and in professional associations have placed freedom of expression under siege. Do we only defend speech that we like? Do we only embrace diversity that we value? Are conservatives permitted to speak and serve if they do not endorse feminist principles? What of other conservative causes—religious fundamentalists, antiaffirmative action, pro-life groups—that offend the liberal sentiments of feminists. Anyone who prizes conservative causes understandably fears being characterized as a woman-hating, victim-blaming misanthrope. In the name of promoting diversity, feminism may be promoting censorship.

From an Integrative Perspective

Feminist therapy has brought an overdue correction to the androcentric biases in diagnosis, assessment, and treatment in mental health. But even corrections can go too far. Prizing the gender of the patient above all else and attributing most psychopathology to social problems goes too far. It begins to sound like the extreme liberalism promulgated in Feminist Theory and Social Problems courses on college campuses.

Integration favors a balanced and comprehensive account of human behavior. Yes, a patient's gender is significant for treatment planning, but so are dozens of other considerations—race, age, sexual orientation, diagnosis, personality, treatment goals, socioeconomic status, stage of change, and so on. Yes, many human problems are caused by social ills, but also by brain chemistry, unrealistic thinking, internal conflicts, family dysfunction, and so on. Privileging gender above all is neither scientifically defensible nor clinically tenable.

Finally, feminist therapy and theory have been developed by and with White women. In the candid acknowledgment of two leading feminists (Brown & Brodsky, 1992, p. 53): "Currently, feminist therapy theory is neither diverse nor complex in the reality it reflects. It has been deficient from the start in its inclusiveness of the lives and realities of women of color, poor or working class women, non-North American women, women over sixty-five, or women with disabilities." A truly comprehensive psychotherapy must integrate the needs of all people, men, women, and children, not only adult mainstream women (Enns, 2010).

A Feminist Analysis with Mrs. C

For most of this century, women like Mrs. C were treated out of context—not the context of marriage and family, but rather the larger social context that dictated roles women could play and rules for feminine behavior. Individual psychopathology was seen as the villain, and there was little appreciation of how women could be victims of a restrictive society.

Take Mrs. C's frigidity, for example. How many men have ever been diagnosed as frigid? Is this because women are weaker in their sexuality? Or is it because women have historically been more oppressed sexually? Look at Mrs. C's father, waiting up for her after a date to question her as if she were accused of a crime. He even had the gall to follow her on a date as if she were a chattel that he had the right to control. Would a father dare to do that to his son? Would he even think to do that to a son?

With a father so preoccupied with his teenage daughter's dating behavior, we must wonder about the possibility of incestuous activity. For most of this century, incestuous concerns were supposed to be a function of childhood fantasy—until feminists pulled the covers off of a dreadful reality. Millions of children, particularly girls, were discovered to be victims of sexual abuse. Psychotherapy would certainly need to explore the real possibility that Mrs. C, like all too many female clients, was using symptoms to cover over traumatic memories. Mrs. C's preoccupation with cleanliness may have been related to early experiences in which she was made to feel dirty and bad. How would one wash away the trauma of having one's innocence soiled and spoiled by abusive behavior?

Of course, Mrs. C's preoccupation with keeping her house clean from germs and worms represents

(continued)

the stereotype that a woman's work is never done. Do men ever have compulsions related to housework? Men frequently have aversions to housework but rarely compulsions. When did Mrs. C's compulsions get out of control? When her oldest daughter developed pinworms and the physician ordered Mrs. C to boil everything—on top of the housework, the child care, the flu, and the pregnancy. Most people still don't realize that only a couple of cultures in the world will allow anyone to have exclusive child care responsibilities for more than 5 or 6 hours at a time. It's emotionally too exhausting. No wonder Mrs. C broke down. She insisted on functioning effectively in a dysfunctional social system.

Did she ever get relief? One child after another, from A to E. Who wouldn't be likely to fail? When it came to having so many children, was she doing her Catholic duty? When it came to having sex, was she doing her wifely duty? When was Mrs. C ever free? Not as a young child, not as a blossoming teenager, not as a young mother, not as a mature wife. Perhaps in the privacy of her shower, she experienced a place free from demands of others, free from control by others. But whatever pleasure she might have sought from the sensation of warm water caressing her body was soon controlled by rituals as rigid as the roles she played as daughter, mother, and housewife.

Mrs. C doesn't need another therapist to tell her what's wrong with her. She certainly doesn't need another man to tell her what to do. Mrs. C needs the freedom of feminist therapy to raise her consciousness about coercive controls that defined her as a daughter, as a mother, as a housewife, and as a dental hygienist. But when was she ever free to be a woman outside the narrow confines of these stereotypical female roles?

Mrs. C doesn't need to be told what to do. She needs to be empowered by a sensitive female psychotherapist to do what *she* wants to do.

Instead of being unilaterally analyzed by a therapist, Mrs. C will co-analyze herself *with* a therapist—a process of mutual discovery and direction. She will gradually discover her authority and soon speak in her own voice. Mrs. C will discover how she can begin to take control of her life through personal strength rather than social weakness. If she is sick of excessive housework, for example, she can choose to say no. If she is angry over being controlled by men—her father, her husband, her previous psychotherapist, or her physician—she can be empowered to restructure her relationships rather than controlling herself through compulsions.

Mrs. C can learn to control her life through hidden strengths rather than over learned weaknesses. An egalitarian women's group or an assertion training group in addition to individual treatment would enhance both her consciousness and her skills.

Once Mrs. C struggles to win back her body and her self, to break out of roles and rules too small for her soul, don't be surprised if such healing is resisted by her husband, her children, her parents, and her priest. Who knows what a liberated woman might choose to do? They no doubt want her free from her neurosis. But do they want her free from the roles and rules that make her a predictable, sacrificial, and controllable woman?

What if Mrs. C decides that to be healthy and whole she needs to be on her own—something she has never experienced? Will she be accused of abandoning her children, opposing her church, dumping her husband? Repressive forces may well exert themselves and tempt Mrs. C to believe that there are only certain roles she is free to play. Feminist theory recognizes that if women are to become free from internalized cultural conflicts, then psychotherapy must help facilitate social change as well as self-change. The personal will also be political for Mrs. C.

Future Directions

As part of the broader movement toward **cultural competence** in psychotherapy (Chapter 14), gender is a critical variable and a central mediator of a client's experience. Women—and men—will be recognized as a special culture that requires tailored formulations and interventions. Psychotherapists will increasingly consider gender context when conducting assessments and devising treatments.

We and others (Brown & Brodsky, 1992; Good & Brooks, 2005) foresee several pressing tasks in the future of gender-sensitive therapies. First, feminist therapy will profit from a central, organizing theory of human behavior and personality. Otherwise, feminist therapy will be seen as a politically correct add-on rather than a full-fledged system of psychotherapy. Second, feminist and male-sensitive therapy will more fully address the needs of children, families, elders, and people with disabilities to make them inclusive. Third, if gender-sensitive therapies are to be considered evidence-based therapies, then controlled outcome studies will need be conducted.

Most urgently, gender-sensitive training opportunities must exist, both in graduate training and in continuing education. The optimal training is not a single, separate course on the Psychology of Women (or Psychology of Men), but rather continuous knowledge infused throughout an engendered curriculum (Bronstein & Quina, 2003). The multicultural lens has, thankfully, extended our vision beyond gender, but let's not forget the 51% of all races and ethnicities who are women.

We also presage escalating social activism on the part of feminist therapists. The overlap between psychotherapy and activism is huge: one is written small and one is written large. The cycle that leads from trauma to transcendence, from confusion to clarity, from helplessness to empowerment is the same. Both are about becoming part of what Martin Luther King called the "beloved community" (Pipher, 2012). Whether the fight concerns environmental destructions, reproductive freedoms, or economic disparities, gender-sensitive practitioners will apply their healing skills to the wider world.

The continuous process is to act as a powerful gadfly, moving the mainstream away from destructive sexist paradigms toward new visions shaped by gender analysis. In the words of Brown and Brodsky (1992, p. 56), feminist therapy

will always be a voice for the least powerful and most oppressed in our cultures; we will always be a source of irritation to whatever complacencies about their good intentions that our colleagues may develop about their work with women and members of other disenfranchised and at-risk groups. We will continually challenge mainstream theories and practices to be more inclusive of human diversity, more questioning of their assumptions, more willing to scrutinize their need to be paternalistic with functioning adult clients.

This perpetual focus, this process of gender-sensitive therapies, will herald their contributions in years to come.

Key Terms

alexithymia
androcentric
androgyny
bibliotherapy
consciousness-raising groups
cultural competence
culturally determined
egalitarianism
empowered consent
empowerment
feminism
feminist therapy
feminization of poverty
fundamental attribution error
gender identity paradigm

gender role strain paradigm
gender socialization
glass ceiling
internalized oppression
male-sensitive therapy
mother blaming
power analysis groups
relational-cultural theory
role conflict
role strain
social liberation
The personal is political

Recommended Readings

Brown, L. S. (2004). *Subversive dialogues: Theory in feminist therapy.* New York: Basic.
Good, G. E., & Brooks, G. R. (Eds.). (2005). *The new handbook of psychotherapy and counseling*

with men (revised ed.). San Francisco: Jossey-Bass.

Jordan, J. V. (2010). *Relational-cultural therapy.* Washington, DC: American Psychological Association.

Jordan, J. V., Walker, M., & Hartling, L. M. (Eds.). (2004). *The complexity of connection: Writings from the Jean Baker Miller Training Institute.* New York: Guilford.

Pollock, R. F., & Brooks, G. R. (Eds.). (1998). *New psychotherapy for men.* New York: Wiley.

Rosewater, L. B., & Walker, L. E. A. (Eds.). (1985). *Handbook of feminist therapy.* New York: Springer.

Worell, J., & Remer, P. (Eds.). (2002). *Feminist perspectives in therapy: Empowering diverse women* (2nd ed.). New York: Wiley.

JOURNALS: *Journal of Feminist Family Therapy; Journal of Men's Studies; Feminist Psychology; Gender & Psychoanalysis; Men and Masculinities; Psychology of Men and Masculinity; Psychology of Women Quarterly; Women & Therapy.*

Recommended Websites

Feminist Therapy Institute:
www.feminist-therapy-institute.org/

MenWeb:
www.menweb.org/

Society for the Psychological Study of Men & Masculinity:
www.apa.org/divisions/div51/

Society for the Psychology of Women:
www.apa.org/divisions/div35/

Stone Center/Wellesley Centers for Women:
www.wcwonline.org

CHAPTER 14

Multicultural Therapies

Lillian Comas-Diaz

Stanley Sue

Beverly Greene

"When I began my studies at the University of Amsterdam, my family of origin and I had family therapy for about 6 months. These were the early years of family therapy, and my family felt very unfamiliar and uneasy in the therapy situation, but endured this ordeal with Calvinist equanimity. Looking back, I am confident that our family therapists felt just as unfamiliar and uneasy and just put up with the situation as well. Careful maneuvering by the therapists and cautious cooperation by my family resulted in the idea that we were making progress, even though all of us felt quite uncertain.

At that time, the American family therapy pioneer Carl Whitaker visited Europe and was invited to do live demonstration sessions in the Netherlands with several families. My family was selected. The therapy language was English; the children translated for each other.

It was a memorable session. No careful maneuvering this time; within an hour Carl Whitaker turned our family upside down. One family member was identified as 'the crucified of the family,' another member's motives were interpreted as 'driven by the fear of death,' and my parents were made aware of the 'benevolent but suffocating regime' they had imposed upon our family. I managed to escape the wrath of this vengeful god, as the entire family felt it, by being completely occupied in translating for my brother and sister.

One session later we informed the family therapists of our decision to terminate. We met only mild resistance on their part.

The point I want to make is that even though American culture and Northern European culture are not very dissimilar, the cultural gap between the two turned out to be very large indeed. Carl Whitaker may be a wonderful family therapist, and from his point of view he must have made some very well-designed interpretations. But the interpretations he gave, however true, we did not understand; the interventions he made, however adequate within his therapy system, only aroused fright and shock; the way he made contact with us, whatever he wanted to convey, was experienced as disrespectful. His therapy felt to us like balancing on the brink of chaos. From the point of view of a Dutch upper-middle-class family, there was no way that this session could have been helpful."

Our Dutch colleague, Dr. Sjoerd Colijn, shared his foregoing experience at a professional conference to demonstrate the presumptive error of importing one culture's system of psychotherapy into another. With the kind permission of his entire family, we offer their illuminating incident as a warning against culture-insensitive treatment and as an introduction to the centrality of multiculturalism in psychotherapy.

A Sketch of Multicultural Pioneers

Historically, most influential contributors to mainstream psychotherapy were middle- or upper-class, White heterosexual males. Because the concept of psychotherapy was European in origin, its sociopolitical values were rooted in Western civilization. Little attention was given to the concerns of minority or marginalized groups. At the time, most psychotherapists believed that their treatments could be applied to all clients, regardless of their race, ethnicity, gender, culture, or sexual orientation. Thus, psychotherapy was originally envisioned as a transcultural process: One size or type would fit all potential patients.

However, it was soon discovered that psychotherapy was created by humans to solve human problems and that any product of human ingenuity is by definition cultural. Psychotherapy is inescapably and inextricably bound to a particular cultural framework (Wohl, 1989). The assumptions of traditional therapies—based on White, middle-class, European culture—do not always match the cultural assumptions of clients of non-European origins, including African Americans, Asian Americans, Latino/Hispanic Americans, and Native Americans. Such traditional therapies may not address the therapeutic needs of such individuals.

Changing demographics signal an ever-increasing need for cultural awareness in all pursuits, but especially those as rooted in interpersonal relations as psychotherapy. African Americans comprise 13% of the U.S. population. The Asian-American population of the United States now comprises 5% and is projected to grow to 10% by mid-century. Latino/Hispanic Americans are the largest (16%) and fastest growing minority group in the United States; more than half of the growth in the total population of the United States between 2000 and 2010 was due to the increase in the Hispanic population. These categories overlap, of course, because individuals choose more than one racial affiliation (U.S. Census Bureau, 2011).

One in 10 Americans are now foreign born, and almost two in 10 defines himself of "immigrant stock" (immigrant and their children). If present trends in immigration and birth rates persist, people of color will no longer be the minority, but the majority, by the year 2050.

To put the matter into a global context, consider the following statistics. If we could, at this time, shrink the Earth's population to a village of precisely 100 people, there would be:

- 57 Asians, 21 Europeans, 14 people from the Western Hemisphere, and 8 Africans.
- 70 non-White people.
- 70 non-Christian people.
- 50% of the entire world's wealth in the hands of only 6 people, with all 6 citizens of the United States.

As the population of the United States (and the world) becomes more diverse, the practice of psychotherapy must follow suit or be left by the wayside. In other words, the **browning of America** changes not only people of color, but also the institution of psychotherapy.

The three multicultural pioneers we feature in this chapter (and picture on the opening page) have been instrumental in changing psychotherapy. All three—a Hispanic American, an Asian American, and an African American—have triumphed over racism and marginalization in their personal lives and have led the profession toward more culturally sensitive practices.

Lillian Comas-Díaz's (1949–) journey to becoming a multicultural psychotherapist vividly demonstrates the confluence of culture, ethnicity, and gender (Comas-Díaz, 2005). A long tradition of healers runs through her veins; her paternal grandmother was a folk healer who solicited help from the Virgin Mary, read gypsy cards, and invoked African Orishas. Traveling to El Norte (the north), her working-class Puerto Rican parents settled in Chicago to earn a living. When Comas-Díaz was born with a cleft palate, they reached out to the host culture. Speaking broken English and carrying empty bags, her parents

negotiated an experimental surgery at the University of Illinois. At age of 6, she traveled "back" to Puerto Rico, tasting culture shock at an early age. She longed for home after leaving the frigid Windy City for the Caribbean tropical island. She realized the pervasive influence of culture on behavior while dreaming in Spanglish. Struggling with physical impediment and cultural translocation, she grounded her identity as a wounded healer. Comas-Díaz returned to the mainland for her doctoral degree, where elitism, racism, and sexism welcomed her in Connecticut.

The sociopolitics in her own life contributed to her advocacy of liberation in psychotherapy. Involving awareness and critical analysis of oppression, the liberation paradigm helped her to become a cultural warrior rescuing identity and working to improve Latinos' psychological and social conditions.

Today, Lillian Comas-Díaz is executive director of the Transcultural Mental Health Institute in Washington, DC, where she is also clinical professor of psychiatry at George Washington University School of Medicine and a psychologist in private practice. Among her multiple contributions have been editing the journal *Cultural Diversity and Ethnic Minority Psychology*, directing Ethnic Minority Affairs for the American Psychological Association, and heading the Hispanic Clinic at the Connecticut Mental Health Center (affiliated with Yale University). Her ethnocultural psychotherapy has been featured in many journal articles, therapy videotapes, and scholarly books (Comas-Díaz, 1994, 2000, 2011; Comas-Díaz & Greene, 1994).

Stanley Sue (1944–) was born in Portland, Oregon, where he enrolled in an all-boys technical high school in order to become a television repairman—for reasons he can no longer remember (Sue, 1994). After a year of such training, he found little interest in what he was learning and later developed a fascination with psychology.

When Sue informed his parents that he wanted to become a clinical psychologist, his China-born father replied, "What is that?" He couldn't believe that people would pay anyone to listen to their problems; his reaction and that of Sue's mother reflected cultural differences. Even now, many Asian Americans are unfamiliar with the profession of psychology. In any event, Sue persisted in pursuing a career in psychology. Then his second oldest brother decided to become a psychologist; his oldest brother became a psychologist and married a psychologist; and his youngest brother also became a psychologist!

As a student, Sue began to read the mental health literature on ethnicity. It struck him that much was unknown about identity development, mental health, and treatment methods with respect to ethnically diverse populations. His early research found that Asian Americans tended to underutilize mental health services in comparison to their population—findings that persist even today. Why did Asian Americans underutilize services? Did they have a low prevalence rate for mental disorders? How could we improve the effectiveness of services to ethnically diverse clients? In his years at the University of Washington, UCLA, and University of California–Davis, Stanley Sue has rigorously pursued these questions in hundreds of articles, chapters, and books.

Today, Sue is professor of psychology at Palo Alto University and director of its Center for Excellence in Diversity. He is former director of the National Research Center on Asian American Mental Health and coauthor (with his psychologist brothers) of the best-selling textbook, *Understanding Abnormal Behavior* (Sue, Sue, & Sue, 2012), which brings a multicultural perspective to the topic.

Beverly Greene's parents grew up in the deep South amidst the extreme conditions of American racial apartheid. As adults, her parents made frequent trips there with Beverly and her siblings to visit relatives, among them a 100+-year-old maternal great-grandmother who came into the country in the early 1860s as a slave.

Greene (1952–) was born in East Orange, New Jersey, the first of four children, and was raised in a multigenerational household with parents, paternal and later maternal grandmothers, and paternal aunt and uncles. She came of age during the civil rights movement and graduated from high school barely a month after the assassination of Martin Luther King, Jr. and just weeks after Robert Kennedy's murder. She attended college at New York University as a member of the first group of Martin Luther King Scholars during the height of the protest against the war in Vietnam, the crusade to free Angela Davis (a jailed Black woman who advocated for social change), and the fight for women's rights. Her abiding commitment to psychotherapy as a tool for social justice was fueled in part by her early experiences with racial discrimination, the visits to her parents' birthplaces, her parents' efforts to prepare their children to manage racism, and the sociopolitical events of those tumultuous times.

Greene is professor of psychology at St. John's University and a psychotherapist in private practice in Brooklyn, New York. Her scholarly work focuses on psychotherapy with culturally marginalized clients, especially on the intersection of gender, color, and sexual orientation (e.g., Greene & Croom, 2000; Jackson & Greene, 2000). Her coauthored textbook, *Abnormal Psychology in a Changing World* (Nevid, Rathus, & Greene, 2010), challenges thousands of students each year to approach psychopathology with a more inclusive and tolerant attitude.

All three multicultural therapists came of age during the turbulent 1960s and the 1970s, when the mental health professions realized that racial minorities' psychological concerns were being neglected. Culturally encapsulated views of minority groups received widespread criticism. The multicultural movement gained momentum as both the American Psychological Association (APA) and the American Association for Counseling and Development (AACD) developed policies and established committees to work with racial and ethnic minority groups more effectively. Training conferences recommended that conducting psychotherapy without cultural sensitivity was to be declared unethical. In 1978, the President's Commission on Mental Health examined, for the first time, the effectiveness of psychotherapy for ethnic minorities. Throughout the 1980s and the 1990s, professional associations incorporated guidelines regarding diversity and multicultural sensitivity into their ethical and training standards.

Before moving further into the chapter, we should comment on the manner in which we conceptualize and present multicultural psychotherapy throughout the book. Multicultural therapy is not simply a system of psychotherapy. Rather, cultural competence should be incorporated into all systems of psychotherapy. For this reason, we have attended to the role of culture in psychotherapy both within each book chapter (in the form of cultural criticisms of each system) and in this separate chapter.

At this point, out of sheer frustration, our students sometimes demand: "Well, is multicultural therapy a separate system of psychotherapy OR a skill set for all practitioners?!" Our reply is an emphatic "Yes!" which usually serves to aggravate the students further! The uncomfortable truth is that multicultural practice is not either/or but both/and. We like to put things into distinct categories, but there is no need to choose one or the other. Our answer and our coverage of multicultural therapy are entirely consistent with multiculturalism itself: let's not assign complex humans to a single box or type.

Theory of Personality

Culture is like the air we breathe. It is largely invisible, but it is ubiquitous, powerful, and life sustaining. Only when someone draws our attention to the air—or when we find the air different or potentially offensive—do we appreciate its existence and clout. Culture is just as invisible and powerful as air.

Culture is the major determinant of personality; each distinct culture includes events and expectations that shape both the group and the individual. **Culture** is an integrated constellation of human knowledge, belief, and behavior that is learned and transmitted to succeeding generations. It binds members of societies through a set of attributions, shared traditions, common beliefs, and norms for living. These characterize a particular class, community, or population. Culture is a matter of intersections—of class, race, ethnicity, gender, age, and sexual orientation—which are diverse and ever changing (Baruth & Manning, 2003).

Cultures are by no means neatly defined categories. Not only do they change constantly, but they are also heterogeneous and subjective creations with fuzzy boundaries. It follows, then, that there is no single, universal theory of personality for multicultural therapy. Instead, there are as many theories of personality as there are cultures. Each subpopulation within a culture may share defining or delimiting features, but a widespread theory of personality does not exist. We require multiple perspectives rooted in, informed by, and sensitive to particular cultures.

In the tradition of an old Asian saying, all individuals are (a) like no other individuals, (b) like some individuals, and (c) like all other individuals. At the individual level (a), our genetic endowments make us all unique biologically, along with our nonshared experiences. At the group level (b), we see both similarities and differences, as each of us is born into a cultural matrix of beliefs, values, and social practices. At the universal level (c), we are all members of the same human race and belong to the same biological species (Sue & Sue, 2003).

Race and **ethnicity** contribute heavily to how we conceptualize culture. Although the terms should not be used synonymously with culture, they constitute two of the most salient aspects of culture for many individuals. Further, it is important to note that race and ethnicity denote distinct processes. Race is a category of persons who are related by a common heredity or genetics, and who are perceived and responded to in terms of external features or traits. On the other hand, ethnicity is shared culture with respect to lifestyles, norms, and values.

As a consequence, individuals sharing a racial group do not necessarily share the same ethnicity. A prime example can be found in one of this book's coauthors. My (JCN) race is part Native-American (Cherokee) but my ethnicity is White from southern New Jersey and Philadelphia.

Race, itself, has two important meanings. First, race is a social construct, a way of grouping people into categories on the basis of perceived physical attributes and ancestry. Second, race is more broadly associated with power, status, and opportunity (American Anthropological Association, 1998). In Western cultures, European or White "race" confers advantage and opportunity, even as improved social attitudes and public policies have reinforced social equality. In this sense, race is a relational and political process that partially defines personality (Smedley & Smedley, 2005).

Many people use a person's racial categorization, such as Black versus White versus Hispanic, to mean racial identity. However, **racial identity** is more broadly defined as the quality of a person's commitment to his or her socially ascribed racial group, based on the perception that one shares a common racial heritage with that group (Helms, 1990). The commitment to one's racial group consists of several factors: personal identity (feelings and attitudes about oneself), reference group orientation (the extent to which one uses the racial group to guide feelings, thoughts, behaviors, values), and ascribed identity (one's deliberate affiliation or commitment to a particular racial group).

Stage theories of racial identity describe it as a developmental process wherein a person potentially, though not necessarily, moves from one level of identity to another. According to stage theorists, we can understand a person's behavior by analyzing his or her identity at the present time. Whether or not one's present level of racial identity development has long-term implications for the individual's personality probably depends on the complex interaction of individual attributes, environmental forces, and personal life experiences (Helms, 1990).

The values of the European-American culture are not embraced by all racial and ethnic groups. For example, European-American culture highly values individual choice, self-sufficiency, and most especially, independence. However, a large number of non-European children are raised with an emphasis on harmony and family reliance. Many Asian Americans, for instance, raise their children to be interdependent within the family unit and expect group members to subordinate their individual needs to the needs of the family and society. Likewise, many African Americans are raised in extended family units and feel strong kinship bonds and a sense of "we-ness" with members of their group. The result is a number of cultural characteristics that are not always shared with members of the dominant culture.

In reality, no individual is a repository of a pure culture. Everyone belongs to multiple groups, each of which exerts different cultural influences. Because of this complexity and interactivity, it is never safe to infer a client's cultural orientation from knowledge of any single group to which he or she is believed to belong.

Attempting to merge so much diversity under a single label may lead mental health professionals to tenuous conclusions about individuals. In doing so, they fall victim to the **myth of uniformity**, the naïve belief that all members of a group will have the same characteristics. There is a fine line between sensitivity

who experienced more frequent and intense racism were more likely to suffer from depression and anxiety, which in turn may contribute to the Black population's higher rate of hypertension (Piet et al., 2012).

To a large extent, success in our society is determined by those in power. Dominant cultures determine the meaning of success, the requisites for success, and how success is measured. Those with privilege and power rarely give up their power voluntarily.

Those with power and privilege frequently believe that they are not discriminatory or prejudiced in principle, but society is structured to preserve their privilege. In terms of race, this often leads to **unconscious racism**, unknown and unintentional expressions of prejudice that lead to discriminatory behaviors. Multiple experimental studies demonstrate the subtle bias due to unconscious racism; up to 80% of Whites in the United States show this bias in their behavior (Dovidio & Gaertner, 2004; Dovidio et al., 2002).

White Americans typically experience difficulty acknowledging their privilege. The difficult but necessary discussions on race-related matters can elicit Whites' guilt about their privileged status, threaten their self-images as fair and nonracist, and suggest that their "unawareness" may perpetuate inequities among people of color (Sue et al., 2007). A spate of e-mails circulating during the 2008 and 2012 presidential elections illuminates White privilege:

- White privilege is when you can get pregnant at age 17 and everyone is quick to insist that your life and that of your family is a personal matter, and that no one has a right to judge you or your parents, even as Black and Latino families with similar challenges are regularly typified as irresponsible and pathological.
- White privilege is when you are a gun enthusiast and do not make people immediately scared of you.

- White privilege is when you can develop a painkiller addiction, having obtained your drug of choice illegally, go on to beat that addiction, and everyone praises you for being so strong, while being an ethnic minority who did the same thing is routinely labeled a drug addict who probably winds up in jail.

Living with the privilege makes it psychologically easier; living underneath the privilege promotes psychological symptoms.

Minority group members may become distressed when they attempt to be successful within the dominant culture while maintaining their identity. Many find that doing so necessitates an understanding of and, to some extent, adherence to cultural values that may clash with their own. Some may even feel forced to idolize the dominant group's culture and denigrate their own. That often produces conflict with their own cultural group and generates interpersonal conflicts and identity crises.

For example, on the one hand, African Americans who try to fit into White cultural norms of success may be viewed as traitors (or "Uncle Toms") by fellow African Americans. On the other hand, African Americans who assert their own heritage through dress, language, and customs may not be successful in terms of the White-dominated employment world. Thus, for minority group members who seek a balance between the two cultures, the "damned if you do" (acculturate) and "damned if you don't" (separate) dilemma almost inevitably prompts conflict.

Psychopathology may stem not only from clashes with the dominant culture, but also from family responses to that dominant culture. Conflicts in minority families frequently revolve around acculturation. **Acculturation** is the cultural modification of an individual or group by adapting to or borrowing traits from another culture. Put simply, individuals are torn between remaining loyal to their family of origin and cultural group, on the one hand, and desiring to experience new ways of thinking and acting, on the other.

Often parental judgments on mainstream culture conflict with those of their children. Although the difficulties of older minority clients stem from acculturation problems, such as role reversal, downward mobility, and discrimination, younger clients experience more conflict with their family over lack of cultural flexibility. Younger minority group members in particular may be more inclined to do things the "American way," refusing to learn or continue to speak their parents' native language or to participate in cultural traditions. This rebelliousness is often viewed by minority parents as disrespect, and they blame American society for their family problems.

Differences in desired acculturation challenge members of minority groups. For those who desire to fully acculturate into the dominant culture, failure to be accepted by the dominant culture's standards can prove devastating. Not only have the individuals been rejected by a group they want to identify with, but they may now also be without their supportive reference group(s). This double rejection can precipitate psychopathology, including substance abuse, depression, and anxiety. For example, Native Americans living on reservations disproportionately abuse drugs and alcohol and their suicide rate is twice the national average (Sue & Sue, 2003).

The impact of culture on psychological health is due more to social inequality than to biological vulnerability, particularly in terms of economic hardships. Poverty is a major risk factor for chronic mental disorders; psychological distress is a direct correlate of economic hardship. Whether one looks at income, education, or employment, as one moves down the socioeconomic ladder, there are more individuals with health problems (Pedersen et al., 2002). Since minority groups are overrepresented among those with a lower socioeconomic

status (SES; U.S. Census Bureau, 2011), problems associated with low SES are disproportionately experienced by members of minority groups. Such problems include disadvantaged school systems, malnutrition, lack of access to health care and child care, and substandard housing.

Many such problems can be attributed, at least in part, to social and political factors, including institutionalized racism. In health care, considerable evidence suggests racial power differentials between clinicians and their patients, as well as clinicians' implicit racial biases and ethnic stereotypes, contribute to the inequitable health care that patients of color receive across the nation (Institute of Medicine, 2003). **Racial disparities in health care**, including mental health care, have barely improved over the years (Lopez et al., 2012). Stated simply, to be a person of color in the United States means to receive worse health care, if one has access to health care at all.

The overriding point is that psychopathology is culturally created, in several significant senses. Psychopathology is behavior that the predominant culture consensually deems unusual or maladaptive. "Abnormality" exists in eye of the beholder, typically a beholder raised in the norms of the privileged group. Psychotherapy itself may even be seen as an instrument of the dominant culture to enforce individualistic cultural values. Moreover, the causes of psychopathology are more often cultural and sociological than biological. Problems do not reside solely within a person; rather, they often lie within society.

Therapeutic Processes

Multicultural psychotherapy is based on one of three perspectives on the ideal therapeutic process. The first, **cultural relativism**, consists of developing culture-specific psychotherapies for each patient group. This transforms psychotherapy by applying culture-specific theories and techniques to the unique sociocultural reality of each group, such as African-American clients, Asian-American clients, Latino/Hispanic-American clients, and Native-Americans clients. The second perspective, **cultural universality**, consists of developing general transcultural therapeutic skills applicable across a wide array of minority groups.

The third perspective, **cultural adaptation**, splits the difference. Research-supported therapies based on cultural universality, such as short-term psychodynamic or cognitive-behavioral therapies, are tailored to the individual cultures of the patient, as in cultural relativism. In this way, culturally adapted therapies enjoy, at once, the nomothetic support of following controlled research and the idiographic sensitivity of tailoring treatment to the patient's cultures (Bernal & Rodriguez, 2012).

Few mental health professionals today embrace only one of these three perspectives. Instead, **multicultural psychotherapy** constitutes a blend of culture-specific, transcultural, and adaptation components (Pedersen et al., 2002). Thus, our coverage of therapeutic processes combines aspects of all three.

Cultural competence in conducting psychotherapy entails invoking several processes throughout treatment and appreciating the sociopolitical context in which treatment is embedded. The therapeutic processes most frequently used in multicultural therapy are consciousness raising, catharsis, and choosing.

Consciousness Raising

Consciousness raising serves many purposes for both the patient and the therapist. It can help patients to understand the oppression and adverse impact of the majority culture, to move from naïveté or acceptance to naming and resistance against oppressive systems, to reflect on self and self-in-culture, and to redefine themselves in a way that promotes pride (Ivey & Brooks-Harris, 2005).

Therapists begin by helping clients to understand how the dominant culture may have oppressed them and shaped their self-views. Negative internalization of the dominant culture separates many clients from their own identity. This liberation of consciousness helps clients to appreciate how oppression operates in their lives. Therapists points out that internal distress is often related to (or a reaction to) external stressors, such as racism and prejudice.

At the same time, clients must face the truth about themselves—that they may hold the norms of the dominant culture in high esteem and may denigrate aspects of their own culture. Eventually, clients come to realize that by turning their backs on their culture, they may have simultaneously alienated themselves and have lost cultural-group support.

Consider the case of a female college student of Chinese descent who presented for treatment suffering from a depressive reaction manifested in feelings of worthlessness and thoughts of suicide. The patient had little contact with members of her own race, outside of her family, and she openly expressed scorn for anything Chinese. She was hostile toward Chinese customs and especially Chinese men, whom she described as introverted, passive, and sexually unattractive. She dated only White men, to the disappointment of her family, but her most recent relationship ended because her boyfriend's parents objected to her race. Although she was not completely conscious of this, the client was having increasing difficulty with denying her racial heritage. The breakup of her relationship had made her realize that she was Chinese and not fully accepted by all segments of society. At first she had denounced the Chinese for her present situation, but later much of her hostility was turned back onto herself. Feeling alienated from her own subculture and not fully accepted by American society, she experienced an identity crisis, resulting in feelings of worthlessness and depression. As this case demonstrates, consciousness raising must help clients understand the devastating effects of prejudice; only then can they begin to rectify cultural alienation (Sue & Sue, 2003).

Consciousness raising may also assist patients in recognizing how their cultural conditioning impedes their acceptance of psychological treatment and implementation of change. In responding to partner violence, for instance, some Mexican women will not seek help because they believe their situation is God's will. Under the same circumstances, some Southeast Asian women may be afraid to confide in clinicians because Hmong tradition requires that, in times of conflict, clan elders must be consulted first. Battered African-American women may have been socialized to believe that seeking psychological treatment is only for Whites (Mitchell-Meadows, 1992). In such situations, a culturally sensitive therapist can help women become aware of these detrimental influences of socialization.

Cultural-competent practitioners assist clients in consciously identifying their individual styles of dealing with racism and in recognizing unhealthy modes. Consider a recently divorced Black medical student who came to therapy complaining of stress-related migraine headaches (Sue & Sue, 2003). He felt that the racist environment of his medical school and one professor in particular were responsible for his problem. He wanted to confront the professor directly and accuse him of racism, but knew that doing so could lead to his dismissal from medical school. Therapy revealed that the patient's choice of strategy was partially related to unresolved feelings of anger over his recent divorce, and the resultant bitterness and vulnerability had overdetermined his choice to confront the professor. As the client began to understand the impact of his divorce, he considered a wider range of options and decided it would be better to file a complaint with the minority affairs office. Although the tension between the client and his professor remained high, the client felt that he had chosen the best option, enabling him to remain in school.

Psychotherapists, in addition to clients, benefit from cultural consciousness raising. Multicultural awareness begins at home: Therapists ought to understand and come to terms with their own feelings about racism and a client's culture. Cultural competence ranges along a continuum (Cross et al., 1989):

- cultural destructiveness: therapist's attitudes and practices are damaging to other cultures
- cultural incapacity: therapist expresses paternalistic attitudes toward culturally diverse groups
- cultural blindness: therapist believes that culture makes no difference
- cultural pre-competence: therapist is aware of cultural competence but unsure of how to proceed
- cultural competence: therapist values and respects cultural differences and, in concert with client, adapts therapy accordingly

In assisting patients in coming to terms with their ethnic identity, therapists must be comfortable discussing their own cultural biases. By continually articulating their own worldview (and evaluating the validity of its sources), therapists become more aware of—and hence more in control of—personal biases. Such awareness of biases contributes to a bidirectional flow of information in session. For example, a therapist may say to a client, "I appreciate your letting me know when I say subtle things in an insensitive way, not realizing I am being biased."

Catharsis

Suppressed anger over discrimination and cultural alienation often comes to the surface once patients comprehend the negative impact of the dominant culture on them. It is typically therapeutic that minority clients express this anger and begin to recognize that it is a normal and justified response.

Whether it be a Latina angry at her loss of status or an African American resentful of racial discrimination, the healthy expression of anger is a vital aspect of therapy. The primary goals of the therapist, in this respect, are to facilitate the client's expression of affect, work through antagonism, and redirect the anger into useful channels.

If the therapist is of a racial minority background, he or she can often serve as a positive role model in teaching the client how to respond to discrimination and anger. Minority therapists can share with clients their own feelings and coping methods. For example, a Native-American therapist who had a difficult time dealing with employment discrimination can share her experiences with clients facing similar circumstances.

But the responsibility is shared by all psychotherapists, not only those from racial or ethnic minority heritages. All therapists should proactively learn about the client's culture and facilitate a corrective emotional experience. By modeling healthy outrage over cultural inequities and by showing genuine respect for all cultures, they display the growth they seek to encourage in clients.

Choosing

After consciousness raising and catharsis comes choices that lead to change. Once patients have acknowledged their oppression and expressed their wounds, they choose how to channel their newfound liberation and pride constructively. "A wounded deer leaps the highest," as Emily Dickinson once wrote.

A critical choice facing clients is how to integrate their sense of self with their cultural group. "How much should I integrate? Which parts of myself and my culture am I willing to sacrifice? How do I cultivate healthy relationships in the face of cultural expectations?" Clients learn to make deliberate choices about these matters,

choices that are compatible with their own values and goals, not only those valued by the dominant society.

An African-American history professor expressed his anger in psychotherapy about not being free to just be a professor. "You Whites can just worry about what's best for your career, but I'm expected to care about what's best for all Blacks, not just what is best for me. I worked all my life to be free to immerse myself in history. But if I'm not heavily involved with Black students, Black faculty, and Black studies, I feel guilty and afraid I'll be seen as a traitor. Do you even have these problems as a White professor?" No, I (JOP) had to admit that, as a White male, I have the privilege of just caring about my profession if that is what I choose to do.

Immigrant clients face choices regarding how to incorporate cultural traditions and roles with the norms of their new country. Clients must choose how much they want to acculturate into their new society and, if desired, determine how they can blend aspects of both cultures without losing central aspects of each. The basic choice for such clients comes down to how to achieve a healthy, comfortable balance. This, of course, is easier said than done.

As patients face decisions regarding the balance between acculturation and retention of minority culture traditions, therapists concentrate on assisting them in dealing with their feelings of uncertainty about the future. Some clients may choose not to identity with the minority group, and their feelings of pain and guilt might be addressed. The therapist can assist clients in working through these feelings and support their decisions. Other clients may decide that they would like to identify with their cultural group, but fear rejection. In these instances, the therapist will work with the client in planning ways to reintegrate with their cultural group and handle rejection if it occurs. The African-American professor had to deal with anger both from some White colleagues whom he could no longer see as often and from Black colleagues who wondered where he had been so long.

Still other clients will select a bicultural identity, and cultural-sensitive therapists may seek to help them to deal effectively with the potential backlash resulting from their choices. Clients need to become aware of the pros and cons of their decisions and how their lives will change. Cooperative planning and mutual problem solving give patients a sense of empowerment.

An inspirational template for active intervention is **liberation psychotherapy** (Friere, 1970, 1973). It challenges the traditional notion of marginality and provides means to eliminate the subordinate status of minority cultures. Awareness of the social context promotes concrete change; working toward freedom forms the base of liberation psychotherapy. We need to actively intervene in order to transform the society in which we live.

Lived examples of liberation abound in the careers of multicultural therapists and in the successes of their clients. Lillian Comas-Díaz directed a Hispanic clinic for underserved clients, Stanley Sue founded a national center for mental health research on Asian Americans, and Beverly Greene initiated a book series on the neglected intersection of gender, color, and sexual orientation. Acting from raised consciousness, clients courageously choose to start a campus multicultural center, run for political office, insist on affordable child care, and introduce cultural sensitivity training at work. All do so in the face of considerable opposition. Talk is not enough to guarantee social justice.

Therapeutic Content
Intrapersonal Conflicts
Anxiety and Defenses
Anxiety about cultural norms is the root of many minority clients' distress. When clients are unable to blend their cultural norms with prevailing norms, anxiety often manifests itself in defensive actions and maladaptive behaviors. When clients are unable to access equal opportunities to decent schools, jobs, and heath care, anxiety becomes an understandable response.

Anxiety takes different forms in cultural contexts. Physical symptoms and complaints, such as headaches and, especially among Latino/Hispanics, visions, are a common and culturally acceptable means of expressing psychological conflict. In many cultures, it is far more acceptable to be physically ill than emotionally distressed. Anxiety also surfaces as acting-out behavior, especially among minority adolescents and family scapegoats.

Self-Esteem
Discrimination ripples across centuries, trapping each new generation in a web of stereotypes and self-fulfilling prophecies. How can people who, for generations have internalized messages about incompetence, be expected to emerge unscathed and psychologically sound? When minorities are constantly bombarded with messages that the dominant culture is best, they begin to accept these messages and denigrate both themselves and their own cultural group—a process known as **internalized racism**. Minorities often begin to idolize the dominant culture and see their own culture and themselves as inferior.

Interpersonal Conflicts
Intimacy and Sexuality
Intimacy—or, more specifically, the loss of intimacy—is central to culturally related problems. Intimacy lies in the deep bonds of family and cultural groups, not only between two lovers. When these bonds are broken, owing mainly to the subtle racism of the dominant culture, an individual feels not only the loss of familial support, but also a loss of self. Re-establishing the bonds of intimacy, or coming to terms with its loss, is crucial to re-establishing the sense of self and self-esteem.

Views of healthy sexuality differ among cultural groups. The safest generalization is that there is no single acceptable perspective on sexuality. Sexual customs must be recognized from the perspective of the culture they reflect; they cannot be judged solely from the dominant European-American point of view. Whereas traditional White European cultures have emphasized men as the "head" of the family and the source of authority, Hispanic-American and African-American family structures are more centered on women as the affective center of relationships.

Communication

Communication problems can occur between the dominant culture and minority cultures as well as within minority groups. The focus of communication difficulties between cultural groups is on expectations, biases, and prejudicial messages. There must be a distinction between healthy communication and destructive communication, such as racial and ethnic slurs. Communication can be good or bad, depending on the context; communication fails when differences between individuals, and individual minority groups, overshadow their similarities.

Communication difficulties within cultural groups, especially within families, manifest themselves in misunderstandings and resentment when communication is lost. Gaps in communication can be corrected only when group members try to understand the needs of those individuals who want to experience a lifestyle and people different from the one in which they were raised. Individuals must also appreciate the values of the group into which they were born. Only when the lines of two-way communication remain open can both parties reach mutual understanding and respect.

Hostility

Hostility among minorities is the expected reaction to years of discrimination and self-depreciation.

Even in 2012 (Associated Press surveys.ap.org), 51% of non-Black Americans express explicit anti-Black attitudes and 52% of non-Hispanic Whites express explicit anti-Hispanic attitudes! Whether it is the Los Angeles riots in response to the acquittal of White police officers for beating an African-American motorist or an uprising among Haitian immigrants denied entrance into the United States, anger is a natural response to oppression. Problems occur when hostility builds and is expressed in maladaptive behaviors. Violence is destroying too many young minority group members. Yet we have to hear and understand their cry: "No justice, no peace." Validating outrage without encouraging destructive hostility is a delicate balance.

Control

For many minorities, the task is not only how to control hostility, but also how to stop being controlled by others, especially being controlled by the biased messages of society. Biased messages control cognitions and actions, preventing minority group members from achieving their potentials. The resolution of control issues, both intrapersonal control of hostility and structured control of social rewards, rests on establishing greater opportunities for individuals and groups.

Individuo-Social Conflicts

Adjustment versus Transcendence

Many minority group members have never fully adjusted to society, so it is even harder for them to transcend it. In Maslow's hierarchy of needs, one must meet security and belongingness needs before achieving self-actualization.

To transcend, minority group members will learn how to avoid internalized racism and to acquire self-esteem. They must not merely adjust to societal conditions, but transcend to a level of positive worth and autonomy not dictated by society. If this means a need to separate at times, then separate they must.

In an invited address to the American Psychological Association, Martin Luther King, Jr., put it this way:

> *I am sure that there are some things in our world to which we should never be adjusted. There are some things concerning which we must always be maladjusted if we are to be people of good will. We must never adjust ourselves to racial discrimination and racial segregation. We must never adjust ourselves to religious bigotry. We must never adjust ourselves to economic conditions that take necessities from the many to give luxuries to the few. We must never adjust ourselves to the madness of militarism and the self-defeating effects of physical violence.*

Impulse Control

One negative stereotype is that particular minority groups manifest frequent problems with impulse control. The fact is that the majority of all racial groups are law-abiding citizens who control impulses just fine. But we should not be surprised that impoverished, alienated people are more likely to act out their outrage. We should not be surprised that young people may act out fantasies to be successful when they have few opportunities to live out their fantasies. Yet psychotherapists need to help individuals appreciate that indiscriminate acting out of impulses is ultimately self-defeating. Validating the feelings behind such impulses while finding more valuable activities for enhancing oneself is the therapeutic key.

Beyond Conflict to Fulfillment

Meaning in Life

For many people, meaning is found in the celebration and continuation of their culture. Family is the fundamental unit of a culture, and family members seek the meaning that comes with marriage, parenting, grandparenting, and other forms of connection. Families celebrate relevant birthdays, anniversaries, and holidays. Schools are designed in part to help families socialize and enculturate their children and prepare them to participate in their culture's economy.

But for minority groups caught between cultures such meaning is not just contextual: it is conflictual. To which culture do I give my loyalty? What if the dominant culture lacks loyalty to my type of family? What if the culture does not permit specific groups to participate in their customs and rituals? Such cultural conflicts can undermine the source of meaning that so many embrace in life. The solution is to help create a more inclusive and connected culture that can be defined by rich diversity rather than narrow prejudices.

Ideal Individual

In the context of cultural differences, we cannot subscribe to the myth of a single ideal individual. Rather, the ideal is one in which minority individuals accept themselves for what they are. Ideal individuals learn to disregard messages that are false and to view the dominant European-American culture for what it truly is—another lifestyle, not the paragon of virtue. Minority individuals respect their own culture and feel free to live in the manner they see fit; they are in control, but not controlled. Above all, ideal individuals understand that cultural diversity is enriching and empowering, a source of value and pride.

Therapeutic Relationship

The establishment of an abiding therapeutic relationship is simultaneously one of the most powerful sources of change and one of the most challenging aspects of multicultural therapies. The therapy relationship is powerful in that clinician empathy, support, and collaboration are the foundation of multicultural therapy. The clinician's task is to listen, care, and validate. The therapy relationship is challenging in that the clinician, frequently of a different race and ethnicity, needs to secure the trust and credibility of the client, who may be understandably hesitant to pursue the talking cure with a clinician representing the dominant, often invalidating culture.

For this reason, psychotherapy with culturally diverse clients adapts the relationship to the individual needs and cultural preferences of each client. The goal is to join the client wherever he/she is. The Asian values of reserve, restraint of strong feelings, and subtlety in approaching problems, for example, will require a different therapy relationship from, say, one with a Western patient with conventional expectations of openness, psychological mindedness, and assertiveness (Leong, 1986). Every therapy relationship should be conceptualized as a multicultural therapy relationship.

Indeed, the very meaning of "psychotherapist" varies by culture. Asian Americans and African Americans typically view the psychotherapist as a physician, whereas Native Americans may call the therapist a "medicine man." Latino/Hispanic Americans may see therapists as folk healers or curanderos, who provide a holistic form of healing (Schaefer, 2004). Because race, ethnicity, and culture mightily influence human behavior, it follows that such forces also impact how minority groups define relationships (Sue & Sue, 2003).

Often, minority clients feel more comfortable with a psychotherapist from their own ethnic background. A same-culture therapist can serve as a role model and can genuinely empathize with the problems of the minority client. However, with so many diverse cultural groups, it would be impractical to expect that there would be a health care practitioner readily available to match each patient's cultural backgrounds.

Since racial/ethnic matching of therapists and patient is not always possible and does not guarantee effectiveness, the responsibility for treating culturally diverse clients is distributed among all psychotherapists. Therapists often find themselves working with clients from cultural backgrounds radically different from their own. This can be a problem for both the client, who may feel misunderstood by the therapist, and the clinician, who may struggle to understand the client's cultural framework and to adapt therapeutic strategies to fit the client's individual needs.

The culture-sensitive therapist will be vigilant for how racial and ethnic differences with the client might affect their relationship and the success of treatment. One way to open this type of conversation might be to say (adapted from Cardemil & Battle, 2003, p. 281):

> I know that this can be a sensitive topic, but I wonder how you feel about working with me being that I am from a different racial/ethnic background?

Then, later:

> I ask because it is my goal to be as helpful as I can and to tailor therapy to your needs. But I realize that there may be times when I cannot fully appreciate your experiences. I want you to know that I am open to discussing this matter and hope that you will let me know if I am not understanding your culture.

Often therapists commit the error of omission in not raising these topics rather than risking an error of commission by initiating such conversations (Cardemil & Battle, 2003).

A positive multicultural relationship may well demand more than ordinary therapist empathy; it may require **cultural empathy** (Pederson et al., 2008). As defined in the Western culture, empathy takes on an individualistic interpretation of human desire and distress. "I understand your personal feelings." Cultural empathy takes on a more inclusive orientation by placing cultural responsiveness at the center. It is a learned ability to accurately understand the client's self-experience from another culture and then to express that understanding back to the client. "I understand your personal feelings *and* your cultural context."

In these cases, true collaboration is required in involving clients to map out treatment goals and to incorporate their cultural preferences. Integrating aspects of the client's culture into treatment shows the therapist's respect for and interest in that culture. And that culture will impact the clients' belief systems about how one approaches health care, how one defines illness, and one's likelihood to use the health care system at all. In short, a multicultural relationship allows for individual change outside the European value system.

Culturally competent therapists will attend to language in the relationship. Whites tend to insert small gaps in conversation to allow for a smooth transition from one speaker to the next. African Americans tend to overlap speech, with one person starting to speak as the other is finishing. Latino Americans overlap to an even greater degree, almost speaking simultaneously. Asian Americans are comfortable with short periods of silence between utterances to recall what was said. Native Americans also use these silences to an even greater degree, to look around and reflect upon what is said (Sue & Sue, 2003).

Problems may arise when the therapist's native language does not match that of the client. Approximately 20% of households speak a language other than English (U.S. Census Bureau, 2011), but the use of translators remains controversial. The clear benefit, particularly during an emergency, is that health professionals understand the client—to some extent, anyway. On the other hand, there are real risks. Translators may distort or misinterpret the client's intent through omissions, additions, and substitutions. The presence of an unfamiliar third party may prove disagreeable to the client. The client may be hesitant to express feelings, while the therapist may be confused or misled by the translation. The use of translators has been associated with misdiagnosis (usually more severe than necessary) and increased dropout rates (Paniagua, 1998). If the psychotherapist decides translation is in the best interest of the client, it should ideally be an individual free of dual roles with the client—that is, not a family member or friend (American Psychological Association, 1991, 1993, 2003).

In empowering their clients, multicultural therapists will frequently adopt different helping roles—as adviser, mentor, change agent, facilitator, consultant, and even as advocate. As **advocates**, psychotherapists work to empower clients for social change. Therapists teach and encourage growth for individual clients as well as society as a whole. When the advocate's values are on the side of the client in a particular conflict, the therapy relationship is certainly strengthened. The therapist, while working with the presenting individual, is also seeking to transform society.

Properly conducted, multicultural therapy is a bilateral learning relationship. Cultural interaction within a personally meaningful and emotionally charged relationship affects the therapist as well as the client (Pedersen et al., 2002). Both come away from treatment with an enduring respect for the grand diversity of cultures.

Practicalities of Multicultural Therapies

Practice of multicultural therapy cannot be reduced to universal prescriptions any more than identical treatments can be applied to clients of all cultures and heritages. The treatment format and therapist team will depend on the culture of the particular client.

Multicultural therapists employ individual, couple, family, and group formats but go even further. Therapists tend to develop a network of change agents that will reverberate throughout the client's life.

In working with a depressed adolescent female of color, for instance, the therapist and client had the client's friends attend a session to enhance her sense of connection. They addressed ways the client could reach out to her family and ask for their support. Subsequent sessions involved discussions of campus and community resources, helping her to take advantage of her university and church. The therapist promoted the client's activism, practicing leadership skills when speaking against oppression. In the multiple context approach—involving friends, family, university, church, and social activism—the client connected to the larger community, developed strengths that would buffer marginalization, secured mentors, and strengthened her own voice in activism against oppression (Querimit & Conner, 2003). If it takes an entire village to raise a child, it probably takes that same village to keep its adults healthy.

Although Western culture (and psychotherapy) tends to be individualistic, many cultures embrace more collectivistic perspectives. Some clients, such as Native Americans, may present to the clinic with their entire families who accompany them to provide support. Dhayani Ywahoo (in Cook, 1997) has said, "In the Native world view, there is no in or out; everyone in the circle is necessary for the benefit of the whole family of human beings and those that walk, crawl, swim, and fly." The practice of multicultural treatment may entail more than a single presenting patient; it may involve contact with families and entire communities.

Part of working in minority cultures may be contact with **traditional or indigenous healers**. Multicultural therapists frequently collaborate with folk healers, either because the client demands it or because the therapist realizes that it is necessary. Such collaboration will probably challenge professional training and socialization that teaches folk healing is quackery. But collaboration will probably teach that folk healing and psychotherapy share much in common and that the former has much to say about spiritual and existential matters (Comas-Díaz, 2005).

Multicultural therapy concerns the content and process of treatment, not its length. The broad goals of cultural sensitivity are compatible with both long-term and short-term therapy. The length of multicultural therapy is really a matter of individual and cultural preferences: different strokes for different folks (and cultures).

Unfortunately, attrition rates in psychotherapy are significantly higher among racial/ethnic minority clients than the general population. It is estimated that 50% of ethnic minority clients terminate after only a couple of sessions with a mental health professional (Paniagua, 1998). With this in mind, brief multicultural therapy must be intentional and not an unwitting result of miscommunication and misalliance.

The upshot is for multicultural therapists and their clients to engage in mutual exploration of preferences from the inception of psychotherapy. One common practice is to acquaint beginning clients with the respective roles of patient and therapist and the nature of the psychotherapy enterprise. These procedures, which fall under the heading of **pretreatment patient preparation**, take a variety of forms, including direct instruction, informational interviews, therapist modeling, video presentations, and role playing. Many patients hold divergent expectations about the processes of psychotherapy and may be uncomfortable with the nature of mental health treatment; pretherapy orientation is designed to clarify these expectations and to mutually define a more comfortable role for the client. Evidence for the positive impact of this preparation is quite plentiful (Levine et al., 1983; Lorion, 1978; Orlinsky & Howard, 1986).

Multicultural therapy demands diversifying the training curriculum beyond the mainstream of contemporary Western thought. A meta-analysis of multicultural education in the mental health professions revealed that such educational interventions are typically associated with positive outcomes, but that interventions explicitly based on theory and research yield outcomes nearly twice as beneficial as those that were not (Smith et al., 2006). Multicultural training should be grounded in theory and research, like other systems of psychotherapy, and should be spread throughout the curriculum, instead of relegated to a single course.

Students must have educational experiences that generate cultural sensitivity and skill. Students need to acquire knowledge of the particular cultures of patients they will be treating, of course, but they should also develop an awareness of inter-ethnic relationships, racism, and the historical, social, and psychological context in which cultural groups have functioned. With this background, even when therapists cannot articulate the cultural context of each patient, they can demonstrate cultural sensitivity and respect (Yutrzenka, 1995).

Psychotherapy with LGBT Clients

Lesbian, gay, bisexual, and transgendered (LGBT) clients constitute a diverse group within themselves. Despite their heterogeneity, however, shared experiences of discrimination and stigma connect LGBT clients with other minority group clients. LGBT clients, like racial/ethnic minority clients, are an oppressed group in society. They have been subjected to detrimental stereotypes, have been slighted and marginalized in psychotherapy research, and have often been underserved or inappropriately served in the mental health system (Sue & Lam, 2002). No matter where we stand, we see similar problems—exclusion, invisibility, and the absence of cultural competence among practitioners (Brown, 2005b). Thus, LGBT clients require psychotherapists who are culturally competent in all sexual orientations.

Although people of color have legally won equal rights in the United States, this is not the case for LGBT people. "The laws of the US do not protect us;

they may, in some cases, endanger us" (Brown, 2005a, p. 364). In numerous states, marriage and adoption are outlawed for LGBT individuals. Some states even forbid domestic partnering. Basically, these laws say that it is still legal to discriminate against people of minority sexual orientations.

Some statistics on the prevalence of legalized discrimination against LGBT in education and in the workplace (Fassinger & Arseneau, 2007):

- In 37 states, LGB students can be legally harassed.
- In 47 states, transgender students can be legally harassed.
- Almost half of sexual minority youth report harassment or violence in school; one third report missing school out of fear for personal safety.
- In 31 states, it is legal to fire someone based on sexual orientation.
- In 39 states, it is legal to fire someone based on gender identity.
- Gay men earn 10% to 32% less than similarly qualified heterosexual men.
- Between 16% and 68% of sexual minorities report experiencing employment discrimination.

LGBT represents a subculture demonized, ignored, and mistreated throughout the history of psychotherapy. Practitioners were often taught to view homosexuality as pathological. This view was formalized in 1952, when homosexuality was classified as a personality disturbance and was listed alongside other sexual deviations, such as pedophilia. In 1968, homosexuality was placed among nonpsychotic mental disorders. The 1973 decision to remove homosexuality from the *Diagnostic and Statistical Manual* (DSM) was a milestone, but it did not end the pathological view.

Although homosexuality is no longer classified as a mental disorder, homophobic attitudes toward LGBT clients persist. Even well-intentioned therapists cannot help but be influenced by society subconsciously. Therapists have long been exposed to a wealth of inaccurate and negative information about LGBT culture, which has rendered it difficult to affirm the identity of LGBT clients (Baruth & Manning, 2003).

Homophobia is not restricted to heterosexuals, however. Being raised in a heterosexist world that continually tells LGBTs that they are wrong or sick, many experience **internalized homophobia**. This refers to a set of negative attitudes toward homosexuality in other persons and toward homosexual features in oneself. LGBT individuals with internalized homophobia receive harsh criticisms from others and from within themselves simultaneously.

Parallel to members of ethnic and racial minorities, LGBT individuals struggle to establish an identity based on their own needs, as compared to the norms of the prevailing heterosexual culture. The individual's acceptance of a homosexual orientation comes at an agonizing cost. Rejected by many peers, estranged from certain family members, and ostracized by society, LGBT clients face stigmatization and discrimination.

Teenagers experiencing same-sex attraction face obstacles that would prove unimaginable to their straight peers. No one tells the straight kids that heterosexuality is just a phase or that they are too young to know yet. As a lesbian client rhetorically asked me (JCN) in a session, "Who even asks a straight kid whether she is sure of her sexual orientation?" Only gays are met with disbelief and dismissal. As the chorus rhetorically sings in the play *Rent,* "How can you connect in an age when strangers, landlords, lovers, your own blood cells betray?"

Many LGBT individuals will find it a lengthy, painful process to privately acknowledge and then publicly affirm their sexual orientation. The stages of gay and lesbian identity formation typically begin with (Cass, 1979):

- *confusion:* where the individual questions his or her sexual orientation

- *comparison:* where the individual accepts the possibility that he or she may be a member of a sexual minority
- *tolerance:* where the individual accepts that he or she is gay or lesbian
- *acceptance:* where the individual has increased contact with other gays and lesbians
- *pride:* where the person finds peace with and prefers his or her sexual orientation

Even for those reaching the gay-pride stage, living in a heterosexist society leads to significant stress. A minority sexual orientation increases risk for a number of stresses, ranging from chronic daily hassles to more serious negative life events (American Psychological Association, 2011). For example, the absence of legal rights and the invalidation of couples' relationships in emergencies (medical insurance for domestic partners, family medical leave policies, hospital visitation rights, medical decision making by partners, to name a few) have been associated with helplessness and depression.

LGBT clients are more likely than their heterosexual counterparts to suffer from anxiety, depression, substance abuse, and suicidal behavior (Cochran et al., 2003; King et al., 2008). These higher rates do not indicate that homosexuality is pathological, but rather that social discrimination and political danger exert a deleterious influence on mental health. In some cases, inadequate coping can be blamed, but the power of discrimination cannot be ignored. For this reason, LGBT clients share a particular set of therapeutic needs that differ from those of people with dominant sexual orientations, even when they share other social markers, such as gender or race.

Awareness of sexual orientation and LGBT concerns in psychotherapy does not subsume all other matters. Laura Brown (2005b, p. 351) phrases this point eloquently when she says, "In order to effectively work with LGB clients, a therapist must be able to avoid making the client's sexual or gender orientation the problem, and rather be able to focus on the distress that brings the client into treatment; at the same time, the therapist must not ignore the salience of the client's LGB identity."

The therapeutic processes used with LGBT clients are essentially the same processes as those used with any culturally marginalized client: consciousness raising, catharsis, and choosing. The hard work of awareness and emoting eventually give way to self-liberation and typically social liberation.

Successful outcomes in psychotherapy with LGBT clients rely heavily on the client-clinician relationship, probably more so than many systems of psychotherapy. A warm, supportive, affirming relationship reduces the detrimental effects of decades of oppression and invalidation. For this reason, a deeply empathic and accepting approach forms the core of working with LGBT clients (Perez et al., 2006). This approach says "I value you, not despite your homosexuality, bisexuality, or gender atypicality, but because of it, because you are human and your gender/sexuality are part of that humanity" (Brown, 2005b).

This proactive stance is evidenced in **gay affirmative therapy**, which celebrates and advocates for the integrity of LGBT. Such treatment is intended to counteract the destructive effects of a homophobic society and promote positive regard for the client. Gay affirmative therapy first emerged in the 1980s and 1990s when gay and lesbian therapists started writing about their own lives, when they realized the need for empowering therapists free of heterosexist bias (Kort, 2004).

Therapists working with LGBT clients should be especially sensitive to language. The term *homosexual* is a clinical term offensive to many gays and lesbians, analogous to referring to African Americans as Coloreds or Negroes (Kort, 2004). The recommended term is *sexual orientation*, not "sexual preference" or "lifestyle." An orientation is constant and unchanging, but a preference is preferred and a lifestyle is chosen (Baruth & Manning, 2003; Kort, 2004).

Reparative therapy and **sexual conversion therapy** constitute the opposite of affirming the LGBT identity; instead, they are designed to change or "convert" LGBT clients "back" to a heterosexual orientation or at least gain control over same-sex behavior (Haldeman, 1994). Such treatments might include structured aversive fantasy, psychodynamic methods, group therapy, and religion-based programs (Lasser & Gottlieb, 2004). Although reparative therapy is still practiced, it is considered in professional circles to be discredited. The evidence for the efficacy of sexual conversion programs is less than compelling (Haldeman, 1994). Several studies have found that the use of reparative therapy negatively predicts beneficial outcomes (Jones et al., 2003). Because same-sex desire is no longer considered pathological, efforts to change sexual orientation are unwarranted and may even prove harmful (Shidlo & Schroeder, 2002).

In fact, the American Psychological Association, American Psychiatric Association, and American Counseling Association have all issued position statements warning practitioners against attempting to change patients' sexual orientation. In 2012, the state of California outlawed therapies that claim to turn gay minors into heterosexuals. California's governor at the time (Jerry Brown) said when signing the legislation into law, "These practices have no basis in science or medicine, and they will now be relegated to the dustbin of quackery."

Heterosexism is founded upon the initial assumption that the client is heterosexual. It can manifest itself in something as simple as the intake form, where questions about relational denominations often exclude LGBT experiences. Most heterosexual therapists are unaware of the power and privilege inherent in being the majority sexual orientation. The experiences of an LGBT individual are nearly unknowable to them. Thus, therapists must keep their sense of privilege from reducing their empathy, by becoming more aware of how heterosexist norms pervade our society. Using the term *marital therapy* (instead of couple therapy), for example, can offend those not granted the legal right of marriage.

In this regard, bisexuals are inadvertently misclassified by most therapists and researchers. Bisexual individuals share a diverse set of experiences and relationships that distinguish them from their gay and lesbian counterparts. The polarization of sexual orientation into heterosexual and homosexual categories has the potential to invalidate bisexuality, leaving it to be inaccurately represented as a transitional state.

Additional reasons for therapists' ineffectiveness with the LGBT population are, first, the lack of reliable information about gays, lesbians, and bisexuals and, second, the influence of a subtle bias against nonheterosexual behaviors (Eubanks-Carter et al., 2005). Psychotherapists feel poorly prepared to serve LGBT clients because LGBT concerns are often neglected in psychotherapy training programs. In a survey of final-year clinical and counseling graduate students, the modal number of LGBT clients seen and the modal number of hours of didactic training on LGBT were both zero (Philips & Fischer, 1998).

In the future, psychotherapy will also become more sensitive to the need for controlled outcome research with LGBT clients. While psychotherapy has generally been shown to be effective with gay men, empirical studies do not allow us to determine whether they fare better, worse, or similar to heterosexual clients (Sue & Lam, 2002). There is little empirical research on the effectiveness of mental health treatments for lesbians and bisexuals or of gay affirmative therapy.

In the future too, attention to sexual orientation will be mainstreamed into psychotherapy rather than ghettoized as a "diverse population."

Changing personal attitudes and behaviors takes time. We may never completely unlearn negative biases, but through effort and education, therapists can learn to recognize those biases and take steps to enhance clinical effectiveness with LGBT clients. A change in one person often leads to a change in the entire system.

Effectiveness of Multicultural Therapies

Conclusions reached in reviews of the literature on race and ethnicity effects in psychotherapy appear to reflect the race of the reviewer (Abramowitz & Murray, 1983). White reviewers tend to minimize the effects of ethnic differences, whereas ethnic minority reviewers tend to emphasize findings in which differences are found.

Several robust conclusions can be drawn, nonetheless. First, many racial and ethnic minorities are underserved in the mental health arena (Lopez et al., 2012; Sue & Lam, 2002). Studies show that Asian Americans/Pacific Islanders and Latino Americans/Hispanics, in particular, underutilize mental health services (Breaux & Ryujin, 1999; Sue et al., 2012). Second, the evidence supports preferences for ethnically similar therapists by members of racial minority groups (Abramowitz & Murray, 1983; Atkinson, 1985). Meta-analyses of relevant studies demonstrate that ethnic minorities definitely tend to prefer ethnically similar counselors over European-American counselors (Cabral & Smith, 2011; Coleman et al., 1995). Third, the research fails to show that ethnic minority therapists achieve better (or worse) treatment outcomes (Atkinson, 1985; Sue, 1988; Sue & Lam, 2002). Meta-analyses show no significant differences with respect to client functioning, treatment retention, or number of sessions attended between client-clinician dyads racially-ethnically matched and those not matched (Cabral & Smith, 2011; Shin et al., 2005).

Few controlled studies have been conducted in the United States on the effectiveness of psychotherapy with culturally diverse populations. Based on the limited evidence, the following conclusions can be drawn (Sue, 1994; Sue & Lam, 2002):

- In no studies have African-American clients been found to exceed White American clients in terms of favorable treatment outcomes. Some investigations have revealed no ethnic differences, and some studies have supported the notion that outcomes are less beneficial for African Americans.
- Research is inadequate to address the question of the effectiveness of psychotherapy with Native Americans.
- Any conclusions about the effectiveness of treatment for Asian Americans would be premature given the limited data (only a handful of outcome studies).
- A meta-analytic review on the effectiveness of psychotherapy with Latinos in the United States produced positive results (Navarro, 1993). A total of 15 studies were identified, with the majority of therapeutic interventions (57%) being conducted in the Spanish language. All treatments showed positive effects beyond no-treatment controls, and the average effect sizes were similar to those reported for mainstream psychotherapies. Although Latinos clearly benefit from multicultural psychotherapy, it remains to be seen if they benefit as much as White Americans.

Several meta-analyses have now been conducted on the burgeoning number of controlled studies on **culturally adapted therapies**—traditional therapies tailored to improve the treatment utilization and outcomes of ethnic minority clients. A meta-analysis of 65 studies, encompassing 8,620 clients, evaluated the effectiveness of culturally adapted therapies versus traditional, nonadapted therapies.

The results revealed a positive effect ($d = 0.46$) in favor of clients receiving culturally adapted treatments (Smith et al., 2011). Cultural "fit" works, not only as an ethical commitment but also as an evidence-based practice.

Mental health services can be adapted in many ways. The most frequent methods of adaptation involve incorporating cultural content/values and using the client's preferred native language. Treatments conducted in clients' native language (if other than English) are twice as effective as interventions conducted in English (Griner & Smith, 2006). Treatments that adapt the meaning of the client's illness so that it is mutually understood by therapist and client within a culturally consonant way also prove more effective (Bernish et al., 2011).

While cultural adaptations of existing therapies are generally effective, the effectiveness of multicultural therapies as a separate system of psychotherapy per se has not been adequately tested with members of minority races, ethnicities, and sexual orientations (Brown, 2005b; Sue & Zane, 2005). Few randomized clinical trials of multicultural therapy have been conducted (Ivey & Brooks-Harris, 2005). The conclusion reached by the President's Commission on Mental Health in the late 1970s is still echoed today, some 40 years later, by the U.S. Surgeon General (2001): The gap between research and practice is particularly acute for racial and ethnic minorities. Outcome research is needed that is inclusive of ethnic minority populations and that is explanatory about the effects of culture in psychotherapy.

Criticisms of Multicultural Therapies
From a Psychoanalytic Perspective

Criticize multicultural therapies? Are you kidding? Politically correct forces have made such criticisms positively dangerous. Even hinting that a multicultural formulation might not be accurate or that a multicultural treatment might not be indicated is to invite the accusation that one is a closet racist or homophobe. In the name of overthrowing a socially oppressive system, multiculturalists have substituted a clinically oppressive system.

Psychology has been replaced by victimology. People do not participate in producing their pathologies. Individuals are strictly victims of abusive stereotypes and discriminatory systems, including families, schools, governments, and corporations. All of these social institutions have conspired to keep racial minorities down.

This worldview is a little paranoid. If it weren't for all those outside forces controlling us and coercing us, we would be free to be happy, healthy, and successful. If we are participating in producing our own problems, then we can participate in discovering our own solutions. But if we are victims of social oppression, then can we ever be free short of a social revolution? Such social analysis certainly has a proper place in academia. But is it appropriate for multiculturalists to advance their political ideology in the name of psychotherapy?

The multicultural movement threatens to discredit traditional, insight-oriented psychotherapy and replace it with identity politics. Multicultural therapy holds that psychopathology is primarily cultural and imposes a rigid framework of racial politics. Let's bring back individual responsibility and insight-oriented psychotherapy.

From a Cognitive-Behavioral Perspective

Multicultural diversity represents one important value in psychotherapy, but only one value. Mandating diversity can have unintended negative effects (O'Donohue, 2005). Ethics codes have incorporated language on cultural sensitivity, but the rationale and research for mandating culturally sensitive practices are not compelling. Should we avoid using demonstrably effective treatments just because they have not been extensively researched with ethnic minority clients? Should we routinely match patients and therapists on ethnicity/race even though there is no evidence that doing so enhances effectiveness? Should we refer a Hispanic/Latino patient from an expert White therapist to a less experienced Hispanic/Latino therapist in the name of multiculturalism? Our primary value should be effectiveness, not diversity.

Speaking of effectiveness, multicultural therapy has not yet been subject to clinical trials research. Where are the controlled studies in which half of the patients are randomly assigned to multicultural therapy and the other half to an alternative therapy? Notice, by contrast, that cognitive-behavioral therapies have already proven effective with ethnic minority children and adults (Horrell, 2008; Miranda et al., 2005).

At some point, political values need to be buttressed by research evidence. That time has come. If multicultural therapy is not soon supported by such evidence, it will remain a political value rather than an evidence-based practice.

From a Humanistic Perspective

Values of equality and diversity evoke compassion. But if we want diversity, what's wrong with individuality? Why does an individual's racial or ethnic group confer identity more than does personality? A humanistic society and a humanistic psychotherapy hold that all individuals are uniquely valuable. No two people are the same. But a group psychology threatens to treat all members of a group the same. In the name of diversity, individuals can lose their identity.

We all value equal opportunity, but many multiculturalists desire something more: equal outcomes. Societies that try to enforce equality of outcomes wind up denying freedom, inhibiting creativity, and suppressing identity. The former Soviet Union was based on a single value system of equality. For the sake of equality and social justice, many other values, including individual freedom, were sacrificed. In the name of anti-oppression, these socialist systems constructed some of the most oppressive institutions in the history of humanity.

One of the grand experiments of the 20th century was to construct cultures that would ensure that everyone had equal outcomes. These experiments were based in part on the belief that all psychopathology was the result of an unjust society. Almost all pathology was seen as the result of oppressive poverty. What were the results of these grand experiments? Yes, it is true that no groups had to live in desperate poverty. But was there any less alcoholism? Was there any less depression? Was there any less oppression? Was there any greater happiness? In the search for social solutions to individual pathologies, these grand experiments ended up producing sick societies.

From an Integrative Perspective

How can we help patients become free from oppressive ideologies if we are dogmatic? How can we empower individuals to be autonomous adults by convincing them that they are victims? How can we help clients affirm their uniqueness if we treat them as part of a group? You want to know the ultimate context: eclecticism.

Eclecticism posits that the context for every individual, African, Asian, Latino, or Anglo, is unique. And each psychotherapy needs to be individually constructed to match the needs of a particular person. In some cases, this involves helping individuals become free from social oppression. In other cases, it means helping them become free from mental obsessions. In yet other cases, it involves treatment of biological depression. When will we learn that no single system has a stranglehold on the truth? Not multiculturalism, not constructivism, not empiricism, not even eclecticism.

Theoretical humility can enhance our humanity. Therapeutic pluralism can best prepare us to treat each individual uniquely. As therapists, we know we cannot predetermine what is right for any individual. No therapist has the omnipotence or the omniscience to decide what is the best way for clients to restructure their lives. Why should we believe we have such wisdom to decide what is the best way to reconstruct entire societies? Of course, we can and should advocate for social changes that will benefit oppressed people, and obsessed people, and depressed people. However, we must do it with the humility of knowing we might be mistaken and someone else just might have a better solution. Just because justice is on our side doesn't mean that truth is.

A Multicultural Analysis of Mrs. C

As a member of the dominant White Christian culture in the United States, Mrs. C might be expected to be free from cultural conflicts. However, Mrs. C's hand washing and other compulsions cannot be truly appreciated outside the context of her controlling culture. Consider, for example, that in a comparative analysis of cultural values, Caucasian Christian Americans rate cleanliness as more important than love. Cleanliness is truly next to Godliness.

Look at how hard Mrs. C worked to be clean. What a shining example she strived to be for her family and her society. Do not underestimate how much Mrs. C was bombarded by television to buy soaps and detergents to keep her and her household clean. As the homemaker, there could be no worse criticism than to have an unclean house and a dirty home. Why else would washing be one of the dominant culture's most common compulsions? It is as if social salvation could come from an immaculate perception of one's self by society.

At the time her compulsions began, one of the dominant culture's most popular soaps was white, of course, and was promoted as 99.44% pure. Pure is what Mrs. C strived to be: pure of
(continued)

any dirt or disease and perhaps pure of any off-color fantasies or feelings. It is as if with her hands Mrs. C was literally praying "Grace of God wash away the sins from my soul!"

What could be the sins of this pristine person? From a cultural perspective, the most critical transgressions would be to violate the ultimate concerns of your culture. The ultimate concern of any culture like any family is to reproduce itself. What a wonderful job Mrs. C was doing. She had learned at a young age that the purpose of sex was to procreate.

As an adult, Mrs. C's primary purpose had become procreation, as if it was her occupation. But then came her preoccupation. How could she possibly keep her hands clean and her home clean with so many children with dirty diapers and dirty hands? Then add in the germs that infect the household with an average child having four or more upper respiratory infections a year when her brood was young. Who wouldn't develop extra anxiety about disease and dirt?

How was Mrs. C. to cope? Only when she was immersed in her shower and washing rituals did Mrs. C feel free from her fears and from all the family and cultural demands that threatened to overwhelm her. If Mrs. C could develop a multicultural perspective, she might discover one of the dirty secrets of her dominant culture. She might learn that the United States is one of the few cultures in the world that require an individual to assume sole responsibility for a child for more than 5 hours a day, day after day. Most cultures accept that such extended mothering and caring becomes exhausting and will overwhelm an individual's ability to cope.

A valuable lesson that can be learned from minority cultures in the United States is that extended families and extended communities provide invaluable social support. But Mrs. C had no such support. She was on her own, and any conflicts would be seen as personal inadequacies rather than social shortcomings. In effect, Mrs. C was being blamed for her culture's problems.

Mrs. C could not even count on Mr. C for much social support. As a child, she had learned in her patriarchal family that the husband controlled the household. One of the vulnerabilities of an oppressive system, however, is that people can learn that if they cannot control through strength, they can control through weakness. If they cannot control through power, they can control through pathology. Gradually, Mrs. C had learned that the way she could count on social support from Mr. C was to hook him into her compulsions. In her showers and related rituals, Mrs. C practiced like a High Priestess, with George as her loyal assistant.

If Mrs. C is to become free from the cultural imperatives of cleanliness, procreation, community isolation, and patriarchal control, she will need to become conscious of how enculturated she has become. Does she choose to have one child after another out of fulfillment or is that a rule imposed on her by her church? Can cleanliness really be next to godliness, especially when you have six young children? Mrs. C needs to learn to counter the commercials of her culture, just like children are learning to counter tobacco and alcohol ads.

Mrs. C. can learn to assert herself in the face of patriarchal and cultural controls so that she can receive the support she needs out of strength rather than weakness. She can substitute interpersonal power for personal pathology, so that she not be expected to provide an unhealthy amount of nurturing and caring for her children.

Part of Mrs. C's power can emerge from catharsis, including anger and outrage over having to sacrifice so much of herself for the sake of cleanliness, procreation, and a patriarchy. Rather than trying to wash away such sinful feelings, Mrs. C. can put such emotions into action. She needs to restructure her family into a unique culture that is healthy for all, including herself.

Mrs. C may benefit from the support of a "natural healer," like a modern pastor, who has been trained in multicultural perspectives. Such a pastor could complement a multicultural therapist to help Mrs. C. accept that sex can be a celebration of life without having to produce life. Such assistance could help Mrs. C decide if values such as love and acceptance are much closer to godliness than is cleanliness. Such assistance could help Mrs. C to see that a healthy culture permits people to express their differences and diversity without them being a threat to society or sanity.

Future Directions

The numerous theoretical shifts in the history of psychotherapy have all maintained a White, Western-European, heterosexual common denominator. In the future, the populations that traditional psychotherapy forgot will not settle for monocultural treatments. The demographic avalanche and the pluralistic nature of society will require multicultural therapies. The future must embrace cultural competence if psychotherapy is to remain relevant for anyone except the ever-smaller White, middle-class population to whom it was traditionally targeted. Without cultural competence, psychotherapists risk becoming irrelevant at best, guilty of cultural malpractice at worst (Hall, 1997).

Pluralism is likely to dominate in the evolution of multicultural therapies (Comas-Díaz, 1992). Pluralism is the condition in which numerous ethnic and racial groups are present and accepted within society, accompanied by the belief that such a condition is desirable. The hope is that pluralism will become the social blueprint, infusing diversity and flexibility into psychotherapy constructs. Existing paradigms will not only be questioned, but modified by pluralistic ones that are less ethnocentric and more inclusive. Many extant "universal" principles of human behavior will be perceived as examples of clinical myopia or cultural imperialism.

One step toward an inclusive psychotherapy is to broaden the meaning of culture to embrace all salient dimensions of personal identity, such as sexual orientation, chronological age, disability status, and so forth. Clearly, LGBT clients, the elderly, and the disabled are subject to the same prejudice and oppression as racial/ethnic minorities. An acronym organizing the factors to be considered in culturally responsive practice (Hays, 1996) forms the slightly misspelled word ADRESSING:

Age and generation

Disability

Religion

Ethnicity

Social status

Sexual orientation

Indigenous heritage

National origin

Gender

In the future, practitioners will indeed be "adressing" the complex **intersectionality of multiple identities** in their assessment and treatment of heterogeneous clients (Nettles & Balter, 2011). Although the content of each category varies, there are many commonalities relating to acculturation-separateness, inclusion-exclusion, and power-oppression. Multicultural therapies will take us deeper into compassion and connection. We will increasingly recognize the existence of intolerance against members of certain disability communities, such as wheelchair users, and certain religious communities, such as Islam after the 9-11 terrorist attacks. The future hope is that we will be increasingly united by tolerance and even celebration of our differences.

The search is on for cultural competence in psychotherapy. Cultural humility, cultural awareness, and cultural skills are highly prized but rarely accomplished in formal training. Many training programs still rely on a single diversity or multicultural course to satisfy the needs of its students (Jackson, 2004). Overall, cultural pluralism is not yet sufficiently reflected in faculty, curriculum, or research of psychotherapy programs.

Of course, attracting more racial and ethnic minorities to the helping professions will bring the browning of America to the heart of psychotherapy. Ethnic minorities are substantially underrepresented at all levels of the educational pipeline. What mental health disciplines have not yet achieved may be accomplished by the government: The national standards on Culturally and Linguistically Appropriate Services (CLAS; minorityhealth.hhs.gov/) require all accredited health care organizations to make their practices more culturally and linguistically accessible in partnership with the communities being served.

The future will probably bring fewer attempts to create specific treatment algorithms for various groups of people (cultural relativism), and instead invite more efforts to take the larger and more genuinely culturally competent stance that all humans constitute diverse intersectionalities of multiple identities (cultural universality and cultural adaptation). That stance will inform equally our work with a Euro-American heterosexual Christian married man as with an African-American lesbian pagan living in a polyamorous relationship (Brown, 2009). That will necessitate all therapists starting with and respecting the client's identities (rather than our own) and privileging his or her preferences (rather than our own) for treatment methods, therapist characteristics, and relationship stances. In that way, cultural competence will not be a special topic, a political interest, or a psychotherapy system; it will become an indispensable clinical competence.

Multiculturalism brings new perspectives and different priorities into the mix of psychotherapy. Existing politics, practices, and privileges will be reevaluated and probably replaced by more inclusive, pluralistic processes. The challenge will be to effectively manage these shifts in ways that are experienced by all as equitable. These enduring shifts will serve to strengthen the field through the full inclusion of worldviews of every culture.

Key Terms

acculturation

advocates

browning of America

cultural adaptation

cultural empathy

cultural relativism

cultural universality

culturally adapted therapies

culture

culture-bound syndromes

ethnicity

gay affirmative therapy

heterosexism

internalized homophobia

internalized racism

intersectionality of multiple identities

lesbian, gay, bisexual, and transgendered (LGBT)

liberation psychotherapy

multicultural psychotherapy

myth of uniformity

pluralism

pretreatment patient preparation

race

racial disparities in health care

racial identity

reparative therapy

sexual conversion therapy

traditional or indigenous healers

unconscious racism

Recommended Readings

Bernal, G., & Rodriguez, M. M. D. (Eds.). (2012). *Cultural adaptations: Tools for evidence-based practice with diverse populations.* Washington, DC: American Psychological Association.

Bieschke, K. J., Perez, R. M., & DeBord, K. A. (Eds.). (2006). *Handbook of counseling and psychotherapy with lesbian, gay, bisexual, and transgender clients* (2nd ed.). Washington, DC: American Psychological Association.

Comas-Díaz, L., & Greene, B. (Eds.). (1994). *Women of color: Integrating ethnic and gender identities in psychotherapy.* New York: Guilford.

Jackson, L. C., & Greene, B. (Eds.). (2000). *Psychotherapy with African American women.* New York: Guilford.

Paniagua, F. A. (2005). *Assessing and treating culturally diverse clients: A practical guide* (3rd ed.). Thousand Oaks, CA: Sage.

Ponterotto, J. G., Casas, J. M., Suzuki, L. A., & Alexander, C. M. (Eds.). (2009). *Handbook of multicultural counseling* (3rd ed.). Thousand Oaks, CA: Sage.

Sue, D. W., & Sue, D. (2012). *Counseling the culturally diverse: Theory and practice* (6th ed.). New York: Wiley.

JOURNALS: *Asia Pacific Journal of Counselling and Psychotherapy; Cultural Diversity and Mental Health; Hispanic Journal of Behavioral Sciences; Journal of the Asian American Psychological Association; Journal of Black Psychology; Journal of Cross-Cultural Psychology; Journal of Gay and Lesbian Mental Health; Journal of LGBT Issues in Counseling; Journal of Multicultural Counseling and Development; Journal of Multicultural Social Work; Transcultural Psychiatry.*

Recommended Websites

APA Presidential Taskforce on Diversity Education:
teachpsych.org/diversity/ptde/index.php

Association for Multicultural Counseling & Development:
www.multiculturalcounseling.org

Parents, Families & Friends of Lesbians and Gays:
www.pflag.org/

Society for the Psychological Study of Ethnic Minority Issues:
www.apa.org/divisions/div45/

Society for the Psychological Study of Lesbian, Gay, and Bisexual Issues:
www.apadivision44.org

CHAPTER 15

Constructivist Therapies
Solution-Focused and Narrative

Insoo Kim Berg

Michael White

Diane had been dumped, unceremoniously and unexpectedly, by her longtime boyfriend in the middle of her senior year in high school. How could he! And dumped for a good friend of hers! Her heart felt like it had been ripped out and thrown on the floor. Diane alternated between grief and rage, one moment sobbing and unable to get out of bed and the next moment fantasizing some murderous payback. How could he! Her first true love, her first sexual partner, her first soul mate.

To make matters worse, Diane's mother seemed as upset as she was. Her mother offered support and comfort; after all, she was a talented psychotherapist committed to lengthy, insight-oriented work. Yet Mom hinted darkly to Diane at home and to me in the referral call of "relational vulnerabilities" and "emotional traumatization" resulting from this breakup. The mother/therapist was expecting many months, perhaps years, of weekly intensive psychotherapy to address the roots of the problem.

But Diane wanted to dig out of her crisis, not dig into the archaeology of her emotional life. When I (JCN) asked her to describe her goals for psychotherapy, she immediately replied, "Not to let this jerk spoil the rest of my senior year. To get back my life." When I invited her to imagine that tonight, after our first session, she went back home and fell asleep and a miracle happened that solved the problems that brought her to therapy, what would she notice that would be different? Diane had her answer ready: "I would get up happy in the morning, planning my day, looking forward to

405

basketball practice, and thinking about my friends." Diane knew the path to her health and how to proceed.

Despite her mother's expectations of months of ponderous psychotherapy, Diane finished her work in just four sessions. She had cried enough in the week between being dumped—which she rechristened "liberation day"—and our first appointment. She called on her considerable skills and resources as a college-bound student to develop a plan to get her life back. Return to basketball, return to friends she had perhaps neglected because of her beau, and most importantly, return to her own interests and identity, separate from her boyfriend. She consumed the best seller *Reviving Ophelia* (Pipher, 1994) in one night, declaring that she too had totally lost her self in a relationship, like many adolescent women. After four sessions in pursuit of solutions, not problems, Diane felt empowered to direct her recovery and to mobilize her resources.

At the close of our final session, just 2 months after we initially met, Diane turned to me and said, "We've really surprised Mom. She was pissed at first that we decided to only meet every two weeks. If she had her way, you would have seen me twice a week. But as much as I love her, sometimes the patient knows what's best for her, not the therapist. And sometimes therapy doesn't have to be so long. I proved that to myself and to Mom."

In this chapter, we cover two newer entries onto the psychotherapeutic scene, which we shall collectively call **constructivist** (Mahoney, 2003; Neimeyer & Mahoney, 1995). These therapies share several features: Both are newer "brief" therapies, often averaging only four or five sessions; both focus on change and resources as opposed to the causes of problems; and both emphasize the client's unique, subjective perspective or self-constructed narrative, as contrasted with an "objective" or consensual reality. Consistent with the brief nature of these therapies, this chapter will be relatively brief as well.

A Sketch of the Construction of Therapies

The major philosophical struggle on college campuses pits **constructivism** against **empiricism**. Constructivism's core claim about knowledge is that the knower does not—indeed cannot—attain knowledge of a reality that is objective or independent of the knower. Reality is not out there to be found; reality is constructed inside each of us. We cannot attain knowledge of how the world really is. All knowledge is relative to the construct, culture, language, or theory that we apply to particular phenomenon.

That is not to deny the reality of concrete objects or a physical existence. Constructivists walk on the same ground and bump into the same walls that everyone does. Constructivism does not equal nihilism, the philosophy which argues that life is without objective purpose or intrinsic value. Real things exist, but they are not the objects of intelligence and language.

Our constructed reality is the result of our culture, perception, and language. We cannot access reality outside language and meaning. As Henry David Thoreau wrote, "It's not what you look at that matters, it's what you see."

We cannot know patients and their problems purely and directly: We can only know our interpretations of patients and their problems. Different theories, different languages, and different cultures result in very different perceptions of the same client and the client's behavior.

Witness Mrs. C, for example. Each therapy system in this book can make a compelling case for its particular construction of Mrs. C and her obsessive-compulsive disorder (OCD). Mrs. C, herself, actively participates in constructing her own reality. Her reality is filled with threatening things, such as underwear, that need to be avoided.

Empiricism holds that given the proper scientific methods, we can discover reliable and valid knowledge about Mrs. C and her OCD. Applying scientific methods can result in an adequate knowledge of the reality in which Mrs. C was socialized, the real causes of her condition, and consequently, the best treatments for overcoming her obsessive-compulsive behaviors. At this point in history we may not have developed all of the scientific technologies we need, such as psychological tests and interpersonal interviews, to reach scientific agreement on the causes and cures for the case of Mrs. C. But we are progressing toward such scientific means for knowing the reality of such complex cases.

By contrast, constructivism holds science is just another social construction. Different scientists at different times in history, studying in different cultural contexts, have constructed different theories of reality. The diversity of theories in this book is not a temporary condition that will disappear as the science of psychotherapy progresses. The diversity of theories is a permanent condition reflecting the complexity and individuality of each client and each knower (McNamee & Gergen, 1992).

An umpire joke vividly demonstrates the difference between the empirical or objective perspective and the constructivist perspective (Hoyt, 2000). Three baseball umpires are arguing about how they call balls and strikes. The first umpire, who prides himself on ethics, says, "I call them as I see them." The second umpire, who believes in objective accuracy, counters with "Not bad, but I call them the way they are." Finally, the third, constructivist ump speaks: "They are nothing until I call 'em!"

Our clients are open to a diversity of alternative interpretations. That is part of what protects their individuality (Held, 1995). They cannot be reduced to a set of universal laws or principles that can account for the uniqueness of personality and psychopathology.

People are like great poems. Each of us who interacts with a person or a poem perceives something different. Literary critics have constructed a multitude of meanings and interpretations for a single poem, such as T. S. Eliot's "The Waste Land." When asked if he meant all of these interpretations when he wrote the poem, Eliot responded "I didn't then, but I do now." Such **postmodern** literary criticism has swept the humanities by storm.

Is psychotherapy a science or an art? Is knowledge about personality, psychopathology, and psychotherapy based on a reality that we can discover? Or are therapists always left with knowing only the language, the theory, and the "reality" that they and their clients construct and interpret together?

The precursors to constructivist psychotherapy can be found in many theoretical orientations (Mahoney, 2003). In the 1950s, George Kelly (1955) developed a cognitive theory of **personal constructs**, seeing humans as curious, amateur scientists who actively construct their worlds. Kelly's fundamental postulate was that "A person's processes are psychologically channelized by the way in which he anticipates events" (1955, p. 46). A person construes or interprets the world by means of his or her personal constructs, not by an objective reality. In the 1970s, Roy Schafer (1976) proposed a new conceptualization and language for psychoanalysis, a constructivist position that emphasized the narrative tradition. Psychoanalysts' interpretations are "useful narratives" as opposed to "the correct interpretation" or the "the truth."

These and other threads of constructivism converged into formal constructivist therapies in the 1990s as the popularity of the postmodern movement in academia filtered into clinical practice. In this chapter we explore two of the most influential therapies based on social constructivism: **solution-focused therapy** and **narrative therapy**. We begin with solution-focused and then examine narrative therapy.

Solution-Focused Therapy
Theory of Personality and Psychopathology

Solution-focused therapy begins with refreshing assumptions. People are healthy. People are competent. People are capable of constructing solutions that improve their lives. Psychotherapy helps people improve their lives by focusing on solutions rather than problems.

Theories of personality and psychopathology focus on causes rather than solutions, problems from the past rather than changes in the future. There is a long-standing belief that therapists and patients need to know the causes of troubling behaviors before they can find solutions for changing those behaviors. However, as constructivism has demonstrated, we can never know the real causes of people's problems. We can construct alternative interpretations. We can apply different theories of personality and psychopathology in attempts to explain people's problems. But we can never know the "reality" of personality and psychopathology. There are respected empiricists, such as many behavior therapists, who reject the entire domain of personality and psychopathology. After a century of searching, personality theories have accounted for relatively little of human behavior.

Furthermore, precious little evidence exists to support the belief that constructing causes leads to better solutions. Not knowing the causes of breast cancer doesn't keep oncologists from curing breast cancer. *Why* someone became a drinker 25 years ago (e.g., peer pressure, stress reduction) may have little to do with *how* the individual is going to change now.

Change is happening all the time. People quit smoking or drinking every day. People overcome depression and anxiety every day. The fact is most problems get solved without psychotherapy, further attesting to individuals' competencies. And few people who solve problems on their own have theories of personality and psychopathology.

What replaces past causes of problems in solution-focused therapy? What can help people, including psychotherapists, shift from a problem-oriented endeavor to a solution-focused enterprise? If the answers are not to be found in the past, then what is left is the present and the future.

What can pull people into a healthier and happier future? Healthier and happier goals. We cannot change our past; we can change our goals. Better goals can break us out of stuck places and can lead us into a more fulfilling future. Rather than learning all types of personality characteristics and psychopathology categories, what effective brief therapists need to know are characteristics of therapeutic goals.

Here are criteria for constructing well-defined goals (Berg & Miller, 1992; Walter & Peller, 1992):

- *Positive.* Instead of having negative goals such as "I am going to get rid of drinking, depression, or anxiety," the goals should be positive. The key word here is *instead. Instead* of drinking, being depressed or anxious, what positive things are you going to do? A simple therapeutic question for setting goals is, "What will you be doing *instead*?"
- *Process.* The key word here is *how.* "*How* will you be doing this healthier or happier alternative?"
- *Present.* Change happens now, not yesterday and not tomorrow. The key phrase here is *on track.* A simple question to help is, "As you leave here today, and you are *on track*, what will you be doing differently or saying differently to yourself?" Today, not tomorrow.
- *Practical.* "How attainable is this goal?" The key word is *attainable.* Clients who want their spouse, employer, parent, or teacher to change are seeking unattainable solutions and will set themselves up for more problems.
- *Specific.* "How specifically will you be doing this?" Global, abstract, or ambiguous goals, such as "spending more time with my family," are not nearly as effective as: "Specifically I will take a 15-minute walk with my wife each evening," "I will volunteer to help coach my daughter's soccer team," or "I will take my son golfing with me on Saturdays."

- *Client control.* "What will *you* be doing when the new alternative happens?" The key word is *you*, the client, because *you* have the competency, the responsibility, and the control to make better things happen.
- *Client language.* Use the clients' words for forming goals rather than the therapist's theoretical language. "I am going to have weekly adult telephone conversations with my father" is more effective than "I am going to resolve my oedipal conflicts with my father."

In place of personality and psychotherapy, in place of problems and the past, psychotherapy proceeds in the present guided by specific positive goals constructed in the client's language and under the client's control.

Therapeutic Processes

Given that people get stuck repeating past patterns because they focus too much on their problems, the goal of therapy is to shift the focus onto solutions in the present that will sustain healthier and happier goals in the future. **Problem talk** maintains a problem focus, so therapeutic change will involve a shift to **solution talk**.

Solution talk and solution-oriented therapy originated in the humble beginnings of the Brief Family Therapy Center (BFTC), a nonprofit treatment center in Milwaukee, Wisconsin. Insoo Kim Berg, MSSW, executive director of the BFTC, was one of the founders of solution-oriented therapy and one of its most influential voices. Starting in the mid-1980s and until her death in 2007, she published 10 books and a multitude of videotapes on the solution-oriented approach. A native of Korea, Berg balanced her Eastern heritage with her Western training in social work. She and her husband, Steve de Shazer (1940–2005), creatively blended consciousness raising and choosing processes of change.

Consciousness Raising

Too many clients enter therapy preoccupied with problems. "I'm depressed all the time." "I can't control my drinking." "My partner and I are always fighting." "I'm a worrywart." "I can't sleep." The natural question would seem to be "Why? Why are you depressed? Why is your drinking out of control? Why are you and your partner always fighting?"

Therapists could apply their favorite theories to construct answers to these causal questions. But is that helpful? They could help clients become even more conscious of their problems and the multitude of past experiences that may have contributed to their problems. Constructing elegant explanations for past events might allow clients and therapists to feel better, but will the clients live better?

Insoo Kim Berg, Steve de Shazer, and solution-focused therapists help clients become more conscious of the exceptions to their problems. "When are the times when you don't feel depressed?" "Oh, when you go to church, and when you play golf, and when you listen to your favorite music." Raising awareness about such **exceptions**—panning for gold, so to speak—can create solutions.

"When have you been most in control of your drinking?" "Oh, when you attended Alcoholics Anonymous (AA) regularly, and when you tended to your spirituality, and when you were around people who cared about you." Are there any clues in such increased consciousness as to how controls over drinking could be reconstructed?

Rare are clients who have no exceptions to their troubles. For those experiencing difficulty identifying positive exceptions to their problems, Berg will ask the **miracle question**. "If by a miracle, you found yourself free from your problems overnight, how would things be different?" Constructing in imagination exceptions to a problem-filled world can help clients become more conscious that their current reality need not be their only reality. The miracle of therapy is to help clients transform their imagined reality into specific attainable goals.

Choosing

The goals we choose determine the future we live. As clients become more conscious of current exceptions to a problem-filled life, they can choose to create more of those exceptions. The client who entered therapy focused on depression can choose to participate in more church functions, exercise more often, and listen to more favorite music, specifically uplifting music. The client focused on alcohol problems can choose to focus on alcohol solutions with immediate goals such as daily AA attendance, reading religious and inspirational materials, and socializing with people who care about him or her.

Here are four guides to therapeutic choices (Walter & Peller, 1992):

1. If it works, don't fix it. Choose to do more of it.
2. If it works a little, choose to build on it.
3. If nothing seems to be working, choose to experiment, including imagining miracles.
4. Choose to approach each session as if it were the last. Change starts now, not next week.

Here are pathways for constructing solutions (de Shazer, 1985, 1988, 1994).

- **Goal focus**. Therapy begins by focusing on present goals that can construct a better future. "What is your goal in coming here?" Goal-forming questions are aimed at breaking the miracle solution into achievable steps. The therapist frames treatment around goals in the present rather than problems from the past. "What brings you here?" is a therapist opening much more likely to encourage clients to continue with problem talk.
- **Solution focus**. "When the problem is solved what will you be *doing* differently?" Is the client ready to begin doing a small piece of it now? If so, start the change immediately.

- *Exception focus.* "How is what you will be doing differently happening some now?" or "When isn't the problem happening?" These are known as **exception-finding questions** that build on the client's strengths.
- *Choice or spontaneity.* Are the problem-free events occurring by choice, deliberately, intentionally? Or are these healthier and happier times occurring spontaneously, accidentally, or unpredictably?

If the exceptions are already under the client's control, then specific goals can be constructed that encourage the client to choose to do more of what helps. If the exceptions are more spontaneous, such as friends dropping by, then the focus is on finding out how such events can occur, such as inviting your friends to stop by.

If the client responds to any of these questions by saying "I don't know," the therapist lets the client know that is a good sign. This process is new to the client. It will help the client to think differently and to begin constructing alternatives that may not have been imagined before.

- *Small changes lead to larger changes.* Follow-up sessions build on the gains and the goals that are constructed early in therapy. As one of my (JCN) clients said, "Changing me is like turning an ocean freighter rather than a speed boat. Slowly, gradually at first. But once I have a new direction, there's no holding me back."
- *Each solution is unique.* Just as each client is a unique individual, so too is each solution unique. Therapists need to be prepared to be surprised. Here is one creative solution constructed by an elderly woman living alone in the center of a city. To help free herself from depression, she joined three churches: Catholic, Baptist, and evangelical! She received three times as much social support, three times as much social opportunities, and much less empty time to get depressed. The fact that

most people construct their lives around only one denomination didn't prohibit her from being ecumenical.

- *Solutions evolve out of conversations.* Whether it is from self-talk or talking in therapy, solutions emerge from dialogues. If therapy encourages us to talk about our same old problems, then we are likely to remain our same old self. Change begins in talking about solutions. If therapy is to be brief, then therapeutic dialogues should focus on solutions as soon as possible.
- *Language is our reality.* Show us a therapist whose language is filled with technical terms about personality and psychopathology, and we will show you a therapist who is prepared to do long-term therapy that repeats the past. Show us a client who talks about practical and personal goals in the present, and we will show you a client whose reality is changing.

These same pathways and principles are used to build solutions with mandated (or involuntary) clients, who are ordered to receive psychotherapy by the legal system (Berg, 1999). Berg first asks the clinician to set aside any personal biases against the mandated client and to set aside what she may have heard or read about the client from others. This mind-set enables the clinician to hear the client's point of view without prejudging. Then, Berg seeks to collaboratively negotiate sustainable solutions and to help the client to assess her own progress toward her own goals. Specific methods will include:

- Discovering the details of what the clients want (goal specification).
- Defining, at a minimum, what the clients think they have to do to satisfy the referring person (a variant of the miracle question).
- Talking in terms of solutions, not problems (solution talk).
- Finding past and recent successes (exceptions).

- Determining what the clients need to do to repeat the exceptions (scaling).
- Asking what are the next small steps to achieve the desirable goal (goal-forming).
- Ascertaining how the clients' significant others would scale the clients' movement toward the goal (scaling by others).
- Assisting the clients in establishing when they have done enough.

Therapeutic Relationship

Because solution-focused therapy is designed to be brief, the therapist plays a more active role in shifting the session as quickly as possible from problems to solutions. The therapist gently but persistently guides clients in exploring their strengths and building solutions. The basic relational strategy is to ignite the clients' initiatives, to help them to see and better use their response-ability (Hoyt, 2000). Once the focus is on solutions, the clients are largely in charge. Clients are the experts on what goals they want to construct in order to create a better future.

Solution-focused clinicians are experts on the process and structure of therapy; clients are experts on their goals and corresponding solutions. The fundamental relationship, then, is like a multidisciplinary collaboration between experts. Each expert, the client and the therapist, contributes to shared solution. The relationship between patient and therapist is purposeful; that is, the patient comes to therapy for a reason and to achieve a purpose. To that end, the multidisciplinary collaborators will also establish criteria that will tell them that they have succeeded and can end treatment.

Brief, strength-based therapies emphasize the client's solutions and the clinician's techniques, not their therapeutic relationship. However, as solution-focused therapies enter the mainstream and are blended with other methods, more attention is being devoted to how the relationship can unstick difficult situations and pave the way to successful solutions (Lipchik, 2002). More focus is being paid to the emotional, interpersonal nature of the multidisciplinary collaboration. Compassion and caring are crucial to any constructivist helping relationship (Mahoney, 2003).

Practicalities

As with multidisciplinary teams collaborating to create solutions, the therapeutic relationship lasts only as long as needed to implement an acceptable solution. Remarkably few therapeutic sessions are scheduled. Time is not wasted on indexing every psychopathology or researching every etiology. In this time-effective therapy, the search is on as soon as possible for solutions. The focus on solutions is tightly maintained throughout treatment.

Solution-oriented treatment is designed to start, not finish, the solution process. As collaborator, the client is competent to continue implementing the solution long after therapy has ended. Starting therapy in such a time-effective manner limits the tendency of clients to become dependent on the expert therapist who can divine the causes of their disorders and apply the best therapeutic solutions within therapy sessions.

Solution-oriented therapy is indeed brief. The average number of sessions hovers between three and five. A study of 275 clients presenting for services at the Brief Family Therapy Center in Milwaukee resulted in the following distribution by length of treatment (DeJong & Hopwood, 1996):

NUMBER OF SESSIONS	NUMBER OF CASES	PERCENT OF CASES
1	72	26
2	80	29
3	47	17
4	31	11
5	20	7
6	10	4
7 or more	15	6

As seen, more than 80% of patients came for 4 or fewer sessions with an average of only 2.9 sessions. In other clinical settings, too, patients receiving solution-focused brief therapy are seen for only two or three sessions on average (Rothwell, 2005).

Solution-focused therapy has been applied to virtually all behavioral disorders and in all therapy formats. Its methods are frequently employed in coaching, education, and substance abuse counseling. In fact, the solution-focused treatment of problem drinking (de Shazer & Isebaert, 2003; Miller & Berg, 1995) shares many commonalities with motivational interviewing (reviewed in Chapter 5). The brief focus is particularly valued for the treatment of mild problems and adjustment disorders (Araoz & Carrese, 1996) but has also been recommended for chronic psychiatric patients (Booker & Blymyer, 1994; Webster et al., 1994). The fundamental concepts—using what is already working, leveraging existing strengths, speaking in solution language, and listening to client beliefs—are applied to inpatient settings with patients historically treated as incompetent.

Although solution-focused therapy was initially launched as a family therapy at the Mental Research Institute in Palo Alto, California (see Chapter 12) and at the Brief Family Therapy Center in Milwaukee, Wisconsin, it is now also widely practiced in the individual format.

Narrative Therapy

Solution-focused therapists hold that clients construct their future by pursuing goals in the present, whereas narrative therapists assert that clients construct their past by telling stories in the present. The past can be changed by constructing new **narratives** or stories. Witness how the history of the United States is being changed by narratives written by and about women, Native Americans, and African Americans whose stories were once omitted from our history books.

A realist or an empiricist might argue that one cannot change the reality of the past. What was, was. Naive answer, reply the narratives. Recognize that "what was" is what history books tell us. You can know history books, but you cannot know history. And history books are being rewritten as more and more people claim their freedom to tell their stories.

Narrative therapists are **antirealists** (Held, 1995). They believe no objective reality exists behind our stories. The "reality" in which we exist is our stories. History and herstory is the reality of each client—unique, personal, subjective, and fortunately, open to change.

Theories of Personality and Psychopathology

Theories of personality and psychopathology are the stories that psychotherapists tell about their clients. Unfortunately, such theories can also be the stories that therapists impose on their clients (McNamee & Gergen, 1992). Such theoretical impositions or interpretations can be oppressive at best and destructive at worst. For too many decades, male therapists tried to convince women that they were plagued by "penis envy." Women's "herstory" concerned "voting envy," "career envy," "salary envy," and "political power envy." For too long childhood sexual abuse was interpreted according to the dominant theory that held that such events were childhood fantasies based on the child's wish fulfillment to have sex with a parent. The professional story about gay and lesbian individuals was that they were DSM disorders—sexual deviants.

No wonder narrative therapists reject empirical theories of personality and psychopathology. It's professional arrogance for therapists to believe that they can tell people who they are. Clients must be free to tell us who they are and who they want to be. Theories are oppressive; they seek to impose one perspective on all people. Theory

masquerading as reality is equally oppressive. There is no reality; there are only stories we tell about reality.

Empirical reality is said to be objective and fixed, so that we can eventually all come to know the same reality. Would that mean that once the "truth" is known about a healthy personality, for example, we would all strive to be the same person? Such psychological cloning of humans should be seen as being as unethical as biological cloning of humans. What the world needs is diversity, not identity. Even identical twins do not have the same identity, the same personality. Each has her or his unique story to tell, just as each client has her or his unique story to tell. If we are to protect the freedom and individuality of our clients, then we start by rejecting an imperial empiricism that would impose the same reality on us all.

One of the wonders of narratives is that they are open, ongoing, never ending. Historical narratives and scientific narratives are open, ongoing, and changing. As our stories change, so too do we change. Look at how our society has transformed as more women, minorities, and other oppressed people have publicly told their stories.

If you want to know your identity, the reality of who you are, don't turn to someone else's theory. Turn to the next chapter in your own story.

In place of theories of personality and psychopathology, narrative therapists encourage us to rely on stories (White & Epston, 1990, 1994). Stories don't mirror life; they shape it. Narrative therapists, like fine literary critics, help us to construct new meanings and new interpretations about who we are, who we have been, and what we can become.

Therapeutic Processes

Because our experience of problems is a function of the stories we have constructed, the resolution of our problems emerges from **deconstructing** our old stories and constructing new ones. Therapeutic narratives must be more consciously constructed as liberating stories.

Michael White (1948–2008), a pioneer of narrative therapy, liberated himself from his original occupation as a mechanical draftsman and constructed a new identity as a social worker with a special interest in family therapy. Following his initial attraction to the cybernetic thinking of Gregory Bateson (Chapter 12), White became preoccupied with the ways people construct meaning and identity. He launched a narrative approach to literary theory, postmodern philosophy, and psychotherapy practice. Before his death in 2008, White's numerous books, including *Narrative Means to Therapeutic Ends* (White & Epston, 1990), and his clinical practice in south Australia integrated the change processes of consciousness raising, choosing, and counterconditioning.

Consciousness Raising

First we need to become conscious of how much of our story has been constructed from the **dominant discourses** in our families and societies (McNamee & Gergen, 1992). Who are the powerful people who tell us how to think and feel about ourselves? Whose language defined sex as bad and high grades as good? Whose stories said that being spontaneous was dangerous and being controlled was safe? Who constructed the reality in which children with high energy and enthusiasm would be diagnosed and drugged for attention-deficit hyperactivity disorder (ADHD), because they couldn't sit still for long hours in boring classes? Whose dominant discourses declared that people who prefer their own company and their own imagination over superficial social discourse are introverted, withdrawn, or antisocial?

In the past, powerful people had the privilege of editing our experiences. Some of them were strong enough to impose meaning on our lives, such as "I'm a weakling; I'm a coward; I'm shy; I'm ugly; I'm a sex object; I'm a problem."

With the support of a narrative therapist we can become aware that when it comes to constructing the story of our lives, we occupy the **privileged position** (White & Epston, 1990, 1994). No predetermined theoretical interpretations are imposed on our personal experiences. No damaging diagnoses will reduce us to a schizophrenic, a bipolar, an obsessive-compulsive, a sexual deviant, an addict, or an ADHD. In narrative therapy, we have the privileged position of both reading and authoring the text of our lives.

As we begin to retell our story, the psychotherapist can help us to perceive ourselves from multiple perspectives. Who in the past would not be surprised that we are getting better and doing better? Was our life always this way? Or were there important changes and stages? As we perceive a changing world in the past, we begin to perceive the possibilities for a changing world in the future.

But first we must become aware of how powerful our Problem has become. As in dramatic storytelling, it helps to have a villain and a victim. Personifying the problem puts it in perspective as an oppressor that demands much of our time and energy and sense of self (White & Epston, 1990, 1994). My Depression is a demon that demands that I listen to sad music, attend depressing dramas, read absurd existential fiction, and tell sad stories. My Addiction insists that I go out late at night to clubs where controls are checked at the door and people get high on suds, sex, and seduction. My Procrastination requires that I am late for every paper and performance and that I rebel against other people's rules by putting off their wishes as long as I possibly can.

By mapping the influence of this key character in our life, we can understand more concretely just how determined we have been by the description, the demands, and the discouragement of our Problems. But we can also look for unique and unexpected outcomes. When did we resist the

Problem's invitation to become part of it? What were the occasions in which we were the hero or heroine, when we defeated our Demon? When were the times we were free from our Problem, where we escaped the dominance and oppression of the Problem? Did we retreat back to the comfort and security of our Problem? Did we escape from freedom, from the responsibility of having to author a novel life?

Choosing

Are we prepared to plot an alternative story? Just as there have been plots against us, to suppress our sexuality or to oppress our originality, so too can we construct plots in our favor. We can choose to overthrow dominant discourses with our own voice, our own words, our personal privilege. Keeping a journal, for example, is a choice asserting that our words matter, our experiences are meaningful. Writing letters to our parents without having to worry about mailing them can free us to give meaning to parts of us that have been omitted for too long. The adult in us, the assertive one in us, the angry one, or the forgiving one, might emerge when we are telling it like it is or like it was.

Michael White trained thousands of narrative therapists to write post-session letters to clients underlining their healthy choices. The letters celebrate clients' unnoticed strengths, overlooked accomplishments, and remarkable heroics. Narrative therapists amplify client "know-hows": their taken-for-granted choices to survive all manner of abuse, ridicule, and trauma (Madigan, 2008).

Counterconditioning

To construct a new story we need new words, new images, and new meanings (Friedman, 1993). To counter our chronic construction, Michael White and narrative therapists encourage the use of poetic and picturesque language. As our language becomes richer, our experience becomes richer. As our words have multiple meanings, our lives have more meaning.

If our lives are too empty, too narrow, or too devitalized, it is because our language is too limited.

Since the narratives we use to describe our experience shape that experience, we can tell ourselves new stories that offer more liberating and healthier possibilities. One method centers on **externalization of the problem** outside of the individual (and the family) in a way that makes the problem the external common enemy. It's the difference between "I am depressed" and "I am struggling with depression." The first says that the problem exists inside oneself; the second says that a problem is located apart and outside. Relocating problems outside helps clients feel more control over their lives and lessens self-blame or guilt about the problem (White, 2007).

In narrative therapy, clients experience aspects of themselves that they never expressed before. A broader range of emotions—anger, excitement, joy, sadness, and outrage—counter the old drab, dreary, monotone meaning that is so depressing. Excitement, anticipation, and wonder are words that can substitute for the tight, repetitive, burdened language of the worrywart. One of the clearest signs that one's self is changing is that one's words are changing. But we should not substitute technical or scientific terms devoid of personal meaning for worn-out words from the past that only express problem meanings.

Not only does narrative therapy encourage clients to assume authorship of their life stories but it also enables them to star in their newly constructed narratives. They are free to rehearse in therapy sessions, where all the anxieties of acting and speaking anew can occur in a safe and accepting place. Clients are then encouraged to launch their performances on other stages: with more accepting friends at first, then with employers or parents who have been experienced as part of the Problem.

One client's parents were taken aback when she began to share the rich dialogue that she had written to them in unmailed letters. She not only talked about her old story, when she had to be "oh so perfect" in her dress, her manners, and her language. Now she expressed herself in a less-than-perfect style, stammering and stopping at times, loud and emotional at other times, colorful and off-color at still other times. After one particularly moving soliloquy expressing her estrangement from herself and her father, her parents actually broke into light applause and into tears. They were changing too.

Therapeutic Relationship

Ideally, each therapeutic relationship is unique: constructed by a particular client and a particular clinician conversing together in a particular time, place, and context (McNamee & Gergen, 1992). The relationship unfolds in their dialogue; it is not predetermined by generic principles based on a standard theory of personality, psychopathology, or psychotherapy. Only in this manner of relating can the client's individuality be respected and protected.

Ideally, nothing more need be said. But in practice, if there are no general guiding principles, then there is nothing that can be taught or learned. Nothing can be generalized from one client to another or even one session to another without some principles or continuity.

The continuity in therapy is constructed from the story clients tell. The narrative therapist's general contribution is to gently guide clients into constructing new editions of their stories that are less limiting and more liberating. The narrative therapist recognizes that we are "making history" and not just "taking history." Poetics more than physics is the relational stance to best examine the warp and weft of human life (Hoyt, 2000).

Contrary to Alexander Pope's famous assurance, hope does *not* "spring eternal in the human breast." Rather, narrative therapists must vigilantly nurture hope in their clients. They do so by expressing faith in the possibilities and preciousness of human life in process. Positive meaning must be endlessly and individually recreated in client struggles and triumphs (Mahoney, 2003). Teaching

the tools of literary criticism is what therapists can contribute to the "reality" of a story. Therapists can help clients construct novel narratives that flow into a freer future. If we want to appreciate the richness of relationships between therapists and clients, then we need to listen to and interpret the multiple meanings of their dialogue.

Although there is no universally correct therapeutic attitude, therapists do strive for what has been called **narrative empathy** (Omer, 1997). Unlike external empathy, which describes the client from the outside and from the point of view of theory, narrative empathy attempts to construe and express the inner emotional logic of the client's problem patterns. The criterion of an empathic narrative is that it elicits a client response of "That's me!"

Practicalities

In light of the uniqueness of each therapeutic relationship, it could seem impossible to describe any common practices for narrative therapy. Although initially introduced in family therapy, narrative therapy is now advanced for children, adults, couples, families, and entire communities (Franklin et al., 2011). Unlike solution-focused therapy, the length of narrative therapy can vary considerably. There is a preference for brief therapy but there is no theory that requires that the co-construction of narratives be a brief process. In practice, sessions are structured by the therapist with the standard 50-minute session the rule rather than the exception. But therapy can overflow the rigid boundaries of this rule because clients continue the narrative process in their journals or letters. Although clients create their own reality, they are expected to pay for their sessions with real money.

Effectiveness of Constructivist Therapies

The newer constructivist therapies have patterned themselves after the older clinical tradition in favoring naturalistic studies and therapist testimonials instead of controlled outcome studies. The founders were far more invested in applying their methods than in researching their effectiveness. As a new psychotherapy on the block, constructivist therapy is in its research adolescence.

Solution-Focused Therapy

An early outcome study (DeJong & Hopwood, 1996) on solution-focused therapy was uncontrolled in design and was not published in a peer-reviewed journal. Nonetheless, the findings convey some sense of the typical practices of the treatment. The study tracked 275 clients who presented for treatment at BFTC.

Two outcome measures were used to gauge treatment success. The first intermediate measure involved the **scaling question** asked by the therapist at each session: "On a scale of 1 to 10, where 10 is 'the problems you came to therapy for are solved' and 1 is 'the problems are the worst they've been,' where are they now on that scale?" On this measure, 26% showed no progress or worsened, 49% showed moderate progress (defined as 1 to 3 points higher on the scaling question), and 25% showed significant progress.

The second measure was obtained by contacting the clients by telephone following treatment and asking whether their treatment goals were met. The data showed that 45% of contacted clients said their goals were met, and an additional 32% said some progress was made toward the goals. The remaining 23% replied that no progress was made. In such an uncontrolled study, of course, we have no reliable comparisons of how many of these clients would have reported success without psychotherapy, with longer therapy, or with another type of therapy.

The first published meta-analysis of solution-focused brief therapy (SFBT) was conducted in 2006 on 21 controlled and uncontrolled studies (Stams et al., 2006). The effect size (d) relative to no treatment was 0.57, indicating a medium effect for SFBT. The effect, however, was not larger than that for treatment as usual ($d = 0.16$).

A subsequent meta-analysis of outcome studies focused on solution-focused therapy in comparison to no treatment or an alternative therapy (Kim, 2008). However, 11 of the 22 studies were unpublished dissertations and only half employed a true experimental design. The studies were grouped into three categories based on the targeted outcome: externalizing problems, internalizing problems, and family or relationship problems. The average effect sizes for all three—internalizing problems ($d = 0.26$), externalizing problems (0.13), and family/relationship problems (0.26)—were quite small, suggesting that SFBT had a modest effect.

A 2012 review of the solution-focused literature located 43 different outcome studies, but, again, many of them were neither controlled nor randomized (www.gingerich.net/SFBT/2012_review.htm). In two better-designed studies of late, SFBT performed as well as short-term psychodynamic therapy with fewer sessions (Gingerich et al., 2012).

The conclusions we draw are that:

- SFBT is superior to no treatment.
- SFBT is frequently briefer and less costly than alternative therapies.
- The effectiveness of SFBT compared to other psychotherapies has been insufficiently investigated in randomized controlled trials (RCTs).
- The early findings from the existing RCTs are equivocal (Corcoran & Pillai, 2009).

Narrative Therapy

Our literature reviews located no RCTs on narrative therapy. It is not included in meta-analyses on the effectiveness of child, adolescent, adult, older adult, or group therapy. Existing studies are largely case reports or qualitative research.

One uncontrolled study investigated the effects of eight sessions of manualized narrative therapy for 47 adults with major depressive disorder. Pre- to posttreatment, the patients experienced considerable improvement in symptom improvement ($d = 1.36$) and less improvement in interpersonal relatedness ($d = 0.62$). Three-month follow-up found maintenance of symptom reduction but not interpersonal gain (Vromans & Schweitzer, 2011). We hope that this early stirring of outcome research will portend further studies on the effectiveness of narrative therapy.

Other Constructive Therapies

In family therapy, reviews of the literature uncovered only a couple of published studies on the effectiveness of constructive family therapy. One study (Besa, 1994) assessed the effectiveness of narrative therapy in reducing conflicts between six sets of parents and children. A larger study of 59 children and their families (Lee, 1997) investigated outcomes in solution-oriented family therapy and reported promising results: 65% success rate over an average of 5.5 sessions. However, the absence of any control group or comparative treatment makes it practically impossible to interpret the results. Neither solution-oriented nor narrative therapy is included in the major reviews of couple and family therapy (Sandberg et al., 1997; Sexton et al., 2003).

Personal construct therapy (PCT) has been applied to a number of clinical problems and contexts since George Kelly published his seminal book on the psychology of personal constructs in the mid-1950s. Two meta-analyses examined the 20-plus studies on the effectiveness of PCT (Holland et al., 2007; Metcalfe et al., 2007). The effect sizes for PCT were a modest 0.38 versus no treatment and a small 0.21 versus active treatments (Holland et al., 2007). Traditional self-reports and behavioral measures tended to yield larger effects than those focused on personal meanings. Clients receiving PCT tended to fare better than those not receiving any treatment but not better or worse than other psychotherapies.

In part, the dearth of controlled outcome studies on constructivist therapies reflect opposition against the empirical studies accepted for publication in "scientific" journals. Such research studies require group designs, standardized measures, manualized treatments, and quantitative analyses that offend constructivist principles. The research definition of evidence relies on objectification of experiences and privileges one conception of evidence over others. The typical research prized by academics and insurance companies does not so much discover truth as it privileges a particular truth compatible with the political needs of the group conducting the research. In the human sciences, there can be no unbiased research that leads to one unassailable truth (Cushman & Gilford, 2000).

Criticisms of Constructivist Therapies
From a Cognitive-Behavioral Perspective

Let us tell you a story about two women who suffered from a morbid dread of developing breast cancer. Several relatives of each woman had died of breast cancer. Personal acquaintances had developed breast cancer. As successful career women, they had delayed having children until their mid-thirties. Each coped with their anxiety and depression by drinking and eating too much and exercising too little. Facing 40, they found their fears increasing and their coping abilities decreasing.

Nan consulted a narrative therapist and told her story. She interpreted her text as having been written primarily by a society that would use science to scare women who placed higher priority on having careers than children. Bad things like breast cancer would happen to such women, especially those who drank too much and dieted too little. With the help of narrative therapy, Nan co-constructed her own story in which a woman was free to fulfill her career first and would not be punished for delaying having children. In this construction, how she coped was her own business, as long as it did not violate anyone else's rights. She finished narrative therapy with a fresh appreciation of her power to tell her story free from fears and negative consequences. Four years later, Nan died of undiagnosed late-stage breast cancer.

Ann consulted a cognitive-behavior therapist who prescribed the evidence-based methods of desensitization, exposure, and cognitive restructuring to reduce her morbid dread. The therapy prepared Ann to face her fears, in part by going for regular mammograms. Ann learned from the scientific literature that alcohol abuse, high-fat diets, and sedentary lifestyles increased risks for breast cancer and many other chronic diseases. With the help of cognitive-behavior therapy, Ann developed healthier habits for coping with emotional distress. She finished therapy doing her best to reduce her risks from breast cancer and other chronic diseases. Two years later, Ann was diagnosed with early-stage breast cancer that was successfully treated with surgery and chemotherapy.

From a Psychoanalytic Perspective

If you do not have a theory of psychotherapy that can do justice to the complexities of personality and psychopathology, then the solution is simple. Deny the reality of personality and psychopathology. Poof—the problem disappears!

Proof? That's another problem that disappears with postmodernism. Only modernists believe in the privileged position of rationalism and empiricism: that through reason and experimentation we can differentiate between reality and fantasy. Postmodernists in the guise of constructivist therapists would have us regress to infantile narcissism. Reject the reality principle! Overthrow the ego! Reason, cognition, and objectivity have no privileged place in helping us or our patients determine what is real and what is not.

The tragic reality of life is that reality is oppressive. It keeps us from being free to fulfill every fantasy. That was the common complaint from patients fixated on wish-fulfilling fantasy. Now we are hearing the same complaint from clinicians seduced by the fantasy that they can fix a lifetime of psychopathology in a brief time. Instant gratification is available for everyone—clients, clinicians, and managed care organizations.

Solution-oriented therapies remind us of Freud's (1917/1966) explanation of the difference between brief psychotherapies and psychoanalysis. Brief treatment seeks to cover up and gloss over something in mental life; psychoanalytic treatment seeks to expose and get rid of something. The former acts like a cosmetic; the latter like surgery. Brief therapy strengthens the repressions, but, apart from that, leaves all the processes that have led to the formation of the symptoms unaltered.

Where will the brief, cosmetic movement in psychotherapy end? Personality and psychopathology have already been deconstructed and dissolved in a brief solution-focused therapy. Next to go will be the psychotherapy itself—deconstructed and dissolved by the reality (or is it the fantasy?) of pharmacotherapy. We can begin constructing this brave new world free from personality, psychopathology, and psychotherapy by putting Prozac in the public water supply or Lexapro in diet sodas.

From a Humanistic Perspective

We applaud constructivism's purpose of attempting to protect individualism from the oppression of totalitarianism. Certainly the 20th century repeatedly witnessed the political and personal pathology that can be imposed on people in the name of reality. Whether that reality is constructed from fascism or communism, racism or sexism, colonialism or imperialism, the results are the same. Privileged people in power who dominate the discourse can impose their universal truths on everyone. We have repeatedly witnessed that those in power can diagnose you as a misfit—a personality disorder, a political prisoner, or simply a problem. How you get treated is up to them.

They can label you or libel you, imprison you or hospitalize you, shock you or drug you, and most of all alienate you.

The challenge for the postmodern clinician is how to protect the particularity of this special person existing in this particular place and time. The problem is that in place of the oppressive generality of the universal truths of science, narrative therapists are left with a single tool. This is the tool of interpretation derived from a literary criticism that holds that each particular reader is free to give new meaning to a text—a poem, a play, or a performance. With this metaphor in mind each individual is deconstructed, discovering what meaning is missing from their dominant discourse. Then a new play or performance is co-constructed through conversations between the client and the clinician.

However, let's examine how dehumanizing this new construction can be. Poems don't feel pain, people do. Words don't worry, women do. Metaphors don't miss emotions, men do. Theories don't make life-enhancing or limiting decisions, individual clients and clinicians do. What is so liberating about becoming adult is that we can now take responsibility for what we say and what we do. In our living, and changing, we are not limited by only one tool of knowing. As creative and constructive as literary criticism can be, it has no privileged position helping me to know who I am and who I will become.

We are reminded again of Abraham Maslow's metaphor that if our only tool is a hammer, then we will treat everything and everyone like a nail. So please don't try hammering away at my real problems as if they were simply poems, merely metaphors, or temporary texts. If you don't have a way of knowing who I am as a real person, then I don't want to know who you are as a psychotherapist.

From an Integrative Perspective

Who says that we must choose between constructivism and empiricism, words and numbers, art and science? As mental health professionals, we have both ways of knowing. Art is the source of our inspiration. Science is the source of our validation.

Plays, poetry, painting, and music can all create a deeper and richer appreciation of humanity. Film and theater, for example, so often make real the struggle of individuals to break out of self-defeating patterns. The images used in poetry and paintings can give new insights into the darker side of ourselves that are often hidden from direct observation. Music gives voice to such a broad range of emotions that we can all experience if we open our ears. These are wonderful ways of knowing and expressing that can enrich our lives.

At the same time, our lives and our work can be equally elevated by discovering scientific principles that can be generalized across problems and across people. Behavioral and cognitive therapies, for example, relieve suffering around the world—quite independent from the question of who told that therapeutic story in which language. Our search for valid principles for progressing through the stages of change, for another example, has enabled us to construct treatment programs that can reach many more people than previously possible (see Chapter 17). Such generalizable principles permit us to approach clients with confidence that we know something special that can help them change.

We don't have to act like "know-nothings" who must discover everything anew with each particular person. Of course, we need to be open to understanding what is of special importance to each individual client and what particular changes would most enhance their lives. However, if we do not have any generalizable knowledge to share, then each client is reduced to trial-and-error learning, which is inefficient and ineffective. Each client would have to reinvent the wheel of change. We in psychology and in education have known for decades that guided learning is much more effective than trial-and-error learning. Clinical ethics dictate that we listen to both our clients and our science.

We can assign a privileged position to those in the arts and humanities who have special talents for constructing a multitude of interpretations for humanity. We can also assign a privileged position to those in the sciences who have the ability to conduct research and test theories. Their scientific methods allow us to reject even our favorite interpretations in favor of alternatives that meet our toughest tests of validation. But no theory, literary or scientific, can meet the test of absolute certainty. As Nietzsche warned, we should not be misled by those who would substitute certainty for truth. Science occupies the privileged position of telling us what is most probably valid and useful given all that we know to date.

Unfortunately, in psychotherapy we often do not possess enough scientific knowledge that can be generalized to a particular person or problem. We are thrown back for now to relying on theoretical interpretations. The privileged position here is the clinician and client struggling together to understand and modify particular problems. Their perspectives are likely to be most helpful when they are informed by the best that the art *and* the science of psychotherapy has to offer.

A Narrative Analysis by Mrs. C

Mrs. C has told and retold her story far too many times. Before therapy, during therapy, and after therapy she repeated her preoccupation with pinworms. Her psychoanalytic therapy kept going backward in time, obsessively paying attention to every detail of her disorder. Seeking to uncover the hidden causes of her OCD deep in her childhood memories, her therapists were missing the forest for the trees. Mrs. C's discourse was her disorder.

The more Mrs. C focused on her childhood, the more she repeated the dominant discourses that were so demanding and discouraging. "Be clean! Be cute! Pick that up. Put that down. Eat your peas. Slowly. Be home on time. Behave! Be good. Be healthy. Be careful! Be neat. Be prompt. Be still."

In narrative therapy it would not take Mrs. C long to discover who had held privileged positions in her past: her patriarchal parents, her pastor, and then her psychotherapists. Her parents and her pastor were obvious, with all of their demands based on predetermined categories of how a good child, a good American, and a good Christian should behave. Her psychotherapists were more subtle, but soon Mrs. C could see that they were repeating the same pattern of imposing their predetermined categories on her: obsessive-compulsive disorder; anal-stage fixations; conflicts over toilet training;

defenses against sexual and aggressive impulses; and the laundry list went on. The language had changed, but the meaning was the same.

A privileged person—a parent, pastor, or psychotherapist—had the power to tell her story. Their paternal, religious, and psychological constructs took precedence over Mrs. C's personal experience. She had no right to interpret their behavior because it was all benign; they were only doing it for her own good.

A narrative therapist would refuse to impose any predetermined meaning on Mrs. C. She doesn't need a detached, theoretical formulation of herself written by a psychotherapist; she deserves a lived, personal story written by herself. She would be encouraged to construct her own story. What fits? What feels good? What was missing from the old stories? Mrs. C would begin to deconstruct the dominant discourse. What meanings were missing? What hidden text was covered and controlled by all the cleaning? Where's the joy? Where is the fun? No spontaneity. No running around. No desires, just demands. No decisions, just disruptions. Startled, Mrs. C could discover that what was missing from such discourse was her self, her soul.

Her narrative therapist would encourage Mrs. C to accept the privileged position of being at the

(continued)

center of her own life. No one needed to tell her what to do, to tell her story and determine what it meant and how it must unfold. Mrs. C could become free to be the author of her own existence. A post-session letter from her therapist might underscore Mrs. C's unnoticed resilience and capabilities under crippling life circumstances.

In her daily journal Mrs. C could begin to write in her own words the multiple meanings that had been omitted, washed away by the dominant discourse; the joy of having her first child, the lust that had gotten lost along the way.

She might decide that her soap opera had run its course. It had lost its vitality. For too long she had tried too hard to buy into what her privileged parents were promoting: "Be clean; be good; behave." She could decide to experience a much fuller range of stories—from comedy to drama; from mystery to history.

Mrs. C might decide to enroll in courses at her local university. Here she could see the world from multiple perspectives. What better way to revitalize her life, to fill the void, than to bring art and music into her existence? What fun it could be to go to the football games with her family! After all, when it came to constructing her own life, she felt like a freshman.

Mrs. C could come to understand why such a curriculum is called "liberal arts." For her, they could be liberating arts. If she had received such an education earlier in her life, she might have seen through her parents' privileged position. She might have realized that their way of constructing life was only one of many. Then she could have been free earlier to begin authoring her own existence.

Fortunately, Mrs. C would discover that it is never too late to reconstruct the world and her self. Combining ideas from across continents and across ages, emotions across religions and philosophies, would all enrich her life. Mrs. C would shift from a profound preoccupation with her problems to a liberating awareness of her humanity. No longer would Mrs. C need to be fixated on the past; by creating her own narrative she would perceive from her own privileged position how open is her story and her self.

Future Directions

Constructivism is one of the dominant discourses in academics, and psychotherapies based on it will probably continue to grow. Indeed, the use of constructive words (words beginning with "construct") nearly doubled in the psychological literature in the past 25 years (Mahoney, 1996). In this chapter we have explored two of the leading examples of constructivist therapy. The gender-sensitive therapies (Chapter 13) and multicultural therapies (Chapter 14) are also constructivist alternatives designed specifically for women, men, and racial/ethnic minorities. Theoretically, there is an unlimited number of therapies that can be created from a constructivist perspective.

Constructivism will increasingly emerge as an enlightened response to the ongoing movement toward **evidence-based practices** in mental health.

This movement advocates practice based on solid, scientific research of a treatment's safety and effectiveness (see Chapter 18). But constructivism will serve as the loyal opposition to this empirical imperialism. In the postmodern spirit, they will challenge, "Who are insurance companies to determine what works for a unique client?" "How can statistics prevail over empathy in a therapy relationship?" "What gives researchers permission to write the stories of individual patients?" "Whose hidden economic and political interests are being served by this movement?" "Why privilege only controlled group studies?" "What about qualitative and narrative research?" They will righteously protest that a controlled research trial is only one fallible, incomplete manner of looking at psychotherapy.

Another direction probably lies in the extensive criticism and deconstruction of traditional DSM diagnosing. Psychiatric diagnoses are merely constructs, not tangible entities; diagnoses are improperly used to confer power to the establishment, not to empower the client's experience (Cosgrove, 2004). Constructivists are abandoning psychodiagnosis in favor of multidimensional assessment that focuses on client strengths and that involves family members who deliberate on possible ways of understanding the individual within his or her context and how best to go on (Gergen, 2001). The privilege historically accorded to the psychotherapist, psychodiagnosis, and psychopathology may gradually give way in the future to the community, consensus, and strengths.

In an era of declining insurance payments for mental health and shrinking institutional resources for health care treatments, the short-term constructivist therapies should prosper. Not all clients have the need, or the money, for extended psychotherapy. Not all professionals have the time, or the opportunity, to provide it either. Narrative and solution-focused treatments fit well with a fast-paced world and get-er-done clients.

In academia, the security of tenure and the principle of academic freedom give faculty the right to teach and write whatever they choose. Few predetermined criteria are imposed on their classroom curricula or their research agendas. In the health care system, however, there is no such security or autonomy. Managed care organizations require numerical outcomes and evidence-based practices. Science, along with business, is becoming a dominant force in health care. Narrative and solution-focused therapists are likely to confront a limiting future that will test their philosophical assumptions. They will need to produce hard empirical data demonstrating that constructivist clinicians can produce cost-effective outcomes with real clients suffering from DSM disorders. The alternative will be to construct practices not covered or controlled by health care systems.

In the future, constructivist therapies will pick the clinical circumstances in which they will be particularly indicated and perhaps consistent with the "objective" outcome research. Solution-focused therapy, for example, seems particularly well-suited to life coaching, crisis management, school counseling, medication adherence, and severe mental illness (Franklin et al., 2011; Rowan & O'Hanlon, 1999). Narrative therapy, for another example, fits well with older patients and **reminiscence therapy**, which have already proven effective for geriatric depression (Pinquart et al., 2007; Scogin et al., 2005).

In the meantime, the philosophical appeal of constructivism, its popularity in academia, and the brevity of solution-focused therapy are likely to appeal to clinicians helping clients develop solutions and rewrite their life stories in an era of short-term psychotherapy.

Key Terms

antirealism	miracle question
constructivism	narrative empathy
constructivist therapies	narrative therapy
deconstructing	narratives
dominant discourses	personal constructs
empiricism	postmodern
evidence-based	privileged position
practices	problem talk
exception-finding	reminiscence therapy
questions	scaling question
exceptions	solution focus
externalization of the	solution-focused
problem	therapy
goal focus	solution talk

Recommended Readings

Berg, I. K., & Miller, S. D. (1992). *Working with the problem drinker: A solution-focused approach.* New York: Norton.

de Shazer, S. (1985). *Keys to solution in brief therapy.* New York: Norton.

de Shazer, S. (1994). *Words were originally magic.* New York: Norton.

DeJong, P., & Berg, I. K. (2013). *Interviewing for solutions* (4th ed.). Pacific Grove, CA: Brooks/Cole.

Franklin, C., Trenner, T. S., McCollum, E. E., & Gingerich, W. J. (Eds.). (2011). *Solution-focused brief therapy: A handbook of evidence-based practice.* New York: Oxford University Press.

Hoyt, M. F. (Ed.). (1998). *The handbook of constructive therapies.* San Francisco: Jossey-Bass.

Mahoney, M. J. (2003). *Constructive psychotherapy: A practical guide.* New York: Guilford.

White, M. (2011). *Narrative practice: Continuing the conversations.* New York: Norton.

White, M., & Epston, D. (1990). *Narrative means to therapeutic ends.* New York: Norton.

JOURNALS: *Constructive Change; Constructivism in the Human Sciences; Journal of Brief Therapy; Journal of Constructivist Psychology: Personal Construct Theory and Practice.*

Recommended Websites

European Constructivist Training Network:
   www.pcp-net.org/ectn/
Dulwich Centre (Narrative Therapy):
   www.dulwichcentre.com.au/
Personal Construct Psychology:
   www.personal-construct.net/
Solution-Focused Brief Therapy Association:
   www.sfbta.org/

CHAPTER 16

Integrative Therapies

Arnold Lazarus

Paul Wachtel

For some students, every exam threatens to overwhelm them with anxiety. No matter how hard they study, they can't be confident. They can't relax. They are convinced that their dreaded anxiety will interfere with their performance. And it usually does. Their debilitating test anxiety can interfere with understanding the exam questions, or it can disrupt retrieval of the correct answers. No matter how bright students are, they almost always perform below their potential.

Highly test-anxious students have trouble sleeping before an exam. The day of a big exam, they may have trouble eating. Their intestinal tracts may flare up. One of their worst fears is that they will block entirely on an exam and will feel absolutely foolish when they turn in an exam that is barely begun. When test anxiety becomes so aversive and debilitating, talented students can drop out of college to escape what one student called "a fate worse than death."

To help such students, we compared two treatments for test anxiety. The first was traditional systematic desensitization that paired deep muscle relaxation with images of exam situations that become increasingly stressful. Over time, these undergraduates learned to counter highly anxious reactions to images of exams with deep muscle relaxation. The second was a novel and integrative treatment called dynamic desensitization. This therapy combines the counterconditioning principles of behavior therapy with images from a psychodynamic interpretation of test anxiety.

According to the psychoanalytic perspective, debilitating test anxiety is rooted in early childhood experiences in which mistakes were met with parental criticism and threats of rejection or other forms of loss of love. Children dependent on their parents' approval are not free to fight back against what they perceive as their parents' demands for perfection. To express their anger would be to risk corporal punishment, emotional abuse, and the prospect of rejection. As students grow older, every exam becomes a test of their self-worth. Every exam threatens to prove their parents' harsh judgments that they are not bright enough, not careful enough, not good enough. Any ambiguity on an exam, the slightest unfairness in wording or grading, can threaten to overwhelm them with anger toward the teacher/parent who is just waiting to make them look bad.

In dynamic desensitization, the undergraduates learned to vividly imagine a series of evaluative situations in which they make a mistake, are berated by a parent or teacher, and are overwhelmed with anxiety and anger, resulting in both humiliation and physical retribution from parental figures. In essence, this therapy integrates behavioral processes and psychoanalytic content.

We were not surprised to find that both forms of desensitization were effective in significantly reducing debilitating test anxiety. In fact, there were no differences between the treatments in terms of immediate effectiveness.

We were pleased to discover, however, that the dynamic desensitization led to significantly more generalization to a broad range of evaluative situations. Not only were students in this integrative therapy coping better with demanding exams, but they were also relaxing more in other situations where they felt they were being evaluated, such as meeting new people, giving a speech, going out on a date, and starting a new job. These students were helping us to advance the integration movement, which seeks innovative methods of combining powerful processes and content from psychotherapy systems traditionally viewed as incompatible.

A Sketch of Integrative Motives

Psychotherapy integration is motivated by a desire to look beyond the confines of single-school approaches to see what can be learned—and how clients can benefit—from other approaches. The objective of doing so is to enhance the effectiveness and efficiency of psychotherapy. The integration movement, as it is now called, is characterized by a spirit of open inquiry and a zest for transtheoretical dialogue (Norcross & Goldfried, 2005).

Rivalry among theoretical orientations has a long and undistinguished history in psychotherapy, dating back to Freud. In the infancy of the field, therapy systems, like battling siblings, competed for attention and affection in a "dogma eat dogma" environment (Larson, 1980). Clinicians traditionally operated from within their own particular theoretical frameworks, often to the point of being blind to alternative conceptualizations and potentially superior interventions.

As psychotherapy has matured, the ideological cold war has abated and integration has emerged. The debates across theoretical systems are less polemic, or at least more issue-specific. The theoretical substrate of each system is undergoing intensive reappraisal, as psychotherapists acknowledge the inadequacies of any one system and the potential value of others.

Integration as a point of view has probably existed as long as philosophy and psychotherapy. In philosophy, the third-century biographer, Diogenes Laertius, referred to an eclectic school that flourished in Alexandria in the second century. In psychotherapy, Freud consciously struggled with the selection and integration of diverse methods. As early as 1919, Freud introduced psychoanalytic psychotherapy as an alternative to classical analysis, recognizing that the more rarefied approach lacked universal applicability and that many patients did not possess the requisite psychological mindedness (Liff, 1992).

Even the Iron Curtain isolating Eastern Europe and the governments there imposing a single system of treatment (Pavlovian conditioning) could not stop psychotherapy integration. From 1950 until 1968 in Czechoslovakia, Ferdinand Knobloch (1996; Knobloch & Knobloch, 1979) created an integrated therapy combining various theories, as well as embracing individual, group, and family modes of treatment. Inspired by the therapeutic community, this integrated psychotherapy predated many contemporary approaches and foreshadowed several contemporary principles of psychotherapy.

Although the notion of integrating therapeutic approaches has intrigued mental health professionals for many decades, it is only within the past 25 years that integration has developed into a clearly delineated area of interest. Indeed, the temporal course of interest in psychotherapy integration, as indexed by both the number of publications and the development of organizations and journals (Goldfried & Newman, 1992), reveals occasional stirrings before 1970, a growing interest during the 1980s, and rapidly accelerating interest from 1990 to the present.

The rapid increase in integrative psychotherapies of late leads one to inquire "Why now?" Many interacting motives have fostered the development of integration (Norcross, 2005):

- *Proliferation of therapies.* Which of 500-plus therapies should be studied, taught, or bought? The hyperinflation of brand-name therapies has produced narcissistic fatigue: "With so many brand names around that no one can recognize, let alone remember, and so many competitors doing psychotherapy, it is becoming too arduous to launch still another new brand" (London, 1988, pp. 5–6). This might

also be called the "exhaustion theory" of integration: Peace among warring schools is the last resort.

- *Inadequacy of any single theory for all patients and problems.* No therapy or therapist is immune to failure. It is at such times that experienced practitioners often wonder if the clinical methods from orientations other than their own might have been more effective. Underlying the ecumenical spirit is the stark realization that narrow conceptual positions and limited clinical methods cannot begin to address the diverse needs and disorders of our patients. Clinical realities have come to demand a more flexible, if not integrative, perspective.

- *External socioeconomic contingencies.* Psychotherapy has experienced mounting pressures from not easily disregarded sources such as policy makers, informed consumers, and insurance companies. Everyone is demanding hard research evidence of effective treatments. Unless they demonstrate accountability, psychotherapists stand to lose prestige, customers, and money. Attacks from outside the mental health professions have started to propel them together. There is something to be said for having the different therapies "hang together" rather than "hang separately."

- *Ascendancy of short-term, problem-focused treatments.* The brief, problem focus has brought divergent therapies closer together and has created variations of different therapies that are more compatible with each other. Integration, particularly in the form of eclecticism, responds to the pragmatic time-limited injunction of "whatever therapy works better— and quicker—for this patient with this problem."

- *Opportunities for therapists to observe and experiment with various treatments.* The establishment of specialized clinics for the treatment of specific disorders—personality disorders, obsessive-compulsive disorders, and eating disorders, to name only a few—have afforded exposure to other therapies, and stimulated some therapists to consider the other therapies more seriously. Treatment manuals have also induced an informal version of "theoretical exposure": Previously feared and unknown therapies were approached gradually, anxiety dissipated, and the previously feared therapies were integrated into the clinical repertoire.

- *Recognition that therapeutic commonalities heavily contribute to treatment outcome.* As discussed in Chapter 1, only about 8% to 12% of outcome is generally accounted for by the specific treatment method. Therapeutic success can be best predicted by common elements of psychotherapy, such as the contributions of the patient, the therapy relationship, and facilitative qualities of the therapist.

- *Development of professional societies for integration.* The creation of professional networks has been both a consequence and cause of interest in psychotherapy integration. Several organizations, principally the Society for the Exploration of Psychotherapy Integration (SEPI), have brought together integration enthusiasts through conferences, networking, and journals. Integrationists and eclectics now have a professional home.

These motives speak to the entire field of psychotherapy moving toward integration. But what motivates individual therapists to embrace integration? From a personal-historical perspective, Robertson (1979) identifies six factors that facilitate the acquisition of an eclectic or integrative stance. The first is the lack of pressures in training to adopt a doctrinaire position and the absence of a charismatic figure to emulate. The second factor, which has been substantiated by research (Norcross, 2005), is length of clinical experience: As therapists encounter complex clients and problems over time, they are more likely to reject a single theory as too simple. A third factor is the extent to which doing psychotherapy is making a living or making a philosophy of life; Robertson asserts that eclecticism is more likely to follow the former. In the words of several distinguished scientist-practitioners (Ricks et al., 1976, p. 401):

> So long as we stay out of the day to day work of psychotherapy, in the quiet of the study or library, it is easy to think of psychotherapists as exponents of competing schools. When we actually participate in psychotherapy, or observe its complexities, it loses this specious simplicity.

The remaining three factors are personality variables: an obsessive-compulsive desire to give order to all the interventions of the therapeutic universe; a maverick temperament to move beyond some theoretical camp; and a skeptical attitude toward the status quo. These personality traits are frequently found in the personal histories of prominent integrative therapists (see Goldfried, 2001, for examples).

Common Factors

There are numerous pathways toward the integration of the psychotherapies; many roads lead to Rome. The most popular routes at present are common factors, technical eclecticism, and theoretical integration (Norcross & Goldfried, 2005). Although all are intent on increasing therapeutic effectiveness by looking beyond the confines of single-school approaches, they do so in rather different ways and at different levels.

The **common factors** approach, as we discussed in Chapter 1, determines the core ingredients that different therapies share in common. The goal is to create more parsimonious and efficacious treatments based on those commonalities. Advocates of common factors argue that commonalities are more important in accounting for therapy outcome than the unique factors that differentiate among therapies. That is, a positive therapy relationship, a hardworking client, and an empathic therapist probably account for more of treatment success than the particular treatment method, be it psychodynamic, experiential, cognitive-behavioral, or systems.

One way of determining common factors is by focusing on a level of abstraction somewhere between theory and technique. This intermediate level of abstraction, known in our transtheoretical model as a **change process**, is a heuristic that guides the efforts of experienced therapists. Marvin Goldfried (1980, p. 996), a leader of the integration movement, posits:

> To the extent that clinicians of varying orientations are able to arrive at a common set of strategies, it is likely that what emerges will consist of robust phenomena, as they have managed to survive the distortions imposed by the therapists' varying theoretical biases.

In specifying what is common across orientations, we may also be selecting what works best among them.

Bruce Wampold has been an ardent and influential supporter of the common factors approach. Relying on his extensive meta-analytic studies of psychotherapy, Wampold (2001; Wampold et al., 1997, 2002, 2010) argues that the research purporting to show that certain psychotherapies produce superior outcomes is misleading, on at least three counts.

First, comparative psychotherapy studies frequently overestimate the effects of particular treatment methods because differences between treatments are due in part to individual therapists. Some therapists are more effective than other therapists. Thus, in clinical trials, true treatment differences must be estimated by taking into account the variation among therapists; ignoring **therapist effects** results in an overestimation of treatment methods. When the respective effects of the treatment and the therapist are separated, Wampold (2001, p. 200) concludes

"a preponderance of evidence indicates that there are large therapist effects … and that the effects greatly exceed treatment effects."

Second, the purported superiority of some therapies is frequently due to comparisons between a treatment intended to be therapeutic and another treatment that is barely a therapy at all. In many randomized clinical trials, the comparison therapies are not intended to be therapeutic; they are not structurally equivalent. The comparison therapy may have no rationale or explanation provided to the client, may be conducted by therapists who are not trained or do not have allegiance to that therapy, may have fewer sessions, and the therapists may be forbidden from using responses that they would normally use. When Wampold compares only bona fide therapies, he consistently finds their outcomes are equivalent. When another set of researchers (Luborsky et al., 2002) similarly examined 17 meta-analyses of comparisons of active treatments with each other, they found only a small and nonsignificant effect. The smallness of the effect size supports the potency of common factors and the **Dodo bird verdict**. Taken from a scene in *Alice in Wonderland*, the dodo bird judges runners in a footrace and declares that "everyone has won and all must have prizes." All tested bona fide psychotherapies work with equal success for the vast majority of disorders.

And third, as we discussed in earlier chapters, Wampold notes that the theoretical allegiance of the researcher reliably exerts a strong influence on therapy outcomes (Luborsky et al., 1999; Wampold, 2001). The literature is replete with examples of studies that favor a particular treatment conducted by advocates of that treatment, whereas studies conducted by advocates of an alternative treatment favor the alternative. In fact, Wampold's own meta-analyses find that the size of the **allegiance effect** is several times as great as the effect for differences among treatment approaches. Given that most investigations of psychotherapies are conducted by researchers with an allegiance to the psychotherapy being investigated, allegiance has to be taken into account in any apparent superiority.

What are the clinical implications of rejecting the medical model that certain psychotherapies are more effective than other psychotherapies for certain disorders? A common factors model of psychotherapy, one rooted in the individual therapist, the therapeutic relationship, and fit between the treatment and the client's values and culture. Clients should choose the best therapist and choose the treatment that best accords with their worldview. Psychotherapists should be trained "to appreciate and be skilled in the common core aspects of psychotherapy" (Wampold, 2001, p. 229). These include empathic listening, developing a working alliance, working through one's own conflicts, understanding interpersonal and intrapsychic dynamics, and learning to be self-reflective about one's work. Therapists should learn as many treatment approaches as they find congenial and convincing. Psychotherapists should also provide clients with an explanation for their disorders that is acceptable to the client, enhance the client's expectations about overcoming his or her difficulties, and offer actions that are helpful to the client.

Barry Duncan, Scott Miller, and Mark Hubble have also been fierce advocates of a common factors psychotherapy. In their aptly titled book, *The Heart and Soul of Change* (2010; Hubble et al., 1999), they demonstrate how commonalities powerfully operate in any behavior change, including individual therapy, medicine, pharmacotherapy, family therapy, and education. They argue that an impartial reading of the outcome research supports four major therapeutic factors:

- Client factors (harnessing naturally occurring change in the client's life, minding the client's competence, and tapping the client's world outside therapy)

- Relationship factors (fostering a positive therapeutic alliance by accommodating the client's readiness for change and embracing the client's view of the alliance)
- Hope and expectancy (facilitating client hope by having a healing ritual, focusing on what is possible, and orienting treatment toward the future)
- Models and techniques (selecting effective methods because they provide structure and offer novel ways of thinking and behaving)

These factors, not theoretical orientations or technical interventions, lie at the heart and soul of change.

Embracing these common factors may lead to a unifying language for psychotherapy and to effective treatments, especially for difficult clients (Miller et al., 1997). More attention to the impact of client factors and the "heroic" aspects of clients will produce more outcome-informed therapy. Instead of assuming that the right theory or method leads to favorable results, psychotherapists should systematically assess their clients' experience of the therapy relationship and treatment success in order to guide psychotherapy (Miller et al., 2005).

These brief (less than a minute) assessments entail straightforward questions about outcome asked of the client every session or every couple of sessions via a four-item self-report instrument. The results are immediately fed back to the therapist (visit www.MyOutcomes.com). This monitoring approach empowers the client, unifies the treatment around change, and results in improvements in outcome. In fact, meta-analyses shows that providing psychotherapists with real-time feedback on client progress during psychotherapy does enhance treatment success, particularly for those clients who are likely to have a negative response (Lambert et al., 2005; Lambert & Shimokawa, 2011). The point is to privilege the client's theory and experience of change, not the therapist's.

Bruce Wampold, Jerome Frank (Chapter 1), and the trio of Miller, Duncan, and Hubble eloquently advance the cause for a more ecumenical, less doctrinaire approach anchored in outcome research. Because we have already introduced common factors in Chapter 1 and will consider them again in Chapter 18, we shall devote the remainder of this chapter to technical eclecticism and theoretical integration.

Technical Eclecticism or Theoretical Integration?

Technical eclecticism seeks to improve our ability to select the best treatment for the person and the problem (Lazarus et al., 1992). This search is guided primarily by research on what has worked best in the past for others with similar problems and similar characteristics. Eclecticism focuses on predicting for whom interventions will work: The foundation is actuarial rather than theoretical.

Proponents of technical eclecticism use procedures drawn from different sources without necessarily subscribing to the theories that spawned them, whereas the theoretical integrationist draws from diverse systems that may be philosophically incompatible. For technical eclectics, no necessary connection exists between metabeliefs and techniques. "To attempt a theoretical rapprochement is as futile as trying to picture the edge of the universe. But to read through the vast amount of literature on psychotherapy, *in search of techniques*, can be clinically enriching and therapeutically rewarding" (Lazarus, 1967, p. 416).

The term *eclecticism* has acquired an emotionally ambivalent, if not negative, connotation for some clinicians because of its allegedly disorganized and indecisive nature. Indeed, it is surprising that so many clinicians admit to being eclectic in their work, given the negative valence the term has acquired (Garfield, 1980).

But these accusations of being "wishy-washy" should be properly redirected to **syncretism**— uncritical and unsystematic combinations (Norcross, 1990; Patterson, 1990). Such haphazard "eclecticism" is primarily an outgrowth of pet techniques and inadequate training, which produce an arbitrary, if not capricious, blend of methods by default. Eysenck (1970, p. 145) characterizes this indiscriminate smorgasbord as a "mishmash of theories, a hugger-mugger of procedures, a gallimaufry of therapies," having no proper rationale or empirical verification. This muddle of idiosyncratic clinical creations is the opposite of effective psychotherapy, which is the product of years of painstaking clinical research and experience. Rotter (1954, p. 14), years ago, summarized the matter as follows: "All systematic thinking involves the synthesis of preexisting points of view. It is not a question of whether or not to be eclectic but of whether or not to be consistent and systematic."

In **theoretical integration**, two or more psychotherapy systems are integrated in the hope that the result will be better than the constituent therapies alone. As the name implies, there is an emphasis on integrating the underlying *theories* of psychotherapy along with the techniques from each. The various proposals to integrate psychoanalytic and behavioral theories illustrate this direction, as well as grander schemes to meld all the major systems of psychotherapy.

Psychotherapists combine many available theories in creating their clinical hybrids. When we asked 187 self-identified integrative psychotherapists to rate their use of six theories (behavioral, cognitive, humanistic, interpersonal, psychoanalytic, systems), the resulting 15 dyads were each selected by at least one therapist (Norcross et al., 2005). The most common combinations are shown in Table 16.1, along with the findings of similar studies conducted in 1976 (Garfield & Kurtz, 1977) and 1986 (Norcross & Prochaska,

Table 16.1 Most Frequent Combinations of Theoretical Orientations

COMBINATION	1976* %	1976* RANK	1986 %	1986 RANK	2005 %	2005 RANK
Behavioral and cognitive	5	4	12	1	16	1
Cognitive and humanistic			11	2	7	2
Cognitive and psychoanalytic			10	3	7	2
Cognitive and interpersonal			4	12	6	4
Cognitive and systems			4	14	6	4
Humanistic and interpersonal	3	6	8	4	5	6
Interpersonal and systems			5	7	4	7
Psychoanalytic and systems			4	9	3	8
Interpersonal and psychoanalytic			4	15	3	8
Behavioral and interpersonal			4	13	2	10
Behavioral and systems			5	7	2	11
Humanistic and psychoanalytic			4	12	2	11
Behavioral and humanistic	11	3	8	4	1	13
Behavioral and psychoanalytic	25	1	4	9	1	14

*Percentages and ranks were not reported for all combinations in the 1976 study (Garfield & Kurtz, 1977).

1988). The typical combination in the late 1970s was psychoanalytic-behavioral; in the late 1980s, the three most popular hybrids all involved cognitive therapy; and in the early 2000s, cognitive therapy dominated the list of combinations. As seen in the table, in conjunction with another therapy system, cognitive therapy occupies the first 5 of 14 combinations and accounts for 42% of the combinations. Over time, the behavioral and psychoanalytic combination (ranked as #1 in the late 1970s) as well as the behavioral and humanistic combination have dropped considerably.

Theoretical integration entails a commitment to a conceptual creation beyond a technical blend of methods. The goal is to create a theoretical framework that synthesizes the best elements of two or more approaches to therapy. Integration, however, aspires to more than a simple combination; it seeks a theory that is more than the sum of its parts and that leads to new directions for practice and research.

How, then, do these two strategies differ? A National Institute of Mental Health Workshop (Wolfe & Goldfried, 1988) and several studies (e.g., Norcross & Napolitano, 1986; Norcross & Prochaska, 1988) have summarized the distinctions between integration and eclecticism. These are shown in Table 16.2. The primary distinction is that between empirical pragmatism and theoretical flexibility. Integration refers to a conceptual or theoretical creation beyond eclecticism's pragmatic blending of procedures. To take a culinary metaphor, the eclectic selects among several dishes to constitute a meal; the integrationist creates new dishes by combining different ingredients.

A corollary to this distinction, rooted in theoretical integration's early stage of development, is that current practice is largely eclectic; theory integration represents a promissory note for the future. In the words of Wachtel (1991, p. 44):

The habits and boundaries associated with the various schools are hard to eclipse, and for most

Table 16.2 Eclecticism versus Integration

ECLECTICISM	INTEGRATION
Technical	Theoretical
Divergent (differences)	Convergent (commonalities)
Choosing from many	Combining many
Applying what is	Creating something new
Collection	Blend
Applying the parts	Unifying the parts
Atheoretical but empirical	More theoretical than empirical
Sum of parts	More than sum of parts
Realistic	Idealistic

of us integration remains more a goal than a constant daily reality. Eclecticism in practice and integration in aspiration is an accurate description of what most of us in the integrative movement do much of the time.

We now examine one exemplar of theoretical integration and one of technical eclecticism—namely, Paul Wachtel's **integrative psychodynamic-behavior therapy** and Arnold Lazarus's **multimodal therapy**.

Integrative Psychodynamic-Behavior Therapy
A Sketch of Paul Wachtel

Paul L. Wachtel (1940–) authored the 1977 classic, *Psychoanalysis and Behavior Therapy: Toward an Integration*, that many believe ushered in an era of sophisticated attempts at theoretical integration. He was formally trained at the graduate and postgraduate levels in psychoanalytic psychotherapy and operated largely from this traditional perspective in his early years, but gradually incorporated behavioral and systemic perspectives into his practice.

An early integrative influence was John Dollard, who taught Wachtel his first psychotherapy course at Yale and was his first therapy supervisor, and who coauthored *Personality and Psychotherapy: An Analysis in Terms of Learning, Thinking, and Culture* with Neil Miller in 1950. This seminal contribution went beyond translating psychoanalytic concepts into behavioral language to synthesizing ideas about neuroses and psychotherapy from the two perspectives in order to create a more unified theory. Dollard and Miller's (1950, p. 3) objective—"The ultimate goal is to combine the vitality of psychoanalysis, the rigor of the natural science laboratory, and the facts of culture"—anticipated Wachtel's own substantial body of work.

His 1977 integrative classic began, ironically, in an effort to write an article portraying behavior therapy as "foolish, superficial, and possibly even immoral" (p. xv). But in preparing his article he was forced for the first time to look closely at what behavior therapy was and to think carefully about it. When he observed some of the leading behavior therapists of the day, including Joseph Wolpe and Arnold Lazarus, much to his astonishment he realized that the particular version of psychodynamic therapy toward which he had been gravitating dovetailed to a surprising extent with what a number of behavior therapists were doing. Wachtel's experience in this regard reminds us that isolated theoretical schools perpetuate caricatures of other positions, thereby avoiding basic changes in viewpoint and expansion in therapy practice. Integration typically occurs only after "desegregation" and interaction occur.

Wachtel found many sources of dissatisfaction with standard psychoanalytic therapy and several strengths in behavior therapy. Psychoanalysis overemphasized the causal role of early experiences, overplayed the role of insight as the agent of change, undervalued the process of extinction as a major source of change, and devoted insufficient attention to the role of social skills. Behavior therapy introduced the possibility of active intervention, highlighted the role of context in determining human behavior, and emphasized empirical validation of procedures. The psychodynamic influence has remained considerable in his thinking, so much so that he still occasionally describes his approach as integrative psychodynamic therapy or integrative relational therapy (Wachtel, 2008). But the compatibility of his interpersonal version of psychodynamic therapy with the social-learning version of behavior therapy is the distinctive feature of his theoretical integration.

Wachtel continues to expand and articulate his integration in his positions as distinguished professor of psychology at the City University of New York, cofounder of the Society for the Exploration of Psychotherapy Integration (SEPI), and workshop leader on several continents. The scope of his perspective has been enlarged by incorporating explicitly relational therapies (Wachtel, 2008) and broader systemic forces (*The Poverty of Affluence*, 1989, and *Family Dynamics in Individual Psychotherapy* with Ellen Wachtel, 1986). His evolution toward a more seamless integration has been aided by his explorations into *Therapeutic Communication* (2011b) and what transpires *Inside the Session* (2011a), the titles of his most recent books which demonstrate that our language as therapists is inevitably a form of intervention.

Theory of Personality and Psychopathology

The centrality of anxiety is a common emphasis of both the psychoanalysts and the behaviorists. To be sure, there are major differences between the two viewpoints in formulating and treating anxiety. But these differences can be recognized as complementary, rather than contradictory. Bridges can be built to connect the chasms that separate them. Moreover, by distinguishing between the original assumptions of psychoanalysis and behavior therapy and their evolving practice, more commonalities can be discovered. These are Wachtel's (1977, 1997) integrative strategies.

What is particularly characteristic of the psychoanalytic perspective is its emphasis on the persisting influence of certain childhood wishes and fears despite later experiences that might be expected to alter them. Repression prevents the desire or fantasy from "growing up," from changing over the course of development.

This is the timeless unconscious or, as Wachtel (1977) calls it, the **woolly mammoth view of psychopathology**—once trapped in ice, it stays perfectly preserved forever. This classical Freudian view of the role of the past in present functioning presents a major obstacle to any effort to reconcile the psychoanalytic and behavioral approaches. But if one reevaluates the conception of the historical dimension in creating the neurosis, then more behavioral explanations (and interventions) of anxiety can be employed. Wachtel tries to do precisely this in arguing against the woolly mammoth view. We are not unalterably frozen in time; we do modify and act on the original fantasy and wishes.

Must neurosis be locked-in remnants of the past that can be changed only by gradually uncovering layer after layer of intrapsychic structure? Or can the presence of these primitive inclinations be accounted for by the way the patient is currently living? And might these inclinations change if the way of living is changed? By arguing in the affirmative to the latter two questions, Wachtel offers an active and interpersonal alternative to classic psychoanalytic thought. It draws heavily on the formulations of Karen Horney, Harry Stack Sullivan, and Erik Erikson. In contrast to the psychoanalytic metaphor of treatment as peeling an onion, Wachtel views it as a blooming rose—an unfolding and self-creating process.

The primitive demands that are seemingly unresponsive to reality turn out, on closer inspection, to be responsive to reality and not to be completely cut off from the ego's perceptual contact with reality. That is why helping people to change the way they live can lead to changes in these seemingly out-of-touch-with-reality intrapsychic attitudes.

An anxiety-ridden, 30-year-old chef whose mother had died when he was an infant had a clinging, passive-dependent relationship with his wife. He looked to her to tell him what to wear, what to eat, what to cook, and what to do in his spare time. This pattern had been tolerable until they had their own children. Now with two young ones hanging on her, the wife was increasingly impatient with what she called her "third child." He was panicky that she was pushing him away, criticizing his clinging, and demanding that he grow up and share the parenting. Was his problem buried deep within his oral-stage psyche with a schema of women who would abandon him unless he held on for dear life? Or was his problem apparent in his repeated pattern of clinging to his wife for parenting and nurturing? The answers are located in the parallel between the client's unresolved intrapsychic conflicts and his current interpersonal behaviors.

Conflicts that dominate a person's life can be understood as following from, as well as causing, the way he or she lives. Intrapsychic conflicts create problematic behavior; problematic behavior creates intrapsychic conflicts. This ongoing etiological process is known as **cyclical psychodynamics**. A person's meek and self-denigrating lifestyle, for instance, may be caused by repressed rage. But a meek and self-denigrating lifestyle may also generate rage. It's a vicious, self-perpetuating cycle. The patient's current way of living both stems from and simultaneously perpetuates his or her problems.

But how are these connections, these continuities, between past and present to be construed? The traditional psychoanalytic imagery is archaeological—layer after layer of residue in hierarchical fashion. The traditional behavioral view emphasizes the conditioning process of generalization from one event to another. The connection between past and present lies in the cyclical re-creation of interpersonal events. To invoke Piaget's notion of **schema**, we assimilate new experiences into older schemata—more familiar ways of viewing and thinking about things. New people and new relationships thus tend to be approached in terms of their similarity to earlier ones.

The core of neurosis is the anxiety invoked and maintained by the client's cyclical psychodynamics. A young woman presents for therapy with a developmental history filled with enormous conflict over sexual activity. This internal conflict has led to intense anxiety over sexual relationships and inhibitions in learning the social skills involved in approaching an individual who interests her. She is caught in a vicious cycle in which intrapsychic conflicts generate anxiety over sexual arousal, which then leads to avoidance of sexual situations. Hence, she is awkward and ineffective in speaking with possible dates; hence, her anxiety intensifies over sexual arousal. Such a cyclical pattern, repeated countless times, is likely to be far more responsible for her current fear of dating and sex than exotic symbolic representations of her anxiety that finally "emerge" in her psychoanalytic sessions.

Therapeutic Processes

That interpersonal events perpetuate neurosis implies a need for active intervention on the part of the therapist in order for neurotic patterns to change. Cyclical psychodynamics value direct intervention in the patient's day-to-day problems in living. Wachtel moves away from the psychoanalytic notion that interpretation is the "pure gold" of psychotherapeutic interventions and from the largely unsupported claim that lifting repression and imparting insight will automatically give way to behavior change. Interpretive efforts aimed at insight into origins or even current motives are but one of many ways of disrupting the destructive circle of events.

The immediate therapeutic implication is, in the title of a published collection of Wachtel's (1987) essays, to combine **action and insight**. Actions and insights are mutually facilitative; ways of understanding clinical phenomena that exclude one or the other are not fully satisfactory. "To put it differently, who we are cannot be separated from what we do; fundamental personality change requires fundamental change in how we handle the events of our daily lives" (Wachtel, 1987, p. vi). It is not a matter of action or insight, or of one first and then the other, but of both together.

True to the spirit of Wachtel's message of synergy among the processes of change, we will consider together his use of the action process of counterconditioning and the insight process of consciousness raising.

The Therapist's Work

The integrative psychodynamic-behavioral therapist adopts both dynamic and behavioral methods. Dynamically, much of the interpretive work is similar to that of the psychodynamic therapists, as presented in Chapter 3. Behaviorally, much of the counterconditioning and skills training is akin to that of behavior therapists, as summarized in Chapter 9. But putting them together produces a synergistic integration, an emerging whole, superior to either alone.

In the treatment of a self-diagnosed case of test anxiety, Wachtel (1991) combined systematic desensitization, imagery, and insight-oriented work to help John overcome his anxiety. The cyclical psychodynamic perspective led the therapist to see as relevant, and as part of a larger pattern, a number of features of John's experience of a licensure test. His concerns about status and humiliation led him to avoid studying and to treat the exam lightly. This, in turn, produced additional anxiety brought on by the unacknowledged sense of being underprepared and by failures on previous administrations of the test. The failures, in turn, heightened his test anxiety and further threatened his status, leading to still further avoidance and more compensatory actions to appear cavalier about the entire matter.

The therapist attended, sometimes alternately and sometimes simultaneously, to John's concerns about status, his shame about those concerns, his need to expose himself to the test-taking cues that generate anxiety, his behavioral avoidance, his study habits, and several other considerations in a complex weave of interventions. Insights from "psychoanalytic" exploration informed the process of systematic desensitization and the metaphors for the imagery procedure, and the results of these two "behavioral" procedures fueled new and deepened insights.

Such a seamless integration of two historically rival theories requires another type of therapist work: building bridges across the chasm that separates psychoanalysis and behaviorism and piercing the stereotypes that obscure commonalities between them. Quite apart from acquiring the technical competencies to conduct each form of therapy, the integrative therapist must complete the arduous mental work of finding the perspectives complementary, not contradictory.

Consider the behavioral methods of systematic desensitization and assertiveness training. Although there are real differences between psychodynamic treatment and systematic desensitization, they are not as hard and fast as typically thought (Wachtel, 1977). If one looks past the rhetoric to what experienced behavior therapists actually do, there are some striking similarities.

Gradual exposure to increasingly threatening images and fantasies characterizes both behavioral and dynamic work. It is usually impossible to proceed directly to the original occurrence of the symptom. Even if one could recapture it, such a direct assault on the target exerts little therapeutic effect. Rather, Freud found that he had to proceed gradually and systematically back from recent occasions until the original event was finally recalled and tolerated. This is, conceptually and methodologically, very similar to systematic desensitization. Under the rubric of "dosing the anxiety," "timing of interpretations," and "allowing the patient to set the pace," dynamic therapists are trained to create conditions just like systematic desensitization. "Wild analysis" and "flooding"—in which clients are confronted prematurely with repugnant images—are frowned on. Psychoanalysts and behaviorists, then, emphasize in practice the same effective components of relaxation, gradual approach, exposure to anxiety cues, and client willingness to trust the therapist and explore fears.

Similarly, endorsement of the essential components of assertion training are shared by behaviorists and psychodynamicists—if they choose to openly examine each other's practices. Patient deficits are identified, in-session "training" is provided, therapist modeling and patient rehearsal are emphasized, and then gradual entries into the real world are encouraged. Assertiveness training becomes in vivo desensitization.

In recent years, Wachtel (1997, 2008) has extended cyclical psychodynamics to the relational world. This extends treatment from the largely intrapsychic world of clients to the larger context in which they live. A fuller, richer therapy results from bringing significant others into the consulting room, employing systemic methods, and facilitating action in the real world.

The tasks of the cyclical psychodynamic therapist, in summary, are to employ interventions traditionally associated with psychoanalytic, behavioral, and relational/systemic approaches, and to do so in a manner that renders them mutually facilitative and their effects synergistic. Both technical competence and integrative commitment are required to meld insight and action.

The Client's Work

Although some psychotherapists find the integrative burden too onerous, clients typically accept the combination of action and insight quite naturally. Conflicts and inhibitions that typically are at the core of the patient's problems lead regularly to behavioral deficits, and patients, as a rule, are interested in both understanding the origins of their difficulties and taking concrete steps to correct them. Probably the only special expectation in cyclical psychodynamics is that patients, with the guidance of the therapist, repeatedly translate insight into action and action into insight. Beyond this, the client's work at any moment will depend specifically on the nature of the "behavioral" or "psychodynamic" intervention.

Therapeutic Content

The cyclical psychodynamic approach was developed to integrate the concepts and methods of diverse perspectives into a coherent view. The theoretical synthesis tries to encompass a full range of observations addressed by its contributory sources and to provide a context for a wide range of clinical interventions (Wachtel et al., 2005). As an integrative effort, the approach does not prescribe specific or unique therapeutic content. Rather, it is a new way of looking at, and working with, clinical phenomena in a more inclusive fashion.

The recurrent content, if one can call it that, is the pervasive role of **vicious cycles** in initiating and maintaining anxiety. Cyclical psychodynamics places emphasis not on the fixation of traumatic experiences but on the vicious cycles set in motion by those experiences and on the ways those cyclical patterns persist into the present. This emphasis on circular processes, both intrapsychic and interpersonal, provides a key to bringing together the individual psychodynamic and family systems approaches (Wachtel & Wachtel, 1986) and to integrating the characterological emphasis of psychoanalytic approaches and the situational emphasis of behavioral approaches (Wachtel, 1977).

Therapeutic Relationship

Psychotherapy is, first and foremost, a human relationship (Wachtel, 1990). The cultivation of the real relationship and analysis of the transference speak to Wachtel's psychodynamic underpinnings, but his interpersonal and integrative variant departs from traditional psychoanalytic perspectives in important ways, principally in the need for more active intervention.

To use Wachtel's (1983, 1987) phrase, "You can't go far in neutral." The classic psychoanalytic stance is limited by therapeutic neutrality and the attendant avoidance of prescriptive action. Minimal intervention typically begets minimal change. The dangers involved in "muddying the waters of transference" and in "contaminating the field" are outweighed by the lost opportunities for creative and direct intervention.

A positively affirmative stance and behaviorally active relationship are required. The therapeutic relationship is both a precondition of change and a process of change and, depending on the presenting problem, perhaps also as a content to be changed (such as shyness). Empathy, genuineness, and respect are combined with in-session behavioral methods and with between-session homework.

The prevailing emphasis on neutrality in some psychotherapeutic camps has also incurred Wachtel's (1983) wrath because many interpretations are unwittingly cast in an accusatory or destructive manner. In *Therapeutic Communication*, he provides principles of respectfully and collaboratively conveying information to the patient.

In the treatment of John's test anxiety, discussed previously, the inquiry into his status concerns—concerns that were initially disavowed—began by addressing his parents' concerns and proceeded only gradually to inviting John to explore his own conflicts in that area. That exploration was undertaken in a way that enabled John to examine those concerns in a manner that permitted him to maintain his self-respect. The path toward acknowledging and assuming responsibility for those concerns led initially through an early disavowing of responsibility (it was his parents' hang-up). This strategy of enabling people to recognize and take responsibility for their experiences by initially placing the responsibility elsewhere is known as **externalization in the service of the therapy**. It is one of several relationship strategies to ensure that interpretations and information enhance, rather than diminish, the client's self-esteem and the therapeutic alliance.

Practicalities

As an integrative perspective, as opposed to a distinct school of psychotherapy, cyclical psychodynamics has relatively little to say about the practicalities of learning and conducting psychotherapy. The typical duration of treatment is longer than a pure behavior therapy but shorter than a pure psychodynamic treatment. Cyclical psychodynamic perspective is not opposed to briefer treatments because it is compatible with and encourages more active interventions. In particular circumstances, time-limited versions have been undertaken, although the course of treatment is typically more than a year (Wachtel et al., 2005).

The approach has been almost exclusively applied to individual, outpatient treatment of neurotic disorders, although the underlying principles have also been applied to family contexts and social criticism. Wachtel's approach is compatible with the adjunctive use of medications to relieve symptoms and is well suited to inviting the cast of characters in the patient's life in for occasional conjoint therapy sessions (Wachtel et al., 2005).

Effectiveness

The clinical experiences of Wachtel and other psychoanalytic practitioners attest to the value of blending more active, behavioral observations with psychodynamic psychotherapy. There is also a significant body of research, largely in social and developmental psychology, that supports the tenets of cyclical psychodynamics, including expectancy effects, self-fulfilling prophecies, and disconfirmation of expectations (Wachtel et al., 2005). However, controlled research and comparative outcome studies on this therapy have not been conducted.

By contrast, outcome research on other forms of psychotherapy integration has been conducted in recent years. A review (Schottenbauer et al., 2005) finds that many different integrative therapies have substantial empirical support, defined as four or more controlled studies. These are acceptance and commitment therapy (Chapter 11), cognitive analytic therapy (Chapter 10), dialectical behavior therapy (Chapter 11), emotion-focused therapy (Chapter 6), eye movement desensitization and reprocessing (EMDR; Chapter 8), mindfulness-based cognitive therapy (Chapter 11), multisystemic therapy (Chapter 12), systematic treatment selection (discussed later in this chapter), and transtheoretical therapy. The latter therapy has been described as "the most thoroughly tested model" of integration (Glass et al., 1992, p. 17) and will be reviewed in Chapter 17. These integrative therapies have been empirically shown to be effective in that they outperform no therapy and placebo therapy, but have not been shown to be superior (or inferior) to conventional, single-theory treatments, with a few exceptions.

What is impressive is the dramatic progress in outcome research on psychotherapy integration of late. What is even more impressive is that these theoretical integrations, once deemed as heretical and impossible, are now widely embraced by psychotherapists of diverse orientations. The fact that these integrative therapies are now claimed by pure-form therapies as their own is a testament to the growing acceptance of integration, a movement fueled by Wachtel's groundbreaking work.

Multimodal Therapy
Sketch of Arnold Lazarus

Arnold A. Lazarus (1932–) approached technical eclecticism from the behavioral tradition, quite a different origin from that of Wachtel. Lazarus was born, raised, and educated in South Africa, where he earned his PhD in 1960 from the University of Witwatersrand in Johannesburg under the tutelage of the behavior therapy pioneer Joseph Wolpe (Chapter 9). Lazarus's dissertation, "New Group Techniques in the Treatment of Phobic Conditions," examined the effectiveness of systematic desensitization in groups and employed objective measures for assessing phobic avoidance.

Although his early training and practice were in behavior therapy, his treatment results and follow-up studies showed that behavioral interventions produced impressive headway but the gains were often not maintained. As early as the late 1950s, Lazarus (1956, 1958) emphasized that problems are best tackled within a broad-spectrum frame of reference and called for a synthesis of various psychoeducational, psychotherapeutic, and pharmaceutical measures. In 1967, he briefly propounded the virtues of technical eclecticism (as opposed to theoretical integration) and specifically recommended the addition of cognitive interventions to the behavioral armamentarium. By this time, he was forcibly distinguishing his broad-spectrum behavior therapy from narrow-band behavior therapy (Lazarus, 1966, 1971a).

But even extending behavior therapy with cognitive methods proved incomplete and unsatisfactory for Lazarus. Scrutiny of his case notes revealed that clients with situational crises or circumscribed problems obtained positive results, but people suffering from obsessive-compulsive disorders, panic attacks, addictions, and other self-destructive tendencies did not. The search for additional interventions led him past behavior and cognition to imagery, sensory, and affective domains.

As a result, in 1973 Lazarus introduced a distinctive approach termed *multimodal* therapy to emphasize comprehensive coverage of all the modalities. His evolution from a pure behavior therapist to an eclectic therapist continues to this day, as he incorporates new techniques into the multimodal repertoire and as he experiments with such notions as matching his therapeutic stance to the individual needs of the client.

Previously located at Stanford, Temple, and Yale universities, Lazarus found a permanent home at the Graduate School of Applied and Professional Psychology at Rutgers University, where he now holds the title of distinguished professor emeritus. His scholarly output is prolific: more than 250 articles and chapters and 18 books, including his classic *The Practice of Multimodal Therapy* (1981/1989a). He offers workshops throughout the world and, in national surveys, is regularly cited by his peers as one of the most influential psychotherapists. He also directs the Lazarus Institute in Princeton, New Jersey. His interpersonal charisma, inculcated in his early South African/English upbringing, and his feisty temperament, forged in his early boxing experiences, coalesce into a powerful and persuasive voice for technical eclecticism.

Theory of Personality and Psychopathology

Predictably, the multimodal theory of personality is broad and inclusive. We are the products of a complex interplay of our genetic endowment, social-learning history, and physical environment. Genetics play a large role in the etiology of mood and schizophrenic disorders. The social-learning triad—classical conditioning, operant conditioning, and vicarious conditioning/modeling—accounts for some disorders, but the majority of clinical disorders seem to emanate from perceived associations rather than actual conditioning. Departing from a pure behavioral perspective toward a more phenomenological and cognitive viewpoint, Lazarus reminds us that people rarely respond automatically to the out there (external stimuli), but respond instead to the in here (internal cognitions) representations of stimuli. While recognizing the existence of a multitude of forces in personality development, the multimodal position underscores the impact of the biological substrate and of learning history broadly conceived.

In matters of personality, we should subscribe to **Occam's razor**—entities should not be multiplied unnecessarily and the simplest of competing theories is preferred. We do not have to look beyond several factors that shape and maintain human personality: associations and relations among events; modeling and imitation; nonconscious processes; defensive reactions; private events; metacommunications; and physical thresholds (Lazarus, 1997). But even here, we do not require a precise, accurate explanation of personality and psychopathology to remedy them.

By the same token, multimodal therapy views psychological disturbances as resulting from numerous, poorly understood influences. Psychopathology is typically a product of one or more of the following: conflicting or ambivalent feelings, misinformation, missing information, maladaptive habits, biological dysfunctions, interpersonal inquietude, negative self-acceptance, external stressors, and existential concerns (Dryden & Lazarus, 1991; Lazarus, 1989b, 2005).

Consider the apparently simple case of specific phobias. The psychoanalytic view, as demonstrated in Freud's well-known study of phobic 5-year-old "Little Hans," holds that phobias nearly always have unconscious significance and usually result from the displacement of hostile or erotic impulses. The behavioral view, as exemplified by Watson and Rayner's (1920) case of the 11-month-old "Little Albert" rendered fearful of furry objects, holds that phobias nearly always have their origins in conditioning and are usually compounded by subsequent avoidance behavior.

The psychological formulations embodied in the benchmark cases of Little Hans and Little Albert are insufficient for multimodal therapy. The dichotomy between the psychoanalytic and behavioral views has retarded clinical progress. More complex conceptualizations and multimodal treatments are required for phobic—and other—behavioral disorders (Lazarus, 1991).

Multimodal therapy, characteristic of eclecticism, is principally concerned with remediating psychopathology, not with explaining it. Behind every technical eclectic is a vague or inclusive theory of personality. We now turn to the content and process of change, a shift in clinical attention that eclectics heartily endorse.

Therapeutic Content

A central premise of multimodal therapy is that patients are troubled by a multitude of specific problems that should be remedied with a similar multitude of specific techniques. Unlike psychotherapists in some other systems, the multimodal therapist neither dictates the particular content to be treated nor forces the client's problems onto a **Procrustean bed**. (You may recall that Procrustes was the legendary Greek innkeeper who placed unsuspecting guests onto a single-sized bed and then trimmed or stretched guests to fit the bed.) Rather, the task of the multimodal therapist is to comprehensively and systematically assess the patient's specific deficits and excesses.

The multimodal assessment template is the **BASIC I.D.**:

B = Behavior
A = Affect
S = Sensation
I = Imagery
C = Cognition
I = Interpersonal relationships
D = Drugs/biology

This acronym serves to target the content for psychotherapy and to guide the therapist in selecting specific and effective interventions for each. All modalities but one can be dealt with directly in treatment. Affect (emotion) can only be worked with indirectly because one cannot elicit or change emotions directly. Affect can be accessed and treated only through behavior, sensation, imagery, cognition, interpersonal relationships, and drugs/biological processes. Although many people seek psychotherapy because they feel bad, the multimodal position is that the most elegant and thorough way of reducing distress is to eliminate the dysfunctional patterns on the other modalities.

Therapeutic Processes

In many systems of psychotherapy, the change processes drive the selection of the therapeutic content. That is, the *how* of therapy determines the *what* of therapy. In multimodal therapy, by contrast, the patient's problems, as cataloged through the multimodal assessment on each domain of the BASIC I.D., in large part determine the change processes to be employed. For this reason, we have departed from our usual chapter outline to address therapeutic content first and therapeutic processes second.

The technical eclecticism of multimodal therapy leads to a wide array of mechanisms of change. The specific mechanisms operating in a given case depend on the selected techniques, which in turn depend on the patient's particular problems. Cutting across all patients and problems, some of the main hypothesized mechanisms of change include the following:

- *Behavior:* Positive reinforcement; negative reinforcement; counterconditioning; extinction; stimulus control
- *Affect:* Acknowledging, clarifying, and recognizing feelings; abreaction
- *Sensation:* Tension release; sensory pleasuring
- *Imagery:* Coping images; change in self-image
- *Cognition:* Cognitive restructuring; heightening awareness; education
- *Interpersonal relationships:* Modeling; developing assertive and other social skills; dispersing unhealthy collusions; nonjudgmental acceptance
- *Drugs/biology:* Identifying medical illness; substance-abuse cessation; better nutrition and exercise; psychotropic medication when indicated

This partial listing of change mechanisms in multimodal therapy overlaps to a great extent with the 10 processes of change discussed in Chapter 17. Feedback, education, corrective emotional experiences, stimulus control, self-liberation, counterconditioning, reevaluation, and contingency management are all prominently represented (although Lazarus does not always use these exact terms).

Missing are social liberation and dramatic relief, the two change processes least frequently employed across the psychotherapies (see Chapter 17). But even here, Lazarus has on occasion reported techniques in his published case histories that incorporate these processes—empowering patients and referring them to organizations devoted to advocating for their social rights in the case of social liberation and promoting intense and draining catharsis in the case of dramatic relief.

Rather than redundantly summarizing here all the change processes used by multimodal therapists, we refer you to the previous chapters in which the respective processes have been defined and illustrated. Counterconditioning and contingency management are most expertly handled by the behavior therapists, cognitive restructuring by the cognitive therapists, helping relationships by the person-centered therapists, and so on. This is in keeping with the multimodal maxim of borrowing any clinical technique from any theoretical framework when it might prove effective in a particular case.

The Client's Work

The work of the client, like that of the therapist, depends to a large degree on the nature of the problem and on the type of techniques employed. The treatment is personalized and goal directed, the person being the client (not the therapist) and the goals largely those of the client. If imagery is one of the techniques selected, then the patient will be instructed in deep relaxation, visualize the scene, relay the experiences to the therapist, and collaborate on some visualization scenes to practice between sessions. If assertiveness training is mutually selected as the **treatment of choice**, then the client will be asked to engage in active role-playing, perhaps purchase and read an assertion book, and attempt homework assignments prior to the next appointment.

Multimodal therapy is an active and comparatively demanding therapy, but it should be far less demanding on the client than on the therapist (Dryden & Lazarus, 1991). The skillful clinician will pace treatment according to the capacities and objectives of the individual client. Clients typically don't feel overwhelmed, but some therapists do.

The Therapist's Work

When properly executed, a day of multimodal therapy is mentally and behaviorally exhausting for the clinician. Psychotherapists who offer the same clinical techniques and relationship stances to virtually all of their patients have it comparatively easy. But customizing all these elements, in each and every case, demands additional energy and considerable competence.

The therapist begins by obtaining information from initial interviews and a multimodal life history inventory (Lazarus & Lazarus, 2005). This information leads to the creation of a **modality profile**—essentially, a BASIC I.D. chart listing the patient's problems by modality. If more information is desired or if treatment impasses occur, then a second-order BASIC I.D. assessment will be performed.

In addition to the modality profiles, another multimodal assessment procedure is the use of **structural profiles**, which are quantitative ratings across the BASIC I.D. Seven-point ratings (1 being the lowest and 7 the highest) are made by clients on each modality; for Behavior, to take the first one, clients are informed "Some people may be described as doers—they are action oriented, they like to busy themselves, get things done, take on various projects" and then asked "How much of a doer are you?" These ratings are then depicted on a graph.

Having compiled this clinical information, the multimodal therapist proceeds, in consultation with the patient, to select the therapeutic procedures and postures indicated for this particular case. Obviously, the therapist's work will depend on the type of procedures and postures elected. A "Glossary of Principal Techniques" employed in multimodal therapy (Lazarus, 1989a) contains no fewer than 39 interventions—and those are only the *principal* ones! The therapist's tasks in implementing Gendlin's (1981) focusing technique as opposed to, say, paradoxical strategy or thought blocking will be quite different indeed.

The primary basis for technique selection is outcome research attesting to that technique's effectiveness. The treatment of bulimia, for example, usually calls for a structured and active program of therapy that involves response prevention and cognitive restructuring. However, the technique must be accommodated to the idiosyncratic characteristics of each individual. If response prevention proves unsuccessful or unacceptable to the patient, then the empty-chair technique or imagery or literally dozens of other interventions will be considered. Selecting a therapy technique is a science, but implementing it is an art.

In working with a young woman who had developed a cat phobia after watching a grisly television program in which feline monsters were possessed by the devil, Lazarus (Dryden & Lazarus, 1991) initially opted for standard desensitization. It is an extensively researched procedure of having the client relax while visualizing cats in the distance getting closer and closer to her. But in this case it did not work. Lazarus recalled a specific technique drawn from neurolinguistic programming (NLP) that seemed relevant, even though he considers NLP to be theoretically unsound and scientifically untenable. The technique consists of imagining the feared object and shrinking it down to a tiny little size that you can then crush. In this case, the technique fit the patient perfectly, and it worked splendidly. As a technical eclectic, Lazarus could employ an NLP technique without subscribing to the entire theory behind it.

To summarize: The work of the multimodal therapist is to conduct a multimodal assessment, determine the treatments of choice, and customize the therapeutic relationship to the needs of that particular client.

Therapeutic Relationship

Multimodal therapy regards the patient–therapist relationship as the soil that enables the techniques to take root, not as the principal means to the end (Lazarus & Fay, 1984). In this respect, multimodal clinicians, like their behavioral colleagues, view the therapeutic relationship as a precondition of change in practically all cases and as a content to be changed in only those cases in which specific interpersonal styles (such as assertion deficits or anger excesses) are identified as problematic in the interactions between the patient and therapist. A warm, caring relationship is the context for change, but only rarely the central process of change. Far more often, patients require alleviation of maladaptive behaviors, faulty cognitions, and other problems throughout the BASIC I.D. with skills training.

Lazarus (1991, 1993) has been particularly critical of the notion that genuine empathy, therapist congruence, and positive regard are the necessary and sufficient conditions for constructive personality change, as Rogers (1957) suggested. For one thing, the empirical research supports neither the necessity nor sufficiency of these facilitative conditions (see Chapter 5). For another thing, offering the identical, unitary (or unimodal) therapeutic relationship to all clients flies in the face of a personalized, custom-made psychotherapy. In Lazarus's (1993, p. 404) words: "They [militant client-centered therapists] do not stop to consider when, and under what circumstances, and with whom, a focused didactic or pedagogic stance should be employed, or when a sphinx-like guru might be made to order." And: "How is it that one of the first things we all learn in Psychology 101 is that individual differences are paramount, that everyone is unique, but when it comes to treating patients, some seem to assume that they all come from identical molds?" (p. 406).

The multimodal therapist modifies his or her participation in the therapeutic process in order to offer the most appropriate relationship for that particular client, as opposed to fitting the person to the treatment. The notion of the **authentic chameleon** is often invoked. A flexible repertoire of relationship styles and stances is required to suit different client needs and expectations. This would include the therapist's level of informality or formality, the degree to which the therapist discloses personal information, the extent to which the therapist initiates topics of conversation, and in general, how often to be directive, supportive, or reflective. "The only don'ts to which we subscribe are (1) Don't be rigid and (2) Don't humiliate a person or strip away his or her dignity" (Lazarus, 1989b, p. 129).

The markers that guide the clinician's interpersonal stances are the client's readiness for change, treatment preferences, and resistance level (Lazarus, 1993). In treating a young woman who was exceedingly timid and offended by loud and pushy people, for instance, he would almost whisper and be excessively polite. But in dealing with a middle-aged woman who described herself as "a wife, mother, homemaker, and part-time legal secretary in that order," he would respond with friendly banter and jesting.

Consider his recollection (Lazarus, 1993, p. 405) of his first session with a challenging, brusque woman, who looked him up and down upon entering his office:

Patient: Why do you have graves outside your office?

Lazarus: (surprised and responding in Rogerian style) I have graves outside my office?

Patient: Look outside the window, dummy!

Lazarus: (looking outside his office window to the two new flower beds which had been installed alongside the front walk) Well, since you ask, I have just buried one of my clinical failures in one grave and the other is earmarked for you if you turn out to be an uncooperative client.

Different relationship stances but all apparently therapeutic for the clients involved. The authentic chameleon changes color and blends into various contexts, but no creature has an infinite range of different hues and shades. If the therapist's style differs markedly from the patient's expectations, positive results are unlikely. When the multimodal therapist is unable or unwilling to match relationship stances to individual clients, a referral is indicated.

The flexibility of relational styles in therapy also applies to relationships outside of therapy. Lazarus (Lazarus & Zur, 2002) maintains that thoughtfully crossing certain nonsexual boundaries with patients can have positive and healing impacts. If invited, he might play a game of tennis with a client or attend a client's party—a move that frequently solidifies positive feelings about the therapy and its outcome. Practitioners who follow a rigid rulebook of proscriptions (as laid down by many licensing boards) might fail to provide the basic humanity from which their clients can gain a sense of genuine acceptance and self-affirmation.

Practicalities

It is decidedly difficult to generalize about a personalized psychotherapy that seeks to tailor-make psychological treatment for each unique patient. The recurrent answer to questions about the length, format, and cost of multimodal therapy is "It depends" (Dryden & Lazarus, 1991).

The length of multimodal therapy tends toward brief. With patients experiencing disorders of moderate severity, the average length seems to be about 30 sessions—more or less; it depends. On the opening page of his book on brief multimodal therapy, Lazarus immediately "cuts to the chase"—an appropriate line given his topic—and inquires: "Anyone can offer brief therapy, but is it possible to provide a course of short-term but comprehensive psychotherapy? My explicit answer is 'Often, yes.'" (Lazarus, 1997, p. 1). His concise multimodal formula begins, first, with determining whether there are significant problems in each of the BASIC I.D. modalities. Second, in concert with the client, select three or four pivotal problems that require specific attention. Third, if so indicated, have the patient receive a physical examination and psychotropic medication. Fourth, whenever possible, apply evidence-based methods to the specific problems.

Effective brief therapy depends far less on the hours you put in than on what you put into those hours. Trying to accomplish more with less places significant demands on the eclectic clinician to rapidly identify problems, cultivate a therapeutic relationship, and intervene with specific methods. This description probably applies to all brief therapies in general, but definitely applies to brief multimodal therapy in particular.

More than most psychotherapy systems, the multimodal approach employs and combines different formats—individual, couples, family, group—with various populations—inpatients, outpatients, children, and older adults. Specialized sex therapy and pharmacotherapy are also offered, as indicated in a given case, relatively often.

Following from technical eclecticism, clinical training should cull effective methods from many sources. This demands that the therapist be continually on the lookout for efficacious procedures, independent of their theoretical heritage, and that the therapist be aware of the research on psychotherapy outcome. More demanding still, the multimodal therapist is committed to acquiring competence in a wide array of clinical techniques and relationship stances. Mentally and emotionally exhausting indeed!

Fascination with abstruse theories undermines the breadth of effective eclectic therapy. Psychoanalytically inclined trainees, for one example, spend too much time exploring mental conflicts rather than promoting action. Family systems aficionados are prone to see the entire forest but not the individual trees. And rigidly cognitive trainees, for a final example, continue to dispute, challenge, and explain when getting nowhere instead of switching modalities. Flexible pragmatism is the key to effective treatment.

Training is available from many systematic eclectics, as well as several multimodal therapy institutes around the country. Personal therapy is not mandatory except in those instances in which the therapist's personal problems are likely to interfere with accurate assessment and effective treatment.

Effectiveness

A couple of outcome studies and several dissertations have examined the effectiveness of multimodal therapy. In the Netherlands, a treatment outcome study involved 84 inpatients suffering from anxiety disorders, the vast majority of whom had received prior treatment without success. Multimodal therapy resulted in substantial improvement and durable 9-month follow-ups (Kwee, 1984; Kwee & Kwee-Taams, 1994). In Scotland, a controlled outcome study on children with learning disabilities compared multimodal treatment to less integrative approaches. The results favored the multimodal therapy (Williams, 1988).

Lazarus himself has conducted several follow-up inquiries on patients receiving multimodal treatment, finding that durable outcomes are in direct proportion to the number of modalities deliberately traversed. It is a multimodal maxim that the more a client learns in psychotherapy, the less likely he or she is to relapse.

The few controlled studies on the effectiveness of multimodal therapy are supportive, but not definitive. Multimodal therapy tries to incorporate state-of-the-art research findings into its open framework, in contrast to yet another system of psychotherapy. But whether scanning the field for better treatment methods increases the clinician's effectiveness remains an open empirical question.

In broader strokes, the outcome research on eclectic psychotherapy comes in three guises. First

and most generally, the entire body of empirical research on psychotherapy informs eclectic treatment selection. A genuine advantage of being an eclectic is the vast amount of research attesting to the efficacy of psychotherapy and pointing to its differential effectiveness with certain types of disorders and patients. Of course, this research only translates into improved outcomes if the psychotherapist is aware of, and adheres to, the research conclusions. Eclectic therapists were early and noisy proponents of evidence-based practice (see Chapter 18).

Second, some controlled outcome research has been conducted on psychotherapy crudely characterized as "eclectic" or "mixed." A comprehensive review of the adult literature (Grawe et al., 1998) located 22 controlled studies covering 1,743 patients treated with diverse therapies described as eclectic: either explicitly no school connection or multiple combinations of methods. In 9 of the 13 comparisons, the eclectic therapy outperformed the control treatment in terms of symptom relief and in 4 of the 6 comparisons in terms of subjective well-being. A comprehensive meta-analysis of the child literature (Weisz, Weiss, et al., 1995) located 20 controlled studies on mixed treatments, which produced a respectable effect size of 0.63 compared to control conditions, a moderate to large effect. The interpretative problem, however, is that we possess little understanding of what these multifarious treatments represent. Perhaps the only conclusions that can be reliably drawn are that coherent "eclectic" and "mixed" psychotherapies outperform no treatment and that these treatments are insufficiently compared to other systems of psychotherapy.

A corrective strategy would be to assess whether more complex and integrative treatments outperform simpler and single-theory treatments. One clever meta-analysis did just that (Stevens et al., 2007). In 14 studies, more complex therapies were compared with less complex treatments. The effect size for the complex therapies was slightly higher (0.15), which translates into an increase in improvement rates from 66% to 81%.

Third and more specifically, ongoing programmatic research supports the effectiveness of a disciplined eclecticism that prescriptively matches different treatments to different people. An exemplar of **prescriptive matching** is Larry Beutler's **systematic treatment selection** (Beutler & Clarkin, 1990; Beutler & Harwood, 2000; Beutler et al., 2005). All the patient qualities that predict differential effectiveness have not yet been determined, but considerable research conducted by Beutler and colleagues indicates that certain patient characteristics point to certain treatments, which if applied, enhance the success of psychotherapy. Different folks need different strokes.

For example, matching therapist directiveness to the client's degree of resistance improves therapy outcome. In 80% of the studies, clients presenting with high resistance benefit more from self-control methods and minimal therapist directiveness, such as motivational interviewing (Chapter 5). By contrast, clients with low resistance benefit more from therapist directiveness and explicit guidance. This strong, consistent finding can be expressed as a large effect size averaging 0.76 (Beutler, Harwood, Michelson, et al., 2011). The clinical implication is to match the level of therapist's directiveness to the patient's level of resistance.

For another example, research has investigated matching treatment to the patient's coping style. Research been devoted primarily to the externalizing (impulsive, stimulation-seeking, extroverted) versus the internalizing (self-critical, inhibited, introverted) coping styles. A meta-analysis of 12 studies, involving more than a thousand patients, revealed a medium effect (0.55) for matching therapist method to patient coping style (Beutler, Harwood, Kimpara, et al., 2011). Specifically, interpersonal and insight-oriented therapies are more effective among internalizing patients, whereas symptom-focused and skill-building therapies are more effective among externalizing patients. This pattern is frequently known for child patients—say, a depressed internalizing girl versus a hyperactive externalizing boy—but less well known for adult patients.

These and other research-supported prescriptive matches can improve the effectiveness of psychotherapy. How directive should a therapist be? Which treatment approach—insight-oriented or symptom-focused—works better? In the integrative tradition, it depends upon the particular client.

Criticisms of Integrative Therapies
From a Psychoanalytic Perspective

Wachtel's integrative psychodynamic-behavioral therapy only has the first half right. His insistence on adding behavioral interventions bespeaks his impatience with the necessarily gradual alteration in deep intrapsychic conflicts. If he seriously expects us to employ behavioral methods, then he must definitely demonstrate, in repeated clinical cases, that their addition contributes anything over and above what we achieve with psychodynamic therapy alone. Keep the original faith!

Lazarus is a cognitive-behaviorist, pure and simple. His methods are too active, too technical, and too dismissive of intrapsychic conflicts and insight-oriented contributions. He delights in bashing classic psychoanalysis in his writings and workshops. Enough said; see our criticisms of cognitive and behavior therapies for details.

From a Cognitive-Behavioral Perspective

Wachtel's integrative psychodynamic-behavioral therapy only has the second half right. His insistence on retaining psychoanalytic metapsychology bespeaks his acceptance of inefficient means to alter learned behavioral problems. If he seriously expects us to employ psychodynamic methods, then he must definitively demonstrate, in controlled outcome studies, that their addition contributes anything over and above what we achieve with behavior therapy alone. Make a clean break with the psychoanalytic psychobabble!

Lazarus anticipated our future early on by augmenting narrow-band behavioral procedures with cognitive techniques. But by contemporary standards, he is a cognitive-behavioral therapist in the guise of a technical eclectic. Take away the BASIC I.D. assessment template and the structural profiles, and you have a self-professed empiricist in the social-learning tradition. Welcome home, Arnie!

Eclecticism usually means that therapists beg, borrow, and steal from the leading systems of psychotherapy. Eclectics rarely create new therapeutic interventions or theoretical constructs. To the extent they are creative at all, it is in the way they put together their bag of tricks rather than in creating new concepts that others can borrow. More controlled research and clinical specificity are needed. We applaud the general thrust of combining the most effective techniques without regard to their theoretical parentage, but the proof of the pudding is in the eating. Keep cooking, and call us when you have something worth consuming.

From a Humanistic Perspective

In title and deed, a psychodynamic-behavioral hybrid disregards humanistic contributions. Combining two theories is barely integrative. We are open to combining theories and methods, but any genuine integration must undoubtedly embrace at least portions of the third force of humanistic psychology.

For us, psychotherapy is an encounter between two people in a helping relationship; for Lazarus, psychotherapy is more a technical enterprise. His clients disappear in his case presentations, partitioned into segments by the BASIC I.D. and then repaired in segments with precise surgical interventions. Nowhere do we have a sense of the person of the client, of how the segments fit together or what sort of functioning whole they constitute (Davis, 1990). The therapeutic relationship is the constant bedrock of our work, but Lazarus's "authentic chameleon" sounds as valid as a genuine phony.

From a Cultural Perspective

As each psychotherapeutic door opens, another closes. There are always trade-offs in the service of psychotherapy integration. In recommending action along with psychic exploration, Wachtel closes off some avenues to deeper meaning and intention. In bringing cognitive and emotional factors into the behavioral purview, Lazarus reduces his appeal to measurable objectives and environmental contingencies (Messer & Winokur, 1980).

Integration also brings with it another problem. A clinical technique is not a disembodied procedure that can be incorporated wholesale from one context to another without consideration of its psychotherapeutic surround. Does an effective technique in one psychotherapy system lose something in the translation and transportation into another system? Does it take on different nuances of meaning and intention in the new context? Would not much of the outcome research on a technique in the previous context need to be reconducted on its effectiveness in the new context? Most contextualists think so (Messer, in Lazarus & Messer, 1991).

Although we applaud Wachtel and Lazarus for conducting couple/family therapy and for recognizing systemic forces, there is little appreciation of culture-sensitive and gender-aware issues in the integration movement (Ivey & Brooks-Harris, 2005). You want psychotherapy integration? Then find methods to integrate the oppressed and disenfranchised into the wealthy resources of our society. That will solve some real problems. Otherwise, you are only including theories and techniques while excluding major groups of people.

A Multimodal Analysis of Mrs. C

Complex cases such as Mrs. C's require a comprehensive and individualized psychotherapy. The breadth and multitude of her problems make her an ideal candidate for the multimodal approach.

We begin by constructing a modality profile that identifies specific excesses and deficits on the client's BASIC I.D. Throughout therapy, we will return to this profile, a list that directs therapeutic interventions and enables ongoing evaluation of treatment. At the beginning of therapy, most of the BASIC I.D. information will be obtained from the initial interview and from the Multimodal Life History Inventory completed by the client before her second interview.

These give rise to a detailed modality profile, which would include the following:

- *Behavior:* Compulsive washing; not cooking and caring for children; physically unkempt; tends to withdraw and isolate herself; avoids dirt
- *Affect:* Anxiety (especially in the presence of dirt and disarray); depression; underlying and unexpressed anger; fear of being institutionalized; periodic hopelessness
- *Sensation:* Out of touch with her body; nervous; panicky if prevented from washing or in the presence of dirt
- *Imagery:* Vivid pictures of parental censure and paternal control; images of pinworms contaminating the C family; pictures herself being hospitalized; "going crazy" when unable to engage in rituals
- *Cognition:* Intrusive thoughts about pinworms; dictatorial demands about cleanliness; perfectionistic; catastrophic thinking; "I'm hopeless and might as well kill myself"
- *Interpersonal relations:* Excessive attempts to control others; marital tensions; avoids sexual encounters; withdrawn from most friends; alienates her children and their friends; resorts to compulsive rituals when confronted
- *Drugs/biology:* Probably out of shape; no mention of regular exercise; may require medication for depression and anxiety

The life history questionnaire would also probably indicate that Mrs. C favors an aggressive, action-oriented therapy that can save her marriage and avoid hospitalization at the state psychiatric facility. Let us presume she responds that her first treatment goal is to reduce her washing time and her related avoidance of dirt. Her expressed preferences and the modality profile—not the therapist's predilections or a global diagnosis of obsessive-compulsive disorder—furnish a blueprint for personalized treatment.

When a client such as Mrs. C experiences problems in almost all spheres of functioning, the more modalities therapy can impact, the more positive will be the outcome. With such deeply entrenched disorders, it is doubtful that Mrs. C would recover to her premorbid level of functioning without a broad-based program.

Where to start? With a problem to which the client accords high priority and for which we have demonstrably effective interventions. The research indicates that her affect, imagery, and behavior problems evoked by pinworms and dirt can best be remedied through a combination of response prevention and systematic desensitization followed by in vivo desensitization. First, Mrs. C will be trained in deep relaxation that she can apply during her anxious moments. She can practice the relaxation response at home with audiotapes. Once this is achieved, we will create hierarchies composed of stimuli related to dirt and pinworms. Part of a hierarchy would include, for example, imagining buying brand-new underwear wrapped in cellophane, followed by touching brand-new underwear, then approaching freshly laundered underwear, and moving toward picking up underwear that are basically clean though worn. Mrs. C will be able to actually approach dirty underwear and limit her washing time only after her anxiety is no longer elicited because it has been counterconditioned by desensitization. With this newfound relaxation response at her disposal and with increasing confidence in her behavioral control, she will begin, step by step, to reduce the amount of time she spends in her daily shower.

Having curtailed her anxiety and attendant rituals, we move on to her irrational cognitions. The available research and Mrs. C's preferences

(continued)

point to cognitive therapy as the treatment of choice. A self-help book devoted to identifying and disputing cognitive distortions, such as *Don't Believe It for a Minute! 40 Toxic Ideas That Are Driving You Crazy* (Lazarus et al., 1993), would be recommended as a homework assignment between therapy sessions. Mrs. C's lowered self-esteem and assertion deficits would suggest a therapeutic relationship characterized by support, empathy, and collaboration.

After several months of weekly or biweekly hardworking therapy sessions, Mrs. C is slowly coming alive behaviorally and cognitively. But her other modalities are still impaired, and we will probably tackle them simultaneously—ever alert to the client's preferences and expectations, of course. Her paucity of sensual sensations and avoidance of sex can best be treated with sensate focusing, followed by the progressive steps of sexual therapy. Didactic information, perhaps in the form of readings from Masters and Johnson's books, will be used to counteract the myths she has inherited from her parents. Some of the sex therapy will occur in the context of conjoint marital sessions, which will also address her controlling style of family interactions. We can experiment with family assertiveness training to help other family members stand up to Mrs. C's unreasonable demands and also to help her express her frustrations more directly.

Depending on her response to the foregoing interventions, we will certainly consider the possibility of a referral for an antidepressant medication, which research has found useful with many patients suffering from similar problems. This is especially true if she is unable to learn deep relaxation or respond to cognitive therapy.

Multimodal therapy, then, will combine the most efficacious psychotherapeutic, didactic, and pharmacological interventions available for this patient in this situation. We try to impact across multiple modalities in helping her acquire a variety of constructive coping responses. If Mrs. C desensitizes herself to dirt, learns to use the relaxation response and realistic thinking as alternatives, asserts herself when angry, and pleasures herself and her husband, she will gradually return to a more rewarding life. In place of obsessive ruminations fostered by passive psychoanalytic musings, Mrs. C will acquire healthier functioning fostered by active, multimodal interventions.

Future Directions

By most accounts, one or more variations of psychotherapy integration will represent the psychotherapeutic Zeitgeist of the 21st century. The confluence of forces that has propelled the integration movement in the past, reviewed earlier in this chapter, will continue to exert enormous pressure toward intertheoretical cooperation and integrative treatment. More than 90% of training programs already expose their students to a specific integrative therapy, with multimodal, common factors, and the transtheoretical model leading the packs (Lampropoulos & Dixon, 2007). Managed care's limitations on insurance reimbursement and the demand for evidence-based practices—arguably the most radical changes ever in the funding of mental health services—will favor short-term, integrative, and prescriptive practice.

Time-limited treatment and psychotherapy integration are definitely simpatico. Virtually every form of brief therapy advertises itself as active in nature, collaborative in relationship, and eclectic in orientation (Hoyt, 1995). Integration is one response to the ascendancy of brief therapies and the resultant pressure to do more (and better) in 6 or 12 sessions with a variety of clientele. Brief therapy and integrative therapy share a pragmatic and flexible outlook that is quite opposite from the ideological one that characterized the previous school domination in the field (Omer, 1993).

The theoretical integrationists and technical eclectics diverge slightly at this juncture as to how the integrative trend will manifest itself. Integrationists predict increasing consolidation of psychotherapy systems, a closer alliance between research and practice, and incorporation of findings from cognitive science and neuroscience. We shall also see continued reliance on research findings in creating integrative approaches and continued consciousness raising about integration for those who working within a single orientation. While maintaining their respective theoretical identities, more psychotherapists will acknowledge the limitations of their own paradigms and will experiment with other methods, thus becoming "de facto integrationists" (Goldfried & Castonguay, 1992, p. 8).

Technical eclectics predictably foresee that the limitations of theoretical integration will be more fully realized in the future and that specific treatments of choice for particular clinical disorders will become standard practice. Lazarus, echoing the aims of many eclectics, hopes that the term "psychotherapy integration" will become redundant and meaningless. As a body of essential knowledge for psychotherapists becomes identified, there should be no competing theories. Evidence-based methods will be taught in all respectable schools, and outcome-informed treatments will be routinely implemented for many disorders. Psychological therapies will be matched increasingly not only to clinical diagnosis but also to transdiagnostic client variables, such as resistance level, coping style, stages of change, and cultural considerations.

Two intertwined challenges will confront psychotherapy integration in the near future. First, the ever-expanding hybrid of cognitive-behavior-acceptance therapies will rival and perhaps overtake the popularity of integrative/eclectic therapies. The addition of the third wave (Chapter 11) to traditional CBT has made it more attractive and complete to many clinicians, leading to direct competition with integration. Second, the integrative

movement prizes theoretical and methodological pluralism, but some prominent scientist-practitioners find all of the pluralism a bit messy and unnecessary. Instead, David Barlow and associates (2010) believe a unified treatment protocol will prove preferable to the loosely organized integrative therapies.

The **Unified Protocol** incorporates the common principles of CBT present in all evidenced-based protocols for specific emotional disorders, and focuses on four core strategies: becoming mindfully aware of emotional experience; reappraising rigid emotion-laden cognitions; preventing behavioral and emotional avoidance; and facilitating exposure to both internal and situational cues associated with emotional experiences. Although integrative in one respect, in another respect it obviously favors the commonalities among cognitive-behavior-acceptance therapies.

As integration matures, it will invariably become "institutionalized" and possibly reified as yet another competing therapy school instead of the open system it was intended to be. Whether or not integration can successfully navigate between the perils of haphazard syncretism, on the one side, and the dangers of ideological institutionalization, on the other, will largely determine its enduring contribution to psychotherapy.

Key Terms

action and insight
allegiance effect
authentic
    chameleon
BASIC I.D.
change process
common factors
cyclical
    psychodynamics
Dodo bird verdict

externalization in the
    service of the
    therapy
integrative
    psychodynamic-
    behavior therapy
modality profile
multimodal therapy
Occam's razor
prescriptive matching

Procrustean bed
psychotherapy
   integration
schema
structural profiles
syncretism
systematic treatment
   selection

technical eclecticism
theoretical integration
therapist effects
treatment of choice
Unified Protocol
vicious cycles
woolly mammoth view
   of psychopathology

Recommended Readings

Beutler, L. E., & Harwood, T. M. (2000). *Prescriptive psychotherapy: A practical guide to systematic treatment selection.* New York: Oxford University Press.

Corey, G. (2012). *The art of integrative counseling* (3rd ed.). Belmont, CA: Brooks/Cole.

Duncan, B. L., Miller, S. D., Wampold, B. E., & Hubble, M. A. (Eds.). (2010). *The heart and soul of change* (2nd ed.). Washington, DC: American Psychological Association.

Lazarus, A. A. (1989). *The practice of multimodal therapy* (rev. ed.). Baltimore: John Hopkins University Press.

Lazarus, A. A. (2006). *Brief but comprehensive psychotherapy: The multimodal way* (2nd ed.). New York: Springer.

Norcross, J. C., & Goldfried, M. R. (Eds.). (2005). *Handbook of psychotherapy integration* (2nd ed.). New York: Oxford University Press.

Wachtel, P. L. (1977). *Psychoanalysis and behavior therapy: Toward an integration.* New York: Basic.

Wachtel, P. L. (1997). *Psychoanalysis, behavior therapy, and the relational world.* Washington, DC: American Psychological Association.

JOURNALS: *Evidence-Based Mental Health; Online Journal of Multimodal & Rational-Emotive Behaviour Therapy; Integrative Psychiatry; Journal of Psychotherapy Integration; Journal of Unified Psychotherapy and Clinical Science* (e-journal).

Recommended Websites

Heart & Soul of Change Project:
   http://heartandsoulofchange.com/
International Center for Clinical Excellence:
   http://centerforclinicalexcellence.com/
Lazarus Institute:
   www.thelazarusinstitute.com
Society for the Exploration of Psychotherapy Integration (SEPI):
   http://sepiweb.org/
Systematic Treatment Selection:
   www.larrybeutler.com/systematic-treatment-selection/

CHAPTER 17

Comparative Conclusions
Toward a Transtheoretical Therapy

The transtheoretical model begins with a comparative analysis of the major systems of psychotherapy within the integrative spirit of seeking the best that each has to offer. As you read—and as we wrote—the preceding chapters, we recognized that each psychotherapy system contains brilliant insights into the human condition.

Each system provides a coherent and compelling construction for understanding human function and dysfunction, once we accept its core assumptions. Most of the systems are inspiring and, we hope, encourage deeper exploration of the theory and its methods. Applying each system to the same complex case of Mrs. C indicates how differently and yet convincingly each can explain and treat the same troubled individual. All of the systems provide practical insights that can be useful within an integrative model of therapy.

Each psychotherapy system also has its shortcomings, however. Most are more rational than empirical in construction. None consistently demonstrate in controlled research a superior ability to predict how people respond in psychotherapy or a superior ability to help people change as a result of psychotherapy. Even when we encountered the apparently superior effectiveness of cognitive, behavioral, and systemic therapies, we soon discovered that such claims were tempered by the investigator's allegiance effect. Many systems focus on theories of personality and psychopathology (*what* to change) rather than processes of change (*how* to change). And, of course, with the exception of the integrative therapies, none of the psychotherapy systems provide templates for the integration of profound insights and beneficial methods from diverse therapies into a more comprehensive model of behavior change.

The net result is an acute confrontation with the dilemma of choosing the type of psychotherapist we might become or the type of psychotherapist we might consult. What further structure can we provide for such a diverse, if not chaotic, discipline?

For starters, we must realize that the way we structure and integrate psychotherapy cannot at this time depend entirely on scientific research. No single system of psychotherapy has cornered the market on effectiveness. As seen throughout this book, research has revealed only a few robust differences in outcome among the evaluated mainstream therapies; "Meta-analytic research shows charity for all treatments and malice towards none" (London, 1988, p. 7). Nor can a purely rational analysis of the theoretical morass provide a definitive answer. At this point in the development of clinical knowledge, the manner in which we integrate psychotherapy systems is largely an imposition of our own intellectual and ethical development.

In this chapter, we introduce two perspectives for understanding the intellectual and ethical development of an integrative theory. We then review the core dimensions of the transtheoretical model—the processes, stages, and levels of change—and apply them to the systems of psychotherapy covered in this book. The transtheoretical relationship, the effectiveness of transtheoretical therapy, and criticisms of it are addressed. Finally, we provide a transtheoretical analysis of Mrs. C and report on the outcome of her psychotherapy.

Developmental Perspectives
Perry's Model

Given the pluralistic nature of knowledge, dedicated individuals will structure knowledge according to their cognitive development. Let us apply William Perry's (1970) model of intellectual and ethical development to the personal view that we are likely to take toward the diverse theories of psychotherapy.

Based on longitudinal research on the intellectual and ethical development of undergraduates, Perry (1970) derived a cognitive stage theory. He identified nine different stages, each representing a qualitatively different mode of thinking about the

nature of knowledge. As several of Perry's stages are primarily transitional, we will focus only on the four stages that represent the most contrasting structures that students impose on knowledge. These four stages of intellectual and ethical development can be summarized as follows:

Dualistic → Multiplistic → Relativistic → Committed

Dualists

In the dualistic stage, the world is seen in polar terms: right/wrong, truth/falsehood, good/bad. Dualistic students are likely to expect that in this chapter the authors as authorities will reveal which single theory of therapy is correct. Dualistic students view themselves as receptacles eagerly waiting to receive the truth.

Dualistic therapists believe they have had the truth revealed to them. Dualists are the true believers who think that a particular therapy system is correct and all others are in error. Research evidence is of little interest because the true system of psychotherapy is already assumed to be known, and research would only document the obvious.

Dualistic therapists can be found in any system of psychotherapy. True-believing psychoanalysts, behaviorists, or humanists are the result not of the structure of their theoretical system, but rather of the structure of their own intellects.

Multiplists

As students develop, they come to accept the diversity and uncertainty in an area such as psychotherapy. At first, the diversity is seen as unwarranted confusion that comes from poorly qualified authorities. "Psychotherapists don't know what the hell they're doing" may be a common complaint of these students. Later, diversity and uncertainty are seen as legitimate, but only as temporary in the development of our knowledge.

The multiplistic therapist thinks that at some point in the future a particular theory of therapy will be proved correct. Multiplists are the true bettors who are convinced that investing their energies in one therapy will pay off in the future when it is eventually proven to be correct.

Relativists

Students in the relativistic stage of intellectual development view knowledge as disconnected from the concept of truth and absolute correctness. Diversity and uncertainty are not temporary; the very nature of knowledge is that it is contextual and relative. The truth about therapy is that it is pluralistic, with a variety of valid alternatives. Relativists are the true eclectics.

The validity of psychotherapy systems is relative to particular issues. Some eclectics see the form of therapy as relative to a patient's specific disorder or symptoms; they would select the best treatment for, say, depression or bulimia. Other therapists see the utility of therapy systems as relative to the patient's personality, whereas others assume that the value of any therapy is relative to the therapist's personality. Other eclectics see the treatment of choice as relative to the client's values, so that they match therapy to values or preferences.

Given the relativistic nature of knowledge, the eclectic thinks that no single psychotherapy theory will ever be found to be the best or the most correct. Some developing psychotherapists find this **relativism** to be tremendously disconcerting. The old guidelines of right/wrong and true/false are lost, and the therapist can face an alienating experience of being lost and alone in a chaotic world of psychotherapy. Such therapists are usually judged to have a low tolerance for ambiguity, although more accurately they have a low tolerance for relativity. The ensuing existential anguish and sense of alienation can precipitate a retreat to the more secure stages of dualism or multiplism.

Although the relativism of eclecticism is a respectable scholarly position, one problem is that the psychotherapist is an activist, not only a

scholar. Seeking to prescriptively match psychotherapies with disorders, personalities, or values is truly an important task of our time. But what does the relativistic therapist do when confronted with a particular patient in need of assistance? The evidence is not always available on which therapies work best with which types of problems or patients. So for now the eclectic is frequently left with decisions on the basis of clinical experience, much of which may well be fact, but some of which is surely folly.

Given the knowledge explosion, does anyone seriously believe that any individual can expect to master all the available theories and techniques of psychotherapy? Many therapists who reach the stage of intellectual relativism begin to comprehend the necessity of personal commitment.

Committed Therapists

The dilemma for the ethical psychotherapist is maintaining intellectual integrity while committing to a personal approach without the security of research evidence in all situations. Realizing that the empirical evidence is not always convincing and that there is little consensus on doing psychotherapy, the clinician is free to make a commitment to a theoretical system that is based on an ethical position—a position of values. The ethical therapist moves beyond the realm of knowing to the realm of acting by affirming, "This is the approach to humanity that I would love to see valid, and I commit myself to trying to validate it." An ethical commitment brings with it a passion to master the particular therapy, to improve it, and to evaluate it.

The ethical therapist is not a dogmatic absolutist. The commitment flows out of an undeniable relativism and entails a humility that derives from the awareness that other therapy systems may be equally valid for other individuals. The psychotherapists prepared to refer clients to other treatments when it is apparent that the client is not progressing or not committing to the therapist's valued approach.

By contrast, the dualistic therapist will work to convert the client in the name of truth, righteousness, and all that is good.

Committed therapists form a community of dedicated professionals who realize that, at this point in our intellectual development, the questions we share are more important than the answers we give. That is, they are centrally concerned with questions of what is the best way to be in psychotherapy; what is the most valuable treatment we can provide for our clients, our colleagues, and our students; and how can we help our clients attain a better life. As intellectual relativists, we know we cannot provide absolute answers to such questions. We value the fact that colleagues are committed to actualizing other alternatives that we ourselves have not chosen.

Werner's Model

Werner's (1948; Werner & Kaplan, 1963) organismic-developmental theory is also instructive for conceptualizing psychotherapists' development of a mature integrative stance (Kaplan et al., 1983; Rebecca et al., 1976). In the first of three developmental stages in learning new information, one perceives or experiences a global whole, with no clear distinctions among component parts. All systems of psychotherapy are uncritically grouped into the catchall category of "therapy." Unsophisticated laypersons and untrained undergraduates probably fall into this category.

In the second stage, one perceives or experiences differentiation of the whole into parts, with a more precise and distinct understanding of components within the whole. Obsessive comparisons and precise contrasts among psychotherapy systems are prized. However, one no longer has a perspective on the whole, and consequently loses the big picture. Many psychotherapy courses, textbooks, and educated practitioners fall into this category.

In the third stage, the differentiated parts are organized and integrated into the whole at a higher level. Here, the unity *and* the complexity of psychotherapy are appreciated. Both the valuable differences and the essential similarities among the schools are recognized.

The Transtheoretical Model

The transtheoretical model strives to surpass the relativism of eclecticism through a commitment to a higher order theory of psychotherapy that, in Werner's terms, appreciates the unity *and* the complexity of the enterprise. Transtheoretical therapists make an epistemological commitment more than an ethical commitment. The commitment is predicated on the belief that the current relativism can be transcended by discovering or constructing concepts that cut across the traditional boundaries of the psychotherapies. The transtheoretical therapist, then, is a relativist operating on an ethical and epistemological commitment.

In the integrative spirit, we set out to construct a model of psychotherapy and behavior change that can draw from the entire spectrum of the major theories—hence the name **transtheoretical**. We were guided by a number of criteria for the model. First, as we have emphasized throughout this book, a sophisticated integration will respect both the fundamental diversity *and* the essential unity of psychotherapy systems. The valuable and occasionally unique contributions of the major systems of psychotherapy must be preserved; reducing all systems to their least common denominator removes their richness and relevance. Second, the model should emphasize empiricism, in that the fundamental variables must be measurable and validated. Why bother with a new model if it is never tested or if it does not produce more compelling outcomes than those already available? Third, we sought a model that could account for how people change without therapy as well as within therapy, as the majority of people with clinical disorders do not seek professional assistance (Veroff & Douvan, 1981a, 1981b). Fourth, the model should prove successful in generalizing to a broad range of human problems, including physical health as well as mental health problems. Fifth and finally, the transtheoretical model should encourage psychotherapists to become innovators, not simply borrowers from other systems.

The transtheoretical model to which we aspire must provide guiding structures for practice and core principles for a comparative analysis. At the same time, it must remain flexible to encourage therapist choice and to incorporate the addition of new psychotherapy systems and research developments.

Processes of Change

The transtheoretical model rests on three core dimensions—the processes, stages, and levels of change. Let us consider each in turn.

The first dimension involves the **processes of change**. As introduced in Chapter 1, processes are the covert or overt activities that people engage in to alter emotion, thinking, behavior, or relationships related to particular problems or patterns of living. The processes were at first theoretically derived in this book's comparative analysis of systems of psychotherapy (Prochaska, 1979) and were later modified on the basis of empirical research on how people change behavior with or without professional treatment (DiClemente & Prochaska, 1982; Prochaska & DiClemente, 1983). The goal, as Einstein emphasized, is to account for the most facts with the fewest principles.

The following 10 processes of change (defined in Chapter 1) have received the most research support:

- *Consciousness raising (education and feedback)*
- *Catharsis/dramatic relief*
- *Self-reevaluation*
- *Environmental reevaluation*
- *Self-liberation*
- *Social liberation*
- *Counterconditioning*
- *Stimulus control*
- *Contingency management*
- *Helping relationship*

We have suggested in this book that the major psychotherapies diverge much more in terms of the content to be changed than in the processes used to change that content. That is, systems of psychotherapy differ on *what* to change but tend to agree on *how* to change. Divergences in content are a function of the multitude of personality theories rather than of a multitude of change processes.

A summary of the change processes advocated by psychotherapy systems shows more convergence than would appear when we are distracted by the content of therapy. Table 17.1 demonstrates where each of the major therapeutic systems fits according to the salient processes of change.

One thing that becomes quickly apparent from Table 17.1 is that the change process with the greatest agreement is consciousness raising. Compared with other processes of change, twice as many therapies include an expansion of consciousness as a central factor in behavior change. Unless major theorists have really missed the mark, this table indicates that considerable research needs to go into exploring which specific methods are most effective in helping people to process information that was previously outside their awareness.

The transtheoretical analysis embodied in Table 17.1 reveals how much psychotherapy systems agree on the processes producing change (the how) while disagreeing on the content to be changed (the what). In other words, different orientations do not dictate the specific methods to use as much as they determine the therapeutic goals to pursue (Beutler, 1983). A consensus on treatments of choice, then, will be attained only when we agree on the target problem to be treated and on the kinds of evidence to be accepted for successful psychotherapy.

Table 17.1 Summary of Psychotherapy Systems According to the Change Processes Assumed to Be the Essence of Therapy

Consciousness raising

1. *Feedback*
   Psychoanalysis
   Psychoanalytic therapy
   Psychodynamic therapy
   Adlerian therapy
   Existential therapy
   Logotherapy
   Reality therapy
   Person-centered therapy
   Motivational interviewing
   Gestalt therapy
   Rational-emotive behavior
      therapy
   Cognitive therapy
   Transactional analysis
   Communication/strategic
      therapy
   Structural therapy
   Bowenian therapy
   Solution-focused therapy
   Narrative therapy
   ACT
   DBT
   Mindfulness therapy
2. *Education*
   Psychoanalysis
   Adlerian therapy
   Interpersonal therapy
   Logotherapy
   Transactional analysis
   Rational-emotive behavior
      therapy
   Cognitive therapy
   Behavior therapy
   Bowenian therapy
   Feminist therapy
   Multicultural therapy
   Multimodal therapy
   ACT
   DBT

Catharsis

1. *Corrective emotional experience*
   Psychoanalytic therapy
   Person-centered therapy
   Gestalt therapy
   Interpersonal therapy
   Implosive therapy
   Satir's family therapy
   Multicultural therapy
   ACT
   DBT
2. *Dramatic relief*
   Gestalt therapy

Conditional stimuli

1. *Counterconditioning*
   Behavior therapy
   Rational-emotive behavior
      therapy
   Cognitive therapy
   EMDR therapy
   Exposure therapy
   Feminist therapy
   Multimodal therapy
   Solution-focused therapy
   ACT
   DBT
2. *Stimulus control*
   Interpersonal therapy
   Behavior therapy
   Multimodal therapy
   ACT

Contingency control

1. *Reevaluation*
   Adlerian therapy
   Rational-emotive behavior
      therapy
   Cognitive therapy
   EMDR
   Multimodal therapy
   ACT
2. *Contingency management*
   Rational-emotive behavior
      therapy
   Behavior therapy
   Multimodal therapy

Choosing

1. *Self-liberation*
   Adlerian therapy
   Existential therapy
   Logotherapy
   Reality therapy
   Motivational interviewing
   Transactional analysis
   Behavior therapy
   Communication/strategic therapy
   Bowenian therapy
   Feminist therapy
   Multicultural therapy
   Multimodal therapy
   Solution-focused therapy
   Narrative therapy
   ACT
   DBT
2. *Social liberation*
   Adlerian therapy
   Structural therapy
   Feminist therapy
   Multicultural therapy

Therapeutic relationship

Psychoanalytic therapy
Adlerian therapy
Existential therapy
Person-centered therapy
Motivational interviewing
Gestalt therapy
Communication therapy
Structural therapy
Feminist therapy
Multicultural therapy
DBT

Consider the psychological treatment of specific phobias. Freud (1919), the intrapsychic master, stressed that if the psychoanalyst actively induced the patient to expose himself or herself to the feared stimulus, "a considerable moderation of the phobia" would be achieved. This observation predates the contemporary consensus on the superiority of exposure and response prevention in alleviating phobic behavior (see Chapter 8). The existing evidence points to the necessity of reducing phobic anxiety and avoidance through exposure to the feared object; this approach, in its many forms, is considered the treatment of choice (Barlow & Beck, 1984). Freud readily understood the process of reducing phobic behavior, but he decided that the desirable content of psychoanalysis—the therapeutic goal—was to make the unconscious conscious (Norcross, 1991).

The table also reveals that psychotherapy systems have largely ignored the impact of common or nonspecific factors in producing change. Anywhere from 10% to 35% of change can be attributed to expectation or placebo (see Chapter 1 and Lambert, 2004). Our assumption is that the critical process of change in placebo groups is that clients have chosen to change. They have made a commitment to change, as affirmed by their continuing attendance at placebo sessions. The placebo sessions provide a public forum for them to make their commitment known, and a public commitment is more likely to be lived up to than is a private decision.

From this point of view the critical question becomes: Just which change processes do people use to solve their own problems? Psychotherapists should not be so arrogant as to believe that people do not solve psychological problems without professional assistance. One strategy of our research program is to study people who successfully change their behaviors on their own. We will soon see how research on self-changers and therapy changers has enhanced the transtheoretical model.

In fact, our studies indicate that people in the natural environment use many different processes of change to overcome problems (Prochaska et al., 1995). Most psychotherapy systems, however, emphasize only two or three processes. One of our positions is that therapists should be at least as cognitively complex as their clients. They should think in terms of a more comprehensive set of change processes and apply techniques to engage each process when indicated.

Stages of Change

The optimal use of change processes involves understanding the stages of change through which people progress. The stages are the second dimension of change that we discovered empirically.

When we tried to assess how frequently people applied the change processes in self-change and psychotherapy, they kept saying that it depended on what point in the course of change we were talking about. At different points they used different processes. In their own words, our psychotherapy patients and self-change volunteers were describing the phenomena we now call **stages of change**. Stages of change had not been identified in any of the major systems of psychotherapy. These stages are a relatively unique contribution from the transtheoretical model.

The stages represent specific constellations of attitudes, intentions, and behaviors related to an individual's readiness in the cycle of change. They provide a temporal dimension, in that change unfolds over time. Each stage reflects not only a period of time but also a set of tasks required for movement to the next stage. Although the time an individual spends in each stage varies, the tasks to be accomplished are assumed to be invariant.

Change unfolds over a series of six stages: **precontemplation**, **contemplation**, **preparation**, **action**, **maintenance**, and **termination**. If change is initially unsuccessful, then people will recycle back into earlier stages. When change is complete and stable, then termination is reached. What follows is a description of each stage and the tasks to be accomplished to progress to the next stage.

Precontemplation

In this stage, there is no intention to change behavior in the foreseeable future. Many individuals in the precontemplation stage are unaware or under aware of their problems. As G. K. Chesterton once said, "It isn't that they can't see the solution. It is that they can't see the problem." Families, friends, neighbors, or employees, however, are often well aware that the precontemplator has problems. When precontemplators present for psychotherapy, they often do so because of pressure from others. Usually they feel coerced into changing by a spouse who threatens to leave, an employer who threatens to dismiss them, parents who threaten to disown them, or judges who threaten to punish them. They may even demonstrate change as long as the pressure is on. Once the pressure is off, however, they often quickly return to their old ways.

Even precontemplators can wish to change, but this is quite different from intending or seriously considering change in the foreseeable future. Items that are used to identify precontemplation on a continuous stage-of-change measure include "As far as I'm concerned, I don't have any problems that need changing" and "I guess I have faults but there's nothing that I really need to change" (McConnaughy et al., 1983). Resistance to recognizing a problem is the hallmark of precontemplation.

Precontemplators are not considering altering their behavior in the foreseeable future and, as a consequence, engage in little change-process activity. In order to move ahead, they need to acknowledge or "own" the problem, increase awareness of the negative aspects of the problem, and accurately evaluate self-regulation capacities.

Contemplation

In this stage, people are aware a problem exists and are seriously thinking about overcoming it but have not yet made a commitment to take action. On the continuous measure these individuals endorse items such as "I have a problem and I really think I should work on it" and "I've been thinking that I might want to change something about myself." Serious consideration of problem resolution is the central element of contemplation.

The essence of the contemplation stage is beautifully communicated in an incident related by Benjamin (1987). He was walking home one evening when a stranger approached him and inquired about the location of a certain street. Benjamin pointed it out to the stranger and provided specific instructions. After readily understanding and accepting the instructions, the stranger began to walk in the opposite direction. Benjamin said, "You are headed in the wrong direction." The stranger replied, "Yes, I know. I am not quite ready yet." This is contemplation: knowing where you want to go, but not being quite ready yet to go there.

People can remain stuck in the contemplation stage for long periods. In one of our self-change studies, we followed a group of 200 contemplators for 2 years. The modal response of this group was to remain in the contemplation stage for the entire 2 years without ever moving to significant action.

Contemplators, then, are evaluating options. To move forward in the cycle of change, they must avoid the trap of obsessive rumination for years—what we call chronic contemplation—and make a firm decision to begin to take action. These small steps of preliminary action, these "baby steps" lead them into the next stage.

Preparation

The preparation stage combines intention and behavioral criteria. Individuals in this stage are intending to take action immediately and report some small behavioral changes, such as smoking five fewer cigarettes or delaying their first cigarette of the day for 30 minutes longer than precontemplators or contemplators. Although they have made some reductions in their problem behaviors, individuals in the preparation stage have not yet reached a criterion for effective action, such as abstinence from smoking, alcohol, or heroin. They are intending, however, to take such action in the very near future. On a continuous measure, they score high on both the contemplation and action scales.

Like anyone on the verge of momentous actions, individuals in the preparation stage need to set goals and priorities. In addition, they need to dedicate themselves to an action plan they choose. Often they are already engaged in change processes that would increase self-regulation and initiate behavior change.

Action

In this stage, individuals modify their behavior, experiences, and/or environment in order to overcome their problems. Action involves the most overt behavioral changes and requires a considerable commitment of time and energy. Modifications of a problem made in the action stage tend to be most visible and receive the greatest external recognition. People, including professionals, often erroneously equate action with change. As a consequence, they overlook the requisite work that prepares changers for action and the huge efforts necessary to maintain the changes following action.

Individuals are classified as being in the action stage if they have successfully altered a problem behavior for a period of 1 day to 6 months. Successfully altering a problem behavior means reaching a specific criterion, such as abstinence. With smoking, for example, cutting down by 50% or changing to lower tar and nicotine cigarettes are changes that can help prepare people for action, but they do not satisfy the criterion for successful action. On a continuous measure, individuals in the action stage endorse statements such as "I am really working hard to change" and "Anyone can talk about changing; I am actually doing something about it." They score high on the action scale and lower on the scales assessing the other stages of change. Modification of the target

behavior to an acceptable criterion and significant overt efforts to change are the hallmarks of action.

People in the action stage require the skills to use the key action-oriented change processes, such as counterconditioning, stimulus control, and contingency management, to interrupt habitual patterns of behavior and adopt more productive patterns. They become aware of the pitfalls that might undermine continued action, whether these are cognitive (abstinence violation expectations), behavioral (apparently irrelevant decisions), emotional (exacerbation of stress or depression), or environmental (lack of reinforcement or spousal support) in nature. In this way, they will acquire effective strategies to prevent lapses or slips from becoming complete relapses.

Maintenance

In this stage, people work to prevent relapse and consolidate the gains attained during action. Traditionally, maintenance has been viewed as a static stage. However, maintenance is a continuation, not an absence, of change. For chronic problems, this stage extends from 6 months to an indeterminate period past the initial action. For some problems, maintenance can be considered to last a lifetime.

Remaining free of the chronic problem and/or consistently engaging in a new incompatible behavior for more than 6 months is the criterion for the maintenance stage. On the continuous measure, representative maintenance items are: "I may need a boost right now to help me maintain the changes I've already made" and "I'm here to prevent myself from having a relapse of my problem." Stabilizing behavior change and avoiding relapse are the hallmarks of maintenance.

Recycling

As is now well known, most people taking action to change behavior do not successfully maintain their gains on their first attempt. Many New Year's resolvers, for example, report 5 or more years of consecutive pledges before maintaining the behavioral goal for at least 6 months (Norcross & Vangarelli, 1989). **Relapse and recycling** through the stages occur for most individuals as they attempt to modify behavior.

Although psychotherapy is typically effective in the short run, relapse is the most common, long-term outcome in the treatment of addictions and serious mental disorders. In a classic review of outcome literature on alcoholics, heroin addicts, and habitual smokers, relapse curves across these different substances showed a strikingly similar pattern. Within 3 months of treatment completion, nearly two thirds of all patients had relapsed, with a majority of these relapses occurring within the first month following treatment termination (Hunt et al., 1971). Early treatment approaches focused on changing behavior but not necessarily on maintaining those changes over time. This resulted in a "revolving door" or recycling in which treatment completers returned to treatment following each relapse (Roberts & Marlatt, 1998).

Relapse prevention (RP) is self-management training designed to avoid recycling and to enhance the maintenance stage (Marlatt & Gordon, 1985). With skills training as the cornerstone, RP teaches clients how to:

- *Understand relapse as a process*
- *Identify high-risk situations*
- *Learn how to cope with cravings and urges to engage in the addictive behavior*

- *Reduce the harm of relapse by minimizing the negative consequences and learning from the experience*
- *Achieve a balanced lifestyle, centered on the fulcrum of moderation (Roberts & Marlatt, 1998)*

We should note in passing that the accumulating research on RP yields positive findings. A meta-analysis was performed to evaluate the effectiveness of RP in 26 studies representing a sample of 9,504 patients (Irvin et al., 1999). Results indicated that RP was generally effective, certainly more so than no-treatment controls, and particularly effective for alcohol and polysubstance use disorders.

Because relapse or recycling is the rule rather than the exception in behavior change, we found that we needed to modify our original stage model. Initially we conceptualized change as a linear progression through the stages; people were supposed to progress simply and discretely through each step. Linear progression is a possible but relatively rare phenomenon with chronic disorders, such as the addictions, mental disorders, and health conditions

Figure 17.1 presents a spiral pattern of how many people actually move through the stages of change. In this spiral pattern, people can progress from contemplation to preparation to action to maintenance, but many individuals will relapse.

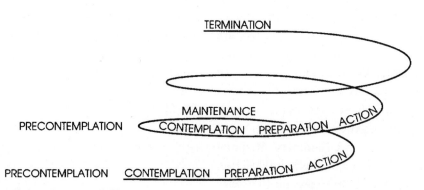

Figure 17.1 The Spiral Pattern of Change

During relapse, individuals regress to an earlier stage. Some relapsers feel like failures—embarrassed, ashamed, and guilty. These individuals become demoralized and resist thinking about behavior change. As a result, they return to the precontemplation stage and can remain there for various periods of time. Approximately 15% of relapsers regress back to the precontemplation stage (Prochaska & DiClemente, 1984).

Fortunately, this research indicates that the vast majority of relapsers—85% of self-changers, for example—recycle back to the contemplation or preparation stage. They begin to consider plans for their next action attempt, while trying to learn from their recent efforts. The spiral pattern suggests that most relapsers do not revolve endlessly in circles and that they do not regress all the way back to where they began. Instead, each time relapsers recycle through the stages, they potentially learn from their mistakes and can try something different the next time around.

Termination

Termination of a problem occurs when a person no longer experiences any temptation to return to troubled behaviors and no longer has to make any efforts to keep from relapsing. Obviously, termination of treatment and termination of a problem are not coincidental. Psychotherapy frequently ends before serious problems terminate entirely. Consequently, it is expected that, for many clinical disorders, patients will return for booster sessions, most often when they feel they may be slipping back from previous gains. Also, because treatment terminates before most problems have reached their termination, clients tend to experience anxiety and distress over the termination of therapy.

Clients in Different Stages

Individuals who seek our professional assistance do not arrive at our doorstep in the identical stage of change. Patients entering treatment

programs at two different outpatient clinics and at a large alcoholism treatment center demonstrated a variety of profiles on the stages-of-change scale (DiClemente & Hughes, 1990; McConnaughy et al., 1989). The type of screening and the particular demands made by the treatment program can influence the numbers of people in different stages who present for help, but it is unlikely that any program would recruit clients only from one stage unless it preassessed stage of change as a selection criterion. For most practitioners and programs, patients represent a heterogeneous group in terms of readiness to change.

A patient's pretreatment stage of change is an important determinant of prognosis. The further along clients are in the stages of change at the beginning of therapy, the more quickly they are likely to progress. When therapy involves two or more clients working together, as in couples treatment, then therapy can be expected to progress most smoothly when each of the clients is at the same stage of change. If one partner is ready for action while the other has not contemplated what change will mean, then treatment will be difficult at best. The therapist is then in the difficult position of being damned by one spouse for moving too slowly or resisted by the other for moving too quickly.

With family therapy, it is almost axiomatic that some of the family members will occupy different stages. Perhaps this is one reason homeostasis as a source of resistance has been such a key concept in systemic perspectives. Getting all family members to the same stage of change at about the same time is no small challenge.

Studies on the Stages

Literally hundreds of published studies have used the stages-of-change measures. We will review here the results of a handful of representative studies on the clinical utility and predictive validity of the stages of change.

The amount of progress clients make during treatment tends to be a function of their pretreatment stage of change. A meta-analysis of 39 studies, encompassing 8,238 patients, found that the stages reliably and robustly predict outcomes in psychotherapy (Norcross et al., 2011). Those beginning in the preparation and action stages do better than those beginning in precontemplation or contemplation. This has been found to be true for brain-impaired patients in rehabilitation programs (Lam et al., 1988), panic-disordered patients receiving antianxiety medication (Beitman et al., 1994), cardiac patients undergoing counseling (Ockene et al., 1992), and Mexican Americans enrolled in community programs for smoking cessation (Gottlieb et al., 1990). This strong stage effect applies immediately following intervention, as well as 12 and 18 months afterward (Prochaska et al., 1993).

In one study, we examined the percentage of 570 smokers who were not smoking over an 18-month period as a function of the stage of change before random assignment to four treatments. The amount of success was directly related to the stage they were in before treatment (Prochaska & DiClemente, 1992). To treat all of these smokers as if they were the same would be naïve; yet that is what we have traditionally done in many treatment programs.

If clients progress from one stage to the next during the first month of treatment, they can double their chances of taking action during the initial 6 months of the treatment. Of the precontemplators who were still in precontemplation at 1-month follow-up, only 3% took action by 6 months; of the precontemplators who had progressed to contemplation at 1 month, 7% took action by 6 months. Similarly, of the contemplators who remained in contemplation at 1 month, only 20% took action by 6 months; of the contemplators who had progressed to the preparation stage at 1 month, 41% attempted to quit by 6 months. These data demonstrate that treatments that help people progress just one stage in a month can double the chances of participants' taking action on their own in the near future (Prochaska & DiClemente, 1992).

Another study (Brogan et al., 1999) demonstrated that the stages of change can predict who remains in psychotherapy. For some time clinicians have known that approximately one quarter of patients prematurely discontinue psychotherapy (Swift & Greenberg, 2012); however, the characteristics of these dropouts have not been reliably known. Premature termination from psychotherapy was predicted using variables traditionally among the best predictors of therapy outcome—client characteristics, such as demographics, and problem characteristics, such as duration and intensity—but these variables had zero ability to predict therapy dropouts. When the stages and processes of change were used, 93% of the premature terminators—as opposed to therapy continuers and early but appropriate terminators—were correctly identified. The stage profile of the 40% who dropped out of therapy was that of precontemplators. The stage profile of the 20% who terminated quickly but appropriately was that of people in the action stage. The stage profile of the therapy continuers was similar to that of contemplators.

A person's stage of change provides prescriptive as well as proscriptive information on the treatment of choice. Action-oriented therapies may be quite effective with individuals who are in the preparation or action stage. These same programs may be ineffective or detrimental, however, with individuals in the precontemplation or contemplation stage.

An intensive action- and maintenance-oriented smoking cessation program for cardiac patients was highly successful for those patients in the preparation and action stages. This same program failed, however, with smokers in the precontemplation and contemplation stages (Ockene et al., 1988). Patients in this special-care program received personal counseling in the hospital and monthly telephone counseling calls for 6 months following hospitalization. Of the patients who began the program in the action or preparation stage, an impressive 94% were not smoking at 6-month follow-up. This percentage is significantly higher than the 66% nonsmoking rate of patients in similar stages who received regular care for their smoking problem. The special-care program had no significant effects, however, with patients in the precontemplation and contemplation stages. For patients in these stages, regular care did as well or better.

Independent of the treatment received, there was a clear relationship between pretreatment stage and outcome. Patients who were not smoking at 12 months included 22% of all precontemplators, 43% of the contemplators, and 76% of those in action or prepared for action at the start of the study.

Integration of Stages and Processes

One of the most powerful findings to emerge from our research is that particular processes of change are more effective during particular stages of change. Thirty years of research in behavioral medicine and psychotherapy converge in showing that different processes of change are differentially effective in certain stages of change. A meta-analysis (Rosen, 2000) of 47 cross-sectional studies examining the relationship of the stages and the processes of change showed large effect sizes (0.70 and 0.80).

The integration of stages and processes of change can serve as an important guide for psychotherapists. Once a patient's stage of change is evident, the therapist would know which processes to apply in order to help that patient progress to the next stage of change. Rather than apply the change processes in a haphazard or trial-and-error manner, therapists can use them in a much more systematic and efficient style.

Table 17.2 diagrams the integration between the stages and processes of change (Prochaska et al., 1995). Specifically, the table shows the change processes used most often during stages of change. Let us now review how this integration can systematically direct psychotherapy.

During precontemplation, individuals use change processes significantly less than people in any other stage. We found that precontemplators process less information about their problems; spend less time and energy reevaluating themselves; experience fewer emotional reactions to the negative aspects of their problems; are less open with significant others about their problems; and do little to shift their attention or their

Table 17.2 Stages of Change in Which Change Processes Are Most Emphasized

STAGES OF CHANGE				
PRECONTEMPLATION	CONTEMPLATION	PREPARATION	ACTION	MAINTENANCE
Consciousness raising Dramatic relief				
	Environmental reevaluation Self-reevaluation			
		Self-liberation		
				Contingency management Counterconditioning Stimulus control

environment in the direction of overcoming their problems. If you don't believe you have a problem, why bother with changing it? In treatment, these patients have been historically labeled resistant or defensive.

What can help people move from precontemplation to contemplation? Table 17.2 suggests that several change processes are most effective. First, **consciousness raising** methods—such as observations, education, and interpretations—can help clients become more aware of the causes, consequences, and cures of their problems. To move to the contemplation stage, clients will become more aware of the negative consequences of their behavior. Often we have to first help clients become more aware of their defenses before they can become more conscious of what they are defending against. Second, the process of **dramatic relief** (or catharsis) provides clients with motivating emotional experiences, such as those used in Gestalt methods like the empty chair. These experiences can release emotions related to problem behaviors. Life events can also move precontemplators emotionally, such as the disease or death of a friend or lover, especially if such events are problem related.

Clients in the contemplation stage are most open to consciousness raising methods, such as feedback, observations, bibliotherapy, and other educational interventions. As clients become increasingly more aware of themselves and the nature of their problems, they are freer to reevaluate themselves both affectively and cognitively. The **self-reevaluation** process includes an assessment of which values clients will try to actualize, act on, and make real, and which they will let die. The more central problems are to clients' core values, the more their reevaluation will involve changes in their sense of self. Contemplators also use **environmental reevaluation**, that is, they deeply consider the effects their behaviors exert on their environment, especially the people they care about most.

Movement from precontemplation to contemplation, and movement through the contemplation stage, involves increased use of cognitive, affective, and evaluative processes of change. To better prepare individuals for action, changes are required in how they think and feel about their problems and how they value their destructive lifestyles.

Preparation indicates a readiness to change in the near future and incorporation of valuable lessons from past change attempts. Preparers are on the verge of taking action and need to set goals and priorities accordingly. They often develop an action plan for how they are going to proceed. In addition, they will make firm commitments to follow through on the action option they choose. In fact, they are often already engaged in processes that would increase self-regulation and initiate behavior change.

Individuals typically begin by taking some small steps toward action. They may use counterconditioning and stimulus control to begin reducing their problem behaviors. Counterconditioning involves substituting healthier alternatives in conditions that normally elicit problems, such as relaxation instead of anxiety or acceptance instead of controlling. Stimulus control involves managing the presence or absence of situations or cues that elicit problems, such as not stopping at a bar after work. Addicted individuals may delay their use of substances each day or may control the number of situations in which they rely on the addictive substances.

As they prepare for the action stage, it is important that clients act from a sense of **self-liberation** or willpower. They need to believe that they possess the autonomy and power to change their lives in key ways. Yet they also need to accept that coercive forces areas much a part of life as is autonomy. Self-liberation is based in part on a sense of **self-efficacy** (Bandura, 1977, 1982)—the belief that one's own efforts play a critical role in succeeding in the face of difficult situations.

The action stage, however, requires more than merely an affective and cognitive foundation. Clients must also be effective with behavioral processes—such as **counterconditioning**, **contingency management**, and **stimulus control**—to cope with those conditions that can coerce them into relapsing. Therapists can provide skills training, if necessary, in behavioral processes to increase the probability that clients will be successful when they do take action.

Successful maintenance builds on each process that has come before, and also involves a candid assessment of the conditions under which a person is likely to relapse. Clients assess their alternatives for coping with such coercive conditions without resorting to self-defeating defenses and pathological responses. Perhaps most crucial is the sense that one is becoming more of the kind of person one wants to be. Continuing to use counterconditioning, contingency management, and stimulus control is most effective when it is based on the conviction that maintaining change maintains a sense of self that is highly valued by oneself and at least one significant other.

To sum up: We have determined that effective behavior change depends on doing the right things (processes) at the right time (stages). Matching the change processes to the patient's stage increases the probability of more successful and seamless psychotherapy.

We have observed two frequent mismatches in this respect. First, some clients (and clinicians) rely primarily on change processes most indicated for the contemplation stage—consciousness raising, self-reevaluation—while they are moving to the action stage. They try to modify behaviors by becoming more aware, a common criticism of classical psychoanalysis: Insight alone does not necessarily bring about behavior change. Second, other clients (and clinicians) rely primarily on change processes most indicated for the action stage—contingency management, stimulus control, counterconditioning—without the requisite awareness, decision making, and readiness provided in the contemplation and preparation stages. They try to modify behavior without awareness, a common criticism of radical behaviorism: Overt action without insight is likely to lead to temporary change (Prochaska, DiClemente, & Norcross, 1992).

Competing systems of psychotherapy have promulgated apparently rival processes of change. However, ostensibly contradictory processes become complementary when embedded in the stages of change. Specifically, change processes traditionally associated with the experiential, cognitive, and psychoanalytic persuasions are most useful during the precontemplation and contemplation stages. Change processes traditionally associated with the existential and behavioral traditions, by contrast, are most useful during the action and maintenance stages.

Research has been highly supportive of the core constructs of the transtheoretical approach and the integration of the stages and processes of change. Longitudinal studies affirm the relevance of these constructs for predicting premature termination and treatment outcome. Comparative outcome studies attest to the value of stage-matched interventions. Population-based studies support the importance of developing interventions that match the needs of individuals at all stages of change (see Prochaska & Norcross, 2002, and Prochaska, Norcross, & DiClemente, 1995, for reviews).

Levels of Change

At this point in our analysis, it may appear that we are restricting our discussion to a single, well-defined problem. However, as we all realize, reality is not so accommodating, and human behavior is not so simple. Although we can isolate certain disorders, these occur in the context of complex, interrelated levels of human functioning. The third core dimension of the transtheoretical approach addresses this issue.

The **levels of change** represent a hierarchical organization of five distinct but interrelated levels of psychological problems that can be addressed in psychotherapy. These levels are:

1. Symptom/situational problems
2. Maladaptive cognitions
3. Current interpersonal conflicts
4. Family/systems conflicts
5. Intrapersonal conflicts

Psychotherapy systems have attributed psychological problems primarily to one or two levels of change and have targeted their methods to these levels. Behavior therapists have focused on the symptom and situational determinants, cognitive therapists on maladaptive cognitions, family therapists on the family/systems level, and psychoanalytic therapists on intrapersonal conflicts. A critical point in treatment occurs when psychotherapists and patients agree on the level to which they attribute the problem and on the level (or levels) they will mutually target to modify the disorder.

What is the key level of content for psychotherapy? The answer depends on the therapist's preferred theory of personality and psychopathology and/or the client's preferred theory of problems. As an integrative model, transtheoretical therapy appreciates the validity of each level. How critical each level is can vary for different clients even when they are presenting with the same disorder.

Consider, for example, three cases of vaginismus, a sexual disorder characterized by the involuntary contraction of the muscles surrounding the vagina when penetration is attempted. Case A recovered by focusing solely on the symptom/situational level and changing the situations under which the couple had sexual relations. Case B, a difficult success, clearly had current interpersonal problems of communication and control that contributed to the maintenance of vaginismus. Case C, a failure, appeared to have critical involvement of family/systems conflicts, with the young woman experiencing her sexuality as still under the control of her mother's rules.

Given five different levels of change, how can psychotherapists proceed systematically across them? In the transtheoretical model, we prefer to intervene initially at the symptom/situational level because change tends to occur more quickly at this more conscious and contemporary level of problems. The further down the hierarchy of levels we proceed, the further removed from awareness and the present the determinants of the problem are likely to be. That is, "deeper" levels involve more unconscious and historical conflicts contributing to the disorder. Thus, the deeper the level that needs to be changed, the longer and more complex psychotherapy is likely to be.

What's more, the further removed in history are the determinants of the problem, the greater the resistance to trying to change those determinants. One of the reasons for increased resistance is that deeper attributions tend to be more threatening to self-esteem than are more surface attributions. It is more threatening, for example, to believe that vaginismus is due to hostility toward a father figure than to believe that the anticipation of painful intercourse elicits fear and involuntary circum vaginal muscle contractions. A transtheoretical guideline is to use the least threatening attributions that can be justified, because our clinical formulations have the potential for producing damage in their own right.

The levels of change, it should be emphasized, are not independent or isolated; on the contrary, change at any one level is likely to produce change at other levels. Symptoms often involve intrapersonal conflicts; maladaptive cognitions often reflect family/system beliefs or rules. In the transtheoretical approach, therapists are prepared to intervene at any of the levels of change, though the preference is to begin at the highest and most contemporary level that clinical assessment and disciplined judgment can justify.

Putting It All Together

In summary, the transtheoretical model advocates for the differential application of the processes of change at specific stages of change according to the identified problem level. In colloquial terms, we have identified the basics of *how* (processes), *when* (stages), and *what* (levels) to change.

Integrating the levels with the stages and processes of change provides a model for intervening hierarchically and effectively across a broad range of therapeutic content.

Three strategies can be employed for intervening across multiple levels of change. The first is that of **shifting levels**. Psychotherapy would typically focus initially on the client's symptoms and the situations supporting the symptoms. If the change processes could be applied effectively at the first level and the patient could progress through each stage of change, psychotherapy could be completed without shifting to a deeper level of analysis. If treating only the situation or symptoms was not effective enough, then therapy would shift to a focus on maladaptive cognitions that are supporting the symptoms. The processes of change would be applied to cognitive content with the goal of progressing through each stage of change. If progress was not sufficient at the cognitive level, then therapy would shift to current interpersonal conflicts. The processes would now be applied at an interpersonal level, with the goal of progressing through each stage of change. The same pattern of successfully progressing through the stages or shifting levels would be followed until the client had sufficiently improved or until the deepest, least conscious, and most resistant intrapersonal conflicts had been analyzed.

The second strategy is to focus on **key levels**. There are certain clear-cut cases in which a high degree of consensual validation would emerge among clinicians regarding the causes of a client's problems. If the available evidence is unambiguous and points to one key level of causality, then the psychotherapist would work first and foremost at this key level of intervention. These cases are relatively easy to formulate once the clinical data are in, though that does not mean that they are necessarily easy to treat.

The third alternative is the **maximum impact strategy**. With complex cases and comorbid disorders, it is sometimes clear that every level is involved as a cause, an effect, or a maintainer of the client's problems. For maximum impact, treatments can be created that engage the patient at each and every level of change. This creates a synergy of change interventions. The maximum impact strategy will be illustrated in the transtheoretical analysis of Mrs. C.

As should now be evident, the length of psychotherapy varies according to both the stage and the level of change, as well as how hard and how well clients work between sessions. Clients who enter treatment prepared to take action can have brief but successful therapies, typically in 6 to 12 sessions. The more defenses patients have to work through and the less successful work they have done before entering treatment, the longer the course of psychotherapy is likely to be, typically ranging from 6 to 24 months.

It follows, then, that clients with problems at the situational and cognitive levels can typically expect comparatively brief treatment. For patients saddled with disorders more deeply embedded in the context of a dysfunctional family of origin or a pathogenic intrapersonal history, psychotherapy will typically take longer. Problems that develop in a current interpersonal relationship are usually of more moderate duration, averaging about 12 months of weekly sessions. Problems that are multilevel in origin usually necessitate longer treatment.

We hope that psychotherapy research will progress to the point where we will know that a specific level of intervention is most effective with particular types of patients afflicted with particular disorders. Research already suggests that about half of the patients with focal phobias can be effectively helped by modifying the situational determinants of their phobias. Research does not suggest, however, what to do with the 50% of phobic patients who drop out or fail to progress at the situational level (Barlow & Wolfe, 1981). Until clear-cut research is available for guiding therapeutic interventions with specific disorders, the transtheoretical model provides an efficient and effective guide for many client presentations.

Theoretical complementarity is the key to integrating the major systems of psychotherapy. Table 17.3 illustrates where leading systems of therapy fit best within the integrative framework of the transtheoretical model. In general terms, the psychoanalytic and experiential psychotherapies

are most useful during the earlier precontemplation and contemplation stages. Existential, cognitive, and interpersonal therapies are particularly well suited to the preparation and action stages. The behavior and exposure therapies, by contrast, are most useful during action and maintenance. Each theoretical persuasion has a place, a differential place, in the "big picture" of behavior change.

Depending on the level and stage we are targeting, different therapy systems will play a more or less prominent role. Behavior therapy and exposure therapy, for example, have developed specific methods at the symptom/situational level for clients who are ready for action. At the maladaptive cognition level, Ellis's rational-emotive behavior therapy and Beck's cognitive therapy are most indicated for clients in the preparation and action stages.

Two prominent psychotherapies missing from Table 17.3 are Carl Rogers's person-centered therapy and multicultural therapy. His system has been most eloquent in articulating and demonstrating the therapeutic relationship as a critical

Table 17.3 Integration of Psychotherapy Systems within the Transtheoretical Model

	STAGES OF CHANGE				
LEVELS	PRECONTEMPLATION	CONTEMPLATION	PREPARATION	ACTION	MAINTENANCE
Symptom/ situational	Motivational interviewing			Behavior therapy EMDR and exposure	
Maladaptive cognitions		Adlerian therapy	Rational-emotive behavior therapy Cognitive therapy Third-wave therapies		
Interpersonal conflicts	Sullivanian therapy	Transactional analysis	Interpersonal therapy (IPT)		
Family/systems conflicts	Strategic therapy	Bowenian therapy		Structural therapy	
Intrapersonal conflicts	Psychoanalytic therapy	Existential therapy	Gestalt therapy		

process of change. Rogers's influence on the transtheoretical approach cuts across the stages and levels of change. Multicultural therapy primarily concerns what content should be addressed in psychotherapy, not how behavior change occurs. Thus, multicultural content also cuts across all stages and levels of change.

Much of psychotherapy research has traditionally been dedicated to determining whether one type of therapy is more effective than an alternative therapy for a specific disorder. Such horse-race contests have resulted in a disappointing abundance of ties (Smith et al., 1980; Stiles et al., 1986; Wampold, 2001). After 50 years of research, we can only partially specify which treatment is best for which type of client with which type of problem.

The transtheoretical model offers a unique means of treatment matching: match to the client's stage and level of change. Because troubled people vary in their readiness to take action on their disorders, then treatments should vary in terms of how much action they demand of clients. Behavior modifiers have been ingenious in their ability to develop action-oriented methods, but these action-oriented methods may be appropriate only for the small percentage of people who are prepared for action at any given time.

A patient and therapist each working at different stages is a recipe for resistance. If the therapist is action-oriented and the client is a precontemplator, then the client will experience the therapist as insensitive and coercive, like a parent pressuring for change when the client isn't convinced that change is needed. Conversely, if the patient is prepared to take action and the therapist relies almost exclusively on consciousness raising and self-reevaluation processes, the client will experience treatment as moving much too slowly, whereas the therapist may perceive the client as acting out.

Similarly, clients who believe that immediate situational changes will improve their symptoms are likely to be resistant to spending much time becoming more conscious of their childhood. Clinicians who depend heavily on situationally focused techniques may experience resistance from patients who are convinced that their phobias are rooted in much deeper levels. A client being treated with systematic desensitization for a social phobia by one of our graduate students complained, "It seems to me that the therapy you are using is like treating a cancer with aspirin."

If psychotherapists can only work effectively at one level of change, then they had better have the luxury of selecting patients who match that level. In choosing a professional, well-informed clients are often implicitly seeking someone who works at a level that they believe is most relevant to their problems. This is a leading reason why some clients prefer behavior therapists, whereas others seek psychoanalytic therapists, and still others seek interpersonal or family therapists. A transtheoretical therapist can be trained to match the needs of a much broader range of clients. Psychotherapists who are well matched to a client's stage and level of change are likely to experience the therapeutic process as progressing reasonably smoothly. Of course, patients can become stuck in a stage, but at least the psychotherapist is aware of not contributing to the stagnation.

A case in point: Many patients stuck in the contemplation stage tend to substitute thinking and reflecting for acting. They become very comfortable with clinicians who prefer contemplation-oriented processes such as consciousness raising and self-reevaluation. But encouraging such clients to go deeper and deeper into more levels of their problems can be **iatrogenic**; that is, the treatment itself can produce negative outcomes, such as feeding into their problems of being "chronic contemplators." At some point, action must be taken. But a therapist who has not been trained to effectively use action-oriented processes might prefer to avoid action in the same way that chronic contemplators avoid action. After years and years of archaeological expeditions into the deepest levels of personality, such patients may yell out like the character on the cover of *The New Yorker* magazine: "Help, I'm being held captive in psychotherapy!"

The Transtheoretical Relationship

The transtheoretical therapist is seen as an expert on how to change—not having all the answers, but being aware of the critical processes and stages of change and offering valuable assistance in this regard. Clients' enormous self-change potential will be tapped in order to effect behavior change. As with any interactive endeavor, a therapeutic alliance must be built in order to accomplish the work. The transtheoretical therapist will be empathic, supportive, and collaborative. However, the nature of support and the therapy relationship will be tailored to the patients' stage of change.

The optimal therapist's stance at different stages can be characterized as follows. With precontemplators, often the role is akin to that of a nurturing parent joining with a resistant and defensive youngster who is both drawn to and repelled by the prospects of becoming more independent. With contemplators, the therapist behaves like a Socratic teacher who encourages clients to achieve their own insights into their condition. With clients in the action stage, the stance is more like that of an experienced coach who has been through many crucial matches and can provide a fine game plan or can review the person's own plan. With clients who are progressing into maintenance, the psychotherapist becomes more of a consultant who is available to provide expert advice and support. As termination approaches in lengthier treatment, the transtheoretical therapist is consulted less and less often as the client experiences greater autonomy and ability to live a life freer from previously disabling problems.

The amount of structure that needs to be provided in a given case also varies with the client's stage of change. Precontemplators need much more help in getting started and dealing with defenses. Contemplators love to engage in consciousness raising and self-reevaluation and can typically do much of the within-session work with minimal structure. Once it comes to taking action, clients vary in how much direction they seek from treatment. Those who have become demoralized about their ability to change usually look to the therapist for guidance on how they can be more effective in their next action attempt. Other clients can be quite creative in applying behavioral processes to modify their situations, cognitions, interpersonal relationships, family systems, and intrapersonal conflicts.

Effectiveness of Transtheoretical Therapy

Over the past 30 years, the transtheoretical model (TTM) has generated vast amounts of research about how people change on their own and in treatment.

Historically, treatments were evaluated by their **efficacy**, the percentage of patients who were successful at posttreatment or follow-up. If a smoking cessation program, for example, generated long-term abstinence rates of 30%, it would be judged to be a 50% better practice than a program generating only 20% abstinence or efficacy. The problem was that the best practices in smoking cessation generated 1% or less participation, even when offered for free (Prochaska, 1996). Such practices exert little impact on the most deadly of addictions. Low participation was the rule rather than the exception for participation with most health and mental health behaviors (Prochaska & Norcross, 2002).

Impact has been defined as the participation rate times efficacy. If the best practice that produces 30% abstinence generates 5% participation, its impact is 1.5%. If an alternative practice that produces 20% abstinence generates 75% participation, its impact is 15%. The apparently less effective practice actually has 10 times as much impact on the population. We will review transtheoretical research designed to produce increasing impacts and to raise the standard for best practices.

Smoking Cessation

Our first treatment research was with smoking, because it is the most deadly of behaviors and because previous treatment had been designed for and tested on only the 20% of motivated smokers in the preparation stage. Consistent across four studies was the finding that the best practice was treatment tailored to the transtheoretical stages of change and the processes of change. These computer-based treatments were at least as effective as computers plus telephone counselors (Prochaska et al., 1993, 2001). These treatments were significantly more effective than action-oriented self-help programs and stage-based self-help manuals (Prochaska et al., 1993; Velicer et al., 1999). These TTM treatments produced significant long-term abstinence rates in a narrow range of about 24% abstinence. These consistent results were found even when more than 80% of populations participated (Prochaska et al., 2001) and more than 80% of the smokers were classified as "unmotivated" (in the precontemplation or contemplation stage). As far as is known, these are the highest impacts produced by any smoking cessation therapy.

In England, the TTM-tailored computer treatments were added to the best practices of midwife counseling for pregnant smokers (Haslam & Lawrence, 2004). The addition of the TTM-tailored treatments produced eight times more impact than person-to-person counseling alone.

Stress Management

With a national population suffering from stress symptoms, we proactively recruited over 70% ($N = 1,085$) to a change program for stress management (Evers et al., 2006). The level of stress would predict that this population would seek health or mental health treatments in the next few weeks. The TTM program involved three tailored communications over 6 months and a stage-based self-help manual. At the 18-month follow-up, the TTM group had over 60% of the at-risk sample reaching action or maintenance compared to 40% for the proactive assessment alone control group.

Compared to studies on smoking cessation, this stress-management intervention produced much more effective action at 6 months in the TTM group (about 60%), and this outcome was maintained over the next 12 months. This treatment also produced significant reductions in depression. This program has received evidence-based status from SAMSHA. (To see a demonstration of this program, go to www.prochange.com/stressdemo.)

Depression

A variety of effective psychotherapies exists for depression. However, there is a service gap for patients who do not receive or respond to traditional psychotherapy because of low treatment receptivity or subclinical syndromes. Three computer-assisted TTM-tailored reports and a workbook tailored to the individual's stage of change addressed the problem of depression in primary care (Levesque et al., 2009).

Primary care patients experiencing major depression or subclinical depression but not receiving treatment ($n = 481$) and primary care patients nonadherent with antidepressant medication ($n = 175$) were randomized to TTM or usual care. The treatment group was significantly more likely than the usual care group to experience a clinically significant improvement in their depression (35% versus 25%). The odds ratio was 1.79, meaning that the patients receiving the TTM-tailored treatments were almost twice as likely to improve as the patients receiving usual care. The largest difference was found among patients suffering major depression (22% versus 6%). That odds ratio was 7.86, meaning that the TTM group was about eight times more likely to improve than usual care. Low-cost, computer-assisted TTM interventions can improve depression outcomes among primary care patients who may not be receptive to traditional treatments.

Multiple Health Behaviors

Six studies applied our best practice of TTM-tailored guides and stage-based self-help manuals to multiple health behaviors. Across all studies, the TTM treatments produced significant impacts on multiple behaviors (Jones et al., 2003; Evers et al., 2006; Prochaska et al., 2004, 2005; Rossi et al., 2003). The interventions also produced abstinence rates for smoking cessation that were in the same narrow 24% range found when the single behavior of smoking was treated. This is among the first body of research that has demonstrated that multiple-behavior treatments can be as effective as treating single behaviors, but the impacts are greater because more behaviors are treated effectively. Other treated behaviors, such as diet and prevention of skin cancer, were even more effective, with the percentages in the action-maintenance stage at long-term follow-up ranging from 25% to 40%.

A recent meta-analysis of tailored communications found that TTM was the most commonly used approach across a broad range of behaviors (Noar et al., 2007). TTM or stages of change models were used in 35 of the 53 studies. Significantly greater effect sizes were found when tailored communications included each of the following TTM constructs: stages of change, pros and cons of changing, self-efficacy, and processes of change. By contrast, interventions that included the non-TTM construct of perceived susceptibility had significantly worse outcomes. Tailoring on non-TTM constructs like social norms and behavioral intentions did not produce larger effect sizes. This genre of research has begun to teach us which variables and treatments produce great outcomes and which do not.

Multiple Domains of Well-Being

With the goal of increasing therapeutic impacts with entire populations, TTM-tailored interventions have expanded beyond multiple health behaviors to multiple domains of well-being. Adopting a World Health Organization (WHO) definition of health as more than the absence of physical or mental illness, we have aimed treatments at enhancing emotional well-being, such as happiness and joy, and life-evaluation, such as thriving rather than suffering (Prochaska et al., 2012).

This program reached out to nearly 4,000 people in 39 states in the United States. The adult population had an average of four chronic conditions and four risk behaviors. They also were well below national averages on emotional and physical well-being, and the majority were struggling rather than thriving. The TTM-tailored telephone counseling and online program produced significantly more individuals than the control group progressing from at-risk to not at-risk for exercise, stress management, diet, and depression. The treatment groups also showed significantly more increases in emotional and physical health. This is an example of how psychotherapy systems can keep raising the bar to help more individuals to feel better and live better.

Bullying and Violence

Bullying may be the number one daily mental health concern of children and adolescents. Tailored interventions based on TTM and delivered over the Internet for middle school and high school students were designed to reduce participation in each of three roles related to bullying (bully, victim, and passive bystander).

Effectiveness trials were completed in 12 middle schools and 13 high schools in the United States. A diverse sample of 1,237 middle school and 1,202 high school students were available for analyses. At follow-up in the middle schools, there was about a 30% reduction in each of the three roles for the treatment groups compared to about 19% in the control group (Evers et al., 2007). In the high schools, there was about a 40% reduction in the treatment groups in each of the roles compared to about 22% in the control group. These programs have received evidence-based status from SAMSHA. Given the relative ease of dissemination, these programs could be applied as stand-alone practices or as part of more intensive interventions.

With male perpetrators of partner violence, TTM-tailored treatments were added to the best practice of mandatory weekly group therapy. At the 6-month follow-up with the first 200 participants, the addition of the stage matching produced significant reduction in violence compared to the weekly group counseling alone. With the addition of TTM tailoring, only 3% of the female partners of the perpetrators had been beaten in the past 6 months compared to 23% of the women whose partners received only the group therapy (Levesque et al., 2009). With the TTM treatment, about twice as many perpetrators had progressed to the action or maintenance stage. Particularly encouraging was that more than twice as many of the perpetrators in the TTM treatment had voluntarily sought additional psychotherapy.

The controlled research on TTM indicates that matching treatments to the client's stage of change significantly improves outcome across disorders. The same studies demonstrate that TTM can produce bigger impacts on entire populations, not only the relatively few patients in the action stage who voluntarily seek mental health services. And the studies establish that treatment can effectively target multiple health behaviors and multiple domains of well-being at the same time in a cost-efficient manner.

Criticisms of Transtheoretical Therapy
From a Psychoanalytic Perspective

Transtheoretical therapists would have you believe that psychoanalysis and insight-oriented therapies are a warm-up for the action-oriented cognitive and behavioral therapies. The contemplation stage is presented as a mere way station for eager patients en route to their final destination of the action stage. Such mischaracterizations do a disservice to patients and the profession.

Psychotherapy is an intense, life-changing experience rooted in a nurturing interpersonal relationship. Its purpose is to change character, the very fabric of our being, over years of treatment. "The examined life," as Socrates put it, would be a more apt description than "contemplation."

The action-oriented bias of TTM shines through in its own research. Brief treatments, self-help materials, and computerized interventions are all directed to eliminating bad habits. We are tempted to speculate on what Freud would say of such "modern revolutions" in mental health, but prefer instead to suggest that transtheoretical therapy take its own medicine. Get to the action stage of understanding that psychotherapy is about the deep exploration of psychic life, not a quick race to termination.

From a Cognitive-Behavioral Perspective

Hundreds upon hundreds of studies have been conducted on the stages of change. The results of those studies reliably indicate that treatments should be tailored to the client's stage or readiness for change. Fair enough, but that's like saying that therapists should adjust their treatments to the client's preferences or goals or personality. Effective therapists already know that.

If TTM is to graduate from an interesting client dimension to a bona fide evidence-based psychotherapy, then we better find some randomized clinical trials (RCTs) on its effectiveness as a psychotherapy for common clinical disorders. And what do we find? A bunch of RCTs conducted on self-help treatments for smoking cessation, addictions, bullying, partner violence, and skin cancer prevention. Where are the RCTs for anxiety, trauma and personality disorders? TTM is an evidence-based self-help treatment for addictions and habits, but it has not crossed that threshold as a psychotherapy (Wilson & Schlam, 2004). Until then, TTM as a psychotherapy for mental health disorders must be relegated to the pile labeled "promising."

From a Humanistic Perspective

TTM is more a theory of behavior change than a theory of psychotherapy. What does it have to offer when people's problems emerge from changes that have been imposed on them, such as the death of a child or other traumas caused by crises, cancer, or crime? What does transtheoretical therapy have to say about acceptance in the face of coercive forces beyond our control? TTM helps people with the courage to change that which they can change, but it fails to help them find the ability to accept that which they cannot change. Transtheoretical therapy also fails to help individuals and therapists to develop the wisdom to tell the difference between what they can change and what they cannot change.

From a Cultural Perspective

Change as progress is so typically a Western and especially an American ideology. Transtheoretical therapists mainly assume that all they need to do is help clients get unstuck and they will freely progress through the rest of the stages of change.

The 20th century raised profound challenges to the belief that historical change and cultural change inevitably represent progression. More people were killed by wars and violence than in all previous centuries combined. Some change is regression.

If progress for entire populations is to occur, then change will need to occur at the cultural level and not just the individual level. Therapeutic interventions must vigorously target sexism, racism, heterosexism, and the other "isms" that permit the privileged powerful to dominate the marginalized and voiceless. The progress that individuals make to enhance their personal freedom can all too readily be reversed if powerful forces continue to run rampant over groups who are assigned to anything less than first-class citizenship.

A Transtheoretical Analysis of Mrs. C

Mrs. C entered psychotherapy stuck in the contemplation stage. The 6 years she spent in psychoanalytic psychotherapy had increased her consciousness about her obsessive-compulsive patterns and personality. She had spent considerable time reevaluating her life. Intellectually, she appreciated how much her life had gotten out of control; but emotionally, it still felt right to protect herself and her family from dirt and disease. As is often the case with obsessive-compulsive clients, Mrs. C isolated much of her emotion from her intellect when reevaluating herself and her symptoms.

Obsessive-compulsive patients are especially prone to getting stuck in the contemplation stage. They are convinced that if they keep thinking enough about a perplexing problem, eventually it will be resolved or enough information will be found that points to a perfect solution. They are seeking certainty as to the causes of their symptoms, when probability is the best that can be provided. Obsessives, like Mrs. C, hate to admit that there can be serious limits to thinking and that many dysfunctions can only be changed by commitments that go beyond reason. The fear of facing the irrational can keep obsessives seeking sufficient information for years, as they shift from one theory to another or from one therapist to another. Of course, some therapists are also afraid of making commitments to action without an obsessive understanding of their clients' problems.

Mrs. C was feeling coerced into action. Her environment was threatening to force changes on her. Her psychotherapist had given up and had decided to terminate treatment. Her family was also giving up on her. Mrs. C overdosed on aspirin to express her depression and anger over the recommendation that she be admitted to a state psychiatric hospital.

Her alternatives for action, then, were to work with me (JOP), to enter the psychiatric hospital, or
(continued)

to follow through on suicide. We hoped Mrs. C would identify with our efforts as potentially the most liberating alternative rather than feeling entirely coerced into cooperating. The fact is that if she felt entirely coerced, she wouldn't cooperate and would resist being changed by someone trying to control her.

At what level should we try to help Mrs. C change? Mrs. C is clearly a complex case. At the symptom and situational level, dirt and disease evoke compulsive hand washing that is probably reinforced by reduction in anxiety. At the cognitive level, Mrs. C believes that she needs to be perfectly clean in order to be perfectly safe and secure. Her maladaptive cognitions include perseverating about pinworms and magnifying the dangers of pinworms entirely out of realistic proportions. She believes that even thoughts or images of dirt and pinworms are awful and unbearable. She also seems to believe that things around her will go out of control if she does not keep up her compulsive rituals.

At the interpersonal level, Mrs. C has mixed relationships at best. She relates ambivalently to her children, as she struggles to protect them from dirt and disease. Her relationship with her husband has deteriorated to the point where it lacks intimacy or sexuality. Their only significant interaction is Mr. C's participation in her morning shower ritual. Mrs. C is conflicted over caring for her family or controlling her family.

At the family/systems level, Mrs. C is still heavily influenced by her mother's rules to be ultraclean and to be hypervigilant about disease, as well as her father's controlling intrusiveness about sex and men. She hails from a family in which she was dominated by her parents but was not free to acknowledge anger and resentment toward their coercive control.

At the intrapersonal level, she appears to be defending against, in psychoanalytic terminology, classic anal impulses. Urges to play with her anus and its products are counteracted by doing the opposite, a reaction formation that entails being perfectly clean. She has trouble letting go, as she hoards cheap jewelry and other junk. She lives a highly constricted life in which she overcontrols her feelings, her sexual urges, and her aggression. To let go of her defenses would threaten to drive Mrs. C crazy.

In TTM, we can begin psychotherapy at the symptom/situational level and shift to deeper levels, if necessary. We can also intervene at a key level of change if one of the levels is clearly the key to her problems. Or we can use the maximum-impact strategy and attempt to produce changes at each level. With a complex case like Mrs. C, where there are multilevel problems, we prefer a maximum-impact strategy.

Even though I (JOP) treated Mrs. C as a psychology intern long before transtheoretical therapy was developed, it is intriguing that much of my early integrative style anticipated my later work. With Mrs. C, for example, psychotherapy involved multilevel interventions. Treatment also included a range of change processes that were indicated for a client moving into action. (Were Mrs. C to present for treatment today, she would also undoubtedly receive one of the new antiobsessive medications.)

At the symptom/situational level, treating Mrs. C as an inpatient enabled the psychotherapist to exert greater influence over stimulus situations that controlled her symptoms. Because her handwashing at home was immediate and automatic, she had little voluntary control over washing. As an inpatient, she would have to sign in at the nurses' station before she could wash and sign in again after completing her washing. This gave an accurate count of her compulsive washings and provided feedback about the effectiveness of our treatment. The signing in also served as a delay during which the nurses could use counterconditioning to help Mrs. C cope with her anxiety, such as talking about it or encouraging her to relax by playing cards, knitting, or watching television. The delays also allowed Mrs. C to use self-liberation and make more conscious decisions to wash or to resist washing. If she resisted washing, the hospital staff could then use contingency management and reinforce Mrs. C for not washing. As therapy progressed, the signing in also served as a stimulus control procedure that

(continued)

controlled how often and how long Mrs. C could remain in washing situations.

A helping relationship was enhanced by meeting twice a week in more person-centered, supportive sessions. In these sessions, Mrs. C could share the many thoughts and feelings generated by her hospitalization and treatment. These sessions also helped Mrs. C identify with therapy, as she experienced her therapist as caring rather than coercive. The more Mrs. C identified with psychotherapy, the more she relied on self-liberation, as she committed herself more fully to taking action to overcome her chronic compulsions.

The comprehensive treatment also entailed exposure sessions three times a week. We used the early form of exposure known as implosive therapy, as described in Chapter 8. The implosive scenes affected almost every level of Mrs. C's problems. The first scene, for example, encouraged Mrs. C to face situations such as dirty underwear filled with pinworms. The anal picnic scene would impact on several levels simultaneously, ranging from symptom stimuli of dirt and disease to intrapersonal desires to act out anal impulses. We also introduced challenges to her maladaptive cognitions of having to be perfectly clean in order to be safe and secure and family/systems themes related to rebellion against parental dominance over toilet training.

The third scene impacted on interpersonal conflicts, especially Mrs. C's ambivalence toward her children. She imagined her children being infected by pinworms because of her carelessness. In the middle of the night, she heard her children complaining to her as they were being bothered by pinworms. Mrs. C ignored their pleas and went to bed feeling free at last from having to care for her children.

The interpersonal level was also addressed through biweekly conjoint sessions for the C family. The family members expressed the considerable anger and resentment toward Mrs. C that had accumulated over the years. For a while it looked as though Mrs. C might not return home, because four of the children were adamant about not wanting her back. As the anger dissipated,

however, Mr. C and the older children helped the younger children reevaluate their mother, because they shared memories of how Mrs. C was before she became obsessed. Individual sessions with Mr. C also helped him to remember the warm feelings that had been buried under all the frustration and resentment.

The family/system conflicts of Mrs. C were most intensely affected by the fourth implosive scene, in which she imagined sinking an ax into her father's bald head. Mrs. C also confronted what psychoanalysts would describe as oedipal conflicts with a father who waited up for her after dates. Of course, these scenes could also impact on intrapersonal conflicts, as Mrs. C imagined releasing some of her most taboo impulses of sex and aggression.

Another implosion scene was directed at intrapersonal conflicts over losing control and going crazy. She imagined running around the house nude, wrecking the house, and then being shipped back to the clinic for disposition. At the clinic, a full staff meeting was held with the family members present. After discussing all the terrible things that Mrs. C had done, the director asked if anyone from the clinic or the family had anything good to say about her. Silence was the only response. Again the question was asked, and again no one spoke. Finally, Mrs. C was sent to the state hospital in a panel truck and placed in an isolated room with a sign on her door: "Hopeless Case: No Visitors Allowed." This scene, in addition, assisted Mrs. C in confronting some of her situational anxieties regarding relapse after returning home from the hospital.

The final implosive sessions involved real unwashed underwear that Mr. C had brought from home. Mrs. C had to reach into the bag with her eyes closed and handle the dirty underwear. This in vivo exposure helped Mrs. C confront not only situational stimuli but also her maladaptive cognitions that magnified out of all proportion the dangers of dirty underwear.

By the end of Mrs. C's 6-week stay in the clinic, the sign-in sheets indicated a dramatic decrease in the frequency and duration of her washing compulsion. The biggest change came after the

(continued)

fourth implosive scene, in which Mrs. C was to imagine physically attacking her father. During this session, Mrs. C was in a psychophysiological lab and was wired to seven different channels for measuring anxiety. As the session progressed, Mrs. C reported that she was having trouble with the scene. She could imagine the scene all right, but she was not feeling emotions as she had in previous scenes. Recognizing her reaction as a form of defensive isolation, I told her to really let go, to strike out with her hand and tell him what a bastard he was, to tell the son of a bitch she was glad he was suffering as he had made her suffer. Suddenly she began hacking away at the table and swearing, sobbing, and shaking. The seven anxiety channels all went off the recording paper, as Mrs. C opened up for the last 15 or 20 minutes of the session. She then went up to her room and, with a nurse present, continued to relive the scene for over an hour with considerable affect expressed. The next morning, she again relived the scene until she felt emotionally drained.

Mrs. C's Outcome

After this intensive course of treatment, Mrs. C looked and felt considerably better. She was now able to pick up such things as a ball of yarn off the floor. She could accept a drink of soda from the same can from which a disheveled youngster had been drinking; previously she would not even get near such an unclean person. Her showers and handwashing were down to average times, and Mrs. C was ready to return home.

Fortunately, Mrs. C's family had been willing to use stimulus control to change their environmental conditions, both for their own sakes and for Mrs. C's. They had been painting, repairing, and redecorating the house, which had come to look like a city dump. On her first weekend home, Mrs. C joined right in and directed the discarding of the junk she had retained for years. Her children and their friends formed a long line, and Mrs. C handed them boxes of dresses, towels, and assorted items to be picked up by the trash truck. Mrs. C genuinely enjoyed the freedom of letting go.

To our surprise, she also let go sexually with her husband more than she ever had in her life.

The first day home, they went up to their bedroom in the daytime, which they had never done before, and really enjoyed making love. Mr. C blurted out spontaneously, "This isn't the girl I married!" A few months later, Mrs. C experienced her first orgasm at the age of 47.

The family was amazed at Mrs. C's newfound freedom. The kids reported her doing things they could never imagine, such as getting down on the floor and playing with them or picking up a cookie off the new rug, brushing it off, and eating it. She was cooking special meals, helping with the cleaning, and allowing her children to have their friends over.

Mr. C said that he was amazed by his wife's improvement but also troubled because he had always thought of himself as better adjusted than she was, whereas now she seemed healthier. I offered him some implosive sessions, but he declined with a smile, saying he could learn to adjust all right.

After some initial enthusiasm at being home and feeling good, there were the predictable setbacks. Mrs. C was generally more tense at home than in the clinic. Part of her anxiety derived from trying to care for six children after having been withdrawn from them for so long. She was especially troubled by her guilt concerning the emotional problems she believed she had helped cause in her second son. Even though her son was receiving psychotherapy, Mrs. C felt that her guilt was authentic, and all she could do was continue her commitment of being available emotionally to her children when they needed her.

Mrs. C experienced some trouble limiting her morning shower to 5 minutes. She felt more anxious in her shower at home, which had been the scene of so many repetitions of her irrational ritual. So I went to the house and imploded Mrs. C in her shower (while she was fully clothed, of course).

Mrs. C also experienced a mild depressive reaction when I left the clinic and our therapeutic relationship was terminated. My supervisor, who continued to see her on a monthly basis, half-jokingly suggested to me that her dramatic

(continued)

improvement seemed to be the result of her having fallen romantically for me and thus trying very hard to please me. I told him that his explanation sounded an awful lot like a "transference cure" explanation for a behaviorist like himself!

The last I heard of Mrs. C was 2 years post-termination. She was continuing to function much more autonomously. Her morning shower was occasionally giving her problems, but what empowered her most was a new job that would not tolerate her being late. There was no denying that Mrs. C could still be characterized as an obsessive-compulsive personality, but her needs for cleanliness and neatness were more under self-control. She had regained sufficient autonomy to reassert the commitment she had made many years before: to share her life with her family rather than wasting it in a compulsion to wash.

Key Terms

action stage
consciousness raising
contemplation stage
contingency
  management
counterconditioning
dramatic relief
dualism
efficacy versus
  impact
environmental
  reevaluation
iatrogenic
key levels strategy
levels of change
maintenance stage
maximum impact
  strategy

precontemplation
  stage
preparation stage
processes of change
relapse and recycling
relapse prevention
  (RP)
relativism
self-efficacy
self-liberation
self-reevaluation
shifting levels strategy
stages of change
stimulus control
termination
theoretical
  complementarity
transtheoretical

Recommended Readings

Connors, G. J., DiClemente, C. C., Velasquez, M. M., & Donovan, D. M. (2012). *Substance abuse treatment and the stages of change* (2nd ed.). New York: Guilford.

DiClemente, C. C. (2002). Motivational interviewing and the stages of change. In W. R. Miller & S. Rollnick (Eds.), *Motivational interviewing* (2nd ed.). New York: Guilford.

Marlatt, G. A., & Donovan, D. M. (Eds.). (2007). *Relapse prevention: Maintenance strategies in the treatment of addictive behaviors* (2nd ed.). New York: Guilford.

Norcross, J. C. (2012). *Changeology*. New York: Simon & Schuster.

Norcross, J. C., Krebs, P. M., & Prochaska, J. O. (2011). Stages of change. In J. C. Norcross (Ed.), *Psychotherapy relationships that work* (2nd ed.). New York: Oxford University Press.

Prochaska, J. O., & DiClemente, C. C. (1984). *The transtheoretical approach: Crossing the traditional boundaries of therapy*. Homewood, IL: DowJones–Irwin.

Prochaska, J. O., Evers, K. E., Castle, P. H., et al. (2012). Enhancing multiple domains of well-being by decreasing multiple health risk behaviors: A randomized clinical trial. *Population Health Management, 15*, 1–11.

Prochaska, J. O., Norcross, J. C., & DiClemente, C. C. (1995). *Changing for good*. New York: Avon.

Prochaska, J. O., Velicer, W. F., Rossi, J. S., et al. (1994). Stages of change and decisional balance for twelve problem behaviors. *Health Psychology, 13*, 39–46.

Recommended Websites

APA Division of Psychotherapy:
  www.divisionofpsychotherapy.org/
HABITS—Health & Addictive Behaviors
  Investigating Transtheoretical Solutions:
  www.umbc.edu/psyc/habits/
Home of the Transtheoretical Model:
  www.uri.edu/research/cprc/

Pro-Change Behavior Systems:
  www.prochange.com
Relapse Prevention:
  **www.pubs.niaaa.nih.gov/publications/
  arh23-2/151-160.pdf**

CHAPTER 18

The Future of Psychotherapy

In this concluding chapter, we extract and amplify important trends in psychotherapy during the 21st century. We begin by reviewing the results of a Delphi poll on the future of psychotherapy commissioned for this book and completed by 70 authorities on psychotherapy. Then, by integrating converging developments articulated in the preceding chapters and in other sources, we sketch a dozen emerging themes for psychotherapy.

A Delphi Poll

What might the future of psychotherapy look like? The volatile and impermanent nature of the discipline has created a pressing need to identify trends that will impact clinical practice, research programs, graduate training, and policy decisions. We would all like to anticipate the face of psychotherapy in 2020 or 2025.

However, trying to predict the future is a risky and difficult pursuit. Only a truly intrepid observer would attempt to differentiate evanescent from potentially important and durable trends in the field (Yalom, 1975). Moreover, many predictions in the uncertain world of psychotherapy tend to be self-fulfilling prophecies or magical wishes.

For these reasons, we secured the consensus of a panel of experts, committed to diverse orientations, on what *will happen* in the future of psychotherapy, not what they personally would like to happen (tempting as that might be). We were principally concerned with the big picture or megatrends confronting the discipline.

We employed a sensitive forecasting method— the **Delphi poll**—to predict the future of psychotherapy over the next 10 years. Named in honor of the ancient Greek oracle, Delphi polling structures a group communication so that a group of experts, as a whole, can grapple with a complex problem. The Delphi panel answers the same questions at least twice. In the first phase, the experts answer the questions anonymously and without feedback. In subsequent phases, the experts are provided with the names and views of the entire panel and given the opportunity to revise their predictions in light of the group judgment.

Consistent with the commonly held notion that "two (or more) heads are better than one," the Delphi poll capitalizes on multiple and interactive expert perspectives. The particular virtues of Delphi methodology are that (1) it consistently provides the closest answer to extremely difficult questions compared to other prognostication techniques; (2) the responses from the second phase are typically less variable and hence less ambiguous than those of the first; and (3) group consensus has been found to be more accurate than individual expert opinion (Ascher, 1978; Fish & Busby, 1996; Linstone & Turoff, 1975; Moore, 1987).

Our Delphi panelists were distinguished mental health professionals who completed two phases of the poll. The panel was composed of participants from our earlier Delphi study (Norcross, Hedges, & Prochaska, 2002) and editors of leading mental health journals. The 70 participants all held a doctorate and had an average of 33 years of postdoctoral clinical experience. The experts represented a diversity of theoretical orientations: integrative/eclectic (29%), cognitive-behavioral (26%), psychodynamic (10%), humanistic/experiential (10%), systems/family systems (4%), and interpersonal (3%).

Our intrepid observers first forecasted the extent to which a variety of psychotherapy systems will be employed over the next decade. All ratings were made on a 7-point, Likert-type scale where 1 = great decrease, 4 = remain the same, and 7 = great increase. Table 18.1 presents the mean ratings of the 31 psychotherapy systems in ranked order.

As seen in Table 18.1, mindfulness therapies, cognitive-behavior therapy, integrative therapy, multicultural therapies, motivational interviewing, and dialectical behavior therapy were expected to increase the most. All achieved average ratings of 5.00 and higher. By contrast, classical psychoanalysis, transactional analysis, Adlerian therapy, and Jungian therapy were expected to decrease the most. The humanistic therapies—Gestalt, existential, and person-centered—were also expected to decrease in professional popularity.

The panelists next predicted the relative change in use of 45 therapy methods. Fully 28 of these 45 interventions were predicted to increase in the next decade (above an average rating of 4.25 on the 7-point scale). Those methods characterized by computer technology (online self-help, smartphone applications, virtual reality, social networking interventions), client self-change (self-help resources, bibliotherapy, self-help techniques, self-control procedures), and skill building (relapse prevention, homework assignments, problem-solving techniques, cognitive restructuring) were forecast to increase the most. Accompanying these high-tech, directive methods were the high-touch, interpersonal processes of fostering the therapeutic alliance, providing interpersonal support, and expressing warmth and caring, all in the top 15. On the other hand, panelists forecasted that aversive conditioning, free association, encounter exercises, dream interpretation, and emotional flooding/implosion would diminish the most.

Our experts also predicted the future popularity of therapy formats. They foresee short-term therapy, psychoeducational groups, crisis intervention, couples/marital therapy, and group therapy as increasing in the future. Two therapy formats were expected to experience no change in the future: conjoint family therapy and individual therapy. Our panel members forecast only one treatment format to decline: long-term therapy.

These experts' composite ratings portend what's hot and what's not in the next decade. In terms of theoretical orientations, mindfulness, cognitive-behavioral, integrative, and multicultural persuasions will thrive, but classical psychoanalysis and humanistic therapies probably will not. The acronyms MI, DBT, and ACT will probably become even more familiar to the next generation of therapists. In terms of methods and modalities,

Table 18.1 Composite Predictions of Psychotherapy Systems of the Future

ORIENTATION	MEAN	SD	RANK
Mindfulness therapies	5.55	0.92	1
Cognitive-behavior therapy	5.48	0.88	2
Integrative therapy	5.23	1.31	3
Multicultural therapies	5.20	1.01	4
Motivational interviewing	5.15	0.92	5
Dialectical behavior therapy	5.13	0.91	6
Eclectic therapy	4.85	1.45	7
Exposure therapies	4.85	1.16	7
Interpersonal therapy (IPT)	4.81	0.87	9
Cognitive therapy (Beckian)	4.79	1.05	10
Acceptance and commitment therapy	4.70	1.09	11
Systems/family systems therapy	4.53	0.88	12
Attachment-based therapies	4.51	1.19	13
Behavior therapy	4.43	0.94	14
Relational therapy	4.18	1.27	15
Experiential therapies	4.02	1.02	16
Narrative therapy	3.94	1.11	17
Solution-focused therapy	3.90	1.12	18
Psychodynamic therapy	3.79	1.22	19
Person-centered therapy	3.59	1.05	20
Humanistic therapy	3.55	1.07	21
Feminist therapy	3.44	1.13	22
Male-sensitive therapy	3.40	1.22	23
Existential therapy	3.00	1.02	24
Eye movement desensitization and reprocessing (EMDR)	2.71	1.11	25
Gestalt therapy	2.65	1.03	26
Reality therapy	2.48	0.78	27
Psychoanalysis (classical)	2.15	1.05	28
Jungian therapy	2.10	0.74	29
Adlerian therapy	1.84	0.68	30
Transactional analysis	1.81	0.72	31

NOTE: 1 = great decrease; 4 = remain the same; 7 = great increase.

the consensus is that psychotherapy will become more reliant on computers, client self-change, interpersonal support, and skill building in the next decade. More directive, problem-focused, and briefer, to be sure. Concomitantly, relatively unstructured, historically oriented, and long-term approaches are predicted to decrease. In terms of therapy formats, psychoeducational groups, couples therapy, and group therapy are seen as continuing their upward swing. The largest transformation is expected in treatment length: Short term remains in, and long term on its way out.

Twelve Emerging Directions

By immersing ourselves in the content of this book and the psychotherapy literature, we have discerned several directions for the future of psychotherapy. Several of these themes represent a continuation of contemporary trends, whereas others portend a future discontinuous with our past. There is little need here to amplify directions that are widely recognized as having come of age, such as brief therapy, psychotherapy integration, and multicultural therapy. Instead, we choose to give voice to a dozen newer directions.

1. Economics of Mental Health Care

We begin our whirlwind tour of the future of psychotherapy by addressing the rhinoceros in the living room: economics. The funding of health care has undergone a revolution in the past 20 years. Managed care now covers more than 85% of the Americans who attain their health benefits through their jobs and that percentage is still increasing.

It would be inaccurate to lump all managed care into a monolithic entity, so let us broadly frame the concern as **industrialization of mental health care**. Following are the common mechanisms of managing psychotherapy:

- Restricting access to mental health treatment (e.g., only "medically necessary" services)
- Limiting the amount of psychotherapy (e.g., 6 to 12 sessions)
- Using lowest cost providers (e.g., master's- and baccalaureate-level therapists)
- Requiring pre-approval for psychotherapy or implementing utilization review (e.g., after six sessions)
- Reimbursing primarily short-term, symptom-focused psychotherapies
- Shifting to outpatient care (e.g., only hospitalize if suicide attempt)

- Requiring referrals through gatekeepers (e.g., only through primary care physicians)
- Restricting patient's freedom of choice in practitioners and treatments
- Denying reimbursement for treatment of certain problems (e.g., personality disorders, couple dysfunction)

Health care is manifesting the two cardinal characteristics of any industrial revolution (Cummings, 1986, 1987). One: the producer—in our case, the psychotherapist—is losing control over the services as this control shifts to business interests. Two: practitioners' incomes are decreasing because industrialization requires cheaper labor.

In one of our studies of psychologists, we discovered that 75% accept some managed care patients and 25% accept none. In fact, the median percentages of managed care patients in psychologists' caseload expanded tenfold—from 5% to 50%—in just 5 years (Norcross et al., 1997b). These are the footprints of a rhinoceros tramping across the landscape of psychotherapy.

Although we do not subscribe to the doomsday prophecies of the demise of psychotherapy, we recognize that in the future, psychotherapy will increasingly be performed in the public marketplace by master's- and baccalaureate-level professionals for briefer intervals. Some clinicians will find opportunities in the transformation, whereas others will curse the change. All will be profoundly influenced by these socioeconomic forces.

2. Evidence-Based Practice

The **evidence-based practice (EBP)** movement is an international juggernaut racing to achieve accountability in all forms of health care. The aim of EBP is to require professionals to base their practice on solid, typically research, evidence in order to improve treatment effectiveness and enhance public health.

EBP in medicine entails the integration of the best research evidence with clinical expertise and patients values (Institute of Medicine, 2001). The American Psychological Association (APA Task Force, 2006) similarly defined EBP as the integration of the best available research with clinical expertise in the context of patient characteristics, culture, and preferences. Compared to evidence-based medicine, the client assumes a more active, prominent position in EBPs in mental health and addictions. As shown in Figure 18.1, EBP occurs at the intersection of three evidentiary sources: best available research; clinical expertise; and patient characteristics, culture, and preferences.

At first blush, there is universal agreement that we should use evidence as a guide in determining what works. It's like publicly prizing mother and apple pie. Can anyone seriously advocate the reverse: non-EBP?

But it is neither as simple nor consensual as that. Defining evidence, deciding what qualifies as evidence, and applying that which is privileged as evidence are complicated matters with deep philosophical and huge practical consequences (Norcross, Beutler, & Levant, 2005). For example, many psychological treatments deigned as evidence-based have never been tested on diverse populations, including ethnic minority, GLBT,

and physically disabled clients. Neither EBPs nor TAUs (treatment as usual) have satisfactorily addressed the various dimensions of human diversity in mental health. For another example, 60% to 80% of EBPs in psychotherapy identified by one organization are cognitive-behavioral treatments. These typically involve skill building, have a specific focus, involve relatively brief treatment, and rarely use traditional assessment measures (O'Donohue et al., 2000).

However, not all patients want, nor do all practitioners embrace, an action-oriented model. With the most deadly of addictions, for example, the Clinical Guidelines for the Treatment of Tobacco (Fiore et al., 2000) recommended a broad range of action-oriented treatments for motivated smokers. But in spite of 6,000 plus research studies, there were no evidence-based treatments for the unmotivated smokers who comprise 80% of all smokers in the United States. Too much of the current evidence comes from efficacy trials that screen out more complicated individuals, such as those in earlier stages of change and those with co-morbidities.

The decision rules to require treatment manuals, to rely on controlled research, to focus on

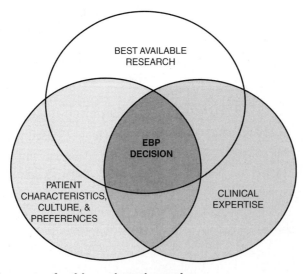

Figure 18.1 The three elements of evidence-based practice

specific disorders, and to validate specific treatment methods have all come under attack. In particular, traditional EBPs tend to minimize the centrality of the therapy relationship, dismiss the effects of the individual therapist, and ignore the complexity of the individual client and his or her context (Norcross, 2011).

Dozens of organizations are already synthesizing evidence and disseminating their respective lists of EBPs in mental health. The American Psychiatric Association (2006), for one, has promulgated more than a dozen **practice guidelines**, on disorders ranging from schizophrenia and anorexia to nicotine dependence. Although not identified as "evidence-based," the guidelines are similar in scope and intent: use the best available knowledge to compile statements of "what works" or "best practices."

The American Psychological Association's Division of Clinical Psychology identified **empirically supported treatments** for adults and has publicized the existence of these treatments to fellow psychologists and training programs. A succession of task forces constructed and elaborated a list of empirically validated, manualized treatments for specific disorders based on randomized controlled studies (Chambless, 1998). In the case of obsessive-compulsive disorder, like Mrs. C's, exposure with response prevention is listed as a "well-established treatment," and cognitive therapy and relapse prevention are listed as "probably efficacious treatments." Subsequent efforts have identified research-supported treatments for older adults, children, couples, and families as well.

Large EBP collaborations are occurring across countries and disciplines. One of the oldest is the Cochrane Collaboration (www.cochrane.org/), founded in Great Britain and named in honor of Archibald Cochrane, a noted British epidemiologist. Another group modeled after the Cochrane Collaboration is the Campbell Collaboration (www.campbellcollaboration.org), named in honor

of the American psychologist and methodologist. Several federal agencies—the Substance Abuse and Mental Health Services Administration (SAMHSA) and the Agency for Health Care Research and Quality, among them—maintain specific centers devoted to the identification and transfer of EBPs in mental health.

Although the desire to base clinical practice on solid evidentiary grounds is old and unanimous, the promulgation of evidence-based treatments has been relatively recent and divisive. What we can say with certainty is that EBP in health care is here to stay. All mental health professions will need to respond to this clarion call by demonstrating the safety, efficacy, and efficiency of their work. In fact, the demands for evidence from various constituencies will escalate in the future.

What we can also confidently say is that EBPs will have profound implications for mental health practice, training, and policy. What is designated as "evidence-based" will increasingly determine what is conducted, what is reimbursed, what is taught, and what is researched. "No research, no reimbursement" will become the mantra of insurance carriers when it comes to paying for psychotherapy. Along with the (mostly) negative influence of the industrialization of health care, there is probably no more issue central to psychotherapists than the emergence of EBP.

3. Therapy Relationship

EBPs and practice guidelines have attempted to enhance the effectiveness of psychotherapy by selecting the best treatment, the best method. But they have done so largely at the neglect of the therapy relationship, which accounts for as much of the success of psychotherapy as the particular method (Norcross, 2011; Wampold, 2008).

Of course, specific delineations between the therapeutic technique and the relationship are nearly impossible in practice. Both are interwoven in the contextual fabric of psychotherapy. Hans

Strupp (1986), a distinguished psychotherapy researcher, offered an analogy to illustrate the inseparability of these constituent elements: Suppose you want your teenager to clean his or her room. Two methods for achieving this are to establish clear standards and to impose consequences. Fine, but the effectiveness of these methods will vary depending on whether the relationship between you and the teenager is characterized by warmth and mutual respect or by anger and distrust. This is not to say that the method is useless, merely that how well it works depends on the relational context in which it is used.

There is virtual unanimity among the reviewers of the outcome research that the therapist–patient relationship is central to success. Cognitive and behavior therapists who previously slighted the curative power of the therapy relationship are now emphasizing it to a far greater extent (Glass & Arnkoff, 1992). In psychoanalytic practice, a decisive shift involves a relative de-emphasis on interpretation and increasing emphasis on the therapist–patient interaction (Chapters 2 and 3).

An interdivisional task force of APA divisions recently published a thorough review of what works in the therapy relationship (Norcross, 2011). The task force concluded that the therapy relationship makes substantial and consistent contributions to outcome independent of the specific type of psychotherapy. Accordingly, practice guidelines should explicitly address therapist behaviors and qualities that promote a facilitative therapy relationship. Efforts to promulgate EBPs without including the relationship are seriously incomplete and potentially misleading.

Based on a series of meta-analyses, the task force concluded that the following elements of the therapy relationship are demonstrably or probably effective:

- Alliance in individual (adult) therapy, child therapy, and family therapy
- Cohesion in group therapy

- Empathy
- Goal consensus
- Collaboration
- Positive regard/affirmation
- Congruence/genuineness
- Collecting client feedback

Each of these relational behaviors, primarily provided by the therapist, predicts and contributes to treatment gains. Without several of them, such as cultivating a positive alliance and collecting client feedback, clients are markedly more likely to prematurely discontinue treatment or experience deterioration.

Although practitioners have appreciated the power of the relationship for generations, the research base is now so strong that we can speak of **evidence-based relationships** as we would of *evidence-based treatments*. The future will ensure that graduate training and treatment manuals sufficiently attend to what seasoned practitioners and grateful patients have always known: It's the relationship that counts.

4. Technological Applications

Until recently, psychotherapy has been relatively immune from the information revolution: Two people speaking to each other in the privacy and immediacy of the consulting room remains the quintessential format. But the information age is dramatically changing psychotherapy in the forms of computer-assisted treatment, telepsychotherapy, virtual reality treatment, and online counseling. In place of, as the old saying goes, psychotherapy only needing two people, an office, and a box of tissues, in the 21st century we might only require one person and a computer.

The Internet is helping to treat behavioral/mental disorders in multiple ways. Websites are providing psychoeducation, screening people for disorders, promoting self-monitoring, providing outcome measures, and functioning reliably without fatigue (Wright & Wright, 1997). Internet applications, increasingly on smartphones, are furnishing self-help guides, clinical assessments, treatment programs, and support groups. **Behavioral e-health** is the popular term that captures the variety of psychological services being delivered over the Internet, ranging from psychoeducational information to psychotherapy (Maheu & Gordon, 2000).

Computer-mediated communications offer distinctive advantages that will contribute to their expanded significance during the next decade. These advantages include:

- The ability to tailor the communication to the individual (by disorder or stage of change, for example)
- Reduced cost compared to face-to-face intervention
- More willingness to reveal embarrassing or sensitive information
- Lower level of commitment needed by program users
- Constant availability with convenient and private access
- Equivalent or better outcomes for children and computer-savy adults
- Greater standardization and precision (Budman, 2000)

No wonder that practitioners are increasingly using and recommending online programs. In 2011, fully 78% of psychotherapists recommended Internet sites to their patients, up from 34% ten years earlier. And almost a quarter of psychotherapists are now recommending particular online treatment programs to patients (Norcross et al., 2013).

Computer therapy for anxiety and depression via the Internet has proven acceptable and practical in several nations, especially in Australia and Britain. In a meta-analysis of 22 studies of computer therapy, the mean effect size was 0.88 compared to a control group. The benefits were evident across major depression, panic disorder,

social phobia, and generalized anxiety. The client acceptability was good, the improvement was maintained for a median of 26 weeks, and the computer treatment was about as effective as face-to-face CBT. Some patients are now thriving on the virtual couch.

At the same time, psychotherapy by telephone, videotelephone, and videoconferencing will escalate. This has been labeled **telepsychotherapy**: psychological treatment conducted by a therapist at a location different from the patient's through bidirectional communication technology supporting real-time interactivity in the audio, audiovisual, or text modalities. A meta-analysis of 12 controlled trials of telephone-administered psychotherapy yielded a large effect size (0.81) for reductions in symptoms from the beginning to the end of treatment and a modest but significant effect size (0.26) compared to control conditions (Mohr et al., 2008). Attrition rates for telephone-administered psychotherapy were considerably lower than rates reported for face-to-face psychotherapy, suggesting that the use of technology does indeed reduce barriers to treatment.

Some clinicians are now conducting psychotherapy from around the country or around the world at any hour of the day—that's what live, online counseling services now offer on the Internet. All you need is a computer, a webcam, and the free Skype software (www.Skype.com). Although fraught with legal, reimbursement, ethical, and logistical concerns (Baker & Bufka, 2011), various forms of telehealth are destined to proliferate. The information revolution is assuredly arriving in psychotherapy.

5. Self-Help Resources

A massive, systemic, and yet largely silent revolution is occurring in mental health today and is gathering steam for tomorrow: **self-help**. People are increasingly changing behavior by themselves, reading self-help books, surfing the Internet for advice and treatment, watching movies and incorporating their cinematic lessons, and attending self-help and 12-step groups (Norcross, 2000).

The self-help movement continues the timeless human quest to conquer behavioral disorders, but the percentages of people engaging in self-help activities are probably now at record highs. Self-help books on every conceivable topic appear at the rate of about 5,000 a year, and they dominate the best-seller lists. In the past year, 5% to 7% of American adults attended a self-help group, and 18% have done so at some point in their lifetime (Kessler et al., 1999). Approximately 80% of all Internet users have sought health care information there (Pew Internet and American Life Project, 2003), with mental disorders and relationship problems leading the list. Call it Emersonian self-reliance, the do-it-yourself-nation, or the Home Depot effect, but the self-help revolution is upon us.

Converging forces contribute to the proliferation of self-help resources. One force is managed care: Brief professional treatment means that adjunctive and ancillary methods must be incorporated to secure sufficient gains. A second force is the widespread availability and lower cost of self-help tools, particularly those online. A third reason is that self-help is typically private and anonymous; in words of self-helpers, "No one will know." Decreased stigmatization and increased privacy of self-help likely play a pivotal role in its popularity.

Another force is its effectiveness. Reviews of the rates at which neurotic patients improve on their own, without professional treatment, found that a median of 43% of people demonstrate improvement (Lambert, 1976). Several meta-analyses on the effectiveness of self-help resources and self-administered treatments find that their effect sizes are nearly as large as therapist-assisted interventions within the same studies (Cuijpers, Donker, et al., 2010; den Boer et al., 2004; Gregory et al., 2004; Menchola et al., 2007). Fears, mild depression, and sleep disturbances seem especially amenable to self-help. And several well-controlled evaluations of 12-step groups for addictive disorders show that they generally perform as effectively as professional treatment, including at follow-up (Morgenstern et al., 1997; Ouimette et al., 1997; Project MATCH Research Group, 1997).

For multiple reasons, then, people in their natural environments and psychotherapists in their consulting rooms use self-help resources. In any given year, for example, 79% of therapists recommend a self-help/support group to patients and 85% recommend a self-help book (Norcross et al., 2013). As was evident in the experts' forecast in our Delphi poll, mental health professionals in the future will increasingly provide clients with information to change on their own and recommend "do-it-yourself" therapies. Self-help, with or without psychotherapy, is the country's de facto treatment for most behavioral disorders.

6. Neuroscience

Advances in **neuroscience** have begun to impact the theory and practice of psychotherapy. In fact, psychotherapy might be called "brain therapy" in the future. And many mental disorders might be redefined as "brain illnesses."

Psychotherapy typically results in detectable changes in the brain and the body (Etkin et al., 2005; Siegel, 1999). In most studies, psychotherapy is similar to medication in normalizing functional abnormalities in brain circuits that give rise to symptoms. Psychotherapy and medication share some common therapeutic effects on the same brain regions. In a seminal and replicated study by Lewis Baxter and colleagues (1992), patients with obsessive-compulsive disorder who were treated with medication or psychotherapy (exposure and response prevention; Chapter 8) showed normalized changes in the functioning of multiple brain regions. An important 2012 study demonstrated that 10 weeks of cognitive-behavioral stress management reversed the pro-inflammatory gene expression in circulating leukocytes among women with breast cancer (Antoni et al., 2012).

Positive human interactions, such as psychotherapy, can create new synaptic connections and release neurotransmitters, helping people respond with increasing resilience and self-soothing abilities. Several neuroimaging studies in mood and anxiety disorders have found that activity in certain brain regions can predict who is most likely to respond positively to treatment. These lines of research remind us that we are treating not only "mental disorders" but literally "brain illnesses" (regardless of what originally caused the disorder).

The brain is the mind is the brain. Separating the mind from the brain may finally come to an end, 400 years after René Descartes launched mind–body dualism (Cozolino, 2003). Many psychotherapists are realizing that all mental processes, even the most complex psychological processes, derive from operations of the brain (Kandel, 1998). Psychotherapy is learning from neuroscience, just as neuroscience is learning from psychotherapy.

As we enter the age of neuroscience, we will learn more about the genetic origins of childhood temperaments and psychological disorders, we will examine the common and specific brain effects of medication and psychotherapy, and we will understand better the neurobiological correlates of early traumatic memories and unconscious processing. We will treat brain illnesses more specifically based on their molecular biology, and we will enhance prevention by identifying powerful biological indicators of vulnerability. The burgeoning field of neuroscience will likely narrow the gap between mind and brain. It may also require a whole new way of thinking about, and talking about, how psychotherapy works.

7. Behavioral Health

Psychotherapy is not immune to fads and fashions. Each decade seems to bring about a renewed interest in certain disorders. In the 1980s, it was eating disorders. In the 1990s, personality disorders and attention-deficit hyperactivity disorder occupied central stage. Addictions and autism seemed to dominate the conversation in the 2000s. The 2010s are highlighting the treatment of physical health problems.

The interest in the psychological consequences and treatment of health problems is directly linked to their lethality: The behavioral problems of smoking and obesity are the two leading causes of death in the United States (Mokdad et al., 2004). In part, the concern is financial. Over 50% of health care costs are due to behaviors (Prochaska, 1996). Smoking, obesity, chronic pain, depression, and anxiety are the five most costly conditions in our society (Loeppke et al., 2009). In part, too, the recent interest is due to recognizing that traditional medical care of chronic health conditions is unsatisfactory. As currently practiced, only 20% of the aforementioned conditions are treated effectively in the population at large. And, in part, the interest is spurred by the effectiveness of psychological treatments for children and adults with chronic medical conditions.

Both objective evidence and our Delphi experts predict psychotherapists will routinely treat the behavioral components of health problems and chronic illnesses in the future. Indeed, psychiatry is remedicalizing itself as a part of mainstream medicine, and organized psychology is redefining itself as a health care profession, as opposed to a mental health profession. The term **behavioral health care** is gradually replacing mental health care in an effort to communicate its broader focus and wider range of disorders treated.

The treatment of health behaviors frequently applies a **stepped care model** (Haaga, 2000). Not all patients require the same intensity of intervention; some may be helped from a self-help DVD, some will benefit from a brief psychoeducational group, and still others will require long-term individual treatment from a highly trained psychotherapist.

Stepped care attempts to maximize the effectiveness and efficiency of resource allocations. Typically, we start with the least costly help, such as a support group and a self-help book. If these work, great. If not, we would step up to a more intensive treatment, for example, a multimedia interactive program delivered over the Internet. If more help is needed we could add telephone counseling. Face-to-face psychotherapy would be saved for the most complicated and severe cases.

Mental health services are emerging as part of the overall health care system, not apart from it. No health care system will work unless behavior is integrated throughout it. Only a biopsychosocial model will address the central roles of lifestyle choices, compliance with medical regimens, and management of chronic diseases. And only psychotherapists are trained to change such behaviors.

The movement to **integrated primary care** has enormous implications for psychotherapy. Behavioral health services will be increasingly provided as part of larger interprofessional group practices and psychotherapists will need a flexible armamentarium of evidence-based relationships and treatments to address a host of mental disorders and medical issues. The traditional 50-minute psychotherapy hour will still exist, but not for most patients.

Therapists will need to know how to simultaneously treat multiple health-risk behaviors. Such patients are at the highest risk for chronic diseases, premature death, lost productivity, and unsustainable health care costs. The traditional wisdom was that it is hard enough to change one behavior, and treating multiple behaviors will overwhelm patients and professionals. But, using TTM-tailored counseling or online programs, we helped a large population make multiple health changes in their exercise, stress management, diet, and depression (Prochaska et al., 2012). With just three 20-minute interactions over 6 months, we enhanced multiple domains of well-being and improved physical and emotional health; a majority of individuals changed from

suffering to thriving. This study is an example of how integrative behavior heath care can be applied briefly to improve multiple health behaviors, both physical and mental.

Such behavioral health care may transform our current system by emphasizing health promotion, by addressing multiple changes simultaneously, and by treating the behavioral causes of chronic diseases, not just the biological symptoms. The future will bring health care for the whole person (Kaslow et al., 2005), and psychotherapists can be right in the middle of it.

8. Proactive Treatment of Populations

Psychotherapy has traditionally taken a passive and narrow approach to patients. Like most health care professionals, psychotherapists initially relate to patients reactively. Therapists wait for individual patients to seek their services. As a result, traditional psychotherapy reaches a minority of people suffering from mental and health disorders.

In the future, psychotherapists will proactively reach out and offer therapeutic services, often to entire populations. **Proactive outreach** will markedly increase the percentage of high-risk and suffering people receiving treatment for behavioral problems.

In the United States, national screening days for depression, anxiety, and eating disorders now reach millions of people annually. In Rhode Island, proactive programs funded by the National Institutes of Health reach out to entire populations suffering from alcohol abuse, depression, obesity, smoking, and stress and offer them treatment matched to their stage of change. With alcohol abuse and depression, patients are screened in primary care practices and then referred for appropriate treatment. With obesity, smoking, and stress, the outreach is done by telephone at home.

In our lab, studies investigated the success of **population-based interventions** (Prochaska, 2004). With a representative sample of 5,000 smokers we proactively offered therapeutic services.

Because only a small minority of this population would be ready to take action, we let them know the services were designed for smokers at every stage of change: the 20% or less in the preparation stage who were ready to act in the next month; the 40% in the contemplation stage who were getting ready to quit in the next 6 months; and the 40% in the precontemplation stage who were not ready to quit. By reaching out to these patients and customizing our clinical communications to their stage of change, we provided services to 80% of them (Prochaska et al., 2001). That results in a quantum increase in our ability to care for this addiction. We replicated these results with an HMO population of about 4,000 smokers (Prochaska et al., 2000) and a population of about 2,300 parents of teenagers with multiple behavior risks (Prochaska, 2004).

In contrast to the traditional paradigm which focuses only on efficacy, a population paradigm focuses on impact. Impact is calculated as efficacy (or success) multiplied by participation. A psychotherapy of 75% efficacy (or success rate) with a 4% rate of population participation yields an impact of 3%. By contrast, a population-based treatment of 30% efficacy with an 80% rate of population participation yields an impact of 24%. In this example, the less effective and less expensive population-based treatment has eight times the impact.

We will begin to think like public health and community advocates: Target the entire population, not only individual patients. Forward-looking therapists will plan for careers that entail more than reactively waiting for distressed patients seeking their services in a private office. In the future, psychotherapists will proactively and effectively impact a much broader range of populations, including those who do not initiate the help-seeking process.

9. Treatment Adaptations

As virtually everyone knows, psychotherapy should be tailored to the individuality of the patient and the singularity of his or her context. The mandate for individualizing psychotherapy was embodied in Gordon Paul's (1967, p. 111) iconic question: "*What* treatment, by *whom*, is most effective for *this* individual with *that* specific problem, and under which set of circumstances?" Every psychotherapist recognizes that what works for one person may not work for another; we seek to create a new therapy for each patient according to the research evidence.

The historical way of individualizing psychotherapy was to select a particular treatment method for the patient's disorder. The Treatment X for Disorder Y approach can indeed be effective, as some therapies make better marriages for disorders than others. Cognitive-behavioral therapies for severe anxiety disorders and parent management training for conduct disorders represent two such examples of match making.

However, such treatment-disorder matching is not always successful (as many tested therapies produce equivalent outcomes) and is usually incomplete. Particularly absent until recently has been tailoring psychotherapy to the entire person of the patient, beyond his or her disorder. As Sir William Osler (1906), father of modern medicine, said: "It is sometimes much more important to know what sort of a patient has a disease than what sort of disease a patient has."

In the future, psychotherapists will increasingly tailor or adapt treatment to the patient's transdiagnostic (across diagnoses) characteristics. The process of creating this optimal fit has been accorded multiple names: **treatment adaptation**, responsiveness, prescriptionism, treatment selection, and differential therapeutics. By whatever name, the goal is to enhance treatment effectiveness by tailoring it to the individual and his or her singular context.

Meta-analyses have shown how to do so in ways that demonstrably improve psychotherapy success (Norcross, 2011). Adapting treatment to the following six patient features are effective: reactance level, stages of change, culture, coping style, preferences, and religion/spirituality. Since we have already discussed most of these in earlier chapters, we shall focus here on the latter two.

Client preferences are frequently direct indicators of the best therapeutic method and healing relationship for that person. Decades of empirical evidence attest to the benefit of seriously considering, and at least beginning with, the treatment and relational preferences of the client. A meta-analysis of 35 studies compared the treatment outcomes of clients matched to their preferred treatment to those clients not matched to their preference. The findings indicated a medium positive effect ($d = 0.31$) in favor of clients matched to preferences. But clients who were matched to their preference were a third less likely to drop out of psychotherapy—a powerful effect indeed (Swift et al., 2011).

Psychotherapy systems are gradually rediscovering their souls. After years of trying to legitimize the discipline by avoiding moral matters, psychotherapists are increasingly integrating spiritual and religious content into treatment. Some patients might request explicitly religious treatment; after all, 80% of the U.S. population is affiliated with a religion and another 10% call themselves "spiritual" (Pew Study, 2012). Psychotherapy might be performed by a clergy person or might occur within a pastoral counseling setting. Or treatment might be conducted by a practitioner who labels himself or herself as a Jewish, Christian, or Muslim therapist.

Other clinicians will adapt treatment to the patient's religion or spirituality, known as **religious-accommodative therapies**. Several meta-analyses have found them effective (Smith et al., 2007; Worthington et al., 2011). The medium effect sizes (0.40–0.60 range) compared to control conditions indicate that religious and spiritually oriented psychotherapies exert beneficial effects on a variety of psychological problems, including depression, anxiety, and eating disorders. What's more, religious-accommodative therapies are typically as effective as secular therapies and typically more effective with highly religious clients who prefer treatments consistent with their religious worldviews.

Research now enables us to confidently adapt psychotherapy to particular clients, in addition to their diagnoses. In the future, effective therapy will be "defined not by its brand name, but by how well it meets the need of the patient" (Weiner, 1975, p. 44). In other words, the question will no longer be "Does the therapy work?" but rather "Does it work *best* for this client?"

10. Positive Psychology

Martin Seligman (2000), one of the parents of **positive psychology**, believes that psychotherapy over the past 100 years has subscribed to a "rotten to the core" notion of human nature. Humans are neurotic, if not evil, deep down. This belief system has led to a half-baked psychotherapy that solely focuses on the alleviation of suffering. By helping clients discover and capitalize on their significant strengths, positive psychology promises a fuller therapy that promotes growth.

Positive psychology aims to build on the strengths and virtues that enable individuals, communities, and societies to thrive. In psychotherapy, this aim translates into clinicians identifying the character strengths and virtues of their patients (Peterson & Seligman, 2004)—an effort that counterbalances the diagnostic preoccupation with psychopathology. It translates into **executive coaching**—assisting managers and other executives to clarify their goals and move toward them. It translates into helping organizations develop responsibility, resilience, justice, optimism, and other institutional strengths. It encompasses dozens of activities that help individuals and communities, not just to endure but also to flourish.

Many of these themes were advanced by humanistic psychologists in the 1960s and 1970s, but positive psychology has repackaged the themes and added novel interventions and scientific evidence. A sampling of methods includes practicing meditation to enhance recovery from schizophrenia, conducting well-being therapy for anxiety disorders, emphasizing the positive features in couples therapy, writing gratitude letters for grief, and using signature strengths in a new way. A meta-analysis of 51 positive psychology interventions, involving 6,018 individuals, revealed that such methods do indeed significantly enhance well-being (ES = 0.29) and decrease symptoms as well (ES = 0.32; Sin & Lyubomirsky, 2009).

In the future, psychotherapists will be expected to both treat psychopathology and promote growth. Take the case of growth following a highly stressful life event. Already there is abundant evidence that people commonly report growth, often by people experiencing even the most traumatic of events (Park & Helgeson, 2006). While treating post-traumatic stress, psychotherapists can simultaneously help patients locate meaning in their tragedy. Such positive meaning can be momentary; however, the patient resources and resilience built as a result of widening the lens can be long-lived (Fitzpatrick & Stalikas, 2008).

11. Integration of Psychotherapy and Pharmacotherapy

Every psychotherapy patient, it seems, has taken or been prescribed a pill to feel less depressed, anxious, inattentive, or disruptive. The use of psychotropic medications has risen dramatically, even alarmingly, particularly among children. In just 10 years, the annual rate of psychotropic medication for children jumped from 1.4% to 4.8% (Martin et al., 2003; Olfson et al., 2002). Overall use of psychoactive medications among adults grew 22% from 2001 to 2010 (www.medcohealth.com), to the point that one in five adults in the United States are taking a psych medication.

Each day, psychotherapists blend their psychological therapies with pharmacological interventions, frequently prescribed by another professional. **Combined treatment** is quickly becoming the rule rather than the exception and, for the more severe disorders, typically proves more effective than either treatment alone. Such appears to be the case, according to the meta-analytic research, for adolescent depression (Calati et al., 2011), adult depression (Cuijpers, van Straten, Hollon, et al., 2010), bipolar disorder (Scott et al., 2007), obsessive-compulsive disorder (Eddy et al., 2004), and psychotic disorders (Sammons & Schmidt, 2002).

The landmark Child/Adolescent Anxiety Multimodal Study (CAMS) is a case in point for combined treatment. CAMS was a NIMH-funded, multisite, randomized controlled trial evaluating the effectiveness of medication (sertraline/Zoloft), CBT, and their combination for children and adolescents suffering from anxiety disorders. At the end of the 12-week treatment, response rates were 81% for combination therapy, 60% for CBT, and 55% for the medication. All therapies evidenced far greater improvement than the placebo, which had a paltry response rate of 24%. The combination therapy, though more costly, was the most effective option (Walkup et al., 2008).

At the same time, combined therapy opens questions and requires decisions on complex care. For example (Beitman et al., 2003; Sammons & Schmidt, 2002):

- When is combining pills and talk therapy contraindicated?
- Should the same professional conduct psychotherapy and prescribe medication for the same patient, or do these interpersonal roles potentially conflict?
- Who is "directing" the patient's care? Surely the informed adult patient in most cases, but what occurs when the patient is a child, incompetent, or in need of immediate hospitalization?
- How are disputes among the psychotherapist, the pharmacologist, and the patient reconciled? When disagreements arise in the

three-way therapeutic contract, say, on the recommended type of medication or psychotherapy, how are the final decisions made?

- How do psychotherapists respond to direct-to-the-consumer advertising TV campaigns that convince many patients that their behavioral disorders are entirely the product of neurotransmitters?
- Can psychotherapists challenge the behemoth of the billion-dollar pharmaceutical industry that thrives on medication sales, frequently at the expense of psychotherapy?

A future characterized by combined treatment raises issues both practical and political. Those knotty issues are here now and will continue to mount as mental health professions try to dissolve the mind–brain barrier.

12. Psychotherapy Works!

The controlled outcome research reviewed in the preceding chapters consistently attests to the effectiveness of those psychotherapies rigorously evaluated to date. Whether one relies on the 7,000+ individual studies or the 700+ meta-analyses, well-developed psychological interventions exert meaningful, positive effects on the intended outcomes. Psychological therapies are robustly effective across settings that range from research-oriented labs to practice-oriented clinics (Shadish et al., 2000). Across all studies, the average effect size for psychotherapy is 0.80, a large effect size in the behavioral sciences (Wampold, 2001, 2008). The average client receiving psychotherapy is better off than 79% of untreated clients. Simply put, psychotherapy is remarkably effective.

A case in point is the effectiveness of psychological treatments in health care systems. Many well-controlled studies demonstrate the success of psychotherapy for behavioral ailments—stress, insomnia, Gulf War illness, and so on—when compared with medication or alternative treatments (Barlow, 2004). These treatments are all matched to specific disorders and to specific patient characteristics. A series of intriguing comparisons between the effects of psychotherapy and the effects of biomedicine (Rosenthal, 1990, 1995) convincingly demonstrated that the typical magnitudes of psychotherapy are of great practical importance, rivaling and exceeding the magnitude of effect often found in biomedical breakthroughs.

Another case in point is the treatment of clinical depression. Popular belief holds that antidepressant medications, particularly the selective serotonin reuptake inhibitors, are plainly the most potent treatment for depression. But, in fact, there is no stronger medicine for depression than psychotherapy (DeMaat et al., 2006; DeRubeis et al., 2005; Imel et al., 2008). The preponderance of scientific evidence shows that psychotherapies are as effective or more effective than medications in treating depression, especially when patient-rated measures and long-term follow-ups are considered. Psychotherapy evidences a lower drop-out rate and a lower relapse rate than pharmacotherapy (DeMaat et al., 2006). This is not to devalue the salutary impact of antidepressant medication or combination treatment; rather, it is to underscore the reliable potency of psychotherapy (Hollon et al., 2005; Munoz et al., 1994).

Nor is this to say that nothing more needs to be researched. On the contrary, we must all do better and must all better understand the active ingredients of successful psychotherapy. The proper agenda for the next generation of psychotherapy research is to investigate which treatments are most effective, the mediating causal processes through which they work, and the therapist characteristics that maximize improvement. Determining what works for whom—the prescriptive mandate—is also part of the research agenda (Roth et al., 2005). The question is no longer whether it works but how it works and how it can be made to work better (Lipsey & Wilson, 1993).

To reiterate the future direction: Practitioners, patients, policy makers, and payers alike will increasingly come to recognize the considerable science supporting the effectiveness of psychotherapy. Effect sizes and probability values, we must remember, translate into vital human statistics: happier and healthier people.

In Closing

Psychotherapy has a short history but, we are confident, a long and prosperous future. Concerned as we are about the possibility of Draconian cuts in payments for mental health services and mental health research, we are equally excited about psychotherapy in the future. Exactly how that future will look in 25 years, or even in 10, is not easy to predict. In some ways, we hope that human behavior will remain as mysterious as it often is but that the wondrous effects of psychotherapy will become more predictable and increasingly widespread.

The creative and committed psychotherapist, like the Roman god Janus, must look simultaneously forward and backward (Rothenberg, 1988). In the Janusian tradition, we hope our efforts in this book have captured the sizable knowledge from our past and have embodied our enthusiastic pursuit of the future.

Key Terms

behavioral e-health
behavioral health care
combined treatment
Delphi poll
empirically supported
  treatments
evidence-based
  practice (EBP)
evidence-based
  relationships

executive coaching
industrialization of
  mental health care
integrated primary
  care
neuroscience
population-based
  interventions
positive psychology
practice guidelines

proactive outreach
religious-
  accommodative
  therapies

self-help
stepped care model
telepsychotherapy
treatment adaptations

Recommended Readings

Beitman, B. D., Blinder, B. J., Thase, M. E., et al. (2003). *Integrating psychotherapy and pharmacotherapy: Dissolving the mind-brain barrier.* New York: Norton.

Grawe, K. (2007). *Neurotherapy: How the neurosciences inform effective psychotherapy.* Mahwah, NJ: Lawrence Erlbaum.

Lopez, S. J., & Snyder, C. R. (Eds.). (2011). *Handbook of positive psychology* (2nd ed.). New York: Oxford University Press.

Nathan, P. E., & Gorman, J. M. (Eds.). (2007). *Treatments that work* (3rd ed.). New York: Oxford University Press.

Norcross, J. C. (Ed.). (2011). *Psychotherapy relationships that work* (2nd ed.). New York: Oxford University Press.

Norcross, J. C., Campbell, L. M., Grohol, J. M., et al. (2013). *Self-help that works* (4th ed.). New York: Oxford University Press.

Norcross, J. C., Hogan, T. P., & Koocher, G. P. (2008). *Clinician's guide to evidence-based practices: Mental health and the addictions.* New York: Oxford University Press.

Prochaska, J. O. (2004). Population treatment for addictions. *Current Directions in Psychological Science, 13,* 242–246.

JOURNALS: *Behavioral Healthcare Tomorrow; Best Practices in Mental Health; CyberPsychology & Behavior; Evidence-Based Mental Health; Health Psychology; Journal of Behavioral Medicine; Journal of Neuroscience; Journal of Technology in Human Services; Journal of Telemedicine and Telecare; Journal of Positive Psychology; Mental Health Services Research;*

Population Health Management; Psychology of Religion and Spirituality; The Scientific Review of Mental Health Practice.

Recommended Websites

Cochrane Collaboration:
www.cochrane.org/
Evidence-Based Behavioral Practice:
www.ebbp.org

International Positive Psychology Association:
www.ippanetwork.org
Research-Supported Psychological Treatments:
www.div12.org/PsychologicalTreatments/ treatments.html
Society for Neuroscience:
apu.sfn.org/
Society of Behavioral Medicine:
www.sbm.org/

An Alternative Table of Contents

Therapies (pp. 192–193) / In Exposure Therapies (p. 215) / In Behavior Therapies (p. 258) / In Cognitive Therapies (pp. 294–296) / In Third-Wave Therapies (pp. 313–314) / In Systemic Therapies (pp. 350–351) / In Gender-Sensitive Therapies (pp. 372–373) / In Multicultural Therapies (pp. 402–403) / In Constructivist Therapies (pp. 422–423) / In Integrative Therapies (pp. 450–451) / In Psychotherapy General (all of Chapter 18)

Topics Missing in This Course Organization

A Sketch of the Founder / Theory of Personality / Theory of Psychopathology / Therapeutic Content / Practicalities of Psychotherapy / Criticisms of the Psychotherapies / Recommended Websites

References

Abbass, A., Kisely, S., & Kroenke, K. (2009). Short-term psychodynamic psychotherapy for somatic disorders: Systematic review and meta-analysis of clinical trials. *Psychotherapy and Psychosomatics, 78,* 265–274.

Abraham, K. (1927). The influence of oral eroticism on character formation. In K. Abramson (Ed.), *Selected papers.* London: Institute for Psychoanalysis and Hogarth Press.

Abramowitz, J. (1996). Variants of exposure and response prevention in the treatment of obsessive-compulsive disorder: A meta-analysis. *Behavior Therapy, 27,* 583–600.

Abramowitz, J. (1997). Effectiveness of psychological and pharmacological treatments for obsessive-compulsive disorder: A quantitative review. *Journal of Consulting and Clinical Psychology, 65,* 44–52.

Abramowitz, J. S., Deacon, B. J., & Whiteside, S. P. (2011). *Exposure therapy for anxiety: Principles and practice.* New York: Guilford.

Abramowitz, J. S., Whiteside, S. P., & Deacon, B. J. (2005). The effectiveness of treatment for pediatric obsessive-compulsive disorder: A meta-analysis. *Behavior Therapy, 36,* 55–63.

Abramowitz, S. I., & Murray, J. (1983). Race effects in psychotherapy. In J. Murray & P. R. Abramson (Eds.), *Bias in psychotherapy* (pp. 215–255). New York: Praeger.

Acarturk, C., Cuijpers, P., van Straten, A., & de Graaf, R. (2009). Psychological treatment of social anxiety disorder: A meta-analysis. *Psychological Medicine, 39,* 241–254.

Acierno, R., Hersen, M., van Hasselt, V. B., et al. (1994). Review of the validation and dissemination of eye-movement desensitization and reprocessing. A scientific and ethical dilemma. *Clinical Psychology Review, 14,* 287–299.

Addis, M. E., & Mahalik, J. R. (2003). Men, masculinity, and the contexts of help seeking. *American Psychologist, 58,* 5–14.

Adler, A. (1917). *Study of organ inferiority and its physical compensation.* New York: Nervous and Mental Diseases Publishing.

Adler, A. (1929). *Problems of neurosis.* London: Kegan Paul.

Adler, A. (1931). Compulsion neurosis. *International Journal of Individual Psychology, 9,* 1–16.

Adler, A. (1936). The neurotic's picture of the world: A case study. *International Journal of Individual Psychology, 3,* 3–13.

Adler, A. (1964). *Social interest: A challenge to mankind.* New York: Capricorn. (Original work published 1929.)

Agras, W. S., Walsh, T., Fairburn, C. G., et al. (2000). A multicenter comparison of cognitive-behavioral therapy and interpersonal therapy for bulimia nervosa. *Archives of General Psychiatry, 57,* 459–466.

Alexander, F., & French, T. M. (1946). *Psychoanalytic therapy.* New York: Ronald.

Alexander, J. F., & Parsons, B. V. (1973). Short-term behavioral intervention with delinquent families: Impact on family process and recidivism. *Journal of Abnormal Psychology, 81,* 219–225.

Alexander, J. F., & Parsons, B. V. (1982). *Functional family therapy: Principles and procedures.* Carmel, CA: Brooks/Cole.

Alford, B. A., & Beck, A. T. (1997a). *The integrative power of cognitive therapy.* New York: Guilford.

Alford, B. A., & Beck, A. T. (1997b). Therapeutic interpersonal support in cognitive therapy. *Journal of Psychotherapy Integration, 7,* 105–117.

American Anthropological Association. (1998). American Anthropological Association Statement on "Race." Retrieved June 11, 2005, from http://www.aaanet.org/stmts/racepp.htm

American Psychiatric Association. (1994). *Diagnostic and statistical manual of mental disorders* (4th ed.). Washington, DC: Author.

American Psychiatric Association. (2000). Position statement on therapies focused on attempts to change the sexual orientation (reparative or conversion therapies). *American Journal of Psychiatry, 157,* 1719–1721.

American Psychiatric Association. (2006). *Practice guidelines for the treatment of psychiatric disorders, Compendium 2006.* Washington, DC: Author.

American Psychological Association. (1991). *Guidelines for psychological practice with ethnic and culturally diverse populations.* Washington, DC: Author.

American Psychological Association. (1993). Guidelines for providers of psychological services to ethnic, linguistic, and culturally diverse populations. *American Psychologist, 48,* 45–48.

American Psychological Association. (2000). Guidelines for psychotherapy with lesbian, gay, and bisexual clients. *American Psychologist, 55,* 1440–1451.

American Psychological Association. (2003). Guidelines on multicultural education, training, research, practice, and organizational change for psychologists. *American Psychologist, 58,* 377–402.

American Psychological Association. (2007). Guidelines for psychological practice with girls and women. *American Psychologist, 62,* 949–979.

American Psychological Association. (2011). *Practice guidelines for LGB clients.* Retrieved from http://www.apa.org/pi/lgbt/resources/guidelines.aspx

Anchin, J., & Kiesler, D. E. (Eds.). (1982). *Handbook of interpersonal psychotherapy.* New York: Pergamon.

Anderson, E. M., & Lambert, M. J. (1995). Short-term dynamically oriented psychotherapy: A review and meta-analysis. *Clinical Psychology Review, 15,* 503–514.

Anderson, W. (1974). Personal growth and client-centered therapy: An information processing view. In D. Wexler & L. Rice (Eds.), *Innovations in client-centered therapy.* New York: Wiley.

Andrews, G., Cuijpers, P., Craske, M. G., et al. (2010). Computer therapy for the anxiety and depressive disorders is effective, acceptable, and practical health care: A meta-analysis. *PLoS One, 5,* e13196.

Andronico, M. P. (Ed.). (1996). *Men in groups: Insights, interventions, and psychoeducational work.* Washington, DC: American Psychological Association.

Ansbacher, H. L., & Ansbacher, R. R. (Eds.). (1964). *Superiority and social interest.* New York: Norton.

Antoni, M. H., Lutgendorf, S. K., Blomberg, B., et al. (2012). Cognitive-behavioral stress management reverses anxiety-related leukocyte transcriptional dynamics. *Biological Psychiatry, 71,* 366–372.

Antonuccio, D. O., Danton, W. G., & DeNelsky, G. Y. (1994). Psychotherapy for depression: No stronger medicine. *Scientist Practitioner, 4*(1), 2–18.

Aos, S., & Barnoski, R. (1998). *Watching the bottom line: Cost-effective interventions for reducing crime in Washington.* Olympia: Washington State Institute for Public Policy.

APA Task Force on Evidence-Based Practice. (2006). Evidence-based practice in psychology. *American Psychologist, 61,* 271–285.

Araoz, D. L., & Carrese, M. A. (1996). *Solution-oriented brief therapy for adjustment disorders.* New York: Brunner/Mazel.

Arkowitz, H., Westra, H. A., Miller, W. R., & Rollnick, S. (Eds.). (2008). *Motivational interviewing in the treatment of psychological problems.* New York: Guilford.

Ascher, W. (1978). *Forecasting.* Baltimore: Johns Hopkins University Press.

Atayas, V. (1977). *Psychology and education of beyond adjustment.* Unpublished manuscript, University of Rhode Island Counseling Center.

Atkinson, D. R. (1985). A meta-review of research on cross-cultural counseling and psychotherapy. *Journal of Multicultural Counseling and Development, 13,* 138–153.

Ayllon, T., & Azrin, N. (1968). *The token economy: A motivational system for therapy and rehabilitation.* New York: Appelton-Century-Crofts.

Aylmer, R. (1978). *Family systems therapy.* Workshop presented at the University of Rhode Island, Kingston, RI.

Azrin, N. H., & Nunn, R. G. (1973). Habit-reversal: A method of eliminating nervous habits and tics. *Behaviour Therapy Research, 11,* 619–628.

Babcock, J. C., Green, C. E., & Robie, C. (2004). Does batterers' treatment work? A meta-analytic review of domestic violence treatment. *Clinical Psychology Review, 23,* 1023–1053.

Bachrach, H. M., Galatzer-Levy, R., Skolnikoff, A., & Waldron, S. (1991). On the efficacy of psychoanalysis. *Journal of the American Psychoanalytic Association, 39,* 871–916.

Baker, D. C., & Bufka, L. F. (2011). Preparing for the telehealth world: Navigating legal, regulatory, reimbursement, and ethical issues in an electronic age. *Professional Psychology: Research and Practice, 42,* 405–411.

Baldwin, S. A., Christian, S., Berkeljon, A., & Shadish, W. R. (2012). The effects of family therapies for adolescent delinquency and substance abuse: A meta-analysis. *Journal of Marital & Family Therapy, 38,* 281–304.

Ballou, M. B. (1990). Approaching a feminist-principled paradigm in the construction of personality theory. In L. S. Brown & M. P. P. Root (Eds.), *Diversity and complexity in feminist therapy* (pp. 23–40). New York: Hawthorne.

Bandura, A. (1969). *Principles of behavior modification.* New York: Holt, Rinehart & Winston.

Bandura, A. (1977). Self-efficacy: Toward a unifying theory of behavior change. *Psychological Review, 84,* 191–215.

Bandura, A. (1982). Self-efficacy mechanism in human agency. *American Psychologist, 37,* 122–147.

Barbato, A., & D'Avanzo, B. (2000). Family interventions in schizophrenia and related disorders: A critical review of clinical trials. *Acta Psychiatry Scandanavia, 102,* 81–97.

Barbato, A., & D'Avanzo, B. (2008). Efficacy of couple therapy as a treatment for depression: A meta-analysis. *Psychiatric Quarterly, 79,* 121–132.

Barber, S. L., Funk, S. C., & Houston, B. K. (1988). Psychological treatment versus nonspecific factors: A meta-analysis of conditions that engender comparable expectations for improvement. *Clinical Psychology Review, 8,* 579–594.

Barkley, R. A. (1991). *Attention-deficit hyperactivity disorder.* New York: Guilford.

Barlow, D. H. (2004). Psychological treatments. *American Psychologist, 59,* 869–878.

Barlow, D. H. (Ed.). (2013). *Clinical handbook of psychological disorders* (5th ed.). New York: Guilford.

Barlow, D. H., & Beck, J. G. (1984). The psychological treatment of anxiety disorders: Current status, future directions. In J. B. W. Williams & R. L. Spitzer (Eds.), *Psychotherapy research: Where are we and where should we go?* New York: Guilford.

Barlow, D. H., Farchione, T. J., Fairholme, C. P., et al. (2010). *Unified Protocol for transdiagnostic treatment of emotional disorders.* New York: Oxford University Press.

Barlow, D. H., Gorman, J. M., Shear, M. K., & Woods, S. W. (2000). Cognitive-behavioral therapy, imipramine, or their combination for panic disorder: A randomized controlled trial. *Journal of the American Medical Association, 283,* 2529–2536.

Barlow, D. H., & Lehman, C. L. (1996). Advances in the psychosocial treatment of anxiety disorders. *Archives of General Psychiatry, 53,* 727–735.

Barlow, D. H., & Wolfe, B. (1981). Behavioral approaches to anxiety disorders: A report on the NIMH–SUNY,

Albany, research conference. *Journal of Consulting and Clinical Psychology, 49,* 448–454.

Barrett-Lennard, G. (1998). *Carl Rogers' helping system: Journey and substance.* Thousand Oaks, CA: Sage.

Barth, J. (1967). *The end of the road.* New York: Doubleday.

Barton, A. (1974). *Three worlds of therapy.* Palo Alto, CA: National Press Books.

Baruth, L. G., & Manning, M. L. (2003). *Multicultural counseling and psycho-therapy: A lifespan perspective* (3rd ed.). New Jersey: Merrill Prentice Hall.

Basco, M. R., & Rush, A. J. (2005). *Cognitive-behavioral therapy for bipolar disorder* (2nd ed.). New York: Guilford.

Bateson, G., Jackson, D., Haley, J., & Weakland, J. (1956). Toward a theory of schizophrenia. *Behavioral Sciences, 1,* 251–261.

Batthyany, A., & Guttmann, D. (Eds.). (2006). *Empirical research in logo-therapy and meaning-oriented psycho-therapy: An annotated bibliography.* Phoenix, AZ: Zeig, Tucker, & Theisen.

Baum, M. (1970). Extinction of avoidance responding through response prevention (flooding). *Psychological Bulletin, 74,* 276–284.

Baxter, L. R., Schwartz, J. M., Bergman, K. S., et al. (1992). Caudate glucose metabolic rate changes with both drug and behavior therapy for obsessive-compulsive disorder. *Archives of General Psychiatry, 49,* 681–689.

Bechtoldt, H., Norcross, J. C., Wyckoff, L. A., et al. (2001). Theoretical orientations and employment settings of clinical and counseling psychologists: A comparative study. *The Clinical Psychologist, 54*(1), 3–6.

Beck, A. T. (1970). The core problem in depression: The cognitive triad. In J. Masserman (Ed.), *Depression: Theories and therapies.* New York: Grune & Stratton.

Beck, A. T. (1976). *Cognitive therapy and the emotional disorders.* New York: International Universities Press.

Beck, A. T. (1988). *Love is never enough.* New York: Harper & Row.

Beck, A. T. (2000). *Prisoners of hate: The cognitive basis of anger, hostility, and violence.* New York: Harper Perennial.

Beck, A. T., Emery, G., & Greenberg, R. L. (1985). *Anxiety disorders and phobias: A cognitive perspective.* New York: Basic.

Beck, A. T., Freeman, A., & Davis, D. D. (2004). *Cognitive therapy of personality disorders* (2nd ed.). New York: Guilford.

Beck, A. T., Rector, N. A., Stolar, N., & Grant, P. (2008). *Schizophrenia: Cognitive theory, research, and therapy.* New York: Guilford.

Beck, A. T., Rush, A. J., Shaw, B., & Emery, G. (1979). *Cognitive therapy of depression.* New York: Guilford.

Beck, A. T., Wright, F. D., Newman, C. F., & Liese, B. S. (1993). *Cognitive therapy of substance abuse.* New York: Guilford.

Beck, J. S. (2011). *Cognitive behavior therapy: Basics and beyond* (2nd ed.). New York: Guilford.

Becker, S. J., & Curry, J. F. (2008). Outpatient interventions for adolescent substance abuse: A quality of evidence review. *Journal of Consulting and Clinical Psychology, 76,* 531–543.

Beitman, B. D., Beck, N. C., Deuser, W. E., et al. (1994). Patient stage of change predicts outcome in a panic disorder medication trial. *Anxiety, 1,* 64–69.

Beitman, B. D., Blinder, B. J., Thase, M. E., et al. (2003). *Integrating psychotherapy and pharmacotherapy: Dissolving the mind-brain barrier.* New York: Norton.

Bem, S. L. (1975). Sex-role adaptability: One consequence of psychological androgyny. *Journal of Personality and Social Psychology, 31,* 634–643.

Bem, S. L. (1977). On the utility of alternative procedures for assessing psychological androgyny. *Journal of Consulting and Clinical Psychology, 45,* 196–205.

Benjamin, A. (1987). *The helping interview.* Boston: Houghton Mifflin.

Benjamin, L. S. (2006). *Interpersonal reconstructive therapy: An integrative, personality-based treatment for complex cases.* New York: Guilford.

Benton, M. K., & Schroeder, H. E. (1990). Social skills training with schizophrenics: A meta-analytic evaluation. *Journal of Consulting and Clinical Psychology, 58,* 741–747.

Berg, I. K. (1999). *Building solutions with mandated clients.* Retrieved from www.brief-therapy.org/insoo_handouts.htm

Berg, I. K., & Miller, S. D. (1992). *Working with the problem drinker: A solution-focused approach.* New York: Norton.

Bergin, A. E., & Lambert, M. J. (1978). The evaluation of therapeutic outcomes. In S. L. Garfield & A. E. Bergin (Eds.), *Handbook of psychotherapy and behavior change* (2nd ed.). New York: Wiley.

Bernal, G., & Rodriguez, M. M. D. (Eds.). (2012). *Cultural adaptations: Tools for evidence-based practice with diverse populations.* Washington, DC: American Psychological Association.

Berne, E. (1964). *Games people play.* New York: Grove.

Berne, E. (1970). *Sex in human loving.* New York: Simon & Schuster.

Berne, E. (1972). *What do you say after you say hello?* New York: Grove.

Berne, E., Steiner, C., & Dusay, J. (1973). Transactional analysis. In R. Jurjevich (Ed.), *Direct psychotherapy* (Vol. *1*). Coral Gables, FL: University of Miami Press.

Bernish, S. G., Imel, Z. E., & Wampold, B. E. (2008). The relative efficacy of bonafide psychotherapies for treating posttraumatic stress disorder: A meta-analysis of direct comparisons. *Clinical Psychology Review, 28,* 746–758.

Bernish, S. G., Quintana, S., & Wampold, B. E. (2011). Culturally adapted psychotherapy and the legitimacy of myth: A direct-comparison meta-analysis. *Journal of Counseling Psychology, 58,* 279–289.

Besa, D. (1994). Evaluating narrative family therapy using single-system research designs. *Research on Social Work Practice, 4,* 309–325.

Beutler, L. E. (1983). *Eclectic psychotherapy: A systematic approach.* New York: Pergamon.

Beutler, L. E., & Clarkin, J. (1990). *Systematic treatment selection: Toward targeted therapeutic interventions.* New York: Brunner/Mazel.

Beutler, L. E., Consoli, A. J., & Lane, G. (2005). Systematic treatment selection and prescriptive psychotherapy. In J. C. Norcross & M. R. Goldfried (Eds.), *Handbook of psychotherapy integration* (2nd ed.). New York: Oxford University Press.

Beutler, L. E., Crago, M., & Arezmendi, T. G. (1986). Research on therapist variables in psychotherapy. In S. L. Garfield & A. E. Bergin (Eds.), *Handbook of psychotherapy and behavior change* (3rd ed.). New York: Wiley.

Beutler, L. E., & Harwood, T. M. (2000). *Prescriptive psychotherapy: A practical guide to systematic treatment selection.* New York: Oxford University Press.

Beutler, L. E., Harwood, T. M., Kimpara, S., et al. (2011). Coping style. In J. C. Norcross (Ed.), *Psychotherapy relationships that work* (2nd ed., pp. 336–353). New York: Oxford University Press.

Beutler, L. E., Harwood, T. M., Michelson, A., et al. (2011). Reactance/resistance. In J. C. Norcross (Ed.), *Psychotherapy relationships that work* (2nd ed., pp. 261–278). New York: Oxford University Press.

Bhar, S. S., Thombs, B. D., Pignotti, M., et al. (2010). Is longer-term psychodynamic psychotherapy more effective than shorter-term therapies? Review and critique of the evidence. *Psychotherapy and Psychosomatics, 79*, 208–216.

Bibring, E. (1954). Psychoanalysis and the dynamic psychotherapies. *Journal of the American Psychoanalytic Association, 2*, 745–770.

Bieschke, K. J., Perez, R. M., & DeBord, K. A. (Eds.). (2006). *Handbook of counseling and psychotherapy with lesbian, gay, bisexual, and transgender clients* (2nd ed.). Washington, DC: American Psychological Association.

Bike, D. H., Norcross, J. C., & Schatz, D. M. (2009). Processes and outcomes of psychotherapists' personal therapy: Replication and extension 20 years later. *Psychotherapy, 46*(1), 19–31.

Binswanger, L. (1958). The case of Ellen West. In R. May, E. Angel, & H. Ellenberger (Eds.), *Existence.* New York: Basic.

Binswanger, L. (1963). *Being-in-the-world: Selected papers of Ludwig Binswanger.* New York: Basic.

Birk, L., Huddleston, W., Millers, E., & Cohler, B. (1971). Avoidance conditioning for homosexuality. *Archives of General Psychology, 25*, 314–323.

Bisson, J., & Andrew, M. (2007). Psychological treatment of posttraumatic stress disorder (PTSD). *Cochrane Database of Systematic Reviews, 3*, CD003388.

Black, A. (1958). The extinction of avoidance responses under curare. *Journal of Comparative and Physiological Psychology, 51*, 519–525.

Blagys, M. D., & Hilsenroth, M. J. (2000). Distinctive features of short-term psychodynamic-interpersonal psychotherapy: A review of the comparative psychotherapy process literature. *Clinical Psychology: Science and Practice, 7*, 167–188.

Bloch, M. H., Landeros-Weisenberger, A., Dombrowski, P., et al. (2007). Systematic review: Pharmacological and behavioral treatment for trichotillomania. *Biological Psychiatry, 62*, 839–846.

Blomberg, J., Lazar, A., & Sandell, R. (2001). Long-term outcome of long-term psychoanalytically oriented therapies: First findings of the Stockholm Outcome of Psychotherapy and Psychoanalysis Study. *Psychotherapy Research, 11*, 361–382.

Bohart, A. C. (1993a). Experiencing: The basis of psychotherapy. *Journal of Psychotherapy Integration, 3*, 51–67.

Bohart, A. C. (1993b). The person-centered therapies. In A. S. Gurman & S. B. Messer (Eds.), *Modern psychotherapies.* New York: Guilford.

Bohart, A. C., Elliott, R., Greenberg, L. S., & Watson, J. C. (2002). In J. C. Norcross (Ed.), *Psychotherapy relationships that work* (pp. 89–108). New York: Oxford University Press.

Bohart, A. C., & Greenberg, L. S. (Eds.). (1997). *Empathy reconsidered: New directions in psychotherapy.* Washington, DC: American Psychological Association.

Bolling, M. Y. (1995). Acceptance and Dasein. *Humanistic Psychologist, 23*, 213–226.

Booker, J., & Blymyer, D. (1994). Solution-oriented brief residential treatment with "chronic mental patients." *Journal of Systemic Therapies, 13*(4), 53–69.

Bootzin, R. R. (2005). Stimulus control instructions for the treatment of insomnia. In G. P. Koocher, J. C. Norcross, & S. S. Hill (Eds.), *Psychologists'*

desk reference (2nd ed.). New York: Oxford University Press.

Bordin, E. S. (1976). The generalizability of the psychoanalytic concept of the working alliance. *Psychotherapy: Theory, Research and Practice, 16*, 252–260.

Bornstein, P. H., & Bornstein, M. T. (1986). *Marital therapy: A behavioral-communications approach.* New York: Pergamon.

Boss, M. (1963). *Daseinanalysis and psychoanalysis.* New York: Basic.

Boss, M. (1983). *Existential foundations of medicine and psychology* (2nd ed.). New York: Jason Aronson.

Boudewyns, P. A., & Hyer, L. A. (1996). Eye-movement desensitization and reprocessing as treatment for posttraumatic stress disorder. *Clinical Psychology and Psychotherapy, 3*, 185–195.

Bowen, M. (1972). On the difference of self. In J. Framo (Ed.), *Family interaction: A dialogue between family researchers and family therapists.* New York: Springer.

Bowen, M. (1978). *Family therapy in clinical practice.* New York: Jason Aronson.

Bowers, T. G., & Clum, G. A. (1988). Relative contribution of specific and non-specific treatment effects: Meta-analysis of placebo-controlled behavior therapy research. *Psychological Bulletin, 103*, 315–323.

Bowlby, J. (1969). *Attachment and loss: Vol. 1. Attachment.* New York: Basic.

Bowlby, J. (1973). *Attachment and loss: Vol. 2. Separation, anxiety and anger.* New York: Basic.

Bowlby, J. (1977). The making and breaking of affectional bonds. I. Aetiology and psychopathology in light of attachment theory. *British Journal of Psychiatry, 130*, 201–210.

Bowman, D., Scogin, F., Floyd, M., & McKendree-Smith, N. (2001). Psychotherapy length of stay and outcome: A meta-analysis of the effect of therapist sex. *Psychotherapy, 38*, 142–150.

Boyd-Franklin, N. (2006). *Black families in therapy* (2nd ed.). New York: Guilford.

Bozarth, J. D. (1984). Beyond reflection: Emergent modes of empathy. In R. E. Levant & J. M. Shlien (Eds.), *Client-centered therapy and the person-centered approach.* New York: Praeger.

Bozarth, J. D. (1991). Person-centered assessment. *Journal of Counseling and Development, 69,* 458–461.

Bradley, R., Greene, J., Russ, E., et al. (2005). A multidimensional meta-analysis of psychotherapy for PTSD. *American Journal of Psychiatry, 162,* 214–227.

Brannon, R., & David, D. S. (1976). The male sex role: Our culture's blueprint of manhood, and what it's done for us lately. In D. S. David & R. Brannon (Eds.), *The forty-nine percent majority.* Reading, MA: Addison-Wesley.

Breaux, C., & Ryujin, D. H. (1999). Use of mental health services by ethnically diverse groups within the United States. *The Clinical Psychologist, 52*(3), 4–15.

Broderick, C. B., & Schrader, S. S. (1991). The history of professional marriage and family therapy. In A. S. Gurman & D. P. Kniskern (Eds.), *Handbook of family therapy* (Vol. 2). New York: Brunner/Mazel.

Brogan, M. M., Prochaska, J. O., & Prochaska, J. M. (1999). Predicting termination and continuation status in psychotherapy using the transtheoretical model. *Psychotherapy, 36,* 105–113.

Bronowski, J. (1959). *Science and human values.* New York: Harper & Row.

Bronstein, P., & Quina, K. (Eds.). (2003). *Teaching gender and multicultural awareness: Resources for the psychology classroom.* Washington, DC: American Psychological Association.

Brooks, G. R. (1995). *The centerfold syndrome: How men can stop objectifying women and achieve true intimacy.* San Francisco: Jossey-Bass.

Brooks, G. R., & Good, G. E. (Eds.). (2001). *The new handbook of psychotherapy and counseling with men* (2 vols.). San Francisco: Jossey-Bass.

Brown, L. S. (1994). *Subversive dialogues: Theory in feminist therapy.* New York: Basic.

Brown, L. S. (2004). *Subversive dialogues: Theory in feminist therapy.* New York: Basic.

Brown, L. S. (2005a). Don't be a sheep: How this eldest daughter became a feminist therapist. *Journal of Clinical Psychology: In Session, 61,* 949–956.

Brown, L. S. (2005b). The neglect of lesbian, gay, bisexual, and transgendered clients.

In J. C. Norcross, L. E. Beutler, & R. F. Levant (Eds.), *Evidence-based practices in mental health: Debate and dialogue on the fundamental questions.* Washington, DC: American Psychological Association.

Brown, L. S. (2009). Cultural competence: A new way of thinking about integration in therapy. *Journal of Psychotherapy Integration, 19,* 340–353.

Brown, L. S., & Ballou, M. (Eds.). (1992). *Personality and psychopathology: Feminist reappraisals.* New York: Guilford.

Brown, L. S., & Brodsky, A. M. (1992). The future of feminist therapy. *Psychotherapy, 29,* 51–57.

Buber, M. (1958). *I and thou.* New York: Charles Scribner.

Budman, S. H. (2000). Behavioral health care dot-com and beyond. *American Psychologist, 55,* 1290–1300.

Budney, A. J., Higgins, S. T., Radonovich, K. J., & Novy, P. L. (2000). Adding voucher-based incentives to coping skills and motivational enhancement improves outcomes during treatment for marijuana dependence. *Journal of Consulting and Clinical Psychology, 68,* 1051–1061.

Bugental, J. F. T. (1965). *The search for authenticity.* New York: Holt, Rinehart & Winston.

Bugental, J. F. T. (1976). *The search for existential identity.* San Francisco: Jossey-Bass.

Bugental, J. F. T. (1987). *The art of the psychotherapist.* New York: Norton.

Bugental, J. F. T. (1990). *Intimate journeys: Stories from life-changing therapy.* San Francisco: Jossey-Bass.

Bugental, J. F. T. (1991). Outcomes of an existential-humanistic psychotherapy: A tribute to Rollo May. *The Humanistic Psychologist, 19,* 2–9.

Bugental, J. F. T., & Bracke, P. E. (1992). The future of existential-humanistic psychotherapy. *Psychotherapy, 29,* 28–33.

Burke, B. L., Arkowitz, H., & Dunn, C. (2002). The efficacy of motivational interviewing and its adaptations: What we know so far. In W. R. Miller & S. Rollnick (Eds.), *Motivational interviewing: Preparing people for change* (2nd ed.). New York: Guilford.

Burke, B. L., Arkowitz, H., & Menchola, M. (2003). The efficacy of motivational

interviewing: A meta-analysis of controlled clinical trials. *Journal of Consulting and Clinical Psychology, 71,* 843–861.

Burns, D. D. (1999). *Feeling good: The new mood therapy* (rev. ed.). New York: Avon.

Burns, D. D., & Nolan-Hoeksema, S. (1992). Therapeutic empathy and recovery from depression in cognitive-behavioral therapy: A structural equation model. *Journal of Consulting and Clinical Psychology, 60,* 441–449.

Bustillo, J. R., Lauriello, J., Horan, W. P., & Keith, S. J. (2001). The psychosocial treatment of schizophrenia: An update. *American Journal of Psychiatry, 158,* 163–175.

Cabral, R. R., & Smith, T. B. (2011). Racial/ethnic matching of clients and therapists in mental health services: A meta-analytic review of preferences, perceptions, and outcomes. *Journal of Counseling Psychology, 58,* 537–554.

Calati, R., Pedrini, L., Alighieri, S., et al. (2011). Is cognitive behavioural therapy an effective compliment to antidepressants in adolescents? A meta-analysis. *Acta Neuropsychiatrica, 23,* 263–271.

Camus, A. (1956). *The rebel: An essay on man in revolt.* New York: Knopf.

Cannon, W. (1939). *The wisdom of the body.* New York: Norton.

Caplan, P. J. (1989). *Don't blame mother.* New York: Harper & Row.

Cardemil, E. V., & Battle, C. L. (2003). Guess who's coming to therapy? Getting comfortable with conversations about race and ethnicity in psychotherapy. *Professional Psychology, 34,* 278–286.

Carkhuff, R. (1969). *Helping and human relations: A primer for lay and professional helpers* (Vols. 1–2). New York: Holt, Rinehart & Winston.

Carr, A. (2009a). The effectiveness of family therapy and systemic interventions for adult-focused problems. *Journal of Family Therapy, 31,* 46–74.

Carr, A. (2009b). The effectiveness of family therapy and systemic interventions for child-focused problems. *Journal of Family Therapy, 31,* 3–45.

Carroll, K. M., Rounsaville, B. J., & Gawin, F. H. (1991). A comparative trial of psychotherapies for ambulatory cocaine abusers: Relapse prevention and inter-personal psychotherapy. *Journal of Drug and Alcohol Abuse, 17*, 229–247.

Carson, R. C., & Butcher, J. N. (1992). *Abnormal psychology and modern life* (9th ed.). New York: Harper Collins.

Cass, V. C. (1979). Homosexual identity formation: A theoretical model. *Journal of Homosexuality, 4*, 219–235.

Castell, B. D., Kazantzis, N., & Moss-Morris, R. E. (2011). Cognitive behavioral therapy and graded exercise for chronic fatigue syndrome: A meta-analysis. *Clinical Psychology: Science and Practice, 18*, 311–324.

Castonguay, L. G., & Beutler, L. E. (Eds.). (2006). *Principles of therapeutic change that work.* New York: Oxford University Press.

Castonguay, L. G., Goldfried, M. R., Wiser, S., et al. (1996). Predicting the effect of cognitive therapy for depression: A study of unique and common factors. *Journal of Consulting and Clinical Psychology, 64*, 497–504.

Cautela, J. (1967). Covert sensitization. *Psychological Reports, 74*, 459–468.

Chambless, D. L. (1998). Empirically validated treatments. In G. P. Koocher, J. C. Norcross, & S. S. Hill (Eds.), *Psychologists' desk reference.* New York: Oxford University Press.

Chambless, D. L., & Gillis, M. M. (1993). Cognitive therapy of anxiety disorders. *Journal of Consulting and Clinical Psychology, 61*, 248–260.

Champney, T. F., & Schulz, E. M. (1983). *A reassessment of the effects of psychotherapy.* Paper presented at the 55th annual meeting of the Midwestern Psychological Association, Chicago, IL. (ERIC document ED237895).

Chen, K. W., Berger, C. C., Manheimer, M. S., et al. (2012). Meditative therapies for reducing anxiety: A systematic review and meta-analysis of randomized controlled trials. *Depression and Anxiety, 29*, 545–562.

Chessick, R. D. (2000). Psychoanalysis at the millennium. *American Journal of Psychotherapy, 54*, 277–290.

Chiesa, A., & Serretti, A. (2009). Mindfulness-based stress reduction for stress management in healthy people: A review and meta-analysis. *Journal of Alternative and Complementary Medicine, 15*(5), 593–600.

Chiesa, A., & Serretti, A. (2011). Mindfulness-based cognitive therapy for psychiatric disorders: A systematic review and meta-analysis. *Psychiatry Research, 187*, 441–453.

Chodorow, N. J. (1978). *The reproduction of mothering: Psychoanalysis and sociology of gender.* Berkeley: University of California Press.

Chodorow, N. J. (1989). *Feminism and psychoanalytic theory.* New Haven: Yale University Press.

Chorpita, B. F., Daleiden, E. L., Ebesutani, C., et al. (2011). Evidence-based treatments for children and adolescents: An updated review of indicators of efficacy and effectiveness. *Clinical Psychology: Science and Practice, 18*, 154–172.

Clark, D. M., & Ehlers, A. (1993). An overview of the cognitive theory and treatment of panic disorder. *Applied and Preventive Psychology, 2*, 131–139.

Clarkin, J. F., Foelsch, P., Levy, K. N., et al. (2001). The development of a psychodynamic treatment for patients with borderline personality disorder: A preliminary study of behavioral change. *Journal of Personality Disorders, 15*, 487–495.

Clarkin, J. F., & Levy, K. N. (2004). The influence of client variables on psychotherapy. In M. J. Lambert (Ed.), *Handbook of psychotherapy and behavior change* (5th ed.). New York: Wiley.

Clarkin, J. F., Levy, K. N., Lenzenweger, M. F., & Kernberg, O. F. (2007). Evaluating three treatments for Borderline Personality Disorder: A multiwave study. *American Journal of Psychiatry, 164*, 922–928.

Clarkin, J. F., Yeomans, F. E., & Kernberg, O. F. (1998). *Psychotherapy for borderline personality.* New York: Wiley.

Clarkson, P. (1992). Burnout: Typical racket systems of professional helpers. *Transactional Analysis Journal, 22*, 153–158.

Cochran, S. D., Sullivan, J. G., & Mays, V. M. (2003). Prevalence of mental disorders, psychological distress and mental health services use among lesbian, gay, and bisexual adults in the United States. *Journal of Consulting and Clinical Psychology, 71*, 53–61.

Coelho, H., Canter, P., & Ernst, E. (2007). Mindfulness-based cognitive therapy: Evaluating current evidence and informing future research. *Journal of Consulting and Clinical Psychology, 75*, 1000–1005.

Cohen, J. (1988). *Statistical power analysis for the behavioral sciences* (2nd ed.). Hillsdale, NJ: Erlbaum.

Colapinto, J. (1991). Structural family therapy. In A. S. Gurman & D. P. Kniskern (Eds.), *Handbook of family therapy* (Vol. 2). New York: Brunner/Mazel.

Colby, K. (1951). On the disagreement between Freud and Adler. *American Imago, 8*, 229–238.

Coleman, H. L. K., Wampold, B. E., & Casali, S. L. (1995). Ethnic minorities' ratings of ethnically similar and European American counselors: A meta-analysis. *Journal of Counseling Psychology, 42*, 55–64.

Coles, M. E., Turk, C. L., Jindra, L., & Heimberg, R. G. (2004). The path from initial inquiry to initiation of treatment for social anxiety disorder in an anxiety disorders specialty clinic. *Journal of Anxiety Disorders, 18*, 371–383.

Comas-Díaz, L. (1992). The future of psychotherapy with ethnic minorities. *Psychotherapy, 29*, 88–94.

Comas-Díaz, L. (1994). An integrative approach. In L. Comas-Díaz & B. Greene (Eds.), *Women of color: Integrating ethnic and gender identities in psychotherapy* (pp. 287–318). New York: Guilford.

Comas-Díaz, L. (2000). An ethnopolitical approach to working with people of color. *American Psychologist, 55*, 1319–1325.

Comas-Díaz, L. (2005). Becoming a multicultural psychotherapist: The confluence of culture, ethnicity, and gender. *Journal of Clinical Psychology: In Session, 61*, 973–982.

Comas-Díaz, L. (2011). *Multicultural care: A clinician's guide to cultural competence.* Washington, DC: American Psychological Association.

Comas-Díaz, L., & Greene, B. (Eds.). (1994). *Women of color: Integrating ethnic and gender identities in psychotherapy.* New York: Guilford.

Combs, A. W. (1988). Some current issues for person-centered therapy. *Person-Centered Review, 3,* 263–276.

Conklin, C. A., & Tiffany, S. T. (2002). Applying extinction research and theory to cue-exposure addiction treatments. *Addiction, 97,* 155–167.

Constantino, M. J., Glass, C. R., Arnkoff, D. B., et al. (2011). Expectations. In J. C. Norcross (Ed.), *Psychotherapy relationships that work* (2nd ed., pp. 354–376). New York: Oxford University Press.

Cook, J. (Ed.). (1997). *The book of positive quotations.* Minneapolis, MN: Fairview.

Cooper, M., O'Hara, M., Schmid, P. F., & Wyatt, G. (Eds.). (2007). *Handbook of person-centered psychotherapy and counseling.* Hampshire, England: Palgrave Macmillan.

Corcoran, J., & Pillai, V. (2009). A review of the research on solution-focused therapy. *British Journal of Social Work, 39,* 234–242.

Corey, G. (2012). *The art of integrative counseling* (3rd ed.). Belmont, CA: Brooks/Cole.

Corrigan, P. W. (1991). Social skills training in adult psychiatric populations: A meta-analysis. *Journal of Behavior Therapy and Experimental Psychiatry, 22,* 203–210.

Corrigan, P. W. (2001). Getting ahead of the data: A threat to some behavior therapies. *The Behavior Therapist, 24,* 189–193.

Cosgrove, L. (2004). What is postmodernism and how is it relevant to engaged pedagogy? *Teaching of Psychology, 31,* 171–177.

Cox, B. J., Endler, N. S., Lee, P. S., & Swinson, R. P. (1992). A meta-analysis of treatments for panic disorder with agoraphobia: Imipramine, alprazolam, and in vivo exposure. *Journal of Behavior Therapy and Experimental Psychiatry, 23,* 175–182.

Coyne, J. C., & Liddle, H. A. (1992). The future of systems therapy: Shedding myths and facing opportunities. *Psychotherapy, 29,* 44–50.

Cozolino, L. (2003). *The neuroscience of psychotherapy: Building and rebuilding the human brain.* New York: Norton.

Craig, E. (1988). Daseinanalysis today: A brief critical reflection. *Humanistic Psychologist, 16,* 224–232.

Craighead, W. E. (1990). There's a place for us, all of us. *Behavior Therapy, 21,* 3–23.

Critchfield, K. L., Karpiak, C., Benjamin, L. S., & Dillinger, R. J. (2012). *Preliminary evidence of effectiveness for Interpersonal Reconstructive Therapy (IRT) in reducing suicide attempts and recurring days in hospital.* Unpublished manuscript, University of Utah Neuropsychiatric Institute.

Crits-Christoph, P. (1992). The efficacy of brief dynamic psychotherapy: A meta-analysis. *American Journal of Psychiatry, 149,* 151–158.

Crits-Christoph, P., & Barber, J. P. (Eds.). (1991). *Handbook of short-term dynamic psychotherapy.* New York: Basic.

Cross, T., Bazron, B., Dennis, K., & Isaacs, M. (1989). *Towards a culturally competent system of care* (Vol. 1). Washington, DC: CASSP Technical Assistance Center.

Cuijpers, P., Donker, T., van Straten, A., et al. (2010). Is guided self-help as effective as face-to-face psychotherapy for depression and anxiety disorders? A systematic review and meta-analysis of comparative outcome studies. *Psychological Medicine, 40,* 1943–1957.

Cuijpers, P., Driessen, E., Hollon, S. D., et al. (2012). The efficacy of non-directive supportive therapy for adult depression: A meta-analysis. *Clinical Psychology Review, 32,* 280–291.

Cuijpers, P., Geraedts, A. S., van Oppen, P., et al. (2011). Interpersonal psychotherapy for depression: A meta-analysis. *American Journal of Psychiatry, 168,* 581–592.

Cuijpers, P., Marks, I. M., van Straten, A., et al. (2009). Computer-aided psychotherapy for anxiety disorders: A meta-analytic review. *Cognitive Behaviour Therapy, 38,* 66–82.

Cuijpers, P., van Straten, A., Andersson, G., & van Oppen, P. (2008). Psychotherapy for depression in adults: A meta-analysis of comparative outcome studies. *Journal of Consulting and Clinical Psychology, 76,* 909–922.

Cuijpers, P., van Straten, A., Hollon, S. D., & Andersson, G. (2010). The contribution of active medication to combined treatments of psychotherapy and pharmacotherapy for adult depression: A meta-analysis. *Acta Psychiatrica Scandinavica, 121,* 415–423.

Cuijpers, P., van Straten, A., Schuurmans, J., et al. (2010). Psychotherapy for chronic major depression and dysthymia: A meta-analysis. *Clinical Psychology Review, 30,* 51–62.

Cuijpers, P., van Straten, A., & Warmerdam, L. (2007). Problem solving therapies for depression: A meta-analysis. *European Psychiatry, 22,* 9–15.

Cummings, N. A. (1986). The dismantling of our health system: Strategies for the survival of psychological practice. *American Psychologist, 41,* 426–431.

Cummings, N. A. (1987). The future of psychotherapy: One psychologist's perspective. *American Journal of Psychotherapy, 61,* 349–360.

Curran, J. P., & Monti, P. M. (Eds.). (1982). *Social skills training.* New York: Guilford.

Curtis, N. M., Ronan, K. R., & Borduin, C. M. (2004). Multi-systemic treatment: A meta-analysis of outcome measures. *Journal of Family Psychology, 18,* 411–419.

Cushman, P., & Gilford, P. (2000). *Will managed care change our way of being?* *American Psychologist, 55,* 985–996.

Daldrup, R. J., Beutler, L. E., Engle, D., & Greenberg, L. S. (1988). *Focused expressive psychotherapy: Freeing the overcontrolled patient.* New York: Guilford.

Dattilio, F. M. (2009). *Cognitive-behavioral therapy with couples and families: A comprehensive guide for clinicians.* New York: Guilford.

Davidson, P. R., & Parker, K. C. H. (2001). Eye-movement desensitization and reprocessing (EMDR): A meta-analysis. *Journal of Consulting and Clinical Psychology, 69,* 305–316.

Davis, J. (1990). Contribution to "The Wallflower." In N. Saltzman & J. C. Norcross (Eds.), *Therapy wars.* San Francisco: Jossey-Bass.

de Beauvoir, S. (1961). *The second sex.* New York: Bantam.

DeJong, P., & Berg, I. K. (2013). *Interviewing for solutions* (4th ed.). Pacific Grove, CA: Brooks/Cole.

DeJong, P., & Hopwood, L. E. (1996). Outcome research on treatment conducted at the Brief Family Therapy Center, 1992–1993. In S. D. Miller, M. A. Hubble, & B. L. Duncan (Eds.), *Handbook of solution-focused brief therapy*. San Francisco: Jossey-Bass.

DelVecchio, T., & O'Leary, K. D. (2004). Effectiveness of anger treatments for specific anger problems: A meta-analytic review. *Clinical Psychology Review, 24,* 15–34.

de Maat, S., de Jonghe, F., Schoevers, R., & Dekker, J. (2009). The effectiveness of long-term psychoanalytic therapy: A systematic review of empirical studies. *Harvard Review of Psychiatry, 17,* 1–23.

de Maat, S., Dekker, J., Schoevers, R., & DeJonghe, F. (2006). Relative efficacy for psychotherapy and pharmacotherapy in the treatment of depression: A meta-analysis. *Psychotherapy Research, 16,* 562–572.

de Maat, S., Dekker, J., Schoevers, R., et al. (2008). Short psychodynamic supportive psychotherapy, antidepressants, and their combination in the treatment of major depression: A mega-analysis based on three randomized clinical trials. *Depression and Anxiety, 25,* 565–574.

den Boer, P. C. A. M., Wiersman, D., & Van den Bosch, R. J. (2004). Why is self-help neglected in the treatment of emotional disorders? A meta-analysis. *Psychological Medicine, 34,* 959–971.

Denes-Radomisli, M. (1976). Existential-Gestalt therapy. In P. Olsen (Ed.), *Emotional flooding*. New York: Human Sciences Press.

DeRubeis, R. J., Hollon, S. D., Amsterdam, J. D., et al. (2005). Cognitive therapy vs medications in the treatment of moderate to severe depression. *Archives of General Psychiatry, 62,* 409–416.

de Shazer, S. (1985). *Keys to solution in brief therapy*. New York: Norton.

de Shazer, S. (1988). *Clues: Investigating solutions in brief therapy*. New York: Norton.

de Shazer, S. (1994). *Words were originally magic*. New York: Norton.

de Shazer, S., & Isebaert, L. (2003). The Bruges Model: A solution-focused approach to problem drinking. *Journal of Family Psychotherapy, 14,* 43–52.

Diamond, G., & Josephson, A. (2005). Family-based treatment research: A

10-year update. *Journal of the American Academy of Child and Adolescent Psychiatry, 44,* 872–887.

DiClemente, C. C. (2002). Motivational interviewing and the stages of change. In W. R. Miller & S. Rollnick (Eds.), *Motivational interviewing: Preparing people for change* (2nd ed.). New York: Guilford.

DiClemente, C. C. (2003). *Addiction and change: How addictions develop and addicted people recover*. New York: Guilford.

DiClemente, C. C., & Hughes, S. (1990). Stages of change profiles in outpatient alcoholism treatment. *Journal of Substance Abuse, 2,* 217–235.

DiClemente, C. C., & Prochaska, J. O. (1982). Self-change and therapy change of smoking behavior: A comparison of processes of change in cessation and maintenance. *Addictive Behaviors, 7,* 133–142.

Didden, R., Duker, P. C., & Korzilius, H. (1997). Meta-analytic study on treatment effectiveness for problem behaviors with individuals who have mental retardation. *American Journal of Mental Retardation, 101,* 387–399.

Didion, J. (1968). *Slouching toward Bethlehem*. New York: Farrar, Straus and Giroux.

DiGiuseppe, R. A., Ford, P., & Esposito, M. A. (2010, August). *Meta-analytic review of efficacy studies of REBT*. Paper presented at the annual convention of the American Psychological Association, San Diego, CA.

DiGiuseppe, R. A., & Tafrate, R. C. (2003). Anger treatments for adults: A meta-analytic review. *Clinical Psychology: Science and Practice, 10,* 70–84.

Dimeff, L., & Koerner, K. (Ed.). (2007). *Dialectical behavior therapy in clinical practice: Applications across disorders and settings*. New York: Guilford.

Dimidjian, S., Hollon, S. D., Dobson, K. S., et al. (2006). Randomized trial of behavioral activation, cognitive therapy, and antidepressant medication in the acute treatment of adults with major depression. *Journal of Consulting and Clinical Psychology, 74,* 658–670.

Dobson, K. S. (1989). A meta-analysis of the efficacy of cognitive therapy for

depression. *Journal of Consulting and Clinical Psychology, 57,* 414–419.

Dobson, K. S. (Ed.). (2009). *Handbook of cognitive-behavioral therapies* (3rd ed.). New York: Guilford.

Dobson, K. S., Hollon, S. D., Dimidjian, S., et al. (2008). Randomized trial of behavioral activation, cognitive therapy, and antidepressant medication in the prevention of relapse and recurrence in major depression. *Journal of Consulting and Clinical Psychology, 76,* 468–477.

Dollard, J., & Miller, N. (1950). *Personality and psychotherapy: An analysis in terms of learning, thinking, and culture*. New York: McGraw-Hill.

Dougherty, D. D., Rauch, S. L., & Jenike, M. A. (2004). Pharmacotherapy for obsessive-compulsive disorder. *Journal of Clinical Psychology: In Session, 60,* 1195–1202.

Dovidio, J. F., & Gaertner, S. L. (2004). Aversive racism. In M. P. Zanna (Ed.), *Advances in experimental social psychology* (Vol. 36, pp. 1–51). San Diego, CA: Academic Press.

Dovidio, J. F., Gaertner, S. L., Kawakami, K., & Hodson, G. (2002). Why can't we just get along? Interpersonal biases and interracial distrust. *Cultural Diversity & Ethnic Minority Psychology, 8,* 88–102.

Dreikurs, R. (1947). The four goals of children's misbehavior. *Nervous Child, 6,* 3–11.

Dreikurs, R. (1948). *The challenge of parenthood*. New York: Duell, Sloan & Pearce.

Dreikurs, R. (1950). Techniques and dynamics of multiple psychotherapy. *Psychiatric Quarterly, 24,* 788–799.

Dreikurs, R. (1959). Early experiments with group psychotherapy. *American Journal of Psychotherapy, 13,* 882–891.

Dreikurs, R., & Stoltz, V. (1964). *Children: The challenge*. New York: Meridith.

Driessen, E., Cuijpers, P., de Matt, S. C. M., et al. (2010). The efficacy of short-term psychodynamic psychotherapy for depression: A meta-analysis. *Clinical Psychology Review, 30,* 25–36.

Drummond, D. C., & Glautier, S. (1994). A controlled trial of cue exposure treatment in alcohol dependence. *Journal of Consulting and Clinical Psychology, 62,* 809–817.

Dryden, W., & Lazarus, A. A. (1991). *A dialogue with Arnold Lazarus: "It depends."* London: Open University Press.

Dublin, J. O. A. (1981). Bio-existential therapy. *Psychotherapy, 18,* 3–10.

Duncan, B. L., Miller, S. D., Wampold, B. E., & Hubble, M. A. (Eds.). (2010). *The heart and soul of change* (2nd ed.). Washington, DC: American Psychological Association.

Dunn, R. L., & Schewebel, A. I. (1995). Meta-analytic review of marital therapy outcome research. *Journal of Family Psychology, 9,* 58–68.

Dush, D. M., Hirt, M. L., & Schroeder, H. E. (1983). Self-statement modification with adults: A meta-analysis. *Psychological Bulletin, 94,* 408–422.

Dush, D. M., Hirt, M. L., & Schroeder, H. E. (1989). Self-statement modification in the treatment of child behavior disorders: A meta-analysis. *Psychological Bulletin, 106,* 97–106.

Dworkin, M. (2005). *EMDR and the relational imperative.* New York: Routledge.

D'Zurilla, T. J., & Nezu, A. M. (1999). *Problem-solving therapy* (2nd ed.). New York: Springer.

D'Zurilla, T. J., & Nezu, A. M. (2006). *Problem-solving therapy* (3rd ed.). New York: Springer.

Eccleston, C., Morley, S., Williams, A., et al. (2002). Systematic review of randomized controlled trials of psychological therapy for chronic pain in children and adolescents, with a subset meta-analysis of pain relief. *Pain, 99,* 157–165.

Eddy, K. T., Dutra, L., Bradley, R., & Westen, D. (2004). A multidimensional meta-analysis of psychotherapy and pharmacotherapy for obsessive-compulsive disorder. *Clinical Psychology Review, 24,* 1011–1030.

Edwards, D. G. (1982). *Existential psychotherapy: The process of caring.* New York: Gardner.

Edwards, D. J. A. (1990). Cognitive-behavioral and existential-phenomenological approaches to therapy: Complementary or conflicting paradigms? *Journal of Cognitive Psychotherapy, 4,* 105–120.

Edwards, M. E., & Steinglass, P. (1995). Family therapy treatment outcomes for alcoholism. *Journal of Marital and Family Therapy, 21,* 475–509.

Eisler, R. M., & Blalock, J. A. (1991). Masculine gender role stress: Implications for the assessment of men. *Clinical Psychology Review, 11,* 45–60.

Ekers, D., Richards, D., & Gilbody, S. (2008). A meta-analysis of randomized trials of behavioural treatment of depression. *Psychological Medicine, 38,* 611–623.

Elkin, I. E., Shea, T., Watkins, J. T., et al. (1989). National Institute of Mental Health Treatment of Depression Collaborative Research Program: General effectiveness of treatment. *Archives of General Psychiatry, 46,* 974–982.

Elkins, D. N. (2009a). The medical model in psychotherapy: Its limitations and failures. *Journal of Humanistic Psychology, 49,* 66–84.

Elkins, D. N. (2009b). Why humanistic psychology lost its power and influence in American psychology: Implications for advancing humanistic psychology. *Journal of Humanistic Psychology, 49,* 267–291.

Ellenberger, H. (1958). A clinical introduction to psychiatric phenomenology and existential analysis. In R. May, E. Angel, & H. Ellenberger (Eds.), *Existence.* New York: Basic.

Ellenberger, H. (1970). *The discovery of the unconscious: The history and evolution of dynamic psychiatry.* New York: Basic.

Elliott, R., Bohart, A. C., Watson, J. C., & Greenberg, L. S. (2011). Empathy. In J. C. Norcross (Ed.), *Psychotherapy relationships that work* (2nd ed., pp. 132–151). New York: Oxford University Press.

Elliott, R., Greenberg, L. S., Watson, J., et al. (2013). Research on humanistic-experiential psychotherapies. In M. J. Lambert (Ed.), *Bergin and Garfield's handbook of psychotherapy and behavior change* (6th ed.). New York: Wiley.

Elliott, R., Watson, J., Goldman, R., & Greenberg, L. (2004). *Learning emotion-focused therapy.* Washington, DC: American Psychological Association.

Ellis, A. (1957a). *How to live with a neurotic.* New York: Crown.

Ellis, A. (1957b). Outcome of employing three techniques of psychotherapy. *Journal of Clinical Psychology, 13,* 344–350.

Ellis, A. (1958). *Sex without guilt.* New York: Grove.

Ellis, A. (1972). Rational-emotive therapy. In R. Jurjevich (Ed.), *Direct psychotherapy: 28 American originals* (vol. 1). Coral Gables, FL: University of Miami Press.

Ellis, A. (1973). *Humanistic psychotherapy: The rational-emotive approach.* New York: McGraw-Hill.

Ellis, A. (1987a). Integrative developments in rational-emotive therapy (RET). *Journal of Integrative and Eclectic Psychotherapy, 6,* 470–479.

Ellis, A. (1987b). Rational-emotive therapy: Current appraisal and future directions. *Journal of Cognitive Psychotherapy, 1,* 73–86.

Ellis, A. (1988). *How to stubbornly refuse to make yourself miserable about anything—yes, anything!* Secaucus, NJ: Lyle Stuart.

Ellis, A. (1991a). Rational-emotive treatment of simple phobias. *Psychotherapy, 28,* 452–456.

Ellis, A. (1991b). The revised ABC's of rational-emotive therapy. *Journal of Rational-Emotive and Cognitive-Behavior Therapy, 9,* 139–172.

Ellis, A. (1992). Group rational-emotive and cognitive-behavioral therapy. *International Journal of Group Psychotherapy, 42,* 63–80.

Ellis, A. (1995). *Better, deeper, and more enduring brief therapy.* New York: Brunnel/Mazel.

Ellis, A. (1999). Why rational-emotive therapy to rational-emotive behavior therapy? *Psychotherapy, 36,* 154–159.

Ellis, A. (2005). Why I (really) became a therapist. *Journal of Clinical Psychology: In Session, 61,* 945–948.

Ellis, A. (2010). *All out!: An autobiography.* Amherst, NY: Prometheus.

Ellis, A., & Dryden, W. (2007). *The practice of rational-emotive behavior therapy* (2nd ed.). New York: Springer.

Ellis, A., & Grieger, R. (Eds.). (1986). *Handbook of rational-emotive therapy* (Vols. 1–2). New York: Springer.

Ellis, A., & Harper, R. A. (1997). *A new guide to rational living* (rev. ed.). North Hollywood, CA: Wilshire.

Ellison, J. A., Greenberg, L. S., Goldman, R. N., & Angus, L. (2009). Maintenance of gains following experiential therapies for depression. *Journal of Consulting and Clinical Psychology, 77,* 103–122.

Enns, C. Z. (2010). Locational feminisms and feminist social identity analysis. *Professional Psychology: Research and Practice, 41,* 333–339.

Epstein, N., & Baucom, D. H. (2002). *Enhanced cognitive-behavioral therapy for couples.* Washington, DC: American Psychological Association.

Erikson, E. H. (1950). *Childhood and society.* New York: Norton.

Estes, W. (1971). Reward in human learning: Theoretical issues and strategic choice points. In R. Glaser (Ed.), *The nature of reinforcement.* New York: Academic.

Etkin, A., Pittenger, C., Polan, H. J., & Kandel, E. R. (2005). Toward a neurobiology of psychotherapy: Basic science and clinical applications. *Journal of Neuropsychiatry and Clinical Neurosciences, 17,* 145–158.

Eubanks-Carter, C., Burckell, L., & Goldfried, M. R. (2005). Enhancing therapeutic effectiveness with lesbian, gay, and bisexual clients. *Clinical Psychology: Science and Practice, 12,* 1–18.

Evers, K. E., Prochaska, J. O., Johnson, J. L., et al. (2006). A randomized clinical trial of a population- and transtheoretical-based stress management intervention. *Health Psychology, 25,* 521–529.

Evers, K. E., Prochaska, J. O., van Marter, D. F., et al. (2007). Transtheoretical-based bullying prevention effectiveness trials in middle schools and high schools. *Educational Research, 49,* 397–414.

Eysenck, H. J. (1970). A mish-mash of theories. *International Journal of Psychiatry, 9,* 140–146.

Fairbairn, W. (1952). *An object relations theory of the personality.* New York: Basic.

Fairburn, C. G., Jones, R., Peveler, R. C., et al. (1993). Psychotherapy and bulimia nervosa: Longer-term effects of interpersonal psychotherapy, behavior therapy, and cognitive behavior therapy. *Archives of General Psychiatry, 50,* 419–428.

Fairburn, C. G., Norman, P. A., Welch, S. L., et al. (1995). A prospective study of outcome in bulimia nervosa and the long-term effects of three psychological treatments. *Archives of General Psychiatry, 52,* 304–312.

Faludi, S. (1991). *Backlash: The undeclared war against American women.* New York: Craun.

Farber, B. A., Brink, D. C., & Raskin, P. M. (Eds.). (1998). *The psychotherapy of Carl Rogers: Cases and commentary.* New York: Guilford.

Fassinger, R. E., & Arseneau, J. R. (2007). I'd rather get wet than be under that umbrella: Differentiating the experiences and identities of lesbian, gay, bisexual, and transgender people. In K. J. Bieschke et al. (Eds.), *Handbook of counseling and psychotherapy with lesbian, gay, bisexual, and transgender clients* (2nd ed.). Washington, DC: American Psychological Association.

Felder, J. N., Dimidjian, S., & Segal, Z. (2012). Collaboration in mindfulness-based cognitive therapy. *Journal of Clinical Psychology, 68,* 187–197.

Feldman, J. M., & Kazdin, A. E. (1995). Parent management training for oppositional and conduct problem children. *The Clinical Psychologist, 48*(4), 3–5.

Fenichel, O. (1941). *Problems of psychoanalytic techniques.* Albany, NY: Psychoanalytic Quarterly.

Fenichel, O. (1945). *The psychoanalytic theory of neurosis.* New York: Norton.

Feske, U., & Chambless, D. L. (1995). Cognitive behavioral versus exposure only treatment for social phobia: A meta-analysis. *Behavior Therapy, 26,* 695–720.

Fiore, M. C., Bailey, W. C., Cohen, S. J., et al. (2000). *Treating tobacco use and dependence: Clinical practice guidelines.* Rockville, MD: U.S. Department of Health and Human Services.

Fish, L. S., & Busby, D. M. (1996). The Delphi method. In D. H. Sprenkle (Ed.), *Research methods in family therapy.* New York: Guilford.

Fisher, P. L., & Wells, A. (2005). How effective are cognitive and behavioral treatments for obsessive-compulsive disorder? A clinical significance analysis. *Behaviour Research and Therapy, 43,* 1543–1558.

Fisher, S., & Greenberg, R. P. (1996). *Freud scientifically reappraised: Testing the theories and therapy.* New York: Wiley.

Fitzpatrick, M. R., & Stalikas, A. (2008). Positive emotions as generators of

therapeutic change. *Journal of Psychotherapy Integration, 18,* 137–154.

Fletcher, R., Freeman, E., & Matthey, S. (2011). The impact of behavioural parent training on fathers' parenting: A meta-analysis of the Triple P-Positive Parenting Program. *Fathering, 9,* 291–312.

Foa, E. B., & Jaycox, L. H. (1999). Cognitive-behavioral treatment of posttraumatic stress disorder. In D. Spiegel (Ed.), *Efficacy and cost-effectiveness of psychotherapy.* Washington, DC: American Psychiatric Press.

Foa, E. B., Keane, T. M., & Friedman, M. J. (Eds.). (2008). *Effective treatment for PTSD: Practice guidelines from the International Society for Traumatic Stress Studies* (2nd ed.). New York: Guilford.

Foa, E. B., & Kozak, M. J. (1986). Emotional processing of fear and exposure to corrective information. *Psychological Bulletin, 99,* 20–35.

Foa, E. B., & Meadows, E. A. (1997). Psychosocial treatments for posttraumatic stress disorder: A critical review. In J. Spence (Ed.), *Annual review of psychology.* Palo Alto, CA: Annual Review.

Foa, E. B., & Rothbaum, B. O. (2001). *Treating the trauma of rape: Cognitive-behavioral therapy for PTSD.* New York: Guilford.

Foa, E. B., Rothbaum, B. O., Riggs, D. S., & Murdock, T. B. (1991). Treatment of posttraumatic stress disorder in rape victims: A comparison between cognitive-behavioral procedures and counseling. *Journal of Consulting and Clinical Psychology, 59,* 715–723.

Foa, E. B., & Wilson, R. (2001). *Stop obsessing! How to overcome your obsessions and compulsions* (2nd ed.). New York: Bantam.

Foa, E. B., Zoellner, L. A., Feeny, N. C., et al. (2002). Does imaginal exposure exacerbate PTSD symptoms? *Journal of Consulting and Clinical Psychology, 70,* 1022–1028.

Fonagy, P., & Target, M. (1996). Predictors of outcomes in child psychoanalysis: A retrospective study of 763 cases at the Anna Freud Centre. *Journal of the American Psychoanalytic Association, 44,* 27–77.

Forfar, C. S. (1990). *Personal communication to the authors.*

Frank, E. (1991). Interpersonal psychotherapy as a maintenance treatment for patients with recurrent depression. *Psychotherapy, 28,* 259–266.

Frank, E., Kupfer, D. J., & Perel, J. M. (1989). Early recurrence in unipolar depression. *Archives of General Psychiatry, 46,* 397–400.

Frank, E., & Spanier, C. (1995). Interpersonal psychotherapy for depression: Overview, clinical efficacy, and future directions. *Clinical Psychology: Science and Practice, 2,* 349–369.

Frank, J. D. (1961). *Persuasion and healing: A comparative study of psychotherapy.* New York: Schocken.

Frank, J. D., & Frank, J. (1991). *Persuasion and healing* (3rd ed.). Baltimore: Johns Hopkins University Press.

Frankl, V. (1963). *Man's search for meaning.* New York: Washington Square Press.

Frankl, V. (1967). *Psychotherapy and existentialism: Selected papers on logotherapy.* New York: Washington Square Press.

Frankl, V. (1969). *The will to meaning.* New York: New American Library.

Frankl, V. (1978). *The unheard cry for meaning.* New York: Simon & Schuster.

Franklin, C., Trenner, T. S., McCollum, E. E., & Gingerich, W. J. (Eds.). (2011). *Solution-focused brief therapy: A handbook of evidence-based practice.* New York: Oxford University Press.

Franks, C. (1984). Can behavior therapy find peace and fulfillment in a school of professional psychology? *The Clinical Psychologist, 28,* 11–15.

Freedman, N., Hoffenberg, J. D., Vorus, N., & Frosch, A. (1999). The effectiveness of psychoanalytic psychotherapy: The role of treatment duration, frequency of sessions, and the therapeutic relationship. *Journal of the American Psychoanalytic Association, 47,* 714–722.

Freeman, A. (Ed.). (1983). *Cognitive therapy with couples and groups.* New York: Plenum.

Freud, A. (1936). *The ego and the mechanisms of defense.* New York: International Universities Press.

Freud, S. (1919). Turnings in the ways of psychoanalytic therapy. *Collected papers* (Vol. 2). London: Hogarth.

Freud, S. (1923). *The ego and the id.* London: Hogarth.

Freud, S. (1925). Character and anal eroticism. In *Collected papers.* London: Institute for Psychoanalysis and Hogarth.

Freud, S. (1930). *Civilization and its discontents.* New York: Norton.

Freud, S. (1933/1965). *New introductory lectures on psychoanalysis.* First German edition, 1933; in *Standard edition* (Vol. 22). London: Hogarth.

Freud, S. (1937/1964). Analysis terminable and interminable. In J. Strachey (Ed.), *Complete psychological works of Sigmund Freud.* London: Hogarth.

Freud, S. (1953). *The interpretation of dreams.* First German edition, 1900; in *Standard edition* (Vols. 4 & 5), London: Hogarth. (Originally published 1900.)

Freud, S. (1965). *Interpretation of dreams* (J. Strachey, trans.). New York: Avon. (Original work published 1900.)

Freud, S. (1966). *Introductory lectures on psycho-analysis* (J. Strachey, trans.). New York: Norton. (Original work published 1917.)

Friedman, S. (1993). *The new language of change.* New York: Guilford.

Friere, P. (1970). *Cultural action for freedom.* Cambridge: Harvard Educational Review Press.

Friere, P. (1973). *Education for critical consciousness.* New York: Continuum International Publishing.

Gabbard, G. O. (Ed.). (2007). *Treatments of psychiatric disorders* (4th ed.). Washington, DC: American Psychiatric Press.

Gabbard, G. O., Litowitz, B. E., & Williams, P. (2012). *Textbook of psychoanalysis* (2nd ed.). Washington, DC: American Psychiatric Publishing.

Gaffan, E. A., Tsaousis, I., & Kemp-Wheeler, S. M. (1995). Researcher allegiance and meta-analysis: The case of cognitive therapy for depression. *Journal of Consulting and Clinical Psychology, 63,* 966–980.

Galatzer, R. M., Bachrach, H., Skolnikoff, A., & Waldron, S. (2000). *Does psychoanalysis work?* New Haven: Yale University Press.

Ganley, A. L. (1988). Feminist therapy with male clients. In M. D. Douglas & L. E. Walker (Eds.), *Feminist psychotherapies: Integration of therapeutic and feminist systems.* Norwood, NJ: Ablex.

Garfield, S. L. (1980). *Psychotherapy: An eclectic approach.* New York: Wiley.

Garfield, S. L. (1992). Eclectic psychotherapy: A common factors approach. In J. C. Norcross & M. R. Goldfried (Eds.), *Handbook of psychotherapy integration.* New York: Basic.

Garfield, S. L., & Kurtz, R. (1977). A study of eclectic views. *Journal of Clinical and Consulting Psychology, 45,* 78–83.

Gaudiano, B. A. (2005). Cognitive-behavior therapies for psychotic disorders: Current empirical status and future directions. *Clinical Psychology: Science and Practice, 12,* 33–50.

Gay, P. (1988). *Freud: A life for our time.* New Haven: Yale University Press.

Gay, P. (1990). *Reading Freud.* New Haven: Yale University Press.

Geller, J. D., Norcross, J. C., & Orlinsky, D. E. (Eds.). (2005). *The psychotherapist's own therapy.* New York: Oxford University Press.

Gendlin, E. T. (1981). *Focusing* (2nd ed.). New York: Bantam.

Gendlin, E. T. (1996). *Focusing-oriented psychotherapy: A manual of the experiential method.* New York: Guilford.

Gerber, L. (1992). Intimate politics: Connectedness and the social-political self. *Psychotherapy, 29,* 626–630.

Gergen, K. J. (1994). *Realities and relationships: Soundings in social construction.* Cambridge, MA: Harvard University Press.

Gergen, K. J. (2001). Psychological science in a postmodern context. *American Psychologist, 56,* 803–813.

Giesen-Bloo, J., van Dyck, R., Spinhoven, P., et al. (2006). Outpatient psychotherapy for Borderline Personality Disorder: Randomized trial of schema-focused therapy vs. transference-focused psychotherapy. *Archives of General Psychiatry, 63,* 649–658.

Gill, M. M. (1994). *Psychoanalysis in transition: A personal view.* Hillsdale, NJ: Analytic Press.

Gillies, D., Taylor, F., Gray, C., et al. (2012). Psychological therapies for the treatment of post-traumatic stress disorder in children and adolescents. *Cochrane Database of Systematic Reviews, 12*, CD006726.

Gilligan, C. (1982). *In a different voice: Psychological theory and women's development*. Cambridge, MA: Harvard University Press.

Gingerich, W. J., Kim, J. S., Stams, G. J. J. M., & Macdonald, A. J. (2012). Solution-focused brief therapy outcome research. In C. Franklin, T. S. Trepper, W. J. Gingerich, & E. E. McCollum (Eds.), *Solution-focused brief therapy*. New York: Oxford University Press.

Glass, C. R., & Arnkoff, D. B. (1992). Behavior therapy. In D. K. Freedheim (Ed.), *History of psychotherapy: A century of change*. Washington, DC: American Psychological Association.

Glass, C. R., Victor, B. J., & Arnkoff, D. B. (1992). Empirical research on integrative and eclectic psychotherapies. In G. Stricker & J. R. Gold (Eds.), *Comprehensive handbook of psychotherapy integration*. New York: Plenum.

Glasser, W. (1975). *Reality therapy*. New York: Harper & Row.

Glasser, W. (1984). *Control theory: A new explanation of how we control our lives*. New York: Harper & Row.

Glasser, W. (1999). *Choice theory: A new psychology of personal freedom*. New York: Norton.

Glasser, W. (2001). *Counseling with choice theory: The new reality therapy*. New York: HarperCollins.

Glover, E. (1925). Notes on oral character formation. *International Journal of Psychoanalysis, 6*, 131–154.

Gold, J., & Stricker, G. (2001). A relational psychodynamic perspective on assimilative integration. *Journal of Psychotherapy Integration, 11*, 43–58.

Goldberg, G. A., & Kremen, E. (Eds.). (1990). *The feminization of poverty: Only in America?* New York: Praeger.

Goldenberg, I., & Goldenberg, H. (2008). *Family therapy: An overview* (7th ed.). Belmont, CA: Brooks/Cole.

Goldenberg, I., & Goldenberg, H. (2013). *Family therapy: An overview* (8th ed.). Belmont, CA: Brooks/Cole.

Goldfried, M. R. (1980). Toward the delineation of therapeutic change principles. *American Psychologist, 35*, 991–999.

Goldfried, M. R. (Ed.). (2001). *How therapists change*. Washington, DC: American Psychological Association.

Goldfried, M. R., & Castonguay, L. G. (1992). The future of psychotherapy integration. *Psychotherapy, 29*, 4–10.

Goldfried, M. R., & Davison, G. (1976). *Clinical behavior therapy*. New York: Holt, Rinehart & Winston.

Goldfried, M. R., & Davison, G. (1994). *Clinical behavior therapy* (rev. ed.). New York: Wiley.

Goldfried, M. R., & Newman, C. (1992). A history of psychotherapy integration. In J. C. Norcross & M. R. Goldfried (Eds.), *Handbook of psychotherapy integration*. New York: Basic.

Goldman, R. N., Greenberg, L. S., & Angus, L. (2006). The effects of adding emotion-focused interventions to the client-centered relationship conditions in the treatment of depression. *Psychotherapy Research, 16*, 536–546.

Goldstein, A. J., de Beurs, E., Chambless, D. L., & Wilson, K. A. (2000). EMDR for panic disorder with agoraphobia: Comparison with waiting list and credible attention-placebo control conditions. *Journal of Consulting and Clinical Psychology, 68*, 947–956.

Gonzalez, J. E., Nelson, J. R., Gutkin, T. B., et al. (2004). Rational emotive therapy with children and adolescents: A meta-analysis. *Journal of Emotional and Behavioral Disorders, 12*, 222–235.

Good, G. E., & Brooks, G. R. (Eds.). (2005). *The new handbook of psychotherapy and counseling with men* (rev. ed.). San Francisco: Jossey-Bass.

Good, G. E., & Robertson, J. M. (2010). To accept a pilot? Addressing men's ambivalence and altering their expectancies about therapy. *Psychotherapy, 47*, 306–315.

Goodyear, R. K., Murdock, N., Lichtenberg, J. W., et al. (2008). Stability and change in counseling psychologists' identities, roles, functions, and career satisfaction across 15 years. *The Counseling Psychologist, 36*, 220–249.

Gopalan, G., Goldstein, L., Klingenstein, K., et al. (2010). Engaging families in child mental health treatment: Updates and special considerations. *Journal of the Canadian Academy of Child and Adolescent Psychiatry, 19*, 182–196.

Gordon, T. (1970). *Parent effectiveness training*. New York: Peter Wyden.

Gordon, T. (1974). *Teacher effectiveness training*. New York: Peter Wyden.

Gotlib, I. H., & McCabe, S. G. (1990). Marriage and psychopathology: A critical examination. In F. Fincham & T. Bradbury (Eds.), *The psychology of marriage: Conceptual, empirical, and applied perspectives*. New York: Guilford.

Gotlib, I. H., & Whiffen, V. E. (1991). The interpersonal context of depression: Implications for theory and research. In W. H. Jones & D. Perlman (Eds.), *Advances in personal relationships* (Vol. 3). London: Jessica Kingsley.

Gottlieb, N. H., Galavotti, C., McCuan, R. S., & McAlister, A. L. (1990). Specification of a social cognitive model predicting smoking cessation in a Mexican-American population: A prospective study. *Cognitive Therapy and Research, 14*, 529–542.

Gould, R. A., Mueser, K. T., Bolton, E., et al. (2001). Cognitive therapy for psychosis in schizophrenia: An effect size analysis. *Schizophrenia Research, 48*, 335–342.

Gould, R. A., Otto, M. W., & Pollack, M. H. (1995). A meta-analysis of treatment outcome for panic disorder. *Clinical Psychology Review, 15*, 819–844.

Gould, R. A., Otto, M. W., Pollack, M. H., & Yap, L. (1997). Cognitive behavioral and pharmacological treatment of generalized anxiety disorder: A preliminary meta-analysis. *Behavior Therapy, 28*, 285–305.

Grawe, K. (2007). *Neurotherapy: How the neurosciences inform effective psychotherapy*. Mahwah, NJ: Lawrence Erlbaum.

Grawe, K., Donati, R., & Bernauer, F. (1998). *Psychotherapy in transition*. Seattle, WA: Hogrefe & Huber.

Greenberg, G. (1977). The family interactional perspective: A study and examination of the work of Don D. Jackson. *Family Process, 16*, 385–412.

Greenberg, L. S. (1995). *Process experiential psychotherapy*. Washington, DC: American Psychological Association.

Greenberg, L. S. (2002). *Emotion-focused therapy: Coaching clients to work through feelings.* Washington, DC: American Psychological Association.

Greenberg, L. S. (2012). Emotions, the great captains of our lives: Their role in the process of change in psychotherapy. *American Psychologist, 67,* 697–707.

Greenberg, L. S., Elliott, R., & Lietaer, G. (1994). Research on experiential psychotherapy. In A. E. Bergin & S. L. Garfield (Eds.), *Handbook of psychotherapy and behavior change* (4th ed.). New York: Wiley.

Greenberg, L. S., & Johnson, S. M. (1988). *Emotionally focused therapy for couples.* New York: Guilford.

Greenberg, L. S., Rice, L. N., & Elliott, R. (1993). *Facilitating emotional change.* New York: Guilford.

Greenberg, L. S., & Watson, J. (1998). Experiential therapy of depression: Differential effects of client-centered relationship conditions and process-experiential interventions. *Psychotherapy Research, 8,* 210–224.

Greenberg, L. S., Watson, J. C., & Lietaer, G. (Eds.). (1998). *Handbook of experiential psychotherapy.* New York: Guilford.

Greenberger, D., & Padesky, C. (1995). *Mind over mood.* New York: Guilford.

Greene, B., & Croom, G. L. (Eds.). (2000). *Psychological perspectives on lesbian, gay and bisexual issues* (Vol. 5). Thousand Oaks, CA: Sage.

Greenson, R. R. (1967). *The technique and practice of psychoanalysis* (Vol. 1). New York: International Universities Press.

Greenspoon, J. (1955). The reinforcing effect of two spoken sounds on the frequency of two responses. *American Journal of Psychology, 68,* 409–416.

Gregory, R. J., Canning, S. S., Lee, T. W., & Wise, J. C. (2004). Cognitive bibliotherapy for depression: A meta-analysis. *Professional Psychology, 35,* 275–280.

Grencavage, L. M., & Norcross, J. C. (1990). Where are the commonalities among the therapeutic common factors? *Professional Psychology: Research and Practice, 21,* 372–378.

Gresham, F. M., Cook, C. R., Crews, S. D., & Kern, L. (2004). Social skills training for children and youth with emotional and behavioral disorders: Validity considerations and future directions. *Behavioral Disorders, 30,* 32–46.

Griffith, J. D., Rowan-Szal, G. A., Roark, R. R., & Simpson, D. D. (2000). Contingency management in outpatient methadone treatment: A meta-analysis. *Drug and Alcohol Dependence, 58,* 55–66.

Griner, D., & Smith, T. B. (2006). Culturally adapted mental health interventions: A meta-analytic review. *Psychotherapy, 43,* 531–548.

Grissom, R. J. (1996). The magical number 762: Meta-analysis of the probability of superior outcome in comparisons involving therapy, placebo, and control. *Journal of Consulting and Clinical Psychology, 64,* 973–982.

Grote, N. K., Bledsoe, S. E., Swartz, H. A., & Frank, E. (2004). Culturally relevant psychotherapy for perinatal depression in low-income ob/gyn patients. *Clinical Social Work Journal, 32,* 327–347.

Guisinger, S., & Blatt, S. J. (1994). Individuality and relatedness: Evolution of a fundamental dialectic. *American Psychologist, 49,* 104–111.

Gunter, R. W., & Whittal, M. L. (2010). Dissemination of cognitive-behavioral treatments for anxiety disorders: Overcoming barriers and improving patient access. *Clinical Psychology Review, 30,* 194–202.

Guntrip, H. (1973). *Psychoanalytic therapy, theory, and the self.* New York: Basic Books.

Gurman, A. S., Kniskern, D. P., & Pinsof, W. M. (1986). Research on the process and outcome of marital and family therapy. In S. L. Garfield & A. E. Bergin (Eds.), *Handbook of psychotherapy and behavior change* (3rd ed.). New York: Wiley.

Haaga, D. A. F. (2000). Introduction to the special section on stepped care models in psychotherapy. *Journal of Consulting and Clinical Psychology, 68,* 547–548.

Haaga, D. A. F., Dryden, W., & Dancey, C. P. (1991). Measurement of rational emotive therapy in outcome studies. *Journal of Rational Emotive & Cognitive Behavior Therapy, 9,* 73–93.

Hahlweg, K., & Markman, H. J. (1988). Effectiveness of behavioral marital therapy: Empirical status of behavioral techniques in preventing and alleviating marital distress. *Journal of Consulting and Clinical Psychology, 56,* 440–447.

Halchuk, R. E., Makinen, J., & Johnson, S. M. (2010). Resolving attachment injuries in couples using emotionally focused therapy: A three-year follow-up. *Journal of Couple and Relationship Therapy, 9,* 31–47.

Haldeman, D. L. (1994). The practice and ethics of sexual conversion therapy. *Journal of Clinical and Consulting Psychology, 62,* 221–227.

Haley, J. (1973). *Uncommon therapies: The psychiatric techniques of Milton Erickson, M.D.* New York: Norton.

Haley, J. (1976). *Problem-solving therapy: New strategies for effective family therapies.* San Francisco: Jossey-Bass.

Haley, J. (1980). *Leaving home.* New York: McGraw-Hill.

Haley, J. (1984). *Ordeal therapy.* San Francisco: Jossey-Bass.

Haley, J. (1986). *The power tactics of Jesus Christ and other essays* (2nd ed.). Rockville, MD: Triangle.

Haley, J. (1990). *Strategies of psychotherapy* (2nd ed.). New York: Norton.

Halgin, R. P., & Whitbourne, S. K. (1993). *Abnormal psychology.* Philadelphia: Harcourt Brace Jovanovich.

Hall, C., & Lindzey, G. (1970). *Theories of personality.* New York: Wiley.

Hall, C. C. I. (1997). Cultural malpractice: The growing obsolescence of psychology with the changing U.S. population. *American Psychologist, 52,* 642–651.

Hammen, C. (1991). The generation of stress in the course of unipolar depression. *Journal of Abnormal Psychology, 100,* 555–561.

Hand, I., Lamontagne, Y., & Marks, I. M. (1974). Group exposure (flooding) in vivo for agoraphobics. *British Journal of Psychiatry, 124,* 588–602.

Hare-Mustin, R. (1987). The problem of gender in family therapy theory. *Family Process, 26,* 15–27.

Hargaden, H., & Sills, C. (2002). *Transactional analysis: A relational approach.* New York: Brunner-Routledge.

Harman, R. (1995). Gestalt therapy as brief therapy. *Gestalt Journal, 18,* 77–85.

Harper, R. A. (1959). *Psychoanalysis and psychotherapy: 36 systems*. Englewood Cliffs, NJ: Prentice Hall.

Harris, A. B., & Harris, T. A. (1990). *Staying OK*. New York: Harper & Row.

Harris, H., & Bruner, C. (1971). A comparison of self-control and a contract procedure for weight control. *Behavior Research and Therapy, 9,* 347–354.

Harris, T. A. (1967). *I'm OK—you're OK*. New York: Harper & Row.

Hartmann, A., Herzog, T., & Drinkman, A. (1992). Psychotherapy of bulimia nervosa: What is effective? A meta-analysis. *Journal of Psychosomatic Research, 36,* 159–167.

Hartmann, H. (1958). *Ego psychology and the problem of adaptation*. New York: International Universities Press.

Hartmann, H., Kris, E., & Loewenstein, R. M. (1947). Comments on the formation of psychic structure. In A. Freud et al. (Eds.), *The psychoanalytic study of the child*. New York: International Universities Press.

Hartshorne, T. S. (1991). The evolution of psycho-therapy: Where are the Adlerians? *Individual Psychology, 47,* 321–325.

Harvey, S. T., & Taylor, J. E. (2010). A meta-analysis of the effects of psychotherapy with sexually abused children and adolescents. *Clinical Psychology Review, 30,* 517–535.

Haslam, C., & Lawrence, W. (2004). Health-related behavior and beliefs of pregnant smokers. *Health Psychology, 23,* 486–491.

Hatcher, C., & Himelstein, P. (Eds.). (1976). *The handbook of Gestalt therapy*. New York: Jason Aronson.

Hay, P. P. J., Bacallchuk, J., Stefano, S., & Kashyap, P. (2009). Psychological treatments for bulimia nervosa and binging. *Cochrane Database or Systematic Reviews, 4,* CD000562.

Hayes, S. C., Follette, V. M., & Linehan, M. M. (Eds.). (2004). *Mindfulness and acceptance: Expanding the cognitive-behavioral tradition*. New York: Guilford.

Hayes, S. C., Luoma, J. B., Bond, F. W., et al. (2006). Acceptance and commitment therapy: Model, processes and outcomes. *Behavioral Research and Therapy, 44,* 1–25.

Hayes, S. C., Strosahl, K., Bunting, K., et al. (2004). What is acceptance and commitment therapy? In S. C. Hayes & K.

Strosahl (Eds.), *A practical guide to acceptance and commitment therapy* (pp. 1–29). New York: Springer.

Hayes, S. C., Wilson, K. G., Gifford, E. V., et al. (1996). Experiential avoidance and behavioral disorders: A functional dimensional approach to diagnosis and treatment. *Journal of Consulting and Clinical Psychology, 64,* 1152–1168.

Hays, P. A. (1996). Culturally responsive assessment with diverse older clients. *Professional Psychology: Research and Practice, 27,* 188–193.

Heard, H. L., & Linehan, M. M. (2005). Integrative therapy for borderline personality disorder. In J. C. Norcross & M. R. Goldfried (Eds.), *Handbook of psychotherapy integration* (2nd ed.). New York: Oxford University Press.

Heidegger, M. (1962). *Being and time*. New York: Harper & Row.

Held, B. S. (1991). The process/content distinction in psychotherapy revisited. *Psychotherapy, 28,* 207–217.

Held, B. S. (1995). *Back to reality: A critique of postmodern theory in psychotherapy*. New York: Norton.

Helms, J. E. (Ed.). (1990). *Black and White racial identity: Theory, research, and practice*. Westport, CT: Greenwood Press.

Hendricks, I. (1943). The discussion of the "instinct to master." *Psychoanalytic Quarterly, 12,* 561–565.

Henggeler, S. W. (2011). Efficacy studies to large-scale transport: The development and validation of MST programs. *Annual Review of Clinical Psychology, 7,* 351–381.

Henggeler, S. W., & Schoenwald, S. K. (2003). Multisystemic therapy. In T. L. Sexton, G. R. Weeks, & M. S. Robbins (Eds.), *Handbook of family therapy*. New York: Brunner-Routledge.

Henggeler, S. W., Schoenwald, S. K., Borduin, C. M., et al. (2009). *Multisystemic therapy for antisocial behavior in children and adolescents* (2nd ed.). New York: Guilford.

Herman, J. L. (1997). *Trauma and recovery*. New York: Basic.

Hettema, J., Steele, J., & Miller, W. R. (2005). Motivational interviewing. *Annual Review of Clinical Psychology, 1,* 91–111.

Heuzenroeder, L., Donnelly, M., Haby, M. M., et al. (2004). Cost-effectiveness of psychological and pharmacological interventions for generalized anxiety disorder and panic disorder. *Australian and New Zealand Journal of Psychiatry, 38,* 602–612.

Higgins, S. T., & Silverman, K. (Eds.). (1999). *Motivating behavior change among illicit-drug abusers: Research on contingency management interventions*. Washington, DC: American Psychological Association.

Higgins, S. T., Silverman, K., & Heil, S. H. (2007). *Contingency management in substance abuse treatment*. New York: Guilford Press.

Hill, K. A. (1987). Meta-analysis of paradoxical interventions. *Psychotherapy, 24,* 266–270.

Hinrichsen, G. A., & Clougherty, K. F. (2006). *Interpersonal psychotherapy for depressed older adults*. Washington, DC: American Psychological Association.

Hoffman, B. M., Papas, R. K., Chatkoff, D. K., & Kerns, R. D. (2007). Meta-analysis of psychological interventions for chronic low back pain. *Health Psychology, 26,* 1–9.

Hoffman, E. (1994). *The drive for self: Alfred Adler and the founding of individual psychology*. Reading, MA: Addison-Wesley.

Hofmann, S. G., Sawyer, A. T., Witt, A. A., & Oh, D. (2010). The effect of mindfulness-based therapy on anxiety and depression: A meta-analytic review. *Journal of Consulting and Clinical Psychology, 78,* 169–183.

Hofmann, S. G., & Smits, J. A. J. (2008). Cognitive-behavioral therapy for adult anxiety disorders: A meta-analysis of randomized placebo-controlled trials. *Journal of Clinical Psychiatry, 69,* 621–632.

Hofmann, S. G., & Spiegel, D. A. (1999). Panic control treatment and its applications. *Journal of Psychotherapy Practice and Research, 8,* 3–11.

Holland, J. M., Neimeyer, R. A., Currier, J. M., & Berman, J. S. (2007). The efficacy of personal construct therapy: A comprehensive review. *Journal of Clinical Psychology, 63,* 93–107.

Hollin, C. R., & Trower, P. (Eds.). (1986). *Handbook of social skills training.* New York: Pergamon.

Hollon, S. D., & Beck, A. T. (1994). Cognitive and cognitive-behavioral therapies. In A. E. Bergin & S. L. Garfield (Eds.), *Handbook of psychotherapy and behavior change* (4th ed.). New York: Wiley.

Hollon, S. D., DeRubeis, R. J., Shelton, R. C., et al. (2005). Prevention of relapse following cognitive therapy vs. medications in moderate to severe depression. *Archives of General Psychiatry, 62,* 417–422.

Hollon, S. D., & DiGiuseppe, R. (2011). Cognitive theories of psychotherapy. In J. C. Norcross, G. R. VandenBos, & D. K. Freedheim (Eds.), *History of psychotherapy* (2nd ed.). Washington, DC: American Psychological Association.

Holroyd, K. A., & Penzien, D. B. (1990). Pharmacological versus non-pharmacological prophylaxis of recurrent migraine headache: A meta-analytic review of clinical trials. *Pain, 42,* 1–13.

Hora, T. (1959). Epistemological aspects of existence and psychotherapy. *Journal of Individual Psychology, 15,* 166–173.

Hora, T. (1960). The process of existential psychotherapy. *Psychiatric Quarterly, 34,* 495–504.

Horne, A., & Kiselica, M. S. (Eds.). (1999). *Handbook of counseling boys and men.* Thousand Oaks, CA: Sage.

Horner, A. (1979). *Object relations and the developing ego in therapy.* New York: Jason Aronson.

Horowitz, L. M., & Strack, S. (Eds.). (2011). *Handbook of interpersonal psychology: Theory, research, assessment, and therapeutic approaches.* New York: Wiley.

Horrell, S. C. V. (2008). Effectiveness of cognitive-behavioral therapy with adult ethnic minority clients: A review. *Professional Psychology: Research and Practice, 39,* 160–168.

Horvath, A. O., Del Re, A., Flückiger, C., & Symonds, D. (2011). Alliance in individual psychotherapy. In J. C. Norcross (Ed.), *Psychotherapy relationships that work* (2nd ed.). New York: Oxford University Press.

Houts, A. C., Berman, J. S., & Abramson, H. (1994). Effectiveness of psychological and pharmacological treatments for nocturnal enuresis. *Journal of Consulting and Clinical Psychology, 62,* 737–745.

Hoyt, M. F. (1995). *Brief therapy and managed care.* San Francisco: Jossey-Bass.

Hoyt, M. F. (Ed.). (1998). *The handbook of constructive therapies.* San Francisco: Jossey-Bass.

Hoyt, M. F. (2000). *Some stories are better than others.* Philadelphia: Brunner/Mazel.

Hubble, M. A., Duncan, B. L., & Miller, S. D. (Eds.). (1999). *The heart and soul of change.* Washington, DC: American Psychological Association.

Hull, C. (1943). *Principles of behavior.* New York: Appleton-Century-Crofts.

Hunot, V., Churchill, R., Teixeira, V., & Silva de Lima, M. (2007). Psychological therapies for generalised anxiety disorder. *Cochrane Database of Systematic Reviews, 1,* CD001848.

Hunt, W. A., Barnett, L. W., & Branch, L. G. (1971). Relapse rates in addiction programs. *Journal of Clinical Psychology, 27,* 455–456.

Huxley, N. A., Rendall, M., & Sederer, L. (2000). Psychosocial treatments in schizophrenia: A review of the past 20 years. *Journal of Nervous & Mental Disease, 188,* 187–201.

Hyde, J. S. (1991). *Half the human experience* (4th ed.). Lexington, MA: Heath.

Hyman, R. B., Feldmart, H. R., Harris, R. B., et al. (1989). The effects of relaxation training on clinical symptoms: A meta-analysis. *Nursing Research, 8,* 216–220.

Imel, Z. E., Malterer, M. B., McKay, K. M., & Wampold, B. E. (2008). A meta-analysis of psychotherapy and medication in unipolar depression and dysthymia. *Journal of Affective Disorders, 110,* 197–206.

Institute of Medicine. (2001). *Crossing the quality chasm: A new health system for the 21st century.* Washington, DC: National Academy Press.

Institute of Medicine. (2003). *Unequal treatment: Confronting racial and ethnic disparities in health care.* Washington, DC: National Academy Press.

Irvin, J. E., Bowers, C. A., Dunn, M. E., & Wang, M. C. (1999). Efficacy of relapse prevention: A meta-analytic review. *Journal of Consulting and Clinical Psychology, 67,* 563–570.

Issakidis, C., & Andrews, G. (2004). Pretreatment attrition and dropout in an outpatient clinic for anxiety disorders. *Acta Psychiatrica Scandinavica, 109,* 426–433.

Ivey, A. E., & Brooks-Harris, J. E. (2005). Integrative psychotherapy with culturally diverse clients. In J. C. Norcross & M. R. Goldfried (Eds.), *Handbook of psychotherapy integration* (2nd ed.). New York: Oxford University Press.

Jackson, D. (1967). The eternal triangle. In J. Haley & L. Hoffman (Eds.), *Techniques of family therapy.* New York: Basic.

Jackson, L. C. (2004). Putting on blinders or bifocals: Using the new multicultural guidelines for educations and training. *The Clinical Psychologist, 57,* 11–16.

Jackson, L. C., & Greene, B. A. (Eds.). (2000). *Psychotherapy with African American women.* New York: Guilford.

Jacobson, E. (1938). *Progressive relaxation.* Chicago: University of Chicago Press.

Jacobson, N. S., & Christensen, A. (1998). *Acceptance and change in couple therapy: A therapist's guide to transforming relationships.* New York: Norton.

Jacobson, N. S., & Margolin, G. (1979). *Marital therapy: Strategies based on social learning and behavior exchange principles.* New York: Brunner/Mazel.

Jacobson, N. S., Martell, C. R., & Dimidjian, S. (2001). Behavioral activation treatment for depression: Returning to contextual roots. *Clinical Psychology: Science and Practice, 8,* 255–270.

Jacobson, N. S., Roberts, L. J., Berns, S. B., & McGlinchey, J. B. (1999). Methods for defining and determining the clinical significance of treatment effects: Description, application, and alternatives. *Journal of Consulting & Clinical Psychology, 76,* 300–309.

Jakobsen, J. C., Hansen, J. L., Simonsen, S., et al. (2012). Effects of cognitive therapy versus interpersonal therapy in patients with major depressive disorder: A systemaic review of randomized clinical trails with meta-analyses and trail sequential analyses. *Psychological Medicine, 42,* 1343–1357.

James, M., & Jongeward, D. (1971). *Born to win.* Reading, MA: Addison-Wesley.

Jensen, C. D., Cushing, C. C., Aylward, B. S., et al. (2011). Effectiveness of motivational interviewing interventions for adolescent substance use behavior change: A meta-analytic review. *Journal of Consulting and Clinical Psychology, 79*, 433–440.

Jensen, J. P., Bergin, A. E., & Greaves, D. W. (1990). The meaning of eclecticism: New survey and analysis of components. *Professional Psychology: Research and Practice, 21*, 124–130.

Johnson, S. M. (2004). *The practice of emotionally focused couple therapy* (2nd ed.). New York: Brunner-Routledge.

Johnson, S. M., Hunsley, J., Greenberg, L., & Schindler, D. (1999). Emotionally focused couples therapy: Status and challenges. *Clinical Psychology: Science and Practice, 6*, 67–79.

Johnson, W. G., Tsoh, J. Y., & Varnado, P. J. (1996). Eating disorders: Efficacy of pharmacological and psychological interventions. *Clinical Psychology Review, 16*, 457–478.

Jones, C., Hacker, D., Cormac, I., et al. (2012). Cognitive behaviour therapy versus other psychosocial treatments for schizophrenia. *Cochrane Database of Systematic Reviews, 4*, CD008712.

Jones, E. (1955). *The life and works of Sigmund Freud* (Vol. 2). New York: Basic.

Jones, H., Edwards, L., Vallis, M. T., et al. (2003). Changes in diabetes self-care behaviors make a difference to glycemic control: The diabetes stages of change (DiSC) study. *Diabetes Care, 26*, 732–737.

Jordan, J. V. (2010). *Relational-cultural therapy*. Washington, DC: American Psychological Association.

Jordan, J. V., Kaplan, A. G., Miller, J. B., Stiver, I. P., & Surrey, J. L. (1991). *Women's growth in connection: Writings from the Stone Center*. New York: Guilford.

Jordan, J. V., Walker, M., & Hartling, L. M. (Eds.). (2004). *The complexity of connection: Writings from the Jean Baker Miller Training Institute*. New York: Guilford.

Kabat-Zinn, J. (1990). *Full catastrophe living: Using the wisdom of your body and mind to face stress, pain and illness*. New York: Bantam.

Kandel, E. R. (1998). A new intellectual framework for psychiatry. *American Journal of Psychiatry, 155*, 457–469.

Kantrowitz, R. E., & Ballou, M. (1992). A feminist critique of cognitive-behavioral therapy. In L. S. Brown & M. Ballou (Eds.), *Personality and psychopathology: Feminist reappraisals*. New York: Guilford.

Kaplan, A. G., Fibel, B., Greif, A. C., et al. (1983). The process of sex-role integration in psychotherapy: Contributions from a training experience. *Psychotherapy: Theory, Research and Practice, 20*, 476–485.

Kaplan, H. S. (1974). *The new sex therapy*. New York: Brunner/Mazel.

Kaplan, H. S. (1987). *The illustrated manual of sex therapy* (2nd ed.). New York: Brunner/Mazel.

Karlin, B. E., Brown, G. K., Trockel, M., et al. (2012). National dissemination of cognitive-behavioral therapy for depression in the department of veterans affairs health care system: Therapist and patient-level outcomes. *Journal of Consulting and Clinical Psychology, 80*, 707–718.

Karpiak, C. P., & Zaboski, B. A. (2013). Lifetime prevalence of mental disorders in the general population. In G. P. Koocher, J. C. Norcross, & B. A. Greene (Eds.), *Psychologists' desk reference* (3rd ed.). New York: Oxford University Press.

Kaslow, F. (Ed.). (1996). *Handbook of relational diagnosis and dysfunctional family patterns*. New York: Wiley.

Kaslow, N. J., Blount, A., & Sue, S. (2005). *Health care for the whole person: Moving toward improved health outcomes*. Washington, DC: American Psychological Association.

Kazantzis, N., Deane, F. P., & Ronan, K. R. (2000). Homework assignments in cognitive and behavioral therapy: A meta-analysis. *Clinical Psychology: Science and Practice, 7*, 189–202.

Kazantzis, N., Whittington, C., & Dattilio, F. (2010). Meta-analysis of homework effects in cognitive and behavioral therapy: A replication and extension. *Clinical Psychology: Science and Practice, 17*, 144–156.

Kazdin, A. E. (1984). Integration of psychodynamic and behavioral psychotherapies: Conceptual versus empirical synthesis. In H. Arkowitz & S. B. Messer (Eds.), *Psychoanalytic therapy and behavior therapy: Is integration possible?* New York: Plenum.

Kazdin, A. E. (1991). Effectiveness of psychotherapy with children and adolescents. *Journal of Consulting and Clinical Psychology, 39*, 785–798.

Kazdin, A. E. (2001). *Behavior modification in applied settings* (6th ed.). Pacific Grove, CA: Brooks/Cole.

Kazdin, A. E. (2005). *Parent management training*. New York: Oxford University Press.

Keen, E. (1970). *Three faces of being: Toward an existential clinical psychology*. New York: Irvington.

Kelly, G. A. (1955). *The psychology of personal constructs* (2 vols.). New York: Norton.

Kempler, W. (1973). Gestalt therapy. In R. Corsini (Ed.), *Current psychotherapies*. Itasca, IL: Peacock.

Kendall, P. C. (Ed.). (2005). *Child and adolescent therapy: Cognitive-behavioral procedures* (3rd ed.). New York: Guilford.

Kendall, P. C., & Braswell, L. (1992). *Cognitive-behavioral therapy for impulsive children* (2nd ed.). New York: Guilford.

Kernberg, O. F. (1973). Summary and conclusions of "Psychotherapy and psychoanalysis: Final report of the Menninger Foundation's Psychotherapy Research Project." *International Journal of Psychiatry, 11*, 62–77.

Kernberg, O. F. (1975). *Borderline conditions and pathological narcissism*. New York: Jason Aronson.

Kernberg, O. F. (1976). *Object-relations theory and clinical psychoanalysis*. New York: Jason Aronson.

Kernberg, O. F. (1984). *Severe personality disorders: Psychotherapeutic strategies*. New Haven: Yale University Press.

Kernberg, O. F., Ellis, A., Person, E., et al. (1993, April). *A meeting of the minds: Is integration possible?* Two-day conference sponsored by the Institute for Rational-Emotive Therapy, New York.

Kernberg, O. F., Selzer, M. A., Koenigsberg, H. W., et al. (1989). *Psychodynamic psychotherapy of borderline patients.* New York: Basic.

Kerr, M., & Bowen, M. (1988). *Family evaluation.* New York: Norton.

Keshen, A. (2006). A new look at existential psychotherapy. *American Journal of Psychotherapy, 60,* 285–298.

Kessler, R. C., Zhao, S., Katz, S. J., et al. (1999). Past-year use of outpatient services for psychiatric problems in the National Comorbidity Survey. *American Journal of Psychiatry, 156,* 115–123.

Kierkegaard, S. (1954a). *Fear and trembling.* New York: Doubleday.

Kierkegaard, S. (1954b). *The sickness unto death.* New York: Doubleday.

Kim, J. S. (2008). Examining the effectiveness of solution-focused brief therapy: A meta-analysis. *Research on Social Work Practice, 18,* 107–116.

King, M., Semlyen, J., Tai, S. S., et al. (2008). A systematic review of mental disorder, suicide, and deliberate self-harm in lesbian, gay, and bisexual people. *BMC Psychiatry, 8,* 70.

Kirschenbaum, H., & Jourdan, A. (2005). The current status of Carl Rogers and the person-centered approach. *Psychotherapy, 42,* 37–51.

Kiselica, M. S. (2003). Transforming psychotherapy in order to succeed with adolescent boys: Male-friendly practices. *Journal of Clinical Psychology: In Session, 59,* 1225–1236.

Klepac, R. K., Ronan, G. F., Andrasik, F., et al. (2012). Guidelines for cognitive behavioral training within doctoral psychology programs in the United States of America: Report of the Inter-Organizational Task Force on Cognitive and Behavioral Psychology Doctoral Education. *Behavior Therapy, 43,* 687–697.

Klerman, G. L., Budman, S., Berwick, D., et al. (1987). Efficacy of brief psychosocial interventions on symptoms of stress and distress among patients in primary care. *Medical Care, 25,* 1078–1088.

Klerman, G. L., & Weissman, M. M. (1991). Interpersonal psychotherapy: Research program and future prospects. In L. E. Beutler & M. Crago (Eds.), *Psychotherapy research: An international review of programmatic studies.* Washington, DC: American Psychological Association.

Klerman, G. L., & Weissman, M. M. (Eds.). (1993). *New applications of interpersonal psychotherapy.* Washington, DC: American Psychiatric Press.

Klerman, G. L., Weissman, M. M., Rounsaville, B. J., & Chevron, E. S. (1984). *Interpersonal psychotherapy of depression.* New York: Basic.

Kliem, S., Kroger, C., & Kosfelder, J. (2010). Dialectical behavior therapy for borderline personality disorder: A meta-analysis using mixed-effects modeling. *Journal of Consulting and Clinical Psychology, 78,* 936–951.

Knapp, B. W. (1999). Transactional analysis: A theory and context for an integrated approach to psychotherapy. *Transactional Analysis Journal, 29,* 92–95.

Knight, R. P. (1941). Evaluation of the results of psychoanalytic therapy. *American Journal of Psychiatry, 98,* 434–436.

Knobloch, F. (1996). Toward integration through group-based psychotherapy: Back to the future. *Journal of Psychotherapy Integration, 6,* 1–25.

Knobloch, F., & Knobloch, J. (1979). *Integrated psychotherapy.* New York: Jason Arasonson.

Kobak, K. A., Greist, J. H., Jefferson, J. W., et al. (1998). Behavioral versus pharmacological treatments of obsessive compulsive disorder: A meta-analysis. *Psychopharmacology, 136,* 205–216.

Kohut, H. (1971). *The analysis of the self.* New York: International Universities Press.

Kohut, H. (1977). *The restoration of the self.* New York: International Universities Press.

Kohut, H. (1979). The two analyses of Mr. Z. *International Journal of Psycho-Analysis, 60,* 3–27.

Koole, S. L., Greenberg, J., & Pyszczynski, T. (2006). Introducing science to the psychology of the soul. *Current Directions in Psychological Science, 15,* 212–216.

Kort, J. (2004). Queer eye for the straight therapist. *Psychotherapy Networker, 28,* 59–61.

Koss, M. P., & Shiang, J. (1994). Research on brief psychotherapy. In A. E. Bergin & S. L. Garfield (Eds.), *Handbook of psychotherapy and behavior change* (4th ed.). New York: Wiley.

Krijn, M., Emmelkamp, P. M. G., Olafsson, R. P., & Biemond, R. (2004). Virtual reality exposure therapy of anxiety disorders: A review. *Clinical Psychology Review, 24,* 259–281.

Kuhn, T. S. (1970). *The structure of scientific revolutions* (2nd ed.). Chicago: University of Chicago Press.

Kurtz, M., & Mueser, K. (2008). A meta-analysis of controlled research on social skills training for schizophrenia. *Journal of Consulting and Clinical Psychology, 3,* 491–504.

Kwee, M. G. T. (1984). *Klinische multimodale gedragstherapie.* Lisse, Holland: Swets & Zeitlinger.

Kwee, M. G. T., & Kwee-Taams, M. K. (1994). *Klinishegedragstherapie in Nederland & vlaanderen.* Delft, Holland: Eubron.

Lackner, J. M., Mesmer, C., Morley, S. J., et al. (2004). Psychological treatments for irritable bowel syndrome: A systematic review and meta-analysis. *Journal of Consulting and Clinical Psychology, 72,* 1100–1113.

Lai, D. T. C., Cahill K., Qin, Y., & Tang, J. L. (2010). Motivational interviewing for smoking cessation. *Cochrane Database of Systematic Reviews, 1,* CD006936.

Lam, C. S., McMahon, B. T., Priddy, D. A., & Gehred-Schultz, A. (1988). Deficit awareness and treatment performance among traumatic head injury adults. *Brain Injury, 2,* 235–242.

Lambert, M. J. (1976). Spontaneous remission in adult neurotic disorders: A revision and summary. *Psychological Bulletin, 83,* 107–119.

Lambert, M. J. (2002). Research summary on the therapeutic relationship and psychotherapy outcome. In J. C. Norcross (Ed.), *Psychotherapy relationships that work.* New York: Oxford University Press.

Lambert, M. J. (Ed.). (2013). *Handbook of psychotherapy and behavior change* (6th ed.). New York: Wiley.

Lambert, M. J., Harmon, C., Nielsen, S. L., et al. (2005). Providing feedback to psychotherapists on their patients' progress: Clinical results and practice suggestions. *Journal of Clinical Psychology: In Session, 61,* 165–174.

Lambert, M. J., & Shimokawa, K. (2011). Collecting client feedback. In J. C. Norcross (Ed.), *Psychotherapy relationships that work* (2nd ed., pp. 203–223). New York: Oxford University Press.

Lampropoulos, G. K., & Dixon, D. N. (2007). Psychotherapy integration in internships and counseling psychology doctoral programs. *Journal of Psychotherapy Integration, 17*, 185–208.

Lantz, J. (1992). Using Frankl's concepts with PTSD clients. *Journal of Traumatic Stress, 5*, 485–490.

Lapworth, P., & Sills, C. (2011). *An introduction to transactional analysis: Helping people change.* London: Sage.

Larson, D. (1980). Therapeutic schools, styles, and schoolism: A national survey. *Journal of Humanistic Psychology, 20*, 3–20.

Lasser, J. S., & Gottlieb, M. C. (2004). Treating patients distressed regarding their sexual orientation: Clinical and ethical alternatives. *Professional Psychology: Research & Practice, 35*, 194–200.

Lazarus, A. A. (1956). A psychological approach to alcoholism. *South African Medical Journal, 30*, 707–710.

Lazarus, A. A. (1958). New methods in psychotherapy: A case study. *South African Medical Journal, 32*, 660–664.

Lazarus, A. A. (1966). Broad spectrum behavior therapy and the treatment of agoraphobia. *Behavior Research and Therapy, 4*, 95–97.

Lazarus, A. A. (1967). In support of technical eclecticism. *Psychological Reports, 21*, 415–416.

Lazarus, A. A. (1971a). *Behavior therapy and beyond.* New York: McGraw-Hill.

Lazarus, A. A. (1971b). Has behavior therapy outlived its usefulness? *American Psychologist, 32*, 550–555.

Lazarus, A. A. (1971c). Where do behavior therapists take their troubles? *Psychological Reports, 28*, 349–350.

Lazarus, A. A. (1976). *Multimodal behavior therapy.* New York: Springer.

Lazarus, A. A. (1981/1989a). *The practice of multimodal therapy.* Baltimore: Johns Hopkins University Press.

Lazarus, A. A. (1989b). Brief psychotherapy: The multimodal model. *Psychology, 26*, 6–10.

Lazarus, A. A. (1991). A plague on Little Hans and Little Albert. *Psychotherapy, 28*, 444–447.

Lazarus, A. A. (1993). Tailoring the therapeutic relationship, or being an authentic chameleon. *Psychotherapy, 30*, 404–407.

Lazarus, A. A. (1997). *Brief but comprehensive psychotherapy: The multimodal way.* New York: Springer.

Lazarus, A. A. (2005). Multimodal therapy. In J. C. Norcross & M. R. Goldfried (Eds.), *Handbook of psychotherapy integration* (2nd ed.). New York: Oxford University Press.

Lazarus, A. A. (2006). *Brief but comprehensive psychotherapy: The multimodal way* (2nd ed.). New York: Springer.

Lazarus, A. A., Beutler, L. E., & Norcross, J. C. (1992). The future of technical eclecticism. *Psychotherapy, 29*, 11–20.

Lazarus, A. A., & Fay, A. (1984). Behavior therapy. In T. B. Karasu (Ed.), *The psychiatric therapies.* Washington, DC: American Psychiatric Association.

Lazarus, A. A., & Lazarus, C. N. (2005). *The Multimodal Life History Inventory.* In G. P. Koocher, J. C. Norcross, & S. S. Hill (Eds.), *Psychologists' desk reference* (2nd ed.). New York: Oxford University Press.

Lazarus, A. A., Lazarus, C. N., & Fay, A. (1993). *Don't believe it for a minute! 40 toxic ideas that are driving you crazy.* San Luis Obispo, CA: Impact.

Lazarus, A. A., & Messer, S. B. (1991). Does chaos prevail? An exchange on technical eclecticism and integration. *Journal of Psychotherapy Integration, 1*, 143–158.

Lazarus, A. A., & Zur, O. (Eds.). (2002). *Dual relationships and psychotherapy.* New York: Springer.

Leahy, R. L. (2003). *Cognitive therapy techniques: A practitioner's guide.* New York: Guilford.

Lebow, J. (1997). The integrative revolution in couple and family therapy. *Family Process, 36*, 1–20.

Lebow, J. (2005). The role and current practice of personal therapy in systemic/family therapy. In J. D. Geller, J. C. Norcross, & D. E. Orlinsky (Eds.), *The psychotherapist's own therapy.* New York: Oxford University Press.

Ledesma, D., & Kumano, H. (2008). Mindfulness-based stress reduction and cancer: A meta-analysis. *Psychooncology, 18*, 571–579.

Lee, C. W., Taylor, G., & Drummond, P. D. (2006). The active ingredient in EMDR: Is it traditional exposure or dual focus of attention? *Clinical Psychology and Psychotherapy, 13*, 97–107.

Lee, M. (1997). A study of solution-focused brief family therapy: Outcomes and issues. *American Journal of Family Therapy, 25*, 3–17.

Leichsenring, F., & Leibing, E. (2003). The effectiveness of psychodynamic psychotherapy and cognitive behavior therapy in the treatment of personality disorders: A meta-analysis. *American Journal of Psychiatry, 160*, 1223–1231.

Leichsenring, F., & Rabung, S. (2008). Effectiveness of long-term psychodynamic psychotherapy: A meta-analysis. *Journal of the American Medical Association, 300*, 1551–1565.

Leichsenring, F., & Rabung, S. (2011). Long-term psychodynamic psychotherapy in complex mental disorders: Update of a meta-analysis. *The British Journal of Psychiatry, 199*, 15–22.

Leichsenring, F., Rabung, S., & Leibing, E. (2004). The efficacy of short-term psychodynamic psychotherapy in specific psychiatric disorders: A meta-analysis. *Archives of General Psychiatry, 61*, 1208–1216.

Leong, F. T. L. (1986). Counseling and psychotherapy with Asian-Americans: Review of the literature. *Journal of Counseling Psychology, 33*, 196–206.

Lerman, H. (1992). The limits of phenomenology: A feminist critique of the humanistic personality theories. In L. S. Brown & M. Ballou (Eds.), *Personality and psychopathology: Feminist reappraisals.* New York: Guilford.

Lerner, H. (1986). *A mote in Freud's eye.* New York: Springer.

Lerner, H. (1988). *Women in therapy.* New York: Jason Aronson.

Levant, R. F. (1990). Psychological services designed for men: A psychoeducational approach. *Psychotherapy, 27*, 309–315.

Levant, R. F., & Pollack, W. (Eds.). (1995). *The new psychology of men.* New York: Basic.

Levant, R. F., & Shlien, J. M. (Eds.). (1984). *Client-centered therapy and the person-centered approach*. New York: Praeger.

Levenson, H. (1995). *Time-limited dynamic psychotherapy: A guide to clinical practice*. New York: Basic Books.

Levesque, D. A., Driskell, M. M., Greene, R. N., Castle, P. H., & Prochaska, J. M. (2009). *Efficacy of a computerized stage-matched intervention for domestic violence offenders*. Manuscript in preparation.

Levine, J. L., Stolz, J. A., & Lacks, P. (1983). Preparing psychotherapy clients: Rationale and suggestions. *Professional Psychology: Research and Practice, 14*, 317–322.

Levitsky, A., & Perls, F. (1970). The rules and games of Gestalt therapy. In J. Fagan & I. Shepherd (Eds.), *Gestalt therapy now*. Palo Alto, CA: Science and Behavior Books.

Levy, K. N., Ellison, W. D., Scott, L. N., & Bernecker, S. L. (2011). Attachment style. In J. C. Norcross (Ed.), *Psychotherapy relationships that work*. New York: Oxford University Press.

Lewandowski, L. M., Gebing, T. A., Anthony, J. L., & O'Brien, W. H. (1997). Meta-analysis of cognitive-behavioral treatment studies for bulimia. *Clinical Psychology Review, 17*, 703–718.

Lewinsohn, P. M., & Clarke, G. N. (1999). Psychosocial treatments for adolescent depression. *Clinical Psychology Review, 19*, 329–342.

Lewinsohn, P. M., Youngren, M. A., & Zeis, A. Z. (1992). *Control your depression*. New York: Fireside.

Lewis, J. M., Beavers, W. R., Gossett, J. T., & Philips, V. A. (1976). *No single thread: Psychological health in family systems*. New York: Brunner/Mazel.

Liddle, H. A. (2009). *Multidimensional family therapy for adolescent drug abuse* [Clinician's manual and DVD]. Center City, MN: Hazelden.

Lidz, T. (1963). *The family and human adaption*. New York: International Universities Press.

Liebman, R., Minuchin, S., Baker, L., & Rosman, B. (1975). The treatment of anorexia nervosa. *Current Psychiatric Therapies, 15*, 51–57.

Lietaer, G. (1990). The client-centered approach after the Wisconsin Project: A personal view on its evolution. In G. Lietaer, J. Rombauts, & R. VanBalen (Eds.), *Client-centered and experiential psychotherapy in the nineties*. Leuven, Belgium: Leuven University Press.

Liff, Z. A. (1992). Psychoanalysis and dynamic techniques. In D. K. Freedheim (Ed.), *History of psychotherapy: A century of change*. Washington, DC: American Psychological Association.

Lincoln, T. M., Wilhelm, K., & Nestoriuc, Y. (2007). Effectiveness of psychoeducation for relapse, symptoms, knowledge, adherence and functioning in psychotic disorders: A meta-analysis. *Schizophrenia Research, 96*, 232–245.

Linden, W., & Chambers, L. (1994). Clinical effectiveness of non-drug treatment for hypertension: A meta-analysis. *Annals of Behavioral Medicine, 16*, 35–45.

Linehan, M. M. (1993a). *Cognitive-behavioral treatment of borderline personality disorder*. New York: Guilford.

Linehan, M. M. (1993b). *Skills training manual for treating borderline personality disorder*. New York: Guilford.

Linehan, M. M. (2000). Marsha Linehan. In G. Hellinga, B. Van Luyn, & H.-J. Dalewijk (Eds.), *Personalities: Master clinicians confront the treatment of borderline personality disorder* (pp. 179–202). Amsterdam: Boom.

Linehan, M. M., Comotois, K., Murray, A., et al. (2006). Two-year randomized controlled trial and follow-up of dialectical behavior therapy vs. therapy by experts for suicidal behaviors and borderline personality disorder. *Archives of General Psychology, 63*, 757–766.

Linstone, H. A., & Turoff, M. (Eds.). (1975). *The Delphi method: Techniques and applications*. Reading, MA: Addison-Wesley.

Lipchik, E. (2002). *Beyond technique in solution-focused therapy: Working with emotions and the therapeutic relationship*. New York: Guilford.

Lipsey, M. W., & Wilson, D. B. (1993). The efficacy of psychological, educational, and behavioral treatment: Confirmation from meta-analysis. *American Psychologist, 48*, 1181–1209.

Littell, J. H. (2008). Evidence-based or biased? The quality of published reviews of evidence-based practices. *Children and Youth Services Review, 30*, 1299–1317.

Littell, J. H., Popa, M., & Forscythe, B. (2005). Multisystemic therapy for social, emotional, and behavioral problems in youth aged 10-17. *Cochrane Database of Systematic Reviews, 4*, CD004797.

Lloyd, G. (1984). *The man of reason: "Male" and "female" in western philosophy*. London: Methuen.

Loeppke, R., Taitel, M., Haufle, V., et al. (2009). Health and productivity as a business strategy: A multiemployer study. *Journal of Occupational and Environmental Medicine, 51*, 411–428.

Loeschen, S. (1997). *Systematic training in the skills of Virginia Satir*. Pacific Grove, CA: Brooks/Cole.

Loevinger, J. (1976). *Ego development*. San Francisco: Jossey-Bass.

London, P. (1986). *The modes and morals of psychotherapy* (2nd ed.). New York: Hemisphere.

London, P. (1988). Metamorphosis in psychotherapy: Slouching toward integration. *Journal of Integrative and Eclectic Psychotherapy, 7*, 3–12.

Lopez, S. J., & Snyder, C. R. (Eds.). (2011). *Handbook of positive psychology* (2nd ed.). New York: Oxford University Press.

Lopez, S. R., Barrio, C., Kopelowicz, A., & Vega, W. A. (2012). From documenting to eliminating disparities in mental health care for latinos. *American Psychologist, 6*, 511–523.

Lorenz, K. (1963). *On aggression*. New York: Harcourt Brace Jovanovich.

Lorion, R. P. (1978). Research on psychotherapy and behavior change with the disadvantaged: Past, present, and future directions. In S. L. Garfield & A. E. Bergin (Eds.), *Handbook of psychotherapy and behavior change* (2nd ed.). New York: Wiley.

Luborsky, L. (1984). *Principles of psychoanalytic psychotherapy*. New York: Basic.

Luborsky, L., & Crits-Christoph, P. (1990). *Understanding transference*. New York: Basic.

Luborsky, L., Diguer, L., Seligman, D. A., et al. (1999). The researcher's own therapy allegiances: A "wild card" in comparisons of treatment efficacy. *Clinical Psychology: Science and Practice*, 6, 95–106.

Luborsky, L., Rosenthal, R., Diguer, L., et al. (2002). The dodo bird verdict is alive and well—mostly. *Clinical Psychology: Science and Practice*, 9, 2–12.

Luborsky, L., Singer, B., & Luborsky, L. (1975). Comparative studies of psychotherapies. *Archives of General Psychiatry*, 32, 995–1008.

Luepnitz, D. A. (1988). *The family interpreted: Feminist theory in clinical practice*. New York: Basic.

Lundahl, B. W., & Burke, B. L. (2009). The effectiveness and applicability of motivational interviewing: A practice-friendly review of four meta-analyses. *Journal of Clinical Psychology*, 65, 1232–1245.

Lundahl, B. W., Kunz, C., Brownell, C., et al. (2010). A meta-analysis of motivational interviewing: Twenty-five years of empirical studies. *Research on Social Work Practice*, 20, 137–160.

Lundahl, B. W., Risser, J. J., Myket, S. B., et al. (2004, July). *Parent-training meta-analysis: 3,592 participants, 61 treatment groups, and 48 control groups*. Poster presented at the 112th annual convention of the American Psychological Association, Honolulu, HI.

Luthman, S. (1972). *Intimacy: The essence of male and female*. Los Angeles: Nash.

Lyhus, K. E. (2003). Integration of EMDR with other therapeutic approaches: A survey investigation. *Dissertation Abstracts International: Section B: The Sciences & Engineering*, 63(10-B), 4912.

Lynn, D. J., & Vaillant, G. E. (1998). Anonymity, neutrality, and confidentiality in the actual methods of Sigmund Freud: A review of 43 cases, 1907–1939. *American Journal of Psychiatry*, 155, 163–171.

Lyons, L. C., & Woods, P. J. (1991). The efficacy of rational-emotive therapy: A quantitative review of the outcome research. *Clinical Psychology Review*, 11, 357–369.

Maddi, S. R. (1978). Existential and individual psychologies. *Journal of Individual Psychology*, 34, 182–190.

Maddi, S. R. (1996). *Personality theories: A comparative analysis* (6th ed.). Pacific Grove, CA: Brooks/Cole.

Madigan, S. (2008, July/August). Dear Michael. *Psychotherapy Networker*, 44–46.

Maheu, M., & Gordon, B. L. (2000). Counseling and therapy on the Internet. *Professional Psychology: Research and Practice*, 31, 484–489.

Mahler, M. S. (1968). *On human symbiosis of the vicissitudes of individuation*. New York: International Universities Press.

Mahoney, M. J. (1991). *Human change processes: The scientific foundations of psychotherapy*. New York: Basic.

Mahoney, M. J. (1996). Constructivism and the study of complex self-organization. *Constructive Change*, 1, 3–8.

Mahoney, M. J. (2003). *Constructive psychotherapy: A practical guide*. New York: Guilford.

Mahrer, A. R. (1989). *Experiential psychotherapy: Basic practices*. Ottawa: University of Ottawa Press.

Mahrer, A. R. (1996). *The complete guide to experiential psychotherapy*. New York: Wiley.

Mahrer, A. R., & Fairweather, D. R. (1993). What is experiencing? A critical review of meanings and applications in psychotherapy. *The Humanistic Psychologist*, 21, 2–25.

Malcolm, J. (1978, May 15). A reporter at large: The one-way mirror. *The New Yorker*, pp. 39–114.

Mallinckrodt, B. (2000). Attachment, social competencies, social support, and interpersonal process in psychotherapy. *Psychotherapy Research*, 10, 239–266.

Malouff, J. M., Thorsteinsson, E. B., Rooke, S. E., et al. (2008). Efficacy of cognitive behavioral therapy for chronic fatigue syndrome: A meta-analysis. *Clinical Psychology Review*, 28, 736–745.

Malouff, J. M., Thorsteinsson, E. B., & Schutte, N. S. (2007). The efficacy of problem solving therapy in reducing mental and physical health problems: A meta-analysis. *Clinical Psychology Review*, 27, 46–57.

Manaster, G. J. (1987a). Adlerian theory and movement. *Individual Psychology*, 43, 280–287.

Manaster, G. J. (1987b). Editor's comments. *Individual Psychology*, 43, 1–2.

Mancebo, M. C., Eisen, J. L., Sibrava, N. J., et al. (2011). Patient utilization of cognitive-behavioral therapy for OCD. *Behavior Therapy*, 42, 399–412.

Mann, J. (1973). *Time-limited psychotherapy*. Cambridge, MA: Harvard University Press.

Mann, J., & Goldman, R. (1982). *A casebook in time-limited psychotherapy*. New York: McGraw-Hill.

Markowitz, J. C. (1997). The future of interpersonal psychotherapy. *Journal of Psychotherapy Practice and Research*, 6, 294–299.

Marlatt, G. A., & Donovan, D. M. (Eds.). (2007). *Relapse prevention: Maintenance strategies in the treatment of addictive behaviors* (2nd ed.). New York: Guilford.

Martin, A., van Hoof, T., Stubbe, D., et al. (2003). Multiple psychotropic pharmacotherapy among child and adolescent enrollees in Connecticut Medicaid managed care. *Psychiatric Services*, 54, 72–77.

Marx, M. H., & Goodson, F. E. (Eds.). (1976). *Theories in contemporary psychology* (2nd ed.). New York: Macmillan.

Maslow, A. H. (1960). Existential psychology: What's in it for us? In R. May (Ed.), *Existential psychology*. New York: Random House.

Maslow, A. H. (1962). Some basic propositions of a growth and self-actualizing psychology. In *Perceiving, behaving, becoming: A new focus for education*. Washington, DC: Yearbook of the Association for Supervision and Curriculum Development.

Massey, S. D., & Massey, R. F. (1989). Systemic contexts for therapy with children. *Transactional Analysis Journal*, 19, 194–200.

Masters, W., & Johnson, V. (1966). *Human sexual response*. Boston: Little, Brown.

Masters, W., & Johnson, V. (1970). *Human sexual inadequacy*. Boston: Little, Brown.

Masterson, J. F. (1976). *Psychotherapy of the borderline adult*. New York: Brunner/Mazel.

Masterson, J. F. (1981). *The narcissistic and borderline disorders: An integrated* developmental approach. New York: Brunner/Mazel.

Maultsby, M. C., Jr., & Ellis, A. (1974). *Techniques for using rational-emotive imagery*. New York: Institute for Rational-Emotive Therapy.

Mausbach, B. T., Roesch, S., & Patterson, T. L. (2010). The relationship between homework compliance and therapy outcomes: An updated meta-analysis. *Cognitive Therapy Research, 34*, 429–438.

Maxfield, L., & Hyer, L. (2002). The relationship between efficacy and methodology in studies investigating EMDR treatment of PTSD. *Journal of Clinical Psychology, 58*, 23–41.

May, R. (1958). Contribution of existential psychotherapy. In R. May, E. Angel, & H. Ellenberger (Eds.), *Existence: A new dimension for psychology and psychiatry*. New York: Basic.

May, R. (1967). *Psychology and the human dilemma*. New York: Van Nostrand.

May, R. (1969). *Love and will*. New York: Dell.

May, R. (1977). *The meaning of anxiety* (rev. ed.). New York: Norton.

May, R. (1981). *Freedom and destiny*. New York: Norton.

May, R. (1983). *The discovery of being: Writings in existential psychology*. New York: Norton.

May, R. (1989). Rollo May: A man of meaning and myth. Interview with F. E. Rabinowitz, G. Good, and L. Cozad. *Journal of Counseling and Development, 67*, 436–441.

May, R., Angel, E., & Ellenberger, H. (Eds.). (1958). *Existence: A new dimension in psychology and psychiatry*. New York: Basic.

Mayet, S., Farrell, M., Ferri, M., et al. (2004). Psychosocial treatment for opiate abuse and dependence. *Cochrane Database of Systematic Reviews, 4*, CD004330.

Mazzucchelli, T., Kane, R., & Rees, C. (2009). Behavioral activation treatments for depression in adults: A meta-analysis and review. *Clinical Psychology: Science and Practice, 16*, 383–411.

McConnaughy, E. A., Prochaska, J., & Velicer, W. (1983). Stages of change in psychotherapy: Measurement and sample profiles. *Psychotherapy, 20*, 368–375.

McCullough, L. (1997). *Changing character*. New York: Basic Books.

McGoldrick, M., Giordano, J., & Garcia-Preto, N. (Eds.). (2005). *Ethnicity and family therapy* (3rd ed.). New York: Guilford.

McGoldrick, M., & Hardy, K. V. (2008). *Re-visioning family therapy: Race, culture, and gender in clinical practice* (2nd ed.). New York: Guilford.

McGrath, E., Keita, G. P., Strickland, B. R., & Russo, N. F. (Eds.). (1990). *Women and depression: Risk factors and treatment issues*. Washington, DC: American Psychological Association.

McKay, M., Wood, C., & Brantley, J. (2007). *The dialectical behavior therapy skills workbook*. Oakland, CA: New Harbinger.

McNally, R. J. (1999). On eye movements and animal magnetism: A reply to Greenwald's defense of EMDR. *Journal of Anxiety Disorders, 13*, 617–620.

McNamee, S., & Gergen, K. J. (1992). *Therapy as social construction*. London: Sage.

McWilliams, N. (2004). *Psychoanalytic psychotherapy: A practitioner's guide*. New York: Guilford.

Meador, B., & Rogers, C. (1973). Client-centered therapy. In R. Corsini (Ed.), *Current psychotherapies*. Itasca, IL: Peacock.

Meichenbaum, D. (1977). *Cognitive-behavior modification*. New York: Plenum.

Meichenbaum, D. (1985). *Stress inoculation training*. New York: Pergamon.

Meichenbaum, D. (1986). Cognitive-behavior modification. In F. H. Kanfer & A. P. Goldstein (Eds.), *Helping people change* (3rd ed.). New York: Pergamon.

Meichenbaum, D. (1996). Stress inoculation training for coping with stressors. *The Clinical Psychologist, 49*, 4–10.

Meichenbaum, D., & Goodman, J. (1969). Reflection-impulsivity and verbal control of motor behavior. *Child Development, 40*, 785–797.

Meichenbaum, D., & Goodman, J. (1971). Training impulsive children to talk to themselves: A means of developing self-control. *Journal of Abnormal Psychology, 77*, 115–126.

Mellinger, G. D., Balter, M. B., Manheimer, D. I., et al. (1978). Psychic distress, life crisis and use of psychotherapeutic medications. *Archives of General Psychiatry, 35*, 1045–1052.

Meltzoff, J., & Kornreich, M. (1970). *Research in psychotherapy*. New York: Atherton.

Menchola, M., Arkowitz, H. S., & Burker, B. L. (2007). Efficacy of self-administered treatments for depression and anxiety. *Professional Psychology, 38*, 421–429.

Messer, S. B., & Warren, C. S. (1995). *Models of brief psychodynamic therapy: A comparative approach*. New York: Guilford.

Messer, S. B., & Winokur, M. (1980). Some limits to the integration of psychoanalytic and behavior therapy. *American Psychologist, 35*, 818–827.

Metcalfe, C., Winter, D., & Viney, L. (2007). The effectiveness of personal construct psychotherapy in clinical practice: A systematic review and meta-analysis. *Psychotherapy Research, 17*, 431–442.

Meth, R. L., & Pasick, R. S. (1992). *Men in therapy: The challenge of change*. New York: Guilford.

Meyer, A. (1957). *Psychobiology: A science of man*. Springfield, IL: Charles C. Thomas.

Michael, K. D., & Crowley, S. L. (2002). How effective are treatments for child and adolescent depression? A meta-analytic review. *Clinical Psychology Review, 22*, 247–269.

Miklowitz, D. J. (2008). Adjunctive psychotherapy for bipolar disorder. *American Journal of Psychiatry, 165*, 1408–1419.

Miller, G., Galanter, E., & Pribram, K. (1960). *Plans and the structure of behavior*. New York: Holt, Rinehart & Winston.

Miller, J. B. (1986). *Toward a new psychology of women*. Boston: Beacon.

Miller, M. D., Cornes, C., Frank, E., et al. (2001). Interpersonal psychotherapy for late-life depression. *Journal of Psychotherapy Practice and Research, 10*, 231–238.

Miller, M. D., Wolfson, L., Frank, E., et al. (1998). Using Interpersonal Therapy (IPT) in a combined psychotherapy/medication research protocol with depressed elders. *Journal of*

Psychotherapy Practice and Research, 7, 47–55.

Miller, R. C., & Berman, J. S. (1983). The efficacy of cognitive behavior therapies: A quantitative review of the research evidence. *Psychological Bulletin, 94,* 39–53.

Miller, S., Wampold, B., & Varhely, K. (2008). Direct comparison of treatment modalities for youth disorders: A meta-analysis. *Psychotherapy Research, 18,* 5–14.

Miller, S. D., & Berg, I. K. (1995). *The miracle method: A radically new approach to problem drinking.* New York: Norton.

Miller, S. D., Duncan, B. L., & Hubble, M. A. (1997). *Escape from Babel: Toward a unifying language for psychotherapy practice.* New York: Norton.

Miller, S. D., Duncan, B. L., & Hubble, M. A. (2005). Outcome-informed clinical work. In J. C. Norcross & M. R. Goldfried (Eds.), *Handbook of psychotherapy integration* (2nd ed.). New York: Oxford University Press.

Miller, S. D., & Hubble, M. A. (2004). Further archeological and ethnological findings on the obscure, late 20th century, quasi-religious earth group known as "the therapists." *Journal of Psychotherapy Integration, 14,* 38–65.

Miller, S. D., Hubble, M. A., & Duncan, B. L. (Eds.). (1996). *Handbook of solution-focused brief therapy.* San Francisco: Jossey-Bass.

Miller, W. R. (1978). Behavioral treatment of problem drinkers: A comparative outcome study of three controlled drinking therapies. *Journal of Consulting and Clinical Psychology, 46,* 74–86.

Miller, W. R., & Moyers, T. B. (2005). Motivational interviewing. In G. P. Koocher, J. C. Norcross, & S. S. Hill (Eds.), *Psychologists' desk reference* (2nd ed.). New York: Oxford University Press.

Miller, W. R., & Munoz, R. F. (1982). *How to control your drinking* (2nd ed.). Albuquerque: University of New Mexico Press.

Miller, W. R., & Rollnick, S. (1991). *Motivational interviewing: Preparing people for change.* New York: Guilford.

Miller, W. R., & Rollnick, S. (2002). *Motivational interviewing: Preparing people for change* (2nd ed.). New York: Guilford.

Miller, W. R., & Rollnick, S. (2012). *Motivational interviewing* (3rd ed.). New York: Guilford.

Miller, W. R., & Rose, G. S. (2009). Toward a theory of motivational interviewing. *American Psychologist, 64,* 527–537.

Miller, W. R., Taylor, C. A., & West, J. C. (1980). Focused versus broad-spectrum behavior therapy for problem drinkers. *Journal of Consulting and Clinical Psychology, 48,* 590–601. doi: 10.1037/0022-006X.48.5.590

Miller, W. R., Yahne, C. E., Moyers, T. B., et al. (2004). A randomized trial of methods to help clinicians learn motivational interviewing. *Journal of Consulting and Clinical Psychology, 72,* 1050–1062.

Miller, W. R., Zweben, A., DiClemente, C. C., & Rychtarik, R. G. (1992). *Motivational enhancement therapy manual: A clinical research guide for therapists treating individuals with alcohol abuse and dependence.* Rockville, MD: National Institute on Alcohol Abuse and Alcoholism.

Minuchin, S. (1970). The use of an ecological framework in child psychiatry. In J. Anthony & C. Kaupernik (Eds.), *The child in his family.* New York: Wiley.

Minuchin, S. (1972). Structural family therapy. In G. Caplan (Ed.), *American handbook of psychiatry* (Vol. 2). New York: Basic.

Minuchin, S. (1974). *Families and family therapy.* Cambridge, MA: Harvard University Press.

Minuchin, S. (1997). *Mastering family therapy: Journeys of growth and tranformation.* New York: Wiley.

Minuchin, S., Baker, L., Rosman, B. L., et al. (1975). A conceptual model of psychosomatic illness in children. *Archives of General Psychiatry, 32,* 1031–1038.

Minuchin, S., Montalvo, B., Guerney, B. G., et al. (1967). *Families of the slums.* New York: Basic.

Miranda, J., Bernal, G., Lau, A., et al. (2005). State of the science on psychosocial interventions for ethnic minorities. *Annual Review of Clinical Psychology, 1,* 113–142.

Mischel, W. (1968). *Personality and assessment.* New York: Wiley.

Mitchell, K. M., Bozarth, J. D., & Krauft, C. C. (1977). A reappraisal of the therapeutic effectiveness of accurate empathy, non-possessive warmth, and genuineness. In A. S. Gurman & A. M. Razin (Eds.), *Effective psychotherapy.* New York: Pergamon.

Mitchell, S. (1988). *Relational concepts in psychoanalysis: An integration.* Cambridge: Harvard University Press.

Mitchell, S. (1993). *Hope and dread in psychoanalysis.* New York: Basic Books.

Mitchell-Meadows, M. (1992). Consider culture when counseling. *APA Monitor, 23*(9), 37.

Mitte, K. (2005a). Meta-analysis of cognitive-behavioral treatments for generalized anxiety disorder: A comparison with pharmacotherapy. *Psychological Bulletin, 131,* 785–795.

Mitte, K. (2005b). A meta-analysis of the efficacy of psycho- and pharmacotherapy in panic disorder with and without agoraphobia. *Journal of Affective Disorders, 88,* 27–45.

Mohr, D. C., Vella, L., Hart, S., et al. (2008). The effect of telephone-administered psychotherapy on symptoms of depression and attrition: A meta-analysis. *Clinical Psychology: Science and Practice, 15,* 243–253.

Mohr, D. V. (1995). Negative outcome in psychotherapy: A critical review. *Clinical Psychology: Science and Practice, 2,* 1–27.

Mojtabai, R., Olfson, M., & Mechanic, D. (2002). Perceived need and help-seeking in adults with mood, anxiety, or substance use disorders. *Archives of General Psychiatry, 59,* 77–84.

Mokdad, A. H., Marks, J. S., Stroup, D. F., & Gerberding, J. L. (2004). Actual causes of death in the United States, 2000. *Journal of the American Medical Association, 291,* 1238–1245.

Monastra, V. J., Lynn, S., Linden, M., et al. (2005). Electroencephalographic biofeedback in the treatment of attention-deficit/hyperactivity disorder. *Applied Psychophysiology and Biofeedback, 30,* 95–114.

Monte, C. F. (1991). *Beneath the mask* (4th ed.). Philadelphia: Holt, Rinehart and Winston.

Monte, C. F., & Sollod, R. N. (2003). *Beneath the mask* (7th ed.). New York: Wiley.

Monti, P. M., Rohsenow, D. J., Rubonis, A. V., et al. (1993). Cue exposure with coping skills treatment for male alcoholics: A preliminary investigation. *Journal of Consulting and Clinical Psychology, 61*, 1011–1019.

Moore, C. M. (1987). *Group techniques for idea building.* Newbury Park, CA: Sage.

Moos, R. H., Finney, J.W., & Gamble, W. (1982). The process of recovery from alcoholism: II. Comparing spouses of alcoholic patients and matched community controls. *Journal of Studies on Alcohol, 43*, 888–909.

Morganstern, K. (1973). Implosive therapy and flooding procedures: A critical review. *Psychological Bulletin, 79*, 318–334.

Morgenstern, J., Labouvie, E., McCrady, B. S., et al. (1997). Affiliation with Alcoholics Anonymous after treatment: A study of its therapeutic effects and mechanisms of action. *Journal of Consulting and Clinical Psychology, 65*, 768–777.

Morin, C. M., Bootzin, R. R., Buysse, D. J., et al. (2006). Psychological and behavioral treatment of insomnia: Update of the recent evidence. *Sleep, 29*, 1398–1414.

Morin, C. M., Hauri, P. J., Espie, C. A., et al. (1999). Nonpharmacologic treatment of chronic insomnia: An American Academy of Sleep Medicine Review. *Sleep, 22*, 1134–1156.

Mosak, H., & Dreikurs, R. (1973). Adlerian psychotherapy. In R. Corsini (Ed.), *Current psychotherapies.* Itasca, IL: Peacock.

Mowrer, O. H. (1947). On the dual nature of learning: A reinterpretation of "conditioning" and "problem-solving." *Harvard Education Review, 17*, 102–148.

Mowrer, O. H. (1961). *The crisis in psychiatry and religion.* New York: Van Nostrand Reinhold.

Mowrer, O. H., & Mowrer, W. M. (1938). Enuresis: A method for its study and treatment. *American Journal of Orthopsychiatry, 8*, 436–459.

Moyers, T. B., & Rollnick, S. (2002). A motivational interviewing perspective on resistance in psychotherapy. *Journal of Clinical Psychology: In Session, 58*, 185–194.

MTA Cooperative Group. (1999a). A 14-month randomized clinical trial of treatment strategies for attention-deficit/hyperactivity disorder. *Archives of General Psychiatry, 56*, 1073–1086.

MTA Cooperative Group. (1999b). Moderators and mediators of treatment response for children with attention-deficit/hyperactivity disorder. *Archives of General Psychiatry, 56*, 1088–1096.

Mufson, L. H., Dorta, K. P., Moreau, D., & Weissman, M. M. (2004). *Interpersonal psychotherapy for depressed adolescents* (2nd ed.). New York: Guilford.

Munoz, R. F., Hollon, S. D., McGrath, E., et al. (1994). On the *AHCPR depression in primary care* guidelines: Further considerations for practitioners. *American Psychologist, 49*, 42–61.

Murtagh, D. R., & Greenwood, K. M. (1995). Identifying effective psychological treatments for insomnia: A meta-analysis. *Journal of Consulting and Clinical Psychology, 63*, 79–89.

Napoli, D. F., & Wolk, C. A. (1989). Circular learning: Teaching and learning Gestalt therapy in groups. *Journal of Independent Social Work, 3*(4), 57–70.

Nathan, P. E., & Gorman, J. M. (Eds.). (2007). *Treatments that work* (3rd ed.). New York: Oxford University Press.

Navarro, A. M. (1993). Effectividad de las psicoterapias con Latinos en los estados unidos: Una revision metaanalitica. *Interamerican Journal of Psychology, 27*, 131–146.

Neimeyer, R. A., & Mahoney, M. J. (Eds.). (1995). *Constructivism in psychotherapy.* Washington, DC: American Psychological Association.

Nelson, T. S., & Thomas, F. N. (Eds.). (2009). *Handbook of solution-focused brief therapy.* Binghamton, NY: Hawthorne Press.

Nestoriuc, Y., & Martin, A. (2007). Efficacy of biofeedback for migraine: A meta-analysis. *Pain. 128*, 111–127.

Nestoriuc, Y., Rief, W., & Martin, A. (2008). Meta-analysis of biofeedback for tension-type headache: Efficacy, specificity, and treatment moderators. *Journal of Consulting and Clinical Psychology, 76*, 379–396.

Nettles, R., & Balter, R. (2011). *Multiple minority identities.* New York: Springer.

Nevid, J. S., Rathus, S. A., & Greene, B. (2010). *Abnormal psychology in a changing world* (8th ed.). Englewood Cliffs, NJ: Prentice Hall.

Newman, C. F., Leahy, R. L., Beck, A. T., Reilly-Harrington, N., & Gyulai, L. (2002). *Bipolar disorder: A cognitive therapy approach.* Washington, DC: American Psychological Association.

Nichols, W. C. (2003). *Family of origin treatment.* In T. L. Sexton, G. R. Weeks, & M. S. Robbins (Eds.), *Handbook of family therapy.* New York: Brunner-Routledge.

Nikelly, A. G. (1996). Alternatives to androcentric bias of personality disorders. *Clinical Psychology and Psychotherapy, 3*, 15–22.

Noar, S. M., Benac, C. N., & Harris, M. S. (2007). Does tailoring matter? Meta-analytic review of tailored print health behavior change interventions. *Psychological Bulletin, 133*, 673–693.

Norcross, J. C. (1985). In defense of theoretical orientations for clinicians. *The Clinical Psychologist, 38*(1), 13–17.

Norcross, J. C. (1987). A rational and empirical analysis of existential psychotherapy. *Journal of Humanistic Psychology, 27*, 41–68.

Norcross, J. C. (1990). An eclectic definition of psychotherapy. In J. K. Zeig & W. M. Munion (Eds.), *What is psychotherapy?* San Francisco: Jossey-Bass.

Norcross, J. C. (Ed.). (1991). Prescriptive matching in Psychotherapy: Psychoanalysis for simple phobias? *Psychotherapy, 28*, 439–472.

Norcross, J. C. (2000). Here comes the self-help revolution in mental health. *Psychotherapy, 37*, 370–377.

Norcross, J. C. (2005). A primer on psychotherapy integration. In J. C. Norcross & M. R. Goldfried (Eds.), *Handbook of psychotherapy integration* (2nd ed.). New York: Oxford University Press.

Norcross, J. C. (Ed.). (2011). *Psychotherapy relationships that work* (2nd ed.). New York: Oxford University Press.

Norcross, J. C. (2012). *Changeology.* New York: Simon & Schuster.

Norcross, J. C., & Beutler, L. E. (1997). Determining the therapeutic relationship of choice in brief therapy. In J. N. Butcher (Ed.), *Personality assessment in managed care: A practitioner's guide.* New York: Oxford University Press.

Norcross, J. C., Beutler, L. E., & Levant, R. F. (Eds.). (2005). *Evidence-based practice in* mental health: Debate and dialogue on the fundamental questions. Washington, DC: American Psychological Association.

Norcross, J. C., Campbell, L. M., Grohol, J. M., et al. (2013). Self-help that works (4th ed.). New York: Oxford University Press.

Norcross, J. C., & Goldfried, M. R. (Eds.). (2005). Handbook of psychotherapy integration (2nd ed.). New York: Oxford University Press.

Norcross, J. C., & Goldfried, M. R. (2006). The future of psychotherapy integration: A roundtable. Journal of Psychotherapy Integration, 15, 392–471.

Norcross, J. C., & Guy, J. D. (2005). The prevalence and parameters of personal therapy in the United States. In J. D. Geller, J. C. Norcross, & D. E. Orlinsky (Eds.), The psychotherapist's own psychotherapy. New York: Oxford University Press.

Norcross, J. C., Hedges, M., & Prochaska, J. O. (2002). The face of 2010: A Delphi poll on the future of psychotherapy. Professional Psychology: Research and Practice, 33, 316–322.

Norcross, J. C., Hogan, T. P., & Koocher, G. P. (2008). Clinician's guide to evidence-based practices: Mental health and the addictions. New York: Oxford University Press.

Norcross, J. C., Karg, R. S., & Prochaska, J. O. (1997a). Clinical psychologists and managed care: Some data from the Division 12 membership. The Clinical Psychologist, 50(1), 4–8.

Norcross, J. C., Karg, R. S., & Prochaska, J. O. (1997b). Clinical psychologists in the 1990s. The Clinical Psychologist, 50(2), 4–9.

Norcross, J. C., & Karpiak, C. P. (2012). Clinical psychologists in the 2010s: Fifty years of the APA Division of Clinical Psychology. Clinical Psychology: Science and Practice, 19, 1–12.

Norcross, J. C., Karpiak, C. P., & Lister, K. M. (2005). What's an integrationist? A study of self-identified integrative and (occasionally) eclectic psychologists. Journal of Clinical Psychology, 61, 1587–1594.

Norcross, J. C., Krebs, P. M., & Prochaska, J. O. (2011). Stages of change. In

J. C. Norcross (Ed.), Psychotherapy relationships that work (2nd ed., pp. 279–300). New York: Oxford University Press.

Norcross, J. C., & Napolitano, G. (1986). Defining our journal and ourselves. International Journal of Eclectic Psychotherapy, 5, 249–255.

Norcross, J. C., & Prochaska, J. O. (1984). Where do behavior (and other) therapists take their troubles?: II. The Behavior Therapist, 7, 26–27.

Norcross, J. C., & Prochaska, J. O. (1988). A study of eclectic (and integrative) views revisited. Professional Psychology: Research and Practice, 19, 170–174.

Norcross, J. C., Saltzman, N., & Guinta, L. C. (1990). Contention and convergence in clinical practice. In N. Saltzman & J. C. Norcross (Eds.), Therapy wars. San Francisco: Jossey-Bass.

Norcross, J. C., VandenBos, G. R., & Freedheim, D. K. (Eds.). (2010). History of psychotherapy: Continuity and change (2nd ed.). Washington, DC: American Psychological Association.

Norcross, J. C., & Vangarelli, D. J. (1989). The resolution solution: Longitudinal examination of New Year's change attempts. Journal of Substance Abuse, 1, 127–134.

Norcross, J. C., & Wogan, M. (1983). American psychotherapists of diverse persuasions: Characteristics, theories, practices, and clients. Professional Psychology, 14, 529–539.

O'Banion, D. R., & Whaley, D. L. (1981). Behavior contracting. New York: Springer.

Ockene, J., Kristeller, J. L., Goldberg, R., et al. (1992). Smoking cessation and severity of disease: The Coronary Artery Smoking Intervention Study. Health Psychology, 11, 119–126.

Ockene, J., Ockene, I., & Kristeller, J. (1988). The Coronary Artery Smoking Intervention Study. Worcester, MA: National Heart Lung Blood Institute.

O'Donohue, W., Buchanan, J. A., & Fisher, J. E. (2000). Characteristics of empirically supported treatments. Journal of Psychotherapy Practice and Research, 9, 69–74.

O'Donohue, W. T. (2005). Cultural sensitivity: A critical examination.

In R. H. Wright & N. A. Cummings (Eds.), Destructive trends in mental health: The well intentioned path to harm. New York: Routledge.

Okajima, I., Komada, Y., & Inoue, Y. (2011). A meta-analysis on the treatment effectiveness of cognitive behavioral therapy for primary insomnia. Sleep and Biological Rhythms, 9, 24–34.

Okun, B. F. (1992). Object relations and self psychology: Overview and feminist perspectives. In L. A. Brown & M. Ballou (Eds.), Personality and psychopathology: Feminist reappraisals. New York: Guilford.

Oldham, J. M. (2002). Development of the American Psychiatric Association Practice guideline for the treatment of borderline personality disorder. Journal of Personality Disorders, 16, 109–112.

O'Leary, K. D., & Wilson, G. T. (1987). Behavior therapy: Application and outcome (2nd ed.). Englewood Cliffs, NJ: Prentice Hall.

Olfson, M., Marcus, S. C., Weissman, M. M., & Jensen, P. S. (2002). National trends in the use of psychotropic medications by children. Journal of the American Academy of Child & Adolescent Psychiatry, 41, 514–521.

Omer, H. (1993). The integrative focus: Coordinating symptom- and person-oriented perspectives in therapy. American Journal of Psychotherapy, 47, 283–295.

Omer, H. (1997). Narrative empathy. Psychotherapy, 34, 19–27.

Oquendo, M., Horwath, E., & Martinez, A. (1992). Ataques de nervios: Proposed diagnostic specific syndrome. Culture, Medicine and Psychiatry, 16, 367–376.

Orlinsky, D. E., & Howard, K. I. (1980). Gender and psychotherapeutic outcome. In A. M. Brodsky & R. T. Hare-Mustin (Eds.), Women and psychotherapy. New York: Guilford.

Orlinsky, D. E., & Howard, K. I. (1986). Process and outcome in psychotherapy. In S. L. Garfield & A. E. Bergin (Eds.), Handbook of psychotherapy and behavior change (3rd ed.). New York: Wiley.

Osborn, A. (1963). Applied imagination. New York: Scribner.

Osler, W. (1906). Aequanimatas. New York: McGraw-Hill.

Ost, L. G. (2008). Efficacy of the third wave of behavioral therapies: A systematic review and meta-analysis. *Behavior Research and Therapy, 46,* 296–321.

Otto, H., & Otto, R. (1972). *Total sex.* New York: New American Library.

Ouimette, P. C., Finney, J. W., & Moos, R. H. (1997). Twelve-step and cognitive-behavioral treatment for substance abuse: A comparison of treatment effectiveness. *Journal of Consulting & Clinical Psychology, 65,* 230–240.

Padesky, C. A., & Beck, A. T. (2003). Science and philosophy: Comparison of cognitive therapy and rational emotive behavior therapy. *Journal of Cognitive Therapy, 17,* 211–224.

Paivio, S. C., & Greenberg, L. S. (1995). Resolving "unfinished business": Efficacy of experiential therapy using empty-chair dialogue. *Journal of Consulting and Clinical Psychology, 63,* 419–425.

Pallesen, S., Mitsem, M., Kvale, G., et al. (2005). Outcome of psychological treatments of pathological gambling: A review and meta-analysis. *Addiction, 100,* 1412–1422.

Paludi, M. A. (1992). *The psychology of women.* Dubuque, IA: Brown & Benchmore.

Paniagua, F. A. (1998). *Assessing and treating culturally diverse clients: A practical guide* (2nd ed.). Thousand Oaks, CA: Sage.

Paniagua, F. A. (2005). *Assessing and treating culturally diverse clients: A practical guide* (3rd ed.). Thousand Oaks, CA: Sage.

Park, C. L., & Helgeson, V. S. (2006). Introduction to the special section: Growth following highly stressful life events. *Journal of Consulting & Clinical Psychology, 74,* 791–796.

Parloff, M. B., Waskow, I. E., & Wolfe, B. E. (1978). Research on therapist variables in relation to process and outcome. In S. L. Garfield & A. E. Bergin (Eds.), *Handbook of psychotherapy and behavior change: An empirical analysis* (2nd ed.). New York: Wiley.

Parsons, T. D., & Rizzo, A. A. (2008). Affective outcomes of virtual reality exposure therapy for anxiety and specific phobias. *Journal of Behavior Therapy and Experimental Psychiatry, 39,* 250–261.

Pascoe, E. A., & Smart Richman, L. (2009). Perceived discrimination and mental health: A meta-analytic review. *Psychological Bulletin, 135,* 531–554.

Patterson, C. H. (1984). Empathy, warmth, and genuineness in psychotherapy: A review of reviews. *Psychotherapy, 21,* 431–438.

Patterson, C. H. (1985). *The therapeutic relationship.* Belmont, CA; Brooks/Cole.

Patterson, C. H. (1990). On misrepresentation and misunderstanding. *Psychotherapy, 27,* 301.

Paul, G. (1966). *Insight versus desensitization in psychotherapy: An experiment in anxiety reduction.* Stanford, CA: Stanford University Press.

Paul, G. (1967). Insight versus desensitization in psychotherapy two years after termination. *Journal of Consulting and Clinical Psychology, 31,* 333–348.

Payne, K. T., & Marcus, D. K. (2008). The efficacy of group psychotherapy for older adult clients: A meta-analysis. *Group Dynamics: Theory, Research, and Practice, 12,* 268–278.

Pearsall, P. (2011). *500 therapies: Discovering a science for everyday living.* New York: Norton.

Pedersen, P. B., Draguns, J. G., Lonner, W. J., & Trimble, J. E. (Eds.). (2002). *Counseling across cultures* (5th ed.). Thousand Oaks, CA: Sage.

Pedersen, P. B., Draguns, J. G., Lonner, W. J., & Trimble, J. E. (Eds.). (2007). *Counseling across cultures* (6th ed.). Thousand Oaks, CA: Sage.

Pederson, P. B., Crethar, H. C., & Carlson, J. (2008). *Inclusive cultural empathy.* Washington, DC: American Psychological Association.

Pelham, W. E., Gnagy, E. M., Greiner, A. R., et al. (2000). Behavioral vs. behavioral and pharmacological treatment in ADHD children attending a summer treatment program. *Journal of Abnormal Child Psychology, 28,* 507–526.

Perez, R. M., DeBord, K. A., & Bieschke, K. J. (Eds.). (2006). *Handbook of counseling and psychotherapy with lesbian, gay, and bisexual clients* (2nd ed.). Washington, DC: American Psychological Association.

Perkins, B. R., & Rouanzoin, C. C. (2002). A critical evaluation of current views regarding eye movement desensitization and reprocessing (EMDR): Clarifying points of confusion. *Journal of Clinical Psychology, 58,* 77–97.

Perls, F. (1947). *Ego, hunger and aggression: A revision of Freud's theory and method.* Winchester, MA: Allen & Unwin.

Perls, F. (1969a). *Gestalt therapy verbatim.* Lafayette, CA: Real People Press.

Perls, F. (1969b). *In and out the garbage pail.* Lafayette, CA: Real People Press.

Perls, F. (1970). Four lectures. In J. Fagan & I. Shepherd (Eds.), *Gestalt therapy now.* Palo Alto, CA: Science and Behavior Books.

Perls, F. (1973). *The Gestalt approach and eye witness to therapy.* Palo Alto, CA: Science and Behavior Books.

Perls, F., Hefferline, R., & Goodman, P. (1951). *Gestalt therapy: Excitement and growth in the human personality.* New York: Dell.

Perry, M. A., & Furukawa, M. J. (1986). Modeling methods. In F. H. Kanfer & A. P. Goldstein (Eds.), *Helping people change* (3rd ed.). New York: Pergamon.

Perry, W. (1970). *Forms of intellectual and ethical development in the college years: A schema.* New York: Holt, Rinehart & Winston.

Persi, J. (1992). Top gun games: When therapists compete. *Transactional Analysis Journal, 22,* 144–152.

Persons, J. B., & Miranda, J. (1995). The search for mode-specific effects of cognitive and other therapies: A methodological suggestion. *Psychotherapy Research, 5,* 102–112.

Pervin, L. A. (1993). *Personality: Theory and research.* New York: Wiley.

Peterson, C., & Seligman, M. E. P. (2004). *Character strengths and virtues: A handbook and classification.* New York: Oxford University Press.

Peterson, C., Semmel, A., vonBaeyer, C., et al. (1982). The Attributional Style Questionnaire. *Cognitive Therapy and Research, 6,* 281–299.

Peterson, C., & Villanova, P. (1988). An expanded Attributional Style Questionnaire. *Journal of Abnormal Psychology, 97,* 87–89.

Petrocelli, J. V. (2002). Effectiveness of group cognitive-behavioral therapy for general symptomatology: A meta-analysis. *Journal for Specialists in Group Work, 27,* 92–115.

Petry, N. M., Martin, B., Cooney, J. L., & Kranzler, H. R. (2000). Give them prizes, and they will come: Contingency management for treatment of alcohol dependence. *Journal of Consulting and Clinical Psychology, 68,* 250–257.

Pew Internet and American Life Project. (2003). *Internet Health Resources.* Retrieved from http://www.pewinternet.org/reports/toc.asp?Report=95

Pew Study. (2012). *"Nones" on the rise: New report finds one-in-five adults have no religious affiliation.* Retrieved from www.pewforum.org/Press-Room/Press-Releases/

Pfammatter, M., Junghan, U. M., & Brenner, H. D. (2006). Efficacy of psychological therapy in schizophrenia: Conclusions from meta-analyses. *Schizophrenia Bulletin, 32,* S64–S80.

Pharoah, F., Mari, J., Rathbone, J., Wong, W. (2011). Family intervention for schizophrenia. *Cochrane Database of Systematic Reviews, 12,* CD000088.

Philips, J. C., & Fischer, A. R. (1998). Graduate students' training experiences with lesbian, gay, and bisexual issues. *The Counseling Psychologist, 26,* 712–734.

Piaget, J. (1952). *The origins of intelligence in children.* New York: International Universities Press.

Piet, J., & Hougaard, E. (2011). The effect of mindfulness-based cognitive therapy for prevention of relapse in recurrent major depressive disorder: A systematic review and meta-analysis. *Clinical Psychology Review, 31,* 1032–1040.

Pieterse, A. L., Todd, N. R., Neville, H. A., & Carter, R. T. (2012). Perceived racism and mental health among Black American adults: A meta-analytic review. *Journal of Counseling Psychology, 59,* 1–9.

Pilling, S., Bebbington, P., Kuipers, E., et al. (2002). Psychological treatments in schizophrenia: I. Meta-analysis of family intervention and cognitive behaviour therapy. *Psychological Medicine, 32,* 763–782.

Pinquart, M., Duberstein, P. R., & Lyness, J. M. (2007). Effects of psychotherapy and other behavioral interventions on clinically depressed older adults: A meta-analysis. *Aging & Mental Health, 11,* 645–657.

Pinsof, W. M. (1995). *Integrative problem-centered therapy.* New York: Basic.

Pinsof, W. M., Wynne, L. C., & Hambright, A. B. (1996). The outcome of couple and family therapy: Findings, conclusions, and recommendations. *Psychotherapy, 33,* 321–331.

Pipher, M. B. (1994). Reviving Ophelia. New York: Putnam. Pipher, M. B. (2012). Therapists as activists. *Psychotherapy Networker, 36,* 69–70.

Pleck, J. H. (1995). The gender role strain paradigm: An update. In R. F. Levant & W. S. Pollack (Eds.), *A new psychology of men.* New York: Basic Books.

Pollock, R. F., & Brooks, G. R. (Eds.). (1998). *New psychotherapy for men.* New York: Wiley.

Polster, E., & Polster, M. (1973). *Gestalt therapy integrated.* New York: Brunner/Mazel.

Polster, M. (1974). Women in therapy: A Gestalt therapist's view. In S. V. Frankl & V. Burtle (Eds.), *Women in therapy.* New York: Brunner/Mazel.

Ponterotto, J. G., Casas, J. M., Suzuki, L. A., & Alexander, C. M. (Eds.). (2009). *Handbook of multicultural counseling* (3rd ed.). Thousand Oaks, CA: Sage.

Power, R. N. (1981). On the process and practice of psychotherapy: Some reflections. *British Journal of Medical Psychology, 54,* 15–23.

Powers, M. B., & Emmelkamp, P. M. G. (2008). Virtual reality exposure therapy for anxiety disorders: A meta-analysis. *Journal of Anxiety Disorders, 22,* 561–569.

Powers, M. B., Halpern, J. M., Ferenschak, M. P., et al. (2010). A meta-analytic review of prolonged exposure for posttraumatic stress disorder. *Clinical Psychology Review, 30,* 635–641.

Powers, M. B., Sigmarsson, S. R., & Emmelkamp, P. M. G. (2008). A meta-analytic review of psychological treatments for social anxiety disorder.

International Journal of Cognitive Therapy, 1, 94–113.

Powers, M. B., Zum Vorde Sive Vording, M. B., & Emmelkamp, P. M. G. (2009). Acceptance and commitment therapy: A meta-analytic review. *Psychotherapy and Psychosomatics, 78,* 73–80.

Prendergast, M., Podus, D., Finney, J., Greenwall, L., & Roll, J. (2006). Contingency management for treatment of substance use disorders: A meta-analysis. *Addiction, 101,* 1546–1560.

Price, J. R., Mitchell, E., Tidy, E., & Hunot, V. (2008). Cognitive behavior therapy for chronic fatigue syndrome in adults. *Cochrane Database of Systematic Reviews, 3,* CD001027.

Prochaska, J. O. (1979). *Systems of psychotherapy: A transtheoretical analysis.* Chicago: Dorsey.

Prochaska, J. O. (1996). A revolution in health promotion: Smoking cessation as a case study. In R. J. Resnick & R. H. Rozensky (Eds.), *Health psychology through the lifespan: Practice and research opportunities.* Washington, DC: APA Books.

Prochaska, J. O. (2004). Population treatment for addictions. *Current Directions in Psychological Science, 13,* 242–246.

Prochaska, J. O., & DiClemente, C. C. (1983). Stages and processes of self-change of smoking: Toward an integrative model of change. *Journal of Consulting and Clinical Psychology, 51,* 390–395.

Prochaska, J. O., & DiClemente, C. C. (1984). *The transtheoretical approach: Crossing the traditional boundaries of therapy.* Homewood, IL: Dow Jones-Irwin.

Prochaska, J. O., & DiClemente, C. C. (1992). Stages of change in the modification of problem behaviors. In M. Hersen, R. M. Eisler, & P. M. Miller (Eds.), *Progress in behavior modification.* Sycamore, IL: Sycamore.

Prochaska, J. O., DiClemente, C. C., & Norcross, J. C. (1992). In search of how people change: Applications to addictive behaviors. *American Psychologist, 47,* 1102–1114.

Prochaska, J. O., DiClemente, C. C., Velicer, W. F., & Rossi, J. S. (1993).

Standardized, individualized, interactive, and personalized self-help programs for smoking cessation. *Health Psychology, 12,* 399–405.

Prochaska, J. O., Evers, K. E., Castle, P. H., et al. (2012). Enhancing multiple domains of well-being by decreasing multiple health risk behaviors: A randomized clinical trial. *Population Health Management, 15,* 1–11.

Prochaska, J. O., & Norcross, J. C. (2002). Stages of change. In J. C. Norcross (Ed.), *Psychotherapy relationships that work.* New York: Oxford University Press.

Prochaska, J. O., Norcross, J. C., & DiClemente, C. C. (1995). *Changing for good.* New York: Avon.

Prochaska, J. O., Norcross, J. C., Fowler, J., et al. (1992). Attendance and outcome in a work-site weight control program: Processes and stages of change as process and predictor variables. *Addictive Behavior, 17,* 35–45.

Prochaska, J. O., Smith, N., Marzilli, R., et al. (1974). Demonstration of the advantages of remote-control aversive stimulation in the control of headbanging in a retarded child. *Journal of Behavior Therapy and Experimental Psychiatry, 5,* 285–289.

Prochaska, J. O., Velicer, W. F., Fava, J. L., et al. (2000). Counselor and stimulus control enhancements of a stage-matched expert system intervention for smokers in a managed care setting. *Preventive Medicine, 32,* 23–32.

Prochaska, J. O., Velicer, W. F., Fava, J. L., et al. (2001). Evaluating a population-based recruitment approach and a stage-based expert system intervention for smoking cessation. *Addictive Behaviors, 26,* 583–602.

Prochaska, J. O., Velicer W. F., Redding, C. A., et al. (2005). Stage-based expert systems to guide a population of primary care patients to quit smoking, eat healthier, prevent skin cancer and receive regular mammograms. *Preventive Medicine, 41,* 406–416.

Prochaska, J. O., Velicer, W. F., Rossi, J. S., et al. (1994). Stages of change and decisional balance for twelve problem behaviors. *Health Psychology, 13,* 39–46.

Prochaska, J. O., Velicer, W. F., Rossi, J. S., et al. (2004). Multiple risk expert systems interventions: Impact of simultaneous stage-matched expert systems for smoking, high fat diet, and sun exposure in a population of parents. *Health Psychology, 23,* 503–516.

Project MATCH Research Group. (1993). Project MATCH: Rationale and methods for a multisite clinical trial matching patients to alcholism treatment. *Alcoholism: Clinical and Experimental Research, 17,* 1130–1145.

Project MATCH Research Group. (1997). Matching alcoholism treatments to client heterogeneity: Project MATCH posttreatment drinking outcomes. *Journal of Studies on Alcohol, 58,* 7–29.

Prout, H. T., & Nowak-Drabik, K. M. (2003). Psychotherapy with persons who have mental retardation: An evaluation of effectiveness. *American Journal of Mental Retardation, 108,* 82–93.

Purdie, N., Hattie, J., & Carroll, A. (2002). A review of the research on interventions for attention deficit hyperactivity disorder: What works best? *Review of Educational Research, 72,* 61–99.

Querimit, D. S., & Conner, L. C. (2003). Empowerment psychotherapy with adolescent females of color. *Journal of Clinical Psychology: In Session, 59,* 1215–1224.

Rabinowitz, F., & Cochran, S. (2001). *Deepening psychotherapy with men.* Washington, DC: American Psychological Association.

Rait, D. (1988). Survey results. *Family Therapy Networker, 12,* 52–56.

Rank, O. (1936). *Will therapy.* New York: Knopf.

Rapaport, D. (1958). The theory of ego autonomy: A generalization. *Bulletin of the Menninger Clinic, 22,* 13–35.

Raskin, N. J. (1992, August). *Not necessary, perhaps sufficient, definitely facilitative.* Paper presented at the 100th annual convention of the American Psychological Association, Washington, DC.

Rebecca, M., Hefner, R., & Oleshansky, B. (1976). A model of sex role transcendence. *Journal of Social Issues, 32,* 197–206.

Rector, N. A., & Beck, A. T. (2001). Cognitive behavioral therapy for schizophrenia: An empirical review. *Journal of Nervous & Mental Disease, 189,* 278–287.

Rehm, L. P. (1984). Self-management therapy for depression. *Advances in Behaviour Research and Therapy, 6,* 83–98.

Reicherts, M. (1998). Gesprachspsychotherapie. In U. Baumann & M. Perrez (Eds.), *Lehrbuch klinische psychologie* (2nd ed.). Bern: Hans Huber.

Reik, T. (1948). *Listening with the third ear.* New York: Farrar, Straus & Giroux.

Reinecke, M. A., Ryan, N. E., & DuBois, D. L. (1998). Cognitive-behavior therapy of depression and depressive symptoms during adolescence: A review and meta-analysis. *Journal of the American Academy of Child and Adolescent Psychiatry, 37,* 1006–1007.

Reisman, D. (1961). *The lonely crowd.* New Haven: Yale University Press.

Reiss, D. (1977). The multiple family group as a small society: Family regulation of interaction with nonmembers. *American Journal of Psychiatry, 134,* 21–24.

Resick, P. A., Monson, C. M., & Rizvi, S. L. (2008). Posttraumatic stress disorder. In D. H. Barlow (Ed.), *Clinical handbook of psychological disorders* (4th ed.). New York: Guilford.

Resick, P. A., & Schnicke, M. (1996). *Cognitive processing therapy for rape victims: A treatment manual.* Newbury Park, CA: Sage.

Rice, L. N. (1988). Integration and the client-centered relationship. *Journal of Integrative and Eclectic Psychotherapy, 7,* 291–302.

Richard, D. C. S., & Lauterbach, D. (2006). *The handbook of exposure therapies.* Oxford: Elsevier.

Ricks, D. F., Wandersman, A., & Poppen, P. J. (1976). Humanism and behaviorism: Towards new syntheses. In A. Wandersman, P. J. Poppen, & D. F. Ricks (Eds.), *Humanism and behaviorism: Dialogue and growth.* Elmsford, NY: Pergamon.

Rimm, D., & Masters, J. (1974). *Behavior therapy.* New York: Academic.

Roberts, A. H., Kewman, D. G., Mercier, L., & Hovell, M. (1993). The power of nonspecific effects in healing: Implications for psychosocial and biological treatments. *Clinical Psychology Review, 13,* 375–391.

Roberts, L. J., & Marlatt, G. A. (1998). Guidelines for relapse prevention. In

G. P. Koocher, J. C. Norcross, & S. S. Hill (Eds.), *Psychologists' desk reference*. New York: Oxford University Press.

Robertson, M. (1979). Some observations from an eclectic therapist. *Psychotherapy, 16*, 18–21.

Robine, J. (1991). Contact, the first experience. *The Gestalt Journal, 14*, 45–60.

Robins, C. N., Helzer, J. D., Weissman, M. M., et al. (1984). Lifetime prevalence of specific psychiatric disorders in three sites. *Archives of General Psychiatry, 41*, 949–958.

Robinson, L. A., Berman, J. S., & Neimeyer, R. A. (1990). Psychotherapy for the treatment of depression: A comprehensive review of controlled outcome research. *Psychological Bulletin, 108*, 30–49.

Rockland, l. H. (2003). *Supportive therapy: A psychodynamic approach*. New York: Basic Books.

Roethlisberger, F., & Dickson, W. (1939). *Management and the worker*. Cambridge, MA: Harvard University Press.

Rogers, C. R. (1939). *The clinical treatment of the problem child*. Boston: Houghton Mifflin.

Rogers, C. R. (1942). *Counseling and psychotherapy*. Boston: Houghton Mifflin.

Rogers, C. R. (1951). *Client-centered therapy*. Boston: Houghton Mifflin.

Rogers, C. R. (1957). The necessary and sufficient conditions of therapeutic personality change. *Journal of Consulting Psychology, 21*, 95–103.

Rogers, C. R. (1959). A theory of therapy, personality, and interpersonal relationships as developed in the client-centered framework. In S. Koch (Ed.), *Psychology: A study of a science*. New York: McGraw-Hill.

Rogers, C. R. (1961). *On becoming a person*. Boston: Houghton Mifflin.

Rogers, C. R. (1970). *Carl Rogers on encounter groups*. New York: Harper & Row.

Rogers, C. R. (1972). *On becoming partners: Marriage and its alternatives*. New York: Delacorte.

Rogers, C. R. (1977). *Carl Rogers on personal power*. New York: Delacorte.

Rogers, C. R. (1980). *A way of being*. Boston: Houghton Mifflin.

Rogers, C. R. (1983). *Freedom to learn for the 80's*. Columbus, OH: Merrill.

Rogers, C. R. (1986). Carl Rogers on the development of the person-centered approach. *Person-Centered Review, 1*, 257–259.

Rogers, C. R. (1987a). Comments on the issue of equality in psychotherapy. *Journal of Humanistic Psychology, 27*, 38–40.

Rogers, C. R. (1987b). Steps toward world peace, 1948–1986: Tension reduction in theory and practice. *Counseling and Values, 32*, 38–45.

Rogers, C. R., & Dymond, R. (1954). *Psychotherapy and personality change*. Chicago: University of Chicago Press.

Rogers, C. R., Gendlin, E., Kiesler, D., & Truax, C. (1967). *The therapeutic relationship and its impact: A study of psychotherapy with schizophrenics*. Madison: University of Wisconsin Press.

Rogers, C. R., & Rablen, R. (1958). *A scale of process in psychotherapy*. Unpublished manuscript, University of Wisconsin, Madison.

Rokeach, M. (1970). Faith, hope and bigotry. *Psychology Today, 3*, 33–38.

Rollnick, S., & Miller, W. R. (1995). What is motivational interviewing? *Behavioural and Cognitive Psychotherapy, 23*, 325–334.

Rosa-Alcazar, A. I., Sanchez-Meca, J., Gomez-Conesa, A., & Marin-Martinez, F. (2008). Psychological treatment of obsessive-compulsive disorder: A meta-analysis. *Clinical Psychology Review, 28*, 1310–1325.

Rose, S. J., & Hartmann, H. I. (2004). *Still a man's labor market: The long-term gender gap*. Washington, DC: Institute for Women's Policy Research.

Rosen, C. S. (2000). Is the sequencing of change processes by stage consistent across health problems? A meta-analysis. *Health Psychology, 19*, 593–604.

Rosenberg, J. (1973). *Total orgasm*. New York: Random House.

Rosenthal, R. (1990). How are we doing in soft psychology? *American Psychologist, 45*, 775–777.

Rosenthal, R. (1995). Progress in clinical psychology: Is there any? *Clinical Psychology: Science and Practice, 2*, 133–150.

Rosenzweig, S. (1936). Some implicit common factors in diverse methods of psychotherapy. *American Journal of Orthopsychiatry, 6*, 412–415.

Rosewater, L. B., & Walker, L. E. A. (Eds.). (1985). *Handbook of feminist therapy*. New York: Springer.

Rosman, B., Minuchin, S., Liebman, R., & Baker, L. (1978, November). *Family therapy for psychosomatic children*. Paper presented at the annual meeting of the American Academy of Psychosomatic Medicine, Atlanta, GA.

Rossi, J. S., Ruggiero, L., Rossi, S., et al. (2003). Effectiveness of stage-based multiple behavior interventions for diabetes management in two randomized clinical trials. *Annals of Behavioral Medicine, 24*(Suppl.), S192.

Roth, A., Fonagy, P., & Parry, G. (2005). *What works for whom? A critical review of psychotherapy research* (2nd ed.). New York: Guilford.

Rothenberg, A. (1988). *The creative process of psychotherapy*. New York: Norton.

Rothwell, N. (2005). How brief is solution-focused therapy? A comparative study. *Clinical Psychology and Psychotherapy, 12*, 402–405.

Rotter, J. B. (1954). *Social learning and clinical psychology*. Englewood Cliffs, NJ: Prentice Hall.

Rouff, L. C. (2000). Clouds and silver linings: Training experiences of psychodynamically oriented mental health trainees. *American Journal of Psychotherapy, 54*, 549–559.

Rowan, T., & O'Hanlon, B. (1999). *Solution-oriented therapy for chronic and severe mental illness*. New York: Wiley.

Rubinstein, G. (1994). Expressions of existential philosophy in different therapeutic schools. *Journal of Contemporary Psychotherapy, 24*, 131–148.

Ryle, A. (1990). *Cognitive analytic therapy*. London: Wiley.

Ryle, A. (Ed.). (1995). *Cognitive analytic therapy: Developments in theory and practice*. New York: Wiley.

Sachse, R. (1990). Acting purposefully in client-centered therapy. In P. J. D. Drenth, J. A. Sergeant, & R. J. Tokens (Eds.), *European perspectives in psychology* (Vol. I). New York: Wiley.

Sammons, M. T., & Schmidt, N. B. (Eds.). (2002). *Combined treatments for mental disorders: A guide to psychological and pharmacological interventions*.

Washington, DC: American Psychological Association.

Sanchez-Meca, J., Rosa-Alcazar, A. I., Marin-Martinez, F., & Gomez-Conesa, A. (2010). Psychological treatment of panic disorder with or without agoraphobia: A meta-analysis. *Clinical Psychology Review, 30*, 37–50.

Sandberg, J. G., Johnson, L. N., Dermer, S. B., et al. (1997). Demonstrated efficacy of models of marriage and family therapy: An update of Gurman, Kniskern, and Pinsof's chart. *American Journal of Family Therapy, 25*, 121–137.

Sandell, R., Blomberg, J., Lazar, A., et al. (2000). Varieties of long-term outcome among patients in psychoanalysis and long-term psychotherapy. *International Journal of Psychoanalysis, 81*, 921–942.

Saner, R. (1989). Culture bias of Gestalt therapy: Made-in-USA. *The Gestalt Journal, 12*, 57–71.

Sartre, J. P. (1955). *No exit and three other plays.* New York: Vintage.

Sartre, J. P. (1956). *Being and nothingness.* New York: Philosophical Library.

Sartre, J. P. (1967). *Existential psychoanalysis.* Chicago: Henry Regnery.

Satir, V. (1967). *Conjoint family therapy.* Palo Alto, CA: Science and Behavior Books.

Satir, V. (1972). *Peoplemaking.* Palo Alto, CA: Science and Behavior Books.

Satir, V., & Baldwin, M. (1983). *Satir step by step.* Palo Alto, CA: Science and Behavior Books.

Satir, V., Stachowiak, J., & Taschman, H. (1977). *Helping people change.* New York: Jason Aronson.

Saunders, T., Drishell, J. E., Johnston, J. H., & Salas, E. (1996). The effect of stress inoculation training on anxiety and performance. *Journal of Occupational Health Psychology, 1*, 170–186.

Scaturo, D. J. (2005). *Clinical dilemmas in psychotherapy.* Washington, DC: American Psychological Association.

Schachter, S. (1971). Some extraordinary facts about obese humans and rats. *American Psychologist, 26*, 129–149.

Schachter, S., & Singer, J. (1962). Cognitive, social and physiological determinants of emotional state. *Psychological Review, 69*, 379–399.

Schaefer, R. (2004). *Racial and ethnic groups* (9th ed.). New Jersey: Prentice Hall.

Schafer, R. (1976). *A new language for psychoanalysis.* New Haven: Yale University Press.

Schneider, K. J. (2007). *Existential-integrative psychotherapy: Guideposts to the core of practice.* New York: Routledge.

Schneider, K. J., Bugental, J. F. T., & Pierson, J. F. (Eds.). (2002). *The handbook of humanistic psychology.* Thousand Oaks, CA: Sage.

Schneider, K. J., Galvin, J., & Serlin, I. (2009). Rollo May on existential psychotherapy. *Journal of Humanistic Psychology, 49*, 419–434.

Schneider, K. J., & May, R. (1995). *The psychology of existence: An integrative, clinical, perspective.* New York: McGraw-Hill.

Schottenbauer, M. A., Glass, C. R., & Arnkoff, D. B. (2005). Outcome research on psychotherapy integration. In J. C. Norcross & M. R. Goldfried (Eds.), *Handbook of psychotherapy integration* (2nd ed.). New York: Oxford University Press.

Schulenberg, S. E., Hutzell, R. R., Nassif, C., & Rogina, J. M. (2008). Logotherapy for clinical practice. *Psychotherapy, 45*, 447–463.

Schwartz, M. S., & Andrasik, F. (Eds.). (2005). *Biofeedback: A practitioner's guide* (3rd ed.). New York: Guilford.

Scogin, F., & McElreath, L. (1994). Efficacy of psychosocial treatments for geriatric depression: A quantitative review. *Journal of Consulting and Clinical Psychology, 62*, 69–74.

Scogin, F., Welsh, D., Hanson, A., et al. (2005). Evidence-based psychotherapies for depression in older adults. *Clinical Psychology: Science and Practice, 12*, 222–237.

Scott, J., Colom, F., & Vieta, E. (2007). A meta-analysis of relapse rates with adjunctive psychological therapies compared to usual psychiatric treatment for bipolar disorders. *The International Journal of Neuropsychopharmacology, 10*, 123–129.

Segal, L. (1991). Brief therapy: The MRI approach. In A. S. Gurman & D. P. Kniskern (Eds.), *Handbook of family therapy* (Vol. 2). New York: Brunner/ Mazel.

Segal, Z. V., Williams, J. M. G., & Teasdale, J. D. (2002). *Mindfulness based cognitive therapy for depression.* New York: Guilford.

Seidenberg, R. (1970). *Marriage in life and literature.* New York: Philosophical Library.

Seidler, G. H., & Wagner, F. E. (2006). Comparing the efficacy of EMDR and trauma-focused cognitive-behavioral therapy in the treatment of PTSD: A meta-analytic study. *Psychological Medicine, 36*, 1515–1522.

Seligman, M. E. P. (1990). *Learned optimism.* New York: Knopf.

Seligman, M. E. P. (2000). Positive psychology: An introduction. *American Psychologist, 55*, 5–14.

Seligman, M. E. P., Abramson, L. Y., Semmel, A., & vonBaeyer, C. (1979). Depressive attributional style. *Journal of Abnormal Psychology, 88*, 242–247.

Serketich, W. J., & Dumas, J. E. (1996). The effectiveness of behavioral parent training to modify antisocial behavior in children: A meta-analysis. *Behavior Therapy, 27*, 171–186.

Sexton, T. L. (2010). *Functional family therapy in clinical practice: An evidence-based treatment model for working with troubled adolescents.* New York: Routledge.

Sexton, T. L., Robbins, M. S., Hollimon, A. S., Mease, A. L., & Mayorga, C. C. (2003). Efficacy, effectiveness, and change mechanisms in couple and family therapy. In T. L. Sexton, G. R. Weeks, & M. S. Robbins (Eds.), *Handbook of family therapy.* New York: Brunner-Routledge.

Sexton, T. L., Weeks, G. R., & Robbins, M. S. (Eds.). (2003). *Handbook of family therapy.* New York: Brunner-Routledge.

Shadish, W. R., & Baldwin, S. A. (2003). Meta-analysis of MFT interventions. *Journal of Marital and Family Therapy, 29*, 547–570.

Shadish, W. R., & Baldwin, S. A. (2005). Effects of behavioral marital therapy: A meta-analysis of randomized controlled trials. *Journal of Consulting and Clinical Psychology, 73*, 6–14.

Shadish, W. R., Montgomery, L. M., Wilson, P., et al. (1993). The effects of family and marital psychotherapies: A meta-analysis. *Journal of Consulting and Clinical Psychology, 61,* 992–1002.

Shadish, W. R., Navarro, A. M., Matt, G. E., & Phillips, G. (2000). The effects of psychological therapies under clinically representative conditions: A meta-analysis. *Psychological Bulletin, 126,* 512–529.

Shadish, W. R., Ragsdale, K., Glaser, R. R., & Montgomery, L. M. (1995). The efficacy and effectiveness of marital and family therapy: A perspective from meta-analysis. *Journal of Marital and Family Therapy, 21,* 345–360.

Shapiro, D. A., & Shapiro, D. (1982). Meta-analysis of comparative therapy outcome studies: A replication and refinement. *Psychological Bulletin, 92,* 581–604.

Shapiro, F. (1995). *Eye movement desensitization and reprocessing: Basic principles, protocols, and procedures.* New York: Guilford.

Shapiro, F. (1997). *EMDR in the treatment of trauma.* Pacific Grove, CA: EMDR Institute.

Shapiro, F. (2002a). EMDR twelve years after its introduction: Past and future research. *Journal of Clinical Psychology, 58,* 1–22.

Shapiro, F. (Ed.). (2002b). *EMDR and the paradigm prism.* Washington, DC: American Psychological Association.

Shapiro, F. (2002c). *Eye movement desensitization and reprocessing: Basic principles, protocols, and procedures* (2nd ed.). New York: Guilford.

Shapiro, F. (2012). *Getting past your past: Take control of your life with self-help techniques from EMDR therapy.* New York: Rodale.

Shapiro, F., & Forrest, M. S. (1997). *EMDR: The breakthrough therapy for overcoming anxiety, stress, and trauma.* New York: Basic.

Shapiro, F., Kaslow, F. W., & Maxfield, L. (Eds.). (2007). *Handbook of EMDR and family therapy processes.* New York: Wiley.

Shedler, J. (2010). The efficacy of psychodynamic psychotherapy. *American Psychologist, 65,* 98–109.

Shepherd, I. L. (1976). Limitations and cautions in the Gestalt approach.

In C. Hatcher & P. Himmelstein (Eds.), *The handbook of Gestalt therapy.* New York: Jason Aronson.

Sherman, A. (1973). *Behavior modification: Theory and practice.* Pacific Grove, CA: Brooks/Cole.

Sherman, J. J. (1998). Effects of psychotherapeutic treatments for PTSD: A meta-analysis of controlled clinical trials. *Journal of Traumatic Stress, 11,* 413–434.

Shidlo, A., & Schroeder, M. (2002). Changing sexual orientation: A consumer's report. *Professional Psychology: Research and Practice, 33,* 249–259.

Shin, S. M., Chow, C., Camacho-Gonsalves, T., et al. (2005). A meta-analytic review of racial-ethnic matching for African American and Caucasian-American clients and clinicians. *Journal of Counseling Psychology, 52,* 49–56.

Shirk, S. R., & Karver, M. (2011). Alliance in child and adolescent therapy. In J. C. Norcross (Ed.), *Psychotherapy relationships that work* (2nd ed.). New York: Oxford University Press.

Shirk, S. R., & Russell, R. L. (1992). A reevaluation of estimates of child therapy effectiveness. *Journal of the American Academy of Child and Adolescent Psychiatry, 31,* 703–708.

Shoham-Salomon, V., & Rosenthal, R. (1987). Paradoxical interventions: A meta-analysis. *Journal of Consulting and Clinical Psychology, 55,* 22–28.

Siegel, D. J. (1999). *The developing mind.* New York: Guilford.

Siev, J., & Chambless, D. L. (2007). Specificity of treatment effects: Cognitive therapy and relaxation for generalized anxiety and panic disorders. *Journal of Consulting and Clinical Psychology, 75,* 513–522.

Silverman, L. H. (1976). Psychoanalytic theory: "The reports of my death are greatly exaggerated." *American Psychologist, 31,* 621–637.

Simoneau, T. L., Miklowitz, D. J., & Saleem, R. (1998). Expressed emotion and interactional patterns in families of bipolar patients. *Journal of Abnormal Psychology, 107,* 497–507.

Sin, N. L., & Lyubomirsky, S. (2009). Enhancing well-being and alleviating depressive symptoms with positive psychology interventions: A practice-friendly

meta-analysis. *Journal of Clinical Psychology: In Session, 65,* 467–487.

Sitharthan, T., Sitharan, G., Hough, M. J., & Kavanagh, D. J. (1997). Cue exposure in moderation drinking: A comparison with cognitive-behavior therapy. *Journal of Consulting and Clinical Psychology, 65,* 878–882.

Skinner, B. F. (1948). *Walden two.* New York: MacMillan.

Skinner, B. F. (1971). *Beyond freedom and dignity.* New York: Vintage.

Skinner, B. F. (1990). Can psychology be a science of mind? *American Psychologist, 45,* 1206–1210.

Sloane, R. B., Staples, F., Cristol, A., et al. (1975). *Psychotherapy versus behavior therapy.* Cambridge, MA: Harvard University Press.

Sluzki, C., & Ransom, D. (Eds.). (1976). *Double bind: The foundations of the communicational approach to the family.* New York: Grune & Stratton.

Smedley, A., & Smedley, B. D. (2005). Race as biology is fiction, racism as a social problem is real: Anthropological and historical perspectives on the social construction of race. *American Psychologist, 60,* 16–26.

Smedslund, G., Berg, R. C., Hammerstrøm, K. T., et al. (2011). Motivational interviewing for substance abuse. *Cochrane Database of Systematic Reviews, 5.* CD008063.

Smedslund, G., Dalsbo, T. K., Steiro, A., et al. (2009). Cognitive behavioural therapy for men who physically abuse their female partner. *Cochrane Database of Systematic Reviews, 3,* CD006048.

Smit, Y., Huibers, M. J. H., Ioannidis, J. P. A., et al. (2012). The effectiveness of long-term psychoanalytic psychotherapy: A meta-analysis of randomized controlled trials. *Clinical Psychology Review, 32,* 81–92.

Smith, C., & Lloyd, B. (1978). Maternal behavior and perceived sex of infant: Revisited. *Child Development, 49,* 1263–1265.

Smith, M. L., & Glass, G. V. (1977). Meta-analysis of psychotherapy outcome studies. *American Psychologist, 32,* 752–760.

Smith, M. L., Glass, G. V., & Miller, T. I. (1980). *The benefits of psychotherapy.*

Baltimore: Johns Hopkins University Press.

Smith, M. T., Perlis, M. L., Park, A., et al. (2002). Comparative meta-analysis of pharmacotherapy and behavior therapy for persistent insomnia. *American Journal of Psychiatry, 159,* 5–11.

Smith, T. B., Bartz, J., & Richards, P. S. (2007). Outcomes of religious and spiritual adaptations to psychotherapy: A meta-analytic review. *Psychotherapy Research, 17,* 643–655.

Smith, T. B., Constantine, M. G., Dunn, T. D., et al. (2006). Multicultural education in the mental health professions: A meta-analytic review. *Journal of Counseling Psychology, 53,* 132–145.

Smith, T. B., Rodriguez, M. D., & Bernal, G. (2011). Culture. In J. C. Norcross (Ed.), *Psychotherapy relationships that work* (2nd ed., pp. 316–335). New York: Oxford University Press.

Snyder, C. R., & Lopez, S. J. (Eds.). (2005). *Handbook of positive psychology.* New York: Oxford University Press.

Snyder, D. K., Castellani, A. M., & Whisman, M. A. (2006). Current status and future directions in couple therapy. *Annual Review of Psychology, 57,* 317–344.

Snyder, D. K., & Whisman, M. A. (Ed.). (2003). *Treating difficult couples: Helping clients with coexisting mental and relationship disorders.* New York: Guilford.

Sollod, R. N. (1978). Carl Rogers and the origins of client-centered therapy. *Professional Psychology, 9,* 93–104.

Solms, M. (2004). Freud returns. *Scientific America, 290*(5), 82–88.

Solomon, L. N. (1990). Carl Rogers's efforts for world peace. *Person-Centered Review, 5,* 39–56.

Solomon, R., Kamin, L., & Wynne, L. (1953). Traumatic avoidance learning. The outcomes of several extinction procedures with dogs. *Journal of Abnormal and Social Psychology, 48,* 291–302.

Sperry, L. (1992). Psychotherapy systems: An Adlerian integration with implication for older adults. *Individual Psychology, 48,* 451–461.

Spiegelberg, H. (1972). *Phenomenology in psychology and psychiatry.* Evanston, IL: Northwestern University Press.

Spiegler, M. D., & Guevremont, D. C. (2003). *Contemporary behavior therapy*

(4th ed.). Pacific Grove, CA: Brooks/Cole.

Spitz, R. (1945). Hospitalism: Genesis of psychiatric conditions in early childhood. *Psychoanalytic Study of the Child, 1,* 53–74.

Stampfl, T. (1976). Implosive therapy. In P. Olsen (Ed.), *Emotional flooding.* New York: Aldine.

Stampfl, T., & Levis, D. (1973). *Implosive therapy: Theory and technique.* Morristown, NJ: General Learning Press.

Stams, G. J. J. M., Dekovic, M., Buist, K., & De Vries, L. (2006). Effectiviteit van oplossingsgerichte korte therapie: Een meta-analyse [Efficacy of solution-focused brief therapy: A meta-analysis]. *Tijdshrift voor gedragstherapie, 39,* 81–94.

Stanton, M. D., & Shadish, W. R. (1997). Outcome, attrition, and family-couples treatment for drug abuse: A meta-analysis and review of the controlled, comparative studies. *Psychological Bulletin, 122,* 170–191.

Steiner, C. (1971). *Games alcoholics play.* New York: Ballantine.

Steiner, C. (1974). *Scripts people live.* New York: Grove.

Steiner, C. (1990). *Scripts people live* (rev. ed.). New York: Grove/Atlantic.

Stetter, F., & Kupper, S. (2002). Autogenic training: A meta-analysis of clinical outcome studies. *Applied Psychophysiology and Biofeedback, 27,* 45–98.

Stevens, S. E., Hynan, M. T., Allen, M., et al. (2007). Are complex psychotherapies more effective than biofeedback, progressive muscle relaxation, or both? A meta-analysis. *Psychological Reports, 100,* 303–324.

Stewart, R. E., & Chambless, D. L. (2009). Cognitive-behavioral therapy for adult anxiety disorders in clinical practice: A meta-analysis of effectiveness studies. *Journal of Consulting and Clinical Psychology, 77,* 595–606.

Stiles, W. B., Barkham, M., Mellor-Clark, J., & Connell, J. (2008). Effectiveness of cognitive-behavioural, person-centred, and psychodynamic therapies in UK primary-care routine practice: Replication in a larger sample. *Psychological Medicine, 38,* 677–688.

Stosny, S. (2010). Lions without a cause. *Psychotherapy Networker, 34,* 26.

Stricker, G. (1988). Supervision of integrative psychotherapy: Discussion. *Journal of Integrative and Eclectic Psychotherapy, 7,* 176–180.

Strupp, H. H. (1971). *Psychotherapy and the modification of abnormal behavior.* New York: McGraw-Hill.

Strupp, H. H. (1986). The nonspecific hypothesis of therapeutic effectiveness: A current assessment. *American Journal of Orthopsychiatry, 56,* 513–520.

Strupp, H. H. (1992). The future of psychodynamic psychotherapy. *Psychotherapy, 29,* 21–27.

Strupp, H. H., & Binder, J. L. (1984). *Psychotherapy in a new key: A guide to time limited dynamic psychotherapy.* New York: Basic.

Stuart, R. (1969). Token reinforcement in marital treatment. In R. Robin & C. Franks (Eds.), *Advances in behavioral therapy.* New York: Academic Press.

Stuart, R. B. (2004). Twelve practical suggestions for achieving multicultural competence. *Professional Psychology: Research and Practice, 35,* 3–9.

Stuart, S., & Roberston, M. (2012). *Interpersonal psychotherapy* (2nd ed.). New York: Oxford University Press.

Sudak, D. M., & Goldberg, D. A. (2012). Trends in psychotherapy training: A national survey of psychiatry residency training. *Academic Psychiatry, 36,* 369–373.

Sue, D., Sue, D. W., & Sue, S. (2012). *Understanding abnormal behavior* (10th ed.). Boston: Houghton Mifflin.

Sue, D. W., Capodilupo, C. M., Torino, G. C., et al. (2007). Racial microaggressions in everyday life: Implications for clinical practice. *American Psychologist, 62,* 271–286.

Sue, D. W., & Sue, D. (2003). *Counseling the culturally diverse: Theory and practice* (4th ed.). New York: Wiley.

Sue, D. W., & Sue, D. (2012). *Counseling the culturally diverse: Theory and practice* (6th ed.). New York: Wiley.

Sue, S. (1988). Psychotherapeutic services for ethnic minorities: Two decades of research findings. *American Psychologist, 43,* 301–308.

Sue, S. (1994). Change, persistence, and enthusiasm for ethnic research. In P. Keller (Ed.), *Academic paths: Career* decisions and experiences of psychologists. Hillsdale, NJ: Erlbaum.

Sue, S. (2003). In defense of cultural competency in psychotherapy and treatment. *American Psychologist, 58,* 964–970.

Sue, S., & Lam, A. G. (2002). Cultural and demographic diversity. In J. C. Norcross (Ed.), *Psychotherapy relationships that work.* New York: Oxford University Press.

Sue, S., Yan Cheng, J. K., Saad, C. S., & Chu, J. P. (2012). Asian American mental health: A call to action. *American Psychologist, 6,* 531–540.

Sue, S., & Zane, N. (2005). Ethnic minority populations have been neglected by evidence-based practices. In J. C. Norcross, L. E. Beulter, & R. F. Levant (Eds.), *Evidence-based practices in mental health: Debate and dialogue on the fundamental questions.* Washington, DC: American Psychological Association.

Sukhodolsky, D. G., Kassinoveb, H., & Gormanb, B. S. (2004). Cognitive-behavioral therapy for anger in children and adolescents: A meta-analysis. *Aggression and Violent Behavior, 9,* 247–269.

Sullivan, H. S. (1953a). *Conceptions of modern psychiatry.* New York: Norton.

Sullivan, H. S. (1953b). *The interpersonal theory of psychiatry.* New York: Norton.

Sullivan, H. S. (1970). *The psychiatric interview.* New York: Norton.

Sullivan, H. S. (1972). *Personal psychopathology.* New York: Norton.

Sulloway, F. J. (1996). *Born to rebel: Birth order, family dynamics, and creative lives.* New York: Pantheon.

Summers, R. F., & Barber, J. P. (2009). *Psychodynamic therapy: A guide to evidence-based practice.* New York: Guilford.

Svartberg, M., & Stiles, T. C. (1991). Comparative effects of short-term psychodynamic psychotherapy: A meta-analysis. *Journal of Consulting and Clinical Psychology, 5,* 704–714.

Swift, J. K., Callahan, J. L., & Vollmer, B. M. (2011). Preferences. In J. C. Norcross (Ed.), *Psychotherapy relationships that work* (2nd ed., pp. 301–315). New York: Oxford University Press.

Swift, J. K., & Greenberg, R. P. (2012). Premature discontinuation in adult

psychotherapy: A meta-analysis. *Journal of Consulting and Clinical Psychology, 80,* 547–559.

Tannen, D. (1990). *You just don't understand: Women and men in conversation.* New York: William Morrow.

Tarrier, N., & Wykes, T. (2004). Is there evidence that cognitive behaviour therapy is an effective treatment for schizophrenia? *Behaviour Research & Therapy, 42,* 1377–1401.

Task Force on Promotion and Dissemination of Psychological Procedures. (1995). Training in and dissemination of empirically validated psychological treatments. *The Clinical Psychologist, 48,* 3–23.

Tausch, R. (1990). The supplementation of client-centered communication therapy with other validated therapeutic methods: A client-centered necessity. In G. Lietaer, J. Rombouts, & R. Van-Balen (Eds.), *Client-centered and experiential psychotherapy in the nineties.* Leuven, Belgium: Leuven University Press.

Taylor, S., Thordarson, D. S., Maxfield, L., et al. (2003). Comparative efficacy, speed, and adverse effects of three PTSD treatments. *Journal of Consulting and Clinical Psychology, 71,* 330–338.

Taylor, T. L., & Chemtob, C. M. (2004). Efficacy of treatment for child and adolescent traumatic stress. *Archives of Pediatric and Adolescent Medicine, 158,* 786–791.

Teasdale, J. D. (1988). Cognitive vulnerability to persistent depression. *Cognition &Emotion, 2,* 247–274.

Teyber, E. (2005). *Interpersonal process in psychotherapy* (5th ed.). Belmont, CA: Brooks/Cole.

Thompson-Brenner, H., Glass, S., & Westen, D. (2003). A multidimensional meta-analysis of psychotherapy for bulimia nervosa. *Clinical Psychology: Science and Practice, 10,* 269–287.

Thorp, S. R., Ayers, C. R., Nuevo, R., et al. (2009). Meta-analysis comparing different behavioral treatments for late-life anxiety. *American Journal of Geriatric Psychiatry, 17,* 105–115.

Tillich, P. (1952). *The courage to be.* New Haven: Yale University Press.

Tinbergen, N. (1951). *The study of instinct.* Oxford: Clarendon.

Tinker, R. H., & Wilson, S. A. (1999). *Through the eyes of a child: EMDR with children.* New York: Norton.

Tolin, D. F. (2010). Is cognitive-behavioral therapy more effective than other therapies? A meta-analytic review. *Clinical Psychology Review, 30,* 710–720.

Tonnesvang, J., Sommer, U., Hammink, J., & Sonne, M. (2010). Gestalt therapy and cognitive therapy—contrasts or complementarities? *Psychotherapy, 47,* 586–602.

Torrey, E. F. (1972). *The mind game.* New York: Bantam.

Town, J. M., Abbass, A., & Hardy, G. (2011). Short-term psychodynamic psychotherapy for personality disorders: A critical review of randomized controlled trials. *Journal of Personality Disorders, 25,* 723–740.

Truax, C. (1966). Reinforcement and non-reinforcement in Rogerian psychotherapy. *Journal of Abnormal Psychology, 71,* 1–9.

Truax, C., & Carkhuff, R. (1967). *Toward effective counseling and psychotherapy: Training and practice.* Hawthorne, NY: Aldine.

Tudor, K. (Ed.). (2002). *Transactional analysis approaches to brief therapy.* Thousand Oaks, CA: Sage.

Tuerk, E. H., McCart, M. R., & Henggeler, S. W. (2012). Collaboration in family therapy. *Journal of Clinical Psychology, 68,* 168–178.

Turner, S. M. (1997). *Behavior therapy for obsessive-compulsive disorder.* Washington, DC: American Psychological Association Videotape Series.

U.S. Bureau of Labor Statistics. (2011). *Highlights of women's earnings in 2010.* Washington, DC: U.S. Government Printing Office. Retrieved from www.bls.gov/cps/cpswom2010.pdf

U.S. Census Bureau. (2008). Retrieved from www.census.gov/Press-release/www/releases/archives/income_wealth/010583.html

U.S. Census Bureau. (2011a). *Census 2010 gateway.* Retrieved September 28, 2012, from http://2010.census.gov/2010census/

U.S. Census Bureau. (2011b). *Native North American Languages Spoken at Home in* the United States and Puerto Rico. Retrieved September 28, 2012, from www.census.gov/prod/2011pubs/acsbr10-10.pdf

U.S. Department of Labor, Women's Bureau. (1997). *20 facts on women workers.* Washington, DC: Author.

U.S. Surgeon General. (2001). *Mental health: Culture, race, and ethnicity.* Rockville, MD: U.S. Department of Health and Human Services.

Usher, C. H. (1989). Recognizing cultural bias in counseling theory and practice: The case of Rogers. *Journal of Multicultural Counseling and Development, 17,* 62–71.

Valasquez, M. M., Maurer, G., Crouch, C., & DiClemente, C. C. (2001). *Group treatment for substance abuse: A stages-of-change therapy manual.* New York: Guilford.

van Balkom, A. J. L. M., van Oppen, P., Vermeulen, A. W. A., et al. (1994). A meta-analysis on the treatment of obsessive compulsive disorder. *Clinical Psychology Review, 14,* 359–381.

van Etten, M. L., & Taylor, S. (1998). Comparative efficacy of treatments for posttraumatic stress disorder: A meta-analysis. *Clinical Psychology and Psychotherapy, 5,* 126–144.

van't Hof, E., Cuijpers, P., Waheed, W., & Stein, D. J. (2011). Psychological treatments for depression and anxiety disorders in low- and middle-income countries: A meta-analysis. *African Journal of Psychiatry, 14,* 200–207.

Veehof, M. M., Oskam, M.-J., Schreurs, M. G., & Bohlmeijer, E. T. (2011). Acceptance-based interventions for the treatment of chronic pain: A systematic review and meta-analysis. *Pain, 152,* 533–542.

Veevers, H. M. (1991). Which child—which family? *Transactional Analysis Journal, 21,* 207–211.

Velicer, W. F., Prochaska, J.O., Fava, J. L., et al. (1999). Interactive versus non-interactive interventions and dose-response relationships for stage-matched smoking cessation programs in a managed care setting. *Health Psychology, 18,* 21–28.

Veroff, J., Douvan, E., & Kulka, R. A. (1981a). *The inner America.* New York: Basic.

Veroff, J., Douvan, E., & Kulka, R. A. (1981b). *Mental health in America.* New York: Basic.

Viswesvaran, C., & Schmidt, F. L. (1992). A meta-analytic comparison of the effectiveness of smoking cessation methods. *Journal of Applied Psychology, 77,* 554–561.

Vittengl, J. R., Clark, L. A., Dunn, T. W., & Jarrett, R. B. (2007). Reducing relapse and recurrence in unipolar depression: A comparative meta-analysis of cognitive-behavioral therapy's effects. *Journal of Consulting and Clinical Psychology, 75,* 475–488.

Vocks, S., Tuschen-Caffier, B., Pietrowsky, R., et al. (2010). Meta-analysis of the effectiveness of psychological and pharmacological treatments for binge eating disorder. *International Journal of Eating Disorders, 43,* 205–217.

Vollestad, J., Nielsen, M. B., & Nielsen, G. H. (2012). Mindfulness- and acceptance-based interventions for anxiety disorders: A systematic review and meta-analysis. *British Journal of Clinical Psychology, 51,* 239–260.

von Bertalanffy, L. (1968). *General systems theory.* New York: George Braziller.

Vromans, L. P., & Schweitzer, R. D. (2011). Narrative therapy for adults with major depressive disorder: Improved symptom and interpersonal outcomes. *Psychotherapy Research, 21,* 4–15.

Wachtel, E. F., & Wachtel, P. L. (1986). *Family dynamics in individual psychotherapy.* New York: Guilford.

Wachtel, P. L. (1977). *Psychoanalysis and behavior therapy: Toward an integration.* New York: Basic.

Wachtel, P. L. (1983). *You can't go far in neutral: On the limits of therapeutic neutrality.* Paper presented at the 40th anniversary celebration of the William Alanson White Institute, New York.

Wachtel, P. L. (1987). *Action and insight.* New York: Guilford.

Wachtel, P. L. (1989). *The poverty of affluence: A psychological portrait of the American way of life.* Philadelphia: New Society.

Wachtel, P. L. (1990). Psychotherapy from an integrative psychodynamic perspective. In J. K. Zeig & W. M. Munion (Eds.), *What is psychotherapy?* San Francisco: Jossey-Bass.

Wachtel, P. L. (1991). From eclecticism to synthesis: Toward a more seamless psychotherapeutic integration. *Journal of Psychotherapy Integration, 1,* 43–54.

Wachtel, P. L. (1997). *Psychoanalysis, behavior therapy, and the relational world.* Washington, DC: American Psychological Association.

Wachtel, P. L. (2008). *Relational theory and the practice of psychotherapy.* New York: Guilford.

Wachtel, P. L. (2011a). *Inside the session: What really happens in psychotherapy.* Washington, DC: American psychological Association.

Wachtel, P. L. (2011b). *Therapeutic communication: Knowing what to say when* (2nd ed.). New York: Guilford.

Wachtel, P. L., Kruk, J. C., & McKinney, M. K. (2005). Cyclical psychodynamics and integrative relational therapy. In J. C. Norcross & M. R. Goldfried (Eds.), *Handbook of psychotherapy integration* (2nd ed.). New York: Oxford University Press.

Wagner-Moore, L. E. (2004). Gestalt therapy: Past, present, theory, and research. *Psychotherapy, 41,* 180–189.

Walker, L. E. A. (1979). *The battered woman.* New York: Harper & Row.

Walker, M. (1990). *Women in therapy and counselling: Out of the shadows.* London: Open University Press.

Walkup, J. T., Albano, A. M., Piacentini, J., et al. (2008). Cognitive behavioral therapy, sertraline, or a combination in childhood anxiety. *The New England Journal of Medicine, 359,* 2753–2766.

Wallerstein, R. S. (1986). *Forty-two lives in treatment.* New York: Guilford.

Walter, J. L., & Peller, J. E. (1992). *Becoming solution-focused in brief therapy.* New York: Brunner/Mazel.

Waltz, T. J., & Hayes, S. C. (2010). Acceptance and commitment therapy. In N. Kazantzis, M. A. Reinecke, & A. Freeman (Eds.), *Cognitive and behavioral theories in clinical practice* (pp. 148–192). New York: Guilford.

Wampold, B. E. (2001). *The great psychotherapy debate: Models, methods, and findings.* Mahwah, NJ: Erlbaum.

Wampold, B. E. (2008). *The great psychotherapy debate: Models, methods, and findings* (2nd ed.). Mahwah, NJ: Erlbaum.

Wampold, B. E., Imel, Z. E., Laska, K. M., et al. (2010). Determining what works in the treatment of PTSD. *Clinical Psychology Review, 8,* 923–933.

Wampold, B. E., Minami, T., Baskin, T. W., & Tierney, S. C. (2002). A meta-(re) analysis of the effects of cognitive therapy versus "other therapies" for depression. *Journal of Affective Disorders, 68,* 159–165.

Wampold, B. E., Mondin, G. W., Moody, M., et al. (1997). A meta-analysis of outcome studies comparing bonafide psychotherapies: Empirically, "All must have prizes." *Psychological Bulletin, 122,* 203–215.

Warren, K., Franklin, C., & Streeter, C. L. (1998). New directions in systems theory: Chaos and complexity. *Social Work, 43,* 357–372.

Watkins, C. E. (1982). A decade of research in support of Adlerian psychological theory. *Individual Psychology, 38,* 90–99.

Watkins, C. E. (1983). Some characteristics of research on Adlerian theory, 1970–1981. *Individual Psychology, 39,* 99–110.

Watkins, C. E. (1992). Adlerian-oriented early memory research: What does it tell us? *Journal of Personality Assessment, 59,* 248–262.

Watson, G. (1940). Areas of agreement in psychotherapy. *American Journal of Orthopsychiatry, 10,* 698–709.

Watson, J. B., & Rayner, R. (1920). Conditioned emotional reactions. *Journal of Experimental Psychology, 3,* 1–14.

Watson, J. C., Gordon, L. B., Stermac, L., et al. (2003). Comparing the effectiveness of process-experiential with cognitive-behavioral psychotherapy in the treatment of depression. *Journal of Consulting and Clinical Psychology, 71,* 773–781.

Watzlawick, P., Beavin, J., & Jackson, D. (1967). *Pragmatics of human communication.* New York: Norton.

Watzlawick, P., Weakland, J. H., & Fisch, R. (1974). *Change: Principles of problem formation and problem resolution.* New York: Norton.

Webster, D. C., Vaughn, K., & Martinez, R. (1994). Introducing solution-focused approaches to staff in inpatient psychiatric settings. *Archives of Psychiatric Nursing, 8,* 254–261.

Weinberger, J. (1995). Common factors aren't so common: The common factors dilemma. *Clinical Psychology: Science and Practice, 2,* 45–69.

Weiner, I. B. (1975). *Principles of psychotherapy.* New York: Wiley.

Weiss, B., & Weisz, J. R. (1995a). Effectiveness of psychotherapy [Letter to the editor]. *Journal of the American Academy of Child and Adolescent Psychiatry, 34,* 971–972.

Weiss, B., & Weisz, J. R. (1995b). Relative effectiveness of behavioral versus non-behavioral child psychotherapy. *Journal of Consulting and Clinical Psychology, 63,* 317–320.

Weissman, M. M., Markowitz, J. C., & Klerman, G. L. (2000). *Comprehensive guide to interpersonal psychotherapy.* New York: Basic.

Weissman, M. M., Markowitz, J. C., & Klerman, G. L. (2007). *Clinician's quick guide to interpersonal psychotherapy.* New York: Oxford University Press.

Weisz, J. R., Donenberg, G. R., Han, S. S., & Weiss, B. (1995). Bridging the gap between laboratory and clinic in child and adolescent psychotherapy. *Journal of Consulting and Clinical Psychology, 63,* 688–701.

Weisz, J. R., Hawley, K. M., & Doss, A. J. (2004). Empirically tested psychotherapies for youth internalizing and externalizing problems and disorders. *Child & Adolescent Psychiatric Clinics of North America, 13,* 729–815.

Weisz, J. R., & Kazdin, A. E. (Eds.). (2010). *Evidence-based psychotherapies for children and adolescents* (2nd ed.). New York: Guilford.

Weisz, J. R., McCarty, C. A., & Valeri, S. M. (2006). Effects of psychotherapy for depression in children and adolescents: A meta-analysis. *Psychological Bulletin, 132,* 132–149.

Weisz, J. R., Weiss, B., Alicke, M. D. & Klotz, M. L. (1987). Effectiveness of psychotherapy with children and adolescents: A meta-analysis for clinicians. *Journal of Consulting and Clinical Psychology, 55,* 542–549.

Weisz, J. R., Weiss, B., Han, S. S., et al. (1995). Effects of psychotherapy with children and adolescents revisited: A meta-analysis of treatment outcome studies. *Psychological Bulletin, 117,* 450–468.

Werner, H. (1948). *Comparative psychology of mental development.* Chicago: Follett.

Werner, H., & Kaplan, B. (1963). *Symbol formation: An organismic-developmental approach to language and the expression of thought.* New York: Wiley.

Westen, D. (1998). The scientific legacy of Sigmund Freud: Toward a psychodynamically informed psychological science. *Psychological Bulletin, 124,* 333–371.

Wexler, D. (1974). A cognitive theory of experiencing, self-actualization, and therapeutic process. In D. Wexler & L. Rice (Eds.), *Innovations in client-centered therapy.* New York: Wiley.

Wheeler, G. (1990). *Gestalt reconsidered: A new approach to contact and resistance.* New York: Gardner.

Wheeler, G., & Backman, S. (Eds.). (1994). *On intimate ground: A Gestalt approach to working with couples.* San Francisco: Jossey-Bass.

Whitaker, C. A., & Bumberry, W. M. (1988). *Dancing with the family: A symbolic-experiential approach.* New York: Brunner/Mazel.

Whitaker, C. A., & Keith, D. V. (1981). Symbolic-experiential family therapy. In A. S. Gurman & D. P. Kniskern (Eds.), *Handbook of family therapy.* New York: Brunner/Mazel.

Whitbread, J., & McGowen, A. (1994). The treatment of bulimia nervosa: A meta-analysis. *Indian Journal of Clinical Psychology, 21,* 32–44.

White, M. (2007). *Maps of narrative practice.* New York: Norton.

White, M. (2011). *Narrative practice: continuing the conversations.* New York: Norton.

White, M., & Epston, D. (1990). *Narrative means to therapeutic ends.* New York: Norton.

White, M., & Epston, D. (1994). *Experience, contradiction, narrative, and imagination.* Adelaide, Australia: Dulwich Centre Publications.

White, R. W. (1959). Motivation reconsidered: The concept of competence. *Psychological Review, 66,* 297–333.

White, R. W. (1960). Competence and the psychosexual stages of development. In M. R. Jones (Ed.), *Nebraska symposium* on motivation. Lincoln: University of Nebraska Press.

Whittal, M. L., Agras, W. S., & Gould, R. A. (1999). Bulimia nervosa: A meta-analysis of psychosocial and pharmacological treatments. *Behavior Therapy, 30,* 117–135.

Wiederhold, B. K., & Wiederhold, M. D. (2005). *Virtual reality therapy for anxiety disorders.* Washington, DC: American Psychological Association.

Wilhelm, S., Tolin, D. F., & Steketee, G. (2004). Challenges in treating obsessive-compulsive disorder. *Journal of Clinical Psychology: In Session, 60,* 1127–1132.

Williams, M., Teasdale, J., Segal, Z., & Kabat-Zinn, J. (2007). *The mindful way through depression.* New York: Guilford.

Williams, T. A. (1988). *A multimodal approach to assessment and intervention with children with learning disabilities.* Unpublished Ph.D. dissertation, Department of Psychology, University of Glasgow.

Wilson, G. T. (1996). Acceptance and change in the treatment of eating disorders and obesity. *Behavior Therapy, 27,* 417–439.

Wilson, G. T. (1999). Cognitive behavior therapy for eating disorders: Progress and problems. *Behaviour Research & Therapy, 37,* S79–S95.

Wilson, G. T., & Schlam, T. R. (2004). The transtheoretical model and motivational interviewing in the treatment of eating and weight disorders. *Clinical Psychology Review, 24,* 361–378.

Winnicott, D. W. (1931/1992). *Through paediatrics to psycho-analysis: Collected papers.* New York: Brunner-Mazel.

Winnicott, D. W. (1965). *The maturational processes and the facilitating environment: Studies in the theory of emotional development.* London: Hogarth.

Wittgenstein, L. (1953). *Philosophical investigations.* New York: Macmillan.

Wittgenstein, L. (1958). *The blue and brown books.* New York: Harper & Row.

Wohl, J. (1989). Integration of cultural awareness into psychotherapy. *American Journal of Psychotherapy, 43,* 343–355.

Woidneck, M. R., Pratt, K. M., Gundy, J. M., et al. (2012). Exploring cultural competence in acceptance and commitment

therapy outcomes. *Professional Psychology: Research and Practice, 43,* 227–233.

Woldt, A. S., & Toman, S. M. (Eds.). (2005). *Gestalt therapy: History, theory, practice.* Newbury, CA: Sage.

Wolfe, B. E., & Goldfried, M. R. (1988). Research on psychotherapy integration: Recommendations and conclusions from a NIMH workshop. *Journal of Consulting and Clinical Psychology, 56,* 448–451.

Wolitzky-Taylor, K. B., Horowitz, J. B., et al. (2008). Psychological approaches in the treatment of specific phobias: A meta-analysis. *Clinical Psychology Review, 28,* 1021–1037.

Wolpe, J. (1958). *Psychotherapy by reciprocal inhibition.* Stanford, CA: Stanford University Press.

Wolpe, J. (1973). *The practice of behavior therapy* (2nd ed.). Elmsford, NY: Pergamon.

Wolpe, J. (1989). The derailment of behavior therapy: A tale of conceptual misdirection. *Journal of Behavior Therapy and Experimental Psychiatry, 20,* 3–15.

Wolpe, J. (1990). *The practice of behavior therapy* (4th ed.). Elmsford, NY: Pergamon.

Worell, J., & Remer, P. (Eds.). (2002). *Feminist perspectives in therapy: Empowering diverse women* (2nd ed.). New York: Wiley.

Worthington, E. L., Hook, J. N., Davis, D. E., & McDaniel, M. A. (2011). Religion and spirituality. In J. C. Norcross (Ed.), *Psychotherapy relationships that work* (2nd ed., pp. 301–315). New York: Oxford University Press.

Worthington, E. L., Jr., & Sandage, S. J. (2002). Religion and spirituality. In J. C. Norcross (Ed.), *Psychotherapy relationships that work.* New York: Oxford University Press.

Wright, J. H., Thase, M. E., Beck, A. T., & Ludgate, G. (Eds.). (1992). *Cognitive therapy with inpatients.* New York: Guilford.

Wright, J. H., & Wright, A. S. (1997). Computer-assisted psychotherapy. *Journal of Psychotherapy Practice and Research, 6,* 315–329.

Wykes, T., Steel, C., Everitt, B., & Tarrier, N. (2008). Cognitive behavior therapy

(CBTp) for schizophrenia: Effect sizes, clinical models and methodological rigor. *Schizophrenia Bulletin, 34,* 523–537.

Yalom, I. D. (1975). *The theory and practice of group psychotherapy* (2nd ed.). New York: Basic.

Yalom, I. D. (1980). *Existential psychotherapy.* New York: Basic.

Yeomans, F. E., Clarkin, J. F., & Kernberg, O. F. (2002). *A primer of transference-focused psychotherapy for the borderline patient.* Northvale, NJ: Jason Aronson.

Yontef, G. (1988). Assimilating diagnostic and psychoanalytic perspectives into Gestalt therapy. *The Gestalt Journal, 11,* 5–32.

Young, A. S., Klap, R., Sherbourne, C., & Wells, K. B. (2001). The quality of care for depressive and anxiety disorders in the United States. *Archives of General Psychiatry, 58,* 55–61.

Young, J. E., Klosko, J. S., & Weishaar, M. E. (2003). *Schema therapy: A practitioner's guide.* New York: Guilford.

Young, K. M., Northern, J. J., Lister, K. M., et al. (2007). A meta-analysis of family behavioral weight-loss treatments for children. *Clinical Psychology Review, 27,* 240–249.

Yutrzenka, B. A. (1995). Making a case for training in ethnic and cultural diversity in increasing treatment efficacy. *Journal of Consulting and Clinical Psychology, 63,* 197–206.

Zeig, J. K., & Munion, W. M. (Eds.). (1990). *What is psychotherapy? Contemporary perspectives.* San Francisco: Jossey-Bass.

Zimmerman, G., Favrod, J., Trieu, V. H., & Pomini, V. (2005). The effect of cognitive behavioral treatment on the positive symptoms of schizophrenia spectrum disorders: A meta-analysis. *Schizophrenia Research, 77,* 1–9.

Zimring, F. (1974). Theory and practice of client-centered therapy: A cognitive view. In D. Wexler & L. Rice (Eds.), *Innovations in client-centered therapy.* New York: Wiley.

Zinker, J. (1977). *Creative process in Gestalt therapy.* New York: Brunner/Mazel.

Zinker, J. (1991). Creative process in Gestalt therapy: The therapist as artist. *The Gestalt Journal, 14,* 71–88.

Name Index

Dutra, L., 203, 204, 250, 495
Dworkin, M., 209
D'Zurilla, T. J., 240, 259

E

Eccleston, C., 288
Eddy, K. T., 203, 204, 250, 495
Edwards, L., 396, 474
Edwards, D. G., 85
Edwards, D. J. A., 102
Edwards, M. E., 341
Ehlers, A., 281, 286
Eisler, R. M., 367
Eliot, T. S., 407
Elkin, I. E., 187
Ellenberger, H., 80, 85, 94, 112
Elliott, R., 133, 152, 161, 164, 165, 166, 170, 171, 365
Ellis, A., 237, 262–273, 276, 282, 283, 293–296
Emery, G., 277, 279, 293, 296
Emmelkamp, P. M. G., 205, 215
Endler, N. S., 204
Engle, D., 166
Epstein, N., 283
Epston, D., 413, 414, 424
Erikson, E. H., 25, 65, 66, 435
Espie, C. A., 253
Estes, W., 236
Etkin, A., 490
Eubanks-Carter, C., 397
Evers, K. E., 473, 474, 475, 481
Eysenck, H. J., 256, 431

F

Fairbairn, W., 66
Fairburn, C. G., 189, 288
Fairweather, D. R., 162
Faludi, S., 354
Farber, B. A., 140
Fassinger, R. E., 394
Faulkner, W., 29
Fava, J. L., 473, 493
Fay, A., 443, 450
Feeny, N. C., 203
Felder, J. N., 307
Feldman, J. M., 249
Fenichel, O., 25, 37, 182
Feske, U., 286
Fibel, B., 456
Finney, J .W., 179, 249, 490
Fiore, M. C., 486
Fisch, R., 352
Fischer, A. R., 397
Fish, L. S., 483
Fisher, S., 44, 50
Fisher, J. E., 486
Fisher, P. L., 204
Fitzpatrick, M. R., 495

Floyd, M., 369
Foa, E. B., 197–198, 200, 202, 215
Foelsch, P., 73
Follette, V. M., 313, 314
Fonagy, P., 41, 180, 252, 342
Forfar, C. S., 160
Forrest, M. S., 206
Frank, E., 177, 182, 188, 193
Frank, J., 8, 19
Frank, J. D., 8, 19
Frankl, V., 103–104, 111, 112
Franklin, C., 340, 416, 423, 424
Franks, C., 256
Freedheim, D. K., 19
Freedman, N., 41
Freeman, A., 277, 283
French, T. M., 39
Freud, A., 38, 50, 53
Freud, S., 21–22, 25, 35, 37, 45, 50, 67, 70, 81, 212, 459
Friedman, S., 415
Friedman, M. J., 215
Friere, P., 388
Fromm, I., 161
Frosch, A., 41
Funk, S. C., 6
Furukawa, M. J., 242

G

Gabbard, G. O., 50
Gaertner, S. L., 383
Gaffan, E. A., 285
Galatzer, R. M., 41, 50
Galatzer-Levy, R., 41
Galavotti, C., 464
Gamble, W., 179
Ganley, A. L., 366
Garcia-Preto, N., 351
Garfield, S. L., 8, 431, 432
Gawin, F. H., 189
Gay, P., 21, 22, 33
Gebing, T. A., 251
Gehred-Schultz, A., 464
Gendlin, E. T., 119, 124, 162, 171, 443
Gerber, L., 361
Gergen, K. J., 407, 413, 414, 416, 423
Giesen-Bloo, J., 73
Gilford, P., 418
Gill, M. M., 42
Gilligan, C., 364
Gillis, M. M., 286
Giordano, J., 351
Glaser, R. R., 341
Glass, S., 251, 288
Glass, C. R., 5, 221, 241, 243, 439, 488
Glass, G. V., 72, 74, 133, 165, 187, 246, 284
Glasser, W., 104–106, 112
Glautier, S., 201
Glover, E., 24

Gnagy, E. M., 251
Gold, J., 41
Goldberg, D. A., 70
Goldberg, G. A., 358
Goldberg, R., 464
Goldenberg, H., 340, 351
Goldenberg, I., 340, 351
Goldfried, M. R., 5, 140, 225, 238, 258, 259, 291, 397, 426–429, 432, 451, 452
Goldman, R. N., 70, 165
Goldstein, A. J., 215
Gonzalez, J. E., 284
Good, G. E., 368, 369, 373
Goodman, J., 239
Goodman, P., 150, 161
Goodson, F. E., 4
Goodyear, R. K., 3
Gordon, T., 126
Gordon, B. L., 489
Gordon, L. B., 165
Gorman, J. M., 287, 497
Gossett, J. T., 347
Gotlib, I. H., 177, 179
Gottlieb, M. C., 396
Gottlieb, N. H., 464
Gould, R. A., 286, 287, 289
Grawe, K., 72, 74, 133, 187, 244, 246, 446, 497
Greaves, D. W., 350
Green, C. E., 290
Greenberg, G., 319, 320
Greenberg, J., 107
Greenberg, L. S., 133, 152, 161–165, 170, 171, 319, 320, 365
Greenberg, R. P., 44, 50
Greene, B., 377, 378, 403
Greene, J., 203, 211, 287
Greene, R. N., 474, 475
Greenson, R. R., 30, 50
Greenspoon, J., 233
Greenwall, L., 249
Greenwood, K. M., 253
Gregory, R. J., 490
Greif, A. C., 456
Greiner, A. R., 251
Greist, J. H., 203, 250
Grencavage, L. M., 5, 6, 8
Gresham, F. M., 248
Grieger, R., 296
Griffith, J. D., 249
Griner, D., 398
Grissom, R. J., 6
Grote, N. K., 193
Guerney, B., 327, 328
Guevremont, D. C., 259
Guinta, L. C., 6
Guisinger, S., 77
Guntrip, H., 49

Subject Index